THE OXFORD HANDBOOK OF

PEACEFUL ASSEMBLY

THE OXFORD HANDBOOK OF

PEACEFUL ASSEMBLY

Edited by

TABATHA ABU EL-HAJ,

MICHAEL HAMILTON,

THOMAS PROBERT,

and

SHARATH SRINIVASAN

OXFORD
UNIVERSITY PRESS

OXFORD
UNIVERSITY PRESS

Oxford University Press is a department of the University of Oxford.
It furthers the University's objective of excellence in research, scholarship,
and education by publishing worldwide. Oxford is a registered trade mark of
Oxford University Press in the UK and certain other countries.

Published in the United States of America by Oxford University Press
198 Madison Avenue, New York, NY 10016, United States of America.

Library of Congress Cataloging-in-Publication Data
Names: Abu El-Haj, Tabatha, editor. | Hamilton, Michael, 1975–editor. |
Probert, Thomas, 1986–editor. | Srinivasan, Sharath, 1974–editor.
Title: The Oxford handbook of peaceful assembly / edited by Tabatha Abu El-Haj,
Michael Hamilton, Thomas Probert & Sharath Srinivasan.
Description: New York : Oxford University Press, 2025. |
Series: Oxford handbooks series | Includes index. |
Identifiers: LCCN 2025002149 (print) | LCCN 2025002150 (ebook) |
ISBN 9780197674871 (hardback) | ISBN 9780197674895 (epub) |
ISBN 9780197674901
Subjects: LCSH: Assembly, Right of. | Freedom of speech. | Civil rights. |
Demonstrations—Law and legislation. | Protest movements.
Classification: LCC K3256 .O94 2025 (print) | LCC K3256 (ebook) |
DDC 323.4/7—dc23/eng/20250118
LC record available at https://lccn.loc.gov/2025002149
LC ebook record available at https://lccn.loc.gov/2025002150

DOI: 10.1093/oxfordhb/9780197674871.001.0001

Printed by Sheridan Books, Inc., United States of America

The Right to Be Remembered: A Dedication to Christof Heyns

A mountain lake with technicolour sunsets in the early days of March 2020. A gorgeously Gothic Swiss hotel in the little town of Glion. A crazily wonderful setting for a few dozen softly spoken lawyers from all over the world, gathered to discuss the universal right of peaceful assembly. Convened by Professor Christof Heyns, members of the UN Human Rights Committee, charged with interpreting one of the foundational human rights instruments, produced a dizzying degree of intellectual interchange that was extraordinary to be part of.

Within a week, as we returned with buzzing heads to our respective homes, we learnt of the surging impact of the coronavirus. The lockdown that followed not only confined our movements but also froze our imaginations, even our recall. I can well remember the energy, the excitement; it was as though the beauty of nature allowed the beauty of ideas to float freely and uninhibitedly amongst us. Yet I cannot remember a single word of what was said. I know that I was called upon to speak on more than one occasion, but I don't even have scribblings of what I said. The organizers tell me from their notes that the main point I made was that we should not seek to cover each and every form of assembly. Historically, the right of peaceful assembly had been associated with the right to petition against injustice. This should always be at the centre of the right and serve as the foundation to meet contemporary political and technological needs and possibilities. To overextend the protective scope beyond this purposive core would carry the risk of diluting the essence of the right.

According to the notes, the other major point I made was that the General Comment we were producing should not end up being too formulaic; instead, it should strongly underline the core values and principles that lie at the heart of both the right of peaceful assembly and the limitations on the right that would be permissible in an open and democratic society.

These notes seem to ring true. And given the nature of the topic and the occasion, I can add three specific things that I would almost certainly have mentioned. The first is how brutal state responses had been in apartheid South Africa. Massacres had been all too frequent. States of Emergency would be declared in which all public gatherings would be banned unless expressly authorized by the police. The police would fire into crowds. Not only did the majority not have the vote, they could not even protest against their disenfranchisement; armed struggle became inevitable. Second, I would have recalled that after going into exile, I had gotten to know the streets of London by marching from Hyde Park to Trafalgar Square denouncing British collusion with the American military in Vietnam or the failure of successive British governments to support sanctions against racist South Africa. Third, I would have touched on a moment some years later when I was a member of the Constitutional Court, and we were approached by the police to give our views on an application of a militant political group to march from the Johannesburg Civic Centre half a kilometre away to the Constitutional Court itself. Perhaps to the surprise of the police, we indicated that we had no problem at all; the protesters could come right to the front doors of the Court. Though only two of us had actually been incarcerated for our participation in the struggle against apartheid, we had all seen how in the past, more repression had only led to more resistance; no wonder that the new Constitution expressly declared the creation of an open and democratic society to be a foundational value. The only caveat that we introduced was that the volume of the slogans, loudspeakers, and musical instruments be not so great as to interrupt the serenity of the Court proceedings and impede their audibility.

If all this is only reconstructive conjecture with a high degree of probability, there is one thing that I can remember through the fog of COVID with total certainty. It was Christof Heyns, the brilliant conjurer of principled and evidence-based debate, setting out the issues with a delightful animation and ensuring that all engaged with them with free-flowing intellectual passion. It was very, very serious, and yet it was fun.

There Christof was, casually dressed, looking more like a rugby player than an internationally renowned law professor, speaking with an accent that owed more to Pretoria than to Yale or Oxford. A great organizer who loved the big picture yet attended meticulously to the tiny detail, he had told me before with a conspiratorial smile how he had consciously chosen a magic mountain to acquire magic resources to enable us to get there and engage in magical discussion.

Christof was a natural democrat. Inclusive by temperament, he enjoyed seeing and hearing everybody taking ideas seriously. He loved observing everyone talking animatedly with each other with equal voice.

Christof himself had been a rebel. Born into a family nestled in the heart of Afrikaner Nationalism, he had broken the cocoon to fight bravely and imaginatively for a universalist understanding of human rights. In everything, from dress to manner to thought, he had defied the strict conformism to which those around him had passively subordinated themselves. Afrikaners had known oppression, and Afrikaners had become oppressors. His highly placed clerical father, known as the moderate Moderator of the Dutch Reformed Church, had been assassinated, almost certainly by a fanatic right-winger. Christof's history as an Afrikaner, democrat, and internationalist gave him an acute sociopolitical sensibility. In turn, this sensibility had been nurtured by a deeply curious disposition, a warm and compassionate heart, and an irrepressible desire to locate and illuminate the central connections that linked up people as human beings. Fascinated by Gandhi's time in South Africa and non-violent resistance, it was no accident that he chose to do his doctorate on 'A jurisprudential analysis of civil disobedience'.

Then, halfway through the COVID period, the terrible news came through. After restrictions on movement had been relaxed, Christof had been walking in the mountains and had suddenly collapsed with a fatal heart attack. Family, friends, and colleagues throughout South Africa and all around the world were stricken. Outpourings of love and admiration came flooding in.

To this day, it is hard to believe that his very special spirit is no longer of this world. His inimitable openness, warmth, style, humour, clarity of expression, and intrinsic humanity will long be with us. His influence lives on in all those who engaged with him, whether as students, colleagues, human rights activists inside and outside international organizations, or just as neighbours, friends, and sporting and musical mates.

Several of the contributors to this book were present at Glion. Most were at some point inspired by Christof. All were heartbroken by his sudden passing. If ever there was an outstanding thinker and doer with a generous heart and a broad vision who earned the right to be remembered, it was Christof Heyns. With love, tenderness, and pride, this book is dedicated to him.

Albie Sachs
Cape Town
November 2023

Contents

Preface

Today, the world is at a critical turning point—gripped by growing wars and conflicts, a harsh climate crisis, and the backsliding of democracy, while an anti-rights agenda is rapidly spreading amid polarization and a severe clampdown on rights and freedoms across the world. In this context, the right to freedom of peaceful assembly is essential as a valuable avenue for people to ensure their voices are heard and their concerns are taken into account by authorities in taking action to reverse this critical situation. It is through this right that all individuals, including those marginalized, can raise their voices, participate democratically, take action, and contribute towards building inclusive and peaceful societies and ensuring fair development, climate justice, and a better future for all.

The right to freedom of peaceful assembly has been instrumental throughout history in advancing the human rights agenda, defending the rights of the marginalized and oppressed, advancing women's equality, and ending colonialism, slavery, and apartheid. The right is the very foundation of our democracies. It allows us to hold governments to account and to contribute to the building of democratic, responsive, and transparent institutions. This right is essential for empowering individuals and groups so they can become their own agents of change and build their collective future.

The mandate of the UN Special Rapporteur on the rights to freedom of peaceful assembly and of association was established in response to the Arab Spring in 2011, as the world witnessed the repression of mass protests with brutal force as people came together to claim democracy, justice, freedoms, and rights.

Since its establishment, the mandate has contributed significantly to the advancement, promotion, and protection of these rights at the national, regional, and international levels. It has contributed to the increased recognition of the enjoyment of the right of peaceful assembly as a right on its own, and of its role in ensuring that political, civil, economic, social, and cultural rights are fulfilled. The mandate has also advanced the promotion of the freedom of peaceful assembly for groups in vulnerable situations and those facing specific challenges and threats, such as women activists, climate change activists, and social movement activists.

Using my mandate, I have carried out extensive work to strengthen the normative framework protecting human rights during peaceful protests. The mandate's regular thematic reports have been an important catalyst for this and have filled gaps, as these rights were often not fully understood, overlooked by the international human rights discourse, and severely restricted by domestic laws and practices. The mandate's reports have addressed new and emerging issues, responding to people's concerns and needs, such as the latest reports on protecting and enabling the right of peaceful assembly in the digital age, in advancing climate justice, of social movements, of informal workers sector, in crisis situations, including in the context of pandemics, and in the times of peace-building and transition. Throughout my time as mandate-holder, I have also highlighted and advanced standards related to the right of children to exercise their legitimate right of peaceful assembly.

General Comment No. 37 on the right of peaceful assembly, adopted by the Human Rights Committee in 2020, is an important milestone. It has reinforced my efforts as mandate-holder and as such, I have consistently advocated and closely collaborated with the Committee for the development of the General Comment and now for its implementation.

The provisions of General Comment No. 37 have provided important standards, which also have been used for the development of key judgments by regional human rights courts. This complements the work of the mandate in advancing the protection of these rights at the regional level, including but not limited to the development of the guidance contained in the recent report 'Protest and Human Rights' of the Inter-American Commission on Human Rights, and the Guidelines on Freedom of Association and Assembly in Africa of the African Commission on Human and Peoples' Rights.

As the right to freedom of peaceful assembly has faced increased restrictions and threats, it has been critical to resist the negative paradigm and reassert that this is a fundamental right that must be facilitated and not controlled or suppressed. Similar to General Comment No. 37, my report on peaceful protest in crisis situations highlighted that peaceful protests should not be portrayed or perceived as a crisis or a threat, and those exercising this right must never be treated as enemies. This report emphasizes the positive role of peaceful protests and encourages states to take peaceful protests as an opportunity for hearing the voices of protesters and addressing their grievances, which are often root causes for conflicts. As I have documented through my mandate, too often, when protest is suppressed and repressed, the avenues of peaceful resolution of differences are hampered, leading to the rise of conflicts and the increase of crisis.

It has also been essential to address the growing instances of the use of force to suppress protests. As such, I have developed at the request of the United Nations Human Rights Council practical tools for law enforcement, which includes the Model Protocol for Law Enforcement Officials to Promote and Protect Human Rights in the Context of Peaceful Protests. This work has helped to translate international norms and standards into practice to ensure accountable, transparent, and human rights-compliant facilitation of peaceful protests. The Model Protocol has emphasized the duty to *facilitate* peaceful protests in a human rights-compliant manner including when using digital technologies. It has moved away from the concept of *management* of assemblies, which has been consistently misunderstood or misused by governments and law enforcement to suppress protests including with the use of excessive force. I have been particularly concerned about the widespread impunity for serious crimes in the context of assemblies. Every year hundreds of people are killed, injured, or disappeared without accountability because of their participation in protest or their work to defend the rights of others. The mandate has reasserted the obligations of states for ensuring accountability of commanders with respect to the failure to prevent violations in addition to issuing unlawful orders, which is also central in the Model Protocol.

It is also increasingly evident that we must strengthen the protection of freedom of peaceful assembly online. Thus, as part of the Model Protocol for Law Enforcement, I have produced the A Principled-based Guidance for the Human Rights Compliant Use of Digital Technologies in the Context of Peaceful Protests. This document provides practical guidance and foundational principles for human rights-compliant use of technologies by law enforcement to facilitate peaceful assemblies, as important focus has been put on accountability for the use of such technologies and ensuring thorough impact assessment before such technology is deployed in the context of protests.

As we celebrate the seventy-fifth anniversary of the Universal Declaration on Human Rights (UDHR), it is important to remember that the right to freedom of peaceful assembly has been recognized as one of the universal and inalienable rights that everyone is entitled to as a human being, and as the foundation of freedom, justice, and peace. This right has also been instrumental in advancing other rights contained in the Declaration, such as the right to self-determination. Moreover, as the UDHR was born after the global wars and immense human suffering, enshrining this right, among the others, is a recognition of the importance of allowing people to assemble freely in order to ensure peaceful co-existence.

I welcome the *Oxford Handbook of Peaceful Assembly* and commend the contributors for their detailed and robust analysis of the right, including its progress over the past ten years. States, the international community, and the United Nations should take into consideration the findings of the Handbook to ensure that the right of peaceful assembly is fully protected and enabled, so people everywhere can enjoy this right for building a peaceful world, respectful of human rights, where no one is left behind, and climate justice becomes a reality for all.

Clément Nyaletsossi Voule
UN Special Rapporteur on the right to freedom of
peaceful assembly and association
Geneva, April 2024

A Note from the Editors

Our decision to depict Tahrir Square on the cover is not to condone the mass sexual violence perpetrated there or in its vicinity. It reflects, instead, a recognition of the complexity and heterogeneity of assemblies. Protests remembered as peaceful by some may not have been for everyone involved.

About the Editors

Tabatha Abu El-Haj is a Professor of Law at Drexel University's Thomas R. Kline School of Law. A scholar of US constitutional law, she is an expert on the First Amendment's rights of peaceable assembly and association. Shaped by her background in the sociology of law, her work takes an interdisciplinary approach. Her prior publications include "The Neglected Right of Assembly" in the *UCLA Law Review* and "Defining Nonviolence as a Matter of Law and Politics" in *Protest and Dissent (Nomos LXII)*. She has taught as a Visiting Professor at the University of Michigan Law School and the University of Pennsylvania Carey Law School.

Michael Hamilton is a Legal Adviser at the International Secretariat of Amnesty International, working on civic space and the right to protest. Previously, he was Associate Professor of Public Protest Law at the University of East Anglia (where he remains a Visiting Associate Professor), and he has taught at the Department of Legal Studies at Central European University and the Transitional Justice Institute at the University of Ulster. He is a founding member, and presently co-Chair, of the OSCE/ODIHR Panel of Experts on Freedom of Assembly and Association.

Thomas Probert has worked as a Research Consultant and a Special Adviser within the UN human rights system, both to the Special Rapporteur on extrajudicial, summary, or arbitrary executions and to the Human Rights Committee. He has also advised the African Commission on Human and Peoples' Rights. In addition to being a senior researcher at the Centre for Human Rights (University of Pretoria), he is a research associate at the Centre of Governance and Human Rights (University of Cambridge). He has also taught at the University of Oxford and the Geneva Academy for International Humanitarian Law and Human Rights.

Sharath Srinivasan is the David and Elaine Potter Professor of International Politics at the University of Cambridge. With expertise in African politics, he researches contentious politics and civic action from a global perspective. His work spans technology and democracy, civil politics in armed conflict, and assemblies and publics. His publications include *When Peace Kills Politics: International Intervention and Unending Wars in the Sudans* (Hurst/Oxford University Press, 2021) and *Publics in Africa in a Digital Age* (co-ed., Routledge, 2021). At Cambridge, he co-directs the Centre of Governance and Human Rights (CGHR) and is a Fellow of King's College.

Contributors

Tabatha Abu El-Haj, Professor of Law, Thomas R. Kline School of Law, Drexel University

Otto Adang, Professor by Special Appointment, Faculty of Behavioural and Social Sciences, University of Groningen; Chair in Public Order Management, Police Academy of the Netherlands

Micah Alpaugh, Professor of History, University of Central Missouri

Cameran Ashraf, Assistant Professor, Department of Public Policy, Central European University; Wikimedia Foundation

Val Aston, Lecturer in Law, Hillary Rodham Clinton School of Law, University of Swansea

Davide Beraldo, Assistant Professor of New Media, Data and Information, Institute for Logic, Language and Computation, University of Amsterdam

Dominic Bryan, Professor of Anthropology, Queen's University Belfast

Steven Cammiss, Associate Professor in Law, Birmingham Law School, University of Birmingham

Stuart Casey-Maslen, Extraordinary Professor, Faculty of Law, University of Pretoria

Iain Channing, Lecturer in Criminology and Criminal Justice Studies, University of Plymouth

Lynette J. Chua, Professor of Law, National University of Singapore

Brian Doherty, Professor of Political Sociology, Keele University

Louise du Toit, Professor of Philosophy, University of Stellenbosch

Rabab El-Mahdi, Associate Professor of Political Science, American University in Cairo

Asli İkizoğlu Erensü, Assistant Professor, Faculty of Arts and Social Sciences, Sabanci University

David Goldberger, Professor Emeritus of Law, Michael Moritz College of Law, Ohio State University

Michael Hamilton, Visiting Associate Professor, University of East Anglia Law School

Graeme Hayes, Reader in Political Sociology, School of Social Sciences and Humanities, Aston University

Tara Houska, Attorney & Land Defender, Couchiching First Nation

John Inazu, Sally D. Danforth Distinguished Professor of Law and Religion, Washington University in St. Louis

James M. Jasper, Professor Emeritus of Sociology, Graduate Center, City University of New York

Susana Kaiser, Professor Emerita of Media Studies and Latin American Studies, University of San Francisco

Yao Li, Assistant Professor, Department of Sociology, Florida State University

Shan-Jan Sarah Liu, Senior Lecturer in Gender and Politics, School of Social and Political Science, University of Edinburgh

Sarah J. Lockwood, Lecturer in Politics, School of Sociology, Politics and International Studies, University of Bristol; Research Affiliate, Institute for Democracy, Citizenship and Public Policy, University of Cape Town

Gregory P. Magarian, Thomas and Karole Green Professor of Law, Washington University in St. Louis

Megan L. Manion, Clinical Lecturer in Law, Lowenstein International Human Rights Clinic, Yale Law School

Ella McPherson, Associate Professor of the Sociology of New Media and Digital Technology, Department of Sociology, University of Cambridge

David Mead, Professor of UK Human Rights Law, UEA Law School, University of East Anglia

Elly Page, Senior Legal Advisor, International Center for Not-for-Profit Law

Marco Perolini, Visiting Fellow, LSE Human Rights, Department of Sociology, London School of Economics and Political Science

Karen J. Pita Loor, Clinical Professor of Law, Boston University School of Law

Thomas Probert, Senior Researcher, Centre for Human Rights, University of Pretoria; Research Associate, Centre of Governance and Human Rights, University of Cambridge

Adrian Randall, Professor Emeritus of English Social History, University of Birmingham

Nick Robinson, Senior Legal Advisor, International Center for Not-for-Profit Law

Orsolya Salát, Associate Professor, Faculty for Social Sciences, Eötvös Loránd University

Yuval Shany, Hersch Lauterpacht Chair in International Law, Hebrew University of Jerusalem

Sharath Srinivasan, David and Elaine Potter Professor of International Politics, University of Cambridge

Stu Woolman, Elizabeth Bradley Chair of Ethics, Governance and Sustainable Development and Professor of Law, University of the Witwatersrand

Anna Zhelnina, Assistant Professor, Department of Interdisciplinary Social Science, Utrecht University

Timothy Zick, Professor of Law, William & Mary Law School

CHAPTER 1

ON ASSEMBLY

TABATHA ABU EL-HAJ, THOMAS PROBERT, AND SHARATH SRINIVASAN

Introduction

WHY assembly? With a tide of protest worldwide since the 2010s, giving focused attention to peaceful assembly seems easily justified. From Occupy and the Arab Spring to #MeToo, Extinction Rebellion and Black Lives Matter (BLM), ours is a protest age. While assembly is central to the politics of our time, both the right of peaceful assembly and assembly as an independent object of study remain rather neglected. Above all, there is an inattentiveness to what assembly is.

A preoccupation with protest and the law surrounding it elides the fact that assembly is a far more extensive and significant phenomenon than its political public form. From our backyards and front rooms to the street, social media platforms, and town squares, from cultural festivities to sit-ins, from marches of millions to those of just a few, we constantly assemble. Beyond a general impulse to congregate, some kinds of gatherings—whether to exchange views, convey a view towards others, or even come together in solidarity, celebration, or grief—play constitutive roles within vibrant and healthy societies. For those of us invested in the advancement of human rights, the assembly of people at key moments, whether in modest-sized sit-ins or in mass rallies, have often punctuated the progress of a variety of causes, ranging from women's suffrage to the anti-apartheid movement, and from justice for domestic violence to Pride.

Assembly lies at the heart of our existence as social beings, at the foundation of our communities and polities, and at the core of our capacity to collectively begin anew to shape our lives and worlds. Yet, no existing book has assembly *qua* assembly as its primary focus, and there is no comprehensive, let alone multidisciplinary, volume on the right of peaceful assembly in international and domestic human rights law. With rare comparative exceptions, the existing literature on the right of peaceful assembly is remarkably sparse.[1] It is mostly limited in geographic scope and often practically oriented towards mobilization or policing.[2] Violent assemblies and their role in social and political revolutions have received extensive attention from scholars. Peaceful assemblies, much less so.[3] And assembly itself, none.

Even in law, the right of peaceful assembly remains overshadowed by the cognate rights of expression and association. Arguably as a consequence, authorities feel justified in containing, if not outright suppressing, assemblies, especially those that are large and most politically potent, in the knowledge that courts are unlikely to intervene, except in the most extreme instances. This state of affairs persists despite the growing engagements with the right by United Nations bodies, regional human rights mechanisms, and other sources of international standards in recent years.

This Handbook places assembly front and centre, as a distinct social, political, legal, and managerial object of inquiry. It seeks to recover and reimagine the meaning of 'assembly' so as to realize its significance. It argues that this significance is present whether assembly manifests in its untamed political power or its innocuous, quotidian forms.

We believe this approach offers considerable returns. Examining how we have protected and managed assemblies informs not only what the law is but also helps us to consider how we ought to protect and facilitate assemblies. Readers are thus offered a comprehensive understanding of the law of assembly, knowledge deepened by being grounded in historical examples of assemblies analysed as events. But the returns of this endeavour are not limited to legal rights analysis: focusing on assembly as an object of study reveals insights into the nature of society, politics, and power, deepening our understanding of both popular sovereignty and institutionalized government. Examining its dimensions from different perspectives and across time facilitates a deeper understanding of what assembly is, eliciting its nuance, ambiguity, complexity, and tension.

Assembly as Assembly

We need to think about assembly on its own terms. Assembly is a far more extensive and significant phenomenon than its political public form. We cannot reduce assembly to political protest or continue to view it exclusively through an individualized rights lens. These approaches lead to a conception of assembly as exclusively expressive or reduce assembly into its associational elements.

While assemblies may be expressive and may include associative dimensions, assembly remains distinct. Assembly need not have an expressive purpose nor need it be the act of a prior association or the precursor to future association. The act of assembling holds value in its own right. Before examining how adopting a rights-based lens may foreclose some of assembly's potential, we must first understand how the value and significance of assembly extends well beyond the scope of those gatherings brought to mind by a relationship to civic freedoms.

Understanding assembly in a foundational and expansive manner militates against the conflation, too often made, between assembly and public political protest. Marches, rallies, sit-ins, and demonstrations are acts of assembly, but assembly is not limited to these phenomena. Nor should we elevate, amongst these protest assemblies, those that have successfully renegotiated the social contract as the apex of the practice. Similarly, scholarship goes awry when it conflates assemblies with social movements or sees assemblies solely as instrumental, focusing on unpacking the ways social movements can galvanize and bring visibility to causes by assembling. Such approaches ultimately define assemblies as 'political' in a narrow, primarily 'expressive', sense: Groups of individuals gather for the purpose of expressing their views on a political or social issue. Protests, thus, have organizers, and organizers have goals.

There can be no doubt that movement-led protest assemblies command attention. Yet this, perhaps, is precisely because of assembly's distinctive qualities. There is an inherent drama to these gatherings. There is a physicality to the weight of opinion expressed by bodies in the street that exceeds that of signatures on a petition. There is a dynamism to the organization that can take place in a protest encampment that exceeds the membership dues and legal articles of an association. The protest movement conception of what assemblies can achieve is therefore limiting. It introduces a fallacy of instrumentalism: that the significance of assemblies lies in the outcomes they foster.

A further limitation of this understanding of assembly is the added, impliedly or not, modifier 'public'. This privileges a more readily observable form of assembly and also brings with it an intentionality: that what matters about assembly is the willingness to put one's identity and body on the line, physically to go out and publicly identify oneself with one's position. But assemblies may occur for a host of other reasons: less overtly political, less public, and without an instrumental purpose to demand or effect change. Such assemblies are not lesser assemblies, even if they may rarely implicate the protection of the right of peaceful assembly.

When we begin to understand assembly on its own terms, beyond and beside expression and association, as not only taking the form of public political protests, we encounter a much wider phenomenon that is a distinctly and integrally valuable aspect of our social, cultural, and political lives across public and private realms. The oft-quoted maxim that human beings are social animals is used to explain various features of human psychology and conjures certain connotations of sociability, gregariousness, affection, and communality. We assemble at weddings and wakes, at sports matches and music performances, in homes and halls. Increasingly, it has been clear that we are assembling, remotely, in many of our activities online.

Indeed, when we see that we spend our lives assembling, assembly's distinctive qualities come into closer view. In acts of assembling, people form senses of belonging and shape and nourish their identities. Assembling is also a physical act. It possesses, as Judith Butler explains, qualities of embodiment. Bodies assembling also often exchange with speech and gesture, the combinations of which contain distinctive affective or emotive qualities that are experienced and felt with meaning. Here, assembled people possess between them a certain capacity to begin doing new things together. This capacity for what Hannah Arendt calls 'natality' is a collective agency, or power, that lies only with the assembled people.

Assembly is also about solidarity. The act of assembling may generate solidarity just as it may express a pre-existing solidarity. This might entail generating political solidarity directed towards others, fostered in a forum in which commonality surges in a very visceral sense. Or alternatively, assemblies and gatherings may be explicitly and reflexively engaged in expressing solidarity, and deriving comfort or support from collective presence ('Pride' parades are so-called for a reason). Importantly, such solidarity, shared values, belonging, and recognition can be achieved from forms of assembly that do not possess a deliberately political valence and may not be in public.

A central claim of this Handbook is that the experience of assembling is of intrinsic value to humans as social and political beings. The assembly lies at the beginning and coming into being of many of our collective experiences.

The 'Right' of Peaceful Assembly

Placing assembly front and centre as a distinct social and political phenomenon also enables us to rethink assembly as a legal and managerial object of inquiry. It is remarkable that all but nine of the United Nations' 193 member states recognize a right to peacefully assemble. The right is also enshrined in several regional and international human rights instruments. Article 21 of the International Covenant on Civil and Political Rights (ICCPR) articulates the right as an affirmative state obligation: 'The right of peaceful assembly shall be recognized'.

Yet the opposite is also true: Notwithstanding near universal recognition, the right protects only a diminished form of assembly, and only in the social or political form that authorities find tolerable. Indeed, the rights framing inherently reinforces a narrow conception of assembly as the public political assembly that authorities find threatening but may tolerate up to a point. The COVID-19 pandemic offers insights into what might be lost by this conception. The pandemic created a different kind of imperative and interest in restricting a broader range of assembly. For epidemiological reasons, governments suddenly became less interested in what motivated people to come together bodily. This occurred at the same time that people suddenly realized how much they valued the opportunity to share space with others for a whole range of purposes. We used online platforms to approximate some of these spaces, with varying degrees of success.

The first-order issue, then, is that the rights framing inherently reinforces a narrow conception of assembly. Codified as an individual 'civil and political right', and qualified as 'peaceful', our attention is diverted and distracted towards the specific, narrower, though undoubtedly significant, political phenomenon that is of particular interest to the state and its relationship with citizens. The right of peaceful assembly covers a circumscribed kernel of a much more foundational and extensive social and political phenomenon.

The problem goes beyond this first-order issue, however. Even accepting that the right, as codified and construed, is tailored to a narrow conception of assembly, its articulation as a qualified right—a right of *peaceful* assembly—when combined with its typical manifestation as an assembly on the public square means it is largely only protected in the social or political forms that authorities find tolerable. The right has been codified to enhance the legitimacy of the dominion of authorities over their subjects, rather than to enhance the human freedom—sociality, autonomy, and instrumental effectiveness—that makes assembly worthy of human rights protection in the first place. Its frailty arises out of the intersection of this narrow articulation of the right and the characteristics of assembly and its policing. Three intersecting factors work to weaken the right: the 'peaceful' constraint, the recognition of a state interest in public order in the public square, and a tendency towards managerialism.

The peacefulness constraint invites authorities to closely manage conduct at assemblies to ensure they remain within the confines of the right. The 'peaceful assembly' as commonly conceived is thus defined by what it is not. It is not a riot or a revolution; it is a legitimate form of political protest. Superficially uncontroversial (since, who, after all, would see an inherent value in protecting violent assembly?), this limit becomes problematic because of the role played by government authorities in drawing lines around what counts as peaceful and their tendency to do so in exclusionary ways that conserve their own power.

Even when violence is not a concern, the exclusion of non-peaceful forms of assembly discursively contrasts the valorized 'peaceful protest' to highly disruptive forms of assembly. In this way, the regulation and taming of assembly—its spontaneity, autonomy, and power—is justified, and highly disruptive forms of assembly are denigrated. Authorities are invited by the very language of the right to engage in significant line drawing. The insistence on the modifier 'peaceful' leads to questions: What needs to be protected? What can we categorically state people are entitled to do? At what point does the interest in public order or the competing interests of others justify restrictions? These questions in turn invite authorities to choreograph assemblies to diminish their disruptiveness, but also their spontaneity.

The space for assembly is thus routinely constricted by 'limitations' embedded within the rights framing. Some—such as the imperatives of public health or public safety—relate to broader expectations we have of the state. But some others significantly (if maybe necessarily) embed exclusionary power. The most explicit in this regard is the expectation that the right only extends to those assemblies that do not compromise 'public order'. While rights bodies and some courts have attempted to define this concept narrowly, it has a capacious ability in the political and public imagination to delegitimize a wide array of potentially valuable assemblies.

The seemingly reasonable proportionality principle that pervades human rights law further constricts the space for assembly. The codification of a proportionality principle in a context where there are inevitably many points of contact between authorities and those exercising their rights in public invites the exercise of discretion. This weighing exercise (in the language of the ICCPR framed as the potential limitation of the right for the sake of the 'protection of the rights and freedoms of others') also invites a hierarchy in which there are certain kinds of assembly (politically salient protest) that can justify far greater disruption to the ordinary lives of other members of the public than, say, a sporting event or a concert that might attract the same number of people.

Flowing from this balancing and from the state's acceptance of a set of positive obligations related to the facilitation of peaceful assemblies comes a third potential cost of the rights framing: managerialism. The combination of the duty to accommodate and facilitate an assembly alongside wider duties of protection owed both to assembly participants and the public at large leads to a significant impulse on the part of the state to seek to manage the potential externalities and risks of mass gatherings.

Thus, assembly is rendered primarily a phenomenon to be contained in ways that balance the interests of those exercising the right with the general societal interest in public order—an approach reinforced by the assumption that assemblies have organizers who can undertake this managerial task. Some of this has been a product of developments in human rights practice, such as encouraging states to move away from 'public order policing' towards 'crowd management'. While this development, with its rejection of rigid conceptions of orderliness, is commendable in many respects, it represents another form of taming, denuding assembly of its unpredictable and spontaneous essence.

Practices such as notification or prior stakeholder engagement meetings, though potentially well-grounded in the experience of risk management and mitigation, do not sit easily alongside the potential for improvisation and innovation of assembly, untamed and unbounded. Developments in policing itself raise similar concerns. The recent watchword for the policing of assemblies has become 'no surprises'—originating from a well-intentioned commitment that the police owe the public clarity about what will happen when or why. While it has been stressed that such a commitment can only be expected in one direction—that assembly organizers have no parallel responsibility to apprise authorities of their intentions (beyond routine notification, where applicable)—it is unclear whether state authorities will ever fully accept the discomforting one-directional legal obligation and the challenges this presents, especially when those assembled reject, in whole or in part, their authority to govern.

Authorization regimes have been found to be incompatible with the enjoyment of the right. Nevertheless, the astute observation made of them by the former UN Special Rapporteur Maina Kiai, that having to ask permission to exercise a right cuts against the very essence of its character as a right, holds equally for other forms of managerialism. The state generally cannot dictate to individuals how they should exercise their rights: when, where, how, or for how long—and individuals should not be expected necessarily to know any of those things in advance.

The tendency towards managerialism—this tendency of the right in practice to be delimited, administered, and choreographed to protect only a diminished form of assembly that authorities find tolerable—is exacerbated by the failure of human rights discourse to clearly articulate assembly's specific added value. Assembly has routinely been grouped together with two other civic freedoms—freedom of expression and freedom of association. These three rights undoubtedly reinforce each other, but assembly discourse has been underdeveloped by comparison. The result is a failure to articulate forms of protection that are specifically tailored to assembly's power and significance. Instead, a logic of pervasive regulation and management has prevailed. The voice given to agents of control and violation in the context of international debates about the right of peaceful assembly is unparalleled in any other associated field.

Placing assembly front and centre reveals the inherent fragility of the right of peaceful assembly. The seemingly reasonable exclusion of non-peaceful forms of assembly from protection creates a logic that justifies regulatory and managerial approaches that can undercut the very sociality, autonomy, and, at times, instrumental effectiveness that make assembly worthy of human rights protection in the first place. This is true even if we take at face value that the right of assembly, as a practical matter, was designed primarily to protect a narrow conception of assembly as public protest.

Whether the right of peaceful assembly's narrowness and fragility is an inherent defect of its design, a product of how it has been construed, or an effect of who decides is an open question worthy of debate. What is clear is that if the right of peaceful assembly is based on an impoverished account of assembly's wider significance to society, the right is invariably going to be construed too narrowly. The state's management and regulation of the right and the curtailment of its potency and potential become somewhat inevitable. It is thus no surprise that the tide of political protest worldwide in recent years has been met with increased legal restrictions and stronger containment by many states.

The fundamental failure, then, is the failure adequately to value assembly. It is only by appreciating the full reach and range of assembly as a historically foundational social, cultural, and political phenomenon that assembly's crucial importance for society is given due value. The paradox of assembly is that it is fundamental to our social lives, a kind of substrate of society, and thus it often goes out of view. What is more visible is a more limited, regulated, and choreographed form. By coming to see assembly only in narrow ways shaped heavily by the management of the right and its relationship to protest, assembly's wider significance is obscured, contributing to the right's greater fragility.

This Handbook

We have articulated two claims about broadening the lens through which we analyse the phenomenon of assembly. The first is that the observable practice of assembling is a far more thoroughgoing, pervasive, and meaningful human activity than the much-heralded public protest assembly. Assembly takes various alternate forms that speak to its intrinsic value to human societies and how it provides diverse benefits to participants beyond the instrumentally political. Reducing assembly to its public protest form, or to its expressive or associational qualities, diminishes assembly's wider significance. The second claim is that studying and thinking about assembly only from the perspective of a 'right' to be enjoyed may ultimately reinforce and replicate logics of regulation that too readily and excessively tame the potential of assembly as a practice. This is in large part because of the way the right has been codified and the way that the register of legal analysis demands a great deal of boundary-drawing: What is and is not 'peaceful'? How should competing equities and rights to 'public space' be balanced? And so forth. Still, understanding the existing right of peaceful assembly is critical—both to the larger project of reimagining it and for human rights advocates and activists working right now.

This Handbook is guided by these two claims. It thus explores the value of assembly beyond its political and protest forms, but also the law of assembly. Each is explored from a broad range of disciplines, including sociology, anthropology, political theory, and history as well as law. Specifically, as regards peaceful assembly, the chapters that follow offer a variety of insights and paths to a more robust construction of the right. The chapters identify and explore many of the logics of regulation, both in the conventional sense (such as notification and policing) but also in less commonly considered venues (such as algorithms and courtrooms). In some instances, reflexive accounts have been written by participants, and several chapters have been written by those engaging professionally with assemblies, either as law enforcement officials or as civil rights attorneys. In addition, we have also commissioned several shorter, more descriptive chapters that have considered historic assemblies as 'events'. These have not been chosen to be representative and are obviously not exhaustive, but they provide many illustrative examples of the themes raised in the other parts of the Handbook.

The Value and Roles of Assembly

As we have noted, peaceful assemblies tend to be understood as political protests that are mostly in public and ones that are often significant in scale and in their contentiousness. It is unquestionable that the protection of the right in those contexts matters greatly to citizen-authority relations. However, assembly's full significance is underappreciated. For one thing, as Tabatha Abu El-Haj argues, our tendency to focus on historic assemblies calling for major social or political change misses how more quotidian assemblies 'sustain and reinforce the capacity for democratic politics'. Assemblies are not merely important because of their instrumental effects or expressive qualities, observed especially in momentous protests. Assemblies hold intrinsic, latent, and constitutive political functions. Both the possibility of effective democratic politics and the proper construction of the right of peaceful assembly demand that we recognize the value of assembly as assembly.

Historicizing the right reveals a more complex relationship between assembly and violence than is typically appreciated. Adrian Randall shows us how, in the English context, the origins of the right lie in the suppression of a period of riotous dissent and participatory politics. This was an unstable time characterized by a more decentralized state and in which citizens had a sense of their sovereign right to make collective claims and take action. Eighteenth-century Englishmen, he tells us, felt entitled to be riotous 'when customary rights and expectations, or livelihoods were threatened'. Participants in disruptive, even violent, assemblies often viewed themselves as 'enforcing rather than breaking the law'—as engaged in self-help when the state failed to deliver its promise. Peaceful assembly arose out of the taming of such politics, at a time when the political franchise was extended to the middle classes and authority was increasingly centralized. Randall argues that peaceful assembly was not a product 'of moral or intellectual improvement but of brute circumstance' and thus urges us to question whether the right of 'peaceful assembly' should be viewed as an unqualified accomplishment. Even so, participants may choose to be peaceful. Micah Alpaugh's discussion of the Women's March on Versailles, France, in 1789 provides a very early example of a gathering where the potentiality of violence must have been quite palpable. However, as he shows, even when drawn into standoffs with authorities, the participants pursued predominantly peaceful protest techniques, and their intervention quite likely prevented widespread bloodshed during a time of incredible political turmoil.

Pushing back on what 'peaceful assembly' has come to mean and what its narrow construal disallows is also a theme taken up by Stu Woolman. Woolman presents the most forceful defence of a limited place for violence within a constitutional right of assembly. He fears that the right of peaceful assembly in its modern constitutional form, in which violence is never justified, risks displacing 'the democratic politics that animates the freedom to assemble, to deliberate and to act collectively as equal citizens'. Drawing upon a critical rereading of Martin Luther King, Jr., Judith Butler, and Hannah Arendt, Woolman asks us to countenance the possibility of the legitimacy of 'the occasional use of force' by outgroups in order to participate in the self-governance of the polity, and decries how too often in the contemporary regulation of peaceful assembly incidental property damage is equated with violence to discredit and delegitimate assemblies. The prospect of violence as a justification for the use of force against assemblies by authorities has a long and troubling history, as exemplified in Iain Channing's account of the Peterloo massacre in Manchester in 1819. Nevertheless, to Woolman's point, Channing shows how the use of excessive force to coerce an assembly will often boomerang back in the longer term to discredit those wielding the power.

This attention to limits and boundaries of what comes to count as assembly is also prominent in Sharath Srinivasan's search for a political theory of assembly. Assembly as a distinctive mode of politics is largely banished in modern political frameworks that are preoccupied with coercive state power, representative government, and individual liberty. Similar to Randall, for Srinivasan, in contemporary political thought and practice 'the right of peaceful assembly' serves to legitimate dominant conceptions of politics that, paradoxically, leave little place for the assembled people. The sporadic protest assembly is tolerated and tamed at the boundary of ordinary politics, but this also pushes assembly as self-government out of bounds. Srinivasan recovers a global history of popular assembly as a mode of self-government distinct from the history of assembly as protest. He uses this to advance a theory of politics in which the full significance of assembly and its distinctive form of political power comes to light.

Yet, assembly's distinctive qualities should not be reduced to modes of doing politics. Resonating with Abu El-Haj's call for greater attention to assembly's non-expressive qualities, John Inazu sheds light on assembly's important role for sustaining pluralism and identity formation in society. Assembly is a vital social activity that plays a distinct role between expression and association, linking the gathering and the group. Dominic Bryan's account, drawn from his own ethnographic observation, of the 12 July parades in Northern Ireland paints a particularly vivid picture of the role of assemblies in manifesting community identities (albeit while highlighting that many of the 'traditions' associated with them may be inconsistent and relatively novel).

A striking feature of assembly is that it can be a type of action, an entity, or a form. The act of assembly can be a strategic choice (amongst others) for contemporary social movements, as Anna Zhelnina and James Jasper explain. Assembly here is a key choice in the repertoire of social movement action that is heavily shaped by strategic trade-offs and dilemmas, as well as by the reaction of others to past action and by contingency and uncertainty in the event. It is also a part of the repertoire of broader protest tactics, interestingly explored by Susana Kaiser in her discussion of the *escraches* movement in Argentina, where the event of the assembly amplifies the documentation and public shaming of the targets of the protest.

The contingency of assembly often relates to the political context within which assembly is enabled or constrained in different ways. For Zhelnina and Jasper, the coercive context of Russian politics in recent decades bears heavily on the dilemmas faced by protesters. Yet Yao Li argues that the tendency to see assembly's promise and possibility in democracies as very different than in authoritarian contexts is problematic. Both the capacity for contentious politics to exhibit violence and the potential for authorities to coercively repress assemblies exist in democracies as much as in authoritarian polities.

Compared to assembling as something that certain actors choose to do, the assembly can be its own entity, in which its members understand themselves to *be* the assembly. If we are to recentre assembly in democratic theory, we must contend with the relationship of the assembled people with popular sovereignty. Perhaps it is the assembly itself that acts in the world. Indeed, as Asli İkizoğlu Erensü's probing examination of refugee protest camps in Germany and South Africa suggests, the assembly may constitute an embodied foundational politics of placemaking—'staging a collective taking of the right to a place in the world'. A grounded understanding of the role of occupying place in how assemblies enact their distinctive sociopolitical significance can be appreciated in two other chapters that consider protest encampments: Tara Houska's personal reflection upon her time among those protesting the Dakota Access Pipeline at Standing Rock, including some of the deliberative decision-making processes involved; and Marco Perolini's discussion of the refugee O-Platz protest in Berlin, emblematic of İkizoğlu Erensü's point about such occupations being a turning point for migrant visibility.

Whether or not it is placemaking, as a distinct form of social and political practice, assembly arises out of past practices, places, and histories. As Sarah Lockwood explains, this is especially so in the context of assembly in the postcolony. For Lockwood, the historical embeddedness of assembly practices in the postcolony motivates a wider call for historicizing how we study the practice of assembly within longer enduring social and political struggles. Rabab El-Mahdi's chapter demonstrates that this kind of reassessment of the role of iconic and transformative assemblies can happen relatively soon after the event. Her chapter, which seeks to problematize some of the accounts of the 2011 protests in Tahrir Square, makes clear how the socially constructed memory of an assembly can influence perceptions and tactics of protest moving forward. Yet this connection between the practice of assembly past, present, and future might be subtle, as Abu El-Haj's insightful analogy of an 'easement' shows in considering how the practice of small assemblies may make momentous assemblies possible (a point also evident from El-Mahdi's account).

Histories of assembly may not only be subtle: They may indeed be silenced. Peaceful assembly is historically gendered, as Sarah Liu argues, and women's constrained participation in assembly is too readily erased or reduced to a focus on women's rights. Looking towards future scholarship on the value and role of assembly, Liu calls for a feminist and intersectional approach, such as that provided by Louise du Toit, in her focus upon the role of women within the Satyagraha movement during Gandhi's protests in South Africa.

Across these contributions, the Handbook decisively intervenes with a demand that if the right of peaceful assembly is to be given its proper due, assembly must be placed more centre stage as an object of study, within a richer and more expansive understanding of the value of assembly and its historical experience.

The Law of Assembly

The law of assembly comprises two interrelated parts: the right of peaceful assembly *and* the practices of governmental management (including planning, surveillance, and policing). Law, in other words, as sociolegal scholars have long argued, comprises both the law of statutes and courts and the law-in-action, implemented by authorities and contested by legal actors. Although we question whether assembly should be understood exclusively through this legal lens, the fact is that the law of assembly matters. The legal register, as we have argued, invites both line-drawing and vague balancing tests that inherently favour the government and, thereby, undermine the freedom of assembly. It thus matters a great deal for individuals around the world where and how these boundaries are drawn.

A number of chapters in the Handbook illustrate this central dynamic of the right: the preoccupation and difficulties in drawing boundaries and how this creates uncertainty and room for discretion that routinely impacts individuals seeking to exercise their right. As Yuval Shany explains, even after we recognize that the right of peaceful assembly need not be confined to political assemblies, many critical questions remain about the boundaries of the right. These include how purposeful or intentional a gathering must be to fall within the legal protection, whether participants must share a 'common expressive purpose', and whether the right is limited to protecting 'public' assemblies—as well as how that concept should be defined. The definition of 'peaceful' also remains contested, including whether it defines coverage (as in only assemblies that are peaceful are covered) or whether it should be construed as a limit on the right (an individual is protected until they cease to act peacefully). And perhaps most pressingly, given the significance of social media, is it critical that participants assemble simultaneously, let alone gather physically?

Various authors take up these particular questions, demonstrating that there are better and worse ways to draw these boundaries. Like Shany, each argues that these open questions must be resolved according to 'the interests and values that underlie the right'. Ella McPherson and Davide Beraldo, for example, each wrestle, from a sociological perspective, with the definition of 'assembly' itself. For McPherson, the worldwide lockdown in 2020 in response to COVID-19 forever put an end to debates about whether online assemblies are assemblies. When all the normal places for assembling were gone for all purposes, we learned that online spaces could provide important fora for assembly, thus freeing us to theorize about digitally mediated assembly. Beraldo's narrative account of Anonymous, 'an "extreme case"' of online assembly makes a similar point. Although Anonymous has many unique features as a digital assembly, including its members' commitment to participate anonymously, it 'surface[s] properties that are, to a certain extent, implicit characteristics of any kind of assembly'. McPherson ultimately considers how the distinct features of digitally mediated assembly should inform the designing of communication technologies, offering a theory of assembly affordances—a method by which to ensure that online spaces remain both available and capable of supporting assemblies. Cameran Ashraf takes a similar approach to the legal regulation of artificial intelligence, noting the ways that the right of assembly is threatened by opaque artificial intelligence systems that moderate content and determine which opportunities for peaceful assembly are allowed to exist online.

Orsolya Salát and David Mead are preoccupied with a different boundary question: How should the law delineate the boundaries of peacefulness? Salát highlights that among our basic human rights, the right of assembly is uniquely constrained by the limit that it be undertaken peacefully and suggests, like Woolman, that this limit should be understood to be intimately entwined with authorities' ambivalence towards assemblies given their association with violence, revolution, and popular sovereignty. With this in mind, she turns to her analytic project, breaking the peacefulness constraint down still further by asking: How should we define 'peacefully'? Whose peacefulness should matter? And what should the threshold for violence be? Mead, meanwhile, turns to the question of when disruption might count as non-peaceful. While 'non-violent but disruptive protest is not per se outside the protective scope of the international law framework', the legality of efforts by authorities to regulate or disperse contentious forms of disruption, such as physical blockages, he notes, depends on how the standard of proportionality analysis is administered.

Yet it is immediately apparent that the state is not a unitary bloc, and courts are not the only let alone, primary, institution in which the legal boundaries of assembly are defined. A range of government actors, beyond courts, exercise significant discretion to draw lines and manage the conduct of assemblies. Any legitimacy-based critique must, therefore, parse more carefully the different pressures operating on specific branches and agencies. In this regard, various authors turn to the onerous regulatory constraints with which executive officials (administrators and police) define the contours within which assembly occurs. Elly Page and Nick Robinson's chapter, more than any other, demonstrates why human rights advocates worry about the inadequacy of the right of peaceful assembly to protect protest movements worldwide. Authoritarian and democratic governments alike, they argue, are increasingly engaged in a range of illiberal legal practices to control demonstrations, including restricting if, where, and when protests occur; criminalizing the activity of non-violent protesters; and targeting the broader ecosystem within which protests occur to undermine their impact. This is consistent with the sociological work in Li's chapter.

Several chapters show that these illiberal practices are enabled by the way in which international and national law provides that competing equities and rights should be balanced. It is the need to undertake these balancing assessments, for example, that nominally justifies notification requirements, whereby organizers are expected to pre-advise an authority of their intention to enjoy a basic human right—a prior regulatory burden which does not have a parallel with respect to any other right. Indeed, from there, it is a small step (at least, for some jurisdictions) to more onerous authorization regimes. In this regard, Michael Hamilton argues, there is a need to recognize the fragility of the distinction between notification and authorization regimes and (echoing C. Edwin Baker) to fundamentally rethink the taken-for-granted acceptance of mandatory notification requirements altogether. Hamilton (like Baker) favours instead the expansion of incentivized voluntary notification schemes, those that operate without threat of sanction.

One additional consequence of a notification regime is opening up sites of contention before an assembly can even take place. Negotiations between organizers and participants about various key dimensions of the proposed assembly, even when undertaken in good faith, are ripe for controversy, as demonstrated by David Goldberger's chapter on the proposed rally of the neo-Nazi National Socialist Party of America in the Chicago suburb of Skokie in 1976. Goldberger describes how the litigation over these negotiations, in which he represented the organizer on behalf of the American Civil Liberties Union, brought huge public attention to the rally as well as a significant counter-protest. In the end, part of the solution to the conflict was an agreement that a limited rally could take place in Marquette Park, drawing upon its traditional role as a public forum—a space in which assemblies of any and all political valences could be held.

The role of spaces with a unique history of assembly plays a critical role in cutting through otherwise inhospitable political contexts, as discussed in Lockwood's chapter on assembly in the postcolony but also evident in Lynette Chua's chapter on the Pink Dot assemblies in Singapore. In that case, the distinctive status afforded to Hong Lim Park, where prior license approval is not needed but where speakers must still avoid sensitive subjects of race and religion, was critical to the emergence of Pink Dot. The park's singular legal status of requiring only notification before assembling created the opportunity for what Chua terms 'pragmatic resistance' on the part of the LGBTQ community.

Timothy Zick and Gregory Magarian wrestle in more specific contexts with this same concern about how to balance competing equities and rights. Zick explores a significantly underdeveloped area of the law of assembly, namely, whether peaceful assemblies should have a right to gather and communicate within the 'sight and sound' of intended audiences. His answer is a resounding yes, urging future courts to recognize that '[t]he question goes to the very heart of the meaningful exercise of rights of assembly'. Magarian turns to a different thorny question: whether the affirmative right of assembly should be understood to include a corresponding right to exclude unwanted participants. In the United States, it does; in Europe, it does not.

Like many of the authors in the Handbook, Zick and Magarian argue that courts should more thoroughly attend to the underlying values of assembly in delineating the contours of the right. Magarian argues that liberal democratic commitments to equal citizenship, pluralism, and collective self-governance counsel against an expansive understanding of the right that includes a right to exclude. Zick, by contrast, argues that because spaces often have vocality—social meanings—the ability to choose the location of a protest not only shapes its communicative power but also advances other interests, including the autonomy interests of the group. The autonomy interests vindicated by sight and sound rights and the inherent tension with the privacy or property rights of others are well-illustrated in Kaiser's chapter.

The critical point is that the law of assembly is not just conceptual. It also manifests in the logic of regulation. Legal preoccupation with boundary setting and balancing expands the managerial control that authorities exercise. This is evident in Mead's discussion of how proportionality analysis has been used to undermine legal protection for disruptive but not obstructive assemblies. It is also what drives Zick's concern that across jurisdictions courts offer limited recognition for sight and sound rights.

Beyond this, what is evident from many of the chapters is that the formal legal regulations concerning assemblies are necessarily open to a great deal of discretion in application. This means that the enjoyment of the right can be highly vulnerable to sudden shifts in regulatory attitude, as might, for example, be the case during moments of high political tension—arguably when assembly and its discursive and expressive benefits are most needed. Megan Manion demonstrates how the right has proved fragile in situations of emergency, principally those declared to counterterrorism, but also, recently, due to the COVID-19 pandemic. She raises an alarm about the risk posed by substantial deference to states in the perpetuation of a constant 'emergency' footing.

As Otto Adang's chapter reveals, however, states do not need a declared state of emergency to justify their restrictions upon the people massed outdoors. States both engender and appear to respond to a latent but persistent fear of the 'mob' among the wider population. Adang argues such perceptions have for a long time found justification in psychology, where it was once maintained that an inherent pathology attributable to crowds made them more susceptible to disorder and violence. These outmoded theories, he argues, were based on conjecture and defy the empirical fact of the absence of violence in the vast majority of crowds. Instead, Adang argues that 'crowd behaviour can only meaningfully be understood in the social context in which it occurs as an intergroup process'.

Whereas the older (and now widely discredited) crowd psychology contributed to policing strategies such as 'escalated force', this social context insight has prompted newer policing approaches that are dedicated to communication. As Thomas Probert argues, it is time to abandon the various grand theories of 'protest policing' (escalated force, negotiated management, strategic incapacitation) that all share the characteristic of implicitly sanctioning the choreographing, rather than facilitating, of peaceful assembly, and to replace them with an approach to policing grounded in General Comment No. 37, which suggests that by and large police should leave assemblies alone, to the greatest extent possible, interfering with them only when necessary, and only in a content-neutral fashion. Probert argues that our analysis should shift to a tactic-by-tactic approach that emphasizes the police's obligation to facilitate assembly. He underscores that officers on the street enjoy a very high level of discretion in choosing appropriate tactics and responding to evolving situations. This can be particularly challenging with respect to peaceful but highly disruptive assemblies of the kind discussed by Mead. Houska's chapter on Standing Rock and Karen Pita Loor's discussion of Black Lives Matter illustrate both some very questionable decisions made by authorities and the way in which they are experienced as opportunities for further resistance.

Emerging from both Adang and Probert's contributions is a strong normative focus on the conduct of the individual within the assembly, rather than the assembly as a whole, for as long as it is feasible to do so. This is very much the approach of international standards concerning the use of force in the context of assemblies, as further explored by Stuart Casey-Maslen. Underlining the significance of the precautionary approach, Casey-Maslen emphasizes the importance of both direct factors, such as training and equipment, and less direct context, such as legal and accountability frameworks. The ultimate goal is to ensure that officers on the ground only use such force as is necessary and proportionate to the prevailing circumstances.

As Channing's chapter on Peterloo demonstrates, the possibility for organized state actors to overreact to the perceived threat of large assemblies has been a challenge for as long as there have been professional police forces. In her chapter about the Black Lives Matter movement and the waves of policing responses, Pita Loor powerfully illustrates how much work needs to be done to bring national practice into line with the norms laid out by Probert and Casey-Maslen. Substantial evidence of police violence towards those demonstrations, Pita Loor argues, justifies stripping officers of their authority to make warrantless arrests of protesters for non-violent misdemeanours, and, more generally, indicates that when courts review officers' actions during protests, the Fourth Amendment 'reasonableness calculus' should shift from whether their action is reasonable to whether it is *reasonable in light of freedom of expression*.

In the context of these sometimes under-constrained law enforcement powers, Casey-Maslen, Probert, and Pita Loor all advert to the threat posed by new weapons technologies. However, as Val Aston's chapter demonstrates, other forms of technological development also have significant implications for the legal questions surrounding the policing of assembly. Surveillance systems designed to monitor public space, from closed-circuit television (CCTV) to facial recognition technologies, are so pervasive that few assemblies are spared the now ubiquitous deployment of police officers holding cameras or watching remotely from behind CCTV. Courts, however, have been decidedly slow to appreciate the complex harms that the visible monitoring of public spaces inflicts on acts of assembly or the process of mobilization, let alone how they burden the right of peaceful assembly.

What is clear is that courts must play an important role in safeguarding the right in the face of this and other challenges. Courts should establish important thresholds for regulatory power and should play a vital role as a check, in retrospect, of the discretion exercised by officers on the street. Unfortunately, as Salát observes from her comparative research, too often courts construe un-peacefulness too broadly, waxing eloquently about the right of assembly while regularly upholding prior bans, dispersals, and even preventative detention. Mead raises similar concerns about recent doctrinal developments in the European Court of Human Rights that risk undercutting protection for disruptive assembly in the future. Steven Cammiss, Brian Doherty, and Graeme Hayes elevate this concern by raising questions about the efficacy of courts in vindicating assembly rights. Their chapter starts by recognizing that courts are not just places of adjudication but are also social spaces. Thus, in the context of protests, courts often become sites for a continuation of the expressive purpose of organizers and participants and thus are part of the long tail of an assembly's impact. Where assembly is designed to be disruptive and to break or contest regulatory limits, participants often view the almost-inevitable trial as the next venue for the kind of pragmatic resistance discussed by Chua. Cammiss, Doherty, and Hayes, however, caution that courts will not necessarily be the venue for the most effective protection or vindication of the right, either as a social spectacle or in terms of their factual or legal finding. Taken together these authors do not offer an encouraging assessment of the current state of the right's protection in international or domestic law. Ironically, the one exception here is policing, where international legal standards provide clear grounds from which to condemn the over-policing of assemblies based on the principles that police tactics must be guided by both content neutrality and a presumption in favour of continued facilitation.

Several authors thus emphasize that a fuller account of the substantive value of assembly *qua* assembly is necessary if the contours of the legal right are to be redrawn in ways that more fully protect peaceful assembly. Boundary determinations should be informed by a fuller recognition of the independent functions and purposes of assembly, as Abu El-Haj and Salát argue. For several, the starting point is to delineate the boundaries between the right of peaceful assembly and the cognate rights of expression and association. Even as all three rights similarly seek to vindicate, in Magarian's words, 'liberal democratic values of equal citizenship, pluralism, and collective self-governance', we must move away from viewing assembly as a lesser, even superfluous, or redundant, right among a broader group of civic freedoms.

Conclusion

The contributions in this volume make an important intervention: enriching our understanding by providing a fuller, wider, and deeper account of the value of assembly while drawing attention to the extent to which the limitations on the right are often interpreted too restrictively. They also offer support for the two basic claims that we have made. They demonstrate that assembling is a far more thoroughgoing, pervasive, and meaningful human activity than the much-heralded public protest assembly. In doing so, they highlight the array of intrinsic benefits it offers participants beyond the instrumentally political. The chapters also support our second claim that a scholarly focus on assembly exclusively through a rights framework may ultimately reinforce and replicate logics of regulation that too readily and excessively tame the potential of assembly as a practice. In particular, they more fully demonstrate what we mean when we say that the rights framing and the specific way *this* right has been codified reinforce a narrow conception of assembly and the scope for its protection. They display the many ways its frailty arises out of the intersection of a narrow articulation of the right and the characteristics of assembly and its policing.

Above all, however, what the chapters in this Handbook show is that by placing assembly front and centre, as a distinct social, political, legal, and managerial object of inquiry, we can begin to develop a deeper understanding of the existing right of peaceful assembly and lay the groundwork for imagining a broader and more robust construction of the right. This is an important intervention at this critical juncture in our new age of protest.

Notes

1. For a comparative account, see Orsolya Salát, *The Right to Freedom of Assembly a Comparative Study* (Oxford: Hart Publishing, 2015). Most existing scholarship that directly attends to assembly tends to be historical or theoretical, or old and ripe for update. See, for example, Jason Frank, *The Democratic Sublime: On Aesthetics and Popular Assembly* (New York: Oxford University Press, 2021); Judith Butler, *Notes Toward a Performative Theory of Assembly* (Cambridge, MA: Harvard University Press, 2015); Antonio Negri and Michael Hardt, *Assembly* (New York: Oxford University Press, 2017); Mabra Glenn Abernathy, *The Right of Assembly and Association* (Columbia: University of South Carolina Press, 1961); Amitai Etzioni, *Demonstration Democracy* (New York: Gordon and Breach, 1970).
2. Jurisdiction-specific literature includes, for example, Roger N. Douglas, *Dealing with Demonstrations: The Law of Public Protest and Its Enforcement* (Sydney: Federation Press, 2004); Jane Duncan, *Protest Nation: The Right to Protest in South Africa* (Pietermaritzburg: University of KwaZulu Natal Press, 2021); David Kretzmer, 'Demonstrations and the Law', *Israel Law Review* 19, no. 1 (1984): 47–153; David Mead, *The New Law of Peaceful Protest Rights and Regulation in the Human Rights Act Era* (Oxford: Hart Publishing, 2010); Peter E. Quint, *Civil Disobedience and the German Courts: The Pershing Missile*

Protests in Comparative Perspective (London: Routledge-Cavendish, 2007); Tabatha Abu El-Haj, 'The Neglected Right of Assembly', *UCLA Law Review* 56, no. 3 (2009): 543–589; John D. Inazu, *Liberty's Refuge: The Forgotten Freedom of Assembly* (New Haven, CT: Yale University Press, 2012); Timothy Zick, *Managed Dissent: The Law of Public Protest* (Cambridge: Cambridge University Press, 2023); Timothy Zick, *Speech Out of Doors: Preserving First Amendment Liberties in Public Places* (Cambridge: Cambridge University Press, 2009). There is also extensive literature on protest policing. See, for example, P. A. J. Waddington, *Liberty and Order: Public Order Policing in a Capital City* (London: UCL Press, 1994); Donatella Della Porta, Abby Peterson, and Herbert Reiter, eds., *The Policing of Transnational Protest* (Aldershot, UK: Routledge, 2006); Vern Neufeld Redekop and Shirley Paré, *Beyond Control: A Mutual Respect Approach to Protest Crowd-Police Relations* (London: Bloomsbury Academic, 2010); Amory Starr, Luis A. Fernández, and Christian Scholl, *Shutting Down the Streets: Political Violence and Social Control in the Global Era* (New York: New York University Press, 2011); Andrea Flores Khalil, *Crowds and Politics in North Africa: Tunisia, Algeria and Libya* (London: Routledge, 2014); Matt Foot and Morag Livingstone, *Charged: How the Police Try to Supress Protest* (London: Verso Books, 2022)—though again, many policing texts are more generally focused on public order policing than on assemblies.

3. The literature on protest is much more wide-ranging, stemming predominantly from scholarship in the field of social movement studies. See, for example, Hank Johnston, *States and Social Movements* (Cambridge: Polity Press, 2011); Felix Kolb, *Protest and Opportunities: The Political Outcomes of Social Movements* (Chicago: University of Chicago Press, 2007); David S. Meyer, *The Politics of Protest: Social Movements in America* (New York: Oxford University Press, 2007); Karl-Dieter Opp, *Theories of Political Protest and Social Movements: A Multidisciplinary Introduction, Critique, and Synthesis* (London: Routledge, 2009); Donatella Della Porta and Dieter Rucht, eds., *Meeting Democracy: Power and Deliberation in Global Justice Movements* (Cambridge: Cambridge University Press, 2013); Donatella Della Porta and Sidney Tarrow, *Transnational Protest and Global Activism* (Lanham, MD: Rowman & Littlefield, 2005); Charles Tilly, *Contentious Politics* (Boulder, CO: Paradigm Publishers, 2007). This literature, however, does not always engage explicitly with the modalities of public assemblies—focusing primarily on mobilization strategies and the opportunities and constraints facing social movements. Monographs on protest action tend to focus on particular forms (Anna Feigenbaum, Fabian Frenzel, and Patrick McCurdy, *Protest Camps* (London: Zed Books, 2013)), logics (Pollyanna Ruiz, *Articulating Dissent: Protest and the Public Sphere* (London: Pluto Press, 2014)), or technologies (Paolo Gerbaudo, *Tweets and the Streets: Social Media and Contemporary Activism* (London: Pluto Press, 2012); Zeynep Tufekci, *Twitter and Tear Gas: The Power and Fragility of Networked Protest* (New Haven, CT: Yale University Press, 2017)), or on particular movements such as environmental activism (Christopher Rootes, *Environmental Protest in Western Europe* (Oxford: Oxford University Press, 2003)) or global anti-capitalism (Christian Scholl, *Two Sides of a Barricade: (Dis)Order and Summit Protest in Europe* (Albany: State University of New York Press, 2012)). There are also a number of country-focused studies, seeking to explain the contextual dynamics of protest under particular types of regime. These include analyses of protest in Russia (Graeme B. Robertson, *The Politics of Protest in Hybrid Regimes: Managing Dissent in Post-Communist Russia* (Cambridge: Cambridge University Press, 2011); Samuel A. Greene, *Moscow in Movement: Power and Opposition in Putin's Russia* (Stanford, CA: Stanford University

Press, 2014)), Israel (Gadi Wolfsfeld, *The Politics of Provocation: Participation and Protest in Israel* (Albany: State University of New York Press, 1988)), Argentina and Ukraine (Olga Onuch, *Mapping Mass Mobilization: Understanding Revolutionary Moments in Argentina (2001) and Ukraine (2004)* (New York: Palgrave Macmillan, 2014)), Northern Ireland (Dominic Bryan, *Orange Parades: The Politics of Ritual, Tradition, and Control* (London: Pluto Press, 2000); Sean Farrell, *Rituals and Riots: Sectarian Violence and Political Culture in Ulster, 1784–1886* (Lexington: University Press of Kentucky, 2000)), and China (Kevin J. O'Brien, ed., *Popular Protest in China* (Cambridge, MA: Harvard University Press, 2008); Teresa Wright, *Popular Protest in China* (Cambridge: Polity Press, 2018)).

PART I

ASSEMBLY

CHAPTER 2

'RIOTOUS ASSEMBLIES'

Protest in Eighteenth-Century England

ADRIAN RANDALL

INTRODUCTION

EIGHTEENTH-CENTURY England was notoriously prone to riot.[1] While all European countries experienced occasional disorder, in England riot seemed both ubiquitous and endemic, something which amazed visitors. Benjamin Franklin, an acute observer, noted:

> I have seen within a year riots in the country about corn; riots about elections; riots about workhouses; riots of colliers; riots of weavers; riots of coalheavers; riots of sawyers; riots of Wilkesites; riots of government chairmen; riots of smugglers, in which custom-house officers and excisemen have been murdered, the King's armed vessels and troops fired at.[2]

That year, 1769, proved particularly troubled, but every decade witnessed similar outbreaks, with few parts of the country remaining 'peaceful' for long. Public events such as fairs, horse races, national celebrations of naval victories, and hangings all drew large and generally peaceful, if unruly, crowds but, when customary rights and expectations, or livelihoods, were threatened, protests could quickly turn into violent resistance. And while this assertiveness of the English crowd surprised visitors, even more so did the apparent failure of the authorities to reassert order. The Comte de Cambis, French ambassador from 1737 to 1740, spoke for many when he recorded his amazement 'at the extent to which popular disturbances in Britain were not punished and law and order were flouted'.[3] This chapter examines why this was so and why the effectiveness and therefore the prevalence of 'riotous assemblies' diminished in the years after 1800.

Law and Order in the Eighteenth Century

The so-called 'Glorious' Revolution of 1688, when an increasingly autocratic monarch, the Catholic James II, was unceremoniously ousted from the throne, ushered in an increasingly fractious era, dominated by foreign wars and growing religious tensions. Bitter party struggles arose between the Whigs, headed by the great magnates and mercantile interests, and the Tories, the self-described opposition 'Country' party, who loathed the foreign adventurism, toleration of Dissenting religion, and rising taxation of the former. The Whigs in turn accused their rivals of 'Jacobitism', treasonable support for a restoration of the Stuart monarchy. As power fluctuated between them, frequent general elections ensued, no fewer than six between 1701 and 1714, each occasioning widespread disorder.

The death, childless, of Queen Anne in 1714, saw the British throne pass to a new, foreign, monarch, George, Elector of Hanover. His arrival was not well received. The day marked to celebrate his coronation as George I brought extensive anti-Hanoverian riots and rumours of an impending Catholic rising, the latter increasing fears that riots might become a threat to the very state itself. George, though speaking little English, was clear that this was intolerable and found ready support amongst the great Whig families for clamping down upon disorder. Once again dominant in Parliament, the Whigs pushed through the Septennial Act of 1715 which abruptly curtailed eligibility for the vote and extended the life of each parliament from three to seven years. Fewer elections and a smaller electorate made for fewer election riots and a stronger central government. And, the same year, they enacted the Riot Act, aimed at 'preventing Tumult and riotous Assemblies'. The Act was to remain in force until its belated repeal in 1919.

The Riot Act, *I George I, st.2, c.5*, reshaped the legal response to disorder. Under the old common law, an assembly of three or more persons assembled with intent to commit disorder constituted merely a misdemeanour. Only when they proceeded to specific acts of violence did this change to a felony. This, proponents of the Act asserted, prevented the authorities from taking preventative action to preserve the peace. Moreover, formerly any prosecution had to show specific criminal acts had ensued and that clear criminal intent had been behind them. The new Act defined 'disturbance of the peace' as an event where 'someone of reasonable courage and firmness would be alarmed', a phrase gloriously vague. Faced with such an event, magistrates were charged to command, 'with a loud voice', that 'All persons being assembled . . . immediately disperse'.[4] If they did not disperse within an hour, or if they proceeded to commit acts of 'felonious violence', itself loosely interpreted, the authorities were indemnified to use force, even lethal force, to disperse them since the effect of defying the Act was treasonable. As Richard Vogler notes, the Act in effect legitimated martial law.[5]

The Act was far from foolproof. However loud and commanding the voice of the magistrate, not all could or would hear him. And the hour's delay risked new people arriving who had not been present at the Proclamation. Occasionally, local authorities delayed for an hour, even when violence had already started, in the mistaken belief that they must wait.[6] Conversely, others assumed that immediate failure to depart, or merely shouting back, constituted defiance. Few prosecutions were eventually brought under the Act. But prosecution was not its purpose. The Act's principal role was to authorize a deadly and immediate recourse to resist rioters. In this it set a pattern for increasingly draconian legislation for the following century. Thus, between 1714 and 1820 successive Parliaments passed no fewer than five hundred new capital statutes. There had been only twenty on the books before. In this way, the Riot Act ushered in a new era of legislative intolerance.[7]

However, if the new Act enabled a more aggressive response to riots, the agencies to effect vigorous suppression of serious disturbance were both limited and inefficient. The key agents charged with preserving order were the justices of the peace.[8] They carried a considerable burden, being charged, inter alia, with maintaining order (policing), dispensing justice from the magistrates' bench at the quarter and petty sessions and undertaking the numerous civil responsibilities which parliaments laid upon them. Most gentlemen landowners and nobles who were not outright opponents of the government were enrolled in each county's justices roll, but the daily work tended to fall on relatively few, generally those from the ranks of the lesser gentry whose lives were focused upon their more immediate locality. The magisterial 'bench' had grown in autonomy since the Civil War (1642–1646) and was not an agency of government or the crown. It epitomized the highly devolved model of the state so cherished by the political rulers of eighteenth-century England whereby the counties and their constituent hundreds and parishes took on roles which in other European countries might be done by the central state.

The justices, however industrious, lacked effective local means for tackling disorders. In most locales, they could only turn to the parish constable, a role which was usually honorary and seen as an unwelcome burden by those tradesmen whose turn it was to carry the constable's staff. While some boroughs maintained their own small quasi-policing 'watch', there were no established local or national police forces. Nor was there any likelihood of there being such. Here memories of the rule of the military during the republican Commonwealth (1649–1660) continued to bite deep. The landed elite had absolutely no intention of handing power to enforce and prosecute legislation to any agency of the centre. The systematizing and codification of the machinery of law which such would entail was anathema.[9] It was far better, they believed, to maintain discretionary justice by the natural rulers of the country, them, even if at times it was not very effective.

Beyond the constables, the justices could in emergencies call upon the militia, raised on a county basis by ballot and mainly filled by men who could not afford to buy their way out. They were trained after a fashion but could neither be assembled nor armed quickly. Nor were they always reliable once embodied.[10] Local volunteer regiments raised in the last decade of the century proved more useful, but their local origin made for potentially long-lasting social fracture should they be used to coerce their neighbours.[11] And in extremis there was always the *posse comitatus* or enrolled special constables, yet both shared the same drawbacks as the militia. Thus, in many instances, the justice found himself relying upon little more than personal authority, self-confidence, and the implicit threat of swingeing sanctions which might come later.

Without effective local agencies, the army became the sole resource available for restoring and maintaining order whenever disturbances broke out. This use of the military was a major innovation. Since the Civil War, no previous regime, save that of James II and then only briefly, had dared to rely upon the army to maintain public order because the intrusion of 'a standing army in the midst of peace' revived fears of absolutism. Their deployment indicated, like the Riot Act, a new emphasis on repression. However, there were never enough troops to go round[12] while trigger-happy soldiers and officers might make a bad situation worse.[13] And, while their bullets and bayonets might suppress riot, once the soldiery departed, the local authorities who had called them in and directed them still had to go on living there. Moreover, whenever the army was deployed for civil order purposes, it had to be housed and fed.[14] Local innkeepers fumed at the imposition of billeting while local ratepayers resented that all the expense of the soldiers' stay fell on them. There was thus a constant tension between those justices who clutched the army as a comfort blanket and those who wanted them gone as quickly as possible. This was not helped when, as sometimes happened, the billeted military created problems of their own.[15]

This mismatch between draconian legislation and feeble enforcement can only be understood by recognizing that these were deliberate choices. MPs in Westminster who regularly added capital statutes to the law proved equally keen to preserve their local independence when it came to maintaining law and order. Within the axes of that paradox there was room for protests to grow and at times evolve into serious disorder.

Causes of Disorder

The weakness of the civil authorities, even if it may have encouraged protest to morph into disorder, does not *explain* disorder. Old histories tended to see riot as simply the brute response to distress, as a form of primitive protest, as evidence of the 'hired mob' or the manifestation of a natural unlawfulness. Most protests were certainly defensive. Yet the members of those proletarian communities most prone to react vigorously to threats to their well-being also shared long memories of the fate of their forebears who had taken direct action, namely, the gallows and the prison. They well knew that protest carried consequences. 'Riot' was their last, not their first response. This was first recognized by Georges Lefebvre and George Rudé[16] but fullest appreciation of the triggers to popular protest came from the work of Edward Thompson and his followers. His magnum opus, *The Making of the English Working Class*, set out to 'rescue' the troublemakers of eighteenth- and early nineteenth-century England from 'the enormous condescension of posterity', but it was his seminal study of eighteenth-century

English food riots[17] which has spawned a rich new seam of historical scholarship into disorder.[18]

Thompson showed that, while food riots certainly occurred at times of high prices, prices themselves were not the triggers per se to market disorder. Only when rapidly rising prices were seen to be the result of profiteering by farmers and dealers might trouble break out. Consumers, he argued, were well aware that food marketing was constrained by law. Successive governments had recognized that provisioning of foodstuffs could not be left to market forces alone and had for centuries decreed that markets, particularly those for grains, must be regulated and controlled. Foodstuffs might only be sold on charter-specified day(s) of the week in public pitching markets whose opening and closing times were fixed, the whole to be overseen by the justices. Dealers were barred from buying directly from the farms or buying crops speculatively before they were gathered. Transgressors were to be prosecuted.

Improvements in agriculture through the century made foodstuffs more plentiful and market regulation tended to fall into desuetude over time. But when shortages, especially sudden shortages, occurred, consumers were vociferous in demanding the protection which regulation ensured. If national government became less interested in this regulatory model as the century passed, the local justices knew well that failure to act, or failure *to be seen to* react, might ignite a veritable tinder box of disorder. Thompson termed the value system which informed popular attitudes to marketing as 'the moral economy of the crowd'. This concept has proved extraordinarily fecund and has been taken up in many and various ways by social historians, anthropologists, and political scientists alike.[19] While subject to critiques, all serious study of disorder must perforce start with his work.

Let us take just one example, that of the food riots which broke out in the woollen-producing districts of Gloucestershire in 1766. These were merely a part of a much wider series of food riots spread over no fewer than twenty-five English counties in that year and the one after.[20] Here disturbances began, as they did in most places, with minor fracas and theft of foodstuffs in the small local markets when customers discovered that prices had suddenly risen and that grain and hence flour were in shorter supply than usual. Stalls were overturned and produce taken, sometimes without payment, sometimes at the price previously available. Consumers believed that the price hike was a piece of chicanery on the part of the vendors because, not only had they seen the grain ripening nicely in the fields, but they had also read in the local newspaper that the harvest promised to be a good one. In this they and the press were seriously misled. A warm end to the summer made the crops look good but they had been damaged earlier in the season by rain and damp. Farmers and dealers recognized that the harvest would be short and began hoarding the grain which was still in their barns and ricks from the previous year's harvest, in the certain knowledge that, once the new deficient harvest was gathered, this would soon be worth a great deal more.

Shortages triggered sudden price rises, while seizures of foodstuffs at market persuaded farmers not to attend the next one, quickly exacerbating the crisis. Soon large crowds were gathering in Stroudwater and marching to neighbouring markets to 'regulate' the price there. While food thefts still occurred, most were willing to pay a sum for food which approximated to that usually charged, the 'just price'. A large crowd marched the sixteen miles to visit Berkley Castle, home of the Lord Lieutenant of the county, to demand that he order proper regulation of the food markets. He promised action and gave them three guineas. Another group marched north to Cirencester, the major grain market of the Cotswolds and base for many larger dealers, but here they were repulsed by the locals. Not discouraged, a week later a huge crowd, numbering over one thousand, assembled and managed by the sound of horns, repeated the route and this time took over the entire market, hauling hidden supplies out into marketplace for a massive sale, again at the 'just price'.

The fact that they paid for what they took, far from home where they were unlikely to be identified, demonstrates their sense that they did not regard themselves as thieves but as 'regulators', their own term, doing the job that authorities should be doing. Nor were all content with delivering this one lesson in civics. While most returned home, a group continued eastwards, 'setting the price' at markets all the way to Lechlade, some twenty-five miles further. And here their efforts seem to have triggered new riots all along the Thames.[21]

Events in Gloucestershire were replicated elsewhere throughout the century and should remind us that, while the law and prosecutors saw, or chose to see, these disorders as 'riot' and their perpetrators as rioters and thieves, this was not the view of those who were engaged in them. They believed that they were enforcing rather than breaking the law: 'Many that are under sentence of death thought they were doing a meritorious act at the very moment they were forfeiting their lives'.[22] Food riots were therefore both protest and activated direct action. Rioters certainly attacked property when resisted, but personal violence was rare and, when it happened, generally stemmed from the actions of millers, farmers, and dealers whose goods were being 'taken'. Moreover, these plebeian 'regulators' could point to the fact that justices across the country, fearful of such consequences, were now actively managing markets and announcing public subscriptions to help the poor, while central government itself had issued proclamations denouncing forestalling, regrating, and engrossing as illegal, charging the magistrates to give them the widest publicity. Stephen Cratchley, hanged for being the horn blower at a 'riot' in Paganhill, spoke for many when he noted 'he little thought his crime had been of so heinous a nature'.[23]

The strong sense of legitimacy exhibited in food riots can be seen replicated in many industrial disputes which led to 'riot'. Numerous acts of Parliament prohibited the formation of workers' combinations and sought to regulate industries vital to the country's economy, in particular the textile industries. But in so doing so, they often indirectly provided protections for workers as well. This was true of the Elizabethan Statute of Artificers which was used to defend apprenticeship from influxes of less 'skilled' and cheaper labour.[24] Regulatory laws stipulated who might and who might not set up as masters or own loom shops. Others banned machines which threatened the quality of production. These Acts were passed to protect the reputation of goods critical for exports, but each provided elements which could be cited to protect workers' trades.

And when disputes threatened major disruption, workers might, with the help of sympathetic justices and gentry, petition Parliament to introduce new laws to provide for independent arbitration on issues such as rates of pay.[25] While such devices rarely worked for long—employers fought to undermine the process—they again both legitimated protest and emphasized the 'independent' role of the local authority as a regulatory and conciliatory agency. Many justices and gentry demonstrated real sympathy for workers in industrial disputes since they had little patience with employers who aggravated industrial relations to the point of disorder or threw labourers onto the poor rates simply to feather their own nests.[26] In such circumstances, direct action to safeguard custom and livelihoods made sense.

Food prices engaged whole working communities in solidarity and industrial workers shared common interests in defence of their trades, but other groups too were more than willing to protest, if necessary by forceful means, to protect their livelihoods, customs, and rights. 'Country people' were generally more passive, living cheek by jowl with gentry and justices, but could be roused to direct action in certain circumstances. The turnpiking of the public highway by trusts empowered through acts of parliament to upgrade the roads in exchange for charging tolls might arouse violent protest since small traders and petty producers found that their passage to market was now costly. In 1727, miners in Kingswood 'Assembled in tumultuous manner', burning down new toll bars on the road to Bristol 'and obstinately persist, if any more are erected, they will serve them in the same manner.' They knew that the common law protected the right of free passage on the highway, describing the trust's act as 'a thing Clandestinely purchas'd', and swore that 'they'll bring no Coal into the City, nor suffer any Turnpikes in their Roads till they are exempted from paying Toll'. They were. And in 1749, when the Bristol authorities petitioned for a new act to prolong their turnpike control, farmers and petty tradesmen of Somerset repeated the destruction of the toll gates and booths, again pointing to the common law to defend free passage. Similar groups in Herefordshire, Gloucestershire, and Yorkshire likewise resisted turnpikes with violence.[27]

And when in 1757, in the face of high food prices and the threat of war with France, the government chose to order a new mass enrolment into the militia, farming people in Bedfordshire, Cambridgeshire, Hertfordshire, Yorkshire, and Lincolnshire all rose in riotous opposition. Fears that those embodied might be sent abroad to fight certainly aggravated popular opposition but the timing of the measure, right in the middle of harvest, and the high-handed way it was enforced proved galling to those eligible to serve.[28] In all these, direct action, shocking to the local authorities, might reasonably be hoped to prove effective.

Finally, we must note that even religious riots and 'political' disorders around elections can be better understood by recognizing that many of those involved were doing so because they believed that somehow their liberties and rights were being threatened.[29] This is true even of the notorious Gordon riots of 1780 and local versions of attacks on Catholic chapels which followed.[30] Religion stirred violent emotions and the cry of 'the Church in danger' had long been used to rouse popular ire against those deemed to be intent on restoring 'foreign' authority over the country and hence threaten popular liberties. We can see similar resistance by local communities facing attempts by politicians to buy constituencies, remove voter rights, or manipulate the electoral process.[31] John Wilkes was to prove exceptionally adept at exciting such deep popular political prejudices in his rambling campaigns in 1768 in defence of 'liberty'.[32]

While historians now recognize the myriad causes and values behind popular disorder, there remains a reluctance to see these having any common basis. Certainly, each dispute and disorder happened in a unique context, but it is possible to identify a common factor which went beyond a simple defence of custom and conditions. Underlying and informing reaction lay a strong sense of entitlement, a belief that the ordinary people had rights and could not be pushed around with impunity. This belief had its basis in the concept of 'the freeborn Englishman' and his ineffable right to resist oppression, by force if necessary.

'Liberty' and the Freeborn Englishman

The concept of the freeborn Englishman was not plebeian in origin. It stemmed from a history where for centuries the great landlords had resisted accretion of power by the monarchy. The cry of liberty in peril had in the seventeenth century been used by them to justify the execution of Charles I, opposition to the Protectorate which followed, and to endorse the ejection of the Catholic James II. When the Elector of Hanover was offered the crown in 1714, it was decidedly on terms which limited royal power.[33] Future kings were in short to be 'constitutional' monarchs.[34]

This naked aristocratic *realpolitik* received powerful intellectual underpinnings from Locke who's seminal *Two Treatises of Government*, published in 1689, argued that it was the right of all to resist and, as necessary overthrow, rulers who threatened their civil liberties.[35] These views were assiduously projected by the elite thereafter. But the landed magnates also well understood that their exercise of power had to be dressed up in ways which would engage the support of the common people, in effect by projecting a new ruling narrative which embraced the people within it. Thus, at every public occasion, such as at celebrations of naval victories, at election time, or at local festivities, the rhetoric of the 'freeborn' Englishman triumphing over autocrats was echoed in some form or other.[36] It was effective. Josiah Tucker lamented, 'Our people are drunk with the cup of liberty'.[37] It was also widely shared. The *Universal Daily Register* echoed in 1785: 'Although many inconveniences arise from an excess of liberty in this country, yet they are so greatly advantageous, that we cannot be too careful to preserve a blessing which distinguishes us from all the world'.[38] As E. P. Thompson noted, 'freedom was the coinage of patrician, demagogue and radical alike'.[39]

If the concept of the freeborn Englishman was clearly self-serving, it also reflected real substance. The ordinary Englishman did indeed enjoy liberties and freedoms which his continental equivalent did not. The Englishman might travel where he wanted, work, trade, and worship where he chose. He enjoyed freedom from arbitrary arrest or house search by agents of the state and could obtain his news from a growing number of regional newspapers of different political persuasions. Even though this was certainly no golden age of commonality, this overarching narrative proved remarkably successful, imbuing and reinforcing a strong sense of 'belonging' but also endowing the common people with a strong sense of their own liberties. Whether their rulers liked it or not, the freeborn Englishman felt confident of his 'rights' and exhibited a truculent determination to preserve his 'liberties'.[40]

This meant that those who ruled were perforce obliged to tolerate a surprising level of disorder or risk undermining their own narrative. Just as their unwillingness to accept any form of organized police made repression and subjugation impossible, so too must the rulers accept a role which appeared, and often had to be, paternal, overtly protective of the lesser orders even at the expense of offending the wealthier.

The crowd had to be engaged openly and at least the pretence of their having a key role had to be acknowledged. This can be seen clearly in the mechanics of contested parliament elections, the key to political power. While the many had no vote, they had to be involved openly in the process to demonstrate its legitimacy. Candidates were obliged to make daily speeches at the hustings, usually facing a large and unruly crowd which enjoyed baiting them and worse. Voting, in the open at hustings, showed everyone who had voted for whom. Finally, the winner would have to make his last speech to an audience now well-lubricated with alcohol and then endure the custom of 'chairing the member', often perched on a sedan chair carried by drunken supporters and liable at any time to be tipped off. All this must be endured with a good grace.[41] The beast could not be tamed but could be pandered to. And, generally, it worked.

The Decline of 'Riotous Assemblies'

While disorder was indeed endemic in eighteenth-century England, if we project forward to the mid-nineteenth century, the picture of the country painted by visitors had changed considerably. Compared to the turmoil which now beset the Continent, mid-nineteenth-century England seemed to be a country both remarkably orderly and stable. Historians have explained this apparent transformation in various ways. Economic historians suggest that rising living standards, courtesy of a rapidly changing economy, and an inexorable shift to an urbanized and industrialized society broke old social bonds. Political historians point to the changing structure of politics after the Great Reform Act of 1832 and to the defeat of Chartism. Fabian and Marxist historians see the shift as related to a new sense of class identity, forged by the experiences of industrialization, finding expression in a new spirit of collectivism which forsook riot for the pursuit of economic and political equality, a process which saw its eventual culmination in the rise of socialism and the Labour Party. All contribute to the idea that the country witnessed nothing less than 'a "modernization of protest" as the patterns of protest appropriate to the "face to face" society of the small market town gave way to the more permanent and larger-scale organizations of urban and industrial life'.[42]

Each of these explanations seem plausible but none provide convincing causation. It is certainly undeniable that the economic and social context of disorder was changing between 1714 and 1850 but that change was neither rapid nor complete. Eighteenth-century England was already a highly industrialized society, having a much higher percentage of working people divorced from the land, and hence dependent upon capitalist markets for both food and work, than in any other European country. Moreover, the material benefits of industrialization for working people were hardly discernible until the early 1820s and thereafter subject to a violent roller coaster of boom and bust which lasted into the mid-1840s. Migrants to the burgeoning industrial towns might have left behind established, if often declining, communities but few towns lacked existing communities of their own into which the newcomers were assimilated.[43] Combination, though illegal, worked just as well in the eighteenth as in the nineteenth centuries for those trades which had a strong bargaining position. And the campaigns for parliamentary reform, the object of sustained working-class protest after 1815, enfranchised only the middle class, leaving the workers firmly outside the political system.

We need to question views which see changes in the forms of protest simply as an aspect of 'progress' and recognize that before 1800, riotous assemblies had proved at least a modestly effective means of getting voices heard and remedial action implemented. While the mills of justice ground slow and took a bitter harvest of those deemed 'leaders', the local justices and sometimes the state itself were forced to pay attention and act, or at least appear to do so. Thus, food riots abruptly curbed profiteering and pressured the landed to take positive steps to ensure the population was fed. Industrial disorders engaged the attention of the justices and ensured that employers who wished to pay in truck, were setting up shops with unapprenticed workers, or who were introducing banned practices or machines were halted, if only temporarily, in their tracks. Direct action brought benefits.

However, two powerful forces were changing the context within which such direct action might provide traction. Firstly, the justificatory narrative of the state which had facilitated these successes was changing. The ideas of Thomas Malthus persuaded many that poor relief merely encouraged the poor to breed, undermining the Christian imperative towards paternal concern.[44] However, the major driver to ideological change came from a new and persuasive economic theory delineated by Adam Smith. His *Wealth of Nations*, published in 1776, effectively overturned older mercantilist models of trade and argued that economic growth was the result of the interaction between the three constituent orders of land, capital, and labour. Left to find their own balance via the agency of the market, Smith argued, they would produce optimal improvement. Regulation and interference by the state simply constrained that process.[45] His ideas chimed with a time of increasing innovation and attracted the attention of leading and coming politicians, not least William Pitt, the Younger, who became Prime Minister in 1783 at the tender age of 24.[46] If the market was the best way to ensure growth, government might be relieved of the burden of regulatory intervention. Gradually, the state began to withdraw from its old paternalist position.[47]

The fruits of this shift were seen first in the food market. Whereas the government's response to the extensive food riots in 1795 had followed the pattern established in earlier major crises, when new riots broke out in the autumn of 1800 and persisted into 1801, the centre refused to endorse the old model. There was no point in seeking to manage food supplies at the local exchanges. Government could not influence the fate of crops during the seasons; while, once harvested, supply and demand would eventually produce optimal outcomes for both seller and buyer. The Home Secretary chastised the authorities in Oxford in 1801 for blaming disorders on 'the offences of forestalling, ingrossing and regrating' and sought to dismiss the town clerk who condoned those who had set the price in the butter market, describing this as 'a violent and unjustified attack in property'. Cornish justices who had pressed farmers to bring food to market at affordable prices were roundly condemned for actions which 'cannot be justified' as it would prevent 'the Employment of Capital in the Farming Line.'[48]

Local authorities struggled to come to grips with this new approach and usually simply reverted to the old ways. They found support from the Lord Chief Justice, Lord Kenyon. Amidst the riots of 1795, he had endorsed common-law prosecutions against those who bought up standing crops, 'this hydra-headed monster. It is your duty, as Justices, to see justice done'. And in 1800 he sought to press the case by using a trial before King's Bench to reinforce market regulation.[49] In this he clearly echoed and reinforced the views which still held sway with majority opinion in the country at large. But on his death the following year he was replaced by Ellenborough, a strong supporter of both laissez-faire and of the need for forceful suppression of protest. The death knell of the old model had sounded, even if it retained some life for a while.

This pattern of a withdrawal of the central state was replicated in the industrial sphere. Parliaments had been increasingly reluctant to create new controls on industry, but practical circumstances of major disorders forced their hands. Thus, as late as 1800 it had been pressed to appease disgruntled weavers in Lancashire with the Cotton Arbitration Act, which established a formal and legally binding process of arbitration by the magistracy in disputes over wages. It proved a dead letter since the justices in Manchester, closely aligned with the cotton trade, refused to play ball. But it was disputes in the woollen industry which proved pivotal. The old staple was covered by no fewer than seventy-eight regulatory Acts which weavers and cloth dresser sought to use to bolster apprenticeship and to resist new technologies. Two Select Committees took copious evidence which clearly articulated the workers' defence of custom, but in 1809 Parliament repealed all regulation, throwing the industry firmly onto market forces.[50] This was the trigger for rapid mechanization of cloth finishing and for the major Luddite disturbances in Yorkshire in 1812. These echoed conflicts in the east Midland framework knitting industry and were followed by extensive Luddite disorder in Lancashire, both tied to demands that government uphold or reinstate regulation.[51]

While a changing attitude towards its old paternalist role was driven by ideology, government reaction to protest was driven by a second, even more powerful, force: fear of social and political revolution. The French Revolution of 1789, initially welcomed in England by almost all, rapidly turned into a nightmare for the propertied classes when the revolution lurched leftwards, King and aristocrats were guillotined, and the revolutionary armies spread out across Europe. Twenty-three years of war followed amid periodic invasion panics. Worse, the rise of a domestic radical movement demanding political reform, a section of which espoused revolutionary aspirations, terrified the rulers of the country who chose to see all forms of protest as evidence of insurrectionary plotting. The response was ever-tightening repression, and, in a direct assault on the rights of the freeborn Englishman, the suspension in 1794 of Habeas Corpus that vaunted touchstone of liberty. In the numerous ensuing panics thereafter, its suspension enabled the state to imprison without trial 'dangerous' protesters. However, it also cut the ground beneath its claims to be safeguarding the constitutional rights of the individual. Even when war came to an end, the mentality and machinery of repression was maintained, as was witnessed in the events around the mass meeting at St Peter's Fields in Manchester in August 1819.[52]

War and inflated fears of invasion created an atmosphere where the government could, with broad public support, rapidly inflate the army, boost recruitment to the militia, and encourage privately raised regiments. A program of rapid barrack-building enabled the augmented army, much of which was always kept at home, to be spread more widely and in safer conditions, providing a ready and forceful defence against future disorders.[53] This was seen most powerfully in the vigorous suppression of Luddism. Martial law was proclaimed, and some 35,000 soldiers dispatched to the north to defend property and hunt down Luddites.[54]

Conclusion

In this changing world, direct action as a form of bargaining grew ever less effective. Repression without concession became the new norm. Here we see the reality of labour 'learning the lessons' of the new century. Any 'modernisation of protest' from disorder to more peaceful petitioning was the consequence not of moral or intellectual improvement but of brute circumstance, namely, a government which cared less about winning hearts and minds and more about simply putting down dissent.

Riotous assemblies did not, of course, disappear. Indeed, disorders were to continue throughout the nineteenth century, particularly in the first half. Some were both serious and extensive.[55] But, whereas in the previous century those protesting did so with half an eye on the justices and half a hope that some form of mediation or governmental intervention might be forthcoming, in the new industrial age such hopes were soon seen to be vain. Now raw labour power alone could be employed, rarely with successful consequences.

For its part, government remained determined to resist any concession towards a return to older ways. This was clearly shown by the eventual, if reluctant, introduction of a police force in 1839, though this too failed to provide the sort of management of the streets hoped for.[56] But other changes also hindered 'collective bargaining by riot'.[57] The incorporation of the middle class into the body politic after the 1832 Reform Act and the reform of local government under the Municipal Corporations Act of 1834 cemented middle class ratepayers firmly into the ranks of 'order'. Those very spaces which had provided the assembly points for protest were increasingly privatized, cut off, or subject to new local bylaws.[58] Meanwhile, the new railway provided an efficient means for speedily relocating both army and police to trouble spots.

The ensuing campaigns for working-class political representation reflected a recognition by popular radicals that a centralizing government decreasingly heeded local pressure. Yet their campaigns for parliamentary reform demonstrated it was impossible to persuade governments which refused to listen. Moreover, entanglement within the political process involved accepting those terms of engagement dictated from above. The authorities, then as now, always demanded 'respectful' protests. These were easier to ignore.

So, while the freeborn Englishman remained alive and truculent into the new century, he rarely now collectively protested his 'liberties' in the ways which had characterized eighteenth-century riotous assemblies.

Notes

1. The discussion of rioting in this chapter draws heavily upon Adrian Randall, *Riotous Assemblies: Popular Protest in Hanoverian England* (Oxford: Oxford University Press, 2006). Supplementary references are provided in the footnotes.
2. Albert H. Smyth, ed., *The Writings of Benjamin Franklin* (New York: Macmillan, 1907), 10, 239.
3. Cited in Jeremy Black, *Robert Walpole and the Nature of Politics in Early Eighteenth Century England* (Basingstoke, UK: Macmillan, 1990), 25.
4. Delivering the formal Proclamation, as set out in the Act, was thereafter known as 'reading the Riot Act'.
5. Richard Vogler, *Reading the Riot Act: The Magistracy, the Police and the Army in Civil Disorder* (Milton Keynes, UK: Open University Press, 1990), 2.
6. This was the case in London in 1780 when the magistrates delayed acting in the face of the early Gordon Riots and in 1830 when the Bristol authorities were slow in responding to the reform riots there.
7. On the 'bloody code', see James A. Sharpe, *Crime in Early Modern England* (London: Longman, 1984), 147–150; and Douglas Hay, 'Property, Authority and the Criminal Law', in *Albion's Fatal Tree: Crime and Society in Eighteenth-Century England*, ed. D. Hay, P. Linebaugh, and E. P. Thompson (London: Allen Lane, 1975), 17–63.
8. On the justices of the peace (or magistrates for short), see Norma Landau, *The Justices of the Peace* (Berkeley: University of California Press, 1984).
9. Hay, 'Property, Authority and the Criminal Law', 24–25. As late as 1823, *The Times* was denouncing reformers' ideas of a national police force as 'an engine . . . invented by despotism': *The Times*, 31 January 1823.

10. On the militia, the best source remains J. R. Western, *The English Militia in the Eighteenth Century* (London: Routledge, 1965).
11. Yeomanry regiments, drawing their volunteers from farmers and the better off middling sort were more reliable but could, as in the case of the Manchester yeomanry in 1819, prove catastrophically aggressive. The generally poorer volunteers to the new foot troops were viewed with some suspicion by the propertied classes. See Randall, *Riotous Assemblies*, 212, 269.
12. Black, *Robert Walpole and the Nature of Politics*, 25, estimates that there were no more than fifteen thousand soldiers stationed at home in the first thirty-five years of Hanoverian rule, and this number did not increase significantly until the 1790s. John Brewer, *The Sinews of Power: War, Money and the English State, 1688-1783* (Cambridge, MA: Harvard University Press, 1990), 63, notes that 'armed force was of very limited value in enforcing authority in England'.
13. The most notorious case was that of Captain John Porteous whose actions triggered widespread disorder and his eventual lynching by the mob in Edinburgh: H. T. Dickinson and Kenneth Logue, 'The Porteous Riot of 1736', *History Today* 22 (1972): 274–281.
14. James Wolfe noted in 1756 that his regiment, sent to Wiltshire to deal with food riots, had ruined half the inns en route since those places, short of food, could only accommodate the troops by 'destruction to themselves'. Cited in Richard Holmes, *Redcoat: The British Soldier in the Age of Horse and Musket* (London: Harper Collins, 2002), 267.
15. Soldiers, short of food, sometimes caused food riots as in Wells and Abingdon in 1794. See Roger Wells, *Wretched Faces: Famine in Wartime England 1763–1803* (Gloucester, UK: Alan Sutton, 1988), 101.
16. Georges Lefebvre, *The French Revolution: From Its Origins to 1793* (London: Routledge & Kegan Paul, 1962); George Rudé, *The Crowd in History* (London: Lawrence and Wishart, 1981) 3, 4. First published in 1964. See also George Rudé, *The Crowd in the French Revolution* and *Wilkes and Liberty* (Oxford: Oxford University Press, 1962).
17. Edward P. Thompson, *The Making of the English Working Class* (London: Gollancz, 1963; Repr., Harmondsworth, UK: Penguin Books, 1968); and E. P. Thompson, 'The Moral Economy of the English Crowd in the Eighteenth Century', *Past and Present* 50 (1971): 76–136. See also his further thoughts on the moral economy in E. P. Thompson, *Customs in Common* (London: Merlin, 1991), ch. V.
18. See A. Randall and A. Charlesworth, eds., *Moral Economy and Popular Protest: Crowds, Conflict and Authority* (Basingstoke, UK: Macmillan, 2000), ch. 1.
19. See e.g. Thomas Clay Arnold, 'Rethinking Moral Economy', *American Political Science Review* 95, no. 1 (2001): 85–95; Andrew Sayer, 'Moral Economy as Critique', *New Political Economy* 12, no. 2 (2015): 261–270 and James Carrier, 'Moral Economy: What's in a Name?', *Anthropological Theory*, 18, no. 1 (2018): 18–35.
20. On food riots see, inter alia, W. J. Shelton, *English Hunger and Industrial Disorders* (Basingstoke, UK: Macmillan, 1973); John Bohstedt, *The Politics of Provisions: Food Riots, Moral Economy, and Market Transition in England, c. 1550–1850* (Aldershot, UK: Ashgate, 2010); Randall, *Riotous Assemblies*, chs 5, 9.
21. Adrian Randall, 'The Gloucestershire Food Riots of 1766', *Midland History* 10 (1985): 72–93.
22. *Hardwicke Mss.* Add. Mss. 35.607, Pitt to Hardwicke, 20 December 1766.
23. *Bath Chronicle*, 15 January 1767. Even when rioters paid the 'just price', this counted as theft under the law.
24. John Rule, *The Experience of Labour in Eighteenth-Century Industry* (London: Croom Helm, 1981), 95–96. This Act, passed in 1563, was repealed in 1814.

25. C. R. Dobson, *Masters and Journeymen: A Prehistory of Industrial Relations 1717–1800* (London: Croom Helm, 1980), 127–130. See also John Rule, 'Industrial Disputes, Wage Bargaining and the Moral Economy', in Randall and Charlesworth, *Moral Economy and Popular Protest*; for example, *29 Geo.II, c.33*, an Act passed to re-establish the duty of the bench to set piece rates for weaving woollen cloth.
26. Adrian Randall, 'The Philosophy of Luddism', *Technology and Culture* 27, no. 1 (1986): 1–17.
27. Robert W. Malcolmson, '"A Set of Ungovernable People": The Kingswood Colliers in the Eighteenth Century', in *An Ungovernable People: The English and Their Law in the Seventeenth and Eighteenth Centuries*, ed. J. Brewer and J. Styles (London: Hutchison, 1980), 85–127; William Albert, 'Popular Opposition to Turnpike Trusts in Early Eighteenth-Century England', *Journal of Transport History*, 3rd Series, 5, no. 1 (1979): 1–17; Michael Freeman, 'Popular Attitudes to Turnpikes in Early-Eighteenth-Century England', *Journal of Historical Geography* 19, no. 1 (1993): 33–47; and Randall and Charlesworth, *Markets Market Culture and Popular Protest*, 46–68.
28. Western, *English Militia*, 291–299.
29. See, in particular, Nicholas Rogers, *Whigs and Cities: Popular Politics in the Age of Walpole and Pitt* (Oxford: Clarendon Press, 1989).
30. The Gordon riots, a sudden emanation of anti-Catholicism in London, have been closely studied. The most recent examinations are by Nicholas Rogers, *Crowds, Culture and Politics* (Oxford: Oxford University Press, 1998), ch. 5 and Colin Haydon, *Anti-Catholicism in Eighteenth-Century England, c. 1714–80* (Manchester, UK: Manchester University Press, 1993). Haydon likens these riots to the 'moral economy riots', sharing a fundamentally conservative nature', 242, 235.
31. See e.g. the case of Lichfield in 1747 in Randall, *Riotous Assemblies*, 191–192.
32. On Wilkes, see George Rudé, *Wilkes and Liberty* (Oxford: Oxford University Press, 1962); John Brewer, *Party Ideology and Popular Politics at the Accession of George III* (Cambridge: Cambridge University Press, 1976); and Rogers, *Crowds, Culture and Politics*.
33. Passed in 1701 in expectation of this transition, the Act of Settlement banned Catholics from the throne while the Act of Succession determined, inter alia, that no foreign wars might be waged without parliamentary approval, that no foreigner might enter Parliament or the Privy Council, and that the King must seek permission from Parliament before leaving the country.
34. Nowhere can this be seen better than in the anthem 'God Save the King', where the original's final verse noted:

    > *Thy Choicest gift in store, On George be pleas'd to pour, Long may he reign;* ***May he defend our laws, And ever give us cause,*** *To say with heart and voice, God save the King.*

    Deference was conditional.
35. Thomas Hobbes, *Leviathan* (1651), ed. C. B. Macpherson (Harmondsworth, UK: Penguin Books, 1968), 346.
36. See, for example, opposition to the new Cider Tax in the west country in 1766 when gentry, press, and the crowd justified resistance with appeals to liberty, including 'Englishmen born, who with freedom are blessed, Will never submit to be basely oppressed', poem in *Felix Farley's Bristol Journal*, 9 April 1776, cited in Randall and Charlesworth, *Markets, Market Culture and Popular Protest*, ch. 4.
37. Josiah Tucker (Dean of Glocester [*sic*]), *Six Sermons on Important Subjects* (Bristol, S. Farley, 1772), 71.

38. *Universal Daily Register* (later *The Times*), 1 July 1785.
39. Thompson, *Making*, 85.
40. The same sense of being 'freeborn' was exported to Britain's American colonies and informed a continuing tendency to riot there. See Paul A. Gilje, *Rioting in America* (Bloomington: Indiana University Press, 1996), chs. 1, 2.
41. This role of the crowd in the wider theatre of Georgian politics is discussed in Linda Colley, *Britons: Forging the Nation, 1707–1837* (New Haven, CT: Yale University Press, 1992), 51–52, and Rogers, *Crowds, Culture and Politics*, 17–8, 24–32, 176–95. Hogarth's painting 'Chairing the Member' (*ca.* 1754) perfectly captures the character of disorderly election theatre.
42. John Stevenson, 'Food Riots in England, 1792–1818', in *Popular Protest and Public Order*, ed. J. Stevenson and R. Quinault (London: Allen and Unwin, 1974), 67, citing Charles Tilly, 'Collective Violence in European Perspective', in *Violence in America: Historical and Comparative Perspectives*, ed. Hugh D. Graham and Ted R. Gurr (Washington, DC: US Government Printing Office, 1969). Stevenson also notes that 'elsewhere rioting had already been overtaken by trade union activity and strikes' (63). Much of the early work of Charles Tilly emphasizes this same teleological direction towards political engagement and 'orderly' trade unionism, each being seen as 'progress', though note a certain rowing back in his later works.
43. Cf Bohstedt, *Riots and Community Politics in England and Wales*, and Andrew Charlesworth, 'From the Moral Economy of Devon to the political Economy of Manchester 1790–1812', *Social History* 18, no. 2 (1993): 205–217.
44. Rev Thomas R. Malthus, *An Essay on the Principle of Population* (1798).
45. Adam Smith, *The Wealth of Nations* (1776).
46. Jennifer Mori, 'The Political Theory of William Pitt the Younger', *History* 83, no. 270 (1998): 234–248.
47. Smith's model of the interrelationship between the three 'constituent orders' was essentially benign. However, after 1800 subsequent political economists such as David Ricardo presented it not as a delicate balance but as a ferocious conflict where only the triumph of capital, chiefly by cutting wage costs and the cost of foodstuffs, could sustain growth. Malthus, equally keen to reduce the burden of the 'unproductive' poor, chose instead to emphasize the landed elite's conspicuous consumption as the essential ingredient to promote growth, an early version of 'trickle down' theory. Neither version saw any likelihood of improving workers' conditions.
48. Randall, *Riotous Assemblies*, 229.
49. Douglas Hay, 'Moral Economy, Political Economy and Law', in Randall and Charlesworth, *Moral Economy and Popular Protest*, 93–122; and Douglas Hay, 'State and the Market in 1800: Lord Kenyon and Mr Waddington', *Past and Present* 100 (1999): 101–162.
50. Adrian Randall, *Before the Luddites: Custom, Community and Machinery in the English Woollen Industry, 1776–1809* (Cambridge: Cambridge University Press, 1991), 241–228.
51. There is now a rich bibliography on Luddism. For a summary, see Randall, *Riotous Assemblies*, 271–302.
52. There is a voluminous literature on early radicalism, insurrectionaries, and government repression in the years from 1791 to 1820. See a useful summary in Frank O'Gorman, *The Long Eighteenth Century: British Political and Social History, 1688–1832* (London: Bloomsbury Academic, 1997), 242–255. On the Peterloo Massacre, see Channing, in this volume.
53. John Fortescue, *History of the British Army* (1899–1930), Vol. IV, 906 states that more than two hundred barracks were eventually built in this period, able to house 146,000 infantry and 17,000 cavalry.

54. Robert Reid, *Land of Lost Content: The Luddite Revolt* (London: Heinemann, 1986), 151–152. The army also deployed a large detachment of the Stirlingshire Militia undercover to seize likely suspects at night, an early 'snatch squad'.
55. This was especially true of the Lancashire power loom riots of 1826 and the agrarian Swing riots of 1830. On the former see David Walsh, 'The Lancashire "Rising" of 1826', *Albion* 26, no. 4 (1994): 601–621. There is an extensive literature on Swing: see, inter alia, Eric J. Hobsbawm and George Rudé, *Captain Swing* (London: Lawrence and Wishart, 1970); Carl J. Griffin, *The Rural War: Captain Swing and the Politics of Protest* (Manchester, UK: Manchester University Press, 2012); Andrew Spicer and Steve Poole, eds., *Captain Swing Reconsidered: Forty Years of Rural History from Below*. Vol 32 (London: Southern History Society, 2010).
56. The 'new' county police forces after 1839 in fact attracted a violent reception in both urban and rural areas. See Robert D. Storch, 'The Plague of Blue Locusts: Police Reform and Popular Resistance in Northern England, 1840–57', *International Review of Social History* 20, no. 1 (1975): 61–90; Adrian Randall and Edwina Newman, 'Protest, Proletarians and Paternalists: Social Conflict in Rural Wiltshire', *Rural History* 6, no. 2 (1995): 220, re the 'Potterne Lambs'.
57. The phrase comes from Eric J. Hobsbawm, *Labouring Men* (London: Weidenfeld and Nicolson, 1964), 7.
58. On the loss of 'space' for radical protests, see Katrina Navikas, *Protest and the Politics of Space and Place, 1789–1848* (Manchester, UK: Manchester University Press, 2016).

Further Reading

Bohstedt, John. *The Politics of Provisions: Food Riots, Moral Economy, and Market Transition in England, c. 1550–1850*. Farnham, UK: Ashgate, 2010.

Charlesworth, Andrew, and Adrian Randall, eds. *Moral Economy and Popular Protest: Crowds, Conflict and Authority*. Basingstoke, UK: Macmillan, 2000.

Colley, Linda. *Britons: Forging the Nation, 1707–1837*. New Haven, CT: Yale University Press, 1992.

Navikas, Katrina. *Protest and the Politics of Space and Place, 1789–1848*. Manchester, UK: Manchester University Press, 2016.

O'Gorman, Frank. *The Long Eighteenth Century: British Political and Social History, 1688–1832*. London: Bloomsbury Academic, 1997.

Randall, Adrian. *Riotous Assemblies: Popular Protest in Hanoverian England*. Oxford: Oxford University Press, 2006.

Rogers, Nicholas *Crowds, Culture and Politics in Georgian Britain*. Oxford: Clarendon Press, 1998.

Thompson, Edward P. *Customs in Common*. London: Merlin, 1991.

Thompson, Edward P. 'The Moral Economy of the English Crowd in the Eighteenth Century'. *Past and Present* 50 (1971): 76–136.

CHAPTER 3

IN SEARCH OF A POLITICAL THEORY OF ASSEMBLY

SHARATH SRINIVASAN

INTRODUCTION

THE assembly, Judith Butler states, 'is already speaking before it utters any words'.[1] What is assembly saying? For Butler, assembly performs and enacts a form of 'we the people', proclaiming to those in power, 'we are still here'.[2] In the contemporary assemblies she analyses in neoliberal late modernity, the transient assembling of bodies enacts a contestation of the dominant political order and delivers a bodily demand for a less precarious life. There remains, however, the more general question: What does any assembly, all assembly, proclaim? This chapter explores how assembly speaks up against dominant frameworks of modern politics. These frameworks too often reduce politics to the state, its monopoly over legitimate violence, and its institutions of representative government. Assembly speaks of another politics where power is not sourced in coercive authority or bureaucratic order and where the capacity to self-govern is not reduced to electoral choices for political representation.

It is telling that when actual assemblies burgeon uncontrollably, they may cause alarm for ruling authorities. Whether protests against pandemic lockdowns in China, racist policing practices in the United States, pension reform in France, or subjugation of women in Iran, in recent years, as in previous eras, 'we are still here' carries the subtitle 'and we're not happy with you, the state and our rulers, and where you are'.

Equally, one group of citizens' assembly may be another group's insecurity. For assembly is unbounded. Assembly, amidst marches, crowds, protests, riots, and revolutions, holds unpredictable potential to bring forth possibilities of an upended, possibly violent, politics that a social contract between citizens and state is seemingly there to prevent. The threat of the masses or the crowd or the 'mob' may strike fear into citizens; fear that, in turn, is often channelled by the state and representative government to justify the policing and curtailing of assembly in the name of public order.

Yet perhaps the greater fear is the political order's existential fear. Deep down, modern state power rests on a precarious piece of foundational propaganda, aptly captured by Michel Foucault in his reading of Thomas Hobbes's treatise on state sovereignty: Leviathan says, of the state, 'It's what you wanted, it is you, the subjects, who constituted the sovereignty that represents you.'[3] Assembly holds the potential to insist otherwise. The greater threat posed by assembly is not violence or disorder but that the assembled people might become 'a law unto themselves' and reject the legitimacy of the state's coercive authority and the inevitability of representative government. In its boldest forms, the assembly embodies popular sovereignty and enacts self-government, reopening the covenant or the state-society contract and revisiting the matter of its consent.

Given its foundational significance for politics, now and in times past, assembly as an object of enquiry receives remarkably scant attention in two dominant traditions in mainstream political theory: realism and liberalism.[4] A focus on the state, coercion, and rule in the political realism tradition, a focus on individual liberty in liberal political thought, and, across both traditions, a presumptive attachment to virtues of representative government, all eschews sustained consideration of the place of assembly in politics. Yet this inattention is itself political. In what they lay focus upon, these traditions work to banish assembly to the limits of 'ordinary' politics.

Assembly, though, has never been as marginal to politics as these political traditions suggest. This chapter recovers a global historical experience of assembly and draws upon a wider set of perspectives in political thought to reappraise assembly's enduring and central importance. This endeavour reveals how assembly matters not merely because of an individual freedom or right or for actualizing a democratic space to protest against the state or to hold it to account but, more vitally, because it manifests a distinctive political horizon of its own. Assembly, notably popular assembly that enacts self-government, exists as political and historical fact long before the juridical state comes to recognize and police the right to peacefully assemble or is required by a community of states to uphold this right.

This volume is about 'assembly'. However, it is largely concerned with the conventional assemblies in modern political orders—protests, demonstrations, ad hoc gatherings of citizens, and so on—and the state's role in upholding and regulating the right of individual citizens to assemble peacefully. By contrast, this chapter scrutinizes the gap between these contemporary transient assemblies of protest and their regulation and the formal institutionalized assemblies of representatives in many countries across the world, a gap in which popular assembly as a form and practice of politics has fallen and faded from view.

Giving renewed attention to popular assembly—assembly as an enactment of popular sovereignty and self-government—compels us to retheorize assembly's role in modern politics and to think differently about the politics of the right of peaceful assembly. By recovering the essence of popular assembly and finding this to be a hidden core of protest assembly, this chapter argues that assembly, as a political form, constitutes, but also calls into question, the boundary of legitimate political order.

The ruling authority's tolerance of sporadic occurrences of non-violent protest assembly and its acquiescence to individual rights to peacefully assemble are, paradoxically, necessary means through which the legitimacy of the state's capacity to coerce and a government's claim to represent are maintained. By legitimating an individualized right to assemble peacefully in protest, the dominant political order concurrently delegitimates more radical notions of popular assembly as self-government and, in so doing, seeks to tame assembly and its radical political promise. Yet assembly, precisely because of its distinctive political power and its historical experience, remains irrepressible.

Assembly in Mainstream Political Thought

Two dominant traditions in political thought—realism and liberalism—give assembly little regard in their understanding of political authority, power, and legitimacy in modern politics. Centred on explaining and justifying state authority and representative government, both traditions banish assembly to the outer limits (and beyond) of politics. Even so, assembly irrepressibly agitates against some foundational presumptions underpinning both traditions. This disregard for assembly has also been the subject of critical rejoinders from perspectives as diverse as post-structuralism, Marxism, and post-colonialism. Such rejoinders expose the uneasy relationship between the tendencies of law, order, and rights towards tyranny and oppression and the irrepressible possibility of assembly as collective resistance.

In the broad school of what might be called political realism, the focus of enquiry is on rule, authority, legitimacy of force, and order. The main actors are the state and who rules the state. In Hobbes's treatise, only when selfish people, caught in the insecure and uncertain tribulations of the state of nature, covenant with each other to give up their transferable rights to a sovereign and submit unconditionally thereafter to the sovereign's use of coercive power as the sovereign sees fit to ensure peace, is political order achieved. Order and security are paramount. Absolute monarchy is Hobbes's preferred sovereign. Other thinkers in the realist tradition place greater emphasis on how the right to rule is maintained rather than presumed. The prince, Niccolò Machiavelli argued, must learn from the centaur, half-man half-beast, and maintain rule through consent but also, when necessary, coercion.[5] While Machiavelli characterized force and consent separately, for Max Weber, writing much later on the modern state, these combine. A monopoly over the *legitimate* use of physical force is the defining quality of state power.[6]

Across this diverse thought, the central concern of politics is to explain the power to rule, including through the capacity for legitimate violence: Why and how might dominant authority legitimately claim such power? A corollary of prescribing or describing modern politics in this way is that violent civil resistance to government rule is disallowed, prevented, and delegitimated.

A key boundary that expresses legitimate state power in realist thought is the boundary between violent and non-violent collective action. Moreover, it is the state that, prospectively, ensures this boundary. The point is this: Tolerating but also policing peaceful assembly is part and parcel of the state's claim to a monopoly on legitimate violence. The very definitional foundation of the modern state finds expression in how the state prospectively polices the boundary of possibly legitimate non-violent assembly versus illegitimate, possibly violent, collective resistance.

Lurking within political realism's preoccupation with politics-as-rule are equally important elitist conceptualizations of political representation that also undercut assembly. Hobbes is credited with putting the age-old thorny question of representation in politics—how can we explain and justify the authority of elites to govern?—on a secular footing tied to the state, eschewing divine authority. The sovereign's unquestionable authority to rule rests on literally representing the Commonwealth and all its members per the acts of their mutual covenants; the sovereign's will is their will.[7] In Hobbes's thought, representation ensures the unity, and thus submission and obedience, of citizens. This allows him to contemplate but reject the democratic assembly of citizens in favour of absolute monarchy. With no recourse to question sovereign authority, this is a decidedly anti-democratic understanding of political representation.

For Weber, the modern state demanded a pragmatic understanding of how 'ruling minorities' and leaders who wield coercive state authority are reconciled with parliamentary democracies.[8] Despite differences, these elitist approaches to representation in realist thought often reduce democracy to an institutional process, retrenching assembly as a mode of expressing popular sovereignty or enacting self-government.[9] The implication is that to the extent assembly manifests or hints at such an alternative politics and challenges elitist representative politics, it exerts troublesome pressure on authority and order. Thus, for realists, not only violent resistance but also non-violent assembly has its limits.

In liberal political thought, the liberty of individuals to assemble is valued, but the political significance of assembly is underplayed. Liberals, since John Locke and John Stuart Mill, have assumed a better human nature than realist thinkers and sought to protect society's possibilities for human flourishing by grounding state authority and institutions of government in individual freedom. Absolute rule is unnecessarily and immorally coercive. Individual liberty and collective freedom require a just foundation for government that makes it duty-bound to protect citizens' rights.

An important early thinker in this tradition, Benjamin Constant, linked modern liberty to political representation.[10] Rather than freedom to participate *in* government, such as for free adult male citizens in Ancient Athens, modern civil liberties and political rights protected individuals *from* the state, including by protecting their right to elect representatives to undertake the *burden* of government. The liberal rationale for representation may be less elitist than in realist thought, but it remains similarly dismissive of assembly and any aspiration of self-government. The right to assemble in the liberal tradition takes on only subordinated significance, primarily in relation to how individuals choose and hold to account elected representatives who are duty-bound to protect their freedom.

For John Rawls, arguably modern political liberalism's most influential thinker, the freedom of assembly serves the priority of individual political liberty ('the right to vote and to be eligible for public office'); it is not a means of collectively enacting popular sovereignty. Freedom of assembly, as a 'basic liberty', is justified primarily in the context of ensuring effective political participation in a system of representative government, understood alongside the importance of liberty of conscience and freedom to deliberate and engage in public discussion.[11] The limited and individualized attention Rawls gives to assembly places no value on it as a form of collective political action that invokes the virtue of popular sovereignty or self-government.

Moreover, in Rawls's totemic effort to give liberalism a fresh egalitarian restatement, perhaps the most important role ascribed to assembly is pre-political, ahistorical, and atomized. In his foundational thinking on the 'original position', he asks: What rules would hypothetical members of a timeless society, ignorant of their social position, capabilities or life course, have reason to accept? This is an assembly of sorts,[12] but it is an other-worldly thought experiment devoid of plural and situated bodies and identities, discursive exchange, or affective relations.

Thus, in such contemporary liberal political philosophy, the abstracted assembly of the original position under a veil of ignorance forecloses the need for future real-world assemblies that manifest political self-government or renegotiate the just society in fundamental ways. Assembly as a form of collective political action is subordinated and popular sovereignty undervalued.

This diminished place of assembly within realist and liberal traditions of political thought that instead privilege order, legitimate coercion, representation, and individual liberty has been critiqued from a number of angles. One such angle, important here, scrutinizes the historical political projects motivating these traditions. In one volume of his collected lectures, *Society Must Be Defended*, Michel Foucault's critical rereading of Hobbes proposes that Leviathan's order is not a response to generalized *warre* between humans in the state of nature but rather a political project to disallow civil resistance in tumultuous seventeenth-century England. Hobbes's state under sovereign order is historically contingent and contested; it is not an answer to primitive war generally but to a specific war's new phase. Hobbes's treatise for civil politics, Foucault proposes, is war by other means, including the means of law and rights.[13] To the extent political order seeks to achieve a reign of peace in civil society, politics might better be understood as the institutionalization and legitimation of the victors' repression of the vanquished.

Foucault's provocations have exaggerations and flaws, not least how the war metaphor disregards more complex and contested relationships between and amongst rulers and the ruled throughout history. However, he does provoke important questions: To what extent should we reread the protection of the individual right of peaceful assembly as essentially the taming of assembly's greater potential to challenge the right to rule of a given political order? Paradoxically, is the granting of the right to peacefully assemble one ingredient in the juridification of brute political power into legitimate authority? Does the right help to establish the legal obligation for citizens to obey coercive state rule and government by representation?

Affirmative answers to these questions might be drawn from surprisingly diverse quarters, from Karl Marx's suspicion of the juridification of individual rights in the face of entrenched class-based inequality[14] to Franz Fanon's decolonial argument for freedom from the occupier's racial oppression through collective violence[15] and, within realist thought itself, Carl Schmitt's sympathetic theory of the partisan who uses irregular violent means that reject the invader's politico-legal 'rules of the game'.[16]

With this critique of the way dominant frameworks of modern politics marginalize assembly, let us turn to developing a grounded survey of the global history of assembly long before the emergence of the 'right' to peacefully assemble. Remembering the lost or diminished historical experience of popular assembly as a mode of self-government that instantiates popular sovereignty motivates and animates the theoretical purpose of this chapter. It provides the basis for advancing a political theory of assembly in relation to the generative work of other scholars who give assembly, as a distinctive form of politics, careful and due attention.

A Global Historical Survey of Popular Assembly

A brisk global historical survey of popular assembly gives assembly a more integral place in politics than is appreciated in political realism and liberalism. An important finding from such an enquiry is the distinction, overlooked in mainstream political traditions, between assembly as a means of protest versus assembly as a form of self-government. Today, assembly is mostly seen through the frame of individualized rights to assemble and to protest in opposition to constituted authority. Popular assembly, by contrast, invokes popular sovereignty and self-government. This need not mean 'direct democracy', though the Athenian assembly looms large in the political imagination. Indeed, this section deliberately expands our historical and political understanding of popular assembly well beyond Ancient Greece. This allows us to recover a longer and wider history of self-government through popular assembly, including alongside or within hierarchical (monarchic or oligopolistic) regimes and exclusionist societies. While assemblies are today often reduced to temporary protests against state action, assembly as a form of self-government is arguably a more heretical and powerful notion. It is a possibility of politics that, in the example of its historical fact extending far back in world history, only comes to be heretical owing to the advent of the modern state and representative government.

We may start our brief survey with Ancient Athens, but only to then look well before, after, and beyond. Notwithstanding notorious exclusions (women, aliens, slaves), democracy in Athens was 'direct' and the popular assembly (*ekklesia*) was open to all eligible citizens. The *ekklesia* had considerable authority to make proposals, take the initiative, and make major decisions concerning the city-state's affairs.

However, we must proceed cautiously. The imaginary of all citizens engaged in 'direct democracy' in the *ekklesia* is oversimplistic. For a start, the *demos* gathered in any specific assembly were always a subset of eligible citizens that varied based on willingness and ability to attend (averaging six thousand of a total population between thirty thousand and fifty thousand). They were also not undifferentiated. Orators were distinguished as political leaders. Besides the assembly, some affairs, including the important work of the council and the courts, were handled by citizens who put themselves forward for selection by lottery, and other vital affairs (war, finance) by citizens who were elected. The council (*boule*) largely set the political agenda for the assembly, and the decisions of the *ekklesia* were subject to scrutiny by the people's courts. In the fifth century BCE, a new body, the *nomothetai*, comprising a subset of the citizenry appointed by lot, was solely authorized with passing general laws; the *ekklesia* could only pass less-determinative decrees. Thus, Manin turns to the role of drawing lots in Athenian direct democracy in appointing the *nomothetai* to contrast with elections under representative government.[17]

The *ekklesia*, the citizens' assembly, enacted the *demos*'s popular sovereignty and embodied Athens's *demo-kratia*. But disabusing ourselves of an idealized and overdetermined understanding of direct democracy in Athens or an anachronistic reading of the Athenian *ekklesia* as solely 'sovereign',[18] while holding on to the distinctive qualities of Athens' assembly, frees us to recover important examples of popular assembly and modes of self-government elsewhere and across time.

From Ancient Athens, we might first travel further back in time, to Mesopotamia in the third millennium BCE. The idea of a 'primitive democracy' in Mesopotamia was famously first proposed by Jacobsen,[19] who sought to unravel precursors to the role of assembly in carrying out judicial functions in post-Imperial Mesopotamian towns (second millennium BCE). The *purham*, an assembly of town folk, carried out this role. Jacobsen argued that the origins of this lay judicial authority were to be found in an earlier, even more 'democratic', period. Gilgamesh, he illuminates from the epic, relied on the consent of elders in assembly, and the town itself, to go into battle. Signs of the political authority of the assembly, Jacobsen further argues, are to be found in earlier Sumerian and Akkadian mythology concerning how their gods, all gathered (including both sexes) in assembly aided by wine and beer, debated, and decided important matters—above all who might be King (and no longer King). Although Jacobsen was criticized for characterizing these practices as 'democracy', since his breakthrough work in the 1940s scholars have found even more substantial evidence of the central role of popular assembly in prehistoric and latter Mesopotamia and its surrounds. Graeber and Wengrow conclude, 'It is almost impossible to find a city anywhere in the ancient Near East that did not have some equivalent to a popular assembly.'[20]

In *The Dawn of Everything*, Graeber and Wengrow advance a provocative thesis in which popular assembly features prominently. Reinterpreting historical and archaeological evidence from well beyond Mesopotamia, including sites such as the abandoned city of Teotihuacan and the indigenous city-state of Tlaxcala in modern-day Mexico, they rebut two common presumptions about pre-modern societies: that hierarchical and absolute rule by overlords was the norm and that urban centres invariably fell under increasingly centralized forms of administration. Instead, they find evidence in many places for the role of popular assemblies in varieties of decentralized self-government, sometimes in spite of, sometimes alongside, kingship, or aristocratic rule. Without necessarily accepting their entire thesis, we can extend this evidence concerning popular assembly further still.

In pre-colonial Africa, one example of the role of assembly in participatory government is the *kgotla* assemblies of the Tswana people (now contemporary Botswana). Tswana government comprised hereditary chieftaincy, but such *kgosi* authority, at multiple levels from the state itself down through to the ward, required the consent of adult males assembled in *kgotla*. 'The king is king by the grace of the people', says the Tswana proverb.[21] In turn, *kgotla* were spaces for consultation and discursive dissent, with strong rhetorical customs attached to them.[22] Villagers, when assembled in *kgotla*, could criticize *kgosi* without fear of reprisal.

Between the fall of the Roman Empire and the rise of city-states in the twelfth and thirteenth centuries, political assemblies were also prominent across Europe.[23] While most comprised elites, some mixed representative and popular elements, such as the *Thing* assembly system that was prominent in medieval Scandinavia and northern Europe prior to the rise of supra-regional Kingdoms. Enacting a distinctive form of decentralized self-government, *Things* comprised freemen, presided over by a speaker or chieftain, who met regularly and legislated on local affairs, chose royal nominees, and decided upon disputes and legal matters. The system assumed particular significance in Iceland and there, in 930 AD, the national *Althing* was founded, an annual legislative and judicial assembly open to all free men and which was the primary legislative institution of national government for three centuries.[24] Although subsequent Norwegian and Danish overrule diminished its significance, the *Althing* remains the foundation of Iceland's democratic republic.

The popular assembly as a means of self-government has also endured elsewhere. For Hansen, a leading scholar of the *ekklesia* and direct democracy in Athens, it is the Swiss *Landsgemeinde*—people's assemblies introduced in the thirteenth century and still in existence in some of the smaller Swiss cantons—that offers the most striking modern parallel.[25] In this contemporary example of direct democracy, major decisions and all statutes are made by popular assembly, in which every adult citizen has the right to speak and to vote. These assemblies comprise thousands of citizens, the largest over ten thousand. Votes are conducted informally by a show of hands wherever possible, presided over by a chairman, or Landammann.

Popular assemblies have often existed as part of more elitist political systems, playing roles that both constitute and check power. In the shifting fortunes and forms of civic republicanism in the city-state of medieval Florence, as Pocock examines, the role of the popular assembly—the *Consiglio Maggiore*—was a matter of intense reflection among influential public intellectuals around the time of the 1494 constitution.[26] The Florentine republic was oligarchic or monarchic in nature, but an abiding question was how to ensure that the popular assembly oversaw and guaranteed the virtues and functions carried out by elected elites so that the former did not cut across the latter but the latter also did not override the former. Whether the many of the *Consiglio* should be reduced to merely electing or nominating from its ranks the 'few' who sought higher office, or whether the popular assembly should play a role in the initiation, deliberation, or assent of laws, as well as hold authority over the basic laws of the political structure to prevent oligopolistic tendencies, was hotly debated. A consistent feature, however, was the desire to protect civic virtue amongst the citizenry writ large, which required ensuring an important place for the popular assembly.

It is striking that practices of popular assembly in the age of democratic revolutions in Europe (1776–1848) were also central to strands of political thought on democracy that developed alongside realism and liberalism. Frank's illuminating recuperation of Jean-Jacques Rousseau's commitment to popular assembly as manifesting the people's sovereign will reminds us of how realist and liberal presumptions around order, rule, representation, and rights in modern politics were, in their day, fundamentally at odds with actual political experience.[27]

Even the modern *right* to peacefully assemble has a history that relates to assembly as self-government, not only to speak up against government. In the pre-independence United States, the right to assemble emerged in the context of colonists seeking to protect their right—exercised through town hall meetings and county assemblies—to self-govern and address their community's concerns.[28] As Bowie neatly puts it, 'The right to assemble at its inception was more than a claim to dissent—it was also a claim to govern. For over a century before 1789, the right to assemble had been invoked to protect the power of people to meaningfully participate in enacting needed legislation.'[29] And while deeply fearful of mobs, Tocqueville would find in the local assemblies at the township level the most vibrant expression of democracy in post-Independence America.[30]

This rich history of popular assembly as self-government contrasts with its contemporary absence. We should be careful not to presume this is a linear, evolutionary, or teleological story. For a start, apart from diverse examples of popular assembly, there is also a long history of politics where self-government is absent and hierarchy, coercion, rule, and exclusion dominate. There has also long been a history of popular assembly interconnected with more elitist forms of recognition, representation, and rule. Recovering popular assembly in world history through space and time points to political variety, not a 'golden age' or even a 'lost treasure'. Instead, the critical concern is to reappraise the significance of how, with the rise of nation-states and political modernity, popular assembly comes to be subordinated.

Two points are clear. The first is that even though it remains relevant to actual politics in specific places and times, popular assembly as self-government gets somewhat lost in modern politics. As Manin states forthrightly at the very outset of his important work on the subject, 'Representative government gives no institutional role to the assembled people'.[31] Popular assembly, pushed beyond institutional limits, instead became *remarkable*. We see this in accounts of self-determining assemblies in Rojava[32] and collective decision-making amongst the Zapatistas.[33] Popular assembly also emerges as remarkable in the context of protest movements, such as in accounts of Occupy,[34] and of revolutionary uprisings during the 'Arab Spring' and in Sudan.[35] All these assemblies blur the distinction between protest power and popular self-rule. In protesting against prevailing authority, they often reclaim popular sovereignty and are acting out self-government.

The second point that this brief historical survey illustrates is that a long-standing tradition of assembly, one in which assembly actualizes notions of popular sovereignty and self-government, remains of foundational importance in our historical political imaginary. This experience and imaginary challenge what dominant political frameworks consider counts, or should count, as politics. Moreover, that challenge also occurs in practice, in the periphery of 'ordinary politics', where protest assembly both enacts and contests ordinary politics' presumptions and its underdetermined boundaries. Understanding this is crucial to how we re-centre assembly in contemporary political theory.

Re-centring Assembly in Contemporary Political Theory

Advancing political theory on assembly in the context of the modern state requires a fundamental reappraisal of the interrelationship between protest assembly and the diminished but historically salient phenomenon of popular assembly that actualizes self-government. Popular assembly that constitutes or seeks to constitute its own political authority remains salient in our world, notwithstanding its marginalization in contemporary politics and mainstream political thought. The promise and power of popular sovereignty and self-government *in* assembly is enacted in momentous times of political protest, such as Occupy; it rises up amidst revolutions and liberation struggles, such as during the Arab Spring; it persists remarkably in some exceptional polities, such as the Swiss *Landsgemeinde*; and it constitutes and binds newly self-determining political communities such as the Rojava and the Zapatista.

Beyond these extraordinary manifestations, popular assembly is always there, at the foundation of diverse polities and political systems, as a human potentiality that implicitly confers yet might also retract political legitimacy in relation to dominant authority. This is not, or not only, a matter of protest or dissent; rather, it is the potential of people to act out and embody their capacity to self-govern and to reclaim popular sovereignty. There might, for the most part, be no good reason or impetus amongst citizens to do so. Pragmatically, popular assembly's prospects in the face of coercive state power, sophisticated parliamentary representative government, and the institutionalized rule of law may also be dim. But assembly's radical potentiality remains foundationally important.

What is assembly saying, then? What might any assembly *potentially* say? Perhaps, 'We are here. We are capable of self-governing. And we are sovereign.' Moreover, assembly that both draws upon historical experience and points towards a radical political horizon increasingly matters in the context of legitimacy crises facing representative democracy. As Pitkin, a pre-eminent theorist of political representation, recognized in her later years, 'the arrangements we call "representative democracy" have become a substitute for popular self-government, not its enactment'.[36] Assembly, including protest assembly, often manifests, and always holds the potential to manifest, this critique. Indeed, the contemporary trend of curtailing protest across many democracies may be more about this threat in the context of representative democracy's legitimacy crisis than a retreat from liberal values and individual rights.

We have noted earlier how, in some dominant frameworks of modern politics, assembly is, quite literally, made peripheral. Yet now we come to appreciate that assembly is never irrelevant. The historical political imaginary of popular assembly and its remarkable contemporary manifestations challenge the coercion–representation–liberty nexus in mainstream political thought and challenge what dominant political traditions consider counts, or should count, as politics.

From the state's and representative government's points of view, assembly serves as their political 'constitutive outside': outside when taking the form of politics 'by other means' that are violent or seditious; outside when claiming to *be* political authority exercising popular sovereignty and enacting self-government; only tipping to inside the bounds of 'legitimate' politics when an episodic form of constituent protest power that affirms the primacy of the state and representative government, even in the very process of criticizing it. Assembly is curtailed to this liminal place in politics, of transient collective political action which, while constitutionally protected (i.e. regulated) when 'peaceful', cannot fundamentally question the coercion–representation–liberty nexus of politics centred on the modern state and representative government.

Advancing a political theory of assembly requires a re-centring of assembly's role as the 'constitutive outside' in modern politics, that always holds potential to tip over and reconstitute politics 'inside'. Such a task begins with explaining this crucial boundary role that assembly plays and then accounting for how and why the demarcation of the boundary is contested in profound ways. It is in the specific contestations over assembly and how the state's attempts to tame and police assembly come into conflict with assembly's distinct form of political power that our political worlds are always taking shape.

This journey to retheorize assembly in this way is aided by engaging with strands of political thought outside of dominant traditions that give more generative significance to the role of assembly in politics. Reading with Judith Butler, Murray Bookchin, and Hannah Arendt, we encounter theorized articulations of another form and experience of politics that fundamentally departs from politics as coercive state authority, representative government, or the protection of individual liberties.[37]

Beyond the critical rejoinders previously discussed, we might first look to prominent treatments of assembly in recent years that take as their subject social movements and protests of the 2010s, especially those in the wake of the global financial crisis of 2008, such as Occupy and Indignados, but also during the 'Arab Spring' uprisings. Here, Judith Butler's *Notes Toward a Performative Theory of Assembly* warrants close consideration as it explicitly engages with political theory.[38] Observing the 'transient critical gatherings' of protest assemblies during a time of neoliberal precarity,[39] Butler lays emphasis on their quality of embodiment—the act of bodies assembling—and its performative, expressive, and signifying characteristics. Besides and beyond speech that occurs within an assembly, bodies assembling perform and enact a popular will that contests their living conditions by delivering a 'bodily demand' to the established political order.[40] From here, Butler also goes further to examine assembly in relation to state sovereignty and political representation in ways that illuminate a fuller theorizing of assembly in politics.

The crucial intervention Butler makes, which resonates with the arguments developed here, is that the assembly, in the embodied actions of assembling, enacts popular sovereignty, as distinct from state sovereignty and representative government. With assembly, the popular sovereignty of a people is formed through acts of self-designation and self-gathering, and precisely in that process, distinguishes and separates itself 'from the very representative regime it legitimates'.[41] Butler implies here that the transient protest assembly derives its political significance from enacting, in the moment, the foundational possibility of popular assembly that claims sovereign power.

Butler then demands that the freedom of assembly must 'precede and exceed any form of government that confers and protects [the] right of assembly'.[42] Their reasons are emphatically clear:

> As long as the state controls the very conditions of freedom of assembly, popular sovereignty becomes an instrument of state sovereignty, and the legitimating conditions of the state are lost at the same time that the freedom of assembly has been robbed of both its critical and its democratic functions.[43]

Yet perhaps this is too demanding and underplays actual politics. It is out of step with what any representative regime knows most of society, most of the time, will accept as legitimate. The state, in ordering social and political life through laws and coercive power, disciplines contemporary assembly to only be critical and democratic up to a point. It is better to understand that the state and representative government tolerate the popular sovereignty of assembly up to a boundary precisely in order to protect their own legitimating conditions. Assembly must be transient and 'peaceful' (however the state polices and demarcates this), never violent, but, crucially, also never claiming to displace representation and state authority with self-government.

Butler posits that the 'freedom of assembly may well be a precondition for politics itself',[44] but they do not scrutinize how dominant political frameworks deny assembly's true freedom by protecting a more reduced and punctuated form. To put it another way, the transient and critical nature of contemporary protest assembly is tolerated but also conditioned by the dominance of coercive state authority and representative government. This boundary condition, held in tension, is arguably central to constituting the *unfreedom* of popular assembly of a more heretically consequential kind. It is the banishing of this form of assembly politics that seeks to enact self-government over representative government that allows our dominant political institutions to present themselves as (the only) politics as we know it.

If Butler places too much emphasis on transient protest assembly at the expense of popular assembly, we may instead look to Murray Bookchin's institutionalist reworking of popular assembly for contemporary politics.[45] Bookchin's communalist project explicitly rejects protest assembly as being sufficient and sees his project as rescuing political action from being reduced to confrontations with authority or 'street theatre'. He decries the reduction of politics to state order and representative government as a gross ahistorical simplification:

> If politics is denatured to mean little more than statecraft and the manipulation of people by their so-called 'representatives,' then a condition that has acquired varying forms of expression in the classical Athenian assembly, popular medieval civic assemblies, town meetings, and the revolutionary sectional assemblies of Paris, is conveniently erased and the multitudinous institutions for managing a municipality become reducible to the behaviour of cynical parliamentarians or worse.[46]

Bookchin's anarchic project calls for confederated and institutionalized municipal popular assemblies which, '[b]y their very existence, could then challenge the legitimacy of the state and statist forms of power. They could expressly be aimed at replacing state power and statecraft with popular power and a socially rational transformative politics'.[47] His vision might appear wildly ambitious and unlikely, or perhaps even naïve and dangerous, yet it is by being grounded in the historical imaginary and experience that it nevertheless retains significance for how assembly should be properly theorized.

While Bookchin's institutional manifesto might risk distracting us from his core premise, that premise is perhaps best captured by Hannah Arendt. For Arendt, the popular assembly *is* politics properly understood. In a political age dominated by the state and representative government, its loss is our loss in the hope of being truly political beings. Yet her reading of the promise in contemporary times of citizens' assembling and acting to claim a *share in* government is arguably tragic: It is extraordinary and irrepressible, yet also fleeting and fragile, precisely because it is not easily institutionalized in political modernity without damaging it.

Freely associating citizens in a public realm arises spontaneously in momentous times but then invariably vanishes as politics gets institutionalized according to dominant logics. Town hall assemblies in the revolutionary United States, the Parisian Communes, early Russian soviets, the Hungarian uprising, Israeli kibbutz, and the post-war American civil rights, anti-war, and student movements, she essays, all manifest elusively powerful collective political action, despite a dominant politics beholden to coercive rule and party-controlled representation. Arendt characterizes these tragically imperilled instances of popular assembly that enact self-government as the council system:

> Since the revolutions of the eighteenth century, every large upheaval has actually developed the rudiments of an entirely new form of government, which emerged independent of all preceding revolutionary theories, directly out of the course of the revolution itself, that is, out of the experiences of action and out of the resulting will of the actors to participate in the further development of public affairs. This new form of government is the council system, which, as we know, has perished everytime and everywhere, destroyed either directly by the bureaucracy of the nation states or by the party machines. . . . the council system seems to correspond to and spring from the very experience of political action.[48]

For Arendt, transient assemblies, such as the civil rights movement, matter not because of the constituent right to protest per se but because the political action entailed in associational political dissent, insofar as it reprises a collective claim to share in government, is essential for reviving and sustaining the historical constitutional founding of a polity.[49] As she says, 'every large upheaval has actually developed the rudiments of an entirely new form of government, which emerged independent of all preceding revolutionary theories, directly out of the course of the revolution itself, that is, out of the experiences of action and out of the resulting will of the actors to participate in the further development of public affairs'.

The theoretical work in this chapter is not primarily normative. The point is not to endorse Bookchin's anarcho-communalist proposals for municipal assembly as self-government, to align with Butler's primary concern with how the freedom of transient assembly must be unfettered to overcome the failures of representative government to tackle neoliberal precarity, or to search with Arendt for politics' 'lost treasure' in the council system. If normative debates are foregrounded, the more fundamental theoretical intervention in these pages might be too easily lost.[50]

Instead, we theoretically advance on popular assembly's historical experience and imaginary and grasp at assembly's distinct political phenomenology. More specifically, we come to appreciate, first, assembly's foundational place in politics, and, second, its distinctive form and power. Rather than critique the unrealism of these normative proposals for politics, we do better to appreciate the force and urgency of their implicit demand: How we can understand what politics is and might be without accounting fully for the role of assembly—including popular assembly that enacts popular sovereignty and self-government—within it?

Dominant political frameworks work to hide the true power of assembly precisely by containing it. Popular assembly is accommodated in modern politics by banishing its institutional relevance and then taming it, as an individual right to peacefully assemble, in order to tolerate a lesser form. Even the rise to prominence of so-called citizen assemblies in numerous countries, for all of their promise, are heavily circumscribed and subordinated institutionally to state power. However, this chapter's historical, empirical, and theoretical recovery of the significance of popular assembly reveals a form of politics that calls into question the shaky assumptions and democratic shortcomings of the modern state, representative government, and notions of political liberty.

Assembly's boundary-constituting role contains within its radical promise. The distinctive power of assembly—that in protest assembly manifests in its unique qualities of unpredictable, embodied, and affective collective agency, but which on a deeper plane arises from a historical experience of popular assembly as self-government—is inherently at odds with dominant frameworks of politics and thus always calling them into question. Assembly always holds the potential to not only contest the boundary of legitimate politics but to upend that politics altogether.

Conclusion

A historically grounded retheorization of the importance of assembly in politics demands that we look well beyond, and deeper within, protest assembly and the individual right to peacefully assemble. In theory as well in practice, a reductive focus on public protest assembly in the margins of ordinary politics is precisely what dominant frameworks of politics encourage. To value assembly and fully account for its significance, we must account more intrinsically and expansively for its distinctive political power. Protest assembly matters because assembly is about much more than protest. Humankind's lived political experience has a richer heritage in popular assembly as self-government. The possibility of this institutional form and its relationship to popular sovereignty represents the heretical possibility and horizon of assembly as protest, as well as its kernel.

Assemblies threaten dominant political order, but not for the reasons usually played up by that order. The usual characterization of the threat posed by protest assemblies is that they might spill over into disorder or even violence, and thus undermine security and individual liberty. However, the greater threat that assembly poses is to presumptions about what politics could or should be.

The greater fear of the state concerns the distinctive *power* of assembly: that it manifests an alternative form of politics and claim on politics. That form of politics has unique qualities. Episodic protest assemblies are unpredictable, often spontaneous and capable of beginning something new. They have strong affective elements and are often characterized by passion, emotion and experiential meaning. They embody political agency and being in a collective form, in turn shaping political identity and belonging. It is striking how these qualities are tamed through the individual right to peacefully assemble, and how they are regulated in the name of public order. All states, to lesser or greater degrees, seek to make protest assembly more predictable, less disruptive, more transient; upholding but regulating an individual right helps to legitimate this.

However, when we look more closely, the threat that assembly's power contains is more significant, and it is especially a threat to representative government. Taken together, the unique qualities of assembling as a mode of action capture a *lived experience* of politics, of being political and of doing politics, one that also connects with a deeper historical experience of popular assembly. Assembly contains a heretical possibility of politics, but it is not utopian. It presents an elementary but profound threat to politics as government by representation. The assembled people experience their capacity to self-determine. They reclaim a tangible sense of the meaning of popular sovereignty. They ask, or at any time might ask, 'Who are we not to have a greater share in governing ourselves?'

Author's Note

The evolution of this chapter owes a great deal to conversations with many people. My sincere thanks to Antoine Sander, Shalini Satkunanandan, Duncan Kelly, Christian Sorace, Thomas Probert, Michael Hamilton, Stu Woolman, Adrian Randall, and, in particular, Tabatha Abu El-Haj for our exchanges that continue to provoke thought and illumination.

Notes

1. Judith Butler, *Notes toward a Performative Theory of Assembly* (Cambridge, MA: Harvard University Press, 2015), 156.
2. Ibid., 25.
3. Michel Foucault, *'Society Must Be Defended': Lectures at the Collège de France, 1975–1976*, Vol. 1, trans. David Macey (London: Picador (Macmillan), 2003), 98.
4. This disregard echoes assembly's marginality in empirical political science, where it is often overshadowed by the attention given to protest, social movements, crowds, and popular revolution.
5. Niccolò Machiavelli, *The Prince*, Quentin Skinner and Richard Price, eds. (Cambridge: Cambridge University Press, 2019). Machiavelli writes, 'You should know, then, that there are two ways of contending: one by using laws, the other, force. The first is appropriate for men, the second, for animals; but because the former is often not sufficient, one must have recourse to the latter' (ibid., 59–60).
6. Max Weber, 'Politics as a Vocation', in *From Max Weber: Essays in Sociology*, trans. and ed. H. H. Gerth and C. Wright Mills (New York: Oxford University Press, 1946), 77–128.
7. Hobbes writes, 'But as men, for the atteyning of peace . . . have made an Artificiall Man, which we call a Common-wealth; so also have they made Artificiall Chains, called Civill Lawes, which they themselves, by mutuall covenants, have fastned at one end, to the lips of that Man, or Assembly, to whom they have given the Soveraigne Power; and at the other end to their own Ears': Thomas Hobbes, *Leviathan: The Matter, Forme, and Power of a Common-Wealth Ecclesiastical and Civil* (Auckland: The Floating Press, 2009), 301. As Pitkin explains, 'By the concept of representation, the person of this sovereign is identified

with the person of the commonwealth, so that all its members are logically bound into the union'. Hanna Pitkin, 'Hobbes's Concept of Representation—II', *American Political Science Review* 58, no. 4 (1964): 902–18, 916.

8. See especially Weber, *Politics as a Vocation*.
9. Weber's work influenced Joseph Schumpeter's democratic elitism. Schumpeter's influential definition of democracy as a political system in which the principal positions of power are filled 'through a competitive struggle for the people's vote' is a cornerstone of 'minimalist' theories of representative democracy.
10. See Benjamin Constant, 'The Liberty of Ancients Compared with that of Moderns', in *Constant: Political Writings*, trans. Biancamaria Fontana (Cambridge: Cambridge University Press, 1988), 308–328.
11. See John Rawls, *A Theory of Justice*, rev. ed. (Cambridge, MA: Harvard University Press, 2009), 223–227.
12. Rawls underscores that the original position must only invoke a timeless, dehumanized, and highly abstract assembly of sorts: 'The original position is not to be thought of as a general assembly which includes at one moment everyone who will live at some time; or, much less, as an assembly of everyone who could live at some time. It is not a gathering of all actual or possible persons. If we conceived of the original position in either of these ways, the conception would cease to be a natural guide to intuition and would lack a clear sense. In any case, the original position must be interpreted so that one can at any time adopt its perspective. . . . The veil of ignorance is a key condition in meeting this requirement'. Ibid., 139
13. Long after the Norman conquest of England, Foucault suggests, the Levellers and the Diggers saw 'the government, the laws, and property statutes are, basically, no more than a continuation of the war, the invasion and the defeat . . . Government means their war against us; rebellion is our war against them'. Foucault, *'Society Must Be Defended'*, 108.
14. See, for example, Karl Marx, 'On the Jewish Question', in *Marx: Early Political Writings*, ed. Joseph J. O'Malley and Richard A. Davis (Cambridge: Cambridge University Press, 1994), 28–56.
15. Fanon proposes that because of the deep racialized violence of colonial domination, collective violence is vital for the colonized to claim popular sovereignty: 'The mobilization of the masses, when it arises out of the war of liberation, introduces into each man's consciousness the ideas of a common cause, of a national destiny, and of a collective history. In the same way the second phase, that of the building-up of the nation, is helped on by the existence of this cement which has been mixed with blood and anger': Frantz Fanon, *The Wretched of the Earth*, trans. Constance Farrington (New York: Grove Press, 1965), 93.
16. Carl Schmitt, *Theory of the Partisan: Intermediate Commentary on the Concept of the Political*, trans. G. L. Ulmen (New York: Telos Press Pub, 2007).
17. Bernard Manin, *The Principles of Representative Government* (Cambridge: Cambridge University Press, 1997). A comprehensive account of the *Ekklesia* is to be found in works by Hansen. See Mogens H. Hansen, *The Athenian Democracy in the Age of Demosthenes: Structure, Principles, and Ideology* (Norman: University of Oklahoma Press, 1999).
18. See especially Hansen, *Athenian Democracy*.
19. Thorkild Jacobsen, 'Primitive Democracy in Ancient Mesopotamia', *Journal of Near Eastern Studies* 2, no. 3 (1943): 159–172. See also Norman Yoffee, *Myths of the Archaic State: Evolution of the Earliest Cities, States, and Civilizations* (Cambridge: Cambridge University Press, 2005).

20. David Graeber and David Wengrow, *The Dawn of Everything: A New History of Humanity* (London: Penguin Books, 2021), 301.
21. John L. Comaroff and Jean Comaroff, 'Postcolonial Politics and Discourses of Democracy in Southern Africa: An Anthropological Reflection on African Political Modernities', *Journal of Anthropological Research* 53, no. 2 (1997): 123–146. Also, Jonas Hjort, 'Pre-colonial Culture, Post-colonial Economic Success? The Tswana and the African Economic Miracle', *The Economic History Review* 63, no. 3 (2010): 688–709.
22. Isaac Schapera, *A Handbook of Tswana Law and Custom*, 2nd ed. (Oxford: Oxford University Press, 1955). Schapera's work on Tswana 'praise poems' illuminates how commoners 'spoke back' to chiefs in *kgotla* with advice and rebuke.
23. See P. S. Bamwell and Marco Mostert, eds., *Political Assemblies in the Earlier Middle Ages* (Turnhout, Belgium: Brepols, 2003).
24. J. L. Byock, *Medieval Iceland: Society, Sagas, and Power* (Berkeley: University of California Press, 1990).
25. Mogens H. Hansen, 'The Athenian *Ecclesia* and the Swiss *Landsgemeinde*', in *The Athenian Ecclesia: A Collection of Articles 1976–1983* (Copenhagen: Museum Tusculanum Press, 1983), 207–226.
26. J. G. A. Pocock, *The Machiavellian Moment: Florentine Political Thought and the Atlantic Republican Tradition* (Princeton, NJ: Princeton University Press, 2016).
27. Jason Frank, *The Democratic Sublime: On Aesthetics and Popular Assembly* (New York: Oxford University Press, 2021). This richly insightful study warrants far more attention than is possible here.
28. Nikolas Bowie, 'The Constitutional Right of Self-Government', *Yale Law Journal* 130, no. 7 (2021): 1652–1745. Thanks to Tabatha Abu El-Haj for pointing me to this article.
29. Ibid., 1661. See also Randall, in this volume, on the role of 'regulators' at a similar time in riotous eighteenth-century England.
30. Tocqueville writes, 'Everyone takes as zealous an interest in the affairs of his township, his county, and of the whole State, as if they were his own, because everyone, in his sphere, takes an active part in the government of society': Alexis de Tocqueville and Henry Reeve, *Democracy in America Volumes I & II* (Auckland: The Floating Press, 2009).
31. Manin, *Principles of Representative Government*, 8.
32. See Can Cemgil and Clemens Hoffmann, 'The "Rojava Revolution" in Syrian Kurdistan: A Model of Development for the Middle East?', *IDS Bulletin* 47, no. 3 (2016): 53–76.
33. See especially the discussion of the Zapatistas movement in Massimiliano Tomba, *Insurgent Universality: An Alternative Legacy of Modernity* (New York: Oxford University Press, 2019), 186–222.
34. See, for example, Butler, *Notes*.
35. See, for example, the role of neighbourhood popular resistance committees in Sudan's revolution, in Sharath Srinivasan, *When Peace Kills Politics: International Intervention and Unending Wars in the Sudans* (London: Hurst, 2021), Postscript.
36. Hanna F. Pitkin, 'Representation and Democracy: Uneasy Alliance', *Scandinavian Political Studies* 27, no. 3 (2004): 335–342, 340.
37. Besides the works on assembly examined here, a growing body of scholarship in radical political theory also challenges dominant political frameworks that cleave to statist and elitist understandings of politics and advances alternative normative and historical arguments that focus on the role of popular, insurgent, and constituent citizen power in politics. Notable recent works include: Tomba, *Insurgent Universality*; Camila Vergara,

Systemic Corruption: Constitutional Ideas for an Anti-Oligarchic Republic (Princeton, NJ: Princeton University Press, 2020); Adriana Cavarero, *Surging Democracy: Notes on Hannah Arendt's Political Thought* (Stanford, CA: Stanford University Press, 2021).

38. Hardt and Negri's *Assembly* is, title notwithstanding, less relevant to the work of retheorizing assembly undertaken here. This is because the authors explicitly forego developing a theory of assembly, instead approaching the concept of assembly 'transversally' in relation to diverse practices and as 'a lens through which to recognize new democratic political possibilities': Michael Hardt and Antonio Negri, *Assembly* (Oxford: Oxford University Press, 2017), xxi.
39. Butler, *Notes*, 7.
40. Ibid., 160.
41. Ibid., 169.
42. Ibid., 160. See also Woolman, in this volume.
43. Butler, *Notes*, 163 (italicised in the original).
44. Ibid., 160.
45. Murray Bookchin, *The Next Revolution: Popular Assemblies and the Promise of Direct Democracy* (London: Verso Books, 2015).
46. Ibid., 50.
47. Ibid., 28.
48. Hannah Arendt, 'Thoughts on Politics and Revolution', in *Crises of the Republic* (Boston: Houghton Mifflin Harcourt, 1972), 231–232.
49. See also Woolman, in this volume.
50. Normative prescriptions provoke pragmatic rebuttals. Even Arendt's manifesto-like proposal for a 'council system' in *On Revolution* was lamented by one of her most ardent intellectual supporters as being seen as 'something of an embarrassment, a curiously unrealistic commitment': Margaret Canovan, *Hannah Arendt: A Reinterpretation of Her Political Thought* (Cambridge: Cambridge University Press, 1992), 237.

Further Reading

Arendt, Hannah. 'Thoughts on Politics and Revolution'. In *Crises of the Republic*. Boston: Houghton Mifflin Harcourt, 1972.

Bookchin, Murray. *The Next Revolution: Popular Assemblies and the Promise of Direct Democracy*. London: Verso Books, 2015.

Butler, Judith. *Notes Toward a Performative Theory of Assembly*. Cambridge, MA: Harvard University Press, 2015.

Frank, Jason. *The Democratic Sublime: On Aesthetics and Popular Assembly*. New York: Oxford University Press, 2021.

Graeber, David, and David Wengrow. *The Dawn of Everything: A New History of Humanity*. London: Penguin Books, 2021.

Tomba, Massimiliano. *Insurgent Universality: An Alternative Legacy of Modernity*. New York: Oxford University Press, 2019.

CHAPTER 4

THE OVERREGULATION OF THE DEMOCRATIC POLITICS OF FREEDOM OF ASSEMBLY

STU WOOLMAN

INTRODUCTION

THIS chapter's core thesis will appear deceptively simple. In short, the overregulation, limitation, and concretization of the right to assembly limits, in critical ways, the democratic politics that animates the precommitment to 'freedom to assemble collectively'.

Let's break that proposition down into several component parts. First, freedom of assembly remains a precondition of the popular sovereignty that the citizens of a just democratic order enjoy. Second, the freedom to engage in this form of collective political action gives the constitutional right of assembly its content and its legitimacy. Third, the legitimacy of a constitutional right or a statutory recognition of this freedom to assemble continues to be a contingent affair long after its formal adoption. Fourth, the recognition of the right as legitimate can be withdrawn by citizens if the legal scaffolding overregulates and unjustly diminishes the political space for collective action. More precisely: If freedom of assembly is to function as a necessary condition for popular sovereignty and collective action within a constitutionally constructed political community, then we cannot restrict its use to such an extent that rights to private property and significant constraints on the right to assemble trump both its benign forms of expression and its less common moderately destructive incarnations in an actual democracy. This last proposition remains consistent with the views of a concatenation of respected theorists (Martin Luther King, Jr., Hannah Arendt, Judith Butler) who vehemently condemn the use of force to bring about political change, but who, given the logic of their own work, are compelled to countenance a commitment to the occasional use of force by second-class citizens who have been effectively excluded from meaningful collective action. Their subsequent inclusion enables such citizens to participate in the self-governance of the polity and to secure the same opportunities for self-actualization that first-class citizens possess.[1]

Several examples might clarify my meaning. Courts have often so narrowly construed the right to assembly such that well-intentioned convenors of a demonstration can be held strictly liable for any property damage that occurs in even the best organized and supervised congregations. Legislatures have placed conditions on the notification process so onerous that executive officials can avoid the necessary grant of approval for an assembly to occur legally. Courts have limited 'public spaces' for constitutionally protected assemblies to such an extent that this form of collective political action loses most of its purchase: If no other citizens can witness or be engaged by an assembly, then the assembly loses its ability to communicate a concern to other members of a polity. Legislatures, executives, and courts have, in tandem, used state-sanctioned violence to thwart collective assembly action. They often do so to ensure that second-class citizens remain second-class citizens—thereby continuing ongoing patterns of (1) destruction of the bodies and physical integrity of demonstrators, or (2) deeply entrenched inequality between those groups that exercise power through the state and those groups that lack access to political levers of power. To appreciate fully the manner in which states fail to honour this precondition of a just democratic order, this chapter begins with an exploration of the content of the 'freedom of assembly'.

The Freedom of Assembly and the Limited Occasion for the Justified Use of Force

As Martin Luther King, Jr. asked, in the face of an intransigent White America: Where do we go from here?[2] In a relatively egalitarian polity, one might argue that other forms of collective action should enable demonstrators to revisit extant constitutional norms and alter them in manner consistent with the actual political purpose of 'the freedom to assemble'. But that just begs King's question of what is to be done in societies that privilege significant aggregations of private property over rough-and-tumble exercises of political power, or what is to be done in societies where inequalities in political power foreclose change initiated by outgroups.

It would be churlish to call into question the virtue of careful expatiations as to how peaceful assembly ought to work. However, this chapter does question one major underlying assumption: namely, that the formal implementation of a constitutional democratic state will bring about the liberal democracy or social democracy to which most of us remain committed.[3] Problems of collective action on the domestic front, and the absence of global political and economic institutions with the coercive power to address wicked problems,[4] prevent most constitutional orders from producing substantively inclusive democracies. Little more than a score of nations qualify as inclusive democracies, fifty are rightly deemed flawed/failed democracies and the remaining majority of countries should be viewed as autocracies (that grant no meaningful space for collective assembly action).[5] Moreover, the pacification of the freedom of assembly through its concretization as a right is a very modern affair, as Tabatha Abu El-Haj writes with regard to US assembly jurisprudence:

> Today's legalized democracy . . . is the product of a particular regulatory transformation. Between 1880 and 1930, states and municipalities used law to increase governmental controls over the full range of nineteenth-century avenues for democratic participation. Prior to that, the practice of democratic politics in the United States was less structured by law and thus more autonomous from formal governmental institutions than it is today.[6]

The recognition of the greater autonomy found in the 'freedom of assembly' is far more likely to be consistent with the desiderata of popular sovereignty upon which the concretized right to assemble rests.

A more controversial proposition turns on this chapter's resistance to a sanctimonious invocation of non-violence in relation to assembly when faced with the foreclosure of the very freedoms that give a state its legitimacy. That last proposition requires further delineation. Following King, Butler, and Arendt, non violence must be the starting point for all forms of collective political action. However, persistent second-class citizenship may occasion the limited use of force to create the conditions for inclusive collective action. At the same time, Frantz Fanon's glorification of violence and total scorched-earth warfare as a mechanism for political change must be rejected: 'Violence is a cleansing force. It frees the native from his inferiority complex and from his despair and inaction; it makes him fearless and restores his self-respect'.[7]

Such violence, as King, Butler, and Arendt contend, cannot be an end in itself. The inevitable result is a warping of the souls of the oppressed and the oppressors, and an acceptance of violence by state and non-state actors when it comes to the realization of political ends. As Kwame Anthony Appiah has pointed out, Fanon did not live to see the putative 'cleansing' effects of his theory of total war.[8] After eight years, France left Algeria defeated. However, for Algerians across the political and religious spectrum, the lasting legacy of the Algerian War of Independence turned out to be the legitimation of unrestricted extreme violence to realize political and economic ends.[9]

When then is force permissible? King's ethics of conviction led him to reject violence—as a matter of virtue. As a practical matter, he viewed violence in the form of riots as a deformed performative act. While riots may fail to pass Judith Butler's test for a performative act that can generate a norm adhered to by all members of the polity, such demonstrations still function as an important form of protest for a group of second-class citizens that continues to be disenfranchised, dispossessed, dehumanized, and dispatched. King marks off the substantial difference in access to the public space for collective action between a people enslaved for 250 years, and denied meaningful emancipation for another century, from any group not subjected to such abnegation of their existence. Yet so entrenched was White supremacy in the United States that King concluded that the double-bind of race and class discrimination meant that any effective appeal could no longer be limited to the eradication of systemic racism in America. It also had to tackle entrenched class-based poverty:

> In the treatment of poverty nationally, one fact stands out: there are twice as many white poor as Negro poor in the United States. . . . fragmentary and spasmodic reforms have failed to reach down to the profoundest needs of the poor. . . . I am now convinced that the simplest approach will prove to be the most effective — the solution to poverty is to abolish it directly by a now widely discussed measure: the guaranteed income.[10]

King's concession that non-violent protest had run up against an implacable wall of Whiteness led him to embrace a class-based solution that might find sufficient common cause between White Americans and Black Americans. This shift towards a guaranteed income for all reflects King's astute appraisal that formal democratic enfranchisement alone would never be enough to alleviate the penury of this discrete and insular minority. A change in tactics was also in the offing. As the epigram at the outset of this chapter reflects, King insisted that urban riots—as a special form of protest—had become a durable and necessary, if not normatively desirable, social phenomena:

> Urban riots must now be recognized as durable social phenomena . . . They are not insurrections. The rioters are not seeking to seize territory or to attain control of institutions. *They are mainly intended to shock the white community.* They are a . . . form of social protest.[11]

Durable and necessary, if not normatively desirable, social phenomena. Nothing else possessed the 'collective power' to 'shock the white community'.

Arendt too can easily be misread as decrying the use of force as a legitimate form of power under almost any set of circumstances.[12] However, force might be deemed justified if conditions meet certain criteria. Read: if it represents and results in a genuine transition from authoritarian politics to civic republicanism.[13] In an inclusive political community committed to civic republicanism, legitimate power reflects the 'human ability not just to act, but to act in concert'. The exercise of legitimate power belongs not to individuals, but to the efforts of a group of coordinated individuals:

> [The American revolutionaries] . . . discovered . . . the 'charms of liberty' . . . only in the very act of liberation. For the acts . . . which liberation demanded from them threw them into public business, where . . . they began to constitute that space of appearances where freedom can unfold its charms and become a visible, tangible reality. . . . It was altogether different with the speech-making and decision-taking, the oratory and the business, the thinking and the persuading, and the *action doing* which proved necessary to drive this claim to its logical conclusion: independent

> government and the foundation of a new body politic. It was through these experiences that those who, in the words of John Adams, had been 'called without expectation and compelled without previous inclination' discovered that 'it is action, not rest, that constitutes our pleasure'.[14]

To bring about this particular charm, Arendt has to commit herself to the use of means—force—that ought not to occur *normally* in daily political life. 'Successful revolutions', a truly empirical and consequentialist moniker, create the space for such triumphant forms of collective action as the debating and the writing of the US Constitution.

Though states are invariably plural in constitution, collective action around shared ends and unifying norms sets the boundaries for legitimate exercises in power by any actor. Unlike power, the constitutive feature of violence is its 'instrumental character'. Violence embraces the use of force to advance parochial concerns or partisan passions designed to exclude certain classes from decision-making that advances the ends of an entire polity. When it comes to *ending* the exclusion of groups or classes of citizens from meaningful participation in the business of public affairs, Arendt's understanding of a government's legitimate exercise of power remains consistent with her own prior commitments to the existence of empirically justifiable conditions for significant changes in government as well as less comprehensive forms of dissent.[15] Successful armed revolutions remain the exception. Like King, Arendt echoes Kant. For Kant, we cannot bring about a kingdom of ends when our actions reflect inflamed passions that eschew reason and employ instrumental processes that reduce others to mere means.[16]

Much like Arendt, Butler's conception of politics, and her theory of assembly, is performative. Thus, no norms (entirely) precede politics. They are brought into being and sustained through collective action and, notably, through collective assemblies.[17] Butler explains this 'coming into being' by summoning up the Arendtian notion of politics as contingent upon public spaces within which people recognize each another as equal citizens and thereafter undertake collective forms of action. The norms that flow from this collective action *only* remain in existence as long as 'the people' remain assembled. The singular advance that Butler makes on Arendt's thinking stems from her insistence on the priority of action to norm-setting. As she explains in *Gender Trouble*, gender comes into being through engagement in a particular practice understood to be, say, feminine without presupposing an ineradicable 'essence' within a group of similarly situated persons.[18] Because norms only secure their purchase through action, the space always exists for resistance to and deviation from prior norms. That space subsists because there's always a gap between an extant norm and its reproduction. Politics continually offers elbow room for different norms to form, to challenge, and to replace dominant political, social, and economic paradigms.

However, Butler argues that Arendt's conceptualization of the political is limited by her failure (1) to acknowledge fully the material conditions required for its actualization and (2) to acknowledge how deeply embedded conditions of exclusion are. Despite its emphasis on collective action, Arendt's account remains wedded to some conception of rationally autonomous individuals. As I argue in *The Selfless Constitution*,[19] we are all radically heterogeneous naturally and socially determined individuals who must contend with competing narratives within ourselves, as well as (1) the similar, competing narratives of others (given our shared facticity), and (2) the various narratives that account for exclusionary practices that foreclose political change. Butler recognizes these constraints on change in *Frames of War*, where she describes 'precariousness' as an unavoidable condition of 'more or less existential' radically heterogeneous naturally and socially embodied beings 'living in a shared world'.[20] Individual human beings will, therefore, always impinge upon the freedom of others. A political community cannot overvalorize its extant freedom at any given moment in time: for it may contain the seeds of progress or continue to be a font for persistent domination by privileged groups.[21] Privileged members of a polity may continually reproduce norms that will lead to different and unequal degrees of precarity. Unequal distributions of precariousness refers to the 'politically induced conditions in which certain populations suffer from failing social and economic networks of support and become differentially exposed to injury, violence, and death'.[22] Butler thereby demarcates a space within which performative collective assembly need not be an entirely peaceful modality for securing equal political, social, and economic standing. However, given Butler's concern with the precarious nature of the corporeal body—whatever its political, social, and economic status—her work may lead her readers to conclude that she opposes any form of force that would jeopardize the precarious existence of the bodily integrity of another. That's just not so.

The seeds of reformation exist in collective assemblies that refuse to be treated as assemblages of marginalized individuals and occasionally resort to performative acts designed, as King notes, to call the domination and the privilege of first-class citizens into question. Whilst King and Butler are justifiably concerned with uses of collection action that deviate from the forms of collective action that would create a political community of equals, Butler's own recognition of the space for the production of new norms provides a gap where at least some form of force—*not intentionally directed at the precarious individual*—can be justified. Butler, like King, identifies occasions that will arise when a collective assembly uses force to call out a privileged elite for its ongoing failure to treat fellow citizens as equals. Butler may resist describing such collective action as legitimate. But the gap in her own theory certainly allows for contestations of power that will boil over into a use of force designed 'to prick the conscience of the king'.

We have thus far drawn the ambit 'freedom of assembly' and delimited a narrow set of exceptions in which the use of force must be recognized as real and 'durable social phenomena'. Such use of force during assembly challenges the subjugation of precariously constituted outgroups by privileged groups that demonstrate little interest in deviating from the status quo. However, these exceptional uses of *force* can never be recognized as thoroughly legitimate forms of entrenched *power*.

The Content of the Right to Assemble, Properly Understood

Is this demanding version of freedom of assembly delineated above actually consistent with the hurly-burly nature of democratic politics, or a politics that aspires to become democratic? Despite the reticence of King, Arendt, and Butler to employ force to generate collective action, their politics ultimately accommodates the sharp elbows that make democracy work, as well as the rare destructive acts within authoritarian or repressive states that enable otherwise politically oppressed groups to create, through a Butlerian transformation, a democratic and inclusive form of self-governance. As I argue in *The Selfless Constitution*, the facticity of our existence, and, therefore, the radical heterogeneity of those naturally and socially *determined* dispositional states which constitute the corporeal individual require other mechanisms for change to occur. They are (1) trial and error (reflexivity) in concert with other members of the polity, and (2) the access to those basic goods that enable an individual to enter the public square without shame and to flourish.[23] Throwing off the shackles that tie us down is no mean feat. Throwing off those shackles often allows us to be who we already are, as Michael Walzer[24] argues, given the radical facticity of our social endowments. Or it may require a significant deviation from a prior value set with respect to certain ways of being, as per Butler's submission. What we want to see, through a concomitant commitment to flourishing and to experimentation, are how novel ways of being in the world will turn out. For that, we need feedback mechanisms and reflexivity within a normative framework of rough egalitarian pluralism.[25] As Arendt notes, dialogue alone in the 'public square' rarely brings about significant reformation of the extant social order; only the active manner in which citizens conduct public business brings about enduring change. That analysis has a direct bearing on how we understand the relationship between the freedom of assembly and the right to assemble:

> Even the right of assembly, which has come to be the most important positive political freedom, appears in the American Bill of Rights as the 'right of people peacefully to assemble', and to petition the government for a redress of grievances. . . . must read: the right to assemble in order to petition. All these liberties . . . are the results of liberation but they are by no means the actual content of freedom, which . . . is participation in public affairs or admission to the public realm.[26]

Assemblies have played a central role in the liberation politics of most nations. Once the battle for liberation has been won, a sense often exists that assemblies ought to diminish in frequency. Must that be so? Mass protests continue to be an important form of political engagement in both advanced and developmental democracies alike. Every sub-public uses assemblies to press their demands upon the broader polity. First, assembly creates the space for speech, listening, agreement and disagreement, and change through collective action. A lone voice is likely to be drowned out. A choir is far more likely to get its message across. Second, power in modern nation-states invariably concentrates in and around large social formations. Meaningful action within and between these large social formations often requires the collective efforts of demonstrators. Third, consider the nature of this particular species of communicative action: physical presence and placards. Expressive conduct makes us human. Only collective action, through expressive conduct, raises humanity above its most primitive form. Only through such collective action with competent and engaged interlocutors can we assert truth claims about the physical world, and moral claims about the social world. Only collective action enables us to wring out of our shared endowments the agreements that define the ends of our polity. Thus, assemblies and gatherings as forums for collective action become the sine qua non of democracy. Fourth, some confuse this indispensability of assemblies for democratic collective action with instrumentality. That gets things back to front. Without communicative collective action, there are no human subjects, no citizens. The relationship between democracy and communicative collective action is best understood in terms of reciprocal effect: communicative collective action is a necessary, but not sufficient, condition of democracy; democracy deepens our capacity for communicative collective action. Finally, by foregrounding communicative collective action, I want to shift our attention away from that chestnut of democratic theory which tells us that although sixty million, say, South Africans can get it wrong, the more we discuss the ideas we seek to put into practice, the better our decisions are likely to be. Assemblies, on the standard account, generate debate and thereby improve our deliberative processes. That they may do—on the margins.[27] They only do so because shared natural and social endowments have already made agreement and disagreement possible. What assemblies really force us to do is attend to situations where abuse or inequality of power has distorted our capacity to engage in communicative collective action, and has valorized the interests of one portion of the polity over another. This last observation suggests why the right to assemble provides an effective means of communication by those outgroups that feel that their demands are not being given serious consideration within the otherwise capacious confines of representative politics.

Size matters. For outgroups, the right to assemble makes democracy visible and counters a politics designed to maintain their isolation. It also serves to place an oppressive, intransigent majority—or autocratic minority—on notice that their ongoing repression is but temporary. Conversely, by allowing a disempowered group to express their disenchantment with a government's decisions, a government's general exercise of political power becomes more legitimate.[28] As I have argued in 'Seek Justice Elsewhere', communicative collective action should enable second-class citizens to create new norms that deviate from dominant norms, and, at the same time allow them to imagine and to enact an alternative, but still comprehensive, vision of the good.[29] However, the state and those private entities wielding power over membership, voice, and exit in dominant communities must provide these *new* communities with the space and the material goods necessary for the members of these new sub-publics to flourish. The remedies contemplated here are borne by the state and private associations responsible for the discrimination and the oppression of these second-class citizens. Without the reparations required for reimagination, the polity leaves these second-class citizens with nowhere to run and nowhere to hide.[30]

While compelling, even these arguments miss much of that which makes assemblies truly dynamic and powerful: the crowd. The crowd draws its power, as Elias Canetti notes, from its erasure of borders between individuals, the gravitational pull that an expanding, living, moving group has on those around it, and the incipient threat of upheaval that causes all around to sit up and take notice. Canetti writes:

> [E]ruption . . . the sudden transition from a closed into an open crowd . . . is a frequent occurrence . . . A crowd quite often seems to overflow from some well-guarded space into the squares and streets of a town where it can move about freely, exposed to everything and attracting everyone. But more important than this external event is the corresponding inner movement: the dissatisfaction with the limitation of the number of participants, the sudden will to attract, the passionate determination to reach all men.[31]

Canetti's observations about crowds suggest why assemblies remain a potent tool. Crowd action—loud, noisy, disruptive, and sometimes dangerous—ought to be viewed, at a minimum, as a direct expression of popular sovereignty, and if so, as a direct challenge to the status quo. Canetti offers one of the better arguments for giving the right to assemble a broad construction. This construction allows communicative collective action to spill over from the legitimate use of *power* into legitimate constitutional uses of *force* designed to call attention to the ongoing oppression of second-class citizens and their perpetual exclusion from meaningful political participation. That last argument for a robust understanding of the right to assemble vouchsafes our precommitments to political freedom and popular sovereignty in a democracy in which the will of the people is not always mediated by political parties or the elites who run the parties and who populate elected political office and the bureaucracies that govern daily interactions. Recognition of this broad ambit of the right to assemble thereby provides a unique space in which citizens can, legitimately, stand outside the political institutions created by the Constitution. For second-class citizens these constitutional spaces allow people to apply pressure on both political and economic institutions that deny them equality before the law or that refuse to provide those basic goods necessary for living a life worth valuing.

The Overregulation of Freedom of Assembly: On Private Property and the Contraction of Public Space

If the contemporary nation-state no longer serves as a viable vehicle for producing an inclusive democracy, then similarly, and relatedly, the orderly, rational, conversational, respectful, and thickly shared moral view of democracy necessary for 'peaceful' protests stands at odds with the hurly-burly, hotly contested, loud, unruly thinly shared view of democracy which undergirds this author's take on freedom of assembly as a political precommitment that gives rise to an expansively understood constitutional right to assemble. This precondition for popular sovereignty ought not to be pacified by courts and legislatures in a manner that too often places a greater value on the constitutional protection of private property and seeks to cabin visceral expression of discontent within denuded public spaces. On occasion, as Arendt and King recognize, these assemblies challenge the prudent path, and attempt to awaken other members of a polity to the abuses and usurpations of the current government. In rare instances, they can mobilize the masses to overthrow a tyrant, or force radical structural change in the processes of governance and significant change in the distribution of those goods necessary for individuals to pursue a life worth valuing. Such change must be understood as far better than waiting to be heard by your oppressor. Recall King's words:

> Urban riots must now be recognized as durable social phenomena . . . They are not insurrections. The rioters are not seeking to seize territory or to attain control of institutions. They are mainly intended to shock the white community. They are a distorted form of social protest.

Some governments lose their right to rule—having broken the social contract that bind citizens to the state.[32] Perhaps an ongoing disruptive campaign that makes a country ungovernable is exactly what justice requires. On other occasions, mass mobilization that upsets activity in the private domain must be vouchsafed when the political order steadfastly resists a shift in the economic rules of the game that create and reinforce second-class citizenship.

Easy cases such as the disruptive mass action designed to end apartheid or the judicial findings of sedition regarding the insurrection on 6 January 2021 at the US Capitol may not provide bright lines that enable us to distinguish between *all* legitimate and illegitimate assemblies. They still illuminate two dimensions of both the democratic politics of freedom of assembly and the constitutional right to assemble. First, they concentrate our minds upon the actual institutions and processes that do not deliver the basic goods that every individual must possess in order to pursue her own comprehensive vision of the good or that prevent any number of second-class citizens from engaging in collective action. Second, disruptive, if distorted, forms of protest are justified when it comes to challenging extremely inequitable and deeply entrenched structures of power.

Related questions surrounding the degree to which extant assembly legislation, executive regulation, and court doctrine fit the democratic politics that ground the freedom of assembly structure the remainder of this section. The first sub-section attempts to assess what has been gained, and lost, through the regulatory transformation of assembly practices. The second sub-section attempts to reconstruct the kind of exercises in popular sovereignty that have been extirpated through both legislation and judicial doctrines that undercut the unique nature of collective action made manifest in large-scale assemblies.

The Price of Peace and the Protection of Private Property

As now seems evident, by modifying the right to assemble with the word 'peaceful', constitutional drafters, legislators, judges, and academic commentators have committed themselves to a means of pacifying public discontent and giving the government of the day solid grounds for suppressing vociferous opposition to its actions. Courts that otherwise seem progressive use 'peaceful' to place an impossible burden on the organizers of assemblies to account for any damage caused during an assembly—whether it is foreseeable or not and even when they have taken every conceivable measure to ensure that a peaceful protest occurs. That, in any event, was the finding of both a High Court[33] and the Constitutional Court of South Africa[34] in a matter in which a small quantum of damage occurred during a demonstration.

Both enigmatic decisions begin with strange characterizations of the facts. In the High Court, Judge Hlophe writes:

> In this particular case, the march was organised *within* a volatile milieu. The protracted industrial action had been acrimonious and had given rise to the deaths of nearly 50 people pursuant to strike-related violence. Furthermore, there had been previous instances of damage to the Cape Town Municipal Council and private property. The plaintiffs are a disparate group of persons. They are brought together by the mutual misfortune of having been victims of the violence . . . perpetuated during [a] march.[35]

Thus, before any legal analysis of the Regulation of Gatherings Act of 1993 ('RGA') or Section 17 of the Constitution[36] begins, the High Court has shoehorned into its decision quite a large number of irrelevant facts—fifty deaths unrelated to the demonstration and prior instances of damage to private property. It is little wonder that Judge Hlophe ignored Section 17 entirely and read the RGA in the most restrictive manner possible. RGA § 11(2) provides a defence against liability for convenors of an assembly against any damage that might occur if they prove the following:

> (a) that he or it did not permit or connive at the act or omission which caused the damage in question; and
> (b) that the act or omission in question did not fall within the scope of the objectives of the gathering or demonstration in question and was not reasonably foreseeable; and
> (c) that he or it took all reasonable steps within his or its power to prevent the act or omission in question.

Given the pre-gathering commitments of the convenors, the local authorities, and the police to ensure a safe and peaceful demonstration, one struggles to understand why the convenors alone ought to be held liable for events that they, the local authorities, and the police did not anticipate and could not control. Firstly, it defies reason to hold convenors liable for events and damage that occurred prior to an appropriately and statutorily compliant assembly. Secondly, whatever 'reasonably foreseeable' damage that might occur during the demonstration was expressly taken into account by the convenors and the local authorities—including property damage. Nevertheless, the High Court concludes that whilst the convenors are allowed to go ahead with a demonstration for which they have taken all reasonably foreseeable precautions, they must still prepare to be held liable for damages that may flow from the event. Section 17 of the Constitution provided little assistance because, on another cramped reading by the High Court, the prior damage and the unforeseen property destruction proved that the gathering had not been peaceful. As I have previously noted:

> [a] generous interpretation of the 'peaceful' proviso is . . . necessary (a) to prevent the state from exploiting this requirement in order to suppress unpopular positions . . . (b) to ensure that if some members of an assembly resort to violence, while the majority of the participants remain peaceful, the assembly remains protected . . . and (c) [to] prevent a peaceful assembly from being hijacked by violent . . . opponents or agents provocateurs.[37]

Judge Hlophe writes in an entirely different spirit:

> It was further contended on behalf of the plaintiffs that the cancellation of a few prospective gatherings is a small price to pay for the protection of the constitutional rights which would be infringed by a riot such as that which occurred in Cape Town on 16 May 2006. I am inclined to agree.[38]

Is this cancellation of assemblies such 'a small price to pay'? If one's conception of the right to assemble is so cramped that only placid middle-class protests against, say, the construction of new nuclear power plants are protected, then yes, the price for exacting strict liability from convenors who hope to put the working conditions of poorly paid labourers back on the bargaining table is indeed small. If so, one might as well flatly state that a constitutional order said to protect and to promote the security, safety, and pursuit of happiness of poorly paid labourers does nothing of the sort. The right to assemble here imposes truly onerous conditions of liability upon convenors when unforeseeable damage to private property adjacent to public spaces occurs. The chilling effect on assembly is beyond question, as is the shrinking of the public square.

If only South Africa's Constitutional Court had appreciated what was at stake. Instead, Chief Justice Mogoeng suggested to counsel, during oral argument, that if their clients could not guarantee that an assembly would not lead to the destruction of property or physical harm to unaffiliated persons, then perhaps they should stay at home. The Constitutional Court doubled down on the High Court's reasoning and held that the apposite sections of the Regulation of Gatherings Act when read with the constitutional right of assembly imposed upon convenors what can only be characterized as strict liability.

The Constitutional Court's decision warrants interrogation on at least four grounds. South Africa experiences roughly 12,000 predominantly peaceful demonstrations and assemblies per annum. But how do 12,000 predominantly peaceful demonstrations present a danger, so clear and imminent, that South Africa's highest court feels obliged to impose a sanction so severe that (x) the impecunious could not risk even a modicum of damage, or (y) established, well-endowed organizations must now think twice before protesting, or more worrisome still, refuse to collaborate with organs of the state responsible for the security of marchers and non-marchers alike? The imposition of strict liability will lead some convenors to refuse to operate within statutory requirements. Protesters will not self-police with their own marshals, and the police will find themselves even more ill-equipped to deal with assemblies. A judgment that increases the likelihood of harm to property is not just a steeper price for 'peace'. It is completely antithetical to the democratic politics of collective action adumbrated here. The Court subjects all recognized organizers of demonstrations to 'strict liability' for damage to person or to property (1) whether such damage was foreseen, and adequate steps were taken, or more disturbingly (2) whether destructive events occurred that were unforeseeable and unpreventable. The Court's reading of 'peaceful' is so out of touch with the history of assembly in South Africa that it must make many drafters of the Constitution rue their decision to put this modifier in the text.

A more compelling reading is on offer: Section 17 of the Constitution should be read to make good on the founding provisions of Section 1 of the Constitution.[39] In *President of the Republic of South Africa v Modderklip*, the Constitutional Court reviewed the refusal of the state (a) to accommodate a large number of landless persons living on state-owned property and (b) to enforce a court order for eviction of those same landless persons from the private property to which they had been shunted. According to the Court, Section 1 of the Constitution (read with Section 34 of the Constitution on the right of access to court) required that the state take 'reasonable steps . . . to ensure that large-scale disruptions in the social fabric do not occur in the wake of the execution of court orders, thus, undermining the rule of law'.[40] The *Modderklip* Court's reading of Section 1 concerns itself with those steps the state must take to turn back the forces of anarchy, entropy, and rebellion. By transforming those forces into something more benign, the Court forestalls an abrogation of the social contract (reflected in the Constitution). Although the *Modderklip* Court describes the circumstances of the eviction case before it as extraordinary, they most certainly are not. With 50 percent of the country's inhabitants living at the upper-bound poverty line, existential crises run the gamut: they encompass access to adequate housing, health, water, education, social security grants, employment, or any combination of those goods necessary to pursue a life worth valuing. We should turn to the *Modderklip* Court, and not the *Garvis* Court, if we want to find the resources necessary to ensure that the collective action anticipated by the freedom of assembly takes place within the ambit of the concretized right to assemble.

Acceptable Unrest and the Use of Force in Assemblies

Two related assumptions underlie the normative claim that assemblies ought to be peaceful: (1) we must always treat others as ends, never solely as means; and (2) we must be able to meet one another as relative equals in the public square when we decide our collective fate. The ideal also assumes a largely inclusive democracy in which power, not force, is the coin of the realm. Even so, as King, Arendt, and Butler concede, unnerving unrest during protests has a role to play when deeply entrenched structural inequalities create second-class citizens who are excluded from collective decision-making and who do not possess those goods necessary to pursue a life worth valuing.

In one nation, call it France, the executive proposes a bill to increase the retirement age from sixty-two to sixty-four. This executive decision sparks widespread disruptions in the capital. When the executive forces the bill through Parliament using a rarely used provision in the Constitution, unruly demonstrations spread throughout the country. Graffiti on walls along the capital's major thoroughfare read 'We will break everything'. The mildly unruly unrest is met with a crackdown by law enforcement that human rights observers decry as reflective of 'the excessive use of force by agents of the state'. The final tally: 1,300,000 million citizens protest, 531 people suffer minor injuries, the police arrest 171 people, the bill becomes law, and the President's popularity plunges to 22 percent.

In an adjacent democracy, call it the Netherlands, farmer-led dissatisfaction over nitrogen oxide emission legislation that would severely curtail the domesticated livestock industry leads to widespread demonstrations by farmers who plant tractors in the middle of highways in order to bring the entire nation to a standstill. The success of these assemblies yields the nation's third largest political party. It currently possesses the power to block future efforts to reign in global warming and to prevent the government from meeting its extant commitments on carbon emissions reduction within the European Union.

What to make of these two examples? In the first case, an elected official took a deeply unpopular decision that elicited strong responses from a large number of citizens (and their representatives), while causing limited property damage. While both sides used force, the institutions of the state remained intact. The unrest ought to be understood as a 'durable social phenomenon' that enabled citizens to express their deep resentment with this end run around popular sovereignty. The second example reflects the growing resistance to initiatives that directly threaten the economic well-being of various sectors of society within a particular country, and within generally inclusive democracies across the globe. Here we see how wicked problems—and the absence of inclusive global political and economic institutions with the coercive power to solve them—play themselves out on a domestic landscape.[41] As King, Arendt, and Butler would contend, the decision to forestall climate change initiatives is hardly baked in. It could change with new elections, or the newly formed parliament could reach a decision via media with the newest party on the block to achieve similar goals. But if the freedom to assemble so that citizens can engage in collective action is to mean anything, then the price of *absolute* peace—no change at all and no costs associated with the collective action undertaken—would be far too steep.

Conclusion

The argument laid out in these pages springs from hope with a dash of pragmatism. Perhaps this author, American-bred, South African abided, shares with King, Arendt, and Butler what Du Bois would call 'double consciousness'. All citizens of 'the Republic', not exactly insiders, but not entirely outsiders. Black. Jewish Immigrant. Queer. They could understand the politics of the country which they inhabit, but still write knowing that they did not yet fully belong. What all three have in common is the unusual belief that freedom of assembly lies at the heart of a just democratic order. For it is as assembled in the public square that all citizens meet as equals—enjoying the same political freedoms and acting in concert to determine their collective fate. All three hold fast to a neo-Kantian conviction regarding the intrinsic worth of all human beings. Each rules out 'violence'—and the instrumental use of others—as a legitimate means of determining how any given polity ought to move forward.

This article of faith is tempered by experience, by the knowledge that privileged groups will use force against others to maintain their privilege. Nor can force be ruled out when it comes to the collective action that groups undertake in the pursuit of genuinely legitimate ends. Given their shared sensibility, King, Arendt, and Butler make space for these inevitable lapses. They emphasize the brief nature of such deviations and the necessity that we proceed, in the right way, the next time the opportunity to choose a course of collective action arises. That's hope with a dash of pragmatism.

This theory of freedom of assembly has certain readily ascertainable consequences for how we ought to construe the right to assemble. Quite often, lawmakers in a democratic order will overregulate the freedom of assembly in a manner that unjustly diminishes the space for this form of collective action. The modifier 'peaceful' should primarily protect the bodily integrity or precarity of non-participants. It ought not to be read in a manner that prevents (1) the most minimal despoiling of private property during assemblies and (2) assemblies on private terrain that function as public fora. Finally, and most importantly, the modifier 'peaceful' often prevents second-class citizens from challenging the overt and the covert structural barriers that prevent them from participating as equals in the assemblies that determine the contours of their lives. So, lest one think that this chapter's restoration of the freedom of assembly to its rightful place at the centre of the pantheon of freedoms is misplaced, think again. Who amongst us would wish to be a second-class citizen excluded from political assemblies, and thereby denied the ability to pursue the dreams and the aspirations that ought to be every person's birthright?

Acknowledgements

I would like to thank Professor Sharath Srinivasan and Professor Tabatha Abu El-Haj for their sustained engagement with both the substance and the form of this chapter. Though all errors remain my own, I have thoroughly enjoyed this shared endeavour.

Notes

1. Immanuel Kant, *Groundwork of the Metaphysics of Morals* (Cambridge: Cambridge University Press, 1785). See also Stu Woolman, 'Dignity', in *Constitutional Law of South Africa*, ed. Stu Woolman, 3rd ed. (Grahamstown, South Africa: NISC, 2023), ch. 36.
2. Martin Luther King, Jr., *Where Do We Go From Here: Chaos or Community* (Boston: Beacon Press, 1967).
3. Stu Woolman, 'Understanding South Africa's Aspirational Constitution as Scaffolding', *New York Law School Law Review* 60, no. 2 (2016): 283–296; Stu Woolman, 'South Africa's Aspirational Constitution and Our Problems of Collective Action', *South African Journal on Human Rights* 32, no. 1 (2016): 156–183.
4. Stu Woolman, *Wrecking Ball: Why Permanent Technological Unemployment, a Predictable Pandemic and Other Wicked Problems Will End South Africa's Experiment in Inclusive Democracy* (Grahamstown, South Africa: NISC, 2021). *Wrecking Ball* identifies a decalogue of existential wicked problems that confront humanity: nuclear proliferation, climate change and pandemics, automation and artificial intelligence, permanent technological unemployment, public/private surveillance, social media distortions, fragmentation of democracies, the inability to cabin private power, and the deepening of autocratic rule. Even if we possessed inclusive global political and economic institutions with the requisite coercive power, the complexity of these problems would vex policymakers. Wicked problems are often intractably convoluted and possess many of the following features: (1) no metric exists to identify the point at which a solution has been discovered; (2) some problems tend to require one-shot responses rather than allow for trial and error; (3) one wicked problem may be a function of another wicked problem; or worse still, wicked problems actually reinforce and accelerate one another; and (4) policymakers often have no margin for error.
5. Ibid.
6. Tabatha Abu El-Haj, 'Changing the People: Legal Regulation and American Democracy', *New York University Law Review* 86, no. 1 (2011): 1–68, 1.
7. Frantz Fanon, *The Wretched of the Earth* (New York: Penguin Books, 1963), 94.
8. Kwame Anthony Appiah, 'Liberation Psychology: How Frans Fanon Came to View Violence as Therapy', *The New York Review of Books* (24 February 2022).
9. Ibid. See Riaydh Sidaoui, 'Islamic Politics and the Military: Algeria 1962–2008', in *Religion and Politics: Islam and Muslim Civilization*, ed. Jan-Erik Lane and Hamadi Redissi (New York: Routledge, 2009), 241.
10. King, *Where Do We Go from Here.*
11. Martin Luther King, Jr., 'The Role of the Behavioral Scientist in the Civil Rights Movement', American Psychological Association Annual Convention (Washington, DC, 1 September 1967).
12. Hannah Arendt, *On Violence* (New York: Harcourt, 1970).

13. Arendt believed that the self-governing American colonies had partially developed her preferred politics of active civic republicanism before their revolution, and restored power to its rightful place by taking active responsibility for the new country's governance after the war. She vehemently opposed the totalizing violence of the Jacobin terror that marred the French Revolution, as well as the fascist and communist revolutions of the twentieth century, that extinguished those political freedoms that make self-governance by engaged citizens possible. Hannah Arendt, *On Revolution* (New York: Penguin Books, 1963); Hannah Arendt, *The Human Condition* (Chicago: University of Chicago Press, 1958); Hannah Arendt, *The Origins of Totalitarianism* (New York: Harcourt, 1951).
14. Arendt, *On Revolution*, 33–34. Arendt juxtaposed the American reverence for the Constitution—a text to which anyone could claim allegiance—against the animating and mystical notion of a 'volk' [people] that limited the possibilities of many European nation-states.
15. Ibid.
16. Kant, *Groundwork of the Metaphysics of Morals*.
17. Judith Butler, *Notes Toward a Performative Theory of Assembly* (Cambridge, MA: Harvard University Press, 2015).
18. Judith Butler, *Gender Trouble: Feminism and the Subversion of Identity* (New York: Routledge, 1990).
19. Stu Woolman, *The Selfless Constitution: Experimentalism and Flourishing as Foundations of South Africa's Basic Law* (Cape Town: Juta, 2013).
20. Judith Butler, *Frames of War: When Is Life Grievable?* (New York: Verso Books, 2009), 3.
21. Ibid., 14.
22. Ibid., 5.
23. Amartya Sen, *Development as Freedom* (New York: Knopf, 1999).
24. Michael Walzer, *Politics and Passion: Toward a More Egalitarian Liberalism* (New Haven, CT: Yale University Press, 2004), 1–10; Michael Walzer, 'On Involuntary Association', in *Freedom of Association*, ed. Amy Gutmann (Princeton, NJ: Princeton University Press, 1998), 64–74.
25. Woolman, *Selfless Constitution*.
26. Arendt, *On Revolution*, 32–34.
27. Stu Woolman, 'Language, Power and the Margin: Eliot's Philosophy of Language, Wittgenstein on Following a Rule, and Statutory Construction in *Mankayi v AngloGold Ashanti*', *South African Law Journal* 129, no. 3 (2012): 434–460.
28. *S v Mamabolo (E TV and others Intervening)* 2001 (3) SA 409 (CC), 2001 (1) SACR 686 (CC), 2001 (5) BCLR 449 (CC) 50.
29. Stu Woolman, 'Seek Justice Elsewhere: An Egalitarian Pluralist Response to David Bilchitz on the Distinction between Differentiation and Domination', *South African Journal on Human Rights* 28, no. 2 (2012): 273–295.
30. Stu Woolman and Courtenay Sprague, 'Nowhere to Run Nowhere to Hide: The Absence of Public Policy on Intimate Partner Violence Abrogates the Rights to Healthcare and Bodily Integrity under the South African Constitution', *Cardozo Journal of Law and Gender* 22, no. 1 (2015): 29–74.
31. Elias Canetti, *Crowds and Power* (New York: Farrar, Straus & Giroux, 1962), 22.
32. Richard Adelstein, "States without Romance" *Public Choice* 152, no. 3/4 (2012): 259–263: 'Government is . . . treated with contempt in most quarters . . . But this . . . loosening of the

people's sense of consent to the contract, . . . has led increasing numbers to look with hostile distrust at anything government attempts to do'.

33. *Garvis v Satawu (Minister for Safety & Security, Third Party)* 2010 (6) SA 280 (Western Cape High Court).
34. *South African Transport & Allied Workers Union & Congress of South African Trade Unions v Jacqueline Garvis* [2012] ZACC 13. Stu Woolman, '"You Break It, You Own It": South African Assembly Jurisprudence after *Garvis*', *Vienna Journal of International Constitutional Law (Vienna)* 9, no. 4 (2015): 548–571.
35. *Garvis I*, 6–7.
36. Section 17 of the Constitution reads: 'Everyone has the right, peacefully and unarmed, to assemble, to demonstrate, to picket and to present petitions'.
37. Stu Woolman, 'Freedom of Assembly', in *Constitutional Law of South Africa*, ed. Stu Woolman, 3rd ed. (Grahamstown, South Africa: NISC, 2023), ch. 43.
38. *Garvis I*, 41.
39. Section 1 of the South African Constitution reads as follows:

    'The Republic of South Africa is one, sovereign, democratic state founded on the following values:

    (a) Human dignity, the achievement of equality and the advancement of human rights and freedoms.
    (b) Non-racialism and non-sexism.
    (c) Supremacy of the constitution and the rule of law.
    (d) Universal adult suffrage, a national common voters roll, regular elections and a multi-party system of democratic government, to ensure accountability, responsiveness and openness.'
40. See *President of the Republic of South Africa v Modderklip Boerdery (Pty) Ltd* 2005 (5) SA 3 (CC), 2005 (8) BCLR 786(CC)('*Modderklip*') 43.
41. Woolman, *Wrecking Ball*.

Further Readings

Arendt, Hannah. *On Revolution*. New York: Penguin Books, 1963.

Arendt, Hannah. *On Violence*. New York: Harcourt, 1970.

Arendt, Hannah. *The Origins of Totalitarianism*. New York: Harcourt, 1951.

Butler, Judith. *Frames of War: When Is Life Grievable?* New York: Verso Books, 2009.

Butler, Judith. *Notes Toward a Performative Theory of Assembly*. Cambridge, MA: Harvard University Press, 2015.

Canetti, Elias. *Crowds and Power*. New York: Farrar, Straus & Giroux, 1962.

King, Martin Luther, Jr. *Where Do We Go From Here: Chaos or Community?* Boston: Beacon Press, 1968.

Marx, Karl. *On the Jewish Question*. Paris: Deutsch–Französische Jahrbücher, 1844.

Nussbaum, Martha. *Women and Human Development: The Capabilities Approach*. New York: Cambridge University Press, 2000.

Waltzer, Michael. *Politics and Passion: Toward a More Egalitarian Liberalism*. New Haven, CT: Yale University Press, 2004.

Woolman, Stu. 'Seek Justice Elsewhere: An Egalitarian Pluralist Response to David Bilchitz on the Distinction between Differentiation and Domination', *South African Journal on Human Rights* 28, no. 2 (2012): 273–295.

Woolman, Stu. *The Selfless Constitution: Experimentalism and Flourishing as Foundations of South Africa's Basic Law*. Cape Town: Juta, 2013.

Woolman, Stu. 'South Africa's Aspirational Constitution and Our Problems of Collective Action', *South African Journal on Human Rights* 32, no. 1 (2016): 156–183.

Woolman, Stu. *Wrecking Ball: Why Permanent Technological Unemployment, a Predictable Pandemic and Other Wicked Problems Will End South Africa's Experiment in Inclusive Democracy*. Grahamstown, South Africa: NISC, 2021.

CHAPTER 5

ASSEMBLY AS POLITICAL PRACTICE

TABATHA ABU EL-HAJ

Introduction

A right of peaceful assembly has long been recognized as critical to the constitutional commitment to self-government. Accrued initially as part of the rights of free-born Englishmen,[1] it was textually enshrined for the first time during the American Revolution, initially in state constitutions and thereafter in the First Amendment to the US Constitution.[2] A distinct right of peaceful assembly is now recognized in numerous instruments of international law.

Despite near-universal recognition of a right of peaceful assembly, both national and international courts have largely failed to articulate its independent value. Instead, the tendency has been to conceive of the value of assembly in primarily expressive terms. 'Assembly, like speech', the US Supreme Court declared during the height of the civil rights movement, 'is . . . essential in order *to maintain the opportunity for free political discussion*, to the end that government may be responsive to the will of the people and that changes, if desired, may be obtained by peaceful means'.[3] Even constitutional courts that formally construe the right of assembly independently from speech and associational rights tend to characterize assembly as 'a medium of communication on issues of a public nature in open societies'.[4] Such statements reflect that the rights of speech, association, and assembly share the common aim of facilitating democratic accountability and responsiveness and the possibility of political, social, and cultural change—and that they reinforce one another in that purpose.

Nevertheless, assembly offers a distinct contribution to the larger political project of self-government. The act of gathering offers its own contributions to politics—contributions that are distinct from any of its expressive or instrumental political functions. This chapter articulates the distinct characteristics of assembly as a form of social and political practice. It lifts up the latent and constitutive political value of assembly to liberal democratic polities, with the purpose of shedding fresh light on how we ought to conceive of the right.[5] In the absence of a fuller accounting of the non-expressive value of assembly, there is a significant risk assembly will be denigrated or delegitimized—both legally and politically.[6]

The chapter further suggests that we should think of public assembly as a political easement—indeed that would be a fairly accurate way of thinking of it given its British constitutional origins.[7] Like all easements, preserving it means using it. In the absence of use, and a belief in an entitlement to usage, the easement disappears and, with it, its latent and constitutive political functions. Monumental political assemblies—Gandhi's Satyagraha, Martin Luther King, Jr.'s March on Washington, and more recently Tahrir Square in Egypt—do not come out of nowhere. As I have argued elsewhere, 'The extraordinary builds on the ordinary'.[8] Historically momentous iterations of assembly build upon ordinary and long-forgotten gatherings—labour protests against Governor Walker in Wisconsin or fuel protests in Burma.[9] Such mundane usages, including ones that are apolitical, are necessary not only to preserve the existence of the easement for those occasions when it proves to be politically very valuable but also to sustain the civic and political capacity for politics.

A full accounting of the value of assembly requires resisting the temptation to define its value by reference to the monumental moments of 'the people outdoors'—the assemblies that led to self-determination or brought forth substantial social and political change. The distinct value of assembly requires an examination of the more prosaic moments of assembly and their distinctive qualities. It is these regular acts of assembly that hold open the path to the transformative, while also laying the foundation for a host of prerequisites to politics. We must articulate these latent and constitutive political functions of assembly and give courts a reason to construe the right to maintain the broad and rugged parameters of the political easement.[10]

Ambiguity of 'Assembly'

'Assembly' can refer to two related, but distinct, phenomenon. An assembly can be an instantiation of popular sovereignty. As Sharath Srinivasan suggests, assembly is a mode of self-government.[11] It is the capacity, or a claim to the capacity, to self-govern without the mediation of formal institutions of representation. This iteration of assembly overthrows feudal, monarchic, and colonial authorities and establishes new political orders.

National and international bodies that name their governing institutions 'general assemblies' are evoking this long-standing conception of assembly—and the legitimacy that flows from its connection to popular sovereignty. Occupy assembled in this mode. With its nightly governance meetings, in occupied public squares, where participants debated politics, using a 'human loudspeaker', the movement symbolically invoked the sovereign people themselves, outdoors and governing. Nikolas Bowie has recently argued that during the American revolutionary period, Samuel Adams consistently spoke of the right of assembly as protecting this iteration of assembly—as protecting Americans' right to self-govern, rather than 'the act of assembling' itself.[12]

There is, however, a more literal sense of assembly: assembly as individuals gathered in the public realm.[13] Assembly in this sense is a form of collective political action within a historically contingent repertoire of political practices.[14] This conception emphasizes that although it has changed in form, assembly has remained in the mix of regular forms of democratic action from the eighteenth century through today—a testament surely to its value. While it often involves literally gathering outdoors for political purposes, neither congregating outdoors nor congregating for political purposes is essential to the practice. Occupy engaged in this sort of assembly as well: It marched through streets, occupied prominent public spaces, caused disruption, and defied permit requirements, and it did so to highlight political grievances with the aim of shifting government policy.

A critical difference between these two conceptions of assembly is their orientation to the right. From the perspective of assembly as popular sovereignty, as the people themselves, 'the freedom of assembly has to precede and exceed any form of government that confers and protects that right of assembly'.[15] Thus, Judith Butler asserts, 'The power to move or be still, to speak and to act, belongs to the assembly prior to, and in excess of, whatever rights a particular government decides to confer or to protect'.[16] The theoretical intuition is simple: If the collective can bring down a state through exercise of the freedom of assembly, the individuals in the crowd cannot be relying on that state for their liberty to do so.[17]

By contrast, from the perspective of assembly as political practice, assembly is just one of a set of protected political practices within the repertoire of liberal democratic politics. Constitutions and international conventions confer the right of peaceful assembly in the same way that they confer the right to vote or freedom of speech. The political potential of assembly does not change the nature of the right.[18] This chapter discusses both assembly and the right of assembly from this latter perspective, arguing that both the power of and the pervasive ambivalence about assembly are products of the tension between its two manifestations.

'Not Merely Speech'

The function and value of assembly to democratic politics are undertheorized. While its expressive value is well articulated, a fuller consideration of assembly and its contribution to self-government has been eclipsed by the focus on expression.

The problem is not that assemblies are not expressive. Assembling is often expressive, including in ways that are not directly tied to speech. As Butler argues, 'Embodied actions of various kinds signify in ways that are, strictly speaking, neither discursive nor prediscursive'.[19] Gathering—the act of convening in particular places at particular times—often sends a clear message (articulate or not).

The problem is rather that a wholly expressive account of assembly leads to its underprotection. As expressive events, assemblies rarely live up to the legal imagination of how speech contributes to democracy. As C. Edwin Baker correctly observed, in legal academia, speech is valuable where it 'bring[s] about change by the (at least partly) rational process of convincing people of ideas or opinions'.[20] Thus, constitutional protection prioritizes speech that 'insures that the individual will have more information and, thus, be able to make a more informed choice'.[21] Yet assemblies are opportunities for rational, transactional politics in only a very marginal sense. When people gather, including when they gather outdoors in the public square for political ends, they rarely, if ever, offer reasoned disquisitions or distinct policy proposals. There is little argument or debate. Instead, they chant. They sing. They hold handmade signs. They make demands—frequently ones that are conflicting, unrealistic, and often incoherent.

When the inconvenience of assembly is balanced against assembly's expressive value, using this measure, its value is easy to discount. As Erik Barendt observes, '[I]t is hard to see what a street procession or mass demonstration contributes to the discovery of truth'.[22] Assemblies are not forums for mediating collective differences through an informed and respectful exchange of ideas or to reflect and reconsider positions after reason-giving.[23] A discursive conception of the value of assembly leads easily to legal debates about whether assemblies can find adequate, less inconvenient alternatives for expressing their views. It also makes it difficult to explain extending robust protection to those who gather without clear political aims. Protection for the right of peaceful assembly fares little better when individual interests in autonomy and liberty are emphasized.

To understand the value of assembly, we must deepen our conception of politics. Democratic politics is more social and relational than the discursive or deliberative account of democracy that prevails in law. 'Speech', as I have argued elsewhere, 'has never been the primary mechanism for demanding responsiveness, nor the most effective means for holding officials responsible for their choices'.[24] While public discourse is important, influencing public decision-making ultimately requires the *exercise* of political rights in concert. Political demands must be formed, and they must then be translated into political power (legislative, executive, or judicial) through political acts. Assembly, as we will see shortly, is distinctly positioned to mobilize people but also to generate and sustain such political action. And this is true even though the causal relationship between assembly and either policy or political reform is contingent and not guaranteed, linear, or immediate.

Assembly as Political Practice

Assembly is a form of political action within the repertoire of democratic practices. It is also, however, a form of social action—one that itself performs a critical function sustaining politics. While an exhaustive accounting of the distinctive contribution of assembly to politics is beyond the scope of this chapter, three underappreciated characteristics of assembly, *qua* social and political action, are worthy of extended discussion.

Assembly as a Social Politics

Assembly is inherently social. The social character of assembly places it as a bridge—a critical throughline—between civic and political life. Prior to any expressive or instrumental political function, there must be an act of assembling. Not only does the capacity to gather arise out of social ties, but gathering reinforces those ties and generates new ties. The social and relational character of assembly also explains why assemblies, great and small, including for nonpolitical ends, reinforce social solidarity.

Assembling arises out of relationships. The very act of gathering relies heavily upon social ties. Someone must invite, and that invitation must be accepted. While certainly there are instances when assemblies arise from media consumption or happenstance, invitations and acceptances, even on social media, generally run through existing social ties.[25] A seminal study of American politics in the 1990s found that individuals were more likely to agree to take political action if the request was made by a friend or an acquaintance, often from a civic group or church—places where people assemble.[26] A seminal study of recruitment to participate in the Freedom Rides during the US civil rights movement reached a similar conclusion.[27] In fact, Mario Diani observes that 'the notion that prior social ties operate as a basis for movement recruitment . . . [is one of] the most established findings in social movement research'.[28]

Acts of assembly also 'grease the wheels' of future civic and political participation.[29] As a peer-to-peer form of politics, assembly both reinforces existing social ties and generates new social ties.[30] Through being part of a group—walking, talking, and engaging with those who share a social experience—individuals gain a sense of a shared experience and of agency when they name that commonality. As Anna Zhelnina and James Jasper observe, '[P]articipants . . . derive pleasure from the assembly itself, a sense of their own power, and confidence that history is on their side'.[31]

Assembling generates social solidarity—a recognition that not only is one part of a group, but that one has strength by virtue of being part of a group, and that the group has power by virtue of being a group.[32] This capacity for assembly to generate a sense of political efficacy and power has long been noted by observers of American politics. Alexis de Tocqueville, as Jeremy Waldron has noted, observed that public assembly provided '"Men . . . the opportunity of seeing each other" and of taking courage from each other's presence, no longer isolated self-consciously in their individual dissident opinions'.[33]

The social solidarity function of the act of assembly, like the importance of social ties to recruitment, is not limited to overtly political assemblies or even to gatherings in public spaces. Candlelight vigils and funerals like assemblies that serve cultural or recreational ends provide meaningful opportunities for the formation of social solidarity around national, ethnic, and religious identities, but also as neighbours. Consider, in this regard, the long history of the ethnic parade, Mardi Gras, and the variety of festivities associated with national holidays such as the Fourth of July, Twelfth of July, and Bastille Day. Pre-existing social ties, in turn, drive decisions to join such events.

Indeed, emphasizing a dichotomy between political and nonpolitical assemblies is a mistake. It is also a mistake to distinguish between public and private (including commercial) assemblies. For one, most assemblies are 'hybrid events'.[34] Political assemblies often have festive and commercial qualities. Pop stars sing while food and 'merch' is sold. Meanwhile, local politicians greet their constituents at Saturday farmers markets and community festivals while issue-oriented groups set up stalls to educate and raise money. For another, the social characteristics of assembly remain even when money is exchanged for inclusion.

Like hybrid events, acts of assembling in private spaces also reinforce social solidarity and civic capacity. Bowling leagues and book clubs, unions and gay social clubs, Boy Scout troops and college sororities all provide critical opportunities to assemble. Not only does the formation and existence of such groups shape and form individual identities, but these acts of gathering (frequently indoors)—even when they are not part of formal associations—create a collective identity and a sense of belonging. Participation in associational events arises from, but also reinforces and generates, new social ties. Such assemblies are 'private' only in the sense that they take place indoors on private property. Politically speaking, they are 'public'—gatherings in the public realm as opposed to in the household or at work—and their social characteristics generate the latent potential for still more civic and political action.

Ritual, humour, and creativity play a critical role in generating feelings of social solidarity.[35] Choices, like the decision in Singapore to encourage attendees at the first Pink Dot event to arrive for a picnic dressed in all shades of pink and later to instruct the crowd to wave pink cardboard fans, balloons, and umbrellas as they stood in various formations, matter.[36] Even relatively inconsequential assemblies are often orchestrated to be clever and humorous in ways that reinforce collective bonds. A protest in Nebraska over a proposed crude oil pipeline project begins with an Apple Pie Brigade as grandmothers line up to bring baked goods to the Governor's residence.[37] Online assemblies produce similar social solidarity functions through similar collective acts of creativity.[38]

Before proceeding, it is important to be clear that social solidarity should not be confused with social homogeneity.[39] Assembly, like association, often takes the form of us not them. In contemporary pluralistic societies, this can reinforce social divisions and political polarization. Still, as John Inazu argues in this volume, '[T]he value of belonging is itself pluralistic: Everyone does not belong together, but everyone belongs somewhere'.[40] And sometimes, assembling can bridge social divisions, as when civil rights marches forge interracial alliances.

Assembling can also help build the organizational infrastructure of politics by sustaining existing civic and political groups and by providing the impetus for forming new ones. Many annual parades and festivities, including the Orange parades discussed by Bryan in this volume, sustain the membership-based civic associations and social clubs connected with them—lodges, brigades, Mummers, and krewes.[41] Historically, assemblies, whether in the form of conventions, pageants, or parades, were an essential part of building organizational capacity. The US National Women's Suffrage Association that met in Washington, DC in 1888, for example, was held forty years after Seneca Falls, New York and led, in turn, to the founding of the International Council of Women.[42]

Assemblies great and small, as exercises of the easement, contribute to democratic politics by creating the conditions necessary to mobilize people to action, but also by generating and sustaining the social precursors of political action. By facilitating and reinforcing social ties, social solidarity, and social organization, assembly lays the foundation for politics and builds latent political power. This capacity derives from the important role social ties play in facilitating civic and political engagement and the important role assembly plays in bringing people together to facilitate or reinforce those ties. It also derives from the sense of social solidarity, of belonging somewhere that assemblies can offer individuals, as Inazu says, and the agentic experience of citizenship that typically follows.

When the UN Human Rights Committee's General Comment No. 37 asserts that '[assembly] constitutes the very foundation of a system of participatory governance based on democracy, human rights, the rule of law and pluralism',[43] it is these functions—derived from the act of assembling itself—to which it is referring. Of course, whether there will be a call for political action and whether that call will be politically successful is contingent. The capacity of even large assemblies to foment political change depends upon bringing a diverse set of groups and interests across social and political divisions on board as well as upon regime type and political environment. This contingency, however, does not diminish the inherent value of the latent political potential that assembly generates.

Assembly as a Politics of Presence

Presence is an essential characteristic of assembly as a political practice. The decision to appear in public is a claim to civic inclusion and recognition. It also provides an embodied experience of citizenship—one that is often empowering. As Butler observes, '[I]t matters that bodies assemble'.[44] Mere presence—before any words are spoken or demands made—constitutes a nondiscursive political claim distinct from whatever participants have to say once they have gathered.[45]

Waldron elaborates on this intuition, writing, 'One doesn't have to be a follower of Wittgenstein to understand the difference between saying and showing. Even if something does not fall into the category of things that cannot be said, still sometimes showing that thing is more powerful, more effective than saying it'.[46] This distinction between the intrinsic and expressive power of assembly, he argues, is captured in the root of the word 'demonstrate':

> One doesn't have to be an etymologist to recognize the common root here, which is '*monstro, monstrare*', a Latin verb meaning 'to show, point out, indicate.' It is the same

> root for 'monstrance' and maybe even 'monster,' whose original meaning lay somewhere between 'exhibit,' 'prodigy,' and 'warning.'[47]

To be sure, a variety of synonyms for demonstrate—assemble, protest, gather, or march—would undercut his specific linguistic argument. Nevertheless, Waldron's underlying point is sound: in coming together to assemble members of society display their presence by standing together, they embody 'we exist.'[48] Presence is a demand for recognition apart from any slogan brandished. As Butler explains, '[W]hen bodies assemble on the street, in the square, or in other forms of public space (including virtual ones) they are exercising a plural and performative *right to appear*, one that asserts and instates the body in the midst of the political field.'[49] Presence, in the particular contexts she describes, has been a demand for recognition of the economic precarity that policies in favour of free trade, among others, have produced.

Assembly as a politics of presence provides an opportunity for groups to demand inclusion. By showing up, walking out, wearing keffiyehs, flying the Palestinian flag, carrying homemade placards, and chanting various slogans (even those that offend others), pro-Palestinian students in 2023 demanded recognition on US campuses. 'We are here too!' they say. The decision to appear in public was as much a claim to civic inclusion and recognition as an expression of a viewpoint. Palestinians exist in Gaza and also in your community.

Full citizenship in a liberal pluralist democracy turns on recognition in the public realm, including in the literal public square.[50] Contests over control of public space are thus critical to both forging, and claiming recognition of, group identities.[51] The democratizing potential of this politics of presence is understood by those at the margins of politics and society. For example, as Asli İkizoğlu Erensü shows, assembling has afforded refugees displaced by conflict an opportunity 'to appear in public as political actors rather than mere humanitarian subjects.'[52] Even when ultimately unsuccessful, assembling has made the refugees' presence visible and disrupted a conception of refugees as voiceless victims for whom others must speak.

This power of assembly, moreover, is not limited to acts of assembling outdoors. It is evident even when the assembling is physically indoors and legally private. Private acts of assembly—meetings of the LGBTQ law students, banquets of a Muslim association in Leigh County, Pennsylvania, or gatherings at clubhouses of the Knights of Labor—can also be symbolic claims for civic and political recognition and inclusion. The claim to citizenship arises from the mere act of appearing in the public realm broadly understood.

Finally, and just as importantly, assembly as presence ensures a small-c experience of citizenship. Joining others, whether at a political march, in a church group, or at a community litter pick, offers an embodied experience of citizenship in which those present share a public-regarding purpose. Assembly brings people together, including those who have known each other before, around causes or activities, generating a new sense of civic community.[53] Acting together even around minimally significant goals (litter picks) can be empowering. This function of assembly points away from the primacy of large-scale political assemblies and undercuts the instinct to see its primary beneficiaries as politically marginalized groups.[54] The experience of small c-citizenship is valuable to all of us, those who are disempowered simply by being unaffiliated especially.

Assembly as a Politics of Disruption

Assembly is a politics of disruption. Even when assemblies comply with notification or permit requirements and abide by limitations placed by authorities on their timing, location, and noise level, outdoor assemblies literally disrupt ordinary routines. Government resources are diverted. Traffic is held up and rerouted. Pedestrians cross the street, and shoppers avoid London on the weekend of the King's Coronation. Such inconveniences, though they loom large in the public imagination, are, however, the least interesting way in which the act of assembling is disruptive.

Assembly as a form of social and political action is disruptive of public narratives, social and economic patterns, political priorities, and, in certain circumstances, political regimes. The Freedom Convoy, in opposition to Canadian COVID-19 policies, offers a stark example of the economic disruption assembly can cause. The three-week blockade disrupted the flow of goods between the United States and Canada and forced automakers on both sides of the border to curtail production. Although this characteristic of assembly is limited to outdoor assemblies with political valence, it is, nevertheless, important to any theorization of the value of assembly as a political practice.

Appearance can itself be disruptive. When assemblies reveal groups or issues, those revelations can change public perception—as when the public was forced in the 1980s to face an AIDS epidemic and the gay community it impacted. Butler has argued that this has been a feature of recent protests highlighting the challenges resulting from global capitalism: The act of appearing together has reframed economic insecurity and poverty as a collective political failing—a 'social condition [that] is both shared and unjust'—thereby disrupting the neoliberal narrative that poverty is a product of individual moral failure, irresponsibility, and dependency.[55] This is a third sense in which assembly is disruptive.

Assembly's disruptive qualities are most salient when the crowd is political, sizable, persistent, and perceived as authentic. Under the right conditions, assemblies can afford citizens a powerful political tool by which to interrupt public narratives and upend political settlements in ways that are not ordinarily available. Spontaneity is often taken as an indicium of authenticity. Several Black Lives Matter (BLM) protests in reaction to George Floyd's murder in 2020 literally drew elected officials, such as Portland Mayor Timothy Wheeler, into the street to speak to members of the crowd. Even without such face-to-face encounters, BLM protests shifted attention from the immediate public health crisis of the pandemic to the broader impact on Black communities of institutions and practices shaped by segregation and racism. Occupy provides another illustration of this phenomenon. Persistent occupations of urban spaces in 2011 introduced into public discourse the juxtaposition between 'the 1%' and 'the 99%'—which became a shorthand for economic inequality. That shorthand found its way into the stump speeches of Democratic candidates, and, over time, addressing economic inequality found its way into the party's official platform. The degree of disruption or its political impact will vary with the particulars, as these examples illustrate.

While some may be tempted to conclude that the political power of disruption is primarily relevant for groups that remain—even after formal grants of suffrage—politically, socially, and economically marginalized, this would be a mistake. One reason this is a mistake is that large persistent crowds can be used to shore up governing narratives and reigning authorities—an observation to which we will return shortly.

The disruptive quality of large assemblies is a product of persistence, size, and authenticity, not disorderliness or inconvenience. The participants in the Women's March in the United States in 2017, for example, were conventionally privileged, and the protests were exceedingly tame by any measure. The event was organized by non-profit organizations; its routes were negotiated with authorities in advance; its participants were amongst the most educated and privileged in the country; and the assembly itself operated well within accepted bounds of peacefulness. Despite this conventionality, the staggering and unexpected outpourings across the country mobilized a wave of anti-Trump organizing that interrupted his political momentum and defined the character of partisan politics for the duration of his term.

The critical point is that the political power of assembly is tied to the disruptive qualities of a politics of appearance, not disorderliness or the spectre of violence.[56] It is time to problematize the conventional wisdom apparent in David Mead's quip in his contribution to this volume, '[t]o misquote Emma Goldman, "if peaceful, tranquil protest changed anything, they'd abolish it"'.[57] This conventional wisdom also explains why large assemblies are often referred to as 'crowds'—and feared as mobs. And it is evident in Waldron's observation that 'something about a demonstration—*any* demonstration—seems to convey at least to its targets and opponents that things *might* get out of hand if its demands are not listened to. Patience is evaporating, it seems to say'.[58]

Indeed, to date, this has been my position: Discordant assembly, while a long-standing practice of liberal democratic politics, comes with an implicit threat of disorder and violence. Even though most assemblies are peaceful that implicit threat is the source of assembly's power; discomfort with the implicit threat of violence drives courts' (and state authority's) ambivalence towards the right.[59]

But it is possible this has been a mistake. Observers, me included, have inadvertently substituted the disorder and associated risk of violence for the actual threat to the state: The political risk that the appearance of what at first looks to be simply a disgruntled and unruly faction will gain legitimacy and build the political power to disrupt what has been taken for granted. We have failed to heed Hannah Arendt's caution against the temptation to equate violence with power.[60] As Arendt astutely observed, violence does not itself create political change. It simply coincides with it: 'The emergence of a new society [is] preceded, but not caused, by violent outbreaks'—just as 'labor pangs . . . precede, but of course do not cause, the event of organic birth'.[61]

With this in mind, let us return to the assembly that ultimately shores up the status quo. When the crowd (especially a large one) appears to support the government (or a populist leader), it manifests its approval and confers legitimacy. This is critical because, as Arendt reminds us, it is well-accepted in political theory that the power of a ruling class is the product of public acceptance—not violence, as she emphasizes.[62] Still, the basic claim that assembly is inherently disruptive is sound. As with all assemblies, the degree of disruption and its political impact varies with the particulars. In some instances, a status-quo favouring crowd will be critical to disrupting whatever threat to the regime prompted its need to be orchestrated. But it will only truly be effective in disrupting that political cycle if it is not too orchestrated; it must be recognizable as an authentic manifestation of support for those in power.

Three important insights about the disruptive properties of assembly as a political practice flow from this example. First, this example reinforces that it is the appearance of the crowd that is the ultimate source of the assembly's political power: Having people show up in support is exactly what a fragile regime needs to shore itself up. Second, it clarifies why size does matter. Political legitimacy turns on numbers: Power (unlike violence) 'always stands in need of numbers', as Arendt also recognized.[63] Third, acts of assembly may be disruptive, even when they appear to reinforce reigning discourses or shore up existing political elites. The appearance of citizens in support of the powers that be interrupts whatever forces might have been threatening them.

Taken together, the example of the assembly that shores up the status quo reinforces the intuition that it has been a mistake to point to disorder and the spectre of violence as the source of the assembly's political power. It is the widespread showing up to take a stand, not violence to persons or property, that fuels the assembly's political power.

Assembly as Political Easement

Assemblies, great and small, reinforce the capacity for democratic politics and thereby hold open the path to political change on a transformative scale. Assembling reinforces social ties and social solidarity, thereby generating the latent potential for widespread civic and political engagement. Assembly also facilitates opportunities to form a collective identity and forge an embodied and agentic experience of citizenship while providing opportunities for individuals and groups to demand civic and political recognition and inclusion. Finally, assembly is a disruptive form of politics. Each of these characteristics of assembly, moreover, is tied to the fact of gathering together. It is the gathering with others that fosters social ties, social solidarity, and a sense of civic and political agency. It is the act of gathering that is empowering, and it is the act of gathering that is disruptive. It is also the act of gathering—especially in great numbers—that ultimately fuels the political power of assembly.

With this in mind, let us return to the earlier suggestion that we should think of public assembly as a political easement in which ongoing usage shapes the landscape for political action. Acts of assembly not only sustain the civic and political capacity necessary for democratic politics, they also ensure that the right of assembly is maintained and that assembly remains a legitimate form of politics. Regular acts of assembling are essential to preserve the ongoing existence of the easement. Assembling also builds into participants an experiential knowledge and memory of a more agentic form of politics—one that is often inspiring in its distinction from much of what constitutes politics in the modern world.

Assembly is also an easement, however, in a second sense. It is not an accident that assemblies are 'the politics of the people outdoors'.[64] Assembling is most politically powerful in those moments when the crowd assembled in the public square appears to shift into a legitimate expression of the sovereign people themselves. The power of assembly, in other words, lies in its potential to awaken the 'sleeping sovereigns', to use Richard Tuck's extremely apt phrase.[65] This, of course, does not happen often.

Not every large crowd on the street demanding political change is an instance of popular sovereignty. Most disruptive crowds do not call into question the legitimacy of the government—or even profoundly object to its right to represent them. They may cry 'illegitimate', but their main claim is 'do better by us'. Butler is thus mistaken when she (and she is not alone) suggests 'assembly [is] a punctual expression of popular sovereignty'.[66] More importantly, her mistake is not epistemological—how do we decide who the people are? It is conceptual: She elides the difference between popular will (public opinion) and sovereignty. Sovereignty, in a democratic state, lies with the people, but only *before* they have given their powers (the bundle of sticks, as lawyers like to describe it) to the government with certain reservations (retaining the sticks associated with rights)—or in the cases of the United States and the European Union, divided these original powers between different governments. Once the transfer has occurred, however, sovereignty as a practical matter lies with the government, and the people are 'sleeping sovereigns'.[67] They are left only with the rights they have reserved.

The threat of assembly to the state—or its power, depending on one's perspective—emerges only when the sovereign wakes: When the appearance of what at first looks to be simply a disgruntled and unruly faction gains legitimacy and transforms into a manifestation of 'we, the sovereign people outdoors'. This transformation requires numbers, persistence, and authenticity, but it also requires a narrative shift: Those assembled must find a way to connect narratively to previous manifestations of popular sovereignty. Once again, the act of gathering is key.

It is the act of gathering that connects us to the past and reminds us that we are sovereign. When people gather in political crowds, they seek to exploit this easement to their original power as they are both reminded of and seek to connect narratively to 'the people themselves'. Thus, Sarah Lockwood observes that 'the ghosts of the anti-colonial past heavily anchor the forms that activism takes in the postcolony', including with respect to locations, dates, and rituals.[68] Rabab El-Mahdi, similarly, describes how in Tahrir Square in 2011, participants discussed their experiences at previous Tahrir sit-ins: 'Some remembered the 30 March 2003 when they managed to camp in the Square following the protests against the US invasion of Iraq. Others were asking older protesters about the 1970s protests'.[69] El-Mahdi describes further how the memory of Tahrir continues to inspire dissatisfied Egyptians. She notes that the phrase '"El-Tahrir Mawgu'd" (Tahrir would always be there)' has come into use to convey 'the threat of public assembly as a powerful antidote against undesirable political outcomes'.[70]

Making the narrative connection to sovereign power depends on the re-enactment of a face-to-face politics of the past and the rituals associated with doing so. The creativity and sass of the posters of the Women's March connect back to the political toasts and the ritual burning in effigy of John Jay for 'selling "American liberty and independence" for "British gold"'.[71] It also ensures that some participants at a future assembly will have memories of having gathered outdoors.

Conclusion

Ambivalence about the place of public assembly and protest in a democratic society is frequently expressed in terms of the proximity between disorder and violence. Yet, this chapter has argued that it is worth reconsidering this conventional wisdom. Not only is violence not central to assembly's power (as Arendt long ago pointed out), but it would now appear that the core ambivalence about assembly arises out of the proximity between ordinary assembly and untamed popular sovereignty.

Assembly as a political practice stands at the boundary between ordinary and extraordinary political processes—between this constitution and the next. Not all instances of assembly are normal, and it is exceedingly difficult to know in advance when the act of assembling will mark the withdrawal of consent to be governed and the beginning of a political transformation. The problem is that the people can revoke their grant of sovereignty and, like a homonym, when that occurs, it often sounds like they are exercising the right of assembly. This makes governments—as well as anyone who is content with the status quo—nervous.

But, and this is the critical point, non-violent protest is *not* an extra-institutional form of politics. It is a political practice that is critical to sustaining the capacity for democratic politics itself. Thus, despite the homonym, we should eschew any suggestion that assembly is a threat to the normal channels of democratic politics.

Similarly, the right of peaceful assembly is not an extra-constitutional right. It is a core reservation. Like the right to vote, the freedom of speech, and the freedom of association, assembly was reserved to enable citizens to demand representation, accountability, and responsiveness within the confines of ordinary democratic politics. Butler is thus mistaken when she asserts that 'the freedom of assembly has to precede and exceed any form of government that confers and protects the right of assembly'.[72] The right of peaceful assembly is one of the rights the sovereigns reserved before they transferred their governing powers and went to sleep. Her apparent dilemma—'Does it make sense for the people to rely on government to protect itself from the government?'—is a product of theorizing about democracy without sufficient attention to its complex institutional structures. The government is not unitary, and it is the competition between governmental institutions that allows for an imperfect negotiation of the fundamental dilemma of all rights.[73]

With all of this in mind, we are now in a better position to understand what it means to construe the right of assembly to preserve the broad and rugged parameter of the easement. First, coverage must be construed expansively. The law should refrain from distinguishing between political and nonpolitical assemblies and recognize how smaller and hybrid gatherings, indoors and out, serve latent and constitutive political functions. Second, assembly as both a politics of disruption and presence indicates the need for greater legal tolerance of the disorder of assembly, including disorder associated with choosing the place. Third, the account offered in this chapter grounds the peacefulness constraint. The lack of protection for violent assembly is not merely a product of the delicacy of liberal sensibilities; it is justified by a recognition that the power of assembly as a political practice does not arise from violence or the risk of violence. Most importantly, courts should distinguish the right of assembly more carefully from the freedoms of speech and association and recognize how the act of gathering drives the distinct contributions of assembly to liberal democratic polities.

Acknowledgements

It is difficult to express how much this chapter owes to, or how much I have learned from, ongoing conversations over the last three years amongst the editors and between and with contributors to this volume, including Dominic Bryan, Ella McPherson, Orsolya Salát, Adrian Randall, and Stu Woolman. I also wish to thank Don Herzog. The chapter reflects an ongoing dialogue with Sharath Srinivasan about assembly and its relationship to law.

Notes

1. See *United States v Cruikshank*, 92 U.S. 542, 551 (1875) ('The right of the people peaceably to assemble for lawful purposes existed long before the adoption of the Constitution of the United States. In fact, it is, and always has been, one of the attributes of citizenship under a free government'). English authorities, to be sure, often denied the existence of the right or construed it narrowly, as when Parliament passed the notorious and repressive 'Six Acts' in 1819. See Channing, in this volume. See also John Phillip Reid, *In a Defiant Stance: The Conditions of Law in Massachusetts Bay, the Irish Comparison, and the Coming of the American Revolution* (University Park: Pennsylvania State University Press, 1977).
2. The amendment, adopted in 1791, was a concession to opponents of the new federal Constitution and their broader conception of the limits of legitimate dissent. See generally Saul Cornell, *The Other Founders: Anti-Federalism and the Dissenting Tradition in America, 1788–1828* (Chapel Hill: University of North Carolina Press, 1999).

3. *Gibson v Florida Legislative Investigation Committee*, 372 U.S. 539, 562 (1963) (Douglas, J., concurring) (emphasis added).
4. Makarau, JJC, in *Democratic Assembly for Restoration and Empowerment and Others v Saunyama No and Others* (2018), ZWCC 9 p. 8 (characterizing the right further as creating a 'space for individuals to coalesce around an issue and *speak with a voice* that is louder than the individual voices of the demonstrators') (emphasis added). With thanks to David Mead for drawing me to this quote.
5. Assemblies (both peaceful and unpeaceful) occur in both liberal and authoritarian regimes (see Li, in this volume). Whether assembly manifests similarly or differently for citizens and subjects of illiberal and authoritarian states is an interesting question that is unfortunately beyond the scope of this chapter.
6. This risk is evident in Jeremy Waldron's observation in the wake of the Black Lives Matter protests of 2020 that 'there is a hierarchy of legitimate action within normal politics' in which 'lobbying, advocacy, and voting have priority' while 'demonstrating is justified . . . when those tactics have failed' and before civil disobedience which is 'a really, really last resort'. 'What Demonstrations Mean', 7 (unpublished manuscript (1 October 2020) on file with author).
7. See Randall, in this volume.
8. Tabatha Abu El-Haj, 'All Assemble: Order and Disorder in Law, Politics and Culture', *University of Pennsylvania Journal of Constitutional Law* 16, no. 4 (2014): 949–1040, 954.
9. Florence Tan, 'Myanmar Protests Stall Fuel Imports, Drive Up Costs', Reuters, 19 February 2021; Steven Greenhouse, 'Delivering Moral Support in a Steady Stream of Pizzas', *New York Times*, 25 February 2011.
10. This chapter like that of Srinivasan, in this volume, seeks to augment the limited literature theorizing assembly *qua* assembly.
11. See Srinivasan, in this volume.
12. Nikolas Bowie, 'The Constitutional Right of Self-Government', *Yale Law Journal* 130, no. 7 (2021): 1652–1745.
13. I use the phrase 'public realm' rather than 'public square' because although this conception of assembly often involves literally gathering outdoors, this is not, as we shall see, its only form.
14. See generally Charles Tilly, *Contentious Performances* (New York: Cambridge University Press, 2008), 5–7.
15. Judith Butler, *Notes Toward a Performative Theory of Assembly* (Cambridge, MA: Harvard University Press, 2015), 160. Butler articulates key nonspeech functions of public assembly, but the analysis is limited insofar as it articulates these values in the context of *a* particular movement.
16. Ibid., 160–161.
17. For some, the argument turns on a distinction between freedoms that pre-exist the state, whether arising out of natural rights or otherwise, and rights granted by the state. Butler, however, does not make this argument since she draws a distinction between the freedom of assembly and the freedom of speech, though both are denoted as 'freedoms of' rather than rights or 'freedoms from' (e.g. torture or cruel and unusual punishments).
18. This point is elaborated upon further in the text accompanying footnote 72.
19. Butler, *Notes*, 8.
20. C. Edwin Baker, 'Scope of the First Amendment Freedom of Speech', *UCLA Law Review* 25, no. 5 (1978): 964–1040, 972.

21. Ibid., 975.
22. Eric Barendt, 'Freedom of Assembly', in *Freedom of Expression and Freedom of Information: Essays in Honour of Sir David Williams*, ed. Jack Beatson QC and Yvonne Cripps, 161–176 (Oxford: Oxford University Press, 2000), 166.
23. William Smith, 'The Boundaries of a Deliberative System: The Case of Disruptive Protest', *Critical Policy Studies* 10, no. 2 (2016): 152–170, 153 (arguing that notwithstanding increasing acceptance of action that is not strictly speaking deliberation, '[t]he broader deliberative turn in democratic theory is associated with the normative claim that policymaking and public debate should, as far as possible, approximate an idea of informed and inclusive dialogue' while characterizing 'behavior as deliberative if it is suitably reflective, respectful, and dialogic').
24. Tabatha Abu El-Haj, 'How the Liberal First Amendment Under-Protects Democracy', *Minnesota Law Review* 107, no. 2 (2022): 529–604, 534.
25. Florence Passy, 'Social Networks Matter. But How?', in *Social Movements and Networks: Relational Approaches to Collective Action*, ed. Mario Diani and Doug McAdam (Oxford: Oxford University Press, 2003), 21–48 (reviewing literature showing that a primary path by which individuals disposed to take political action are connected to opportunities to do so is through social ties).
26. Sidney Verba, Kay Lehman Schlozman, and Henry E. Brady, *Voice and Equality: Civic Voluntarism in American Politics* (Cambridge, MA: Harvard University Press, 1995).
27. Doug McAdam, 'Recruitment to High-Risk Activism: The Case of Freedom Summer', 92 *American Journal Sociology* 92, no. 1 (1986): 64–90; see also Doug McAdam and Ronnelle Paulsen, 'Specifying the Relationship between Social Ties and Activism', *American Journal Sociology* 99, no. 3 (1993): 640–667.
28. Mario Diani, 'Introduction: Social Movements, Contentious Actions, and Social Networks: "From Metaphor to Substance"?', in Diani and McAdam, *Social Movements and Networks*, 1–18, 7.
29. See Tabatha Abu El-Haj, 'Friends, Associates and Associations, Theoretically and Empirically Grounding the Freedom of Association', *Arizona Law Review* 56, no. 1 (2014): 53–116, 77.
30. A systematic review of fifty-seven longitudinal studies of collective action and protests between 1967 and 2015 finds participation in protests often leads to the formation of new relationships and friendships and extended involvement in and sustained commitment to political and social movements. Sara Vestergren, John Drury, and Eva Hammar Chiriac, 'The Biographical Consequences of Protest and Activism: A Systematic Review and a New Typology', *Social Movement Studies*, 16, no. 2 (2017): 203–221.
31. See Zhelnina and Jasper, in this volume.
32. Zhelnina and Jasper, for example, explain that '[m]arches, rallies, and occupations can make participants feel good about themselves even when their external impact is small, uncertain, or declining' and go on to argue that peaceful protests 'give participants a taste of efficacy, of what it means to join others in demanding—if not always attaining—their moral goals'. Ibid., 116, 135.
33. Waldron, 'What Demonstrations Mean', 22 (citing Alexis de Tocqueville, *Democracy in America*, vol. I, ed. Joseph Epstein (New York: Bantam Books, 2000), 221).
34. Robert J. Sampson, *Great American City: Chicago and the Enduring Neighborhood Effect* (Chicago: University of Chicago Press, 2012), 184–186.

35. There is a long tradition of sociological and anthropological research, developing the insights of Emile Durkheim, that emphasizes the importance of social solidarity in holding society together and addresses the relationship of ritual to social solidarity.
36. See Chua, in this volume.
37. Mary Pipher, 'Lighting a Spark on the High Plains', *New York Times*, 18 April 2013, at A27.
38. Chua, in this volume, also includes a description of the elaborate and ritualized Pink Dot assembly that took place online during the COVID-19 pandemic when Singapore had a complete ban on in-person assemblies. See also McPherson and Beraldo, in this volume. Beraldo's description of Anonymous, in particular, emphasizes the role of playful tropes.
39. See John D. Inazu, *Confident Pluralism: Surviving the Thriving through Deep Difference* (Chicago: University of Chicago Press, 2016).
40. See Inazu, in this volume.
41. This is noteworthy given that face-to-face, membership-based civic associations, while once prominent in the United States and Europe, have largely disappeared in other areas of life, arguably with negative consequences for democracy. See generally Theda Skocpol, *Diminished Democracy: From Membership to Management in American Civil Life* (Norman: University of Oklahoma Press, 2003).
42. See Liu, in this volume.
43. UNHRCttc, General Comment No. 37—Article 21: Right of Peaceful Assembly (17 September 2020), 1, UN Doc. CCPR/C/GC/37.
44. Butler, *Notes*, 7–8.
45. Ibid., 8.
46. Waldron, 'What Demonstrations Mean', 18.
47. Ibid.
48. Ibid., 18–21, 24.
49. Butler, *Notes*, 11 (emphasis added).
50. Joseph Raz, 'Free Expression and Personal Identification', *Oxford Journal of Legal Studies* 11, no. 3 (1991): 303–324.
51. Timothy Zick, 'Recovering the Assembly Clause', *University of Texas Law Review* 91, no. 2 (2012): 375–403, 394 (noting that assembly facilitates recognition by 'allow[ing] otherwise marginalized individuals to be present with others and to communicate specific identity claims to the state and to the general public').
52. See İkizoğlu Erensü, in this volume.
53. Vestergren et al., *The Biographical Consequences of Protest and Activism*, 210–211.
54. These various contributions to citizens' experience of and engagement with democracy that derive from assembly as a practice of presence are hardly recognized in law. Even General Comment No. 37's guide to authorities does not clearly articulate them.
55. Butler, *Notes*, 16.
56. I use the term 'appearance' rather than 'presence' in this subsection to distinguish the fact of appearance from the import of appearance. 'Presence' is associated with recognition. This is not to deny that presence cannot occur without appearance. I also use the term 'violence' narrowly to denote significant violence to persons or property as distinct from merely unlawful action.
57. See Mead, in this volume.
58. Waldron, 'What Demonstrations Mean', 11.
59. See e.g. Abu El-Haj, 'All Assemble'.

60. Hannah Arendt, 'On Violence', in *Crises of the Republic* (New York: Harcourt, Brace Jovanovich, [1969] 1972), 105–198, 150–152.
61. Ibid., 113.
62. Ibid., 151; see also ibid., 140 ('All political institutions are manifestations and materializations of power [as opposed to violence]; they petrify and decay as soon as the living power of the people ceases to uphold them. This is what Madison meant when he said "all governments rest on opinion," a word no less true for the various forms of monarchy than for democracies').
63. Ibid., 141, 143 (arguing further that '[p]ower is never the property of an individual; it belongs to a group and remains in existence only so long as the group keeps together').
64. Tabatha Abu El-Haj, 'Defining Nonviolence as a Matter of Law and Politics', in *Protest and Dissent (Nomos LXII)*, ed. Melissa Schwartzberg (New York: New York University Press, 2020), 201–236, 204.
65. Richard Tuck, *The Sleeping Sovereign: The Invention of Modern Democracy* (Cambridge: Cambridge University Press, 2016).
66. Butler, *Notes*, 174.
67. Butler makes the same mistake when she discusses voting and argues that '[as] democratic theorists have argued for some time, elections do not fully transfer sovereignty from the populace to its elected officials'. Ibid., 161. Once again, the mistake is conceptual, even legal. Constitutions transfer sovereignty, not elections.
68. See Lockwood, in this volume.
69. See El-Mahdi, in this volume.
70. Ibid., 5.
71. Simon P. Newman, *Parades and the Politics of the Street: Festive Culture in the Early American Republic* (Philadelphia: University of Pennsylvania Press, 1997), 99.
72. Cf. Butler, *Notes*, 160.
73. Liberal democracies are established by institutional arrangements—not a speech act. The nonunitary institutional structure of the government accounts for why the reserved rights (for the most part) do protect *from* oppression by the government even as those rights are enforced by the government. Institutionally fracturing power allows that sometimes the people's right of assembly (like its right to vote and speak freely) will be protected by the judiciary; other times, by the police and military and their refusal to unleash violence against the people; and so forth.

Further Reading

Abu El-Haj, Tabatha. 'All Assemble: Order and Disorder in Law, Politics and Culture'. *University of Pennsylvania Journal of Constitutional Law* 16, no. 4 (2014): 949–1040.

Baker, C. Edwin. *Human Liberty and Freedom of Speech*. Oxford: Oxford University Press, 1989.

Bowie, Nikolas. 'The Constitutional Right of Self-Government'. *Yale Law Journal* 130, no. 7 (2021): 1652–1745.

Butler, Judith. *Notes Toward a Performative Theory of Assembly*. Cambridge, MA: Harvard University Press, 2015.

Butler, Judith. 'Protest, Violent and Nonviolent'. In *Antidemocracy in America: Truth, Power, and the Republic at Risk*, ed. Eric Klineberg, Caitlin Zaloom, and Sharon Marcus, 233–240. New York: Columbia University Press, 2019.

Inazu, John D. *Confident Pluralism: Surviving and Thriving Through Deep Difference*. Chicago: University of Chicago Press, 2018.

Inazu, John D. *Liberty's Refuge: The Forgotten Freedom of Assembly*. New Haven, CT: Yale University Press, 2012.

Schwartzberg, Melissa, ed. *Protest and Dissent (Nomos LXII)*. American Society for Political and Legal Philosophy. New York: New York University Press, 2020.

CHAPTER 6

ASSEMBLY, PLURALISM, AND IDENTITY

JOHN INAZU

INTRODUCTION

THE right of assembly is often viewed as a protection for expressive events like protests and demonstrations. It is certainly this, but its scope extends well beyond the gathering itself to the group that precedes the gathering. As General Comment No. 37 to the International Covenant on Civil and Political Rights observes, 'an associative element' is 'inherent to' the right of peaceful assembly.[1] Article 20(1) of the Universal Declaration of Human Rights (UDHR) suggests an even closer link, recognizing a singular 'right to freedom of peaceful assembly and association'.[2] Assembly is perhaps most obscured in the constitutional law of the United States, which recognized a textual right of assembly in the First Amendment in 1791 and added a non-textual right of association almost two hundred years later.[3] Since introducing a right of association in 1958, the US Supreme Court has all but forgotten the right of assembly—in fact, it hasn't taken a case on the right assembly in more than forty years.[4] In the United States, protections for groups fall under the largely undeveloped right of association; meanwhile, protests are governed almost exclusively by free speech law. But severing the expressive gathering from the group that precedes the gathering ignores the interconnectedness between gathering and group, particularly when it comes to notions of pluralism and identity. While current US law sees gatherings principally as speech and groups principally as associations, the history and theory of the right of assembly—both domestically and globally—suggests that gatherings and groups cannot be so easily severed from one another.

Beginning with the US context and moving to international observations, this chapter suggests that 'assembly' properly encompasses both expressive gatherings and the groups that precede them. The connection between the two highlights the significance of assembly to pluralism and identity.

The Roots of Assembly in the United States

When the First Congress debated the Bill of Rights, Thomas Hartley of Pennsylvania argued with Elbridge Gerry of Massachusetts about whether the First Amendment should include a right of assembly. The House of Representatives was considering language specifying that 'the people shall not be restrained from peaceably assembling and consulting for their common good'.[5] Hartley supported this language, arguing that assembly should extend to 'every thing that was not incompatible with the general good'.[6] Gerry responded that Hartley was 'contend[ing] for nothing' if he meant to say that the people 'had a right to consult for the common good' but 'could not consult unless they met for that purpose'.[7]

The final wording of the Assembly Clause does not limit the right to gathering only for the purpose of the common good.[8] Properly understood, the right of assembly enables groups of people to pursue different notions of the common good. It allows for what Justice Robert Jackson once called 'the right to differ'.[9]

It is through this right to differ that people develop and act upon the beliefs and practices that not only form who they are but also inevitably cause friction in a pluralistic society. That friction imposes costs, including exclusion and instability. But there are also the enormous benefits of facilitating a genuine pluralism within which people can pursue their identities and beliefs on their own terms.

Assembly Is Inherently Relational

Assembly is the only right in the First Amendment that requires more than one person to be exercised. While speech, press, petition, and religion (at least in some religious traditions) can be exercised individually, assembly requires at least two people. The right of assembly thus anchors a relational dimension in the First Amendment and reinforces the importance of groups within the protections established under our constitutional framework. In other words, protection for groups existed in the freedom of assembly itself—well before the US Supreme Court created a separate right of association.

The verb 'assemble' presupposes a noun—an assembly. People usually form a group of some kind before they assemble in public. Moreover, while some assemblies occur spontaneously, most do not. In fact, the expressive or outwardly 'political' dimensions of assembly often follow relationships: Labour protests grow out of formal and informal cohesion around labour unionism, religious activism is often rooted in congregations, and political protests are often planned in coffee shops, neighbourhood associations, and online groups. As Nancy Rosenblum has observed, the expressive dimensions of an assembly are 'often unintended [and] unpredictable'.[10] This is 'why democratic justifications for freedom of association are inseparable from the moral uses of pluralism overall' and the groups that enact those moral uses.[11]

I have argued elsewhere that the political history of the United States reveals three characterizations of assemblies: dissenting (those that oppose the government-enforced consensus), public (those that advocate for political space separate from the government), and expressive (those that exhibit adherence to belief or practice).[12] Most of these emerge out of relationships. The importance of informal association that precedes expressive collective action can be seen in civil rights organizing,[13] the suffragist movement,[14] the modern labour movement,[15] and the gay rights movement,[16] amongst others. The theoretical underpinnings of the judicially recognized right of association also demonstrate the importance of these informal and inchoate stages of assembly. Relationships that blossom into fully formed bonds of trust and care begin with informal and undefined connections. The social dimensions of assembly rooted in informal gatherings are as intuitive as they are necessary, both for the protesters in the streets and planners in the coffee shops.

Forming Identity Together

A key aspect of the right of assembly is that it facilitates the formation of collective identity and belief within a social practice—with other people who have joined together in what Tocqueville called 'the art of pursuing in common the objects of common desires'.[17] In fact, the associational ties fostered by assembly 'let people make their own definitions of community'.[18] As the philosopher Charles Taylor has observed: 'I am a self only in relation to certain interlocutors: in one way in relation to those conversation partners who were essential to my achieving self-definition; in another in relation to those who are now crucial to my continuing grasp of languages of self-understanding'.[19]

The identity-forming dimensions of assembly can be found not only in relatively small groups but also in much larger ones. This is one of the problems with Kenneth Karst's distinction between 'intimate' and 'non-intimate' associations.[20] When the US Supreme Court adopted Karst's approach in its 1984 decision, *Roberts v United States Jaycees*,[21] it highlighted that intimate associations are capable of 'cultivating and transmitting shared ideals and beliefs', can 'foster diversity and act as critical buffers between the individual and the power of the State', provide 'emotional enrichment from close ties with others', and that help 'safeguard[] the ability independently to define one's identity that is central to any concept of liberty'.[22] But many non-intimate associations perform some or all of these functions and otherwise enable people to discover and shape their individual and collective identities.

Karst himself recognized the ways that non-intimate associations could contribute to identify formation. He defined intimate association as 'a close and familiar personal relationship with another that is in some significant way comparable to a marriage or family relationship'.[23] But he noted that '[a]n intimate association, *like any group*, is more than the sum of its members; it is a new being, a collective individuality with a life of its own'.[24] Indeed, 'the shared sense that "we" exist as something beyond "you" and "me" '[25] manifests even in much larger groups. Think, for example, of the emotional and relational dynamics underlying claims like 'Our team won!' or 'We lost a hard-fought campaign'.[26]

The right of assembly recognizes the expressive and intimate potential of all of these different groups. But it is also the case that the collective self-understanding and identity of an active assembly is ever changing. Alasdair MacIntyre has explained why this is true of any social practice:

> When an institution—a university, say, or a farm, or a hospital—is the bearer of a tradition of practice or practices, its common life will be partly, but in a centrally important way, constituted by a continuous argument as to what a university is and ought to be or what good farming or what good medicine is. Traditions, when vital, embody continuities of conflict.[27]

The coming together of individuals in assemblies thus regularly creates new forms of identity individually and collectively.[28]

The failure to recognize these dimensions of assembly leads to doctrinal confusion and under-protection. US case law is a caution. Since the *Jaycees* decision, the US Supreme Court has offered scant guidance on how to draw the lines between intimate and non-intimate associations.[29] The Court's failure to clarify its doctrinal line drawing has left some groups entirely unprotected by the right of association, including groups that almost certainly foster collective and individual identity.[30]

The Limits of Assembly

The First Amendment's right of assembly includes a textual constraint: Assemblies must be 'peaceable'. But this constraint still leaves open questions about the nature and limits of peaceability, which may go beyond violence-based limitations, especially in the context of groups. For example, at some point, the power granted to those controlling the membership requirements of an assembly may be limited because society recognizes that the external harms of its exclusionary and expulsive membership policies are too great.[31] In the United States, the paradigmatic example of this limitation came against White-controlled assemblies (including businesses, schools, and neighbourhood associations) that discriminated against Black Americans.[32] Since the dismantling of Jim Crow, courts have struggled to determine which other assemblies should be similarly constrained by government power.[33]

Constraints on exclusion and expulsion represent one side of the membership limit of assembly. The other side of this limit is the right of any member to exit the assembly—an assembly that compelled its members to remain against their will would not be a peaceable one.[34] In most cases, the exit right is formally and functionally available to members, who must decide whether the present and future mission and values of the assembly align with their own sense of meaning and identity. This alignment need not be complete; in fact, as MacIntyre demonstrates, an important part of any assembly is the way its members shape its common life through ongoing argument and conflict.[35] But at some point, members of an assembly may discover that they no longer see themselves as part of an internal reform effort, at which point exit may be their preferred alternative.

In some assemblies—particularly those whose practices and procedures are largely outside public view—exit rights are harder to guarantee.[36] This has been the case, for example, with insular religious communities that maintain geographic, cultural, and educational separation from surrounding communities.[37] In those situations, state authorities must balance honoring the integrity and autonomy of private assemblies while also ensuring that members of those assemblies have joined voluntarily, remain voluntarily, and are aware of their right to exit at any time.[38]

Finally, the right of assembly will always confront limits at the boundaries of tolerable social action. No society is fully pluralistic, which is to say that every society sets limits on 'the right to differ'. In most cases, these limits will restrict action but not always advocacy. For example, the constitutional protections for assembly will extend to groups that advocate for, but do not practice, currently illegal conduct like the use of certain drugs or communist government rule. But even some purely expressive assemblies will be prohibited. The United States will not allow the St. Louis chapter of Al Qaida or the New York branch of the Cult of Human Sacrifice.[39]

The Importance of Belonging

The right of assembly is properly seen as a check on government,[40] a protection for protest and dissent,[41] and an indispensable part of governing the factions that emerge in a pluralistic society.[42] But assemblies also provide a sense of belonging to many if not most people in society. Importantly, the value of belonging is itself pluralistic: Everyone does not belong together, but everyone belongs somewhere. And that means respecting the many groups that emerge to fulfil this sense of belonging—some open and welcoming, others closed and inhospitable to outsiders; some that make sense to us and others that seem incomprehensible; some that we find normatively attractive and some that we see as morally compromised.

Over the past few decades, commentators have expressed concern over the weakened sense of belonging. Writing in 1998, Rosenblum observed declining membership in 'beneficial groups' combined with 'the proliferation of associations whose norms and purposes are antiliberal or undemocratic'.[43] Rosenblum underscored related concerns about 'political mistrust', 'pervasive contempt for major institutions', and 'even clinical depression'.[44] And just two years later, Robert Putnam worried that too many Americans were 'bowling alone'.[45]

Today, the challenges that Rosenblum identified have only increased. Membership in religious organizations is plummeting.[46] People live, work, and play with greater political homogeneity.[47] And the advent of the internet has spawned hundreds of new antiliberal and undemocratic groups and efforts.[48] Perhaps the greatest challenge of the past generation, however, has been the loss of trust in institutions, the fraying of a sense that 'we' have a stake in groups and organizations greater than ourselves, whether social, religious, or political. As Yuval Levin has observed, 'Many of our struggles seem rooted in relational problems. Loneliness and isolation, mistrust and suspicion, alienation and polarization—these are the characteristic maladies of this era. But because they are failures of sociality, they too often fall into the blind spots of our individualist culture'.[49]

Online Assembly, Identity, and Privacy

Increasingly, assemblies critical to identity and belonging are forming online: through social networks, clubs, workplaces, interest groups, churches, and gaming communities. In fact, while early studies assumed 'that face-to-face relationships are inherently superior to online relationships',[50] online relationships are increasingly significant to a growing number of people. At least for some people, 'virtual relationships are more real than real-world ones'.[51] Moreover, many of us do not neatly divide our interpersonal interactions between online and offline, which means that the protections and guarantees in one domain can affect our interactions and relationships in another.[52]

Like their offline counterparts, online assemblies advance political, religious, and other expressive goals that require protection from state interference. As Ilia Siatitsa notes, the UN Special Rapporteur on the Rights to Freedom of Peaceful Assembly and Association has 'emphasized that shutdowns and the blocking of entire websites constitute an extreme and disproportionate measure that cannot be justified in any circumstances' and observed the need to protect those exercising their right of peaceful assembly 'in both physical and digital spaces'.[53] Siatitsa also notes that these intrusions begin with privacy violations: 'A violation of the right to privacy, more often than not, is not an end in itself; it rather offers the means for infringing on other rights. In that sense, it often becomes the enabler for infringing on, amongst others, freedom of assembly'.[54]

The significance of online privacy is heightened by the blurring of professional and personal identities. Take, for example, a teacher of young children. A generation ago, that teacher could have pursued two distinctive identities at work and in her free time. But today, the teacher who blows off steam or lets down her guard on the weekend risks having her words and actions captured on social media—either inadvertently posting to her own account or appearing on someone else's account. And the drink in hand or joke in poor taste can't naturally be limited solely to her 'private life' if the parents or administrators come across the social media post. This reality creates a great deal of pressure for a young teacher who has signed up for a job but not a lifestyle. And it increases the importance of fostering and protecting offline assemblies that can function as 'safe spaces'.[55] These assemblies will not only protect informal and arguably ill-advised words and actions from public view; they will also enable the pursuit of new friendships and ideas outside the public eye. Importantly, they will allow trusted members to try out new ideas and ask genuine questions without fear of public judgement.

Guarantees of privacy, of course, are not without risks. When the government allows words and practices to unfold in secret, it risks the possibility of harms including criminal conspiracies, abusive relationships, involuntary associations, and coercive indoctrination. Any meaningful privacy guarantee in large and diverse societies will result not only in the risks of these harms but in some cases their actual occurrence. Societies and governments can and should address egregious abuses of privacy and secrecy, but they should usually do so in response to established harm, only acting preemptively in rare situations where evidence strongly suggests a future harm.[56]

Glimpses of a More Robust Right of Assembly in US Doctrine

The modern US Supreme Court has insufficiently accounted for the important implications of assembly to pluralism, identity, and non-expressive communication. In fact, the Court hasn't addressed the assembly clause at all in more than forty years. Part of the reason for its neglect is traceable to an odd historical error that limited the scope of assembly. The interpretive error originated in an 1886 Supreme Court opinion, *Presser v Illinois*. Relying on an earlier case, Justice William Woods wrote that the First Amendment protected the right to assemble only if 'the purpose of the assembly was to petition the government for a redress of grievances'.[57] Woods's assertion clearly misstates both the wording and intent of the First Amendment, but it was adopted in decades of ensuing scholarship.[58]

The consequences of this misstep continue today. In 2018, a federal court in Minnesota rejected a First Amendment claim after concluding 'there is no free-standing right to free assembly'.[59] Two years later, a federal court in Kentucky addressing an assembly claim raised against a COVID-related restriction concluded that 'courts typically evaluate free speech, assembly and petition claims under the same analysis'.[60] In fact, every recent case involving the right of assembly has turned to an analysis under either free speech public forum doctrine or the right of expressive association.

The Supreme Court has never corrected its error in *Presser*, but there are signs that it might be close to doing so.[61] In 2021, three Justices examined the issue during oral argument in an important case involving disclosure of membership lists of private organizations, *Americans for Prosperity v Bonta*.[62] Questioning the lawyer for the petitioners, Justice Kavanaugh asked: 'Do you agree on the text of the First Amendment that the freedom to peaceably assemble is distinct from the freedom to petition the government for a redress of grievances'?[63] Justice Barrett followed later with a related question about the right of assembly,[64] and Justice Kagan also referenced an amicus brief arguing that the Court consider the implications for the right of assembly in this case.[65] The Court's opinion in *Bonta* failed to acknowledge the importance of assembly or clarify its earlier error in *Presser*. Justice Thomas's concurrence, however, noted that 'the text and history of the Assembly Clause suggest that the right to assemble includes the right to associate anonymously'.[66]

International Observations

International law, by contrast, more clearly articulates the interconnectedness between group and gathering. Article 20(1) of the UDHR states: 'Everyone has the right to freedom of peaceful assembly and association'.[67] The International Covenant on Civil and Political Rights (ICCPR) splits assembly and association into two separate articles that follow one after the other. ICCPR Article 21 guarantees '[t]he right of peaceful assembly'[68] and Article 22 states that '[e]veryone shall have the right to freedom of association with others'.[69] In both the UDHR and the ICCPR, assembly precedes association.

Although neither the UDHR nor the ICCPR defines 'assembly,' one scholar writing in the international context suggests that an assembly is 'an intentional gathering by two or more people (including in private and online/virtual spaces)'.[70] As in the US context, international law links assembly not only to association but also to expression.[71] In fact, international law recognizes 'the full protection of peaceful assembly is possible only when other, often overlapping, rights are also protected, notably freedom of expression, freedom of association and political participation'.[72]

Nevertheless, the conflation and confusion in the US context has also been observed in the international context. As Michael Hamilton has observed, 'The right of peaceful assembly is often cast in instrumental terms—serving either expressive or associational ends, or both. Such reasoning, however, relegates "assembly" to a second-tier status, denying its independent value and evading enquiry into its autonomous sphere'.[73] Recognizing the importance of assembly apart from these other rights, in international law as in US law, depends on strengthening its connections to pluralism and identity—and ultimately, relationships. Hamilton suggests that 'the key insight is that the communicative function of an assembly (if indeed there is one) may be secondary to its social and relational value—and it is here that the autonomous sphere of assembly begins to come into view'.[74] This intuition is buttressed by General Comment No. 37 to the ICCPR, which recognizes that '[t]he right of peaceful assembly has an intrinsic value'.[75] Or, as Timothy Zick has noted in the US context, 'Assembly is protected in its own right; it stands on its own bottom'.[76]

Conclusion

The right of assembly in the US context continues to be muddled by judicial confusion around the related rights of speech and association. Although there are hints that the US Supreme Court might revive the independent significance of assembly, the doctrinal shift has not yet occurred. In the international context, the right of assembly risks a similar diminishment if disconnected from the related rights of expression and association. The importance of assembly in anchoring and strengthening these correlative rights remains important. As the UN Human Rights Committee suggests, assemblies 'may create opportunities for the inclusive, participatory, and peaceful resolution of differences'.[77] This peaceful resolution of differences lies at the core of well-functioning societies that recognize the importance of both pluralism and identity to the citizens that comprise them.

Acknowledgements

Thanks to Ridge Hughbanks and Alice Gorman for research assistance.

Notes

1. UNHRCtte, General Comment No. 37—Article 21: Right of Peaceful Assembly (17 September 2020) UN Doc. CCPR/C/GC/37, 4. 'The full protection of the right of peaceful assembly is possible only when other, often overlapping, rights are also protected, notably freedom of expression, freedom of association and political participation'. Ibid., 9.
2. Universal Declaration of Human Rights, UNGA Res. 217A(III), 10 December 1948 (UDHR), article 20(1). The International Covenant on Civil and Political Rights recognizes '[t]he right of peaceful assembly' in Article 21 and that '[e]veryone shall have the right to freedom of association with others' in Article 22. International Covenant on Civil and Political Rights, 999 UNTS 171, 16 December 1966 (ICCPR), articles 21, 22.
3. *NAACP v Alabama ex rel. Patterson*, 357 U.S. 449 (1958). For an in-depth history of the constitutional right of association, see John D. Inazu, 'The Strange Origins of the Constitutional Right of Association', *Tennessee Law Review* 77, no. 3 (2010): 485–562.
4. *NAACP v Claiborne Hardware Co.*, 458 U.S. 88 (1982).
5. Congressional Register, 15 August 1789, vol. 2, quoted in Neil H. Cogan. *The Complete Bill of Rights: The Drafts, Debates, Sources, and Origins* (New York: Oxford University Press, 1997), 145.
6. Ibid.
7. Ibid.
8. I explore this observation in greater detail in John D. Inazu, *Liberty's Refuge: The Forgotten Freedom of Assembly* (New Haven, CT: Yale University Press, 2012).
9. *West Va. St. Bd. of Educ. v Barnette*, 319 U.S. 624 (1943).

10. Nancy Rosenblum, *Membership and Morals: The Personal Uses of Pluralism in America* (Princeton, NJ: Princeton University Press, 2000), 191.
11. Ibid. These 'moral uses of pluralism' emerge in the inchoate and informal stages of associations—when relationships are built, ideas generated, and social bonds strengthened. See Tabatha Abu El-Haj, 'Friends, Associates, and Associations', *Arizona Law Review* 56, no. 1 (2014): 55 (noting how various political movements 'gained momentum through social networks—formal and informal, grassroots and astroturf, embodied and virtual').
12. John D. Inazu, 'The Forgotten Freedom of Assembly', *Tulane Law Review* 84, no. 3 (2010): 570–571.
13. John Hope Franklin and Alfred A. Moss, Jr., *From Slavery to Freedom: A History of African Americans* (7th ed., New York: McGraw-Hill, 1994), 377 (describing '"moments of informality" spread across clubs, literary parties, and other events that created "a cohesive force"' among the leaders of the Harlem Renaissance).
14. Linda J. Lumsden, *Rampant Women: Suffragists and the Right of Assembly* (Knoxville: University of Tennessee Press, 1997), 3 (detailing suffragist gatherings organized around banner meetings, balls, swimming races, potato sack races, baby shows, meals, pageants, and teatimes).
15. See Marion Crain and John Inazu, 'Re-Assembling Labor', *University of Illinois Law Review* no. 5 (2015): 1793 (discussing examples of Fast Food Forward and OUR Wal-Mart, among others). See also ibid., 1791 (observing that the 'focus on outward expression overlooks the critical importance of the group's formation and mobilization process and the role that this process plays in constructing the long-term identity of the movement').
16. Brief of Gays & Lesbians for Individual Liberty as Amicus Curiae in Support of Petitioner, *Christian Legal Soc'y v Martinez*, 561 U.S. 661 (2010) (No. 08-1371), 2010 WL 530513, at *11 (describing 'gay social and activity clubs, retreats, vacations, and professional organizations' that fostered 'exclusively gay environments in which to feel safe, to build relationships, and to develop political strategy').
17. Alexis de Tocqueville, *Democracy in America* (London: Saunders and Otley, 1835). See also Theodore M. Mills, *The Sociology of Small Groups* (Hoboken, NJ: Prentice-Hall, 1967), 2 ('[Groups] are units composed of two or more persons who come into contact for a purpose and who consider the contact meaningful.'); Timothy Zick, 'Recovering the Assembly Clause', *University of Texas Law Review* 91 (2012): 393–394 ('Freedom of assembly also serves various emotional and psychological functions. The act of assembly creates a sense of solidarity or common cause. It excites and energizes individuals, whether they gather to knit scarves, play soccer, pray, or participate in marches or protests. It fosters personal and civic pride by providing outlets and venues for the pursuit of common causes. Freedom of assembly does not simply allow individuals to develop their own identities. It allows otherwise marginalized individuals to be present with others and to communicate specific identity claims to the state and to the general public.').
18. Kenneth L. Karst, 'The Freedom of Intimate Association', *Yale Law Journal* 89, no. 4 (1980): 688.
19. Charles Taylor, *Sources of the Self: The Making of Modern Identity* (Cambridge, MA: Harvard University Press, 1992), 36. Taylor suggests that '[a] self exists only within' what he calls 'webs of interlocution'. Ibid., 35. The collective nature of assemblies also brings political and expressive benefits. See e.g. *Rumsfeld v Forum for Acad. & Institutional Rts., Inc.*, 547 U.S. 47 (2006) ('The right to speak is often exercised most effectively by combining one's voice with the voices of others.'); *Citizens against Rent Control v City of Berkeley*,

454 U.S. 290, 294 (1981) ('[B]y collective efforts individuals can make their views known, where individually, their voices would be faint or lost'). But as Tabatha Abu El-Haj has noted, even these political and expressive benefits are rooted in relationships. See Abu El-Haj, 'Friends, Associates, and Associations', 73 (noting that effective political participation 'depends far less on associations as incubators of ideas than on associations as incubators of relationships').

20. Karst, 'Intimate Association', 624.
21. *Roberts v U.S. Jaycees*, 468 U.S. 609 (1984). *Roberts* also announced a separate category of expressive association: 'a right to associate for the purpose of engaging in those activities protected by the First Amendment—speech, assembly, petition for the redress of grievances, and the exercise of religion'. Ibid., 618.
22. Ibid., 618–619.
23. Karst, 'Intimate Association', 629. Karst elaborated: 'The connecting links that distinguish such an association from, say, membership in the PTA may take the form of living in the same quarters, or sexual intimacy, or blood ties, or a formal relationship, or some mixtures of these, but in principle the idea of intimate association also includes close friendship, with or without any such links'. Ibid. The practical limits of some forms of intimacy may support general distinctions between 'small' and 'large' groups, but the constitutional line-drawing has proven to be exceedingly difficult. I have criticized this doctrinal innovation as insufficiently theorized and ultimately artificial insofar as many groups that courts have subsequently deemed 'non-intimate' nevertheless fulfil the same intrinsic and instrumental purposes as intimate ones. See Inazu, *Liberty's Refuge*, 136–140.
24. Karst, 'Intimate Association', 629.
25. Ibid.
26. I recall this phenomenon vividly in my own life while I was in basic training with the US Air Force. During that time, an Air Force pilot was shot down over Bosnia and Herzegovina and spent a week evading enemy forces until he was rescued. We had no idea who this guy was—we were college students marching and doing pushups in the middle of Texas. But the thick sense of 'we' forged by shared words, rituals, and a sense of belonging made us feel a part of every day of the rescue operation. And when we learned of the pilot's successful rescue, we celebrated as if it had been our own.
27. Alasdair MacIntyre, *After Virtue: A Study in Moral Theory* (South Bend, IN: University of Notre Dame Press, 1984), 222.
28. See generally Luke Sheahan, *Why Associations Matter: The Case for First Amendment Pluralism* (Lawrence: University of Kansas Press, 2020).
29. See generally Inazu, *Liberty's Refuge*, 141–149.
30. See e.g. *Chi Iota Colony of Alpha Epsilon Pi Fraternity v City Univ. of N.Y.*, 502 F.3d 136, 149 n.2 (2d Cir. 2007) (noting that the trial court had determined, for purposes of a preliminary injunction, that a fraternity was not an intimate association); *Christian Legal Soc'y v Martinez*, 561 U.S. 661 (2010) (concluding that the associational claim of a Christian student group 'merges' with its free speech claim).
31. I have argued elsewhere that these limits should be tied to an 'anti-monopolistic' principle that limits the protections of assembly when a private noncommercial group 'prospers under monopolistic or near-monopolistic conditions' to the detriment of others. Inazu, *Liberty's Refuge*, 14, 166–175.
32. See e.g. *Runyon v McCrary*, 427 U.S. 160 (1976) (prohibiting nonreligious, racially discriminatory private schools under the Civil Rights Act of 1866). Justice Stewart noted that from

the freedom of association 'it may be assumed that parents have a First Amendment right to send their children to educational institutions that promote the belief that racial segregation is desirable, and that the children have an equal right to attend such institutions. But it does not follow that the practice of excluding racial minorities from such institutions is also protected by the same principle'. Ibid. 176.

33. See e.g. *Doe v Kamehameha Schs./Bernice Pauahi Bishop Est.*, 470 F.3d 827, 829 (9th Cir. 2006) (en banc) (upholding a private school's Hawaiian-only admissions policy against a section 1981 challenge); *Boy Scouts of Am. et al. v Dale*, 530 U.S. 640 (2000) (upholding Boy Scouts' decision to revoke membership of a gay scoutmaster).
34. This intuition is also reflected in Article 20 of the UDHR, which provides that 'No one may be compelled to belong to an association'. UDHR, article 20(2).
35. MacIntyre, *After Virtue*, 222.
36. See e.g. Avigail Eisenberg and Jeff Spinner-Halev, *Minorities within Minorities: Equality, Rights and Diversity* (New York: Cambridge University Press, 2015).
37. Ibid.
38. An example is the Hutterites, which require members to pool their money upon joining the group but provide no financial support to those who choose to leave the group. See Jeff Spinner-Halev, *Surviving Diversity: Religion and Democratic Citizenship* (Baltimore: Johns Hopkins University Press, 2000).
39. Cf. Karst, 'Intimate Association', 627 ('The freedom of intimate association, like other constitutional freedoms, is presumptive rather than absolute. In particular cases, it may give way to overriding governmental interests. The freedom does not imply that the State is wholly disabled from promoting majoritarian views of morality. What the freedom does demand is a serious search for justifications by the State for any significant impairment of the values of intimate association. And, like the First Amendment, which is one of its doctrinal underpinnings, it rejects as illegitimate any asserted justification for repression of expressive conduct based on the risk that a competing moral view will come to be accepted').
40. Inazu, *Liberty's Refuge*, 1–7.
41. Rosenblum, *Membership and Morals*, 14 ('[T]he heart of liberal democracy has been to guard against the tutelary or manipulative intent of authorities, particularly political authorities, who want to mold minds, call up moral sentiments, or exact displays of virtue and enthusiasm'.).
42. John Inazu, *Confident Pluralism: Surviving and Thriving through Deep Difference* (Chicago: University of Chicago Press, 2016), 34–65.
43. Rosenblum, *Membership and Morals*, 4.
44. Ibid., 29.
45. Robert Putnam, *Bowling Alone, the Collapse and Revival of American Community* (New York: Simon & Schuster, 2000).
46. Ryan Burge, *The Nones: Where They Came from, Who They Are, and Where They Are Going* (Minneapolis, MN: Fortress Press, 2021). See also Gregory Smith, 'About Three-in-Ten Adults Are Now Religiously Unaffiliated', Pew Research Center, 14 December 2021, https://www.pewresearch.org/religion/2021/12/14/about-three-in-ten-u-s-adults-are-now-religiously-unaffiliated/.
47. Bill Bishop, *The Big Sort: Why the Clustering of Like-Minded America Is Tearing Us Apart* (New York: Houghton Mifflin Harcourt, 2009).
48. Bolane Olaniran and Indi Williams, 'Social Media Effects: Hijacking Democracy and Civility in Civic Engagement', in *Platforms, Protests, and the Challenge of Networked*

Democracy, ed. John Jones and Michael Trice (Cham: Springer Nature, 2020), 77–94. See also Adrian Shahbaz, 'The Rise of Digital Authoritarianism', *Freedom House*, 2018, https://freedomhouse.org/report/freedom-net/2018/rise-digital-authoritarianism.

49. Yuval Levin, *A Time to Build: From Family and Community to Congress and the Campus, How Recommitting to Our Institutions Can Revive the American Dream* (New York: Basic Books, 2020).
50. Robert LaRose et al., 'Reformulating the Internet Paradox: Social Cognitive Explanations of Internet Use and Depression', *Journal of Online Behavior* (2001), http://old.behavior.net/JOB/v1n2/paradox.html.
51. Robin Fretwell Wilson, 'Sex Play in Virtual Worlds', *Washington & Lee Law Review* 66, no. 3 (2009): 1152.
52. I make this point in John D. Inazu, 'Virtual Assembly', *Cornell Law Review* 98, no. 5 (2013): 1112 ('There is a more pragmatic reason for extending constitutional protections to online groups: the dynamic line between online and offline frustrates attempts to draw significant distinctions. Many of us use online connections to sustain relationships that begin offline.').
53. Ilia Siatitsa, 'Freedom of Assembly under Attack: General and Indiscriminate Surveillance and Interference with Internet Communications', *International Review of the Red Cross* 102, no. 913 (April 2020): 192.
54. Ibid., 190.
55. Ashutosh Bhagwat and John Inazu, 'Search for Safe Spaces', *Inside Higher Ed* (21 March 2017) (tracing the history of safe spaces).
56. This tension is reflected in the law's uncertainty with criminal conspiracy doctrine. See e.g. John Inazu, 'Unlawful Assembly as Social Control', *UCLA Law Review* 64, no. 1 (January 2017): 2–52. See also Steven R. Morrison, 'The System of Modern Criminal Conspiracy', *Catholic University Law Review* 63, no. 2 (2014): 379–388.
57. *Presser v Illinois*, 116 U.S. 252, 267 (1886).
58. Inazu, *Liberty's Refuge*, 39–40.
59. *First Lutheran Church v City of St. Paul*, 326 F. Supp. 3d 745, 767 (D. Minn. 2018).
60. *Ramsek v Beshear*, 468 F. Supp. 3d 904, 908 (E.D. Ky. 2020).
61. In a 1991 dissent, Justice Scalia observed that the First Amendment 'has not generally been thought to protect the right peaceably to assemble only when the purpose of the assembly is to petition the Government for a redress of grievances'. *Chisom v Romer*, 501 U.S. 380, 409 (1991).
62. *Ams. for Prosperity Found. v Bonta*, 141 S. Ct. 2373 (2021).
63. *Bonta*, Oral Arg. Tr. at 36:2–6.
64. Ibid., 39:5–7.
65. Ibid., 61:15–20.
66. *Bonta*, 141 S. Ct. at 2390 (Thomas, J., concurring).
67. UDHR, article 20(1). See also Human Rights Act of 1998, article 11 for the UK equivalent, 1, UK ST 1998 c. 42 Sch. 1(I) 1, article 11.
68. Footnote 3 to General Comment No. 37 on the ICCPR notes that '184 of the 193 State Members of the UN recognize the right to peaceful assembly in their constitutions'. UNHRCtte, General Comment No. 37, note 3.
69. ICCPR, articles 21, 22.
70. Michael Hamilton, 'The Meaning and Scope of "Assembly" in International Human Rights Law', *International and Comparative Law Quarterly* 69, no. 3 (July 2020): 524.

71. 'Although enumerated in separate articles of the UDHR (Articles 19 and 20), freedom on opinion, expression, assembly, and association (collectively, expression rights) are inextricably linked. Expression rights are both essential for good government and central to the affirmation of the dignity of every individual. They are accordingly the hallmark of a free and open society'. Global Citizenship Commission, 'Implementation of Human Rights', in *The Universal Declaration of Human Rights in the 21st Century: A Living Document in a Changing World*, ed. Gordon Brown (Cambridge: Open Book, 2016), 2:86, http://www.jstor.org/stable/j.ctt1bpmb7v14.
72. UNHRCtte, General Comment No. 37, 1; see also Office for Democratic Institutions and Human Rights of the Organization for Security and Co-operation in Europe (OSCE/ODIHR) and European Commission for Democracy through Law (Venice Commission) Guidelines on Freedom of Peaceful Assembly, 3rd ed. (2020) CDL-AD(2019)017rev: (C)(5). Strasbourg/Warsaw, 15 July ('There is a close and symbiotic link between freedom of peaceful assembly and freedom of association. Freedom of assembly is essential for the normal activities of many associations (such as trade unions), and an enabling environment for associations facilitates the exercise of freedom of peaceful assembly. Furthermore, what may begin as a mobilization or gathering of like-minded individuals might evolve into an association over time. As such, the associational value of an assembly can be just as important as its communicative or expressive purpose'.).
73. See Hamilton, 'Meaning and Scope of "Assembly"', 525.
74. Ibid., 531.
75. UNHRCtte, General Comment No. 37, 102.
76. Timothy Zick, 'Recovering the Assembly Clause', *Texas Law Review* 91 (2012): 398.
77. UNHRCtte, General Comment No. 37, 1.

Further Reading

Abu El-Haj, Tabatha. 'The Neglected Right of Assembly'. *UCLA Law Review* 56, no. 3 (2009): 543–589.

Bhagwat, Ashutosh. 'Associational Speech'. *Yale Law Journal* 120, no. 2 (2011): 978–1030.

Hamilton, Michael. 'The Meaning and Scope of "Assembly" in International Human Rights Law'. *International and Comparative Law Quarterly* 69, no. 3 (July 2020): 521–556.

Inazu, John D. *Confident Pluralism: Surviving and Thriving through Deep Difference*. Chicago: University of Chicago Press, 2018.

Inazu, John D. *Liberty's Refuge: The Forgotten Freedom of Assembly*. New Haven, CT: Yale University Press, 2012.

Zick, Timothy. *Managed Dissent: The Law of Public Protest*. New York: Cambridge University Press, 2023.

CHAPTER 7

STRATEGIC ASSEMBLIES

Trade-offs and Dilemmas for Social Movements

ANNA ZHELNINA AND JAMES M. JASPER

Introduction

Protesters always have a variety of strategies and organizational forms to choose among, depending on their resources; their supporters and allies; their targets and opponents; available cultural references; recent events; and other cognitive, physical, and political constraints. In the modern world, social movements have become a common choice (or set of choices) for those wishing to protest and change some condition, but they are not the only one, and they have not always been available as a recognizable form. According to Charles Tilly,[1] the modern social movement as we think of it today arose in Britain in the late eighteenth century to take advantage of emerging national political arenas, primarily parliament (but see Randall, in this volume). With social movements, aimed at persuading various other players, peaceful assemblies took on greater prominence. In some ways, assemblies are the defining activity of the contemporary social movement.[2]

Peaceful assemblies are by definition not violent, but they can be disruptive. Sometimes their influence comes from that disruption, or at least from the threat of disruption. Beyond that, there are assemblies that switch from peaceful to violent, often for reasons out of the control of their organizers. However, their usual intended message is, 'we are strong but well intentioned'. Because assemblies send messages to multiple players—whether corporations, elected officials, news media, police or armies, those who approve, those who disapprove—their organizers often face trade-offs in the impacts they have on these other players. The desired effect on one player may entail an undesired or unanticipated effect on another player. What plays well with one's own followers may play poorly with the authorities. Gains and losses frequently come packaged together.[3] When assembly organizers and other decision-makers recognize those underlying strategic trade-offs, they must grapple explicitly with corresponding dilemmas about whether and how to assemble.

Planning and mobilizing people for marches, rallies, occupations, and other peaceful assemblies is what most contemporary social movements spend much of their time doing, and individual activists know a great deal about how to pull them off. Assemblies have become such a familiar performance in many societies, and relatively easy to accomplish, in what are therefore called 'social-movement societies', that they can lose some of their power to impress, menace, or attract attention.[4] When social movements' 'repertory of action' is limited and unsurprising, so that other players know what to expect and how to respond, peaceful assemblies lose some of their power to promote social change.

In this chapter we look at the trade-offs and dilemmas involved with peaceful assemblies as a strategy or tactic for social movements, leading to different kinds of gains and losses, relying on strategic interaction theory.[5] Although primarily a synthetic essay, we use the case of Russia, in the months following the 2011 elections, for illustrations.

Alternative Audiences

Peaceful assemblies are intended to send messages to one or more audiences. Foremost in many cases is their own participants, who may derive pleasure from the assembly itself, a sense of their own power, and confidence that history is on their side—all important strategic assets. Marches, rallies, and occupations can make participants feel good about themselves even when their external impact is small, uncertain, or declining. Even a social movement in its final stages can generate good feelings that a subsequent movement can utilize. Drawing on Durkheim, Randall Collins[6] points to the emotional energy that crowds can generate. (He also insists that interaction rituals can fail, and deflate participants, for instance when the assembly is smaller than expected or is mistreated by the police.)

Tilly[7] believed that the central message that protesters try to convey to others is about their own character and capacity, what he called WUNC displays (for moral worth, unity, numbers, and commitment). In the modern world, moral worth usually implies non-violent activities. The other three traits suggest strength, broadcasting that this is a movement to be taken seriously. In character theory, strength and morality are the defining features of heroes, and social movements often present themselves as heroes able to protect victims from villains.[8]

Tilly did not clearly distinguish the possible audiences for WUNC displays. In his view, the most obvious audience consisted of the various arms of the state, above all the legislators who formulate laws and executives who implement them. Movements focused on demanding legal rights, access, and other collective benefits from the state include most of the major movements of the last two hundred years, especially revolving around race, class, and gender. Groups of outsiders must gain entry to the polity by proving themselves worthy. Jeff Alexander[9] lists a number of traits that groups of citizens are supposed to have to signal their worthiness: They should be active, autonomous, rational, reasonable, calm, self-controlled, realistic, and sane.

In addition to legislators and the movement itself, another inevitable audience is the 'forces of order'; the police, armies, bureaucrats, even elected representatives who look bad when there is disorder in the streets (even though disorder is sometimes in the eye of the beholder). Regardless of a movement's aims, the forces of order have their own goal, as the term implies. So repression and suppression are less likely when a movement remains peaceable. The police are not independent of other state players, especially in more authoritarian systems where they have less professional autonomy. We return to the issue of the policing of peaceful assemblies later in this chapter (see also Probert, in this volume).

Another audience consists of the targets whose practices the protesters hope to change, such as polluting industries, sexist churches, or bakers who refuse to work for same-sex couples. As we will discuss in a moment, the message for targets may be moral disapproval or it may suggest something more threatening. The state itself is the target for many movements, and sometimes the police in particular. This makes the state in its various forms both umpire and contestant.

Finally, the general public, along with the media that reach them, are often thought to be the primary audience for assemblies, not only to change their lives but also in the hope that they form supportive opinions that might then influence politicians.[10] Bystanders may literally be those along the route of a march, or more mediated, distant observers.[11] Social movements are not always trying to change opinions but to mobilize those who already support them, attracting them to assemblies or other actions. In some cases, protesters encourage members of the public to change their consumption habits, avoiding the products of offending companies. Corporate boycotts frequently succeed, although this may be less by influencing individual shoppers than by attracting institutional allies such as universities, states, and religious groups, or through companion tactics such as assemblies.[12]

Naughty or Nice?

We begin to see how assembly organizers can have different goals in mind for different audiences. A protest group may wish to highlight either its strength or its goodness at the expense of the other trait. It may hope to threaten and intimidate on the basis of its strength, putting the question of its goodness on hold. It faces the naughty-or-nice dilemma[13]: A movement's aggressive actions can coerce or frighten opponents into immediate concessions, but they typically tarnish its long-run moral reputation with authorities and the general public. It appears more powerful but less respectable. The naughty option makes more sense when the immediate gains are highly valued and difficult for other players to reverse later. Aggressive groups may work to repair their reputations later, if possible (it is usually not),[14] but they may instead bring down so much repression that they are effectively destroyed as a player. As Piven and Cloward[15] observed, poor people's movements lack the resources to do that reputation work; their only power lies in their disruptive capacities (see also Mead, in this volume).

Protesters' pre-existing attributes, such as socio-economic status, gender, or racial composition, shape public perceptions of whether their assemblies are dangerous or aggressive. Peay and Camarillo[16] found that 'the racial composition of a demonstration can elicit dramatically different responses from onlookers'. In their US survey experiment, participants more often expected all-Black protests to turn violent than more diverse demonstrations. Perceived 'naughtiness' derives from character work as well as from actual tactical choices. Ironically, protesters can sometimes ignore public perceptions if they believe those attitudes will not change no matter what they do, as with the Black Panthers who cared about their reputation in local Black communities not the wider White community. (We also expect the definition of what is considered aggressive and inappropriate behaviour to vary across cultures and nations.) Notoriously, police may act differently depending on their stereotypes about protesters.

Among other naughty tactics, protesters can turn to means other than peaceful assemblies: sabotage, arson, hostage-taking, explosions, airplane hijackings, and more. They may also deploy aggressive assemblies such as riots, although peaceful assemblies occasionally become less peaceful through interactive dynamics. But when they move away from persuasion and towards coercion, protesters can shade into different operations, becoming criminal gangs or armed rebellions instead of social movements. Even if they do not see themselves as criminals or rebels, their opponents can portray them that way based on any small deviations from non-violent assembly.

Other Trade-offs and Dilemmas

Naughty or nice is not the only strategic trade-off/dilemma that organizers of assemblies face. A related dilemma pits ends against means: Some goals can only be attained (or can more easily be attained) through unethical means. Jasper[17] dubs this the dirty hands dilemma. In the opinion of some, torture is an example—although others deny its efficacy in producing useful information, denying the dilemma altogether. In using informants or spies, agents of order dirty their hands but gain what they consider information useful to their objectives. 'Dirty hands' suggests that peaceful assemblies may have some limits because they insist on clean hands; those who desire abrupt change such as revolution may instead need to go further and get their hands dirty. Non-violence is a widely held moral value, a 'taste in tactics',[18] but it restricts the available protest actions in ways that can make a social movement less effective (see Woolman, in this volume).

Choices of tactics can also embroil organizers in the extension dilemma: The larger the group you mobilize (whether for one event or as an ongoing movement network), the stronger you appear, but the harder it becomes to control what they all do. The larger the group, the more disagreements arise over tactics and goals. Communication becomes more difficult. Schisms threaten. Large numbers can be mobilized for peaceful assemblies, in part because they are (usually) less controversial and in part because participants can implicitly harbour conflicting goals and hopes. Different factions need not even march near one another. More targeted tactics, such as legal suits or sabotage, can only be carried out by smaller, more coherent groups. The rules of an arena determine who—what kind of player—can participate.

Social movements generally try to amplify the reach of their messages through positive media coverage. This involves both extension and naughty-or-nice dilemmas. Gatherings get attention when they are huge, or at least larger than expected, but they may not have much focus in their messages because of their size. They also garner attention when they do unusual or aggressive things: photogenic giant puppets, say, or human blockades and arrests. But that attention is not always positive; in fact, they are sometimes treated as criminals. Getting media attention and getting positive attention are quite different.[19] Sobieraj[20] takes a strong position against media-obsessed strategies, for instance, seeing them as a distraction from other activities.

Peaceful assemblies vary enormously, starting with how peaceful they are and how peaceful others perceive them to be. Some groups try to convey their non-threatening intentions, by sitting or kneeling, by praying or singing hymns; others convey more menace through marching and shouting, often in areas where they are not especially welcome. Nighttime assemblies are usually more threatening than daytime assemblies, except for silent, non-marching ones such as vigils. Assemblies and other players often contest the meanings of naughty and nice.

Another variation involves the extent to which an assembly is aimed at reaching external audiences versus satisfying participants, in the 'Janus dilemma'.[21] Private assemblies have been dubbed 'free spaces', in which those hoping for social change can try out ideas and practices without fear of immediate repression.[22] Free spaces also help build bonds among insiders, reinforcing relevant and useful collective identities. But too much internal focus, while perhaps satisfying to many participants, distracts from an impact on the external world.

In a long, uneven historical process, protest has become less costly in most Western democracies. Numerous citizens know how to advertise, rent buses, arrange marshals, and negotiate with the police over parade routes, civil disobedience, and arrests. Meyer and Tarrow[23] have said that we now live in a 'social movement society', where protest has become a normal political tactic. People can also add their name to an online petition—a kind of 'virtual assembly'—without leaving their desks or couches. In these circumstances, peaceful gatherings become less of a proof of commitment; they risk so little. Movements themselves can change from an 'expression of profound discontent' into a 'conventional form of involvement' with older and better educated participants, as a study of an immigrant rights protest in Texas demonstrates.[24]

But we should not exaggerate how easy assembling has become. As we said, some stereotyped groups are expected to be disruptive, so the police treat them differently, more aggressively. And some issues are treated more forcefully, including protests against policing and international meetings such as the G8 (or G7 or G10, etc.) summits. Authoritarian regimes view even the most peaceful assemblies as a threat, so they are banned and violently suppressed.

Reactions

The planning, the decisions, and especially the impacts of peaceful assemblies depend on the reactions of other players, especially targets and opponents. Politics unfolds as an unending dance of interactions among many players. States, with their many component players, are the primary player whose reactions affect all stages of assemblies.

Our Russian example shows how, in many nations, movement organizers of peaceful assemblies risk a great deal. The largest protests can trigger the greatest repression, and often sharp reversals.[25] Moscow was among the world cities shaken by large-scale protests in 2011, in this case triggered by widely discussed electoral fraud during parliamentary elections of 4 December 2011. Between those elections and the presidential elections of 4 March 2012, rallies in Moscow attracted up to 120,000 people, a number not seen since Perestroika. The protesters denounced falsified election results and demanded new elections, aiming ultimately for the democratization of the regime.

Protests against electoral fraud emerged in cities across the country, but public and media attention centred on Moscow. Organizers invested the most effort in maximizing the size of rallies there: People from other cities travelled to Moscow to show 'numbers'. Being in Moscow also mattered because of the proximity of Moscow's rally locations to government offices and decision-makers. Spatial proximity matters not only symbolically; it also affects the demonstrations' ability to attract and influence public opinion.[26]

Surprised and scared by the protest, Russia's national government implemented a variety of techniques to prevent large crowds from gathering in symbolically important places in Moscow, with further tightening in the following years. It limited protesters' ability to demonstrate their numbers and commitment—to national media, but also to international media, who expect to see and are more likely to report on large, spectacular crowds than small and visually less impressive events. In the kind of seesaw typical of protest, the gain of extensive mobilization triggered a backlash and a loss in the form of tightened rules. This example shows a couple of different dilemmas that assembly organizers and social movements face. In maximizing the size and visibility of an assembly, one risks coming across as too threatening to opponents (in this case, the authoritarian political regime, which grew increasingly paranoid after the events of 2012). Compromises and negotiations, on the other hand, may pacify the powerful opponent, but it also may be less effective in putting pressure on that opponent. There is also a dilemma with a temporal dimension at play here: Protesters try to balance the needs of the moment (assembling a large crowd, displaying solidarity, and nurturing a sense of collective efficacy) and the long-term goals of the movement (including movement survival and minimizing possible repression from the opponent in the future).

In Moscow, the repression tended to divide the movement as intended. Moscow's protesters usually applied to the city government for proper permits to hold their rallies in specific places, choosing central, symbolic locations. In their view, this made participation safer, so that more people would join. Radicals, on the other hand, criticizing the cautious option in naughty-or-nice, insisted that people have the right to gather wherever they want and that asking for permissions concedes too much power to the illegitimate regime. These disagreements often led to confusion and to several rallies being announced in different places at the same time.

The extension dilemma often interacts with the naughty-or-nice dilemma. More broadly in strategic engagements, questions about *who* we are interact with questions about what we *do*; in this case the larger the movement the less radical it was willing to be. One radical group, Strategy 31, consisted of experienced activists, many of whom were aggressive in their selection of places for protest: They chose the most visible and symbolically important locations in Russian cities to hold their rallies on the thirty-first day of any month with thirty-one days. They called for disobedience and rallies in places that protesters chose without the city's permission. But ordinary, first-time protesters were afraid to attend 'unsanctioned' rallies, limiting potential numbers. Other movement leaders, interested in large rallies and familiar crowd pictures for the media, chose to negotiate to allow for wider participation.

In Moscow, protesters constantly debated where to protest and whether to openly disobey the authorities who tried to push them outside the symbolically important city centre to marginal—symbolically non-existent—places. Places and political meanings attached to them can increase or reduce the symbolic significance of assemblies beyond sheer numbers (see also Zick, in this volume, and Robinson and Page, in this volume). Gilbert[27] argues, for example, that 'the protest marches of Las Madres de la Plaza de Mayo in Buenos Aires from 1977 onwards worked as a challenge to the dominant meanings of place', because the plaza had been built to signify the authority of the state which the silently walking women were undermining.

The difficult choice between increasing participation and displaying power and commitment generated lengthy discussions and infighting among movement leaders who represented different political ideologies and agendas. They were only loosely connected by their shared rejection of Putin's corrupt and increasingly repressive regime, and they disagreed on how, where, and under which slogans to protest. Although the rallies they managed to assemble were impressive by Moscow standards, the constant infighting had a demoralizing effect. Other research finds that larger rallies, while attracting more media attention, also make it more difficult for activists to agree on a common message and agenda. The media are likely to report on and amplify the internal disputes and infighting, leading ordinary participants and potential supporters to feel alienated and disappointed.[28] Witnessing a protest can make the public feel empowered, but also fearful of state repression,[29] and depending on the feeling, the targets can become more (if feeling empowered) or less (if feeling threatened) supportive of the movement.

Governments may try to undermine a movement's claims to large numbers by staging their own counter-protests. In Russia, pro-government youth movements' rallies started in December 2011 and took place at the same time as the opposition rallies. The first was organized by the youth branch of United Russia, 'The Young Guard'. College students (and later, public employees) were bused from other towns to Moscow to participate. The game of calculations immediately began: The official numbers from the city police tended to under-count and downplay the opposition's protests and to inflate the numbers of pro-Kremlin demonstrations, while the opposition tried to come up with its own counts and denounced the pro-Kremlin rallies as staged and fake (uncommitted and unworthy).

Governments are not the only players targeted by social movements that have the power to fight back.[30] Corporations, for example, actively respond to criticism in order to defend their reputations, pushing back against activists' negative campaigning. They sometimes go further: International investors in countries experiencing strikes and unrest have sued those countries for lost profits.[31] Protesters can take advantage of the fact that companies compete with one another, experience internal shifts in leadership, and are sensitive to reputational gains and losses; sustained activist efforts targeting specific corporations have been shown to increase the responsiveness of these players to movement demands.[32] Protesters' largest gains often come when their targets make some kind of strategic mistake in responding.[33]

Policing Peaceful Assemblies

Those who organize and attend peaceful assemblies probably interact with the police more than with any other players. The police and other forces of order are charged with monitoring and controlling the assemblies, usually with the goal of keeping them peaceful. Many scholars have examined the policing of protest, describing a continuum (see also Probert, in this volume). At one end repressive policing treats protesters as criminals to be prevented, contained, discouraged, and hurt if necessary; terms such as 'kettling' and 'corralling' suggest that protesters are unthinking natural forces rather than humans.[34] At the other extreme, the police treat protesters as players with whom they can communicate and negotiate, as normal citizens with potentially valid grievances.[35] In much of Europe the pendulum possibly swung towards negotiated policing in the 1990s but has since swung back towards more repressive approaches. In response, the UNHR Council issued a comment that 'explicitly requires governments and their police forces to exercise a "significant degree of toleration" towards protestors, even when the protestors' actions disrupt business and economic activity'.[36]

Police face many of the same dilemmas as protesters. Foremost, as we just suggested, they can be naughty or nice to protesters: Attacking peaceful protesters can disperse them on that day, but public indignation may strengthen their numbers for the next day of gatherings. The reputations of the police or army can be damaged among those who make funding decisions. The explosion of cell-phone videos of police actions has made this dilemma acute for police everywhere, although without always shifting their calculations or actions. Videos can produce intense indignation, perhaps more than words or still images can.[37]

But the dilemma begins long before the face-to-face interactions on the day of the assembly, and continues afterwards. There are choices about what arms and equipment the police should buy: military-level vehicles and weapons, along with heavy riot gear, suggest they see protesters as lethal opponents. Training engrains habits, such as de-escalation, in officers. Planning and deployment of officers (how many, where, with what command structure) allow some types of interactions to occur but prevent others. Communication between police and assembly leaders and between police and other forces of order also affect what happens during assemblies. After the assemblies, too, police make decisions about arrests, charges, and court strategies. There are more aggressive and less aggressive steps along all these pathways.

Both police and protesters prepare strategies and plans in advance of the event, but they also make tactical decisions during the event, sometimes to implement the plans but sometimes ignoring or violating them. They must respond to each other's actions moment to moment in ways no one can entirely foresee.

By synchronizing hundreds of bits of online video, Anne Nassauer[38] reconstructed a number of peaceful marches that turned violent. Even though they are a small proportion of peaceful marches, her main finding is that neither the intentions and plans of the organizers nor those of the police determine outcomes, but rather micro-interactions between the players do. Often, things go wrong for the police, such as malfunctioning radios, overly long shifts, thirst and hunger; poor communication and control among the police leave individual officers on edge. A second factor is what Nassauer calls spatial incursions, when one side enters the public space that the other side considers to be 'its' territory. Peaceful assemblies are about the symbolic occupation of public spaces, so these boundaries are highly charged. Protesters, for instance, may wonder why a police car has been parked along 'their' route, or the police are alarmed if protesters push down barriers and enter 'their' space. The combination of police mismanagement and spatial incursions can lead to violence because police feel powerless and vulnerable rather than in control. They lash out.

There are other paths to violence, Nassauer finds. One occurs when one side begins to mistrust the intentions of the other, through poor communication and lack of information. In all cases, tension and fear replace the joy of crowds that are more typical of peaceful assemblies. People on both sides tense up, stop smiling, and glance around nervously. In these situations, a number of things can trigger the first violent blow: lines of protesters and police start to break up, a protester falls and so is vulnerable, police outnumber or surround small groups of protesters. When they feel this kind of dominance, the police can release tension by striking out.[39] They can also release tension at the end of a hard day by enforcing nighttime curfews with force.

To return to our example, Moscow's government changed its policing tactics over the course of the 2012 protests. Initially, most of the rallies were peaceful as the police did not try to 'clear' the city centre too aggressively. Later the city government began to prevent protesters from gathering in their desired locations, changing the plans previously agreed upon, increasing tensions, and provoking face-offs with the riot police.

Rising tensions climaxed in the 'riot' of 6 May 2012. On that day, police prevented the 'March of Millions' from following the agreed-upon route. Possibly with the intervention of provocateurs among the protesters, the march escalated into multiple clashes with the police, resulting in mass arrests and injuries. More than thirty people, charged with organizing and participating in public disorders, received harsh sentences in trials meant to set an example, now known as 'Bolotnoye delo' (Bolotnaya case, named after the square where the rally was supposed to have taken place). The show trials made protesters look aggressive ('naughty') in the eyes of the undecided public and scared away many potential participants.

The increased repression and new restrictions on assemblies did not deter all the protesters but made them change their tactics in response. An Occupy-style camp, '#OccupyAbai,' lasted several days along one of Moscow's central boulevards. Protesters also came up with new forms of marching that did not formally fit the 'rally' format and so did not require difficult negotiations with the city: sympathetic writers and journalists led 'Walks with the Writers' along central streets, framing them as 'excursions', which nonetheless attracted thousands of people and blocked the streets. Similar events included camps, flashmobs, and motor rallies.

In a situation when the classic and recognizable forms of public protest became costly and dangerous, protesters turned to creative alternatives not formally falling under the legal restrictions: solitary picketing, protest actions disguised as public events, 'nanomeetings' of toys with banners, and other artistic formats.[40] These small-scale and seemingly non-threatening actions, however, are less visible and attractive to the media, especially the international media, and they are more difficult to keep track of. Recent anti-war resistance in Russia, after the brutal crackdown on the attempts of rallies and marches, has again turned to these quiet and small-scale forms of protest—which are mostly ignored by the international media. Although authoritarian isolationist regimes such as the current Russian one may not care much about how the international media represent the events in their country, this representation and acknowledgement mean a lot to the protesters. Visibility and appreciation keep the mobilizing emotions going, helping the movement's resilience and survival.

Assemblies are shaped by constant interactions between organizers and other strategic players, sometimes over many years but sometimes over minutes or hours. The police are always an influential player, but others are as well.

Strategic Centrality

Around the world, peaceful assemblies are recognized as a key ingredient of human rights and social change. For that reason states are forever trying to curtail or channel the rights and practices of assembly, just as activists are forever trying to expand them (although see Srinivasan, in this volume on how states use assemblies to legitimate themselves). Even relatively liberal democratic regimes try to channel and control assemblies. These gatherings are both a satisfying end in and of themselves, a central human capacity, and a means to other ends. They are vital to communication, but even more to the public expression of a group's basic values. It is difficult to imagine social-justice movements that do not assemble from time to time, even under conditions of extreme repression.

But they are a strategic or tactical *choice*, alongside other ways to advance one's ends. More precisely, they impose a continuing *series* of choices, even during the assemblies themselves but more obviously in the prior organization they require. They also impose decisions on other strategic players, sometimes difficult decisions.[41] They are part of ongoing strategic interactions, with players of various kinds responding to each other.

A decision to do one thing is also a decision not to do others. As social media make public gatherings easier to mobilize, that very ease may undermine other protest tactics. The online attention economy transforms how movements operate and how they generate public attention[42] and centres spectacular assemblies as a tactical choice. When activists rely predominantly on networks and organizations to generate protests, they also develop connections to political parties and other powerful players, the quiet back door for negotiations at the same time as noisy public gatherings continue. The good cop alongside the bad. The gatherings put pressure on targets and authorities, while the backstage discussions allowed settlement. Social movements operate in a variety of strategic arenas, of which assemblies in the form of street gatherings are only one.

Our recurrent Russian example is an increasingly authoritarian regime, which we can see unfolding step by step partly in response to protest. Moscow in June 2012 further amended the Federal Law 'On Meetings, Rallies, Demonstrations, Marches and Pickets' to make protest harder and costlier. To curb the protest activity that had shaken the regime in 2011–2012, the amendment increased the fines for violating the rules of organizing and participating in public protests, and specified locations where public events were entirely forbidden (railways and railway stations, territories near the residencies of the president, courts, etc.). It also allowed the city administration to decide whether each particular place is suitable for a rally, giving them almost unfettered power to reject any locations suggested by activists. In 2014, additional amendments threatened serial violators of the law with added criminal charges. Even if assembly organizers manage to achieve some short-term goals (e.g. participants showing up in numbers and mobilizing popular support), these gains can backfire in the long term. Their powerful opponents, states, can change the rules of engagement that would make it legal to repress or limit assemblies. States learn these techniques from one another, observing the development of protest and reaction in other countries.[43]

Whether peaceful protests are diluted because they are too easy—a couple of keystrokes on a device, or disappear because they become too costly, one of their impacts is to give participants a taste of efficacy, of what it means to join others in demanding—if not always attaining—their moral goals. Della Porta[44] argues that protest events must be 'eventful' for the participants themselves: Protects have 'cognitive, affective and relational transformative impacts on the very movements that carry them out'. During the events, she writes, 'organizational networks develop; frames are bridged; personal links foster reciprocal trust'. This is why assemblies are both ends and means for further action.

As we said, some of the interactions between protesters and their targets or governments unfold over many years, but they still tend to follow the path of mutual responses of one player to another. This is how the structures of arenas are built up over time. Each round of interaction sets new parameters to future ones.

Conclusion

Our discussion of a few of the dilemmas that social movements face in deciding to use assembly as an action suggest a rough typology of trade-offs. Some dimensions have to do with navigating obstacles that assemblies face: Are they legal or illegal, safe or risky? Others have to do with social movements' own choices: Are their assemblies aggressive or not, rule-breaking or not? Are their assemblies as large and inclusive as possible, or are they focused on a narrow grievance or group? And are they more focused on influencing the actions, beliefs, and feelings of outsiders or of participants? Assembly organizers can navigate these trade-offs in different ways and at different times, through both internal decisions and reactions to other players.

Peaceful assemblies are usually a 'nice' strategy compared to other possible actions social movements might pursue. Social movement scholars have long debated the advantages and disadvantages of choosing 'disruptive' tactics,[45] which reflect the options of the naughty-or-nice dilemma we identified above. The aggressive option may bring quick results by intimidating opponents,[46] but if repeated, such 'naughty' actions may blemish the player's reputation and cost them public support and allies. Still, a player may choose aggressive tactics and hope that the quick gains will outweigh the long-term losses, perhaps taking advantage of the mobilizing power of short-run emotions, such as anger and outrage, which can quickly mobilize large numbers of people to pressure elites.[47] The effects of aggressive tactics depend on how other players respond: Different strategies are appropriate for different situations. When politicians or other targets are unresponsive to the movement, assertive tactics may pay off, but if they are already sympathetic, trying to threaten them with aggressive actions may alienate them.[48] Peaceful tactics tend to run fewer risks.

Most scholars of social movements live in a milieux where non-violence is considered a basic value or taste in tactics, so it is easy to forget that peaceful assemblies have costs and risks as well as potential benefits. Like all strategic decisions, they carry complex trade-offs, as we have seen. Those trade-offs and dilemmas themselves change continually due to new laws, policies, resources, and more: The Russian government tightened its grip on civil activities, in contrast to earlier protesters in many affluent countries who gradually gained protections. Losses can be reversed; gains can be eroded: the rules of the game change.

We can imagine how the Russian interaction over assemblies could have gone the other way, with gains for the rights of assembly. But we also understand why it unfolded as it did, due to many factors and strategies that president Putin used to protect and aggregate power. Contemporary authoritarians watch and learn from each other, especially in the use of new technologies. The progressive metanarrative behind theories of human rights, protest, and even history itself—in which the direction of progress is largely given—is in doubt.

If all strategic decisions carry trade-offs and dilemmas, usually with a long list of potential costs, benefits, and risks of each choice, it is typically activists themselves who are better able to assess those outcomes than scholars who observe and sometimes advise them. Scholars might attain a loftier historical perspective, it is true, finding distant cases that are similar in many ways and drawing conclusions from them. But no two cases are the same, if for no other reason than the institutional and social learning that occurs over time. What is more, strategic trade-offs are often quite detailed and subtle, so that there is no obviously correct choice in many or most cases. If a choice is obvious to activists, it will be obvious to opponents as well, whose preparation can turn a potential advance into a trap.

Acknowledgements

For excellent comments on an earlier draft, we would like to thank the editors and workshop participants, especially Sarah Liu.

Notes

1. Charles Tilly, 'Parliamentarization of Popular Contention in Great Britain, 1758-1834', *Theory and Society* 26, no. 2/3 (1997): 245–273.
2. We use social movement and protest movement interchangeably here, seeing them as networks of individual and group players who cooperate on actions such as assemblies, with shared goals and some sense of themselves as a player. Assemblies are actions, not players.
3. James Jasper et al., *Gains and Losses: How Protestors Win and Lose* (New York: Oxford University Press, 2022).
4. David Meyer and Sidney Tarrow, eds., *The Social Movement Society: Contentious Politics for a New Century* (Lanham, MD: Rowman & Littlefield, 1997); Pippa Norris et al., 'Who Demonstrates? Antistate Rebels, Conventional Participants, or Everyone?', *Comparative Politics* 37, no. 2 (2005): 189–205.
5. James Jasper and Jan Willem Duyvendak, eds., *Players and Arenas* (Amsterdam: Amsterdam University Press, 2015); Jasper et al., *Gains and Losses;* Jan Willem Duyvendak and James Jasper, eds., *Breaking down the State* (Amsterdam: Amsterdam University Press, 2015).

6. Randall Collins, *Interaction Ritual Chains* (Princeton, NJ: Princeton University Press, 2004).
7. Charles Tilly, *Contentious Performances* (Cambridge: Cambridge University Press, 2008).
8. James Jasper et al., 'Character Work in Social Movements', *Theory & Society* 47, no. 1 (2018): 113–131.
9. Jeffrey Alexander, *The Civil Sphere* (New York: Oxford University Press, 2006), 57.
10. Katherine McFarland Bruce, 'LGBT Pride as a Cultural Protest Tactic in a Southern City', *Journal of Contemporary Ethnography* 42, no. 5 (2013): 608–635.
11. Hahrie Han and Dara Z. Strolovitch, 'What the Tea Party and Occupy Wall Street Illuminate about Bystander Publics as Proto-Players', in Jasper and Duyvendak, *Players and Arenas*, 275–294.
12. James Jasper, *The Art of Moral Protest. Culture, Biography, and the Creativity in Social Movements* (Chicago: University of Chicago Press, 1997) (see chap. 11); Gay Seidman, *Beyond the Boycott: Labor Rights, Human Rights, and Transnational Activism* (New York: Russell Sage, 2007).
13. James Jasper, 'A Strategic Approach to Collective Action: Looking for Agency in Social-Movement Choices', *Mobilization: An International Quarterly* 9, no. 1 (2004): 9.
14. Matthew Feinberg et al., 'The Activist's Dilemma: Extreme Protest Actions Reduce Popular Support for Social Movements', *Journal of Personality and Social Psychology* 119 (2020): 1086–1111.
15. Frances Fox Piven and Richard A. Cloward, *Poor People's Movements: Why They Succeed, How They Fail* (New York: Vintage, 1977).
16. Periloux C. Peay and Tyler Camarillo, 'No Justice! Black Protests? No Peace: The Racial Nature of Threat Evaluations of Nonviolent #BlackLivesMatter Protests', *Social Science Quarterly* 102, no. 1 (2021): 198.
17. James Jasper, *Getting Your Way* (Chicago: University of Chicago Press, 2006), 70.
18. Jasper, *Art of Moral Protest.*
19. Edwin Amenta and Neal Caren, *Rough Draft of History: A Century of US Social Movements in the News* (Princeton, NJ: Princeton University Press, 2022).
20. Sarah Sobieraj, *Soundbitten: The Perils of Media-Centered Political Activism* (New York: New York University Press, 2011).
21. Jasper, *Getting Your Way*, 125.
22. Sara M. Evans and Harry C. Boyte, *Free Spaces: The Sources of Democratic Change in America* (New York: Harper and Row, 1986); Francesca Polletta, '"Free Spaces" in Collective Action', *Theory and Society* 28, no. 1 (1999): 1–38.
23. Meyer and Tarrow, *Social Movement Society*.
24. James A. McCann et al., 'The Changing Contours of the Immigrant Rights Protest Movement in the United States: Who Demonstrates Now?', *The Forum* 14, no. 2 (2016): 169–190.
25. James Jasper and Jane Poulsen, 'Fighting Back: Vulnerabilities, Blunders, and Countermobilization by the Targets in Three Animal Rights Campaigns', *Sociological Forum* 8 (1993): 639–657.
26. Kenneth T. Andrews et al., 'The Legitimacy of Protest: Explaining White Southerners' Attitudes toward the Civil Rights Movement', *Social Forces* 94, no. 3 (2016): 1021.
27. David Gilbert, 'The Geographies of Protest Marches', in *The Street as Stage: Protest Marches and Public Rallies since the Nineteenth Century*, ed. M. Reiss (New York: Oxford University Press, 2007), 47.

28. Sophia J. Wallace et al., 'Spatial and Temporal Proximity: Examining the Effects of Protests on Political Attitudes', *American Journal of Political Science* 58, no. 2 (2014): 436.
29. Hema Preya Selvanathan and Brian Lickel, 'Empowerment and Threat in Response to Mass Protest Shape Public Support for a Social Movement and Social Change: A Panel Study in the Context of the Bersih Movement in Malaysia', *European Journal of Social Psychology* 49, no. 2 (2019): 230–243.
30. Jasper and Poulsen, 'Fighting Back'.
31. Laura Edwards, 'Marching for Justice: Conflicting Perspectives of Peaceful Assemblies in International Investment Law and International Human Rights Law Social Movements around the World', *Yale Journal of International Affairs* 16 (2021): 58–73.
32. Brayden G. King, 'A Political Mediation Model of Corporate Response to Social Movement Activism', *Administrative Science Quarterly* 53, no. 3 (2008): 395–421; Mary-Hunter McDonnell et al., 'A Dynamic Process Model of Private Politics: Activist Targeting and Corporate Receptivity to Social Challenges', *American Sociological Review* 80, no. 3 (2015): 654–678; Sarah A. Soule, 'Targeting Organizations: Private and Contentious Politics', in *Rethinking Power in Organizations, Institutions, and Markets*, ed. D. Courpasson, D. Golsorkhi, and J. J. Sallaz (London: Emerald Group, 2012), 261–285.
33. Jasper and Poulsen, 'Fighting Back'.
34. Alex S. Vitale, *The End of Policing* (New York: Verso Books, 2017).
35. Donatella della Porta and Herbert Reiter, *Policing Protest: The Control of Mass Demonstrations in Western Democracies* (Minneapolis: University of Minnesota Press, 1998).
36. Edwards, 'Marching for Justice', 3.
37. Kristen L. Miller and James Jasper, 'Indignation: Immoral Shocks, Moral Actions', in *Emotions in Culture and Everyday Life*, ed. Michael Hviid Jacobsen (London: Routledge, 2023), 183–198.
38. Anne Nassauer, *Situational Breakdowns: Understanding Protest Violence and Other Surprising Outcomes* (New York: Oxford University Press, 2019).
39. Randall Collins, *Violence: A Micro-Sociological Theory* (Princeton, NJ: Princeton University Press, 2008).
40. Christian Fröhlich and Kerstin Jacobsson, 'Performing Resistance: Liminality, Infrapolitics, and Spatial Contestation in Contemporary Russia', *Antipode* 51, no. 4 (2019): 1146–1165.
41. Majken Jul Sørensen and Brian Martin, 'The Dilemma Action: Analysis of an Activist Technique', *Peace & Change* 39, no. 1 (2014): 73–100.
42. Zeynep Tufekci, '"Not This One": Social Movements, the Attention Economy, and Microcelebrity Networked Activism', *American Behavioral Scientist* 57, no. 7 (2013): 848–870; Thomas Poell and José van Dijck, 'Social Media and New Protest Movements', in *The SAGE Handbook of Social Media*, ed. Jean Burgess, Alice Marwick, and Thomas Poell (London: Sage, 2018), 546–561.
43. Stephen G. F. Hall and Thomas Ambrosio, 'Authoritarian Learning: A Conceptual Overview', *East European Politics* 33, no. 2 (2017): 143–161.
44. Donatella della Porta, 'Eventful Protest, Global Conflicts', *Distinktion: Journal of Social Theory* 9, no. 2 (2008): 30.
45. William A. Gamson, *The Strategy of Social Protest* (Homewood, IL: Dorrsey, 1975); Piven and Cloward, *Poor People's Movements.*
46. Piven and Cloward, *Poor People's Movements.*
47. Jasper et al., *Gains and Losses.*

48. Edwin Amenta, *When Movements Matter: The Townsend Plan and the Rise of Social Security* (Princeton, NJ: Princeton University Press, 2006); Fabio Rojas, 'Social Movement Tactics, Organizational Change and the Spread of African-American Studies', *Social Forces* 84, no. 4 (2006): 2147–2166.

Further Reading

Collins, Randall. *Violence: A Micro-Sociological Theory*. Princeton, NJ: Princeton University Press, 2008.
Della Porta, Donatella, and Herbert Reiter. *Policing Protest: The Control of Mass Demonstrations in Western Democracies*. Minneapolis: University of Minnesota Press, 1998.
Evans, Sara M., and Harry C. Boyte. *Free Spaces: The Sources of Democratic Change in America*. New York: Harper and Row, 1986.
Jasper, James M. *Getting Your Way*. Chicago: University of Chicago Press, 2006.
Jasper, James M., and Jan Willem Duyvendak, eds., *Players and Arenas*. Amsterdam: Amsterdam University Press, 2015.
Jasper, James M., Luke Elliott-Negri, Isaac Jabola-Carolus, Marc Kagan, Jessica Mahlbacher, Manès Weisskircher, and Anna Zhelnina. *Gains and Losses: How Protestors Win and Lose*. New York: Oxford University Press, 2022.
Meyer, David S., and Sidney Tarrow, eds., *The Social Movement Society: Contentious Politics for a New Century*. Lanham, MD: Rowman & Littlefield, 1997.
Nassauer, Anne. *Situational Breakdowns: Understanding Protest Violence and Other Surprising Outcomes*. New York: Oxford University Press, 2019.
Tilly, Charles. *Contentious Performances*. Cambridge: Cambridge University Press, 2008.

CHAPTER 8

BEYOND REGIME TYPES

Assemblies, Repression, and Political Impacts

YAO LI

Introduction

PEACEFUL assemblies include a wide range of activities, such as sit-ins, strikes, rallies, and peaceful protests, both offline and online. Discussion of these activities has been extensive in scholarship on collective action, social movements, and civil resistance. Thus far, most research on assemblies in democracies—especially, Western democracies—centres on 'tame' forms of contention and reform movements,[1] whereas scholarship on assemblies in non-democratic settings largely focuses on 'radical' contention and revolutionary movements.[2] That said, the distinction of contentious politics between democratic and authoritarian regimes has become blurred in the past few decades. Disruption, unpredictability, and sometimes violence have appeared in a great many events of assemblies in Western democracies. Meanwhile, self-limiting and moderate forms of protests can be prevalent in authoritarian contexts. This chapter critically surveys the growing scholarship on diverse forms of assembly and state responses and interrogates the following questions: How do assemblies differ or parallel between democratic and authoritarian regimes? How do state repressive reactions to assemblies vary within and across regimes? Do the political implications of assemblies on regimes differ by type? How should we understand assemblies and repression across borders?

As this chapter highlights, assemblies in democracies and non-democracies share similarities in the forms of state repression they encounter. Covert, subtle forms of repression are extensively applied in many liberal democracies; such forms of repression are employed in non-democratic regimes as well. Moreover, in both types of regimes, state coercion can be selective. Assemblies by racial and ethnic minorities and other marginalized populations tend to suffer more forceful responses in a country, no matter the regime type. That said, the scope and level of repression differ across regimes: Authoritarian regimes have a worse record and practice in violating the rights of assembly.

Regarding the political implications of assembly, not all movements and assemblies that grow within democratic regimes are beneficial to democracy; by the same token, protests in non-democracies do not necessarily all bode ill for authoritarian regime stability. Put differently, the political effects of protests on regimes can be diverse in both types of regimes, depending on the kinds of contention, the state's response, and their interaction.

What's more, transnational activism—varying across different political spectrums—is on the rise. Increasingly, transnational movements are met with repression and countermovement at the international level. Not only can state control transcend national boundaries and target diaspora communities, but individual states can collaborate with other states—as when democracies ally with non-democracies—to exert control abroad.

Given these trends, this chapter contends that the dichotomous understanding of assembly and state reactions across regime types—democracy versus non-democracy—has become increasingly untenable. While regime types may still matter, they work in more subtle ways than much of the existing literature suggests. A more nuanced understanding requires moving beyond regime types to scrutinize not only differences but also commonalities between how regime types respond to assembly, including disparities in the deployment of repression against certain social groups within a state. It also demands more attention to activism and repression across borders.

Types of Assemblies across Regimes: A Dichotomy?

An established position in social movement scholarship is that protest in Western democracies has changed from more risky and contentious forms in the 1960s to more predictable and tamer forms in the 1990s and beyond, when assemblies only rarely broke laws or violated normative boundaries. According to this perspective, social movements and assemblies have become more common and routinized, with disorder becoming rarer in protest events.[3] While violent confrontations between protesters and law enforcement at times break out, protest has become a routine way of political bargaining. Hence, a concept of 'movement society'[4] has been coined to describe the normalization and institutionalization of protest in these countries.[5]

While research on assemblies in democracies—especially, Western democracies—largely examines reform movements,[6] most scholarship on assemblies in non-democratic settings centres on unarmed revolutions and/or fights for maximalist objectives, such as regime change or secession.[7] Since the late 1970s, the overthrow of regimes in the face of mass assemblies and uprisings have proliferated in authoritarian or hybrid regimes, as seen in Iran and Ukraine.[8] While these movements may not ultimately lead to democratization, they share similarities in their most pressing objective: regime change.

In this way, scholarship has tended to characterize assemblies in democratic and authoritarian regimes in a dichotomous manner. As scholars argue, most of contention in democratic countries is *contained* by formal institutions (such as the legal system) which channel conflict, whereas nondemocracies lack institutions for peacefully tolerating open resistance and therefore contention largely takes clandestine or *transgressive* forms (such as clandestine resistance and armed struggles).[9]

Nevertheless, the neat dichotomy of contention in democracies and non-democracies has become less tenable with the increase in disruptive and violent protests in Western democracies and with the rise of self-censored protests in non-democracies. In the democratic setting, for example, from the 1999 Seattle World Trade Organization (WTO) protest to the 2007 German G8 summit to the 2010 Toronto G20 summit, a ritualization of physical confrontations between protesters and police started to become a routine feature of policing protests against neoliberal globalization in North America and Europe.[10] Clashes between protesters and law enforcement also featured in other assemblies across a wide range of causes, including the anti-austerity movement in Greece in 2010, the French Yellow Vest movement in 2018, the Catalan independence movement in Spain in 2019, and anti-lockdown protests in the UK in 2021.

Advanced democracies have also witnessed a rise in extreme right-wing movements and their use of violence (especially towards minority populations) in recent decades.[11] In the United States, for example, far right, White supremacist and right-wing militia groups frequently resort to extreme strategies to make their claims. In the two years after the January 6 Capitol attack of 2021, it was estimated that at least 610 armed demonstrations—overwhelmingly held by right-wing actors—took place around the United States, and such demonstrations were six and a half times more likely to turn violent or destructive than unarmed ones.[12]

On the other hand, self-disciplined and more moderate forms of contention are growing in authoritarian regimes in the post-Cold War era. Under some circumstances, an authoritarian state can abound with 'regime-engaging' protests, in which disgruntled citizens recognize regime legitimacy and endeavour to engage the state in negotiation, with the purpose of gaining state intervention, support, or concessions.[13] In China, for example, many protests are 'boundary-spanning' (neither clearly transgressive nor clearly contained), mingling lawful tactics with disruptive but not quite unlawful actions[14] or linking legal challenges to injustice with extra-legal forms of civil disobedience and collective protest.[15] Yet, while pushing the envelope, Chinese protesters are conscious of the 'red lines' drawn by the authoritarian government and often practice self-censorship, refraining from violence or questioning the one-party state authority. Likewise, before the Arab Spring, mobilization in Egypt largely took 'regime-loyal' and 'tolerated' forms, not seeking to overthrow the regime.[16] Self-limiting protests that avoid direct confrontation with incumbents are also seen in other countries, such as Jordan, Morocco, and Singapore.[17]

In the dynamic interactions between authorities and protesters, such moderate forms of contention may move over time towards a more transgressive direction. In fact, contentious politics is usually part of an ongoing process of 'tactical interaction', in which collective action involves an evolving interplay between the disgruntled and authorities, produces a chess-like sequence of interactions between the two (see also Zhelnina and Jasper, in this volume).[18] On the one hand, specific modes of state response shape and influence particular patterns of contention. For example, to avoid harsh crackdown by the Chinese government on *organized* collective contention, some activists have adopted innovative tactics such as 'disguised collective action' in which organizations coach aggrieved citizens to make individual rights claims instead of engaging in risky collective protests.[19] Facing variegated forms of repression, Jordanian activists have resorted to tactical adaptations by transforming softer repression into opportunities for communication with authorities and by publicizing harder forms repression through protests and their alliance networks.[20] On the other hand, recent years have also seen governments stifle contention by infiltrating movements to provoke violence, vilifying resisters as rioters, amongst other means. Such state reactions further affect the direction and form of contention.

State Repression within and across Regime Types

In terms of state coercion of assembly, the spotlight has long been on authoritarian regimes. However, democracies also employ a variety of tactics to stifle dissent. In particular, sophisticated and less visible forms of repression are extensively applied and even normalized in a liberal democracy. Equally, like democracies, non-democratic regimes have also increased the use of covert, subtler means of coercion. Notably, across regime types, not all groups are equal in the face of state repression. Assemblies by racial and ethnic minorities and other marginalized populations tend to be targeted in democratic and authoritarian regimes alike. The parallels of repression across regime types therefore cautions against overstating the regime-type bifurcation.

The forms of state repression—no matter regime type—are diverse. Some of them are covert (e.g. wiretapping) whereas others are overt (e.g. arrests); some are deployed directly by the state, whereas others are by third parties; some are harsh (such as shootings), whereas others are 'softer' (such as erecting barricades). Sometimes, punishments are done through legal procedure by criminalizing attendees or organizers of assemblies, whereas at other times states resort to extra-legal means such as extrajudicial detention. States also invoke national security measures or other frames to stigmatize and delegitimize protesters. Furthermore, authorities increasingly take advantage of new technologies to monitor dissidents and hinder mobilization. Pre-emptive measures to control contention or to restrict citizens' rights to assemblies are another important part of the repression repertoire. In brief, when challenges to the status quo take place, authorities—no matter the regime type—generally employ some form of repressive action to counter or eliminate the behavioural threat, a trend captured by Christian Davenport's 'Law of Coercive Responsiveness'.[21]

State Repression of Assembly in Democracies

The policing of protests in Western democracies before the 1970s was characterized as the 'escalated force' model, in which police often over-enforced the law, exhibited little tolerance of community disruption caused by assemblies, and employed force to clamp down on protests.[22] Yet, between the 1970s and 1990s, the style of protest policing in these societies altered to a different approach labelled 'negotiated management', in which police showed more tolerance of minor community disruptions, gave attention to the protection of the rights of protesters, and stressed negotiation and communication with movement organizers to minimize the potential for disorder and violence.[23]

Indeed, in today's democratic world, deadly crackdowns on protests—like the 1970 shootings of anti-war protesters at Kent State University in the United States—have become rare. However, scholarship contends that a third policing strategy termed 'strategic incapacitation'—which includes the employment of surveillance, pre-emptive arrests, and less-lethal weapons to selectively disrupt or incapacitate protesters and emphasizes the extensive control of space to isolate and contain disruptive protesters actual or *potential*—has been developed since the late 1990s.[24] In contrast to negotiated management, under this new style of policing, force—arrests and the employment of weapons—is no longer used as a last resort and police have become less tolerant of community disruption, placing a lower priority on the protection of citizen rights. Moreover, police are employing increasingly militarized responses to dissenters who refuse to or are *expected* not to cooperate.[25] For instance, in Germany, police ritualized the use of massive intervention against anti-nuclear protesters.[26] Harsh responses also occurred in the policing of 1999 Seattle WTO mass demonstration, in which police used tear gas, pepper spray, and rubber bullets to attack anyone who got in the way. In the 2011 Occupy Wall Street movement, abusive and unlawful policing practices—such as violent late-night raids on peaceful encampments and unjustified closure of public space—were found to be 'alarmingly evident'.[27] More recently, in the case of the French Yellow Vest Movement, law enforcement repeatedly used controversial weapons like LBDs (rubber-bullet launchers) against largely peaceful protesters, which caused hundreds of injuries such as eye and limb losses and cranial damages.[28] Mass arrests are also part of aggressive policing repertoires in democracies.

Democratization does not necessarily lead to more toleration of assemblies. In some post-communist Eastern European countries, anti-regime protests before 1989 were conceived as a legitimate means of political expression; yet, once the old, non-democratic regimes had been toppled, assemblies started to be seen as illegitimate and were increasingly delegitimized by the liberal elite and mainstream media as a counter-productive activity that has no place in a democratic polity.[29] In Hungary, for example, merely half a year after the first elections in 1990, the democratically elected government responded violently to taxi blockades caused by increased fuel prices.[30]

In addition to heavy-handed coercion, subtler means of repression are employed by democratic states to infringe on rights to assembly. Such means include but are not limited to pre-protest disruptions, surveillance, infiltration, stigmatization, intimidation, unusual punishment to arrested dissidents, bribing protest leaders, legal repression, and outsourcing violence. As an example, US authorities have announced bans on protest in certain areas before scheduled demonstrations taking place.[31] After the September 11, 2001 attacks in the United States, many Western States also increased the use of preventive detention, technological surveillance of protest, and informants and infiltrators to gather intelligence on political activists and protest movements.[32] Particularly, the deployment of covert surveillance has become extensive and normalized both in policing thought and operational practice.[33] Meanwhile, authorities often accuse protesters of 'incivility' or even frame dissidents as 'terrorists' to justify coercion.[34] To intimidate participants, groups of police in militarized costumes and posture have been found to patrol neighbourhoods in which activists are meeting and organizing.[35]

Furthermore, arrested protesters may be held in unusual or illegal conditions (even deprived of legal rights to counsel) and subject to cruel punishment (such as excessively tight handcuffs, beatings in custody, and sexual abuse).[36] Authorities have even offered bribes to leaders of social movement organizations to bring the organization's aspirations and activities to levels acceptable to authorities.[37] Regarding legal repression, on the heels of the 2020 George Floyd protests, the majority of US states passed new bills criticized for violating rights of lawful assembly as they would increase penalties for protesters while granting some immunity to drivers who hit protesters.[38] Government officials in democratic states, such as India, may also outsource violence to third parties (e.g. thugs) to stifle popular resistance.[39]

Finally, authorities often treat assemblies by different social and political groups differently in democratic societies. Here, race and ethnicity matter. Scholars have found that ethnic or racial majority movements are significantly less likely to face repression than ethnic minority movements, whereas minorities are much more likely to be viewed as radical and extremist.[40] In the United States, Black Lives Matter protests, albeit overwhelmingly peaceful,[41] were met by tear gas, police in riot gear, and mass arrests throughout the summer of 2020, whereas White supremacist events are routinely underpoliced, as seen in the 'Unite the Right' rally in 2017 and the January 6 insurrection at the US Capitol by supporters of President Trump in 2021.[42] The seemingly cosy relationship between law enforcement and leaders of right-wing assemblies is consistent with the police's long history of toleration of, and sometimes alliance with, right-wing positions, including those that validate White supremacy and open expressions of racism. Hence, as P. A. J. Waddington argues, 'confrontational or nonconfrontational policing is a reflection of the politics of inclusion and exclusion'.[43]

Similarly, protests by social groups such as foreigners, immigrants, young people, and extreme leftists have been found to be more likely to encounter repressive policing in

Western democracies.[44] When handling protest, police officers pass an implicit judgement on the demonstrators' legitimacy according to the perceived characteristics of protesters and their organization, thereby discriminating 'good' protesters (e.g. working people who have lost their jobs through no fault of their own) against 'bad' ones (e.g. young protesters who are believed to be ill informed and easily manipulated by others). Relatedly, ideology and politics affect policing. When protest control is tied to 'national security' (such as fighting terrorism) or when a dissent group (such as communists) is defined as 'the enemy', the assembly tends to receive severe treatment. Examples include the mass arrests (more than 1,800 arrests) during the 2004 Republican National Convention (RNC) protest where policing was coupled with an anti-terror agenda[45] and the overtly repressive tactics against communists in Florence, Italy.[46] Generally speaking, constituencies that have a sizable potential base of public support tend to be treated with more leniency than are groups without comparable support, since public attitude is a major concern in policing civil disobedience.

In short, democracies can use a combination of overt and covert, harsh and softer means to impose control on dissidents and assembly participants. Transitioning to democracy does not automatically guarantee increased tolerance towards protests. The ritualization of using certain repressive strategies and disparities in policing of protests by different social groups calls into question the style of 'negotiated management'.

State Repression of Assembly in Authoritarian (or Hybrid) Regimes

Authoritarian regimes may resort to extreme forms of repression such as mass killings against assembly participants. The bloody clampdown on the 1989 Tiananmen movement in China, along with the subsequent repression of its historical memory, is noteworthy. In 2022, in Kazakhstan, President Tokayev authorized a shoot-to-kill order for police and the military in the face of nationwide demonstrations, causing massive casualties.[47] In Iran, protests sparked by the death of Mahsa Amini in 2022 led to the killing of 517 protesters during unrest as of early 2023.[48] Indeed, authoritarian regimes often employ all the coercive measures at their disposal, including going beyond the law to stifle resistance:[49] They make unlawful arrests, hold dissidents in extra-judicial detention, and deploy non-state agents (or thugs) to impose protest control.[50] The recent massive internment of Uyghurs and other Muslims in Xinjiang, China, in extra-legal 'political education centres' follows rising Uyghur unrest in the region.[51]

Nonetheless, harsh, open repression is also costly and risky for rulers,[52] as domestic dissidents can be radicalized and governments can be subject to international sanctions. The brutal crackdowns in South Africa, particularly, the suppression of the 1976 Soweto uprising, inspired a growing number of multilateral and bilateral sanctions that isolated the country's apartheid regime.[53] Learning from history and from one another, authoritarian states have become more circumspect in using overt, naked forms of force against peaceful protesters and civil society groups.[54] Some authoritarian countries have even granted limited space for public expression of discontent and political participation,[55] while adding subtler, less visible forms of coercive measures to their repertoire. Many of these measures are not too different from those taken up in democracies.

Since the end of the Cold War, incumbents in non-democracies have increased their toolkit of repression. These subtle means of repression include pre-emptive arrests, harassment, intimidation, stigmatization, surveillance, and legal criminalization.[56] Another politically savvy approach to repression is to infiltrate assemblies and divide them from within.[57] In the internet era, states also take advantage of digital technologies to rally their own supporters, divide the public, and spread misinformation and propaganda.[58] Additionally, the state can sponsor countermovements in their own territories or beyond to thwart public assemblies.[59] For instance, the youth movement Nash was organized by the Russian authorities to thwart the Orange Revolution in Ukraine.[60] Furthermore, authorities may deny employment, scholarships, or university entrance to assembly activists.[61] Officials can also put pressure on protesters' relatives, advisors, and so on, to neutralize mobilization.[62]

Both high-profile, forceful repression and less visible, more sophisticated coercion are important components of an authoritarian regime's repertoire to contain and stifle assemblies. Whereas the former is often a response to an imminent and threatening challenge, the latter is frequently aimed at preventing such challenges from emerging in the first place.[63] In this regard, state coercive *capacity* is a critical factor that influences state selection of the various forms of repression. When a state replaces its internally fragmented and socially exclusive security force with a unitary coercive apparatus with broadly embedded, socially inclusive intelligence networks, it enhances its capacity for domestic surveillance and pre-emption—thereby enabling the state to target challengers and protesters selectively and to decrease state violence.[64] On the other hand, regimes that rely heavily on the military to maintain their grip on power risk being overthrown by the same security forces that may grow to be too powerful.[65]

Authoritarian states, no less than democracies, are often selective in repression across social groups. As Charles Tilly argues, the repressiveness of a government, no matter its regime type, is always *selective* by types of collective action and actors.[66] Regimes may tolerate activities taken by some groups that they forbid by others. In Park Chung Hee's dictatorship in 1970s South Korea, the state treated protests by secular students more harshly than those by other group members.[67] By contrast, Indonesian student protesters were often tolerated in the 1980s, while the country's military force was slaughtering members of East Timorese and Acehnese resistance movements.[68] Likewise, while authoritarian Muslim countries like Morocco treated protest activities by committed Islamists in a harsh manner, they granted students and secular human rights activists some space to demonstrate during the 2000s.[69] In Turkey, the government provides citizens of the Kurdish or Armenian minorities much less civil space than those of Turkish ethnicity.[70] In China, protests by Uyghurs or Tibetans—no matter their claims—are often treated as seeking independence or autonomy by authorities, rendering activism that would be normal in Han areas off limits for the two ethnic minorities.[71] In brief, ethnic minorities with tense relations with authoritarian regimes are often treated more harshly. Selective repression may also result from a conscious divide-and-rule strategy to prevent the linking-up of different social groups and creating discord amongst protest groups.

Although coercion is used to handle assemblies in both democratic and authoritarian contexts, the scope and intensity of repression differ across regime type.[72] In other words, the permitted space for assembly is substantially conditioned by regime type: Some tactics are extraordinarily difficult in some contexts but not others. In more democratic contexts, activists can focus their concerns on recruitment, publicity, and assembly outcomes, whereas for activists in authoritarian regimes repression is hanging like a Sword of Damocles.

Efforts and measures to counter power abuse in protest control also differ across regime type. In liberal democracies such as the United States, proactive political litigation is usually employed as a method to challenge constitutional violations and police misconduct, whereas such counter measures are rare in non-democracies. Given a weak rule of law in authoritarian regimes, the abuse of power in state repression is more common and authorities can adopt a wider range of unlawful repression, from extra-legal detention facilities to hiring thugs to do the 'dirty work'. Still, as demonstrated in this section, the repertoire of state management of contention shows a growing convergence amongst regimes. In particular, today's autocrats have increased the use of subtler repression when handling assemblies and unrest, while those in power in democratic states have increasingly returned to more blatant forms of repression.

The Diverse Political Impacts of Assemblies on Regimes

Popular protests are frequently associated with the downfall of authoritarian regimes. Research on democratic transitions has, in particular, highlighted the vital role of public assembly in destabilizing authoritarian states and promoting democratization. Yet, as discussed below, growing unrest in non-democracies does not necessarily impact regime stability in a negative manner. On the other hand, movements and assembly that grow within democratic regimes are not invariably constructive to democracy.

Strengthening Regimes

When social movements and assemblies are treated as an essential element of normal politics in Western democracies,[73] they may contribute to regime resilience (see also Srinivasan, in this volume). As scholars argue, when liberal democratic states can incorporate social movements and their organizations within the existing institutional arrangements, this can improve the flexibility and adaptability of regime responses to the complexity of society, reducing the chance of riots and public disturbances.[74]

A weak version of the contention-absorbing effect can take place in non-democratic regimes. Authoritarian regimes such as China's do not have the kind of robust institutions that exist in liberal democracies for handling contention, but some *informal* norms (or unwritten rules) may work in this capacity by providing an extra-legal space for certain types of assemblies, serving as a social safety valve, helping channel street protests to the negotiation table, and stimulating self-censorship amongst the aggrieved, which promotes conflict resolution through dialogue and thus helps shore up regime stability.[75] Thus, rising protests in the country does not automatically signal regime decline.

Weakening Regimes

While public assemblies thrive in democratic societies, their existence alone does not guarantee the consolidation or advancement of democracy. Some kinds of assemblies are indeed vital for the reinvigoration and innovation of democracy, with examples including the civil rights movement and the women's movement. Nonetheless, not all movements that grow within democratic regimes turn out to be democratic, which is what Sidney Tarrow calls the 'dilemma of democratic recession'.[76] A prime example here is the 'stop-the-steal' movement in the United States in the wake of the 2020 election of President Joe Biden. The movement, rejecting the election result and taking aim at the electoral system, was a direct attack on US democracy. While the mobilization failed to achieve its immediate goal—reinstating President Donald Trump—it led to a substantial decline in trust of the US electoral system, especially amongst Republican voters, threatening future democratic elections.[77]

In non-democracies, anti-regime assemblies can pose a challenge to regime stability, sometimes contributing to regime change. Quantitative evidence shows that non-violent anti-regime campaigns were more successful than violent campaigns in causing political change.[78] Explanations on the effectiveness of civil resistance include its mobilization advantage over violent insurgencies and its role in promoting defection by government supporters (such as security forces). Nevertheless, scholars have cautioned against idealizing civil resistance or over-emphasizing its effectiveness.[79]

Assemblies and Repression beyond Borders

Amidst growing global interconnectedness, activism has transcended national boundaries, as exemplified in transnational assemblies and coalitions against wars, neoliberalism, human rights abuses, and climate change. In 2003, six to ten million people from sixty countries held assemblies against the imminent invasion of Iraq by the United States and its allies, making the events 'a major new threshold in the transnational coordination of contentious politics'.[80] Since 2005, the Global Climate Justice movement has organized Global Day of Action for Climate Justice, establishing itself as one of the most extensive contemporary transnational movements.[81] Moreover, by naming and shaming abusers, transnational advocacy networks have brought international attention and pressure to bear on behalf of the aggrieved.[82] For instance, diaspora communities have mobilized against their home countries, exposing atrocities that these regimes seek to hide and placing pressure on third parties—such as host-country governments, the media, and international organizations—to intervene.[83]

Transnational activism and mobilization have been critically linked to the availability and use of information and communication technologies (ICTs) such as the internet. Social media mobilization has considerably shaped the development of assemblies and movement coalitions since the late 1990s[84] (see also McPherson, in this volume).

While most studies focus on transnational activism on the left, right-wing transnational activism is growing with globalization. Gaining support from powerful states and international institutions, right-wing transnational networks have waged countermovements against progressive activism and sometimes succeed in producing backlash against existing norms and state policy.[85]

To counter transnational activism, states and the international organizations have gradually limited the access of non-governmental organizations to some policy arenas relevant to international negotiations; even the UN has become more closed to participation from civil society actors and social movements.[86] Both repressive measures and subtler tactics such as 'legitimation' and 'co-optation' have been deployed by elites to impose control and curb opposition abroad.[87] Hence, repression often extends beyond national borders. Transgressional repression, or attempts by autocrats to punish, deter, undermine, and silence activism in the diaspora, can make home-country activism a high-risk endeavour for diaspora members.[88] Through violence, exile, threats, and surveillance, and by harming dissidents' relatives at home, transgressional repression impacts diaspora members' activism, even after they settle in democratic countries.

Conclusion

Through examining assemblies and state coercive reactions across political contexts and regime types, this chapter illustrates how the patterns and repertories of both contention and repression are diverse and complex. It shows how their dynamic interactions can lead to varied implications on regime resilience. Critical changes in the post-Cold War era have illuminated that the distinctions of assemblies, state reactions, and the political impact of assemblies are becoming increasingly blurred across different types of regimes. Notably, the convergence in state repression across regime types as well as transnational protests challenge statist thinking on contentious politics. New scholarship needs to think beyond regime types.

First, additional research is needed to quantitatively document the level and scale of protests involved with disruption and violence in democracies as well as to identify factors, mechanisms, and dynamics leading to the breach of the 'movement society' thesis. For example, scholars have explained the movement society thesis by the role of *formal* institutions in channelling contention.[89] Why are protests becoming less contained? What has happened to those institutions? In addition to the formal institutions, what else matters in explaining these changes? For instance, in China, unwritten rules or informal norms play a role in promoting conflict resolution through dialogue and containing contention.[90] Would *informal* norms provide an alternative useful perspective to understand contentious politics in Western democracies as well? That is, might the erosion of informal norms governing the interactions between protesters and authorities be an explanation for the growing disruption and unpredictability in assemblies in the West?

Relatedly, more research should be undertaken to scrutinize commonalties in state reactions to assemblies and protests between democracies and non-democracies. As this chapter shows, both regime types rely on a wide array of methods—including covert and indirect means—to manage and neutralize dissent and contention. Repression in both regime types is also selective, as certain social groups become easier targets or suffer harsher treatment. Thus, relying on regime type to categorize state reactions to resistance is insufficient. Future research should explore to what extent different regimes converge on coercive reactions and why.

Finally, the surging transnational assemblies and their repression further push us to think beyond national boundaries. More research is necessary to survey and scrutinize the pattern, mechanism, dynamics, and impact of activism and repression at the global level. In particular, more attention should be devoted to right-wing transnational movements, examining how their relationship with those in power differ from left-wing transborder movements and investigating the political, social, and economic implications of right-wing activism. Additionally, scholars still need to learn more about extra-territorial authoritarian practices of repression. Such practices are not only conducted by authoritarian states but also by democracies or through alliances between democracies and non-democracies. Further thinking in these directions would not only contribute to more in-depth and comprehensive understanding of assemblies within and across political contexts but also have broader implications for the study of democracy and authoritarianism.

Acknowledgements

I appreciate valuable comments from Sharath Srinivasan, Tabatha Abu El-Haj, James M. Jasper, Thomas Janoski, and participants in Contributor Workshops of this volume.

Notes

1. Sidney Tarrow, *Power in Movement: Social Movements and Contentious Politics* (Cambridge: Cambridge University Press, 2022).
2. Doug McAdam, Sidney Tarrow, and Charles Tilly, *Dynamics of Contention* (Cambridge: Cambridge University Press, 2001).
3. Howard Ramos and Kathleen Rodgers, *Protest and Politics: The Promise of Social Movement Societies* (Vancouver: UBC Press, 2015).
4. David S. Meyer and Sidney G. Tarrow, 'A Movement Society: Contentious Politics for a New Century', in *The Social Movement Society: Contentious Politics for A New Century*, ed. David S. Meyer and Sidney G. Tarrow, vol. 1 (Lanham, MD: Rowman & Littlefield, 1998), 1–28.
5. John D. McCarthy and Clark McPhail, 'The Institutionalization of Protest in the United States', in *The Social Movement Society: Contentious Politics for a New Century*, ed. David Meyer and Sidney Tarrow, vol. 1 (Lanham, MD: Rowman & Littlefield, 1998), 83–110.
6. Tarrow, *Power in Movement*.
7. Erica Chenoweth and Maria J. Stephan, *Why Civil Resistance Works: The Strategic Logic of Nonviolent Conflict* (New York: Columbia University Press, 2011).
8. Mark R. Beissinger, *Nationalist Mobilization and the Collapse of the Soviet State* (Cambridge: Cambridge University Press, 2002); Charles Kurzman, 'Structural Opportunity and Perceived Opportunity in Social Movement Theory: The Iran Revolution of 1979', *American Sociological Review* 61, no. 1 (1996): 153–170.
9. Charles Tilly, *Regimes and Repertoires* (Chicago: University of Chicago Press, 2006); Charles Tilly and Sidney Tarrow, *Contentious Politics*, 2nd ed. (Oxford: Oxford University Press, 2015).
10. Donatella della Porta and Olivier Fillieule, 'Policing Social Protest', in *The Blackwell Companion to Social Movements*, ed. David A Snow, Sarah Anne Soule, and Hanspeter Kriesi (Oxford: Blackwell Publishing, 2004), 217–241.
11. Ruud Koopmans and Susan Olzak, 'Discursive Opportunities and the Evolution of Right-Wing Violence in Germany', *American Journal of Sociology* 110, no. 1 (2004): 198–230.
12. ACLED and Everytown, 'Updated Armed Demonstration Data Released a Year after the 6 January Insurrection Show New Trends' (Armed Conflict Location & Event Data Project, 5 January 2022), https://acleddata.com/2022/01/05/updated-armed-demonstration-data-released-a-year-after-the-6-january-insurrection-show-new-trends/.
13. Yao Li, *Playing by the Informal Rules: Why the Chinese Regime Remains Stable despite Rising Protests* (Cambridge: Cambridge University Press, 2019), 17.
14. Kevin J. O'Brien, 'Neither Transgressive Nor Contained: Boundary-Spanning Contention In China', *Mobilization: An International Quarterly* 8, no. 1 (2003): 51–64.
15. David Zweig, 'Can New Political Institutions Manage Rural Conflict', in *Chinese Society: Change, Conflict and Resistance*, ed. Elizabeth J. Perry and Mark Selden (London: Routledge, 2010), 123–147.
16. Holger Albrecht, *Raging against the Machine: Political Opposition under Authoritarianism in Egypt* (New York: Syracuse University Press, 2013).
17. Joel Beinin and Frédéric Vairel, 'Introduction: The Middle East and North Africa beyond Classical Social Movement Theory', in *Social Movements, Mobilization, and Contestation in the Middle East and North Africa*, ed. Joel Beinin and Frédéric Vairel (Stanford, CA:

Stanford University Press, 2011), 1–26; Lynette J. Chua, *Mobilizing Gay Singapore: Rights and Resistance in an Authoritarian State* (Singapore: NUS Press, 2014).

18. Doug McAdam, 'Tactical Innovation and the Pace of Insurgency', *American Sociological Review* 48, no. 6 (1983): 736.
19. Diana Fu, 'Disguised Collective Action in China', *Comparative Political Studies* 50, no. 4 (2017): 499–527.
20. Dana Moss, 'Repression, Response, and Contained Escalation Under "Liberalized" Authoritarianism in Jordan', *Mobilization: An International Quarterly* 19, no. 3 (2014): 261–286.
21. Christian Davenport, 'State Repression and Political Order', *Annual Review of Political Science* 10, no. 1 (2007): 1–23.
22. Donatella della Porta and Herbert Reiter, 'Introduction: The Policing of Protest in Western Democracies', in *Policing Protest: The Control of Mass Demonstrations in Western Democracies*, ed. Donatella della Porta and Herbert Reiter (Minneapolis: University of Minnesota Press, 1998), 1–32.
23. McCarthy and McPhail, 'The Institutionalization of Protest'.
24. Patrick F. Gillham, 'Securitizing America: Strategic Incapacitation and the Policing of Protest since the 11 September 2001 Terrorist Attacks', *Sociology Compass* 5, no. 7 (2011): 636–652.
25. Lesley Wood, 'Uncooperative Movements, Militarized Policing, and the Social Movement Society', in *Protest and Politics: The Promise of Social Movement Societies* (Vancouver: UBC Press, 2015), 139.
26. della Porta and Fillieule, 'Policing Social Protest'.
27. Sarah Knuckey, Katherine Glenn, and Emi MacLean, 'Suppressing Protest: Human Rights Violations in the U.S. Response to Occupy Wall Street' (New York: NYU School of Law and Fordham Law School, 2012).
28. US Department of State, 'France 2019 Human Rights Report', 2019.
29. Julia Szulecka and Kacper Szulecki, 'Between Domestic Politics and Ecological Crises: (De)Legitimization of Polish Environmentalism', *Environmental Politics* 31, no. 7 (2022): 1214–1243.
30. Áron Buzogány, 'From Democratization to Internationalization', in *Social Movement Studies in Europe: The State of the Art*, ed. Olivier Fillieule and Guya Accornero, vol. 16 (Oxford: Bergahn Books, 2016), 403–418.
31. Jennifer Earl, 'Introduction: Repression and the Social Control of Protest', *Mobilization: An International Journal* 11, no. 2 (2006): 129–143.
32. Nathan Stephens Griffin, "Everyone Was Questioning Everything': Understanding the Derailing Impact of Undercover Policing on the Lives of UK Environmentalists', *Social Movement Studies* 20, no. 4 (2021): 459–477.
33. Bethan Loftus, 'Normalizing Covert Surveillance: The Subterranean World of Policing', *British Journal of Sociology* 70, no. 5 (2019): 2070–2091.
34. Ruth Braunstein, 'Boundary-Work and the Demarcation of Civil from Uncivil Protest in the United States: Control, Legitimacy, and Political Inequality', *Theory and Society* 47, no. 5 (October 2018): 603–633; Colleen Carroll Mihal, "The Domestic War on Terror: Surveillance, Media and Police Militarization at Protests" (PhD diss., University of Colorado at Boulder, 2015).
35. Amory Starr, Luis A. Fernandez, and Christian Scholl, *Shutting down the Streets: Political Violence and Social Control in the Global Era* (New York: New York University Press, 2011).
36. Jennifer Earl, 'Information Access and Protest Policing Post-9/11: Studying the Policing of the 2004 Republican National Convention', *American Behavioral Scientist* 53, no. 1 (September 2009): 44–60; Knuckey et al., 'Suppressing Protest'.

37. Christian Davenport, *How Social Movements Die: Repression and Demobilization of the Republic of New Africa* (New York: Cambridge University Press, 2015), 62.
38. Chan S. Suh and Sidney G. Tarrow, 'Suppression by Stealth: The Partisan Response to Protest in State Legislatures', *Politics & Society* 50, no. 3 (2022): 455–484.
39. Lynette H. Ong, *Outsourcing Repression: Everyday State Power in Contemporary China* (Oxford: Oxford University Press, 2022).
40. Braunstein, 'Boundary-Work'; Christian Davenport, Sarah A. Soule, and David A. Armstrong II, 'Protesting while Black? The Differential Policing of American Activism, 1960 to 1990', *American Sociological Review* 76 (2011): 152–178.
41. Erica Chenoweth, 'This Summer's Black Lives Matter Protesters Were Overwhelmingly Peaceful, Our Research Finds', *Washington Post*, 23 October 2020, https://www.washingtonpost.com/politics/2020/10/16/this-summers-black-lives-matter-protesters-were-overwhelming-peaceful-our-research-finds/.
42. David Cunningham, 'Policing White Supremacy: Asymmetry and Inequality in Protest Control', *Social Problems* 71 (2024): 58–76.
43. P. A. J. Waddington, 'Controlling Protest in Contemporary Historical and Comparative Perspective', in *Policing Protest: The Control of Mass Demonstrations in Western Democracies*, ed. Donatella Della Porta and Herbert Reiter (Minneapolis: University of Minnesota Press, 1998), 139.
44. della Porta and Reiter, 'Introduction'; Suzanne Staggenborg, 'Social Movement Communities in the Movement Society', in *Protest and Politics: The Promise of Social Movement Societies*, ed. Howard Ramos and Kathleen Rodgers (Vancouver: UBC Press, 2015), 155–172.
45. Earl, 'Information Access'.
46. Waddington, 'Controlling Protest'.
47. Jim Heintz, 'Kazakhstan Says 164 Killed in Last Week's Protests', AP News, 9 January 2022, https://apnews.com/article/europe-russia-kazakhstan-almaty-e8041ebee995d41050e6919eaocdca64.
48. Reuters, 'Iran Hangs Two Men Accused of Killing Security Agent during Protests', euronews, 8 January 2023, https://www.euronews.com/2023/01/08/iran-women-execution.
49. Li, *Playing by the Informal Rules*.
50. Xi Chen, 'Origins of Informal Coercion in China', *Politics & Society* 45, no. 1 (March 2017): 67–89; Ong, *Outsourcing Repression*.
51. Manfred Elfstrom and Yao Li, 'Contentious Politics in China: Causes, Dynamics, and Consequences', *Brill Research Perspectives in Governance and Public Policy in China* 4, no. 1 (2019): 1–90.
52. Daron Acemoglu and James A. Robinson, *Economic Origins of Dictatorship and Democracy* (New York: Cambridge University Press, 2006).
53. Audie Klotz, *Norms in International Relations: The Struggle against Apartheid* (Ithaca, NY: Cornell University Press, 2018).
54. William J. Dobson, *The Dictator's Learning Curve: Inside the Global Battle for Democracy* (New York: Anchor Books, 2013).
55. For example, Dawn Brancati, 'Democratic Authoritarianism: Origins and Effects', *Annual Review of Political Science* 17, no. 1 (2014): 313–326.
56. Manfred Elfstrom, *Workers and Change in China: Resistance, Repression, Responsiveness* (Cambridge: Cambridge University Press, 2021). Yao Li, 'Official Framing—Portraying the Implementation of an Unpopular Policy as Responsive Governance', *Social Movement*

Studies 21, no. 5 (2022): 571–589; Moss, 'Repression, Response, and Contained Escalation'; Graeme B. Robertson, *The Politics of Protest in Hybrid Regimes: Managing Dissent in Post-Communist Russia* (New York: Cambridge University Press, 2011).

57. Erica Chenoweth, 'The Future of Nonviolent Resistance', *Journal of Democracy* 31, no. 3 (2020): 69–84.
58. Jennifer Earl, Thomas Maher, and Jennifer Pan, 'The Digital Repression of Social Movements, Protest, and Activism: A Synthetic Review', *Science Advances* 8, no. 10 (2022): 1–15; Rongbin Han, *Contesting Cyberspace in China: Online Expression and Authoritarian Resilience* (New York: Columbia University Press, 2018); Margaret E. Roberts, *Censored: Distraction and Diversion inside China's Great Firewall* (Princeton, NJ: Princeton University Press, 2018).
59. Mark R. Beissinger, 'Social Sources of Counterrevolution', in *Ruling by Other Means: State-Mobilized Movements*, ed. Grzegorz Ekiert, Elizabeth J Perry, and Xiaojun Yan (Cambridge: Cambridge University Press, 2020).
60. Maya Atwal and Edwin Bacon, 'The Youth Movement Nashi: Contentious Politics, Civil Society, and Party Politics', *East European Politics* 28, no. 3 (2012): 256–266.
61. Steven Levitsky and Lucan A. Way, *Competitive Authoritarianism: Hybrid Regimes after the Cold War* (Cambridge: Cambridge University Press, 2010).
62. Qiangqiang Luo, Joel Andreas, and Yao Li, 'Grapes of Wrath: Twisting Arms to Get Villagers to Cooperate with Agribusiness in China', *China Journal* 77 (2017): 27–50.
63. Yao Li and Manfred Elfstrom, 'Does Greater Coercive Capacity Increase Overt Repression? Evidence from China', *Journal of Contemporary China* 30, no. 128 (2021): 186–211.
64. Sheena Chestnut Greitens, *Dictators and Their Secret Police: Coercive Institutions and State Violence* (New York: Cambridge University Press, 2016).
65. Milan W. Svolik, *The Politics of Authoritarian Rule* (Cambridge: Cambridge University Press, 2012).
66. Charles Tilly, *From Mobilization to Revolution* (New York: McGraw-Hill College, 1978), 106.
67. Paul Chang and Alex Vitale, 'Repressive Coverage in an Authoritarian Context: Threat, Weakness, and Legitimacy in South Korea's Democracy Movement', *Mobilization: An International Quarterly* 18, no. 1 (2013): 19–39.
68. Vince Boudreau, 'Precarious Regimes and Matchup Problems in the Explanation of Repressive Policy', in *Repression and Mobilization. Vol. 21*, ed. Christian Davenport, Hank Johnston, and Carol Mueller (Minneapolis: University of Minnesota Press, 2005), 33–57.
69. Quintan Wiktorowicz, *Islamic Activism: A Social Movement Theory Approach* (Bloomington: Indiana University Press, 2004); Tilly, *Regimes and Repertoires*.
70. Tilly and Tarrow, *Contentious Politics*.
71. Elfstrom and Li, 'Contentious Politics in China'.
72. Christian Davenport and David Armstrong, 'Democracy and the Violation of Human Rights: A Statistical Analysis from 1976 to 1996', *American Journal of Political Science* 48, no. 3 (2004): 538–554.
73. For example, David S. Meyer, *The Politics of Protest: Social Movements in America* (New York: Oxford University Press 2015).
74. Marco G. Giugni and Florence Passy, 'Contentious Politics in Complex Societies: New Social Movements between Conflicts and Cooperation', in *From Contention to Democracy*, ed. Marco G. Giugni, Doug McAdam, and Charles Tilly (Lanham, MD: Rowman & Littlefield, 1998), 81–108.
75. Li, *Playing by the Informal Rules*.
76. Tarrow, *Power in Movement*, 252.

77. Terry Gross, "'Stop the Steal' Has Moved beyond Trump. Now It's Threatening Future Elections', NPR, 28 July 2022, https://www.npr.org/2022/07/28/1114224368/stop-the-steal-has-moved-beyond-trump-now-its-threatening-future-elections.
78. Chenoweth and Stephan, *Why Civil Resistance Works.*
79. Alexei Anisin, 'Debunking the Myths behind Nonviolent Civil Resistance', *Critical Sociology* 46, no. 7–8 (November 2020): 1121–1139; David S. Meyer, 'How the Effectiveness of Nonviolent Action Is the Wrong Question for Activists, Academics, and Everyone Else', in *Social Movements, Nonviolent Resistance, and the State*, ed. Hank Johnston (Abingdon, UK: Routledge, 2019), 151–161.
80. Thomas Smits and Ruben Ros, 'Does Transnational Contention Lead to Transnational Memory? The Online Visual Memory of the February 2003 Anti-Iraq War Protests', *Social Movement Studies* 22, no. 1 (2023): 23–45.
81. Christopher Chase-Dunn and Paul Almeida, *Global Struggles and Social Change: From Prehistory to World Revolution in the Twenty-First Century* (Baltimore: Johns Hopkins University Press, 2020).
82. Margaret E. Keck and Kathryn Sikkink, *Activists beyond Borders: Advocacy Networks in International Politics* (Ithaca, NY: Cornell University Press, 1998).
83. Dana Moss, 'Voice after Exit: Explaining Diaspora Mobilization for the Arab Spring', *Social Forces* 98, no. 4 (2020): 1669–1694.
84. Stefania Vicari, 'Networks of Contention: The Shape of Online Transnationalism in Early Twenty-First Century Social Movement Coalitions', *Social Movement Studies* 13, no. 1 (2014): 92–109.
85. Richard Price and Kathryn Sikkink, *International Norms, Moral Psychology, and Neuroscience*, Elements in International Relations (Cambridge: Cambridge University Press, 2021).
86. Jackie Smith, Samantha Plummer, and Melanie M. Hughes, 'Transnational Social Movements and Changing Organizational Fields in the Late Twentieth and Early Twenty-First Centuries', *Global Networks* 17, no. 1 (2017): 3–22.
87. Gerasimos Tsourapas, 'Global Autocracies: Strategies of Transnational Repression, Legitimation, and Co-Optation in World Politics', *International Studies Review* 23, no. 3 (2021): 616–644.
88. Dana Moss, *The Arab Spring Abroad* (New York: Cambridge University Press, 2021).
89. Tilly and Tarrow, *Contentious Politics.*
90. Li, *Playing by the Informal Rules.*

Further Reading

Beinin, Joel, and Frédéric Vairel. *Social Movements, Mobilization, and Contestation in the Middle East and North Africa*. Stanford, CA: Stanford University Press, 2011.

Chen, Xi. *Social Protest and Contentious Authoritarianism in China*. Cambridge: Cambridge University Press, 2012.

Chenoweth, Erica, and Maria J. Stephan. *Why Civil Resistance Works: The Strategic Logic of Nonviolent Conflict*. New York: Columbia University Press, 2011.

Davenport, Christian. *How Social Movements Die: Repression and Demobilization of the Republic of New Africa*. New York: Cambridge University Press, 2015.

della Porta, Donatella, and Herbert Reiter. *Policing Protest: The Control of Mass Demonstrations in Western Democracies*. Minneapolis: University of Minnesota Press, 1998.

Ekiert, Grzegorz, Elizabeth J. Perry, and Xiaojun Yan. *Ruling by Other Means: State-Mobilized Movements*. Cambridge: Cambridge University Press, 2020.

Diana Fu, *Mobilizing without the Masses: Control and Contention in China*. Cambridge: Cambridge University Press, 2018.

Levitsky, Steven, and Lucan A. Way. *Competitive Authoritarianism: Hybrid Regimes after the Cold War*. Cambridge: Cambridge University Press, 2010.

Li, Yao. *Playing by the Informal Rules: Why the Chinese Regime Remains Stable despite Rising Protests*. Cambridge: Cambridge University Press, 2019.

McAdam, Doug, Sidney Tarrow, and Charles Tilly. *Dynamics of Contention*. Cambridge: Cambridge University Press, 2001.

Meyer, David. *The Politics of Protest: Social Movements in America*. New York: Oxford University Press, 2015.

Moss, Dana. *The Arab Spring Abroad*. New York: Cambridge University Press, 2021.

O'Brien, Kevin J., and Lianjiang Li. *Rightful Resistance in Rural China*. New York: Cambridge University Press, 2006.

Robertson, Graeme B. *The Politics of Protest in Hybrid Regimes: Managing Dissent in Post-Communist Russia*. New York: Cambridge University Press, 2011.

Tarrow, Sidney. *Power in Movement: Social Movements and Contentious Politics*. New York: Cambridge University Press, 2022.

Tilly, Charles. *Regimes and Repertoires*. Chicago: University of Chicago Press, 2006.

Tilly, Charles, and Sidney Tarrow. *Contentious Politics*, 2nd ed. New York: Oxford University Press, 2015.

CHAPTER 9

A FEMINIST CRITIQUE OF PEACEFUL ASSEMBLY

SHAN-JAN SARAH LIU

Introduction

In late 2022, following the death in custody of twenty-two-year-old Mahsa Amini after she was arrested by the Iranian police for not wearing her hijab 'correctly', countrywide demonstrations took place in Iran with women at the forefront. Some women took off their hijabs and chanted 'Death to the dictator' while some others ripped off their headscarves and tossed them into public fires. Although this was not the first time Iranian women had led revolutionary protests, such mobilization still holds significance for the role of women in and the impact of women on peaceful assembly, especially in an authoritarian regime where peaceful assembly is usually not allowed and entails great risks.

Women's participation in peaceful assembly dates back over a century ago. Yet while most studies of peaceful assembly examine specific forms, types, and tactics, such as protest, seldom does research focus on the role of gender in peaceful assembly. Second, although there is some focus specifically on women's rights-focused assembly, such as the suffragist movement, there is a lack of scholarly attention on women's involvement in peaceful assembly for general causes.

Studies of assembly tend to be androcentric by treating men's experiences with peaceful assembly as the default, arguably because political institutions and processes are traditionally masculine. Such an androcentric view means that the experiences with peaceful assembly captured in traditional studies mostly reflect experiences of men. It also means that women's roles in assemblies are too easily erased despite their presence. For example, although women were also involved in the civil rights movement in the United States in the 1960s, they were rarely visible in public media or prominent in dominant accounts of the movement. Their leadership was unrecognized despite being the cornerstone for micro-mobilizing—connecting local communities with the national movement.[1] Martin Luther King, Jr. and other men became the face of the movement while Black women made plans, held meetings, offered tactics, and organized boycotts.

A narrow approach that neglects the importance of gender and other identities limits our understanding of peaceful assembly. Increasingly, however, scholars have begun to pay attention to the role of gender in peaceful assembly to address this gap. In one strand of work, scholars examine how peaceful assembly as a right, a practice, and an institution is historically gendered. For instance, many polities, even democratic ones, historically banned women from engaging in public affairs. Even when prohibitions were slightly lifted, such as for American women to partake in some public events, elites and the mainstream media worried about the consequences of such liberation.[2] Moreover, even in polities where official bans were absent, women were usually discouraged from organizing for political causes as politics has been considered a man's game.

Another strand of scholarship investigates how such gendering shapes the engagement of women in peaceful assembly. This strand focuses in part on the differences between women's and men's propensity to participate in peaceful assembly. Historically, women participate less in peaceful assembly and protest regardless of where they are.[3] This is so even though women often had access to peaceful assembly during periods when they were barred from engaging in politics electorally. In other words, historically women might have had more access to protest than to other forms of democratic action but still participated in public assembly less than their men counterparts. Moreover, in addition to evaluating how women and men differ in the motivation, frequency, and propensity to partake in various forms of peaceful assembly, scholars are increasingly taking a step further to examine the subjective, differential experiences with peaceful assembly of women and men.[4]

While research on peaceful assembly is increasingly emphasizing the role of gender, it is imperative to note that not all of this scholarship is guided by feminist epistemologies.[5] That noted, this chapter takes a feminist approach to reviewing existing scholarship on gendered peaceful assembly and offers new directions for further expansion of this strand of literature. The chapter focuses on two dimensions of scholarship: (1) how peaceful assembly has traditionally been a gendered process and (2) how women's and men's experiences with peaceful assembly differ.

Drawing from Shany's argument in this volume that the UN Human Rights Committee's definition of peaceful assembly in General Comment No. 37 as 'gathering by persons for specific purposes, principally expressive ones' is broader and possibly preferable to the narrower definition in the ODIHR/Venice Commission Guidelines, this chapter uses a feminist lens to consider a variety of activities as peaceful assembly. It evaluates existing scholarship and offers critiques for what is currently lacking. The chapter argues that future research should take a feminist approach particularly by asking more questions about the types, forms, and processes of peaceful assembly.[6] Asking these questions allow scholars to capture the participation of the previously ignored or marginalized individuals in peaceful assembly, ensuring that the studies of who and how people participate in peaceful assembly are comprehensive.

This chapter starts with an overview of the roots of women-led peaceful assembly. Based on personal expertise and familiarity, this discussion is approached with a focus on the US context, recognizing that the origins of such peaceful assembly will differ across contexts.[7] The chapter then examines the role of gender in peaceful assembly. Specifically, it investigates the gendering of peaceful assembly as a political institution and process and gender-based differential experiences. It finally concludes by offering some thoughts on future directions, including taking an intersectional approach and considering online peaceful assembly, of this field of study.

The Origins and Development of Women-Led Peaceful Assembly

Scholarship shows that women continue to participate in politics less than men. Recent studies show that electoral participation might be the only form of political action in which women partake equivalently to, if not more than, men in most democracies.[8] Based on this current understanding of gender gaps in political participation (an extension from and overlap with peaceful assembly), one might assume that historically women were excluded from all forms of peaceful assembly. However, this has not always been the case. Although women were officially excluded from electoral politics as they did not have suffrage, in many countries they could collectively organize and mobilize in other ways, such as holding meetings and protests. Such freedom to assemble peacefully and participate politically via actions other than electoral participation gave women an opportunity to fight for gender equality, which eventually led to their right to vote.

Throughout early US history, for example, women played an active role in peaceful assembly. As different US states were revising constitutions between 1830 and 1860, official conventions were held. These conventions gave women an opportunity to assemble peacefully for various causes. Some women were abolitionists and gathered around these conventions to oppose slavery. At the same time, other women recognized the importance of women's rights and held their own conventions. The convention held by Elizabeth Cady Stanton and Lucretia Mott in Seneca Falls, New York in 1848 marked the beginning of mass organizing efforts of peaceful assembly for women's rights. Two years after the Seneca Falls convention, it was clear that women's rights issues were also intertwined with abolitionist issues. Moreover, instead of and in addition to expressing beliefs of rights to only other women activists, women began to mark a visible and public presence in raising awareness on issues concerning all and not just women. A group of women gathered in Salem, Ohio in 1850, advocating for equal rights 'without distinction of sex or color'.[9] This convention differed from other conventions where 'women occupied the floor and debated resolutions and gave speeches while men sat quietly in the gallery'.[10] Prior to this convention, women might be able to attend conventions through which they expressed political interests but were rarely given the floor to express their opinions.

Women's peaceful assembly for equal rights occurred in this period and laid an important foundation for the international feminist movement that fought for suffrage and other social transformations, which spread to other parts of the world towards the end of the nineteenth century and the beginning of the twentieth century.[11] Women from nine countries (Canada, Finland, France, India, Ireland, Norway, the United Kingdom, and the United States) met in Washington, DC in 1888 for the US National Women's Suffrage Association. Subsequently, the International Council of Women (ICW) was formed with the goal to bring together women from across the globe to address women's issues. The ICW provided a platform for women to share ideas and strategies for organizing for women's rights.

Not all women activists at the time (or at any time in other points of history) shared the same visions. For example, the ICW, which included women activists from across the world, did not think suffrage for women was the most important issue, nor did it directly advocate for enfranchisement. On the contrary, women activists in the United States believed that being enfranchized would empower them, allowing them a say in the political decision-making process. Dominated by middle-class American agendas,[12] women in the United States established networks and structures to address political issues, especially the ones that were relevant to women, specifically suffrage for women.[13]

As a result, the women's movement in the United States split from the international parent when US feminist activists were determined to put enfranchisement as the focus of their movement. Some members separately left the ICW and established the International Alliance of Women (IAW) to focus on a singular issue, which was suffrage for women across the world. Women activists were successful in the United States in 1920 in achieving ratification for the Nineteenth Amendment for all states for extending suffrage to American women.

The suffrage movement developed and depended on several core practices of peaceful assembly to achieve its goals. Suffragists established private associations through their own relationships and networks. Then larger meetings were held, and organizations were established, which eventually planned and led public gatherings and conventions. Women who attended these conventions were then able to organize and encourage others to partake in public demonstrations and marches to pressure the government to extend suffrage to women. All these pioneering efforts in peaceful assembly eventually led to women's (electoral) participation in politics beyond peaceful assembly.

Women's peaceful assembly expanded to new concerns after the extension of suffrage was achieved with women's right to vote. As World War I broke out and women activists became aware of the impact of the war, they began to shift their focus on organizing for peace—an issue salient to all and not just women. Women organized international peace conferences in the Hague in 1915 and in Zurich in 1919 with the goal to promote peace and equality for women.[14] The political climate gave women an opportunity to participate in global politics and enabled them to raise global awareness on inequalities and injustices for women. By the end of the World War II, women in fifty-five countries were granted suffrage, many in existing democracies, showing that transnational alliances of women activists could help women win political rights and enhance their political status. As women activists across the globe utilized peaceful assembly as well as other tactics and forms of political action to achieve their goal, they also moved beyond assembling for women's issues but also other general issues.

Peaceful Assembly as a Gendered Process

Nineteenth-century women in Western democracies had some access to the public square where they could assemble and were able to present politically in civil society through civic associations. This access, as we have seen, proved critical to their fight for electoral inclusion. Nevertheless, the extent to which women, then and now, can partake in association and assembly, and their experience when they do participate, is largely gendered. There is a limit to what women can and cannot do in participating in peaceful assembly and there is a gender hierarchy that dictates who has more power.

The irrefutable starting point is that we live in a gendered culture in which there is almost a universal belief that women are subordinate.[15] We should not be surprised therefore to find that peaceful assembly, itself, is gendered. Gender inequalities exist across most contexts, cultures, and regimes. While the gender structure and culture vary across contexts, in much of the world, patriarchy dominates how women should act, including politically. The differential treatments of women are largely attributed to women's reproduction, as well as the labour and responsibilities that come with their reproduction.[16] While historically women were expected to stay in the private sphere and contribute to domestic labour through childbirth and caretaking, it is additionally complicated when race and class are taken into account. For example, working-class women might be expected to both work outside the home as well as be the primary caretakers at home. Mostly, though, women's reproduction puts them in a second-class status that constrains them from engaging in most public affairs. Thus, despite exceptions, peaceful assembly as a facet of gendered political culture more generally, has traditionally been exclusionary for women; this exclusion has also been classed and racialized.

Second, this gender hierarchy raises important implications for how we have previously comprehended women's leadership in peaceful assembly. Oftentimes women's leadership is overlooked. Women have been leaders in peaceful assembly across the globe; however, unless they organize for women's movements, they are rarely seen (see, for example, du Toit, in this volume, on the role of women in the anti-colonial Satyagraha march of 1913 in South Africa). For example, mothers in Argentina who protested the disappearance of their children gained much attention,[17] but such recognition was associated with their motherhood (conversely, Kaiser, in this volume, argues that Escraches turned motherhood into a political activity in public). Accounts of assemblies for general causes often neglect women's efforts. Other notable movements where women's roles have been under-recognized include the People Power movement in the Philippines[18] and the anti-nuclear power movement in Japan[19]—both movements in which women were heavily involved.

The lack of attention to women's leadership in assemblies is particularly striking in political and social movements because not only do women often do the groundwork, including reaching out to the community and serving as liaison between the local community and the national movement, they also offer advice on strategies and tactics. Many of these movements would perhaps not have succeeded without these women, yet history does not adequately remember them.[20] An exception where a woman leader receives the recognition she deserves is perhaps Kenyan activist Wangari Maathai, the Nobel Peace Prize winner for the Green Belt environmental movement she founded. Thus, research that pays more attention to the role of gender in peaceful assembly from a feminist perspective, not only focusing on women's issues or women's roles as mothers, provides a more holistic and nuanced picture of the process and impact of peaceful assembly.

Gendered Experience of Peaceful Assembly

As established, peaceful assembly allows people to come together to collectively express and pursue their shared ideas. Nevertheless, studies of public assembly assume men's experiences as the default—the gendered experience of public assemblies is invisible in a second sense. Regardless of where peaceful assembly takes place—in the public or private—a substantial body of research shows that gender gaps exist in how people experience peaceful assembly. Gendered experiences with public assembly are also not limited to the past or to the United States. Significant gender gaps in collective action (attending a community meeting and joining others to raise an issue) are also found in sub-Saharan Africa. Even when socioeconomic factors are considered, most sub-Saharan African countries still experience a difference between how women and men engage in participation, including peaceful assembly.[21] This gender gap is apparent starting from a young age. Even in Germany where gender development has been advanced, differences still exist—adolescent women have lower confidence in their personal and political skills, resulting in their lower political engagement.[22]

Biographical availability in the context of social movements is 'the absence of personal constraints that may increase the costs and risks of movement participation', and this might help to explain the gender differences in experiences of assembly.[23] That is, the gender attributions, roles, and responsibilities assigned to women influence how they participate in peaceful assembly as it requires time, energy, capital, and networks[24]—not something many women can afford. Extant studies show that socioeconomic class, marital status, number of children, employment, and so on are all indicators of biographical availability that mediate the likelihood of one to partake in social movements. Fulfilling traditional gender roles, such as being carers (mothers and wives), women have less time and energy to participate in public affairs, making them less biographically available. Moreover, the experience of participation might also involve risks. For example, using data from 330 people who applied to be a part of the 1964 Mississippi Freedom Summer project, McAdam[25] shows that women took on greater risks to participate as they experienced sexual harassments and were assigned secretarial tasks whereas men were often treated as leaders and assigned important tasks. Therefore, those with more financial means (e.g. those who can afford to take off from work to protest) and those who face fewer threats (e.g. those who are less likely to experience danger) are more biographically available to engage in social movements.

The concept of biographical availability can also apply to peaceful assembly. As peaceful assembly is not an individualistic act but rather collective action, the extent to which peaceful assembly requires time, energy, capital, and networks to organize dictates how gendered women's experiences of assembly might be. For instance, historically, married women with children have been less likely to participate in collective action than their men counterparts who share similar characteristics because often they are primary carers.[26] Coffé and Bolzendahl's[27] study on eighteen democracies also suggest that these biographical availability indicators continue to determine the gender gaps in collective action.

As women may participate less in peaceful assembly due to their biographical availability, the patriarchal gender norms might also explain why women are underrepresented, as well as invisible in assembly. For example, women in Spain are significantly less likely to participate in political parties, trade unions, human rights associations, environmental associations, and peace movements than are men. The only aspect of peaceful assembly where the Spanish outshine men are in feminist or women's groups.[28] This finding shows that women are often sidelined in actions taken for peaceful assembly, unless they focus specifically on women's issues. Movements also furthered gender roles by expecting women to perform motherly duties.[29] For instance, women who participated in social movements were assigned menial tasks.[30]

These gender-based differential experiences of assembly may also determine how likely women are to participate again in assembly in the future. The consistent assignment of women to feminine roles in assemblies reduces women's political efficacy and often prompts them to withdraw.[31] In other words, the gender gaps in protest are not innate or simply caused by prior factors but rather significantly a product of how experiences of assembly are gendered by society's expectations of how women and men should behave. Thus, women might have a difficult time envisioning themselves involved in peaceful assembly, especially if it is a hostile environment. Consequently, women might be more inclined to focus on women's issues when organizing and participating in peaceful assembly as research shows consistently that social movements that centre on women's issues or have feminist agendas are organized by and involve women activists.[32]

Nevertheless, women's experiences of assembly and their participation are dynamically and interactively related. While women's efforts often begin with a focus on women's issues rather than general issues, they may at times eventually expand to political engagement across a wide range of issues. Although women's presence has not always been visible, women have also historically played a major role in peace movements.[33] Their anti-war agenda might be due to the loss of lives of husbands and sons—the socially ingrained motherly nature might have been one of the motivating factors for women to promote global peace. In certain contexts, such as Japan, where women's propensity to protest is generally low, women are particularly active in opposing nuclear power plants.[34] Again, Japanese women's involvement in the anti-nuclear movement could be due to their desire to protect the future generations. However, as more recent data show that women and men across the globe might have similar propensity to participate in assembly, it is also important to note that peaceful assembly that focuses on women's issues could also lead the saliency of other issues, as well as garner support from beyond women. The Women's March in 2017, which spurred other organizing efforts against Trumpism,[35] is an example of peaceful assembly. One caveat remains, though, which is that educated, middle-class White women who might have had more time on their hands than less-educated, working-class, non-White women were primary protagonists in anti-Trump women's organizing.[36] Moreover, despite the narrative of spontaneity and grassroots, the heavy lifting organizational work for the Women's March was also done by well-funded non-governmental organizations (NGOs). The paid positions within the NGOs also explain availability of those who had the means to organize for peaceful assembly.

These findings suggest that various dimensions of accessibility and experience of peaceful assembly play important roles in women's involvement. This empirical evidence also illustrates that the cost of collective action—a unique aspect of peaceful assembly, in contrast to individualism in electoral politics—must lower to encourage women's participation. Additionally, the findings also suggest that in certain conditions where women and men experience peaceful assembly differently, women might voluntarily opt out of the process.

Intersectionality in Peaceful Assembly

Not only are experiences with peaceful assembly gendered, but they are also intersectional.[37] Dating back to the Suffrage movement, Black women also fought for the right to vote but were often excluded.[38] When Black women were being shunned by the defrauded voting registration system or experienced violent threats for wanting to vote, White women activists saw that as a race problem—not an issue the suffragettes could address.[39] In recent years, since the third wave of the feminist movement, scholars have begun to take intersectionality into account. Subsequently, scholars have increasingly examined how gender intersects with other axes of identity in shaping one's experiences with peaceful assembly. Scholars have also found that besides gender, race and class, for example, shape political participation. More importantly, by taking intersectionality into consideration, scholars can show the intersectional challenges that minoritized participants face.[40]

Scholarship on peaceful assembly has a long way to go in its understanding about the intersectional experience of assembly. Several questions remain. For example, what new insights could intersectional approaches to peaceful assembly offer? How might organizers of peaceful assembly overcome the challenges, especially if they aim to achieve intersectionality? Currently, scholarship that takes an intersectional approach primarily focuses on gender and race, but we should also broaden our way of thinking by also examining sexuality, disability, and citizenship. For example, while some scholarship examines LGBTQ+ (Lesbian Gay Bisexual Transgender and Queer) participation in the undocumented immigrant youth movement,[41] more studies are needed to investigate the role of sexuality in peaceful assembly. Such an understanding would allow us to understand how recognizing the various dimensions of oppression could empower youth and create a boomerang effect, leading to the promotion of LGBTQ+ inclusivity amongst immigrants.

The inclusion of social movement activists with multiple oppressed identities illustrates that there is an urgency to move towards intersectionality in social movement research.[42] There are further questions to address. For instance, how might peaceful assemblies enact intersectionality? Is it possible to envisage peaceful assembly promote intersectionality by being more inclusive and by paying attention to people with multiple minoritized identities? Conversely, might there be limitations of using intersectionality as a framework when we analyse peaceful assembly? For instance, how intersectionality is understood in the Global North might differ from that in the Global South. We should also consider how we could further ensure that our feminist approach is inclusive in a transnational context. Overall, more research needs to be conducted to examine how peaceful assembly is gendered as well as intersectional, because such an approach could lead to important implications for how we understand how the development of human rights and the solidification of democracy.

Reconceptualizing Peaceful Assembly with a Feminist Lens

All these findings prompt us to reconsider whether our conceptualizations of peaceful assembly are up to date, especially whether they are inclusive and feminist. Traditionally, we understand peaceful assembly to be a gathering of people for specific purposes. Falling in this definition include activities such as protest, peaceful demonstrations, rallies, meetings, and so on. Yet, these conventional forms of political actions could exclude those who do not have the resources, capital, time, and energy to attend such types of assemblies.

The gendered experience of public assembly extends to forms of assembly that take place in the privatized public sphere, such as online assembly. Activists with minoritized identities have increasingly strategized and utilized other avenues for peaceful assembly, such as online activism.[43] New technology has thus broadened the definition and possibility of peaceful assembly (see McPherson, in this volume, and Ashraf, in this volume). People nowadays also gather virtually—what is being discussed, organized, and mobilized online has huge implications for changes that could be made in contentious politics including for the gendered experience of such politics.

Some early studies from Latin America showed that participation increased in the context of new media and digital communication technology.[44] Meanwhile, many might have anticipated and hoped that online activism, taken place quasi-privately, would allow those without the biographical availability to participate publicly in politics and thus provide a more inclusive forum for women. The verdict remains out. Particularly, although the internet does appear to increase political participation for all users, studies in the Middle East suggest it does not differentially increase women's participation in protest.[45] These inconclusive findings suggest that more research needs to be done to enhance our understanding of what feminist peaceful assembly online could look like and where it might take place. Moreover, information consumption and political participation are beneficial for building a healthy democracy.[46] If this assumption is not supported by or only applicable to certain contexts, then we need to think of other avenues through which women could partake in peaceful assembly so that it might be less gendered.

While online peaceful assembly has provided a new meaning and mode of action for political gatherings and contentious politics in recent years, it also has led to much attention on data security and state surveillance.[47] In the digital era, several platforms, such as Zoom, Microsoft Teams, and Skype, are used to conduct meetings. However, the data security on many platforms raises new risks of domination and denial of rights. For example, some platforms are owned by Chinese enterprises where the data are feared to route back to the Chinese Communist Party (see also Ashraf, in this volume, and Aston, in this volume). Therefore, how safe discussions are on such online platforms is an important question, which has significant gendered and racialized implications. The Chinese Communist Party's recent crackdown on the #MeToo movement in China, which arrested only women, illustrates the need to examine how gender plays a role in not just how individuals participate in online assembly but also the impact on who can safely participate and who cannot. If the goal is to be inclusive by providing alternative platforms and avenues to meet for peaceful assembly, platform takedowns, shutdowns, and surveillance are critical feminist issues to consider.

While gatherings for specific purposes can occur almost anywhere on the internet, including publicly accessible social media platforms such as X (formerly known as Twitter), research shows that women experience a significantly higher rate of violence in these spaces.[48] The threat of such violence makes engaging in political affairs daunting for women in new ways.[49] Research needs to further examine how such violence affects women's propensity to engage in online assembly. Equally, more critical praxis research is required to examine how alternative online spaces for peaceful assembly can be fostered that allows women, especially women with multiple marginalized identities, to safely participate.

Conclusion: Where Do We Go from Here?

This chapter starts with providing a discussion on the origins and developments of women-led peaceful assembly and an overview of extant research on peaceful assembly that considers gender. It then shows that scholarship largely suggests that peaceful assembly is a gendered process and institution and that participants often experience differential treatments depending on their gender. Examining how peaceful assembly has traditionally been a gendered process, the chapter critiques how current scholarship fails to recognize the efforts and contributions of women activists and leaders, and how this undermines a comprehensive picture of how we comprehend peaceful assembly. The chapter also proposes applying the concept of biographical availability in studying peaceful assembly, and, using a feminist perspective, it challenges our current operationalizations of 'peaceful assembly' as a concept by advocating for broadening our definitions and measures of peaceful assembly. Importantly, the chapter also raises questions on how a feminist perspective encourages us to include the activities of those who are less visible and that occur in the private space. Investigating how women's and men's experiences with peaceful assembly differ, the chapter calls for future scholarship to take an intersectional approach to bring nuanced insights into our current understanding of peaceful assembly.

While recent scholarship pays increasing attention to the role of intersectionality with a feminist lens, what intersectionality and feminism mean for our understanding of peaceful assembly might differ across contexts. As feminist scholars, how can we ensure that the academy creates greater space for diversity in research on assembly? Political science as a field is still dominated by men political scientists from the Global North. Specifically on the studies of peaceful assembly, androcentric and Eurocentric views are usually the guiding principles, raising questions about how individuals in other parts of the world partake in peaceful assembly.

Specifically, future research should take a transnational feminist perspective by including more studies on/from the Global South—an important area that has been previously ignored. Again, the focus and inclusion of scholarship on/from the Global South enables the field to capture the voices of those who have been underrepresented. Achieving a truly comprehensive picture of peaceful assembly allows us to ensure that the conclusions we have drawn thus far on scholarship from and on the Global North are not biased.

Establishing a safe space for transnational feminist scholars, especially those from the Global South, remains a crucial need. Employing a transnational feminist approach, with the lens from the Global South, could help us achieve nuanced insights into how peaceful assembly might be gendered across contexts. For instance, paying attention to how grassroots organization for peaceful assembly works across world contexts is crucial as research shows that the costs for women to organize locally are lower. Thus, examining peaceful assembly at the local, grassroots level could help us be more inclusive and in turn help us comprehend how democratic institutions could be transparent, trustworthy, and effective if they were to include the (invisible) efforts of women building from the ground up. As history shows that advances in democracy and human rights often start with the grassroots efforts,[50] including feminist efforts, we need to understand these struggles and fights transnationally from a less Eurocentric/American-centric, and androcentric perspective.

Recent decades have witnessed gender progress in peaceful assembly. Scholars have also increasingly paid attention to the role of gender in shaping how peaceful assembly occurs and makes an impact. Nevertheless, there is room to grow to enhance our understanding of how peaceful assembly is gendered and how this shapes the experiences of women and men differently, particularly of women with multiple minoritized identities. Such a comprehension can help efforts to improve democratic political structures and perhaps equally importantly to forge a world that is more inclusive.

Acknowledgements

I thank the editors and the other contributing authors of this volume for their critical feedback, which helped improve this chapter significantly.

Notes

1. Belinda Robnett, 'African-American Women in the Civil Rights Movement, 1954–1965: Gender, Leadership, and Micromobilization', *American Journal of Sociology* 101, no. 6 (1996): 1661–1693.
2. John D. Inazu, *Liberty's Refuge: The Forgotten Freedom of Assembly* (New Haven, CT: Yale University Press, 2012).
3. Alan Schussman and Sarah A. Soule, 'Process and Protest: Accounting for Individual Protest Participation', *Social Forces* 84, no. 2 (2005): 1083–1108; Sarah Henderson and Alana S. Jeydel, *Participation and Protest: Women and Politics in a Global World* (New York: Oxford University Press, 2007); Hannah Pfanzelt and Dennis C. Spies, 'The Gender Gap in Youth Political Participation: Evidence from Germany', *Political Research Quarterly* 72, no. 1 (2019): 34–48; Maria Grasso and Katherine Smith, 'Gender Inequalities in Political Participation and Political Engagement among Young People in Europe: Are Young Women Less Politically Engaged than Young Men?', *Politics* 42, no. 1 (2022): 39–57.

4. Shan-Jan Sarah Liu and Lee Ann Banaszak, 'Do Government Positions Held by Women Matter? A Cross-National Examination of Female Ministers' Impacts on Women's Political Participation', *Politics & Gender* 13, no. 1 (2017): 132–162; Pamela Paxton, Melanie M. Hughes, and Tiffany D. Barnes, *Women, Politics, and Power: A Global Perspective* (Lanham, MD: Rowman & Littlefield, 2020); Jane Jaquette, *The Women's Movement in Latin America: Participation and Democracy* (London: Routledge, 2018); Katrine Beauregard, 'Women's Representation and Gender Gaps in Political Participation: Do Time and Success Matter in a Cross-National Perspective?', *Politics, Groups, and Identities* 6, no. 2 (2018): 237–263; Sarah Shan-Jan, 'Are Female Political Leaders Role Models? Lessons from Asia', *Political Research Quarterly* 71, no. 2 (2018): 255–269.
5. Brooke A. Ackerly and Jacqui True, *Doing Feminist Research in Political and Social Science* (London: Bloomsbury, 2019).
6. See e.g. Shan-Jan Sarah Liu, 'Studying Feminist Governance: Methods and Approaches to the Field', in *Handbook of Feminist Governance*, ed. Marian Sawer et al. (London: Edward Elgar, 2023), 100–111.
7. My limited understanding and access to scholarship written in languages other than English also demonstrates the need to be more inclusive of scholarship from the non-English-speaking world.
8. Filip Kostelka, André Blais, and Elisabeth Gidengil, 'Has the Gender Gap in Voter Turnout Really Disappeared?', *West European Politics* 42, no. 3 (2019): 437–463; Shan-Jan Sarah Liu, 'Gender Gaps in Political Participation in Asia', *International Political Science Review* 43, no. 2 (2022): 209–225.
9. Inazu, *Liberty's Refuge*, 33.
10. Ibid.
11. Jutta Joachim, 'Local-Global-Local: Women's Global Organizing', in *The Oxford Handbook of Gender and Politics*, ed. Georgina Waylen et al. (New York: Oxford University Press, 2013), 462–484.
12. Heidi E. Rademacher and Kathleen M. Fallon, 'The Historical Roots of a Global Feminist Perspective and the Growing Global Focus among U.S. Feminists', in *The Oxford Handbook of U.S. Women's Social Movement Activism*, ed. Holly J. McCammon et al. (online ed., Oxford: Oxford Academic, 2017), accessed 11 January 2023, https://doi-org.ezproxy.is.ed.ac.uk/10.1093/oxfordhb/9780190204204.013.9.
13. Myra Marx Ferree and Carol M. Mueller, 'Feminism and the Women's Movement: A Global Perspective', *The Blackwell Companion to Social Movements*, ed. David Snow (London: Blackwell, 2004), 576–607.
14. Rademacher and Fallon, 'Historical Roots of a Global Feminist Perspective'.
15. Sherry B. Ortner, 'Is Female to Male as Nature Is to Culture?', *Feminist Studies* 1, no. 2 (1972): 5–31.
16. Heather McKee Hurwitz and Verta Taylor, 'Women's Cultures and Social Movements in Global Contexts', *Sociology Compass* 6, no. 10 (2012): 808–822.
17. Rita Arditti, *Searching for Life: The Grandmothers of the Plaza de Mayo and the Disappeared Children of Argentina* (Berkeley: University of California Press, 1999).
18. Dette Pascual, 'Organizing "People Power" in the Philippines', *Journal of Democracy* 1, no. 1 (1990): 102–109.
19. Ulrike Wöhr, 'Gender and Citizenship in the Anti-Nuclear Power Movement in 1970s Japan', in *Gender, Nation and State in Modern Japan*, ed. Andrea Germer, Vera Mackie, and Ulrike Wöhr (London: Routledge, 2014), 250–274.

20. Carmen Ramos Escandón, 'Women and Power in Mexico: The Forgotten Heritage, 1880–1954', in *Women's Participation in Mexican Political Life*, ed. Victoria E. Rodriguez (London: Routledge, 2019), 87–102.
21. Hilde Coffé and Catherine Bolzendahl, 'Same Game, Different Rules? Gender Differences in Political Participation', *Sex Roles* 62, no. 5 (2010): 318–333.
22. Hannah Pfanzelt and Dennis C. Spies, 'The Gender Gap in Youth Political Participation: Evidence from Germany', *Political Research Quarterly* 72, no. 1 (2019): 34–48.
23. Doug McAdam, 'Gender as a Mediator of the Activist Experience: The Case of Freedom Summer', *American Journal of Sociology* 97, no. 5 (1992): 1211–1240.
24. Victoria Gilbert, 'When Women Walk: Armed Groups and Women's Protest Participation during the Syrian Conflict', *The Middle East Journal* 76, no. 1 (2022): 93–114.
25. McAdam, 'Gender as a Mediator of the Activist Experience'.
26. Kay Lehman Schlozman, Nancy Burns, and Sidney Verba, 'Gender and the Pathways to Participation: The Role of Resources', *Journal of Politics* 56, no. 4 (1994): 963–990.
27. Coffé and Bolzendahl, 'Same game, Different Rules?'.
28. Laura Morales, 'Political Participation: Exploring the Gender Gap in Spain', *South European Society and Politics* 4, no. 2 (1999): 223–247.
29. Jenny Irons, 'The Shaping of Activist Recruitment and Participation: A Study of Women in the Mississippi Civil Rights Movement', *Gender & Society* 12, no. 6 (1998): 692–709.
30. Darren E. Sherkat and T. Jean Blocker, 'The Political Development of Sixties' Activists: Identifying the Influence of Class, Gender, and Socialization on Protest Participation', *Social Forces* 72, no. 3 (1994): 821–842.
31. Ibid.
32. Karen Beckwith, 'Beyond Compare? Women's Movements in Comparative Perspective', *European Journal of Political Research* 37, no. 4 (2000): 431–468.
33. Ruth Roach Pierson, ed., *Women and Peace: Theoretical, Historical and Practical Perspectives* (London: Routledge, 2019); Sandi E. Cooper, 'Women's Participation in European Peace Movements: The Struggle to Prevent World War I', in *Women and Peace: Theoretical, Historical and Practical Perspectives*, ed. Ruth Roach Pierson (London: Routledge, 2019), 51–75; Jennifer Thomson, 'The Women, Peace, and Security Agenda and Feminist Institutionalism: A Research Agenda', *International Studies Review* 21, no. 4 (2019): 598–613.
34. Aya H. Kimura, 'Citizen Science in post-Fukushima Japan: The Gendered Scientization of Radiation Measurement', *Science as Culture* 28, no. 3 (2019): 327–350.
35. Marie Berry and Erica Chenoweth, 'Who Made the Women's March?', in *The Resistance: The Dawn of the Anti-Trump Opposition Movement*, ed. David S. Meyer and Sidney Tarrow (New York: Oxford University Press, 2018), 75–89.
36. Leah E. Gose and Theda Skocpol, 'Resist, Persist, and Transform: The Emergence and Impact of Grassroots Resistance Groups Opposing the Trump Presidency', *Mobilization: An International Quarterly* 24, no. 3 (2019): 293–317.
37. Intersectionality is rooted in Black feminist ideologies and originated from the United States. An intersectional approach in academic research requires attention to multiple axes of identity and understanding of how they work in relations with power, inequality, and oppression.
38. Willie J. Epps Jr. and Jonathan M. Warren, 'Sheroes: The Struggles of Black Suffragists', *The Judges' Journal* 59, no. 3 (2020): 10–15.

39. Brent Staples, 'When the Suffrage Movement Sold Out to White Supremacy', *New York Times*, 2 February 2019.
40. Celeste Montoya, 'Intersectionality and Social Movements: Intersectional Challenges and Imperatives in the Study of Social Movements', *Sociology Compass* 15, no. 8 (2021): Article e12905.
41. Veronica Terriquez, 'Intersectional Mobilization, Social Movement Spillover, and Queer Youth Leadership in the Immigrant Rights Movement', *Social Problems* 62, no. 3 (2015): 343–362.
42. Zakiya Luna, Sujatha Jesudason, and Mimi E. Kim, 'Turning toward Intersectionality in Social Movement Research', *Mobilization: An International Quarterly* 25, no. 4 (2020): 435–440.
43. Charlotte Pearson and Filippo Trevisan, 'Disability Activism in the New Media Ecology: Campaigning Strategies in the Digital Era', *Disability & Society* 30, no. 6 (2015): 924–940.
44. Sebastián Valenzuela et al., 'Social Media in Latin America: Deepening or Bridging Gaps in Protest Participation?', *Online Information Review* 40, no. 5 (2016): 595–609.
45. Nadya Hajj, Patrick J. McEwan, and Rebecca Turkington, 'Women, Information Ecology, and Political Protest in the Middle East', *Mediterranean Politics* 24, no. 1 (2019): 62–83.
46. Philipp Lorenz-Spreen et al., 'A Systematic Review of Worldwide Causal and Correlational Evidence on Digital Media and Democracy', *Nature Human Behaviour* 7 (2023): 74–101.
47. See e.g. Nadia Nabila Mohd Saufi et al., 'From Civic Space to the Internet: Legislating Rights to Peaceful Assembly during Pandemic', *Environment-Behaviour Proceedings Journal* 7, no. SI11 (2022): 29–34; Kristopher E. G. Kinsinger, 'Restricting Freedom of Peaceful Assembly during Public Health Emergencies', *Constitutional Forum* 30 (2021): 19.
48. Ruth Lewis, Michael Rowe, and Clare Wiper, 'Online Abuse of Feminists as an Emerging Form of Violence against Women and Girls', *British Journal of Criminology* 57, no. 6 (2017): 1462–1481.
49. Angelia Wagner, 'Tolerating the Trolls? Gendered Perceptions of Online Harassment of Politicians in Canada', *Feminist Media Studies* 22, no. 1 (2022): 32–47; Emily Harmer and Rosalynd Southern, 'Digital Microaggressions and Everyday Othering: An Analysis of Tweets Sent to Women Members of Parliament in the UK', *Information, Communication & Society* 24, no. 14 (2021): 1998–2015.
50. Temma Kaplan, *Crazy for Democracy: Women in Grassroots Movements* (London: Routledge, 2016).

Further Reading

Beyer, Judith, and Aijarkyn Kojobekova. 'Women of Protest, Men of applause: Political Activism, Gender and Tradition in Kyrgyzstan'. *Central Asian Survey* 38, no. 3 (2019): 329–345.

Billard, Thomas J. 'Together We Rise: The Role of Communication and Community Connectedness in Transgender Citizens' Civic Engagement in the United States'. *Mass Communication and Society* 25, no. 3 (2022): 335–360.

Coffé, Hilde, and Selin Dilli. 'The Gender Gap in Political Participation in Muslim-Majority Countries'. *International Political Science Review* 36, no. 5 (2015): 526–544.

Conway, M. Margaret. 'Women and Political Participation'. *PS: Political Science and Politics* 34, no. 2 (2001): 231–233.

Corredor, Elizabeth S. 'Unpacking "Gender Ideology" and the Global Right's Antigender Countermovement'. *Signs: Journal of Women in Culture and Society* 44, no. 3 (2019): 613–638.
Eschle, Catherine. *Global Democracy, Social Movements, and Feminism*. London: Routledge, 2018.
Evans, Elizabeth, and Eléonore Lépinard. *Intersectionality in Feminist and queer Movements: Confronting Privileges*. London: Taylor & Francis, 2019.
Jackson, Sarah J., Moya Bailey, and Brooke Foucault Welles. *# HashtagActivism: Networks of Race and Gender Justice*. Cambridge, MA: MIT Press, 2020.
Jaquette, Jane S. 'Conclusion: Women's Political Participation and the Prospects for Democracy'. In *The Women's Movement in Latin America: Feminism and the Transition to Democracy in Latin America*, ed. Jane S. Jaquette, 223–238. London: Routledge, 2018.
Joo, Yunjeong. 'Same Despair but Different Hope: Youth Activism in East Asia and Contentious Politics'. *Development and Society* 47, no. 3 (2018): 401–422.
Matthews, Tasia. 'The Politics of Protest and Gender: Women Riding the Wings of Resistance'. *Social Sciences* 11, no. 2 (2022): 52.
Naples, Nancy, ed. *Community Activism and Feminist Politics: Organizing across Race, Class, and Gender*. London: Routledge, 2012.
Nazneen, Sohela, and Awino Okech. 'Introduction: Feminist Protests and Politics in a World in Crisis'. *Gender & Development* 29, no. 2–3 (2021): 231–252.
Sackey, Emmanuel. 'Disability and Political Participation in Ghana: An Alternative Perspective'. *Scandinavian Journal of Disability Research* 17, no. 4 (2015): 366–381.
Taylor, Verta, and Nancy Whittier. 'Analytical Approaches to Social Movement Culture: The Culture of the Women's Movement'. *Social Movements and Culture* 4 (1995): 163–187.

CHAPTER 10

HISTORY AND ASSEMBLY IN THE POSTCOLONY

SARAH J. LOCKWOOD

INTRODUCTION

IN 2015, students protesting at the University of Cape Town held up signs linking their demand for free university education to an education-related protest that had taken place more than forty years previously in the Gauteng township of Soweto. When asked, one of the protesters explained: 'This is our Soweto moment. They stood up for our right to education in 1976, and today we are doing the same thing. The struggle continues'.[1] And links like this between contemporary and historical protest assemblies are far from uncommon. For example, during Black Lives Matter protests in Liverpool in 2020, placards were seen bearing slogans and sayings from key figures in the civil rights movement of the 1950s and 1960s,[2] while the Women's March on Washington in 2017 was peppered with signs alluding to earlier struggles for the rights of women.[3]

Despite the clear influence that past protests have on contemporary assemblies, however, much of the academic work on protest overlooks the role that history plays in shaping and guiding later behaviour, often insisting instead 'on the newness of their expressive forms', and leaving underexplored the various links that might exist.[4]

There are some notable exceptions of course. Charles Tilly, for example, famously argued that history helps to shape contemporary opportunities for protest, by providing activists with familiar tools and actions for use (repertoires of contention), as well as creating political opportunities or barriers for mobilization more broadly.[5] Sidney Tarrow, similarly, focuses on the important influence of history in his work *Power in Movement*,[6] while Karl Marx observed in *The Eighteenth Brumaire of Louis Bonaparte* that revolutionaries throughout time have always 'conjure[d] up spirits of the past to their service and borrow[ed] from them names, battle cries and costumes in order to present the new scene of world history in this time-honored disguise and this borrowed language'.[7]

Even in these works, however, the role of history often remains thinly discussed, limited to generalities, and focused primarily on the ways in which history impacts *forms* of assembly, with other elements of protest and the protest environment (such as the issues protested and the ways in which these are framed) overlooked. Moreover, as Tilly[8] himself often bemoaned, these works have tended not to be engaged with much by other scholars, with at best occasional mentions that history might be important seeping into academic discussions.[9]

This determined focus on the new to the exclusion of the old, however, leaves many questions around protest unanswered—and indeed unanswerable. For example, why is it that students protesting high university fees in Cape Town, South Africa, in 2015 carried placards referring to a protest that took place in a different city almost forty years previously? Why do so many protests in the United States involve a march to the Lincoln Memorial in Washington? And why did protests in Egypt during the Arab Spring draw on the language of decolonization, when decolonization officially happened decades earlier? History is important. And without it, we cannot fully understand where movements come from, how they develop, why they take the forms they do, and what it is that they require to be successful.

The ways in which earlier movements continue to shape and reshape contemporary protest generally needs further attention, but this need is particularly critical for protest in the postcolony. Discussion of the 'interconnectedness between different protest "moments" or constellations' across time 'remains extremely thin if not absent'[10] in postcolonial studies—a gap that is particularly glaring given how much the 'terrain of struggle' in the postcolony differs from the 'Northern contexts of traditional social movement theory'.[11]

This chapter contributes to filling this lacuna in the literature by examining the ways in which historically important anti-colonial assemblies continue to influence protest in the postcolony today.[12] Specifically, it argues that anti-colonial movements influence contemporary protests in ways far broader than the traditional Tilly-esque focus on forms and repertoires. While these are certainly an important part of the story, this chapter argues that anti-colonial movements also influence the issues that are protested, as well as the ways in which these issues are presented and framed. Additionally, historic anti-colonial assemblies have also provoked a number of social and political arrangements which, while they are not part of contemporary collective action itself, channel and influence these protest assemblies in important ways. These include often draconian police practices, official views around the legitimacy of assembly, and rules of association.

While similar historical dynamics may influence assembly in the Global North, moreover, this chapter argues further that there is something distinct about the way that anti-colonial movements influence contemporary protest in the postcolony. This is because the dominance of colonial arrangements and the anti-colonial movements make it particularly difficult for activists today to break free from their influence. Ultimately, this chapter argues that the ghosts of the anti-colonial past heavily anchor the forms that activism takes in the postcolony, making it impossible to fully understand contemporary activity without studying and understanding these historical influences. This does not mean that innovation and change is completely absent, however, and the chapter ends by considering some of the ways in which contemporary movements are seeking to move beyond the influences of the past, as well as the possibilities and limitations they face in doing so.

A brief discussion of the term 'postcolonial', as it will be used in this chapter, is necessary before proceeding. The term is a complex and contested one, combining as it does a temporal and a theoretical dimension.[13] Even when it is restricted to the temporal dimension (as it is here), it is not entirely clear quite what should be included and excluded given the long global history of empires, domination, colonialism, and conquest.[14] In this chapter, 'postcolonial' is taken to be a period term, designating the period in any given country which comes after the end of colonial rule in the twentieth century. It is largely taken to be coterminous with the term the 'Global South', while recognizing that there are many who would seek to either expand or restrict that geographic area.[15] And, of course, even with these self-imposed restrictions, the complexity does not completely disappear. In the case of South Africa, for example, which forms a central case study in this chapter, at least three possible dates have been suggested as marking the start of the postcolonial period.[16] In 1931, the British Government granted South Africa dominion status. The country officially became a republic and formally independent of Britain in 1961. And finally in 1994 the country held its first fully democratic elections, ending decades of brutal rule by a White minority. In this chapter I follow postcolonial theorists, such as Edward Said[17] and Anne McClintock,[18] in seeing apartheid as a form of colonialism, and thus seeing the country's first fully democratic elections in 1994 as the key dividing line between the colony and postcolony.[19]

Issues

The first way in which the assemblies of the anti-colonial era continue to influence protest today is through their continuing impact on both the issues protested and the ways in which these issues are discussed and framed.

At perhaps the most obvious level, many protests taking place across the postcolonial Global South explicitly see themselves as continuing the decolonial challenge—fighting to finish the transformation that the earlier movements and assemblies worked towards. Movements such as the Landless Workers' Movement in Brazil or the Hirak Movement in Algeria, for example, draw attention to the limitations of the postcolonial transformation, and explicitly aim to change aspects of the status quo which they argue have their roots in the colonial project, and which continue to detrimentally affect the lives of so many people.[20] As Simukai Chigudu, a founding member of the Rhodes Must Fall movement at Oxford University, states: 'Colonialism . . . never really ended' and there still exists a great need to 'slay the racist ideologies that still [hold] sway' around the world.[21]

Protests demanding the removal of statues or changes to the names of locations and buildings, similarly, often position themselves explicitly as the heirs to the assemblies of the anti-colonial period, fighting to continue a process of decolonization begun often decades earlier.[22] In Namibia in 2020, to provide just one example, protests demanding the removal of the statue of colonial German officer Curt von François in Windhoek highlighted the role he had played in a brutal colonial process, and tied calls for the removal of his statue to broader demands to remove colonial remnant spaces in the city, challenge White supremacy, and push the decolonial transition further.[23] And similar demands have been made in many other countries, including South Africa[24] and India.[25]

Moreover, even movements which ostensibly focus on more contemporary issues, with limited links to earlier anti-colonial demands, often still explicitly reference anti-colonial movements in their framing of issues, positioning their demands in relation to these earlier assemblies. During the Arab Spring, for example, crowds in Egypt and elsewhere in the region described contemporary ruling families as having 'colonized' their countries, positioning their resistance and using 'the same kind of anticolonial protests' to call for change as their parents and grandparents had done against the earlier colonial powers.[26]

And this makes sense for several reasons. First, as many postcolonial scholars and activists have pointed out, even where issues appear, on their face, entirely unrelated to the colonial past, the long shadow of colonialism means that they often have their roots in, or at least links to, some of the same issues that the liberation and anti-colonial movements were fighting against.[27] In the case of the Arab Spring, for example, the oppressive and autocratic rulers being challenged by many of the movements were, in large part, 'the political legacy of colonial rule', making it logical to associate calls for their removal with calls for continued decolonization.[28] The #EndSARS protests that began in 2020 in Nigeria, similarly, while focused ostensibly on protesting contemporary police brutality carried out by the Special Anti-Robbery Squad (SARS)—a unit founded in the postcolonial period—linked many of its claims to the need to push the goals of the anti-colonial movements further. Activists argued that the contemporary problems with brutality in the Nigerian police force have their roots in the police violence of the colonial era, making it essential to consider these longer-term dynamics.[29] Indeed, Nigerian feminist Damola Aluko went so far as to say that full 'liberation is not possible in Nigeria without the abolition of the police' because of the role that police forces played in the colonial era and the continued legacy of this in the country today.[30]

Contemporary protest movements also have another reason to want to link their activity to the assemblies and movements of this earlier time. Liberation movements and anti-colonial assemblies are some of the most influential and valorized protests in recorded history, widely viewed as legitimate, even in the colonizing countries that were their targets. Contemporary movements, therefore, often reach back to these past events and actors to shore up their own legitimacy, positioning themselves as the heirs of this past struggle in order to help gain support.

To provide just one example, the Economic Freedom Fighters (EFF), a political party in South Africa, which was formed in 2013, routinely claims to be the legitimate heir to great freedom fighters of the past, including Nelson Mandela, Solomon Mahlangu, and Steve Biko.[31] Despite the fact that these individuals never had any association with the contemporary political party, the EFF is keen to position itself as continuing their struggle, using their anti-colonial credentials to bolster legitimacy for a young party which has often struggled with image problems.[32] As part of this, they regularly accuse the African National Congress (ANC), the party perhaps best associated with the anti-apartheid liberation movement, as sellouts, and politicians who have been blinded by 'colonialist decorum', while claiming that they (the EFF) are the real heirs of the anti-apartheid struggle.[33]

This does not mean that all postcolonial protests seek to, or need to, link themselves to anti-colonial movements through issues or framing. Many protests around the world are small and very locally focused (e.g. protests over whether or not to place speed bumps on well-travelled roads, or the quality of sanitation in a specific community). These generally lack links to historic movements or issues beyond the immediate. Even here, however, there is always the potential for the ghosts of the anti-colonial past to blow into town in the postcolony, with even small and local issues having the potential to become wrapped up in the language and concepts of decolonization. Protests around the quality of sanitation in small communities in South Africa, for example, are often quickly swept up by political parties and the media into broader debates around justice in the post-apartheid era.[34] Sometimes this is done by the protesters themselves, seeking a bigger stage and more attention for their frustrations, but often it is done as much by the media and wider public, seeking to fit these local complaints into a larger, readily comprehensible, and also politically useful, framework.

And it is here that we find the first big difference between the influence of history on protests in the postcolony and those elsewhere. For, while issues from the past *might* continue to influence protests in the Global North today,[35] plenty of protests and social movements appear relatively unencumbered by the experiences and issues of past protest. Indeed, scholars have even developed the term 'new social movements' to describe what is seen as a new wave of activism in the Global North, distinct from the protests of previous decades, and focused primarily on issues related to human rights and values.[36] While these value-based movements often also exist in the Global South, of course, here they are less likely to be seen as something new, and far more likely to be linked to broader goals of decolonization and the anti-colonial movements of the past. In Zimbabwe, for example, the LGBTQ + movement (often seen in the Global North as a paradigmatic example of a new social movement) has long had to confront claims that homosexuality is a colonial import to the country, forcing the movement to articulate its demands, at least in part, in terms of colonialism and decolonization.[37] While activists in the postcolony may seek to move away from the liberation movements of the past, therefore, they are almost inevitably forced to draw on and engage with them as they do so. Pushed to renegotiate the meaning of decolonization, challenge new issues, and conceptualize new ways of being, but always in conversation with the ghosts of these past assemblies.

Forms and Repertoires

As well as continuing to influence the issues protested in the postcolony, the experiences of anti-colonial movements also continue to reverberate in terms of the forms and repertoires that postcolonial assembly takes. This is not, in and of itself, unique to the postcolony. As Tilly famously observed, 'at any particular point in history . . . [activists] learn only a rather small number of alternative ways to act collectively', and once these forms are learned, shared, and acted out, they tend to be repeated going forward, with new forms appearing relatively rarely.[38] In many countries in the Global South, however, the assemblies that took place during anti-colonial struggles were particularly significant and influential, and it is not surprising, therefore, that their influence on contemporary protest has an unusual hold.

Sites of protest, for example, are often chosen precisely because of their historical resonance, with contemporary protesters continuing to gather in sites and at locations made famous by, or of importance to, earlier movements. Having gained symbolic significance, as many sites did during liberation movements, continuing to hold events in or near these locations can be a powerful way of amplifying messages and increasing the impact of collective action. In South Africa, for example, the township of Soweto—made famous by the 1976 student uprising—continues to act as a key site of contention today, with political and civil society leaders often attending or launching protests there, and parties like the EFF launching manifestos and political campaigns on this symbolic ground. The Zócalo in Mexico City, and the Plaza de Mayo in Argentina, similarly, have long been important locations of protest, acting as focal points for independence movements and contemporary assemblies alike.[39]

In the postcolony, moreover, the historical importance of these sites of protest also intersects in important ways with the continuing dominance of the decolonial issue discussed above. For movements and activists who claim to be continuing the decolonial struggle, holding contemporary events in locations that have a symbolic significance to the anti-colonial movements of the past can be used to make a particularly powerful claim around the unfinished nature of liberation.

In addition to spaces, particular dates associated with previous struggles also often continue to resonate in the postcolony. In South Africa, for example, 21 March, which is officially known as Human Rights Day, commemorates the 1960 Sharpeville massacre, when a protest against the apartheid-era pass laws resulted in the police opening fire on a crowd, killing sixty-nine. Along with 16 June (the anniversary of the Soweto uprising, now commemorated as Youth Day), these dates are routinely used as nationwide protest days. As a South African community activist explained: 'These days are powerful days. They have meaning and memory. They are good days for protest'.[40] Of course, the existence of symbolically important protest days is not unique to the postcolony—for example, annual Labour Day protests and strikes are common across much of Europe—but countries with a recent history of intense struggle are likely to have more of these days, providing a wider range of resonant dates that keep past struggles alive and help to shape contemporary ones.

As well as locations and dates, moreover, the *forms* that contemporary protest takes are also often heavily influenced by repertoires and well-known events associated with the protests of earlier periods. To return to the South African context once more, toyi-toyi, a form of Southern African dance which became a defining feature of anti-apartheid protests, continues to be a central activity at protests today.[41] In fact, the dance is so central to protest activities in contemporary South Africa that civil society organizations known for protest have released albums of 'music to toyi-toyi to'.[42] Meanwhile in neighbouring Zimbabwe, the government has banned toyi-toyi altogether as part of its crackdown on civil dissent.[43] As with the influence of important dates and locations, this influence of history on forms is not unique to protest in the postcolony, but it does seem to have an unusually dominant poignancy there. As a well-known youth activist in Johannesburg explained: 'When you protest in places like London you can pick and choose how you want to do it. If you march or you sit or you barricade everyone knows it is a protest. In South Africa though there must be toyi-toying. Without the toyi-toying it cannot be a protest. It is not possible'.[44]

In sum, dates, locations, and forms from the protest past, while important everywhere, appear to have a greater significance in the postcolony than in Global North, constraining protest in important ways and strongly affecting the repertoires we see. While new forms can and do appear, of course, activists in the postcolony are typically heavily influenced by existing perceptions of what legitimate protest looks like, with less opportunity to innovate and develop new approaches beyond this than is perhaps the case in the Global North.

Social Arrangements

Finally, in addition to influencing the issues protested and the forms and repertoires used, assemblies of the anti-colonial era also exert influence on what Tilly referred to as 'social arrangements': things that are not part of the collective action itself, but which 'channel it to some degree'.[45] These include police practices, laws of assembly, and rules of association. Such social arrangements are critical because they affect who protests and whose protests are seen as legitimate, as well as how protests are organized and policed.

To begin with police practices: The colonial institutions of justice, order, and control that were inherited by newly independent states across much of the Global South tend to ensure that the right to assembly in the postcolony remains complex, constrained, and contested. Modes of control and imprisonment have always been key strategies of colonialism, and although moments of independence offer opportunities to rethink the forces of law and order, all new regimes 'inherit deep structures of thinking and acting from the old'.[46] As a result, it is not uncommon for postcolonial policing to retain strong similarities with the forms of policing that were previously used to oppose anti-colonial movements, such as the use of extreme force, a tendency to overreact to the presence of large groups of people, and the idea of assembly as a threat to the body politic—as fundamentally 'criminal instead of political and revolutionary'.[47]

In many ways, these inherited structures of control are the most striking way in which the anti-colonial era continues to influence postcolonial protest and assembly. For, while policing was obviously not identical in every colony, the tendency for policing to turn excessively violent and for colonial authorities to develop increasingly repressive tools is often seen as a defining feature of policing in colonial empires.[48] While every country around the world struggles with questions of how to police protest (see Probert, this volume), postcolonial regimes typically have unusually controlling and repressive practices and tendencies, inherited from earlier colonial structures, which limit and challenge the concept of public assembly as a political practice in important ways.

In addition to influencing police practices, colonial and anti-colonial experiences also strongly influence views of protest legitimacy in the postcolony. Many of these states came in to being, at least in part, as the result of collective action, assembly, and protest, and, as a result, they might be expected to be pro-assembly. In reality, however, the situation is often far more complex. For some postcolonial states, the awareness of the power of protest to delegitimate and even topple state authority leaves them eager to constrain protest in all its forms, in order to limit any sort of popular challenges to the status quo. As Mbembe states, across much of the postcolonial world challenge is 'forbidden'—controlled through the invention of 'entire constellations of ideas . . . cultural repertoires and powerfully evocative concepts' as well as, where necessary 'the systematic application of pain'.[49]

In other places, however, most notably countries run by former liberation movements, such as Zimbabwe, South Africa, Botswana, and Namibia, blanket repression of protest is more challenging. For former liberation movements, who often rode into power on the back of a wave of popular protest, protest and civil resistance tend to be seen as highly legitimate across society—with struggle credentials often lauded among leading politicians.

Nevertheless, as the moment of liberation recedes into the historical past, these ruling parties often struggle with the idea that they are now the legitimate targets of protests, rather than the true voice of the people, leading to a complicated love-hate relationship with civil unrest. In South Africa, for example, while the ruling ANC party boasts a proud history of protest and assembly during the anti-apartheid era, and continues to organize and support protests today, it also has a tendency to label protests that oppose or challenge it as illegitimate, and even to threaten protest leaders with charges of sedition or treason.[50] In Zimbabwe, similarly, despite the country being a State Party to the 1966 International Covenant on Civil and Political Rights, which recognizes the right of peaceful assembly, the right to protest is even more contentious, with opposition protests subject to often draconian bans and extreme levels of violence.[51]

Contributing to these tensions around protest legitimacy, moreover, many former liberation movements continue to try to position themselves as a, if not *the*, key training ground for activists and protesters (as they were during the anti-colonial era), using their past experiences to train up new activists in their image, and in support of their goals. During the #FeesMustFall protests, for example, sites of protest such as the University of Cape Town experienced often intense tussles for control of events between the old-guard movements (such as the ANC and the South African National Civics Organization) and newer movements such as Fees Must Fall, Rhodes Must Fall, and Patriarchy Must Fall.[52] Indeed, at various times the Fees Must Fall movement was actually accused of treason by the ANC Youth League, with tensions reaching a fever pitch as the ANC Youth League were repelled from taking over and leading the movement.[53] This does not mean the old-guard movements are obsolete, however, and the ANC and its affiliates, in particular, maintain a strong relevance in political and social life across South Africa. Indeed, events since #FeesMustFall have seen many former Fees Must Fall activists move over to represent the ANC and the ANC Youth League in formal politics, using the #FeesMustFall experience as a 'struggle credential'—something that is highly prized in post-apartheid South African politics, but increasingly difficult for younger politicians, born after the anti-apartheid struggle, to gain or demonstrate.[54]

Moments of Innovation and the Influence of the Postcolonial Perspective

This chapter has shown the various and distinct ways in which postcolonial assembly is strongly influenced by the assemblies and experiences of the anti-colonial era. From the issues that are protested, to the forms that protests take, and the ways in which states respond, the influence of these earlier movements is undeniable. However, protest in the postcolony is not a prisoner of its history, and the important role that history plays should not be taken to mean that there is and can be no innovation.

To begin with form and repertoire, for example, an insightful example of changes taking place in the postcolony can be seen with the so-called fallism movements. First developed in South Africa in March 2015, fallism (as it has become known) 'initiated a new form of global socio-political protest, which spread in cities worldwide and was characterized by spatial practices of occupying, modifying and pulling down monuments in public space'.[55] The original fallist movement began on 9 March 2015, when Chumani Maxwele, a student at the University of Cape Town, threw a bucket of human excrement at a statue of Cecil Rhodes on the university campus.[56] His action was supported by a group of students and professors, and rapidly grew into a wider protest movement known as Rhodes Must Fall, which called for the statue to be removed as part of a broader move to transform the campus and remove remnants of White supremacy and colonization.

Over the following months and years, the concept of 'fallism' spread rapidly around the world, including to the Global North, often through social media, and began to be used for other movements in South Africa (such as Fees Must Fall and Patriarchy Must Fall), as well as to guide movements and assemblies in countries ranging from the United Kingdom[57] to the United States[58] and Brazil.[59] These were not the first times that statues have been pulled down, of course. For example, British imperial statues were famously toppled in 1776 when the United States attained independence, as were Tsarist statues in the October Revolution of 1919. And monuments have also been explicitly targeted in contemporary military conflicts, such as Iraq and Syria among others. 'Fallism', however, has become recognized as a new form of contemporary urban activism, aimed not just at destroying statues but also at contesting and transforming public spaces as part of a wider struggle by marginalized and oppressed groups for social recognition and inclusion.[60] Monuments in these moments are attacked as 'symbols', which 'reinforce racism, oppression, discrimination and intolerance with a view of transforming the city into a place of heterogeneity, equality and social justice'.[61] Fallism has been, therefore, a moment in which protest in the postcolony—with its strong historical influences and the ever-lingering presence of the continuing decolonial project—speaks back to the wider world, introducing a new form of protest, but one intimately tied to the experiences and goals of earlier anti-colonial movements.

Pushing innovation further, moreover, while the issues that are protested across the postcolonial world are often heavily influenced and even constrained by the narrative around the importance of continuing the decolonial struggle, many young activists today seek to broaden what decolonization means, explicitly seeking to move beyond what was sought and achieved in the past. In Nigeria, for example, some scholars have read aspects of the #EndSARS movement as an 'indictment of the older generations of Nigerians', arguing that contemporary youth are seeking not simply to push the decolonial project further, but also to reconsider what it means and to reinvent it.[62] While the movement was initially about protesting police brutality committed by the Nigerian Special Anti-Robbery Squad (SARS), it quickly became linked to a broader set of goals around police brutality and systemic injustice. These were linked, in turn, to the need to continue the decolonial struggle. And then, gradually over time, a newer question of intersectionality within the decolonial struggle emerged.[63] Feminists and queer activists spotlighted the ways that injustice, police brutality, and other aspects of continuing oppression impact the lives of women and the LGBTQ + community in Nigeria, drawing attention to the ways in which this has been overlooked by the anti-colonial narratives of older generations. While working within the framework of decolonization, therefore, activists introduced new elements to the concept, and pushed the movement to include not just the removal of lingering colonial aspects in daily life, but also a reconsideration of what it means for all Nigerians to be free.

In Namibia, similarly, activism since 2020 has often sought to move beyond what it sees as the identity politics of the anti-colonial struggle, seeking instead to develop an intersectional activism in which participants 'consciously juxtapose colonial memory with a living vision for the future' that rejects the intersectional inequalities and injustices which postcolonial ruling elites have promoted.[64]

And the influence of the postcolonial perspective is often of particular importance in these moments of innovation—offering a significant opportunity for assembly to move in new directions. Perhaps the clearest example of this in recent years has been seen during the fallist movements discussed above, where discussions have often centred as much on creating a 'new intellectual, political and emancipatory space' to explore questions of decolonization and assembly as on the removal of physical statues.[65] Assembly, for fallist movements, therefore, is not only about bringing around direct change to space and social conditions, but also about opening up new conversations in which the experiences of the marginalized and oppressed are centred and taken seriously, and new ways of thinking, educating, and living can be experienced and debated. In this sense, assembly in the postcolony is not just in conversation with the protests and assemblies of the past; it is also in conversation with postcolonial discussions and debates that are taking place outside the world of assembly.[66] Indeed, as Peter Barry argues: 'If the first step toward a postcolonial perspective is to reclaim one's own past, then the second is to begin to erode the colonialist ideology by which that past had been devalued'.[67] This erosion requires debate, discussion, and the dismantling of the rigid definitions and understandings of both colonialism and protest assembly itself.

While protest and assembly have long been focused on achieving immediate social and political goals, therefore, many postcolonial assemblies, such as fallism, recognize that although these practical goals may be important, something far more radical is needed to really change the status quo and bring about an end to White supremacy and the lingering effects of colonization.[68] These movements recognize that assembly and protest have a critical role to play, not just as a way to bring about change once the goals are agreed upon, but also as a space in which the very goals of decolonization and liberation can be discussed and debated. Rather than just fighting for freedom or questioning authority, postcolonial discussions around assembly move beyond these questions to ask not just who has authority or freedom, but what authority and freedom are and mean at their very core. While assembly in the postcolony might, therefore, be heavily influenced and even constrained by what has come before, the conversations that take place around it inflect far more radical and alternative ideas of the meaning, practice, and ambition of assembly. By highlighting not just the lingering effects of colonialism, but actively seeking to use assembly to discuss alternatives and imagine new and radical futures, protest in the postcolony exists not just as a means of bringing about change, but as a space in which to debate what change even means. In this sense, the postcolony can be seen as a production field,[69] a site in which new knowledge is created and new action writ into the historical experience, which can then be contextualized, reproduced, evaluated, and amended, albeit always in conversation with the past.[70]

CONCLUSION

The influence of history on protest has long been noted by scholars of social movements,[71] but the literature still lacks a detailed understanding of the ways in which earlier assemblies influence activity in the modern day. This chapter provides an initial attempt to fill this lacuna by examining the ways in which a specific set of historical assemblies—anti-colonial movements—influence protest in the postcolonial world today. Drawing on a rich set of examples, it argues that anti-colonial protests influence contemporary protests in ways far broader than the literature has traditionally assumed—affecting not only the forms that protest takes, but also the issues protested and the social and political arrangements that channel protest. Crucially, while some of these connections between past and present may be important globally, this chapter argues further that there is something distinct about the way that anti-colonial movements influence contemporary protest in the postcolony. Specifically, it argues that the dominance of colonial arrangements and anti-colonial movements in the postcolony make it particularly difficult for activists today to break free from their influence, leaving it impossible for us to fully understand contemporary activity without studying and understanding these historical influences. This does not mean that innovation and change are completely absent, however, and the chapter ends by considering some of the ways in which contemporary movements are seeking to move beyond the influences of the past, as well as the possibilities and limitations they face in doing so. It highlights particularly the influence of postcolonial theory in this regard, and the ways in which engagement with postcolonial theory can enable protests in the postcolony to become sites of production and innovation. Future research could fruitfully examine many of these aspects in more detail, with a particular focus on teasing out the mechanisms through which these historical moments have their influence.

NOTES

1. Interview with the author, 21 October 2015.
2. Kay Jones, 'Black Lives Matter—The Voices behind the Placards', *National Museums Liverpool—Stories*, 2020, https://www.liverpoolmuseums.org.uk/stories/black-lives-matter-voices-behind-placards.
3. 'Thousands Participate in Women's March on Washington', *Detroit Free Press*, 2017, https://eu.freep.com/story/news/local/michigan/2017/01/21/womens-march-washington/96847348/.
4. Mark Muhannad Ayyash and Ratiba Hadj-Moussa, eds., *Protests and Generations: Legacies and Emergences in the Middle East, North Africa and the Mediterranean* (Leiden, The Netherland: Brill, 2017), 1.
5. Charles Tilly, 'Contentious Repertoires in Great Britain, 1758–1834', in *Repertoires and Cycles of Collective Action*, ed. Mark Traugott (Durham, NC: Duke University Press, 1995), 15–42.

6. Sidney Tarrow, *Power in Movement: Social Movements, Collective Action and Politics* (New York: Cambridge University Press, 1994).
7. Karl Marx, *The Eighteenth Brumaire of Louis Bonaparte* (1852), 1.
8. Tilly, 'Contentious Repertoires.
9. See e.g. John D. McCarthy and Mayer N. Zald, 'Resource Mobilisation and Social Movements: A Partial Theory', *American Journal of Sociology* 82, no. 6 (1977): 1212–1241; Doug McAdam, '"Initiator" and "Spin-Off" Movements: Diffusion Processes in Protest Cycles', in *Repertoires and Cycles of Collective Action*, ed. Mark Traugott (Durham, NC: Duke University Press, 1995), 217–239; and Rory McVeigh and Christian Smith, 'Who Protests in America: An Analysis of Three Political Alternatives—Inaction, Institutionalized Politics, or Protest', *Sociological Forum* 14, no. 4 (1999): 685–702.
10. Ayyash and Hadj-Moussa, *Protests and Generations*, 1.
11. Marcel Paret, 'Violence and Democracy in South Africa's Community Protests', *Review of African Political Economy* 42, no. 143 (2015): 55.
12. While the title of this volume refers specifically to 'peaceful' assembly, this chapter focuses on assembly more broadly, in recognition of the fact the notion of peaceful protest is a complex and contested one. The labelling of gatherings as either peaceful or violent is overly simplistic, and the decision to label an assembly as one or the other often has as much to do with the interests of those doing the labelling as with the actions of those involved. This chapter, as many others in this volume, does not limit its study to peaceful assembly, therefore, but rather explores protests and the public activities of social movements and activists more broadly.
13. Manfred Liebel, 'Postcolonial Theories from the Global South', in *Decolonizing Childhoods: From Exclusion to Dignity* (Cambridge: Cambridge University Press, 2021), 53–73.
14. Stuart Hall, 'When Was "The Post-Colonial"? Thinking at the Limit', in *The Postcolonial Question*, ed. Iain Chambers and Lidia Curti (London: Routledge, 1995).
15. Ibid.
16. Marshall T. Maposa, 'The Representation of the Temporal Notion of Post-Colonial Africa in South African History Textbooks', *Journal for Transdisciplinary Research in Southern Africa* 14, no. 2 (2018).
17. Edward Said, *Orientalism* (New York: Vintage Books, 1978).
18. Anne McClintock, 'The Angel of Progress: Pitfalls of the Term "Post-Colonialism"', in *Colonial Discourse and Post-Colonial Theory: A Reader*, ed. Patrick Williams and Laura Chrisman (London: Routledge, 1994).
19. See also Maposa, 'Representation of the Temporal Notion of Post-Colonial Africa in South African History Textbooks'.
20. Akosua Adomako Ampofo, 'Re-Viewing Studies on Africa, #Black Lives Matter, and Envisioning the Future of African Studies', *African Studies Review* 59, no. 2 (2016): 7–29; Simran Anjari, 'From Black Consciousness to Black Lives Matter: Confronting the Colonial Legacy of Colourism in South Africa', *Agenda*, 2023, https://doi.org/10.1080/10130950.2022.2166240; Hamza Hamouchene, 'The New Algerian Revolution and Black Lives Matter—A Fanonian Perspective', *The Transnational Institute*, 27 October 2021; David Meek, *The Political Ecology of Education: Brazil's Landless Workers' Movement and the Politics of Knowledge* (Morgantown: West Virginia University Press, 2020); Nisha Thapliyal, '"Legitimate but Not Legal": Learning Power in the Landless Workers Movement (MST), Brazil', *New Directions for Adult and Continuing Education*, 2019, no. 164 (2019): 11–22.

21. Simukai Chigudu, '"Colonialism Had Never Really Ended": My Life in the Shadow of Cecil Rhodes', *The Guardian*, 14 January 2021.
22. Roseanne Chantiluke, Brian Kwoba, and Athinangamso Nkopo, eds., *Rhodes Must Fall: The Struggle to Decolonise the Racist Heart of Empire* (London: Zed Books, 2018).
23. Heike Becker, '"Youth Speaking Truth to Power": Intersectional Decolonial Activism in Namibia', *Dialectical Anthropology* 47 (2023): 71–184.
24. Chantiluke et al., *Rhodes Must Fall: The Struggle to Decolonise the Racist Heart of Empire.*
25. Paul M. McGarr, '"The Viceroys Are Disappearing from the Roundabouts in Delhi": British Symbols of Power in Post-Colonial India', *Modern Asian Studies* 49, no. 3 (2015): 787–831.
26. Josh Sanburn, 'Square Roots: How Public Spaces Helped Mold the Arab Spring', *TIME*, 17 May 2011.
27. Ayyash and Hadj-Moussa, *Protests and Generations*; Adam Branch and Zachariah Mampilly, *Africa Uprising: Popular Protest and Political Change* (London: Zed Books, 2015).
28. Jacqueline S. Ismael and Shereen T. Ismael, 'The Arab Spring and the Uncivil State', *Arab Studies Quarterly* 35, no. 3 (2013): 229.
29. Florence O. Orabueze et al., 'Reminiscence on #EndSARS Protests of 2020 in Nigeria', *Rupkatha Journal on Interdisciplinary Studies in the Humanities* 13, no. 1 (2021): 1–15.
30. Bernard Dayo, 'Can Nigeria's #EndSARS Protests Lead to Police Abolition?', *Al Jazeera*, 23 October 2020.
31. Zach Goldhammer, 'The Coded Clothes of South Africa's Economic Freedom Fighters', *The Atlantic*, 1 August 2014.
32. Ibid.
33. Ibid.
34. Steven Robins, 'The 2011 Toilet Wars in South Africa: Justice and Transition between the Exceptional and Everyday after Apartheid', *Development and Change* 45, no. 3 (2014): 479–501.
35. For example, recent protests around the rights of women in the United States clearly draw and build on earlier suffrage and women's rights movements. Marie Berry and Erica Chenoweth, 'Who Made the Women's March?', in *The Resistance: The Dawn of the Anti-Trump Opposition Movement*, ed. David S. Meyer and Sidney Tarrow (Oxford: Oxford University Press, 2018), 75–89).
36. Nelson A. Pichardo, 'New Social Movements: A Critical Review', *Annual Review of Sociology* 23 (1997): 411–430.
37. Rosie Goldsmith, 'Homosexual and Hated in Zimbabwe', BBC News, 12 August 1998.
38. Tilly, 'Contentious Repertoires, 27.
39. Fernando Bosco, 'Place, Space, Networks, and the Sustainability of Collective Action: The Madres de Plaza de Mayo', *Global Networks* 1, no. 4 (2002): 307–329; Benjamin Bross, *Mexico City's Zócalo: A History of Constructed Spatial Identity* (London: Routledge, 2021).
40. Interview with the author, 21 March 2016.
41. Omatayo Jolaosho, 'Singing Politics: Freedom Songs and Collective Protest in Post-Apartheid South Africa', *African Studies Review* 62, no. 2 (2019): 6–29.
42. Hayde Bangerezako, 'Music to Toyi-Toyi To', *Mail and Guardian*, 28 May 2007.
43. Peta Thornycroft, 'Now Zimbabwe Police Ban Toyi-Toying', *The Mercury*, 26 October 2004.
44. Interview with the author, 16 June 2016.
45. Tilly, 'Contentious Repertoires, 26.

46. Jonny Steinberg, 'Crime Prevention Goes Abroad: Policy Transfer and Policing in Post-Apartheid South Africa', *Theoretical Criminology* 15, no. 4 (2011): 349–364.
47. Sabelo J. Ndlovu-Gatsheni, 'Why Are South African Universities Sites of Struggle Today?', *The Thinker* 70 (2016).
48. Emmanuel Blanchard, Marieke Bloembergen, and Amandine Lauro, eds., *Policing in Colonial Empires* (New York: Peter Lang, 2017).
49. Achille Mbembe, 'Provisional Notes on the Postcolony', *Africa: Journal of the International African Institute* 62, no. 1 (1992): 4.
50. Erin Bates, 'NPA Says It Will Not Hesitate to Prosecute Crimes Including Sedition and High Treason', *Business Day*, 21 July 2021; Rapule Tabane, 'South Africa: Protesters Face Sedition Charges', *Mail and Guardian*, 20 May 2005.
51. Dewa Mavhinga, 'Zimbabwe Bans Demonstrations in Harare', *Human Rights Watch*, 2 September 2016, https://www.hrw.org/news/2016/09/02/zimbabwe-bans-demonstrations-harare; Thornycroft, 'Now Zimbabwe Police Ban Toyi-Toying'.
52. Sizwe Mpofu-Walsh, 'Fallism's Faultlines: The Paradoxes of "Fees Must Fall"', *African Arguments*, 16 June 2021.
53. S'Thembile Cele, 'ANCYL Leader: "#FeesMustFall Is Treason"', *City Press*, 31 January 2016.
54. Mpofu-Walsh, 'Fallism's Faultlines'.
55. Sybille Frank and Mirjana Ristic, 'Urban Fallism: Monuments, Iconoclasm and Activism', *City: Analysis of Urban Change, Theory, Action* 24, no. 3–4 (2020): 552.
56. Nick Shepherd, 'After the #fall', *City: Analysis of Urban Change, Theory, Action* 24, no. 3–4 (2020): 565–579.
57. Haroon Siddique and Clea Skopeliti, 'BLM Protestors Topple Statue of Britsol Slave Trader Edward Colston', *The Guardian*, 2020.
58. Mary Niall Mitchell, '"We Always Knew It Was Possible': The Long Fight against Symbols of White Supremacy in New Orleans', *City: Analysis of Urban Change, Theory, Action* 24, no. 3–4 (2020): 580–593.
59. Renato Cymbalista, 'What to Do with the Bandeirantes: A Challenged Monument in São Paolo, Brazil', *City: Analysis of Urban Change, Theory, Action* 24, no. 3–4 (2020).
60. Frank and Ristic, 'Urban Fallism'.
61. Ibid., 556.
62. Orabueze et al., 'Reminiscence on #EndSARS Protests of 2020 in Nigeria', 2.
63. Ololade Margaret Faniyi, 'A Herstory of #Endsars: Nuances of Intersectionality in Nigeria's Movement against Police Brutality' (Master's thesis, Ohio, Bowling Green State University, 2023), http://rave.ohiolink.edu/etdc/view?acc_num=bgsu1680039616528603.
64. Becker, '"Youth Speaking Truth to Power"', 71.
65. Frank and Ristic, 'Urban Fallism'.
66. Kishan Swaroop Rana, 'Exploring the Elements of Postcolonialism and Its Exponents', *The Creative Launcher* 6, no. 5 (2021): 44–52.
67. As quoted in Rana, 'Exploring the Elements of Postcolonialism and Its Exponents', 44.
68. Paul Maluleka, 'Fallism as Decoloniality: Towards a Decolonised School History Curriculum in Post-Colonial-Apartheid South Africa', *Yesterday and Today* 26 (2021).
69. Karl Maton, *Knowledge and Knowers: Towards a Realist Sociology of Education* (London: Routledge, 2014).
70. Maluleka, 'Fallism as Decoloniality'.
71. See e.g. Richard Flacks, 'Knowledge for What? Thoughts on the State of Social Movement Studies', in *Rethinking Social Movements: Structure, Meaning and Emotion*, ed. Jeff Goodwin and James M. Jasper (Lanham, MD: Rowman & Littlefield, 2004), 135–154; Marx, *The Eighteenth Brumaire of Louis Bonaparte*; Tilly, 'Contentious Repertoires.

Further Reading

Ayyash, Mark Muhannad, and Ratiba Hadj-Moussa, eds. *Protests and Generations: Legacies and Emergences in the Middle East, North Africa and the Mediterranean*. Leiden, The Netherlands: Brill, 2017.

Becker, Heike. '"Youth Speaking Truth to Power": Intersectional Decolonial Activism in Namibia'. *Dialectical Anthropology* 47 (2023): 71–84.

Bosco, Fernando. 'Place, Space, Networks, and the Sustainability of Collective Action: The Madres de Plaza de Mayo'. *Global Networks* 1, no. 4 (2002): 307–329.

Bross, Benjamin. *Mexico City's Zócalo: A History of Constructed Spatial Identity*. London: Routledge, 2021.

Frank, Sybille, and Mirjana Ristic. 'Urban Fallism: Monuments, Iconoclasm and Activism'. *City: Analysis of Urban Change, Theory, Action* 24, no. 3–4 (2020): 552–564.

Liebel, Manfred. 'Postcolonial Theories from the Global South'. In *Decolonizing Childhoods: From Exclusion to Dignity*, 53–73. Cambridge: Cambridge University Press, 2021.

Mitchell, Mary Niall. '"We Always Knew It Was Possible": The Long Fight against Symbols of White Supremacy in New Orleans'. *City: Analysis of Urban Change, Theory, Action* 24, no. 3–4 (2020): 580–593.

Shepherd, Nick. 'After the #fall'. *City: Analysis of Urban Change, Theory, Action* 24, no. 3–4 (2020): 565–579.

CHAPTER 11

REFUGEES, FREEDOM OF ASSEMBLY, AND THE RIGHT TO HAVE A PLACE IN THE WORLD

ASLI İKİZOĞLU ERENSÜ

INTRODUCTION

REFUGEE protests have gained greater visibility across Europe in the twenty-first century. Asylum-seekers and refugees have responded through protest to the securitization of asylum (i.e. the perception of asylum-seekers as potential security threats and associated state practices of restriction of mobility as well as containment within reception facilities), to the de-legitimatization of asylum-seeking with the invention of the figure of the 'bogus asylum-seeker', and to the European Union's attempts at large to prevent asylum-seekers from arriving in Europe instead of seeking protection in their regions of origin. The early 2010s constituted a threshold, arguably even a peak, in refugee activism in Europe, overlapping with the Arab Spring that began in 2011. Throughout 2012 and 2013, refugees were able to mobilize themselves in multiple countries, including Germany, Austria, the Netherlands, Belgium, France, and Italy.[1] These refugee mobilizations paved the way for the 'summer of welcome' in 2015, when ordinary citizens challenged the discourse of a 'refugee crisis' and demanded the reception of refugees, stepping in to provide shelter and other forms of assistance at times when states seemed unable or unwilling to do so.

Refugee activism consists of different modalities, including but not limited to assemblies. While refugee activism is examined from multiple analytical frameworks, such as social movement studies;[2] critical citizenship studies,[3] which include conceptualizations of urban citizenship;[4] and autonomy of migration,[5] specific attention has not been paid to what the practice of assembly affords to refugee activism. This chapter addresses the significance of freedom of assembly for refugees. Yet, in doing so, it also aims to contribute to scholarly understanding of the significance of freedom of assembly for all, regardless of status or possession of papers, and its role in enabling democratic politics.

Refugees have a right of peaceful assembly under international and national laws—a right that is granted to them based on their status, a right that is sanctioned and protected by states which also condition its exercise. Yet, the term 'freedom of assembly' is preferable to 'the right of peaceful assembly' as it highlights the fact that by assembling, refugees are not merely exercising a right given to them but enacting a broader struggle to take the right to have rights (see also Woolman, this volume). Hannah Arendt's famous explication of the right to have rights connects it with 'a right to a place in the world, which makes opinions significant and actions effective':[6] a place where one would be heard, recognized, and responded to by peers. The right to have rights is implicated with the creation of such a place, especially if it has been lost as in the case of refugees.

Accordingly, I understand refugee assemblies as eventful gatherings where the right to a place in the world is enacted. Refugee assemblies pull together multiple senses of place: (1) a physical sense of place as they occupy public spaces during assembly; (2) a global sense of place as the place of assembly is tied up with the global governance of refugee mobility; (3) a local sense of place as many refugee assemblies make demands about leaving, reaching, or remaining in particular places, which either bolster or erode refugees' capacity to realize their right to a place in the world; (4) a legal sense of being in place as many refugee assemblies concern access to legal status; (5) a political sense of place as assembling enables refugees to appear in public as political actors rather than mere humanitarian subjects, to declare that humanitarian authorities cannot represent refugees and to assert their own decision-making capacity; (6) a social sense of place as mutual relations of support develop between refugees, and between protesters and spectators, which help sustain the assembly; (7) a phenomenological sense of place as the assembly experience facilitates belonging; (8) a processual sense of place as refugees make place through assembly; and (9) a foundational sense of place as the assembly embodies a potential re-shaping of the boundaries of the demos it addresses.

Reading refugee assemblies in the light of place-making acquires additional import when we consider that anti-refugee assemblies are also staged as place-defending. Anti-refugee sentiment continues to be on the rise in Europe, overtaking the summer of welcome, and is expressed by way of various demonstrations, marches, and assemblies among other activities. The increased frequency of anti-refugee assemblies not only put a brake on refugee assemblies but also reminds us that assembly as a mode of political activism does not always serve progressive ends. Yet, when thought together, refugee and anti-refugee assemblies attest to the significance of assembly in contesting, making, defending, and re-drawing place and the boundaries of the demos.

To be sure, refugees do not only assemble in protest, nor do they resist only by assembling. On the one hand, mixed migration flows, which include asylum-seekers and refugees, assemble in preparation for border crossings and establish informal encampments.[7] They also assemble virtually for purposes of information-sharing, assistance, and solidarity.[8] On the other hand, refugees resist in different ways; individually, every day, and imperceptibly, or in bursts of more public and publicized events. Collective protest by way of assembly is only one form of refugee resistance amongst others. Saunders and Al-Om[9] even caution that one should not have a publicity bias and prioritize collective protest events in understanding refugee resistance. Heeding these cautionary remarks, the scope of this chapter is nevertheless limited to assemblies for collective protest.

This chapter works through two refugee assemblies, one in Germany and one in South Africa. I refer to all participants in these assemblies as refugees because this is how they self-identified: as persecuted people with a right to international protection. Yet, legally, they could hold different statuses: asylum-seekers in the process of status determination, failed asylum-seekers whose claims have been rejected (some of whom may be in an appeals process), and people given subsidiary or humanitarian protection statuses that fall short of refugee recognition. National and/or international authorities usually tap into these legal differences when de-legitimizing or dispersing an assembly. The two assemblies covered here are neither meant to be seen as representative of all refugee assemblies nor meant to be seen as uniquely significant events. Both assemblies respond to refugees' emplacement by the international refugee regime and their claim to have a place in the world on their own terms. Yet, the differences between these assemblies shed light on the different senses of place mentioned above, and different aspects of place-making through assembly. Before turning to these assemblies, and in order to clarify the stakes of refugee assemblies, the chapter begins by introducing the socio-political context within which refugee assembly as enacting a right to a place in the world occurs, namely, a context in which humanitarianism, and the international refugee regime backed by it, de-politicizes refugees, disallowing their capacity for self-representation and decision-making.

Humanitarianism, Refugees, and a Regime of (Non)-Representation

In an oft-cited article, Malkki refers to refugees as 'speechless emissaries',[10] who want to but are not allowed to speak on their own terms under humanitarian structures. She argues that humanitarian interventions end up de-politicizing refugees, whereby 'refugees stop being specific persons and become pure victims in general'.[11] Relegation to an abstract, universal, suffering subject effectively silences refugees-as-historical-actors. Such silencing is not merely an unfortunate or unintended by-product of humanitarianism; it lies at the core of refugee protection. In the words of Malkki again: 'The ideal construct, the "real refugee" [is] imagined as a particular kind of person: a victim whose judgment and reason ha[s] been compromised by his or her experiences . . . a figure who could be deciphered and healed only by professionals, and who [is] opaque even (or perhaps especially) to himself or herself'.[12] A relation of protection almost necessarily implies that refugees 'need someone [else] to speak for them'.[13]

Scrutinizing the Refugee Convention definition of a refugee as a person with a 'well-founded fear of persecution', Nyers[14] draws attention to the understanding of fear in political theory as an emotion that clouds reasoning and incapacitates human agency. People (in a state of nature in Hobbes's conceptualization) need a sovereign entity to keep danger away, thereby dissolving fear and restoring the fearful to their agency.[15] In the case of refugees, if fear clouds the reasoning of the fearful, somebody other than the fearful, who in contradistinction can reason without hindrance, will need to assess and decide whether the fear is well-founded, that is, based in objective conditions rather than subjective impulses.[16] Nyers argues that such an understanding of fear has substantial consequences for refugee protection. On the one hand, it introduces a hierarchy to refugee protection, by differentiating between the fearful and the one who can reason about the extent and validity of the fear in question. On the other hand, fear serves to keep refugees outside the sphere of politics, where to deliberate, speak, and act, one already needs to be unencumbered by feelings of fear.

Both humanitarianism's and the Refugee Convention's definition of a refugee thus tend to construct refugees as victims who need trustees to represent their interests as if they are children. Yet, in the face of such critique, the UN High Commissioner for Refugees (UNHCR) has for some time promoted refugee participation in the governance of camps. Scholars have been quick to argue that this is part of a larger package of 'responsibilising' refugees for camp administration under neoliberal frameworks of resilience, rather than a call for genuine, democratic engagement in camp life.[17] UNHCR may also work with refugee representatives in camps, who then act as channels of communication between the refugee agency and the rest of the camp residents.[18] However, when refugees contest (through assemblies, boycotts, and other means available in the camps) the terms of participation and representation that they are allowed, they become 'troublemakers'.[19] Both UNHCR and host governments are prone to approach such politicization as threatening to camp order, at times even constituting a national security threat. This may lead to camp 'failures', because of which camps may be evacuated.[20] Refugee participation and self-representation in their own governance can only be tolerated within the parameters set by governing authorities, be they UNHCR officials or host state officials.

For urban refugees, assembling in front of or near UNHCR country offices is a much-used method of protest. In these assemblies, protesters most often condemn the agency for not representing who it should represent and in ways that it should represent them, and they begin to represent themselves. For example, a group of people displaced from Sudan but not recognized as refugees by the UNHCR organized a sit-in in Cairo in 2005. While they claimed themselves to be rightful refugees, they questioned the UNHCR's decision-making power over who gets to be counted as a refugee and accordingly granted protection and care.[21] The agency dealt with their protest by de-legitimizing them as not refugees and re-asserting itself as the only authority that would know who a refugee is, disavowing the contestability of this governmental label.[22] In this protest, as in others, the relations of representation that the UNHCR seemed willing and able to honour were 'founded on a relationship of unequal power of political decision-making'.[23] Refugee assemblies against the UNHCR therefore contain a central tension: Even when they begin by demanding inclusion in the population the agency purports to represent, in assembly, they break from such representation (even if temporarily) since the protesters enact equality—with those holding legal refugee status, and more importantly with those who determine access to legal refugee status.

Refugee assemblies should thus be understood against this background. The logic of humanitarianism and the international refugee regime treats refugees as people whose political agency has been voided through displacement and who therefore need others to represent them. Through assembling, refugees first re-claim a political sense of place: a place from which they appear as capable of political action, a place from which they challenge the knowledge produced on them and the power wielded over them based on this knowledge,[24] a place from which they demand to participate in decisions otherwise taken on their behalf.

A Regime of Distribution and Refugee Assembly as Place-Making

The international refugee regime is as much about partitioning and distributing refugees in the world's space as it is about deciding who a refugee is. Where should refugees go? Which ones should be allowed to pass into the Global North? Within the North, how should states share refugees? Receiving states also develop their own understandings of which country of origin produces people more deserving the status of refugees. Looking into Italy's North African Emergency, declared as a response to the mobilities induced by the Arab Spring, Garelli and Tazzioli identify Italy's partitioning of the asylum-seekers who arrive on its shores: 'Tunisians therefore clandestines' and 'Libyans as war refugees'.[25] Yet another partitioning within asylum-seekers from Libya was also made, whereby fleeing the war in Libya was not sufficient cause to be granted a refugee status if one was not a Libyan national. Those other Africans who were working in Libya when the war struck were sorted out according to their countries of origin, which some had left a long time ago, in assessments of refugee status. Garelli and Tazzioli name such partitioning of asylum-seekers as 'the moral geography of asylum'. Accordingly, moral geographies of asylum reveal how space is used to assign differentiated moral responsibility and thereby lead to diverging 'legal and physical emplacements' for people claiming their right to asylum.[26] The refugee assembly in Hamburg, discussed next, is an example of how refugees posit their own moral geographies while enacting their right to a place in the world, against the enforced emplacements of national and international refugee regimes.

Lampedusa in Hamburg, and Assembling to Remain

In May 2013, a march took place from the main train station in Hamburg, Germany, to the City Hall. A group of refugees had named themselves *Lampedusa in Hamburg* and demanded to meet the mayor. They were war refugees from Libya: not only Libyan nationals but also many sub-Saharan Africans who had worked and lived in Libya and escaped the war and NATO intervention there in 2011. They had first arrived on the Italian island of Lampedusa in the Mediterranean Sea and were housed in Italy's reception centres for eighteen months, only to be released onto the streets, with a humanitarian protection status. Some refugees tried to live in Italy but could neither find work nor shelter given Italy's economic conditions. Many came to Germany and spread to different German cities.[27] However, German authorities claimed that they were under Italy's responsibility and had no legal right to remain in Germany. Germany's refusal was based on the European Union's Dublin regulations,[28] which stipulate that the country of first entry, where fingerprints are taken, is the country from which refugees should seek protection.[29] The mayor of Hamburg did not talk to *Lampedusa in Hamburg* on that day. Yet, in various demonstrations in the city all the way into 2015, the refugees continued to assemble against their emplacement by the Dublin regulations, calling for a new order of refugee mobility within the European space.

Through multiple assemblies, marches, and attempted occupations, *Lampedusa in Hamburg* claimed a political sense of place, from which they advanced their own moral geography of asylum and sought to re-distribute moral responsibility towards them from Italy to Germany. For this, they mobilized their vulnerability[30] by publicly exposing how their Dublin-based emplacement made their lives unliveable and barred their access to a liveable life. They could not subsist in Italy; they could subsist in and socially contribute to Germany, but their Italian papers did not permit them to legally work there, so they had to seek shelter in churches, or live or congregate on the streets. Yet, such mobilization of vulnerability went hand in hand with the establishment of a new kind of sociality within assembly that provided support.[31] In occupied parks, squares, and pavements, assembled refugees might cook, clean, and sleep together; they might sing and read together; they might coordinate daily social life, sanctioning and punishing certain behaviour; they might collectively ensure the safety of their shared space; they might share belongings and information; they might help and care for one another; they might talk and argue with each other and try to reach joint decisions on matters of common concern. In the case of refugee assemblies, such prefigurative socialities are especially significant in the sense that (mutual) relations of support supersede and replace (hierarchical) relations of protection.

This shift from relations of protection to relations of support was observable in the kind of response *Lampedusa in Hamburg* demanded from the city's citizens. Against the hierarchy inherent in protection, whereby the protector does not merely 'shield . . . from harm or danger' but 'extend[s] patronage' to those in need of protection,[32] the protesters sought to enter into relations with Hamburg's activists on the basis of a fundamental equality. At the time in Germany and in Hamburg, different activist groups had already recognized the need to allow asylum-seekers and refugees to self-organize. Activists would accordingly refrain from trying to represent or speak on behalf of *Lampedusa in Hamburg*; they rather provided support for self-mobilization[33] against the governmental mechanisms that render lives precarious (which may cross the citizen-non-citizen divide especially with regards to available housing for the urban poor). Such relations of support, which facilitated the repetition and sustenance of multiple assemblies, also assisted *Lampedusa in Hamburg* to build a social sense of place. If through assembly *Lampedusa in Hamburg* sought political equality, relations of support became the social and material conditions of possibility for such equality.

Lampedusa in Hamburg demanded legalization of their status in Germany. Kesby suggests that in the context of international law, 'a place in the world' delineates a relation between 'physical and legal space' such that one's physical location matches their legal location, as in being a lawful resident of a state.[34] When one is out of place, one is physically present where one legally cannot be. Yet, in struggling to align their physical and legal locations, *Lampedusa in Hamburg* went beyond demanding a simple application of the law and attempted a change in how the laws worked. They not only challenged the Dublin regulations (which denied them legitimate presence in Germany) but also put forth alternative scales of legal recognition. This was evident in how they resisted to go through the federal process of refugee status determination and instead framed a collective right to remain in the city based on Section 23 of the German Residence Act. Section 23 gave the power to the city state of Hamburg (in consultation with the Interior Ministry) to grant group recognition to remain for humanitarian reasons. *Lampedusa in Hamburg* thus opened the existing laws and regulations up to public debate for failing to deliver justice.

Indeed, Butler argues that assemblies wedge an *interval* into time: 'When the legitimacy of a regime or its laws is called into question but when no new legal regime has yet arrived to take its place'.[35] Remaining in assembly is to hold this interval open, with the hope that the current order comes under enough pressure to give way. The interval will hang between, in Benhahib's terminology, jurisgenerativity (the structuration by the existing law of 'an extralegal universe . . . [where] new vocabularies for public claim-making' become available) and jurispathy (when the state uses the same law to dole out violence).[36] It is in this embodied interval (i.e. the assembly) that refugees appear differently—not as humanitarian subjects on behalf of whom asylum laws and regulations have already spoken, not even as people who can speak for themselves (although this is crucial for their re-humanization), but as potential lawmakers. Thus, place-making through assembly is never merely about carving space for oneself in an existing milieu, a kind of fitting in, but involves the questioning, probing, and transgressing of the boundaries of the demos that the assembly addresses. A refugee assembly embodies a potential (re)founding of the demos, a flash-forward into the materialization of that potential. It contains a 'new beginning', whereby actors exercise 'the freedom to call something into being, which did not exist before, which was not given, not even as an object of cognition or imagination, and which therefore, strictly speaking, could not be known'.[37]

More often than not, the beginning is stopped in its tracks, and the pre-existing boundaries of the demos are re-instated. The interval that *Lampedusa in Hamburg* opened was closed down by 'acts of re-taking', which 're-bound . . . political spaces and subjects in ways that are consistent with the political categories of sovereignty (state, citizen, refugee etc.)'.[38] If political activity 'shifts a body from the place assigned to it',[39] sovereign re-takings then return the body to their preordained place. The refugees involved in *Lampedusa in Hamburg* in the end did not receive a collective right to remain in the city based on Section 23 of the German Residence Act. To counter this claim, the Hamburg Senate offered *Duldung*, a German status which would tolerate their presence in the city, temporarily suspend their deportation, and grant limited basic rights. In the meantime, their refugee status could be determined by German federal authorities, potentially reversing their acknowledgement in Italy. The Senate dealt the protesters a further blow by convincing the church network, which acted in solidarity with *Lampedusa in Hamburg*, to promote this plan. This led to an internal split in the group; some members who were closer to the church network decided to go through individual interviews for status determination by German authorities. As a result, their collective claim to group recognition was undermined. Concurrently, as Syrian refugees arrived in Europe in 2015, attention and support of civil society turned to them, taking away from the attention and support given to Libyan war refugees. *Lampedusa in Hamburg* was brought back into the fold of refugee governance, refused to be seen as equal parties in the decision-making process over their status, and reminded that they should wait to be given a place in the world and not dare to take it by themselves.

Yet, it is unfair and unhelpful to expect refugees to finish what they have begun against all odds.[40] Despite failing to achieve their goals, *Lampedusa in Hamburg*'s story of tentative self-determination and exercise of the freedom of assembly to make a place in the world on their own terms remains illustrative. It gives us insight into the multiple senses of place mobilized and enacted in assembly: a political sense of place from which *Lampedusa in Hamburg* addressed the local and national publics, and a legal sense of place from which they engaged in lawmaking. Coupled with a social sense of place filled with relations of support, assembly thus enabled refugees involved in *Lampedusa in Hamburg* to develop a sense of belonging and home-making in the city, which may have continued even after the group's dissolution (see Perolini, this volume).

Greenmarket Square and Assembling to Leave

The refugees involved in *Lampedusa in Hamburg* assembled to demand to remain in Germany. In other cases, refugees believe they are neither protected nor can establish relations of support where they are. They might then assemble to demand to leave and be allowed to go elsewhere. Several countries are not party to the Refugee Convention, not granting refugees full recognition, rights, or a pathway to citizenship. In those countries, refugees may only be temporarily tolerated, whether in camps or in cities. Even when there exists a possibility of some form of legal integration or differential inclusion, refugees may continue to face discrimination, social exclusion, and exploitation, undercutting any sense of protection. In South Africa, even though the country is a signatory to the Refugee Convention, refugees found themselves unable to access protection and they protested to leave in October 2019, targeting the UNHCR for failing to provide them with a solution.

In September 2019, several cities in South Africa (especially Johannesburg and Pretoria) experienced widespread xenophobic unrest, which included the looting of foreign-owned businesses and physical attacks against foreigners.[41] The country's unemployment rate of 30 per cent was believed to fuel these xenophobic sentiments, as some South Africans felt they competed with foreigners for both jobs and government services and accused them of increasing crime. At least twelve people (most of them South Africans) got killed in the ensuing events. This was not the first time that xenophobia erupted into violent rioting in South Africa. A similarly shocking series of events had taken place in 2008, and repeatedly resurged in further events afterwards.

The riots in 2019 caused fear and distress among foreign nationals living in South Africa, including asylum-seekers and refugees. South Africa processes the highest number of asylum claims in southern Africa. As of 2021, around 267,000 people of concern to the UNHCR resided in the country, coming from the Democratic Republic of Congo, Burundi, Angola, Rwanda, Somalia, and Zimbabwe.[42] In October 2019, a month after the xenophobic rioting, refugees began protesting in front of the UNHCR offices in Cape Town and Pretoria. The police forcibly dispersed the protest in Pretoria soon after protesters tried to enter inside the UNHCR office. The protesters in Cape Town, on the other hand, managed to sustain their sit-in for almost six months in 2019 and 2020.[43] They started out by camping at the entrance of the UNHCR office for weeks, eating and sleeping there. When the police removed them (in a manner that was condemned by international human rights groups for its disproportionate violence), protesters occupied the other side of Greenmarket Square, neighbouring the UNHCR office. Some were subsequently given shelter in the nearby Central Methodist Church. The protesters demanded to be resettled outside of South Africa, moved to safer countries on the grounds that they did not feel safe where they were. The UNHCR in turn encouraged reintegration in South Africa and stated that, alternatively, they could choose voluntary repatriation. Resettlement was not an option.[44] The protesting refugees repeatedly refused to return to the communities among which they lived, citing fears that their neighbours did not want them and could even pose a threat to their safety.

While refugees refused their current place, they continued to engage in place-making on two levels. On the one hand, they intervened into the moral geography of asylum, which distributes refugees across the world, and sought a different re-distribution. They challenged the availability and sufficiency of protection in the country of their emplacement and disputed the UNHCR's ability to know what was safe for them. Asking for a solution outside of South Africa, they were seeking a place for themselves on a global scale. Their assembly stood in the middle of a South African city but was situated in a world where refugee mobilities are globally governed.

On the other hand, the response given to their assembly by citizens, civil society actors, and the South African government re-made the city and South Africa as a particular kind of place by re-drawing the boundaries of its demos. While different non-governmental organizations (NGOs) sympathized with the protesters, they were unable to meet them in their political activism. For instance, the head of an NGO, which provided protesters with food, hygienic products, and medical assistance during their prolonged assembly, stated that their demands of resettlement were 'unrealistic'. This led the protesters to ask the NGO to stop their services.[45] In media reports, refugees were sometimes portrayed as causing disorder just so they could be allowed to go to Europe or North America. In these portrayals, refugees did not appear as political actors trying to partake in decisions regarding their futures but were seen as troublemakers not deserving of an equal voice.

In early 2020, protesters were eventually cleared off Greenmarket Square by the police. Their assembly's dissolution came about, in part, by the deepening of a conflict between two internal factions, in a manner similar to the *Lampedusa in Hamburg* case. After the protest was cleared, the protesters were taken to the areas of Bellville and Wingfield in greater Cape Town municipality where they were to be housed in tents as part of South Africa's COVID-19-related public health measures.[46] In October 2022, more than five hundred people remained in tent areas even though the sites were meant to be temporary. The tent areas created internal conflict between governmental authorities, especially after COVID-19 measures were relaxed, as South Africa has no encampment policy for refugees.[47] In this legal quagmire, residents were to choose between two options: either return to their countries of origin (by April 2021, 121 had chosen to repatriate)[48] or re-integrate in South Africa. In the meantime, (at least) forty-one people alongside three protest leaders and spokespersons were deported (with one first serving jail time).[49]

While protesters were thus kept together en masse, they could no longer appear as an assembly as they were excluded from public space and from making their demands public. Some news media instead referred to protest leaders as 'ringleaders' and the then Home Affairs Minister portrayed the rejection of their asylum claims as proof that their protest was already not justified.[50] The association of protesters with criminality and abuse of the asylum system through unfounded claims went hand in hand with the reduction of their assembly to a mob. The presentation of non-citizen gatherings as mobs serves to 'downplay the political dimension of their struggles for movement and . . . thwart[s] the possibility of a multiplicity becoming a collective political subject'.[51]

Mobs and assemblies are indeed placed at opposite poles in democratic theory. Mobs take their strength from their numbers and are prone to violence. They lead to de-individuation (see Adang, this volume), whereby participants begin to act like they are one body. Mobs are also considered apolitical because their demands are regarded as irrational and/or ambiguous. While the demos and their assemblies are 'perceived as the orderly force that democracies needed to foster and to sustain, the mob [is understood as] the antinomy of the demos, the excess and unrest that could only be perceived as threatening for democratic forces'.[52] In contradistinction to a conceptualization of assemblies as healthy and necessary components of a functioning democracy, mobs are a matter of law enforcement and public order.

Some migration scholars resist such de-legitimization and criminalization of non-citizen collective action through the figure of the mob. Tazzioli,[53] for instance, highlights how (migrant) mobs are in fact produced by migration policies; they are what remains after migration policies partition people on the move into different governable categories. In the South African case, Moyo and Zanker[54] explain that country officials have been increasingly (1) migrantizing refugees in policy discourse and legal regulation, that is, conflating asylum-seekers in need of protection with undocumented/irregular migrants, thereby delegitimizing asylum; (2) associating asylum-seekers and refugees with criminality, law-breaking, and public order disruption through such conflation; (3) thereby fuelling xenophobic sentiments against refugees and asylum-seekers; and (4) putting the blame for their problems in accessing protection on them rather than questioning the role of government policies and practices (including backlogs, problems with renewal of permits, and legal changes). Such a policy environment may have played a role in the production of the collectivity that officials then referred to as a mob in the Greenmarket Square case. Yet, Tazzioli[55] argues that being in excess to governmental categorization and policymaking is what gives (migrant) mobs their political character, rather than placing them outside politics.

Aradau and Huysmans[56] similarly re-appropriate the (migrant) mob as a collective force of democratizing politics of mobility. When migrants and refugees make claims on the basis of rights, the workings of the law in adjudicating these claims 'individualise and thus particularise collective demands',[57] and often simply reproduce the existing governmental classifications and exclusions, as we have seen in the case of *Lampedusa in Hamburg*. Against these limitations of the law, the (migrant) mob asserts blanket equality, demands a re-organization of the relations between the citizenry and its others, and 'functions . . . as a "check" upon the democratic practices of rights (by challenging who is a subject of rights and which agents and institutions are allowed to be rights mediators)'.[58] The (migrant) mob in this way becomes vital to the ongoing democratic transformation of the citizenry and is brought back into the realm of politics. In such conceptualizations, any attempts to police a boundary between the assembly and the mob also break down.

Conclusion: The Future for Refugee Assemblies

If one way to emphasize the role of non-citizen collective action in democratizing the politics of mobility is to recover the (migrant) mob as a democratic force, another way to this end could be to insist on naming such collective action as assemblies per se and highlighting the assembly qualities of such action. On the one hand, the practice of assembly is still very closely associated with the citizenry. From ancient Greece, where citizens assembled to directly govern their city states (see Srinivasan, this volume), to citizens' assemblies of the twenty-first century where groups of citizens deliberate together matters of public concern and take part in decision-making more directly than they could by selecting representatives,[59] the word 'assembly' connotes citizen participation and empowerment (against disenfranchisement). Accordingly, a refugee assembly could be considered an act of citizenship in the sense that refugees act as if they are citizens when they gather in assemblies, despite the fact that they do not hold membership status.[60] When a group of undocumented migrants (sans-papiers) in France occupied a church in protest in Paris in 1996, the renowned French philosopher Etienne Balibar contended that sans-papiers had reminded citizens that citizenship 'is not an institution nor a status, but a collective practice' of 'stimulating new forms of activism and renewing old ones'.[61] In democracies, he declared, 'people must always conquer the right to speak, their visibility and credibility, running the risk of repression'.[62] Therefore, this was a case of non-citizens teaching citizens what citizenship was about.

On the other hand, migration scholarship would also advise against uncritically applying criteria used for making sense of citizen assemblies (such as 'visibility, agency, and collective public mobilization') as 'yardsticks' with which to measure non-citizen collective action,[63] and caution against the risk of prioritizing more visible protest events at the expense of more common, more mundane and more sustained practices of everyday resistance. In explaining migrant (and refugee) struggles, Casas-Cortes et al. differentiate between 'more or less organized struggles in which migrants openly challenge, defeat, escape or trouble the dominant politics of mobility' and 'daily strategies, refusals, and resistances through which migrants enact their (contested) presence—even if they are not expressed or manifested as 'political' battles demanding something in particular'.[64] For Casas-Cortes et al., while the first kind of struggles necessitate 'the emergence of their subjects on the "scene" of the political', the second kind 'are not perceptible in the ordinary regime of visibility and do not fit into established paradigms of political representation'.[65]

There thus appears to be an opposition between eventful and everyday resistance in non-citizen struggles. Assemblies undeniably have eventful characteristics, not least in terms of their increased visibility, the related media attention they can garner, the measure of collective organization they need, and their heightened consequences for participants (such as detention and/or deportation in the case of migrants and refugees). Analysing assemblies as events has its merits, especially if one conceives that a protest is eventful by being transformative not only of the socio-political structures that it targets but also of its participants (for instance, by empowering new actors, changing their self-understanding, and building new relations between actors).[66]

This chapter focused on two assembly events; however, it examined them less as events than as practices of place-making. Spatiality is significant to migrant and refugee lives, both in the everyday as they strive to make new homes and make new cities their own and in protest as they use public spaces to make their demands public.[67] The arguments here aim to transcend any simple opposition between eventful resistance and everyday resistance by not limiting assemblies to their immediate spatialities and temporalities, whereby a linear 'process of claims-making . . . [is] followed by one or another (negative or positive) institutional resolution'.[68] 'A place in the world' is a multifaceted, multilayered notion and the power of assemblies lies in their ability to activate and harness this multiplicity across different scales and temporalities.

Instead of pitting eventful/visible and everyday/invisible non-citizen resistances against each other, a more integrated take allows us to view assemblies in a different light. While an assembly is visible in the sense of being publicly seen (even exposed to law enforcement), we cannot assume, as De Genova et al. warn us, that a struggle is 'truly "visible" or "invisible" in any simple sense' without first scrutinizing 'the political hierarchies of visibility that make something appear more or less visible or invisible within the dominant sociopolitical imagination'.[69] An assembly may be visible in the sense of being seen and it may be audible in the sense of being heard, but this by itself does not mean what they say or do will be registered as significant or effective by the rest of the political community. Gündoğdu explains, following Rancière,[70] that 'it is not known in advance whether "a sonorous emission" will be "understood as speech, capable of enunciating what is just," or simply as "a noise signaling pleasure or pain, consent or revolt" '.[71] Thus, as eventful as they are, assemblies have degrees of visibility and audibility based on the extent to which what they say is understood to be relevant and what they do is understood to be meaningful by their audiences. Though there is no guarantee, a place in the world opens when an assembly can transform noise into an embodied address of others.

Refugee assemblies can then be thought of as staging a collective taking of the right to a place in the world. Yet, the phrase 'refugee assembly' could soon turn into an anachronism. With the increased use of detention for purposes of immigration control across the world, asylum-seekers and refugees among other migrants are also being denied the possibility of engaging in collective action (though they may continue to resist individually).[72] In such spaces, they are not only isolated from the public eye but may also be separated from one another in solitary cells. However, even when tucked away from the public, asylum-seekers may create new ways to fall within their sight and sound (see Zick, this volume, on an assembly's right to be within sight and sound of intended audiences). During the COVID-19 pandemic, Italy resorted to quarantining ships it suspected of carrying irregular migrants and asylum-seekers at sea. Some of those stuck on the ships were able to communicate with the outside world, especially with activists in solidarity with their plight in Italy. According to Denaro and Boccagni,[73] using their phones they sent pictures and videos documenting their conditions on board, which were then circulated by their Italian counterparts over social media. They inquired about what rights they could each access from their place on a ship, contacted legal counsellors via messaging, and were even able to give them power of attorney to work on their behalf by sharing photos of handwritten petitions. This provides a powerful example to how digital communication technologies can support taking collective action to reach a targeted audience. Future research will thus have to focus both on what effectively prevents refugee assemblies from taking place, such as increasing detention practices, and on what refugees do to still find ways to appear in public and claim a place in the world.

Notes

1. Katrin McGuaran and Kees Hudig, 'Refugee Protests in Europe: Fighting for the Right to Stay', *Statewatch Journal* 23, no. 3/4 (2014): 28–33; Matthew Willner-Reid, 'Emergence and Decline of a Protest Movement: The Anti-Deportation Campaign for Afghan Asylum Seekers in Belgium', *Journal of Refugee Studies* 28, no. 4 (2015): 505–522; Martina Pasqualetto and Fabio Perocco, 'For Dignity, against Racism: The Struggles of Asylum Seekers in Italy', in *Stuck and Exploited: Refugees and Asylum-Seekers in Italy between Exclusion, Discrimination and Struggles*, ed. Francesco Della Puppa and Giuliana Sano (Rome: Edizioni Ca'Foscari, 2021), 215–235.
2. Donatella Della Porta, ed., *Solidarity Mobilizations in the 'Refugee Crisis': Contentious Moves* (London: Palgrave Macmillan, 2018); Sieglinde Rosenberger et al., eds., *Protest Movements in Asylum and Deportation* (Cham, Switzerland: Springer, 2018); Pierre Monforte, *Europeanizing Contention. The Protest against 'Fortress Europe' in France and Germany* (New York: Bergahn Books, 2014); Federico Oliveri, 'Struggles at the Boundaries of Neoliberal Citizenship: Theorizing Immigrant-Led Movements in Contemporary Europe', in *An Anthology of Migration and Social Transformation*, ed. Anna Amelina et al. (Cham, Switzerland: Springer, 2016), 263–279.
3. Imogen Tyler and Katarzyna Marciniak, 'Immigrant Protest: An Introduction', *Citizenship Studies* 17, no. 2 (2013): 143–156; Ilker Ataç, Kim Rygiel, and Maurice Stierl, 'Introduction: The Contentious Politics of Refugee and Migrant Protest and Solidarity Movements: Remaking Citizenship from the Margins', *Citizenship Studies* 20, no. 5 (2016): 527–544.
4. Harald Bauder, 'Possibilities of Urban Belonging', *Antipode* 48, no. 2 (2016): 252–271.
5. Heather Johnson, 'These Fine Lines: Locating Noncitizenship in Political Protest in Europe', *Citizenship Studies* 19, no. 8 (2015): 951–965.
6. Hannah Arendt, *The Origins of Totalitarianism* (New York: Harcourt, 1951), 296.
7. Thom Davies et al., 'Informal Migrant Camps', in *Handbook on Critical Geographies of Migration*, ed. Katharyne Mitchell, Reece Jones, and Jennifer L. Flori (New York: Edward Elgar, 2020), 220–231.
8. Nicos Trimiklinotis et al., 'Mobile Commons and/in Precarious Spaces: Mapping Migrant Struggles and Social Resistance', *Critical Sociology* 42, no. 7–8 (2016).
9. Natasha Saunders and Tamara Al-Om, 'Slow Resistance: Resisting the Slow Violence of Asylum', *Millennium: Journal of International Studies* 50, no. 2 (2022): 524–547.
10. Liisa Malkki, 'Speechless Emissaries: Refugees, Humanitarianism and Dehistoricization', *Cultural Anthropology* 11, no. 3 (1996): 377–404.
11. Ibid., 378.
12. Ibid.
13. Ibid., 388.
14. Peter Nyers, *Rethinking Refugees Beyond States of Emergency* (New York: Routledge, 2006).
15. Ibid., 53.
16. Nyers does not mean to suggest that the refugee's capacity for reasoning is totally annulled by fear; in the end the refugee claimant will still need to prove the likelihood of their persecution.

17. Suzan Ilcan and Kim Rygiel, '"Resiliency Humanitarianism": Responsibilizing Refugees through Humanitarian Emergency Governance in the Camp', *International Political Sociology* 9, no. 4 (2015): 333–351.
18. Clara Lecadet, 'Refugee Politics: Self-Organized "Government" and Protests in the Agame Refugee Camp (2005-2013)', *Journal of Refugee Studies* 29, no. 2 (2016): 187–207; Naohiko Omata, 'Unwelcome Participation, Undesirable Agency? Paradoxes of De-Politicisation in a Refugee Camp', *Refugee Survey Quarterly* 36, no. 3 (2017): 108–131.
19. Simon Turner, 'Negotiating Authority between UNHCR and "the People"', *Development and Change* 37, no. 4 (2006): 759–778.
20. Elizabeth Holzer, 'A Case Study of Political Failure in a Refugee Camp', *Journal of Refugee Studies* 25, no. 2 (2012): 257–281.
21. Carolina Moulin and Peter Nyers, '"We Live in a Country of UNHCR"—Refugee Protests and Global Political Society', *International Political Sociology* 1, no. 4 (2007): 356–372.
22. Ibid.
23. Michael Hardt and Antonio Negri, *Assembly* (New York: Oxford University Press, 2017).
24. Moulin and Nyers, 'We Live'.
25. Glenda Garelli and Martina Tazzioli, 'Arab Springs Making Space: Territoriality and Moral Geographies for Asylum Seekers in Italy', *Environment and Planning D: Society and Space*, 31 (2013): 1004–1021.
26. Ibid., 1013.
27. Simone Beate Borgstede, '"We Are Here to Stay". Reflections on the Struggle of the Refugee Group "Lampedusa in Hamburg" and the Solidarity Campaign, 2013–2015', in *Migration, Squatting and Radical Autonomy: Resistance and Destabilization*, ed. Pierpaolo Mudu and Sutapa Chattopadhyay (London: Routledge, 2017), 162–179; Martin Bak Jørgensen, '"A Goat That Is Already Dead Is No Longer Afraid of Knives": Refugee Mobilizations and Politics of (Necessary) Interference in Hamburg', *Ethnologia Europaea* 49, no. 1 (2019): 41–57; Susi Meret and Waldemar Diener, 'We are Still Here and Staying! Refugee-Led Mobilizations and Their Struggles for Rights in Germany', in *Citizens' Activism and Solidarity Movements*, ed. Birte Siim et al. (London: Palgrave, 2019), 137–166; Matthew Sparke and Katharyne Mitchell, 'Lampedusa in Hamburg and the "Throwntogetherness" of Global City Citizenship', in *Doreen Massey: Critical Dialogues*, ed. Marion Werner et al. (New York: Agenda, 2018), 215–231.
28. Short for 'Regulation establishing the criteria and mechanisms for determining the Member State responsible for examining an asylum application lodged in one of the Member States by a third-country national' (www.unhcr.org/media/dublin-regulation).
29. There exists a developing literature on refugees' resistance and refusal of Dublin regulations. Contestation does not always take visible and collective forms but continues in less visible, individual ways. See, for instance, Fazila Bhimji, 'Contesting the Dublin Regulation: Refugees' and Migrants' Claims to Personhood and Rights in Germany', *Intersections* 2, no. 4 (2016): 51–68.
30. Judith Butler, *Notes towards a Performative Theory of Assembly* (Cambridge, MA: Harvard University Press, 2015).
31. Ibid., 84.
32. Jef Huysmans, 'Agency and the Politics of Protection: Implications for Security Studies', in *The Politics of Protection: Sites of Insecurity and Political Agency*, ed. Jef Huysmans et al. (London: Routledge, 2006), 15.
33. Meret and Diener, 'We Are', 2019.

34. Alison Kesby, *The Right to Have Rights: Citizenship, Humanity and International Law* (New York: Oxford University Press, 2012), 14.
35. Butler, *Notes Toward*, 75.
36. Seyla Benhabib, *Exile, Statelessness and Migration: Playing Chess with History from Hannah Arendt to Isaiah Berlin* (Princeton, NJ: Princeton University Press, 2018), 121.
37. Cristina Beltran, 'Going Public: Hannah Arendt, Immigrant Action, and the Space of Appearance', *Political Theory* 37, no. 5 (2009): 595–622.
38. Moulin and Nyers, *We Live*.
39. Jaques Rancière, *Dis-agreement: Politics and Philosophy*, trans. J. Rose (Minneapolis: University of Minnesota Press, 1999), 30.
40. Benhabib, *Exile, Statelessness*.
41. Human Rights Watch, *'They Have Robbed Me of My Life': Xenophobic Violence against Non-nationals in South Africa*, 17 September 2020, https://www.hrw.org/report/2020/09/17/they-have-robbed-me-my-life/xenophobic-violence-against-non-nationals-south.
42. UNHCR, *Fact Sheet: South Africa Representation and Multi-Country Office*, January–March 2021, https://reporting.unhcr.org/sites/default/files/South%20Africa%20fact%20sheet%20January-March%202021.pdf.
43. Sisonke Mlamla, 'Refugees in SA Hoping to Get Solution from UNHCR Soon', IOL, 18 October 2019, https://www.iol.co.za/news/south-africa/western-cape/refugees-in-sa-hoping-to-get-solution-from-unhcr-soon-35275666.
44. Anne Juliane Ulrike Görgmeier, 'Between a Rock and a Hard Place: Exploring Xenophobia and Voluntary Refugee Repatriation in South Africa' (MPhil diss., University of Cape Town, 2020).
45. Kaylynn Palm, 'Gift of the Givers Withdraws Services from Refugees after Being Told to Leave', Eyewitness News, 7 November 2019, https://ewn.co.za/2019/11/07/gift-of-the-givers-withdraws-services-from-refugees-after-being-told-to-leave.
46. Brendan Magaar, 'Three Years Later Plight of Protesting Refugees Worsens', *Weekend Argus*, 8 October 2022, https://www.iol.co.za/weekend-argus/news/three-years-later-plight-of-protesting-refugees-worsens-d77e2e7c-de7c-4390-86ed-331052bd4112.
47. Nomzamo Yuku, 'Blame game as to who must account for the refugees and councillor wants them out'. *Weekend Argus*, 4 March 2023, https://www.iol.co.za/weekend-argus/news/blame-game-as-to-who-must-account-for-the-refugees-and-councillor-wants-them-out-c0513d49-88e4-48fe-96f4-52532de69645.
48. Tarryn-Leigh Solomons, 'No such thing as refugee camps in SA, says Motsoaledi'. IOL Politics, 20 April 2021, https://www.iol.co.za/news/politics/no-such-thing-as-refugee-camps-in-sa-says-motsoaledi-b95da83e-712d-4c7d-b70f-f43fe4e4910f.
49. Mwangi Githahu, 'Clock ticking for Cape refugees to either reintegrate or be deported'. Cape Argus, 21 April 2021, https://www.iol.co.za/capeargus/news/clock-ticking-for-cape-refugees-to-either-reintegrate-or-be-deported 088c0299-d714-4e18-a4de-3946bf55d7a9
50. Aphiwe Deklerk, 'Ringleaders of Cape Town refugee protests kicked out of SA'. Times Live, 19 April 2021, https://www.timeslive.co.za/news/south-africa/2021-04-19-ringleaders-of-cape-town-refugee-protests-kicked-out-of-sa/.
51. Martina Tazzioli, 'The government of migrant mobs: Temporary divisible multiplicities in border zones', *European Journal of Social Theory* 20, no. 4 (2017): 473–490, 483.
52. Claudia Aradau and Jef Huysmans, 'Mobilising (Global) Democracy: A Political Reading of Mobility between Universal Rights and the Mob', *Millenium: Journal of International Studies* 37, no. 3 (2009): esp. 597.

53. Tazzioli, *The Government of Migrant Mobs.*
54. Khangelani Moyo and Franzisca Zanker, 'No Hope for the 'Foreigners': The Conflation of Refugees and Migrants in South Africa', *Journal of Immigrant & Refugee Studies* 20, no. 2 (2022): 253–265.
55. Tazzioli, *The Government of Migrant Mobs.*
56. Aradau and Huysmans, *Mobilising (Global).*
57. Ibid., 602.
58. Ibid., 603.
59. Carole Pateman, 'Participatory Democracy Revisited', *Perspectives on Politics* 10, no. 1 (2012): 7–19.
60. See Tyler and Marciniak, 'Immigrant Protest: An Introduction'; and Ataç et al., 'Introduction: The Contentious Politics of Refugee and Migrant Protest and Solidarity Movements'.
61. Étienne Balibar, *What We Owe to the Sans-Papiers*, Speech given at French Filmmakers' Union, Paris, March 1997.
62. Ibid.
63. Maribel Casas-Cortes et al., 'New Keywords: Migration and Borders', *Cultural Studies* 29, no. 1 (2015): esp. 82.
64. Ibid., 80.
65. Ibid., 81–82.
66. Donatella Della Porta, 'Eventful Protest, Global Conflicts', *Distinktion: Scandinavian Journal of Social Theory* 9, no. 2 (2008): 27–56
67. Ilker Ataç '"Refugee Protest Camp Vienna": Making Citizens through Locations of the Protest Movement', *Citizenship Studies* 20, no. 5 (2016): 629–646.
68. Casas-Cortes et al., *New Keywords*, 82.
69. Nicholas De Genova et al., 'Minor Keywords of Political Theory: Migration as a Critical Standpoint', *EPC: Politics and Space* 40, no. 4 (2022): esp. 798.
70. Rancière, *Dis-agreement: Politics and Philosophy*, 23.
71. Ayten Gündoğdu, *Rightlessness in an Age of Rights: Hannah Arendt and the Contemporary Struggles of Migrants* (New York: Oxford University Press, 2015), 191.
72. Ibid.
73. Chiara Denaro and Paolo Boccagni, 'Migration, Borders and "De- bordering" in Pandemic Times: Voices as Interlocution from Quarantine Ships in Italy', *Journal of Borderlands Studies*, advance online publication, https://doi.org/10.1080/08865655.2022.2108110.

Further Reading

Ataç, Ilker, Kim Rygiel, and Maurice Stierl, eds. *The Contentious Politics of Refugee and Migrant Protest and Solidarity Movements: Remaking Citizenship from the Margins.* London: Routledge, 2017.

Beltran, Cristina. 'Going Public: Hannah Arendt, Immigrant Action, and the Space of Appearance'. *Political Theory* 37, no. 5 (2009): 595–622.

Benhabib, Seyla. *Exile, Statelessness and Migration: Playing Chess with History from Hannah Arendt to Isaiah Berlin.* Princeton, NJ: Princeton University Press, 2018.

Butler, Judith. *Notes towards a Performative Theory of Assembly.* Cambridge, MA: Harvard University Press, 2015.

De Genova, Nicholas, Martina Tazzioli, Claudia Aradau, and Brenna Bhandar. 'Minor Keywords of Political Theory: Migration as a Critical Standpoint'. *EPC: Politics and Space* 40, no. 4 (2022): 781–875.

Della Porta, Donatella, ed. *Solidarity Mobilizations in the 'Refugee Crisis': Contentious Moves*. London: Palgrave Macmillan, 2018.

Gündoğdu, Ayten. *Rightlessness in an Age of Rights: Hannah Arendt and the Contemporary Struggles of Migrants*. New York: Oxford University Press, 2015.

Holzer, Elizabeth. *The Concerned Women of Buduburam: Refugee Activists and Humanitarian Dilemmas*. Ithaca, NY: Cornell University Press, 2015.

Honig, Bonnie. *Democracy and the Foreigner*. Princeton, NJ: Princeton University Press, 2001.

Huysmans, Jef, Andrew Dobson, and Raia Prokhovnik, eds. *The Politics of Protection: Sites of Insecurity and Political Agency*. London: Routledge, 2006.

McNevin, Anne. *Contesting Citizenship: Irregular Migrants and New Frontiers of the Political*. New York: Columbia University Press, 2011.

Moulin, Carolina, and Peter Nyers, '"We Live in a Country of UNHCR"—Refugee Protests and Global Political Society'. *International Political Sociology* 1 (2007): 356–372.

Nyers, Peter, and Kim Rygiel, eds. *Citizenship, Migrant Activism, and the Politics of Movement*. London: Routledge, 2012.

Rosenberger, Sieglinde, Verena Stern, and Nina Merhaut, eds. *Protest Movements in Asylum and Deportation*. Cham, Switzerland: Springer, 2018.

Stierl, Maurice. *Migrant Resistance in Contemporary Europe*. New York: Routledge, 2019.

PART II

PEACEFUL ASSEMBLY AS A RIGHT

CHAPTER 12

THE DEFINITION OF PEACEFUL ASSEMBLY

YUVAL SHANY

INTRODUCTION

THE definition of what constitutes a peaceful assembly predetermines the scope of protection afforded by the right of peaceful assembly, and which individual and societal interests and values the right would be able to uphold. The interests and values that underlie the right explain, in turn, the kind of protections available, and the specific exceptions from protection which existing laws may allow. Although the definition of peaceful assembly is important from both a theoretical and practical perspective, its importance need not be overstated: the fact that a gathering or a collective message does not fall within the scope of 'peaceful assembly', as defined in international human rights law (IHRL), does not mean that it is not protected by other provisions of IHRL, such as freedom of expression or association. Still, these alternative protections may be sub-optimal in nature since they lack some of the specific procedural guarantees and nuanced balancing, which exist in connection with the right of peaceful assembly.

The term 'peaceful assembly' is not defined in IHRL treaties, nor is it common to find a definition for the term 'assembly' in national constitutional texts.[1] In some national constitutions, the notion of peacefulness is explicitly linked to absence of arms.[2] In some others, the right of peaceful assembly is associated with demonstrations;[3] and yet in others, it is tied to the term 'petition'.[4] It is against this background of a lack of a clear definition in domestic constitutional law and international law, that the work of IHRL bodies seeking to elaborate the contents of state obligations to implement the right of peaceful assembly assumes particular significance.

This chapter focuses on the manner in which two IHRL bodies have recently defined the term 'peaceful assembly' and thus the scope of protection afforded by the right of peacefully assembly. These are the Human Rights Committee, which dedicated a recent general comment—General Comment No. 37 (2020)[5]—to the right of peaceful assembly, and the European Commission for Democracy through Law (Venice Commission) and the Office for Democratic Institutions and Human Rights of the Organization for Security and Co-operation in Europe (OSCE/ODIHR), which published an update to its Guidelines on Freedom of Peaceful Assembly in 2019.[6] In preparing these two documents, both bodies engaged in extensive discussions—including comments from the public and consultations between them—on the definition of the term 'peaceful assembly' and its conceptual underpinnings. Commentary and debate also extended to the term's associative, expressive, and participatory dimensions, and its application to the online domain. Such discussions provide an important background to the documents the two IHRL bodies produced.

In this chapter, I survey and analyse the positions adopted by the Human Rights Committee and ODIHR/Venice Commission on key aspects of the definition of the term 'peaceful assembly'. The chapter also discusses the implications of the interpretative choices made by the Committee and ODIHR/Venice Commission, as far as they concern the scope of protection afforded to the right of peaceful assembly. I start by discussing the relationship between the associative, expressive, and political components of the right of peaceful assembly and move on to describe specific interpretative choices relating to the purposeful gathering requirement, as well as specific issues relating to online assemblies and conditions for 'peacefulness'.

Associative, Expressive, and Participatory Rights and Interests

The right of peaceful assembly is analytically situated at the crossroads of several other human rights, which share with it certain features and justifications. There is little question that it involves a collective act—that is, a purposeful gathering of individuals—which constitutes a form of *association*, albeit one that is loose in nature, informal in its manner of organization, and temporary in its duration. Indeed, the right of peaceful assembly shares with the freedom of association the protection of similar individual and collective interests: enabling individuals to enjoy the sense of solidarity and community spirit (*commūnitas*) that derives from belonging to a group, the valuable inter-personal social interactions that being in a group facilitates, and the social empowerment that derives from being part of a larger group.[7]

Peaceful assemblies often also involve an act of collective expression.[8] Many assemblies involve a communicative dimension and facilitate expression of ideas and opinion by assembly participants.[9] To the extent that the expression is collective in its nature—in that the same messages are shared or endorsed by all or most assembly participants—the assembly helps in amplifying its resonance. The size of the assembly, its frequency, and other features allow participants and observers to assess the extent of public support the expression in question enjoys.[10]

The justifications for protecting the right of peaceful assembly draw historically primarily from the justifications for protecting freedom of expression,[11] although not all assemblies involve a clear expressive dimension.[12] Indeed, some purposeful gatherings may be part of mundane social activities, such as a family dinner, celebration, or funeral, or they may serve a functional objective, such as participating in a beach clean-up operation or forming a search party. The justifications for protecting such non-expressive purposeful gatherings may be similar to the justifications appertaining to freedom of association, although, here too, there is no full overlap between the scope of the right and its underlying justifications. In fact, most peaceful assemblies do not have the formal and long-term characteristics that would enable them to qualify as an 'association', as that term is understood under many domestic laws.[13] Neither does the organization of peaceful assemblies necessarily involve existing associations, such as trade unions, political parties or civil society organizations.

The overlap between the right of peaceful assembly and its two related rights (freedom of expression and association) is particularly pronounced in the case of political assemblies—that is, assemblies that combine a relatively robust associative dimension (e.g. a clear sense of a common purpose and a long-term agenda) and a prominent expressive function involving a specific political message often in the form of a petition, demand or remonstration—that merit particularly strong legal protection. Such peaceful assemblies not only fulfil important associative and expressive interests, but also play an important role in the political life of the communities in which they take place or with which they interact. They provide opportunities for expressing criticism or support for government policies, raising awareness to specific societal problems, or facilitating resistance to power, which may take the form of changing voting patterns in elections and inside parliament, civil disobedience, and direct action. Whereas in extreme cases, such assemblies may morph into violent action and involve riots and revolution (which are not protected under the right of peaceful assembly), more often, they play the opposite role of providing a non-violent outlet for public anger and dissatisfaction with the government or social order of the day.[14] The political participation aspect of political assemblies provides a third link between the right of peaceful assembly and recognized rights under IHRL—the right to take part in the conduct of public affairs.[15]

The ability to influence public discourse and to provide feedback to politicians through the amplification of expression afforded by mass demonstrations and other forms of gathering renders peaceful assemblies an important avenue for political participation, over and beyond taking part in periodic elections.[16] In addition, as mentioned above, peaceful assemblies serve as an effective safety valve for releasing political pressures, which is another one of their non-violent democracy-supporting features.[17] At the same time, the ability to channel the societal energy found in peaceful assemblies to political resistance serves as an important informal check on governmental power, limiting—over and beyond the operation of more formal systems of institutional checks and balances found in modern democracies—the ability of governments to infringe individual and group rights and harm their interests.[18] The central role played by peaceful assemblies in the political life of many countries justifies classifying the right of peaceful assembly as a political right, which operates in close connection with other political rights—freedom of association and expression—as well as with the aforementioned right to take part in public life (which some regard as comprising a fledgling right to democracy).[19]

It is this combination of political power attached to collective speech and action generated or mediated through peaceful assemblies, the possible application of such power to specific political objectives, and, more generally, fear of crowds, which has made peaceful assemblies the target of extensive governmental regulatory attention, often in the form of legal restrictions on the time, place, size, and contents of assemblies.[20] In fact, the right of peaceful assembly has emerged as a key political right under IHRL both because of its effectiveness in facilitating political change and due to persistent efforts by governments to impose strict limits on the holding of peaceful assemblies.[21]

The definition of what constitutes a 'peaceful assembly' under IHRL instruments, such as the International Covenant on Civil and Political Rights (ICCPR) and the European Convention on Human Rights (ECHR),[22] involves an effort to identify forms of assembly which should be internationally protected. This implies that certain human activities which have assembly-like features would be *ab initio* deprived of legal protection under the right of peaceful assembly, even before the invocation by governments of any permissible ground for restricting them.

A key question which arises in this regard pertains to the aforementioned relationship between freedom of assembly and other political rights. Whereas political assemblies—that is, peaceful assemblies involving political speech by members of political organizations—are most likely to attract restrictive governmental regulation, this does not necessarily imply that other, apolitical assemblies should not also be protected. Such apolitical peaceful assemblies may still involve important human interests of the individuals participating and interacting therein, which implicate some of the most basic conditions for leading a meaningful life in every society in the world,[23] and which are not protected by any other human right. Furthermore, governmental regulation of peaceful assemblies does not always distinguish between different forms of peaceful assembly and some governments target, in a sweeping manner, all forms of gathering in order to nip in the bud any potential for political resistance.[24] Arguably, the scope of the protection afforded in IHRL to the right of peaceful assembly should be determined not only in view of the importance of the protected right, but also in view of the scope of restrictions, which are actually imposed by states on the ability of individuals to hold peaceful assemblies: When confronting sweeping restrictions that are designed to effectively curb political assemblies through excessively restricting all types of assemblies, the need to afford effective protection to the right of peaceful assembly—even if it only were to cover political assemblies—would justify a broad scope of protection, which would encompass both political and apolitical assemblies. Such a broad scope of protection would instrumentally shield political assemblies against unjustified regulation.

Peaceful Assemblies as Purposeful Gatherings

As indicated in the introduction, domestic constitutional law and IHRL instruments tend not to define what constitutes a peaceful assembly. Still, such definitions can be derived—to some extent—from domestic legal instruments, which regulate the exercise of the right of peaceful assembly.[25] Furthermore, delineation of the scope of the right of peaceful assembly, like every other human right, should arguably be responsive both to moral claims and considerations that justify protecting the relevant individual and societal interests (these moral claims and considerations may involve diverse values and normative theories justifying the interests of individuals and societies in holding peaceful assemblies and the imposition of correlative duties on states),[26] as well as be sensitive to actual threats directed or expected to be directed against the ability to exercise the said right, which often manifest themselves as a history of oppression and injustice.[27]

Whereas the associative, expressive, and participatory dimensions of peaceful assemblies provide a particularly strong moral justification, from the vantage point of both the individual and society, for recognizing a human right that would allow individuals to gather purposefully for expressive motives relating to a political objective, apolitical assemblies might also be worthy of protection given the intrinsic and instrumental significance of such gatherings for human and societal welfare (e.g. as a means to enjoy culture, practice religion, access education, and engage in family life) and the risk posed to both political and apolitical assemblies by sweeping governmental regulation.

The different rationales for protecting the right of peaceful assembly underlie a choice between a broad articulation of the right of peaceful assembly that would be responsive to all the relevant interests threatened by assembly-limiting government regulation and a narrow articulation which would cover only the most important or valuable forms of exercise of the right. The latter narrow articulation might involve the simultaneous exercise of a number of human rights—peaceful assembly, expression, and political participation—a combination that is more likely to attract governmental regulation than apolitical assemblies. In other words, the act of delineating the right of peaceful assembly entails a choice between over-inclusiveness and under-inclusiveness.

The two sets of normative instruments at the centre of the present chapter—the ODIHR/Venice Commission Guidelines and General Comment No. 37 of the Human Rights Committee—reflect, to some extent, such a choice. Whereas General Comment No. 37 opted for a potentially over-inclusive definition of the right from the perspective of the most important moral justifications for its existence, the ODIHR/Venice Commission Guidelines arguably risk being under-inclusive in certain critical respects.

The ODIHR/Venice Commission Guidelines offer the following—non-exhaustive[28]—definition:

> For the purposes of the Guidelines, an 'assembly' means the intentional gathering of a number of individuals in a publicly accessible place for a common expressive purpose. This includes planned and organised assemblies, unplanned and spontaneous assemblies, static and moving assemblies.[29]

Yet, the Guidelines also identify areas of special concern, which deserve focused attention and protection:

> These Guidelines are concerned primarily with the protection of gatherings held to express an emotion, idea or opinion relating to matters of public interest or concern, including those that address political, cultural or social issues and those that seek to send a message to the public or relevant decision-makers.[30]

General Comment No. 37 appears to define an assembly more broadly as a 'gathering by persons for specific purposes, principally expressive ones'.[31] Like the Guidelines, the General Comment covers under the concept of a purposeful gathering both pre-planned and spontaneous assemblies.[32]

The two definitions offer a delicate balancing exercise between the physical dimensions of the act of gathering and the purpose of the act. Both recognize that there is little reason to protect through IHRL the random gathering of individuals in bus station queues or their functional gathering in supermarket lines. This is because the act of gathering—and the aforementioned individual and social benefits that are typically associated with purposeful congregation (e.g. a sense of belonging, inter-personal interaction, empowerment, and expression of solidarity)—is not the aim of the congregating individuals. Rather, in those scenarios, the act of gathering constitutes a side effect of the pursuit of another aim (e.g. queuing to ride the bus or to pay the cashier).

The two definitions, however, acknowledge implicitly that purposeful gatherings can play an important role in peoples' lives, even when they do not involve the dissemination of a collective message of a political nature. These include, as mentioned above, participation in religious meetings and cultural events, inter alia. Arguably, such purposeful gatherings deserve protection because of their important contribution to human and societal welfare outside the context of politics.[33]

Where the two definitions do differ, however, is with respect to peaceful assemblies without an expressive purpose (e.g. family gatherings or social events). The broad definition found in the General Comment covers such gatherings—perhaps because Committee members deemed such activities independently worthy of protection, and were concerned that they too may be adversely affected by sweeping laws against public and private gatherings.[34] By contrast, the ODIHR/Venice Commission Guidelines exclude non-expressive assemblies altogether from the scope of the Guidelines (while noting that such assemblies may be protected nonetheless under IHRL, including possibly under aspects of the right of peaceful assembly which the Guidelines do not address).[35]

Still, even drafters of the General Comment seem to recognize that assemblies that serve to generate or propagate expressions should enjoy a heightened level of protection, probably because they also implicate freedom of expression. Such an elevated status can be surmised from the use of the term 'principally' in paragraph 4 of the General Comment. The ODIHR/Venice Commission Guidelines go even farther in that they 'primarily' operate to protect collective expressions relating to 'matters of public interest or concern' and those which 'seek to send a message to the public or relevant decision makers' (i.e. involve political contents or constitute a form of protest).[36] Such collective expressions are, arguably, worthy of particular attention because they implicate not only the right of peaceful assembly and freedom of expression, but also a third human right—the right to take part in public life.

One may criticize the choice of the drafters of the two documents to focus attention on protections that should be afforded to peaceful assemblies involving expressive or political purposes. Arguably, the fact that such assemblies are already protected by freedom of expression, and possibly also by the right to participate in public life, renders the additional protection of the same activity on the basis of the right of peaceful assembly somewhat superfluous.

One effective reply to such criticism is that expressive assemblies—and, even more so, political assemblies—are more likely to encounter restrictive governmental regulation, when compared to other peaceful assemblies. The special attention therefore matches the special threat which accompanies the holding of expressive, and, in particular, political assemblies. Furthermore, the protection afforded by the right of peaceful assembly to expressive or political assemblies is not redundant; rather, such additional protection may be particularly effective since it involves closely tailored procedural and substantive norms (e.g. on pre-assembly notification or choice of sight and sound) that delineate the rights and obligations relating to the exercise of freedom of peaceful assembly under IHRL. The protection afforded through reliance on the more general tests found in other rights, such as freedom of association, freedom of expression, and the right to participate in public life, is less granular, by way of comparison to the right of peaceful assembly:[37] For instance, when confronting government-imposed measures to reroute a protest march, the invocation of freedom of expression may be less effective than the invocation of the right of peaceful assembly, since the former protects primarily the contents of the collective expression (which can still, allegedly, be made effectively in the alternative route) and the latter specifically protects the protesters choice of route (through the 'sight and sound' principle).

Still, to my mind, the advantages of focusing the right to freedom of assembly only on expressive assemblies are outweighed by the disadvantages of excluding non-expressive assemblies from the scope of protection, or conveying the message that they are less worthy of attention (as the ODIHR/Venice Commission Guidelines might appear to do). This is especially so, since the borderline between expressive and non-expressive assemblies is sometimes hard to draw (e.g. a music concert involving protest songs),[38] and because government regulation may target both forms of gathering.[39]

Another aspect of the definition of 'peaceful assembly' in respect of which the ODIHR/Venice Commission and the Human Rights Committee took different positions, perhaps stemming from the different treatment by the Guidelines and General Comment of non-expressive assemblies, relates to the location of the assembly in question. The Guidelines focus on assemblies taking place in 'a publicly accessible place' (a term which may include locations, such as shopping centres, which are privately owned but open to the general public),[40] whereas the definition of peaceful assembly found in General Comment No. 37 does not contain such a limitation. In fact, the General Comment stipulates that 'gatherings in private spaces fall within the scope of the right of peaceful assembly',[41] and many of the gatherings protected by the General Comment, such as family gatherings and social events, take place in private settings and invite protection there as well.[42] The difference in approach between the two documents may have practical implications even for some types of political assemblies. For example, demonstrations against forced evictions or mineral extractions, which take place on the privately owned eviction or extraction site, could be covered by one definition, but not by the other.

As a practical matter, however, these differences may amount to not much more than variations in the methodology for dealing with limitations on the right of peaceful assembly. Whereas the ODIHR/Venice Commission's potential under-inclusiveness towards what constitutes a peaceful assembly might effectively exclude *ab initio* certain peaceful assemblies from the scope of protection afforded under the right to peaceful assemblies, the Human Rights Committee's potential over-inclusiveness might lead to the same result through invocation of the language on restrictions in connection with regulation of peaceful assemblies (e.g. in the second sentence of article 21 of the ICCPR).[43] The General Comment notes, for example, with relation to peaceful assemblies held on private property that 'the interests of others with rights in the property must be given due weight' in the analysis of whether any restrictions are justified.[44] This implies that the question of right of access to private land will be factored in the analysis of the necessity and proportionality of any restrictions imposed by the state on the exercise of the right of peaceful assembly in such situations, possible resulting in a small gap in legal outcomes between the approach of the Guidelines and that of the General Comment.

Other Definitional Issues

Three further interpretative choices merit fuller discussion at this stage: whether or not multiple participants must be gathered in the same place at the same time, the implications of that question for the possibility of online assembly, and questions of 'peacefulness'.

A Gathering of More Than One Person in the Same Time and Place

Notwithstanding some differences in their focus and method of analysis, in many respects the approach of the Guidelines is similar to that of the General Comment. For example, both instruments place a quantitative requirement for eligibility to enjoy the right of peaceful assembly—a gathering of more than one person. The ODIHR/Venice Commission Guidelines allude to 'a gathering of a *number* of individuals',[45] and General Comment No. 37 states that 'the notion of an assembly implies that there will be more than one participant in the gathering'.[46] The Human Rights Committee notes, however, that a single protester would enjoy protections under other provisions of the ICCPR (e.g. freedom of expression).[47]

An important interpretative question that arises in this connection is whether a collective protest or other purposeful activity of an expressive nature that does not involve the simultaneous gathering of individuals in the same place and at the same time falls under the definition of peaceful assembly. Such collective activity may include vigil protests, comprising a series of single persons protesting in consecutive order in the same place,[48] or activities involving individuals engaged in collective protests occurring at the same time but in different places.[49] Several rationales for protecting the right of peaceful assembly—the individual interest in purposeful gathering (e.g. a sense of belonging, empowerment, and expression of solidarity) and the social significance of such collective protest acts—support the inclusion of coordinated activities of more than one person within the definition of 'peaceful assembly' despite their lack of contemporaneousness or concentration in physical space. While such an approach admittedly stretches the natural meaning of the term 'gathering', it is not inconceivable. The decision of the European Court of Human Rights to include informal 'walkabouts' under the protection of article 11 of the ECHR, due to the 'coordinated and purposeful' nature of the activity, is arguably supportive of such a broad approach.[50]

Online Assemblies

Online assemblies present yet another definitional challenge, relating to the outer boundaries of what constitutes a 'gathering' in the context of a 'peaceful assembly'. To be sure, some forms of online activity easily fall within the scope of protection afforded to the right of peaceful assembly. This includes organizing, advertising, and broadcasting on online platforms an offline assembly—all activities which potentially transpose an offline assembly into a hybrid one.[51]

More difficult questions arise in connection with the extent to which an exclusively virtual gathering is a form of gathering, inviting legal protection as a 'peaceful assembly'. It seems rather plausible to maintain that a gathering of two or more individuals at the same time and in the same virtual space, such as on an online platform like a Zoom call, a Twitter space or the metaverse, should be covered by the definition of peaceful assembly given the purposeful and coordinated nature of the act of virtual gathering, which often also involves collective expression. Analogous considerations would seem to apply to the concentration in one physical space (such as projecting images on the wall of a public building) of live videos or live holograms of individuals participating in the event from different locations.[52] Such an approach seems to be supported by General Comment No. 37, which referred to the possibility that online assemblies—whether conducted wholly or partly online—would be covered by article 21 of the ICCPR,[53] and by the ODIHR/Venice Commission Guidelines, which provide that '[i]n this evolving sphere, the possibility that assemblies may occur wholly online cannot, therefore, be excluded'.[54]

The boundaries of what constitutes an assembly could be extended even further, however, in relation to virtual participation in an asynchronic fashion involving the 'gathering' of pre-recorded messages in one online 'location', or the participation, not in real time, in an online event. Here too, one may claim that the associative rationale and other potential interests underlying, in certain cases, the right of peaceful assembly (e.g. expressive and participatory) are met, and that online assemblies should be recognized as particular forms of purposeful gathering held under the special conditions and unique features of digital space.[55] This is especially the case where the purposeful gathering in an 'event' has an interactive dimension, allowing participants to communicate with one another around the common activity, and when the act of participation is noted by inside and outside observers (e.g. through 'likes', 'shares', 'views', or the use of a common hashtag), in a manner that amplifies the collective expression made in the online event in ways similar to participation in a physical assembly. Admittedly however, the boundaries between 'asynchronic assemblies' and other collective forms of expression are blurry, and an examination of the centrality of the component of purposeful gathering in the 'location' for the 'event' would have to be reviewed on a case-by-case basis.

Not every collective activity which takes place online, however, can be or should be regarded as an online assembly attracting the protections attendant to the right of peaceful assembly, in the same way in which not every collective activity occurring in the physical world (e.g. strike or class action) is regarded as a peaceful assembly. An example of an online activity which most probably should not enjoy the status of a peaceful assembly is an online petition, whose offline equivalent—a written petition or joint letter—would not have been considered as an assembly in the offline world. Such collective expression would still be protected, of course, by freedom of expression.

Still, the endless variety of online activities and the difficulties in drawing analogies from the online to the offline world introduces significant problems of distinguishing between coordinated and purposeful online activities, which should or should not be regarded as peaceful assemblies. And it remains to be seen how the caselaw of IHRL monitoring bodies will develop to deal with borderline cases of online activity, particularly those that involve certain virtual forms of gathering but have no close analogies in the offline world and whose specific contours would no doubt continue to evolve with the future evolvement of digital technology.

One specific claim that was made in this connection by civil society actors during the discussions before the Human Rights Committee concerning General Comment No. 37 was that the Committee should consider some collective direct actions, such as hacktivism or trolling, as potentially covered by the right of peaceful assembly.[56] This proposal raises some difficulties as, in the offline world, comparable activities such as coordinated acts of civil disobedience (such as tax resistance) or customer boycotts, would not typically be regarded as 'assemblies'. Furthermore, questions may arise in relation to the peacefulness of some direct action strategies, such as DDoS (distributed denial of service) attacks that entail harm to computer systems, websites, and supported services.[57]

Non-violent Assemblies

A final critical definitional issue dealt with by the Guidelines and the General Comment involves the peaceful nature of protected assemblies. The peacefulness condition is important not only because curbing violence provides a possible justification for restricting *ab initio* the scope of the right of peaceful assembly, but also because resort to violence is incompatible with the notion of political participation, which serves as a central rationale for protecting political assemblies, and is premised on a view of participatory politics as an alternative to political violence.[58] In other words, assemblies can be regarded as important social institutions in the political life of the nation, only to the extent that they generally adhere to a vision of politics as a peaceful process of collective decision-making in relation to the exercise of public power and resource allocation.[59]

The dividing line between peaceful and violent assemblies is often unclear, in law and practice.[60] This is because the term 'violence' has been understood in law to covers a spectrum of conduct which includes, on the one hand, mild forms of social disruption, such as verbal abuse, mere pushing and shoving, and physically stopping traffic,[61] and, on the other hand, extreme attacks, such as resorting to the use of lethal weapons and mob lynching. Furthermore, violence may be sporadic—that is, practiced by a small number of participants in an otherwise peaceful assembly (at times, in response to provocations by law enforcement officials or counter-demonstrators)—or extensive, that is practiced by large numbers of participants or orchestrated or advocated by the organizers of the assembly.

In General Comment No. 37, the Human Rights Committee narrowly construed the non-peaceful exception, and included within the definition of peaceful assembly gatherings featuring sporadic and low-level violence.[62] Furthermore, it introduced a presumption against considering an assembly as violent in nature,[63] and has opined that even the carrying of weapons or the wearing of masks by participants in the assembly would not necessarily result in the reversal of said presumption.[64] Essentially the same approach is found in the ODIHR/Venice Commission Guidelines,[65] which also emphasize that violence cannot be equated with breaking the law.[66]

Conclusion

The definition of 'peaceful assembly' determines the scope of the protection afforded to the right of peaceful assembly under IHRL. Two IHRL bodies have recently published comprehensive documents on the right of peaceful assembly—the Human Rights Committee, which produced General Comment No. 37, and the ODIHR/Venice Commission, which updated its Guidelines on Freedom of Peaceful Assembly. Both normative projects are significant in that they involved highly regarded bodies of experts, which engaged in extensive deliberations while formulating the relevant legal documents, including cross-consultations among themselves. The two documents they produced provide us with a rather authoritative picture regarding the 'state of the art' on the right of peaceful assembly under IHRL.

Review of the General Comment and the Guidelines reveal some important differences with respect to their scope and focus. The Guidelines focus on expressive assemblies and, in particular, on political assemblies. This reflects the insight that such assemblies are most likely to attract restrictive governmental regulation. The General Comment, on the other hand, is more inclusive in its scope of coverage and includes both expressive and non-expressive assemblies. Arguably, such breadth of coverage is justified by the fact that expressive assemblies are already protected by freedom of expression and political assemblies also by the right to take part in public affairs. It is rather the act of purposeful gathering—and the human welfare and societal interests attached to it (e.g. a sense of belonging, inter-personal interaction, and empowerment)—that the right of peaceful assembly should arguably protect first and foremost. At the end of the day, however, the two approaches—which involve some analytical trade-offs between breadth and depth—appear to complement and reinforce one another, providing students of IHRL and IHRL practitioners rich, comprehensive, and precise normative reference points concerning the scope of the right of peaceful assembly and its substantive contents.

Acknowledgements

The author was a member of the Human Rights Committee during the preparation and adoption of General Comment No. 37. Part of the research for this chapter was conducted with the support of ERC Grant No. 101054745: the Three Generations of Digital Human Rights (DigitalHRGeneration3), https://3gdr.huji.ac.il/.

Notes

1. See e.g. US Const., 1st Amend.; Indonesian Convention, article 28; Const. of Nigeria, article 40; Const. of the Republic of Poland, article 57; Canadian Charter of Rights and Freedoms, article 2(c); Const. of the People's Republic of China, article 35; Const. of Japan, article 21.

2. See e.g. Indian Const., article 19 ('peaceably and without arms'); Basic Law of the Federal Republic of Germany, article 8 ('peacefully and unarmed'); Const. of the Italian Republic, article 17 ('Citizens have the right to assemble peaceably and unarmed'); Const. of Brazil, article 5(XVI) ('all persons may hold peaceful meetings, without weapons').
3. See e.g. Const. of the Portuguese Republic, article 45 ('1. Citizens have the right to meet peacefully and without arms, even in places that are open to the public, without the need for any authorisation. 2. All citizens are accorded the right to demonstrate'); Const. of the Republic of South Africa, article 17 ('Everyone has the right, peacefully and unarmed, to assemble, to demonstrate, to picket and to present petitions'); Const. of the Kingdom of Morocco, article 29 ('The freedoms of reunion, of assembly, of peaceful demonstration, of association and of syndical and political membership [appartenance], are guaranteed').
4. See e.g. US Const., 1st Amend. ('Congress shall make no law respecting an establishment of religion, or prohibiting the free exercise thereof; or abridging the freedom of speech, or of the press; or the right of the people peaceably to assemble, and to petition the Government for a redress of grievance'); Const. of the Republic of South Africa, article 17; Const. of the United Mexican State, article 9 ('The right to peacefully associate or assembly for any licit purpose cannot be restricted. Only citizens of the Republic may take part in the political affairs of the country. No armed meeting has the right to deliberate. Meetings organized to make a petition or to submit a protest to any authority cannot be considered as unlawful, nor be broken, provided that no insults are uttered against the authority and no violence or threats are used to intimidate or force the decision of such authority'); Const. of the Republic of Philippines, article 3(4) ('No law shall be passed abridging the freedom of speech, of expression, or of the press, or the right of the people peaceably to assemble and petition the government for redress of grievances'); Constitution of the Russian Federation, article 31 ('Citizens of the Russian Federation shall have the right to assemble peacefully, without weapons, hold rallies, meetings and demonstrations, marches and pickets').
5. UNHRCtte, General Comment No. 37—Article 21: Right of Peaceful Assembly (17 September 2020) UN Doc. CCPR/C/GC/37.
6. Office for Democratic Institutions and Human Rights of the Organization for Security and Co-operation in Europe (OSCE/ODIHR) and European Commission for Democracy through Law (Venice Commission) Guidelines on Freedom of Peaceful Assembly, COE Doc. CDL-AD(2019)017rev. (2020).
7. Cf. George Kateb, 'The Value of Association', in *Freedom of Association*, ed. Amy Gutmann (Princeton, NJ: Princeton University Press, 1988), 35, 38–39.
8. Edison Lanza, Report of the Special Rapporteur on freedom of expression of the Inter-American Commission on Human Rights, *Protest and Human Rights Standards on the Rights involved in Social Protest and the Obligations to guide the response of the State*, 19. OAS Doc. OEA/SER.L/V/II (2019).
9. See e.g. Michael Hamilton, 'The Meaning and Scope of "Assembly" in International Human Rights Law', *International & Comparative Law Quarterly* 69, no. 3 (July 2020): 521–556, 528 (describing the relationship between freedom of expression and freedom of assembly as a 'seemingly umbilical attachment').
10. See e.g. UNHRCtte, General Comment No. 37, 1.
11. See e.g. Ashutosh Bhagwat, 'The Democratic First Amendment', *Northwestern University Law Review* 110, no. 5 (Fall 2016): 1097–1124, 1109.
12. See e.g. Hamilton, 'Meaning and Scope', 530.

13. See e.g. *Conservative and Unionist Central Office v Burrell*, [1981] EWCA Civ 2, at 2 ('I infer that by 'unincorporated association" in this context Parliament meant two or more persons bound together for one or more common purposes, not being business purposes, by mutual undertakings, each having mutual duties and obligations, in an organisation which has rules which identify in whom control *of* it and its funds rests and upon what terms and which can be joined or left at will. The bond of union between the members of an unincorporated association has to be contractual'); Loi du 1er juillet 1901 relative au contrat d'association (France) ('L'association est la convention par laquelle deux ou plusieurs personnes mettent en commun, d'une façon permanente, leurs connaissances ou leur activité dans un but autre que de partager des bénéfices. Elle est régie, quant à sa validité, par les principes généraux du droit applicables aux contrats et obligations'). See also John D. Inazu, 'The Strange Origins of the Constitutional Right of Association', *Tennessee Law Review* 77, no. 3 (Spring 2010): 485–562, 558–559 (discussing the different protections afforded under US law to expressive and intimate associations).
14. See e.g. Richard Thompson Ford, 'Protest Fatigue', in *Protest and Dissent (Nomos LXII)*, ed. Melissa Schwartzberg (New York: New York University Press, 2020), 161, 185.
15. International Covenant on Civil and Political Rights (ICCPR), article 25 (16 December 1966) 99 UNTS 171.
16. See e.g. Dalton, Russell J. 'Political Action, Protest, and the Functioning of Democratic Governance', *American Behavioral Scientist* 66, no. 4 (April 2022): 533–550, 545; Ibrahim J. Gassama, 'Ballots and Bullets: The Right to Democratic Governance in International Law after the Egyptian Coup', *Wisconsin International Law Journal* 32, no. 4 (December 2014): 621–674, 655.
17. See e.g. David Feldman, 'Protest and Tolerance: Legal Values and the Control of Public Order Policing', in *Liberal Democracy and the Limits of Tolerance: Essays in Honor and Memory of Yitzhak Rabin*, ed. Raphael Cohen-Almagor (Ann Arbor: University of Michigan Press, 2000), 43, 46.
18. See e.g. Thorbjørn Jagland, "Report by the Secretary General of the Council of Europe, State of Democracy, Human Rights and the Rule of Law: Populism—How Strong Are Europe's Checks and Balances?" (Strasbourg: Council of Europe, 2017), 8.
19. See e.g. Sigrid Boysen, 'Remnants of a Constitutional Moment: The Right to Democracy in International Law', in *The Cambridge Handbook of New Human Rights: Recognition, Novelty, Rhetoric*, ed. Andreas Von Arnauld, Kerstin Von der Decken, and Marti Susi (Cambridge: Cambridge University Press, 2020), 465.
20. See e.g. Roger Douglas, *Dealing with Demonstrations: The Law of Public Protest and Its Enforcement* (Sydney: Federation Press, 2004), 11.
21. See e.g. Michael Hamilton, 'To Facilitate and Protect: State Obligations and the Right of Peaceful Assembly in International Human Rights Law', *Asia-Pacific Journal on Human Rights and the Law* 12, no. 1 (May 2020): 5–34, 6.
22. European Convention on Human Rights (ECHR), 4 November 1950, ETS 5.
23. For a discussion of 'universal human interests' as a basis for recognizing human rights, see John Tasioulas, 'On the Foundations of Human Rights', in *Philosophical Foundations of Human Rights*, ed. Rowan Cruft, S. Matthew Liao, and Massimo Renzo (Oxford: Oxford University Press, 2015), 45, 50.
24. See e.g. UNHRCtte, Concluding Observations on Second Periodic Report: Thailand, UN Doc. CCPR/C/THA/CO/2 (2017), 39–40.

25. Michael Hamilton is right, however, in cautioning against 'reverse engineering' the scope of the right from the scope of limitations on its free exercise and in noting that some assemblies do not merit any form of regulation. Hamilton, 'Meaning and Scope', 525. Still, the fact that a gathering is regulated as a form of assembly is a strong indication about the scope of definition used by the relevant state.
26. See e.g. Rainer Forst, 'The Justification of Human Rights and the Basic Right to Justification: A Reflexive Approach', *Ethics* 120, no. 4 (July 2010): 711–740, 725–726.
27. For a discussion, see e.g. Charles R. Beitz, *The Idea of Human Rights* (Oxford: Oxford University Press, 2009), 1.
28. OSCE/ODIHR—Venice Commission, Guidelines on Freedom of Peaceful Assembly, 41 ('For the purposes of these Guidelines, an "assembly" means the intentional gathering of a number of individuals in a publicly accessible place for a common expressive purpose. While this definition captures the core protective scope of the right to freedom of peaceful assembly, *it is not an exhaustive definition*') (emphasis added).
29. OSCE/ODIHR—Venice Commission, Guidelines on Freedom of Peaceful Assembly, 18.
30. Ibid., 42.
31. UNHRCtte, General Comment No. 37, 4.
32. Ibid., 14.
33. Note that religious gatherings would also be protected by the right to manifest one's religion and to worship (ICCPR, article 18; ECHR, article 9).
34. See UNHRCtte, Concluding Observations on Second Periodic Report. See also Regulation 7 of the Health Protection (Coronavirus Restrictions) (England) Regulations 2020, https://www.bangkokpost.com/world/1895065/singapore-to-ban-gatherings. The broad approach of the Human Rights Committee is shared by the UN Special Rapporteur on Freedom of Assembly and Association. Maina Kiai, *Report of the Special Rapporteur on the Rights to Freedom of Peaceful Assembly and of Association* (2012) UN Doc. A/HRC/20/27, 24 ('An "assembly" is an intentional and temporary gathering in a private or public space for a specific purpose. It therefore includes demonstrations, inside meetings, strikes, 8 processions, rallies or even sits-in. Assemblies play a vibrant role in mobilizing the population and formulating grievances and aspirations, facilitating the celebration of events and, importantly, influencing States' public policy').
35. OSCE/ODIHR—Venice Commission, Guidelines on Freedom of Peaceful Assembly, 12–14, 41. A similar approach has been taken by the African Commission on Human and Peoples' Rights. African Commission on Human and Peoples' Rights, Guidelines on Freedom of Association and Assembly in Africa (2017), 9, https://www.icnl.org/post/tools/guidelines-on-freedom-of-association-and-assembly-in-africa ('Assembly refers to an act of intentionally gathering, in private or in public, for an expressive purpose and for an extended duration. The right to assembly may be exercised in a number of ways, including through demonstrations, protests, meetings, processions, rallies, sit-ins, and funerals, through the use of online platforms, or in any other way people choose').
36. OSCE/ODIHR—Venice Commission, Guidelines on Freedom of Peaceful Assembly, 42.
37. Hamilton, 'Meaning and Scope', 534. It may be noted that, in practice, IHRL bodies often refrain for reasons of 'judicial economy' from finding violations of both freedom of expression and the right of peaceful assembly. See e.g. Communication No. 1839/2008, *Komarovsky v Belarus*, Views of the UNHRCtte, adopted 25 October 2013, 9.5.
38. See, for instance, Scheinin's observation on the difference between gathering to express a view and gathering to hear a view. Martin Scheinin, 'How to Improve the Human

Rights Committee Draft General Comment on Freedom of Assembly,' Just Security, 13 February 2020.

39. See e.g. UNHRCtte, Concluding Observations on Second Periodic Report.
40. OSCE/ODIHR—Venice Commission, Guidelines on Freedom of Peaceful Assembly, 18. But see OSCE/ODIHR—Venice Commission, Guidelines on Freedom of Peaceful Assembly, 1 ('The right to freedom of peaceful assembly protects the many ways in which people gather together in public and in private'). As indicated, the Guidelines focus their attention on public gatherings, while not excluding the possibility that certain other gatherings, including on private property, would also be protected.
41. UNHRCtte, General Comment No. 37, 57.
42. This may also apply in certain cases to religious gatherings in private settings. See e.g. *Saladdin Mammadov, Rashad Niftaliyev and Sadagat Abbasova v Azerbaijan*, Views of the Human Rights Committee of 15 October 2020, UN Doc. CCPR/C/129/D/2928/2017 (2020). The Committee found admissible the claims under article 21 of the ICCPR, relating to unjustified interference with a private gathering, but did not rule on the merits of these claims, having already found a violation of another provision of the Covenant (detention of participants in the gathering in violation of article 9).
43. ICCPR, article 21 ('No restrictions may be placed on the exercise of this right other than those imposed in conformity with the law and which are necessary in a democratic society in the interests of national security or public safety, public order (ordre public), the protection of public health or morals or the protection of the rights and freedoms of others').
44. UNHRCtte, General Comment No. 37, 57. See also ECtHR, *Navalnyy v Russia*, judgment of 15 November 2018, 98. Cf. *Shell Nederland Verkoopmaatschappij B.V. v Stichting Greenpeace Nederland*, District Court of Amsterdam judgment of 5 October 2012.
45. OSCE/ODIHR—Venice Commission, Guidelines on Freedom of Peaceful Assembly, 18.
46. UNHRCtte, General Comment No. 37, 13.
47. Ibid.
48. Note that General Comment No. 37 does allude to 'candlelit vigils' as a form of assembly, without referring to the contemporaneous or asynchronic nature of such vigils. Ibid., 6.
49. See e.g. observing a day of silence on university campuses—https://www.glsen.org/dayofsilence.
50. See *Navalnyy v Russia*, 108.
51. UNHRCtte, General Comment No. 37, 10, 13, 34; OSCE/ODIHR—Venice Commission, Guidelines on Freedom of Peaceful Assembly, 20, 45, 66.
52. See e.g. Jethro Mullen, 'Virtual Protest: Demonstrators Challenge New Law with Holograms,' CNN, 12 April 2015, https://edition.cnn.com/2015/04/12/europe/spain-hologram-protest/index.html.
53. UNHRCtte, General Comment No. 37, 6, 10, 13.
54. OSCE/ODIHR—Venice Commission, Guidelines on Freedom of Peaceful Assembly, 45. See also ibid., 68.
55. See e.g. Michael Hamilton, Ella McPherson, and Sharath Srinvasan, 'Deal with Me, Here I Stand!': Presence, Participation and the Equal Protection of Online Assemblies,' in *A Life Interrupted: Essays in Honour of the Lives and Legacies of Christof Heyns*, ed. Frans Viljoen et al. (Pretoria: Pretoria University Law Press, 2022), 327, 339. See also the contributions of Ashraf, in this volume; Beraldo, in this volume; and McPherson, in this volume.
56. See Michael Hamilton et al., *The Right of Peaceful Assembly in Online Spaces: A Comment on the Revised Draft General Comment 37 on Article 21 (Right of Peaceful Assembly) of the*

International Covenant on Civil and Political Rights (2020), 6, https://www.ohchr.org/sites/default/files/Documents/HRBodies/CCPR/GCArticle21/ACADEMIA-Hamilton-Dixon-Young-McPherson-Srinivasan-Elean.docx.

57. See e.g. Joshua McLaurin, 'Making Cyberspace Safe for Democracy: The Challenge Posed by Denial-of-Service Attacks', *Yale Law & Policy Review* 30, no. 1 (Fall 2011), 211, 229.
58. Anyssa Bellal and Louise Doswald-Beck, 'Evaluating the Use of Force During the Arab Spring', *Yearbook of International Humanitarian Law* (2011), 3, 12. *Cf.* ECtHR, *Yazar v Turkey*, judgment of 9 April 2002, 49.
59. The Human Rights Committee did clarify however that whereas resort to violence can remove participants from the protection of the right of peaceful assembly, other rights continue to remain available to participants in such assemblies. UNHRCtte, General Comment No. 37, 9.
60. *Cf.* Tabatha Abu El-Haj, 'Defining Nonviolence as a Matter of Law and Politics', in *Protest and Dissent (Nomos LXII)*, ed. Melissa Schwartzberg (New York: New York University Press, 2020), 201–236. Also see Salát, in this volume.
61. For a discussion of the relationship between traffic disruption and the conditions for a peaceful assembly, see Hamilton, 'To Facilitate and Protect', 27–28.
62. UNHRCtte, General Comment No. 37, 15–19.
63. Ibid., 17. *Cf.* OSCE/ODIHR—Venice Commission, Guidelines on Freedom of Peaceful Assembly, 46, 49.
64. UNHRCtte, General Comment No. 37, 20.
65. See e.g. OSCE/ODIHR—Venice Commission, Guidelines on Freedom of Peaceful Assembly 50–51.
66. Ibid., 48.

Further Reading

African Commission on Human and Peoples' Rights. Guidelines on Freedom of Association and Assembly in Africa (2017).

Gutmann, Amy, ed., *Freedom of Association*. Princeton, NJ: Princeton University Press, 1988.

Hamilton, Michael. 'The Meaning and Scope of "Assembly" in International Human Rights Law'. *International & Comparative Law Quarterly* 69, no. 3 (July 2020): 521–556.

Hamilton, Michael, Ella McPherson, and Sharath Srinvasan. 'Deal with Me, Here I Stand!': Presence, Participation and the Equal Protection of Online Assemblies'. In *A Life Interrupted: Essays in Honour of the Lives and Legacies of Christof Heyns*, ed. Frans Viljoen et al., 327–346. Pretoria: Pretoria University Law Press, 2022.

Human Rights Committee. General Comment No. 37: The Rights to Peaceful Assembly. UN Doc. CCPR/C/GC/37 (2020).

Kiai, Maina. *Report of the Special Rapporteur on the Rights to Freedom of Peaceful Assembly and of Association*, 24. UN Doc. A/HRC/20/27 (2012).

Schwartzberg, Melissa, ed. *Protest and Dissent (Nomos LXII)*. New York: New York University Press, 2020.

Venice Commission and OSCE/ODIHR. Guidelines on Freedom of Peaceful Assembly. COE Doc. CDL-AD(2019)017rev. (2020).

CHAPTER 13

PEACEFUL INTENTIONS, PEACEFUL CONDUCT

ORSOLYA SALÁT

Introduction

Freedom of assembly is the only fundamental right which has a restrictive adjective added to it: namely, peaceful. This chapter claims that this fact is in itself cause for wonder, quite apart from any actual interpretation given to the peacefulness requirement. It is a cause for wonder because it lends an air of suspicion to either assemblies or the drafters of human rights texts, or, most likely, to both. What is so special about assemblies that mandates such a restriction? And does it follow then, as literal interpretation would command, that other rights, which are not qualified by a requirement of 'peacefulness', can be exercised unpeacefully? Beyond the question of the comparison with other rights, the problem with peacefulness as a limit on assembly is that it is unclear whose peacefulness counts or what the threshold for peacefulness should be.

The first question that necessarily arises is: *Why* is it different with assembly? Why did the relevant drafters feel the need to include such a qualification exactly and to do so only for freedom of assembly? Two related (if speculatory) explanations come to mind immediately. Let me call the first one the 'fear from the mass mind' and the second one 'the liminal nature' of assemblies.

The suspicion towards a hypothesized 'mass mind' is inherited from the early days of mass psychology. Gustave LeBon, William McDougall, and Sigmund Freud shared, despite their significant disagreements, an aversion towards masses, for they considered them irrational (even feminine!), manipulable, unfree—thus, all in all, dangerous to the peaceful coexistence of intelligent and free men, and not particularly something to be respected and promoted.[1] In a quest to explain the horrors of World War II and, in particular, the Holocaust, many researchers in their footsteps thought that being in the mass contributed to increased hostility towards outsiders, loss of self-control ('deindividuation'), a tendency to violence and anomia, authoritarianism, and so on.[2]

Partly based on these studies, partly trying to re-validate them, however, more current strands in social psychology suggest a rationality and norm-based interpretation of crowds, and have definitely given up the idea of the existence of a mass mind.[3] This history and trend is discussed in Adang (in this volume). Along similar lines, the vast field of social movements studies see gatherings of people as following rational goals, which start out of real or perceived grievances, and use rational means and methods forming part of a larger dynamic of contentious politics (see Zhelnina and Jasper, in this volume).[4] The urge to include peaceful into the guarantee of freedom of assembly thus seems to be consonant with earlier assumptions in crowd psychology, assumptions which have largely lost their validity.

A second possible explanation for why freedom of assembly was explicitly limited to peaceful assemblies lies in what can be called the 'liminal' nature of assemblies. I suggest here to approach the object of freedom of assembly as something in between revolutions and pogroms, on the one hand, and organized political deliberation in the parliament or some other legislative body, on the other. I use pogrom here as a catchword for group violence against actual persons, and revolution as something which leads to a regime change.

Both a pogrom and a revolution start out of assemblies. Law surely wants to prevent the first, and is not necessarily eager to promote the second either, although histories of most countries value at least some past revolutions. At the same time, at a minimum, constitutional democracy is not without a certain self-reflection and alertness about the inherent deficiencies of the constitutional-democratic edifice. Institutionalized democracy alone is not self-correcting and is not automatically responsive to the will of the people. Fundamental rights, including freedom of assembly and the right to protest, are corrective devices in that regard as well.

Consequently, constitutional thinking is not alien to the idea of including more radical freedoms than it would be deemed 'reasonable' in a perfect world. Quite to the contrary, fundamental rights allow for conduct beyond the conventional or usual. The proportionality test and similar fundamental rights tests and standards, which require that fundamental rights be restricted only when there is an explicit justification showing a pressing social need or an important government interest, afford spheres of freedom *beyond* what would seem reasonable by common sense. If that is so with regard to general fundamental rights theory, then it is worth thinking over how it is applied to the fundamental right which captures the social and political nature of human existence and is closest to political action: freedom of assembly.

The following will discuss on this basis some of the fundamental tenets of freedom-of-assembly jurisprudence related to the question of unpeacefulness. It analyses guiding principles and their application by way of illustrative examples in some jurisdictions, mostly, but not exclusively, Germany, France, and the European Court of Human Rights ('ECtHR' or 'Strasbourg Court'). It claims that there is a contrast between the elevated talk we see when it comes to general principles and rationales of freedom of assembly, and the actual interpretation given when courts review regulations related to freedom of assembly, particularly prior bans, dispersals, and preventive detention of 'would-be unpeaceful' protesters. A last subsection before the conclusion sheds light on some examples of what I call 'unpeacefulness by stealth'—that is, situations in which limits unrelated to violence in any way result in the same legal situation as if an assembly had been deemed unpeaceful, permitting bans and dispersals.[5] That is notably the main function of the peacefulness requirement, and that is why stakes are high: If an assembly is found or, more often, is predicted to be(come) unpeaceful, then the exercise of the right can be prevented or stopped entirely. The would-be unpeaceful assembly can be fully prevented, which is a proper prior restraint unheard of in other areas of quintessential political rights.

Principles or the Grand Theory of Freedom of Assembly

Courts usually provide rationales or reasons for protection of fundamental rights during their interpretation (i.e. principled answers to the question of the significance of the right in question). Rationale-based interpretation aligns well with a kind of functionalist or purposive understanding of rights common in much of comparative constitutional and human rights law, which aims to discover the purpose of a rights guarantee and interpret restrictions for permissibility from the angle of the purpose. While such interpretation also has its special risk—notably, in some cases, turning rationales of protection into justifications for limits—it is widely accepted as a method of interpretation.

Such judicial rationales in the case of freedom of assembly seem to accord this right a rather high status and great importance. The ECtHR extols the freedom of assembly as one of the foundations of democratic society. As to the aim, the ECtHR specifically emphasizes that in the exercise of the right to freedom of assembly, the participants not only seek to express their opinion, but to do so together with others.[6] This high importance is also apparent in some judicial talk regarding necessary 'tolerance' of the externalities of assemblies on the part of authorities.[7] The Human Rights Committee similarly sees freedom of assembly as not only about collective expression, but also about exercising individual autonomy in solidarity with others, and thus being a fundamental prerequisite of participatory and inclusive democracy.[8] An 'old' and at times well-regarded court, the US Supreme Court has in principle long considered freedom of assembly to be inherent 'in the republican form of government'.[9] This appears to confirm some sort of crucial structural role assemblies are supposed to fulfil, implying that self-governance is neither exhausted nor sustainable alone by the voting process or by institutionalized politics or, although this is exactly not mentioned a lot lately, freedom of speech.[10]

The German Constitutional Court goes even further in stating that freedom of assembly is a 'moment [a component, literally] of original, untamed, direct democracy',[11] where the protester 'displays his personality in a direct way', 'takes up a position in the real sense of those words and testifies to his point of view'.[12] Assemblies contribute to the 'formation of political will and opinion in a representative democracy'[13] and constitute 'a necessary condition of a political early warning system'.[14]

Thus, assembly seems to be everything to everyone all at once: it is crucial since it is a form of direct democracy;[15] it is crucial since it mediates between institutionalized politics and ordinary people's actual grievances; and it is crucial since assemblies are the place where human personality and the individual human body itself directly appear in society.

For these reasons, freedom of assembly is the kind of fundamental right that ought to be overprotected or protected beyond the seemingly reasonable: It has the character to enlarge the horizon of everyday politics, which may otherwise petrify until it breaks. We would rather let grievances and even conflicts surface than suppress them. The fundamental right to freedom of assembly in this sense, as many authors have noted, possesses a transcendent quality, pointing towards something beyond the ordinary (see Srinivasan, in this volume).[16] The transcendent element leads to the insight that under certain circumstances, 'unpeaceful' political action is legitimate (see Woolman, in this volume), as quasi-universal historical consciousness cherishing revolutions and some normative[17] and empirical[18] studies testify.

Scope or Limit?

Before we can consider how courts define peacefulness, we must address the prior question of where peacefulness is located in the doctrine. There seems to be confusion (and, at times, well-meaning silence) about whether the peacefulness requirement belongs to the scope of the right or places a limit on the exercise of the right. Literal interpretation is rather clearly on the side of it delimiting the scope, demanding that only peaceful assemblies fall under the protection of the right. However, rights interpretation is flexible enough to override literal interpretation, or at least weaken it if it would go counter to the purpose or rationale of the right.

The advantage of being a limit rather than a determinant of the scope is that restrictions can only be justified if they conform to some rights standard, typically to the proportionality standard. Whereas if something is not even covered by a right, there are no limitations on state power to regulate or disperse. One reason for the presumption in favour of a broad scope of fundamental rights is that it allows for the full discussion and hopeful rationalization and theorization of the right and its limits in question. In accordance with the 'broad scope' view, freedom of religion extends to non- and a-religious worldviews or simply questions of conscience; freedom of speech to symbols, artworks, singing, or even access to documents of public interests; and privacy or liberty rights to abortion, same-sex marriage, data protection, euthanasia, and so on.

With regard to freedom of assembly, in one case, tellingly, the opposite happened however: The African Charter[19] does not textually limit the protection of freedom of assembly to peaceful assemblies, but the Committee, nevertheless, has read peacefulness into the scope of the right.[20] Such an extraordinary interpretative move—restricting a right *beyond the text*—is very unlikely to happen with any other right.

Opposite tendencies also appear, even if not to such an extent. The German Federal Constitutional Court, for instance, while not claiming that peacefulness is not a determinant of scope, ends up in the substantive argumentation to require ultimately that it be subject to the proportionality principle. This happens through an emphasis on individual responsibility. Police have to step up first against individual troublemakers, and dispersal is only allowed if such an intervention fails or is insufficient. Dispersing the whole assembly needs to conform to constitutional standards and proportionality.[21] Thus, assemblies can in theory be dispersed for unpeacefulness only after examining whether the dispersal is justified by the limits of freedom of assembly, including that it be proportionate. This brings the peacefulness review close to the normal review on the justifiability of a limit on a right.

In a similar vein, the ECtHR takes a rather close look at the unpeacefulness claims of governments, at least since the *Stankov* decision.[22] Often, peacefulness is examined as one pertaining to the limit, even if the person successfully incited violence, and the state was found to be justified in stepping up against it.[23] As it decides in individual cases, the individual's role is assessed, and that often requires looking closely into the details, such as '(i) whether the assembly intended to be peaceful and whether the organisers had violent intentions; (ii) whether the applicant had demonstrated violent intentions when joining the assembly; and (iii) whether the applicant had inflicted bodily harm on anyone'.[24] Establishing whether freedom of assembly is applicable to the complainant in the given case ultimately gets close to usual rights review at least as to its details.

Substantive Aspects of Unpeacefulness: What Peace?

Peace is an interpretative concept, which then needs a special construction in relation to freedom of assembly. A few distinctions arise though at first glance. While peacefulness for the purposes of assembly law is neither the mere absence of active civil war nor the general quiet of the cemetery, there is a temptation to equate it to analogous notions in domestic law. Public peace (öffentlicher Friede) comes to mind in German law, or breach of the peace in English common law. Intuitive as it may seem, constitutional or international human rights notions cannot be simply derived from concepts in ordinary law because that defies the purpose and idea of fundamental rights. This simple logic is still not fully spelled out and executed throughout human rights law.

The ECtHR regularly and explicitly states that unlawfulness does not equal unpeacefulness, with the consequence that simply unlawful assemblies cannot be dispersed or otherwise drastically restricted.[25] A similar consideration underlies a

German doctrine, whereby assemblies do not have to give notice if there is no organizer (spontaneous assemblies) or may do so later if the event to which they react happened later than the time window open for advance notice (urgent assemblies).[26]

Also, courts, especially lately, tend to claim that the notion of assembly has to be given an autonomous (constitutional or international) meaning,[27] which thus cannot be derived from notions of ordinary domestic criminal or civil law. Nonetheless, there is no general prohibition, or even questioning, of the reliance on ordinary law even at the ECtHR or the Germany High Court. This is especially apparent in the—often mindless—transposition of criminal law limits on freedom of expression to contexts involving the freedom of assembly, as will be visible from the examples that follow.

What is more, in jurisdictions where there is greater suspicion towards judicial interpretation and less constitutionalization of rights, interpretation on the basis of ordinary law is even seen as unproblematic. French law and legal scholarship are particularly keen on such constructions, and illustrate very well how the peacefulness requirement in the international human rights sense can be de facto replaced by speculations about future disturbances of public order.

French law does not explicitly operate with a peacefulness requirement for textual and historical reasons.[28] This, however, does not mean that legal protection extends to unpeaceful assemblies, quite to the contrary. Among offences against the public peace, a specific provision called *attroupement* can be found. An *attroupement* is a gathering of persons that is 'capable (susceptible) of troubling public order'.[29] *Attroupements* can be dispersed by force after two summons.[30] Thus, in practice, the notion of *attroupement* is closest to unpeacefulness in its function. Public order is defined as 'good order, public security, public cleanliness/health and public calm'[31] (i.e. absolutely nothing even close to violent acts).[32] Some in the literature claim to derive the notion of demonstration from the negation of *attroupement* (i.e. a gathering which is not susceptible of causing disturbances of public order).[33] This is a regulatory definition,[34] which then shows how a legal order less sensitive to constitutional or human rights considerations can water down unpeacefulness to disorderliness under domestic law.

In contrast, German constitutional interpretation takes pains to clarify the substance of peacefulness as an autonomous constitutional norm. The federal law on assemblies and processions allows for a preliminary ban where there is evidence that the organizer, or their supporters, strive for a violent or subversive course.[35] Some commentators have suggested—à la française, one is tempted to say—that the constitutional requirement of peacefulness should be interpreted from the law on assemblies, and claim that a peaceful assembly is one which does not take a 'violent or subversive' turn.[36] The German Constitutional Court, however, does not follow this 'statute-directed' legal thinking, and defines unpeacefulness on its own more narrowly, requiring 'acts of a certain dangerousity, such as aggressive excesses against persons or things or other violent acts [Gewalttätigkeiten]', stressing that 'a mere obstruction [Behinderung] of third persons'[37] does not turn an assembly unpeaceful.

Meanwhile, according to the ECtHR, freedom of assembly extends to 'all gatherings except those where the organisers and participants have [violent] intentions, incite violence or otherwise reject the foundations of a democratic society'.[38] The court thus added a category alongside the ones related to violence: rejection of the foundations of democratic society. This is logical in the sense that human rights cannot entail an entitlement to the destruction of the very system of human rights, but it is also worth observing that this is not as such about *peacefulness*. In a case where protesters blocked the Parliament because it had not adopted a promised electoral reform, the ECtHR found that this requirement was not fulfilled: 'A gathering of politicians, civil activists, and ordinary citizens contesting the progress of legislative reforms aimed at enhancing the democratic processes in the country, even if it used an obstructive form of protest, should not necessarily be deemed to constitute a rejection of the foundations of a democratic society'.[39]

Therefore, it seems that in the substantive sense, some relation to violence is required by the ECtHR just as by the German court: Simple obstruction, hindrance, or disturbance does not suffice. However, in both jurisdictions the target of violence can be either persons or objects. In that sense, the notion is not as narrow as possible. The French approach, given its broad definition of unpeaceful as disorderly, is far less protective by default: disturbance of public order is sufficient for both a ban and dispersal.

Before, however, making too much of the relative narrowness of the peacefulness requirement in German law, it is important to keep in mind that several other ways remain open to ban and disperse assemblies. These include the ban of assemblies within so-called pacified districts around constitutional organs of the Federation[40] or other specific prior bans on place and time related to the Holocaust and the Nazi rule,[41] or even preventative detention of supposed troublemakers, who are then physically prevented from participating in an assembly due to their arrest. Most of these bans are accepted by the ECtHR as well.[42] These bans operate *without* regard to a prospect of imminent violence. I discuss some of them in the section 'Unpeacefulness by Stealth: Violations of Dignity, Crime Prevention', but only after having discussed certain other contextual aspects of unpeacefulness related to assessing or determining violence.

Collectivity Threshold: From the Conduct of the Many to the Intent of the Few

Even if a jurisdiction defines the substantive criterion of unpeacefulness narrowly, it may be overly relaxed in its contextual aspects, and, thus, ultimately under-protect assembly. First, a question arises as to the threshold for when an assembly becomes unpeaceful. Second, there is the question of how we are to tell whether an assembly would in fact turn unpeaceful. What means can be used and what cues can be taken into account to predict future unpeacefulness?

The first question raises the issue of how to demarcate individual violence from violence of the assembly as a whole. Whose violence counts? And how much is required? The ECtHR,[43] General Comment No. 37,[44] and the guidelines of the African Commission on Human and Peoples' Rights[45] all state in one way or the other that isolated violent acts do not render the assembly as such unpeaceful. Sheer hindrance, annoyance, or even giving offence do not suffice; rather systematic and widespread violence is required. If unpeacefulness indeed were limited to such cases, then the chapter might be superfluous. However, widespread actual violence, let alone widespread violence against *persons*,[46] turns out to be by far not the only case of unpeacefulness.

The German court, for instance, adds to its own systematicity requirement that non-violent protesters shall not show *solidarity* with the violent 'elements' and, in particular, that organizers have to *explicitly disavow* violence.[47] In other words, in themselves non-violent solidarity gestures of co-participants towards violent participants bring the assembly closer to the threshold of unpeacefulness, as does the (by definition non-violent) failure of the organizers to expressly disavow the violent conduct of some participants.

The switch from violence of the participant (individual) to violence of the assembly (collective) thus may happen by non-violent actions or omissions: Violence of some accompanied by non-violent sympathy of others brings the whole assembly closer to unpeacefulness. Courts also regularly state that the organizers ought not to have violent intentions, and it is this concern that underlies the above-mentioned German duty of disavowal. The ECtHR also specifically includes violent intentions and incitement to violence in the peacefulness analysis.

The question is whether such broadened understanding of unpeacefulness is justified. Under general First Amendment doctrine, it is not (another question is whether that is applied in all cases to assemblies—we know it is not).[48] *Brandenburg v Ohio*[49] only allows for intervention where the violence is imminent—simple intent does not suffice, and there are reasons for it. The violent intent of organizers does not turn the assembly violent. Similarly, incitement to violence on the part of organizers does not necessitate that protesters would actually commit violence during the assembly or later. Neither intent as such nor incitement is in itself coercive. Violent intentions are not 'aggressive acts'—intent is not action. Incitement to violence as such is expression motivated by a state of mind, and not violence itself.

Still, incitement to violence is one form of unpeacefulness according to the ECtHR, whose views are illustrative and also authoritative in many jurisdictions. Incitement to violence is by definition not violent. But it sounds logical: Protesters shall not incite violence, as nobody should. Incitement to violence is a crime, and for a reason, why should protesters be exempt from it?

The question is nonetheless wrongly posed: If protesters incite to violence, then the police are free (mandated) to initiate proper criminal proceedings against them as always. Freedom of expression of the protester can be legitimately restricted if they choose to engage in incitement to violence.

However, here it functions as a limit on the rights of *others*: freedom of assembly of non-inciters, since it authorizes advance bans and dispersals of the entire assembly. This is one of the examples of the problems that arise where restrictions taken over from freedom-of-expression law are automatically extended to freedom of assembly without any independent justification, as if there was only one right (expression) and only one rights holder (the inciter) involved here.

The problem with this reasoning is that we are not only preventing incitement to violence—a proportionate restriction on the freedom of expression of the inciter—when we ban an assembly in advance, or disperse it. We are preventing the exercise of *another* fundamental right, and, more importantly, another fundamental right of *others* as well: freedom of assembly. In fact, the justification for limiting freedom of expression is taken over to limit freedom of assembly as well. The incitement rule which is justified with regard to freedom of expression is extended to a different right and to a multiplicity of rights holders, by reading it into freedom of assembly.

The criminalization of incitement to violence does not prevent the exercise of freedom of expression, it only makes it costly. Should you decide to incite, you will incur punishment. The conflation of unpeacefulness with incitement to violence, however, prevents the exercise of freedom of assembly. Unpeaceful assemblies may be banned in advance or dispersed on the spot by force. You may be punished extra if you disregard the ban or dispersal order, but the point here is that your—often only probable—incitement to violence counts twice: once for the purposes of freedom-of-expression restriction, and once for the purposes of freedom-of-assembly restriction. Moreover, in the latter case, it authorizes immediate and actual state (police) violence, what is more, even against protesters who have not committed a crime, and not just the start of a judicial procedure. A participant who has not incited to violence may be subject to severe immediate police measures resulting in harm to life and limb.

Therefore, it cannot be light-heartedly accepted that the violent intentions of organizers (or whoever in the assembly) deprives a would-be assembly of its peaceful character. There really *is* no mass mind. This is not to say that the state ought to tolerate incitement to violence if it is performed in the context of an assembly: Quite to the contrary, the state has every right to arrest, and start criminal proceedings against anyone inciting to violence at an assembly or prior to it. If, however, the whole assembly could be prevented or dispersed because of someone's incitement to violence, then the hypothetical unpeacefulness of someone(s)—and technically not even that of the inciter—is equalized with unpeacefulness of the assembly.

One person's freedom of expression should not be permitted to swallow everybody's freedom of assembly. Instead of starting criminal proceedings against a suspect, the exercise of a fundamental right is suspended for everybody else. In case of dispersal, the judgement of the police as to the incitement prompts immediate exercise of state violence. In case of advance ban, in order to prevent a potential future act of incitement, the exercise of freedom of assembly by non-inciters is prevented. This unitary treatment of inciters and everyone else casts doubts on any talk of individual responsibility, and systematicity as a threshold for unpeacefulness, and thus basically hollows out the independent right to freedom of assembly.

Predicting Violence from Intentions of Organizers

Apart from the question of whose violence matters, there is the question of what evidence should be considered in assessing the likelihood of future violence and whether it is even possible to make such predictions.

Figuring out whether organizers intend to commit violence proves to be extremely difficult in practice. Express advocacy of violence is rare. No organizer will declare in advance that their intention is to 'Attack the parliament!' or 'Attack the chamber of commerce!' Realistically, organizers with violent intentions do not give advance notice and adhere to a ban if it has been issued.

In the absence of explicit violent intentions, police or courts—in the case of review, if a speedy judicial review is granted at all—construe the implicit intent of some (the organizer or organizers) as indications of future actual violence by many (the organizers and some participants, if the systematicity requirement is not to be deprived of its meaning). This requires a kind of speculation that is nearly impossible to falsify and thus affronts the idea of a fundamental right. Such speculation underwrites a sanction for crimes never committed, in disregard of not only doctrines against prior restraint (note that the *only* area where freedom of expression doctrines do not apply to assemblies is prior restraint), but also of the fundamental principle *nulla poena sine crimine* (no punishment without a criminal act).

Individualization and Preventative Detention

One approach international human rights law takes to ensure that only unpeacefulness of the assembly, and not unpeacefulness of a participant, removes legal protection is to introduce measures which consistently focus on the individual troublemakers. Individual responsibility has thus found its way into assembly jurisprudence. Police are to stand up first against individuals who are violent, and not against the entire gathering. The entire gathering is to be dispersed only if violence is systematic or widespread, and only after proper summons. In other words, before dispersal, it must be clear to individuals intent on non-violence that they should leave.

This approach raises the question: Should some kind of individualization be introduced in the risk assessment phase as well (i.e. prior to the assembly)? Some countries appear to have taken that route, and begun to implement individual(ized) preventative detention of protesters who are judged to bring a risk at an upcoming assembly.

Preventative detention of individuals in order to save the gathering from dispersal may look like a good idea from the perspective of preserving as much freedom of assembly for as many as possible. Still, in practice it is a rather dubious business, mainly for the reason that there necessarily is too much discretion involved in such risk assessment, and police keen on maintaining order will almost automatically overuse this mandate.

Similar considerations apply here as with regard to violent intent of the organizer. If the would-be participant explicitly advertises that they will commit violent actions, then it may not be so hard to justify preventative detention for the duration of the assembly, since the state has a legitimate interest in preventing even individual violence. But that will be the rarest of cases. Moreover, given that authorities generally want to prevent individual violence even when it is not explicitly advertised in advance, states will infer from other cues that violence is to be expected should the detention not be executed.

Some courts have tried to set clear limits on the evidentiary basis for preventative detention (for more on preventative detention see Probert, in this volume). The ECtHR has held that while preventative detention is justifiable under certain circumstances, authorities must have specific knowledge of 'the place and time of the imminent commission of the offence and its potential victim(s)' and the individual must have been notified and given an opportunity to desist.[50] The court found these criteria had been fulfilled when a registered football hooligan (a 'gang leader'), after having been ordered not to commit violent acts at an upcoming football play, slipped away from the group which was to be escorted by police from the football stadium, hid in the ladies room and called another person presumably in order to continue organizing the planned brawl.[51] Such strict, concrete, and personalized conditions, together with an imminence requirement, and limits on the length of the detention, could indeed be a solution to preserve as much freedom of assembly of the non-violent as possible.

In practice, however, it is more likely that courts will adopt the approach of German (or, some Länder in Germany) and French courts which permit authorities regularly to engage in preventative detention without having shown an actual and imminent risk of violence. In these jurisdictions, actual violence *at previous demonstrations* has become the standard for the risk assessment at future demonstrations, as that was the case with G8 protesters in Germany.[52] Past violence on its own should not be taken as a predictor of future behaviour: that is the determinism of the 'dangerous person' who does not change: once a bad person, always a bad person. Such view is simply inconsistent with any philosophy of human rights.

What is more, it seems that the German threshold for preventative detention may be even lower. Recently, climate activists took up a form of protest by glueing their hands to the road—that is, engaging in 'merely obstructive', but not unpeaceful, conduct. Still, Bavarian authorities asserted this justified their preventative detention for thirty (!) days,[53] and this all despite the very clear guidelines in the matter of preventative detention from both Karlsruhe and the Strasbourg Court. If police can preventatively detain all protesters so that they do not glue themselves to the road at some point in the next thirty days, then the police have prevented the assembly as such, instead of saving a violent assembly from dispersal.

In a similar vein, French police increasingly have been allowed to make use of arrests for apparently preventative purposes[54] as recent cases and a report of the ombudsperson for the detained show.[55] This has been true even though the measures are in clear violation of Strasbourg doctrine, and amount to serious violation of not only freedom of assembly but the sheer right to liberty.

The increase in rights protection that may have been gained by individualization in the context of policing actual assemblies is forfeited when applied to risk assessment. Even when principles governing preventative detention ahead of an assembly are relatively straightforward (as is the case in Europe), the police, bent on preventing disorder or obstruction at any cost, cannot be trusted to apply them consistently. As a rule, preventative measures have chilling effect on the exercise of freedom of assembly.

Unpeacefulness by Stealth: Violations of Dignity, Crime Prevention

Many jurisdictions invoke other grounds—differently labelled—to ban and disperse assemblies in advance as if the assembly had been deemed unpeaceful. Most often, this involves dignity violations (a purely deontological claim, not requiring a showing of actual consequential harm), or just crime prevention as such. In such cases, we see a relaxed notion of unpeacefulness sliding through the back door. Unpeacefulness is functionally replaced by other concerns, which authorize advance bans in circumstances where not even the remote possibility of violence, along the previously discussed lines, exists.

Regarding dignity, the famous Holocaust denial decision of the German Constitutional Court needs to be mentioned,[56] not least because it is widely endorsed. There the organizers were required to guarantee that no Holocaust denial would occur at a meeting, where a famous Holocaust denier, David Irving had been invited to talk. The Court reconfigured the issue as to be judged solely under freedom of expression, instead of freedom of assembly, and decided that Holocaust denial could be constitutionally criminalized. Whatever the merit of the reasoning in terms of freedom-of-expression doctrines—I personally believe it is still the best analysis of the problem of hate speech—the judgment had absolutely no regard for freedom of assembly. The last sentence asserts that the same considerations apply to freedom of assembly as to freedom of expression; therefore, nothing else would result from examining the case from the angle of freedom of assembly.[57] It does not even pose the question whether the federal law on assembly, which allows for prior ban of an assembly where a crime could be committed, conforms to the constitution or not. Instead, the decision just takes for granted that if the criminalization of an expression is constitutional, then the prevention of assembly where such expression may occur, is also constitutional. This is the same technique as explained with regard to incitement to violence above: instead of remaining within the framework of freedom of expression and launching a criminal procedure against the speaker advocating Holocaust denial, the entire assembly is prevented. The speaker's freedom of expression swallows everyone's freedom of assembly.

A similar logic is applied in French law with regard to dignity, although there it is understood that dignity is part of public order. In administrative law, public order was interpreted as including the protection of human dignity. On this basis, the French court held that a (consensual) 'dwarf throwing performance' could be banned in advance,[58] and upheld a prior ban on an assembly where an extreme right-wing organization wanted to distribute pork soup called 'Gallic soup' ostensibly to the homeless, but aiming at excluding Jews and Muslims.[59] The Conseil d'Etat argued that its decision took 'into consideration the risks of reactions to what is intended as a demonstration capable of undermining the dignity of persons deprived of the proposed assistance [i.e. the soup] and of causing disturbances of public order as well'.[60] It is unclear from the reasoning of these decisions whether the violation of human dignity on its own amounts to disturbances of public order and thus suffices to justify the ban, or the logic is that the violation of human dignity gives reasons to anticipate the occurence of public disorder.

Conclusion

A number of principles follow from the above. To begin with, the theory of peacefulness needs to be rethought in a more realistic and systematic framework. Courts must clarify the distinction between unlawful and unpeaceful assemblies. They need to develop a narrow notion of unpeacefulness, and, most importantly, they need to refrain from letting freedom of expression swallow the independent right to freedom of assembly: Transposing limits of an individual's freedom of expression to everyone's freedom of assembly is an illegitimate construction that disregards an autonomous and independent right.

Legal scholarship, judges, and legislators have to dispense with remaining suspicions about a mass mind, deindividuation, and other outdated notions of early crowd psychology, long discarded by relevant scholarship, and stand by what they preach about the importance of freedom of assembly.

We need to be realistic about violent protesters: If a group's main purpose is to create violent disorder, harm to life and limb, in short, wreak havoc, they will not give advance notice or if they do, no prior ban will stop them. The function of the advance notice needs to be taken seriously: it is about practical issues of distributing public resources, guaranteeing that ambulances can get through or have alternative routes, rerouting traffic, and facilitating the exercise of other fundamental rights, balancing between demonstration and counter-demonstration, and so on. There is no reason why the whole theory of advance notice has to be construed on the basis of the unrealistic case of future violent protesters giving advance notice.

The systematicity requirement needs to be taken seriously. Dispersal on the spot ought only to be possible in case of active violence on the part of a significant number of protesters who cannot otherwise be stopped by policing, and advance ban ought to be possible only in case the violence is the explicit or at least clearly established aim of the gathering as a whole. Preventative detention of individuals needs to be either categorically prohibited or reserved for cases where violent intent, actual preparatory steps, and proper warning have been confirmed.

The peacefulness requirement cannot function as a qualifying principle that allows freedom of assembly to become 'freedom of expression minus' or 'speech that can be censored'. Finally, there is no reason why freedom of assembly ought to be exercised in a more peaceful manner, whatever it means, than any other right. The peacefulness requirement has a place in a systematic and rule-of-law–based interpretation of fundamental rights only if the same requirement were to apply to other rights as well. Thus, the peacefulness requirement either needs to be read out of legal texts on freedom of assembly, or read into the scope of all rights—in short, given an interpretation which overlaps with what anyway would be a *limit* on the exercise of any and all fundamental rights. Some of these developments are already underway in some judicial interpretations, but much less so in the actual regulation and policing of assemblies. Judicial intepretation all too often does not do justice to the importance and meaning of freedom of assembly as avowed by the very same courts.

Acknowledgements

The author wishes to thank especially Tabatha Abu El-Haj and Michael Hamilton for their invaluable effort and suggestions in the writing process, and also the participants of the workshop on the *Oxford Handbook of Peaceful Assembly*, including Ella McPherson, David Mead, Thomas Probert, and Stu Woolman.

Notes

1. Gustave Le Bon, *The Crowd. A Study of the Popular Mind* (New York: MacMillan, 1896); William McDougall, *The Group Mind* (Cambridge: Cambridge University Press, 1920);

Sigmund Freud, *Massenpsychologie und Ich-Analyse* (Leipzig, Germany: Wien, Zürich, Internationaler Psychoanalytischer Verlag, 1921).

2. E.g. Leon Festinger, A. Pepitone, and T. Newcomb, 'Some Consequences of De-individuation in a Group', *Journal of Abnormal and Social Psychology* 47, no. 2 (1952): 382–389; Henri Tajfel, 'Experiments in Intergroup Discrimination', in *Intergroup Relations. Essential Readings*, ed. Michael A. Hogg and Dominic Abrams (Philadelphia: Psychology Press, 2001), 178–186; Philip G. Zimbardo, 'The Human Choice: Individuation, Reason, and Order vs. Deindividuation, Impulse and Chaos', in *Nebraska Symposium on Motivation*, vol. 17, ed. William J. Arnold and David Levine (Lincoln: University of Nebraska Press, 1969), 237–307; Marylinn B. Brewer, 'Ingroup Bias in the Minimal Intergroup Situation. A Cognitive-Motivational Analysis', *Psychological Bulletin* 86, no. 2 (1979): 307–324.
3. E.g. Tom Postmes and Russell Spears, 'Deindividuation and Antinormative Behavior: A Meta-Analysis', *Psychological Bulletin* 123, no. 3 (1998): 238–259; Steven Reicher, Russell Spears, and Tom Postmes, 'A Social Identity Model of Deindividuation Phenomena', *European Review of Social Psychology* 6, no. 1 (1995): 161–198.
4. Charles Tilly, *Social Movements, 1768-2004* (Boulder, CO: Paradigm Publishers, 2004); Charles Tilly and Sidney Tarrow, *Contentious Politics* (Boulder, CO: Paradigm Publishers, 2006).
5. There is no place here to discuss limits placed on assembly, or what I elsewhere call the modality of freedom of assembly, such as limits on the time, the place, and the manner of assembly, which can result in the same or nearly the same suspension of assembly rights. See Orsolya Salát, *The Right to Freedom of Assembly: A Comparative Study* (Oxford. Hart Publishing, 2015), chs. 6–8. These limits abound in many countries, and famously also in the United States, but as they technically do not fully and categorically prevent the exercise of the right, they have been left out here. Further research is needed to critically assess the danger they pose to freedom of assembly and to establish whether they work as handy substitutes of the peacefulness review. See Hamilton, Robinson, and Page, in this volume.
6. ECtHR *Primov v Russia*, App. No. 17391/06, (12 June 2014), 91.
7. ECtHR, *Oya Ataman v Turkey*, App. No. 74552/01 (5 December 2006).
8. UNHRCtte, General Comment No. 37—Article 21: Right of Peaceful Assembly (17 September 2020) UN Doc. CCPR/C/GC/37, 1.
9. *DeJonge v Oregon*, 299 U.S. 353, 364 (1937) (citing *United States v Cruikshank*, 92 U.S. 542, 552 (1875)).
10. For more on the sad fate of freedom of assembly in the United States, see Tabatha Abu El-Haj, 'The Neglected Right of Assembly', *UCLA Law Review* 56, no. 3 (2009): 543–589; John D. Inazu, 'The Forgotten Freedom of Assembly', *Tulane Law Review* 84, no. 3 (2010): 565–612.
11. BVerfGE 69, 315, 347 (Brokdorf, 1985) (quoting Konrad Hesse, Grundzüge des Verfassungsrechts der Bundesrepublik Deutschland (14th ed., 1984): 157).
12. Ibid., 69, 315, 345, as translated by http://www.utexas.edu/law/academics/centers/transnational/work_new/german/case.php?id=656.
13. Ibid. 69, 315, 347.
14. Ibid.
15. I am critical of this direct democracy rationale (cf. Salát, *Right to Freedom of Assembly*, 48–49), but it demonstrates the zealous awe with which courts approach freedom of assembly.
16. This is similar, but not exactly the same as claimed by Judith Butler (or Hannah Arendt): 'the freedom of assembly has to precede and exceed any form of government that confers

that right of assembly'. Judith Butler, *Notes Toward a Performative Theory of Assembly* (Cambridge, MA: Harvard University Press, 2015), 160.

17. E.g. C. A. J. Coady, *Morality and Political Violence* (New York: Cambridge University Press, 2008); Vincenzo Ruggiero, *Understanding Political Violence. A Criminological Analysis* (Maidenhead, MA: Open University Press, 2006).
18. E.g. Charles D. Brockett, *Political Movements and Violence in Central America* (New York: Cambridge University Press, 2005).
19. Art 11, African [Banjul] Charter on Human and Peoples' Rights, adopted 27 June 1981, OAU Doc. CAB/LEG/67/3 rev. 5, 21 I.L.M. 58 (1982), entered into force 21 October 1986.
20. § 70 African Commission on Human and Peoples' Rights, Guidelines on Freedom of Association and Assembly in Africa, 2020, https://africandefenders.org/wp-content/uploads/2020/09/ACHPR-Guidelines-english.pdf.
21. BVerfGE 69, 315, 360 *et seq.*, Roman Herzog, Kommentar zu Article 8 in Maunz-Dürig Grundgesetz (Roman Herzog, Theodor Maunz, Günter Dürig eds., München, Beck, 2013) at Rn. 117, Helmuth Schulze-Fielitz, Kommentar zu Article 8 in Grundgesetz. Kommentar Vol. I (Horst Dreier ed., 3rd ed., 2018, Tübingen, Germany: Mohr Siebeck) at Rn. 110.
22. ECtHR, *Stankov and the United Macedonian Organisation Ilinden v Bulgaria*, App. Nos. 29221/95, 29225/95 (2 October 2001).
23. E.g. ECtHR, *Osmani and others v Former Yugoslav Republic of Macedonia*, App. No 50841/99 (11 October 2001).
24. ECtHR, *Gülcü v Turkey*, App. No. 17526/10 (19 January 2016) 97.
25. E.g. *Oya Ataman v Turkey*, App. No. 74552/01 (5 December 2006); *Bukta and Others v Hungary*, App. No. 25691/04 (17 July 2007).
26. BVerfGE 85, 69, 75.
27. ECtHR, *Tatár and Fáber v Hungary*, App. Nos. 26005/08, 26160/08 (12 June 2012).
28. For more detail on the different types of assemblies and their legal status in French law, see Salát, *Right to Freedom of Assembly*, 20–25.
29. Penal Code, Article 431-3.
30. Code of Internal Security, Article L211-9.
31. Code général des collectivités territoriales, Article L2212-2.
32. While it is sometimes alleged that actual intervention is authorized only in the case of 'real danger of serious troubles to public order', this real-danger criterion only shows up in the legal norm on banning weapons to a demonstration (Code de la sécurité intérieure, Article L211-4) not with regard to banning and dispersing the demonstration itself (Code de la sécurité intérieure, Article L211-3). Cf Matthieau Jublin, Manifestations et maintien de l'ordre par la police: que dit le droit? 2019, https://www.tf1info.fr/societe/manifestations-et-maintien-de-l-ordre-par-la-police-que-dit-le-droit-2110138.html.
33. Hubert G. Hubrecht, 'Le droit français de la manifestation', in *La manifestation*, ed. Pierre Favre (Paris: Presses de Sciences Po, 1990), 184.
34. Cf. Michael Hamilton, 'The Meaning and Scope of Freedom of Assembly in International Human Rights Law', *International & Comparative Law Quarterly* 69, no. 3 (2020): 521–556.
35. § 5. Nr. 3. Versammlungsgesetz in der Fassung der Bekanntmachung vom 15 November 1978 (BGBl. I S. 1789), das zuletzt durch Artikel 6 des Gesetzes vom 30 November 2020 (BGBl. I S. 2600) geändert worden ist.
36. Hans D Jarass, 'Kommentar zu Art. 8', in *Grundgesetz für die Bundesrepublik Deutschland. Kommentar*, 17th ed., ed. Hans D. Jarass, Martin Kment, and Bodo Pieroth (Munich: Beck,

2022), Rn. 9; Philip Kunig, 'Kommentar zu Art. 8', in *Grundgesetz-Kommentar I*, 5th ed, ed. Ingo von Münch and Philip Kunig (Munich: Beck, 2000), Rn. 23.

37. BVerfGE 104, 92, 106 (Sitzblockaden III, 2001).
38. ECtHR, *Kudrevičius and Others v Lithuania*, App. No. 37553/05 (15 October 2015), 92.
39. ECtHR, *Makarashvili and other v Georgia*, App. Nos. 23158/20, 31365/20, 32525/20 (1 September 2022).
40. Gesetz über befriedete Bezirke für Verfassungsorgane des Bundes vom 8 December 2008 (BGBl. I S. 2366), das durch Artikel 151 der Verordnung vom 19 June 2020 (BGBl. I S. 1328) geändert worden ist.
41. Article 15 of the Federal Law on Assembly, Versammlungsgesetz in der Fassung der Bekanntmachung vom 15. November 1978 (BGBl. I S. 1789), das zuletzt durch Artikel 6 des Gesetzes vom 30 November 2020 (BGBl. I S. 2600) geändert worden ist.
42. See also the acceptability of UK bans for a certain territory and a certain time: ECommHR, *Christians against Racism and Fascism (CARAF) v the United Kingdom*, App. No. 8440/78 (admissibility, 16 July 1980).
43. E.g. *Kudrevičius and Others v Lithuania*.
44. UNHRCtte, General Comment No. 37, 19.
45. ACHPR, Guidelines on Freedom of Association and Assembly in Africa, May 2017, 70.b.
46. For reasons of space, there is no separate discussion on violence against things and violence against persons, but it is not hard to see that there is an important difference between the two. Things are not equal to persons.
47. Wolfgang Hoffmann-Riem, Kommentar zu Article 8 in *Kommentar zum Grundgesetz für die Bundesrepublik* (AK-GG), ed. Erhard Denninger et al. (Neuwied, Germany: Hermann Luchterhand Verlag, 2001); Kunig, 'Kommentar zu Article 8', Rn. 24.
48. Tabatha Abu El-Haj, 'All Assemble: Order and Disorder in Law, Politics, and Culture', *University of Pennsylvania Journal of Constitutional Law* 16, no. 4 (2014): 949–1040.
49. *Brandenburg v Ohio*, 395 US 444 (1969).
50. Article 5 § 1 (b) ECHR. See the key case: ECtHR, *S.V. and A. v Denmark* [GC], App. Nos. 35553/12, 36678/12, and 36711/12 (22 October 2018), 83, referring to ECtHR, *Schwabe and M. G. v Germany*, App. Nos. 8080/08, 8577/08 (1 December 2011), and ECtHR, *Ostendorf v Germany*, App. No. 15598/08 (7 March 2013).
51. *Ostendorf*, 93–100.
52. Julia Muller, 'The Arrest of G8 Protesters: The Contested Legitimacy of Preventive Detention', *German Yearbook of International Law* 55 (2012): 649–658.
53. Poscher et al., Gewahrsam als letztes Mittel gegen die 'Letzte Generation?', *VerfBlog*, 24 November 2022, https://verfassungsblog.de/gewahrsam-als-letztes-mittel-gegen-die-letzte-generation/, https://doi.org/10.17176/20221125-001637-0.
54. In English, see e.g. https://www.lemonde.fr/en/france/article/2023/05/03/french-pension-protests-report-denounces-violations-of-fundamental-rights-during-arrests_6025319_7.html.
55. See Enquête sur les mesures de garde à vue prises dans le contexte des manifestations contre la réforme des retraites, 3 May 2023, https://www.cglpl.fr/wp-content/uploads/2023/05/Enqu%C3%AAte-GAV-manifestation_lettre-ministre-de-lint%C3%A9rieur-et-rapport.pdf.
56. BVerfGE 90, 241 (Karlsruhe 1994).

57. 'Für eine Überprüfung der angegriffenen Entscheidungen am Maßstab von Art. 8 Abs. 1 GG gelten dieselben Erwägungen. Aus diesem Grundrecht kann daher kein anderes Ergebnis folgen'. BVerfGE 90, 241 (Holocaust denial, 1994), Rn. 53.
58. Conseil d'État, Ass., 27 October 1995, Commune de Morsang-sur-Orge, Recueil, 372; RFDA 1995, conclusions Frydman ('*lancer des nains*').
59. Conseil d'Etat, ord. réf., 5 January 2007, n° 300311. Recueil Dalloz, 2007, 307 ('*soupe au cochon*').
60. One line in the reasoning of the 'Pork soup' decision seems to point into this direction: 'Considérant que l'arrêté contesté prend en considération les risques de réactions à ce qui est conçu comme une démonstration susceptible de porter atteinte à la dignité des personnes privées du secours proposé et de causer ainsi des troubles à l'ordre public'.

Further Reading

Abu El-Haj, Tabatha. 'The Neglected Right of Assembly'. *UCLA Law Review* 56, no. 3 (2009): 543–589.

Duffy-Meunier, Aurélie, and Thomas Perroud. 'La liberté de manifestation dans l'espace public en droit comparé'. *Jus Politicum* 17 (2017): 339–376. https://juspoliticum.com/article/La-liberte-de-manifestation-dans-l-espace-public-en-droit-compare-1148.html.

Hamilton, Michael. 'The Meaning and Scope of "Assembly" in International Human Rights Law'. *International & Comparative Law Quarterly* 69, no. 3 (2020): 521–556.

Inazu, John D. 'The Forgotten Freedom of Assembly'. *Tulane Law Review* 84, no. 565 (2010): 565–612.

Mead, David. *The New Law of Peaceful Protest: Rights and Regulation in the Human Rights Act Era*. Oxford: Hart Publishing, 2010.

CHAPTER 14

DISRUPTIVELY ASSEMBLING

DAVID MEAD

Introduction

As this chapter was being finalized in January 2023, the UK Government announced plans for further restrictions on peaceful but disruptive protests, creating new offences of causing serious disruption through 'locking on', tunnelling, or obstructing major transport works. The proposals, in the (now) Public Order Act 2023, were aimed at the current wave of XR/environmental protests such as roadblocks and slow-walking.[1] About the same time, residents in Kroonstad and Boksburg, South Africa took to the streets, closing off roads by burning tyres to protest about local electricity blackouts,[2] while a few days earlier German police commenced the eviction of protesters who had occupied a site in Westphalia, to object to newly granted permission for coal extraction.[3]

With disruptive forms of protest on the rise, the chapter offers a timely discussion of the extent to which human rights law protects the right to assemble disruptively.[4] Dictionary definitions of 'disrupt' are illuminating. Variously, we are told that it means '[t]o break or burst asunder; . . . shatter; to separate forcibly' (OED), 'to prevent . . . from continuing as usual or as expected' (Cambridge), and that a 'disruption' is a 'disturbance . . . interruption . . . [or] upheaval' (Chambers).[5] It is not then simply a synonym for 'obstruction'. Instead, we might equate disruption with prevention or, simply, rendering an activity less easily performed. Disruption can take many forms, but the two most salient forms, in the context of assembly, are physical blockage—either by people or objects—and environmental, such as noise.

We will see that assemblies remain protected in law by human rights or constitutional guarantees even if they become disruptive. It was not always so, with courts conflating disruption with a lack of peacefulness, and so outside the scope altogether. This essentially remains the position in the United States: 'The [Supreme] Court's failure to clearly articulate that non-violent disruptive assembly is constitutionally protected, when combined with rote acceptance of advance regulation of outdoor assembly and the sheer volume of regulation governing access to and use of public spaces, renders the scope of the right of peaceable assembly today shockingly thin'.[6]

The problem for us is this: How far does, or should, the law tolerate restrictions on disruption—what should and can a state do when faced with, to think of just one recent example, environmental activists entering sports arenas to demonstrate against climate change? Should a state be able to create specific, tailor-made offences that allow for substantial penalties? How should the balance be struck, and between what or whose competing interests and rights? This chapter looks at international human rights standards, trying to elicit a common doctrinal framework from the cases. The concluding words offer some thoughts of a more conceptual or socio-legal nature. The chapter is foregrounded on the necessity of a fair measure of disruption within a vibrant polity. To misquote Emma Goldman: 'If peaceful, tranquil protest changed anything, they'd abolish it'.

International Human Rights Norms and Principles

Other contributors to this Handbook have noted the importance of the right freely and peaceably to assemble, and its foundational instrumentalism, contributing to a healthy, sustainable democracy. Authority for this proposition can be found almost anywhere, in both judgments and 'soft law' guidance from the UN and the Venice Commission.[7] Makarau JCC put it this way in the Zimbabwe Constitutional Court in 2018:

> [The right] creates space for individuals to coalesce around an issue and speak with a voice that is louder than the individual voices of the demonstrators . . . demonstrations bring visibility to issues of public concern more vividly than individually communicated complaints or compliments to public authorities. Demonstrations have thus become an acceptable platform of public engagement and a medium of communication on issues of a public nature.[8]

Its importance has led courts to adopt a twin-track interpretative understanding: the scope of the primary right should not be interpreted restrictively, and clawbacks or qualifications should be subjected to rigorous scrutiny.[9]

As is probably also very well known, both the European Convention on Human Rights (ECHR) and the International Covenant on Civil and Political Rights (ICCPR), through interpretation by their adjudicatory bodies, respectively, now ensure that the right to assemble peacefully extends to protect those who take part in disruptive but non-violent protests, demonstrations, and assemblies. If that were not the case, the right would be emasculated almost to extinction. It was not always thus. In this part, I track the lineage of that principle, culminating in the current requirement that state institutions show tolerance even, for (most) disruptive assemblies. Thereafter, I will move on to discuss two important developments which might gainsay that position. The first is Strasbourg's invocation of what is at the core of Article 11, and the second is the ways in which other rights might countervail the expansive protection of the right to assemble peacefully. Both of these developments appear on track to re-sanction the constraint or regulation of disruptive assemblies.

Is There a Right to Assemble Disruptively?

Early ECHR cases featured states parties arguing that disruption was synonymous with non-peacefulness such that disorder, or even the risk of disorder eventuating, would be enough to remove protesters from the ambit of Article 11's protection. Those claims met with a measure of success. As I noted in 2010, there was a tendency to elide 'disruption' with 'disorder'.[10] Cases before the Commission such as *G & E v Norway* (a Laplander protest for four days outside Parliament), *GS v Austria* (an unauthorized demonstration on a public road by utilizing two trestle tables), *S v Austria* (a case of 'excessive noise'), and various German sit-in cases at US Air Force airbases would fall under that rubric. In *G & E*, for example, the Commission found that the interference with protesters' rights could reasonably be considered necessary to protect public order: 'A demonstration by setting up a tent for several days in an area open to public traffic must necessarily cause disorder'.

This remains essentially the approach taken in the United States today: '[A]uthorities routinely disperse nonviolent crowds, exploiting the fact that the [Supreme] Court has never squarely held that non-violent disruptive assemblies cannot be dispersed for merely unlawful acts'.[11] Functionally, disruption is synonymous with non-peacefulness such that disorder (or risk) let alone 'imminence of mere law-breaking removes individuals or groups from constitutional cover'.[12]

By contrast, there has been a marked change in approach on the part of the European Court of Human Rights (ECtHR) in the past decade or so. It now gives short shrift to such attempts. So, in *Schwabe & MG v Germany*, the Court held that:

> Even if there is a real risk of a public demonstration resulting in disorder as a result of developments outside the control of those organising it, such a demonstration does not as such fall outside the scope of Article 11(1), but any restriction placed on such an assembly must be in conformity with [Article 11(2)].[13]

Of more general application internationally, extending beyond the European *éspace juridique*, UN General Comment No. 37 puts it like this:

> Their scale or nature can cause disruption, for example of vehicular or pedestrian movement or economic activity. These consequences, whether intended or unintended, do not call into question the protection such assemblies enjoy. To the extent

> an event may create such disruptions or risks, these have to be managed within the framework of the Covenant.[14]

The Human Rights Committee further noted that 'while peaceful assemblies can sometimes be used to pursue ideas or goals that are contentious and their scale or nature can cause disruption, for example of vehicular or pedestrian movement or economic activity, this has to be tolerated, unless it imposes a disproportionate burden'.[15]

To summarize, the generally accepted international norm now is that the antonym of a protected 'peaceful protest' is not a disruptive protest but instead is one 'characterized by widespread and serious violence'.[16] An individual does not cease to enjoy the right of peaceful assembly as a result of sporadic violence or other punishable acts committed by individual participants in the course of the demonstration, if the individual in question remains peaceful in their own intentions or behaviour.[17] Indeed, peaceful assemblies in some cases can be inherently or deliberately disruptive yet still not lose protection. They might in fact require a significant degree of toleration. 'Public order' and 'law and order' are not synonyms, and prohibitions of 'public disorder' should not be used unduly to restrict peaceful assemblies.[18]

The Need for Toleration

These welcome assertions of principle do not mean that disruptive assemblies must always be permitted. This is a critical point to note. It simply means this: A non-violent but disruptive protest is not per se outside the protective scope of the international law framework. Disruption no longer goes to the primary question of engagement—does this action 'implicate' the protective guarantee of the Convention?—but is instead properly seen as a factor in determining the proportionality of any restrictions under Article 11(2)/21(2).

The UN Human Rights Committee (HRC) put it very recently in these terms:

> It is in the nature of assemblies that they sometimes disrupt the daily exercise of rights such as freedom of movement. This has to be tolerated, unless it imposes a disproportionate burden, in which case detailed grounds for limitations must be provided. Claims that an assembly will result in the undue disruption of traffic and the movement of pedestrians must be substantiated to allow for a full assessment.[19]

For example, the police might well be expected—as an aspect of the positive duty to facilitate the exercise of the right—to minimize the disruption by sensible and appropriate traffic management measures. A diversion through alternative thoroughfares in order, if necessary, to accommodate the organizers' legitimate interests in assembling within sight and sound of their target audience might be appropriate.[20] In *Iyakkam v State of Tamil Nadu*, the Madras High Court, for example, has said that where 'anti-social elements' might may take advantage of the situation, then the police should respond by imposing conditions to 'thwart' their ability to infiltrate and disrupt the course of the meeting.[21]

General Comment No. 37, with its wider international application, too speaks of tolerance for disruptive assemblies:

> Only in exceptional cases may an assembly be dispersed. Dispersal may be resorted to if the assembly as such is no longer peaceful, or if there is clear evidence of an imminent threat of serious violence that cannot be reasonably addressed by more proportionate measures such as targeted arrests. . . . An assembly that remains peaceful but which nevertheless causes a high level of disruption, such as the extended blocking of traffic, may be dispersed, as a rule, only if the disruption is 'serious and sustained'.[22]

That principle of tolerance for disruptive protests and assemblies which are domestically (administratively) unlawful—because, say, the organizers have not complied with notification requirements—but which cause inconvenience for everyday life is by now well established by the ECtHR.[23] Indeed, disruption is to be expected as an ordinary and inevitable incident of certain forms of public political activity, deserving what we might term 'graduated tolerance'.[24] The Zimbabwe High Court in *Dzamara and Others v Commissioner General of the Police* (in 2016) had this to say:

> Freedom of assembly and the right to demonstrate are fundamental freedoms, which should be enjoyed with minimum hindrances whenever possible. Where there has not been any unlawful conduct, dispersal of a demonstration held without notification may be a disproportionate restriction on freedom of peaceful assembly. . . . Any dispersal of such meeting must meet the lawful proportionality test.[25]

This requires restraint from using force when dealing with disruptive assemblies and protests.[26] It might well extend to exerting control on private security guards as they take measures against disruptive demonstrators.[27] A peaceful demonstration should not, in principle, be rendered subject to the threat of criminal sanctions or the deprivation of liberty.[28]

That said, intentionally structuring a demonstration to cause greater disruption than is ordinarily incidental and inevitable 'cannot enjoy the same privileged protection under the Convention as political speech or debate on questions of public interest or the peaceful manifestation of opinions'.[29] While states might enjoy a wide margin of appreciation in such circumstances, this is not an unlimited discretion to take any measures they consider appropriate.[30] Nonetheless, examples of responses the ECtHR has considered proportionate in recent years—and thus lawful—include:

- A three-month suspended sentence and €1500 fine for a go-slow motorway blockade lasting a handful of hours;[31]
- Ten-day custodial sentence for obstructing tree felling;[32]

- Sixty-day custodial sentence suspended for one year, alongside an order (lasting for that year) not to leave their places of residence for more than seven days without the authorities' prior agreement following a three-day obstruction of major roads in Lithuania.[33]

In *Chernega*, the Court identified factors integral to assessing the proportionality: Was it possible to protest for some period at least non-obstructively? Had the demonstrators used alternative mechanisms to participate politically, such as petitioning? Had substantial public attention already, or at least by the time of interference, been attracted? Had the demonstrators sought to utilize judicial remedies?[34] Considering whether or not those assembling had sufficient opportunity to manifest their views while not decisive, was also important in *Knezevic*.[35] There, the state was found to have shown tolerance enough when, after twenty days, a stage and food stands were removed from a protest event in the park opposite parliament.

What Is at the Core of the Right to Assemble Peacefully?

One important but problematic juridical development by the ECtHR has been the introduction of the concept of what is and is not at the 'core' of the right, in the *Kudrevicius* case.[36] This has the potential to alter the scope of protection in one of two ways. Mainly, it expands the leeway offered to states when dealing with disruptive assemblies and protests—lessening the need for tolerance. In extremis, it suggests (though this has never been put into operation) removal of such protection at the outset. In effect, such assemblies and protests are equated with not being peaceful.

Activities 'at the core' are, according to the ECtHR, deserving of greater protection, requiring greater tolerance and intervention by state agents. The Court does not at any stage define what *is* at the core; rather, it is content to conclude which activities are not. In *Kudrevicius*, the Court opined, 'physical conduct purposely obstructing traffic and the ordinary course of life in order to seriously disrupt the activities carried out by others is not at the core' of the freedom protected by Article 11.[37] In doing so, it expanded on its notion of 'reprehensible act' introduced in *Ezelin v France*:[38]

> [T]he intentional serious disruption, by demonstrators, to ordinary life and to the activities lawfully carried out by others, to a more significant extent than that caused by the normal exercise of the right of peaceful assembly in a public place, might be considered a 'reprehensible act' within the meaning of the court's case-law. Such behaviour might therefore justify the imposition of penalties, even of a criminal nature.[39]

What is not clear is whether *Kudrevicius* has loosened the necessity of 'sporadic violence or other punishable acts'.[40] Does 'reprehensible conduct' still imply a measure of free-standing criminality—as was, after all, the situation in *Kudrevicius*? The farmers were variously convicted of administrative offences and of inciting riot. Or is 'intentional serious disruption . . . to ordinary life' without involving any violence now enough to constitute 'reprehensible conduct'?[41] If so, that would have consequential implications for any assessment of 'necessity' carried out under Article 11(2), rendering state interventions easier to justify by affording a more expansive margin of appreciation. Critical too to the disposition was the target. Disruption was not a side effect but a tactic aimed at exerting political pressure.[42] Interestingly, the Court elided disruption aimed directly at preventing an activity of which protesters disapproved (as in *Steel v UK*[43]) and, as here, the 'physical blocking of another activity . . . which had no direct connection with the object of their protest'.[44]

Secondly, the Court went further and implied that it could envisage *some* disruptive sit-in protests as falling outside Article 11: 'Nevertheless, the Court does not consider that the impugned conduct of the demonstrations for which the applicants were held responsible was of such a nature and degree as to remove their participation in the demonstration from the scope of protection of the right'.[45] Clearly, some disruptive protests have not been ruled out by the ECtHR as excessive, but it would surely take quite an effort. Here, the protesting farmers intentionally blocked several major national highways, including with tractors, for more than forty-eight hours, and in circumstances where there was nothing to suggest a sudden political event, calling for an immediate reaction . . . yet did not fall outside.[46] It is, thus, a reasonable conclusion that the vast majority of disruptive or obstructive protests are not outside the ambit of the guarantee, and so proportionality of the response, of the toleration is the touchstone.

We can extract a couple of points from the case law of the ECtHR on disruptive occupations or sit-ins.[47] First, a state that responds to a (reasonably) long-term occupation by disbanding it but without criminal sanction is likely to pass muster with the Court. We can see this as long ago as 1996, in *Cisse v France*, involving an occupation of a church by asylum seekers to draw attention their collective plight—though whether that was because there was no criminal sanction or because of the length of the occupation, nearly two months, we cannot know.[48] Secondly, short-lived and/or small-scale occupations rarely justify serious sanction, especially where the only domestic offence is a failure to give prior notice. In *Bumbes v Romania*, B handcuffed himself to the barriers, blocking access to the parking area of the government's headquarters to protest a controversial mining project.[49] He had not provided the necessary three-day notification. His conviction constituted a disproportionate interference with his rights under Article 10: His protest was peaceful, only involved four people, and was quickly disbanded. The Court reasoned that the national authorities did not show sufficient tolerance for the political speech and placed disproportionate emphasis on the failure to give prior notice for the assembly. By contrast, the twelve-day sentences in *Makarashvili v Georgia* for a two-day obstruction of the national Parliament by blockading the entrances constituted 'reprehensible conduct' and was not considered disproportionate.[50] The custodial sanction for the administrative offence of disobeying the lawful orders of the police was not imposed for having organized and/or participated in the protests, but for having blocked the road during the police attempts to reopen access to the Parliament building, and was imposed for a relatively short duration.[51] Thirdly, anything except a token penalty for all bar more serious disruptions will be disproportionate. Most obviously, we see this in *Taranenko*, where sentences of three years' imprisonment, suspended but replaced with three years' probation for the forty or so members of a political party that occupied the President's Administration building in Moscow for an hour or two were disproportionate.[52] Much lesser convictions—between five and ten days of administrative detention—also constituted violations under Article 11 in *Annenkov*.[53] There, market stallholders refused to leave overnight, and staged overnight sit-ins for several nights.

Countervailing Rights

That international human rights law confers a right to assemble and cause a measure of deliberate disruption is clear. We now need to consider a supplementary question about legal scope and the doctrinal framework. The ECtHR and UN Human Rights Committee have also had to grapple with the question whether there might be countervailing rights at stake, such as the right peacefully to assemble versus the right to privacy in one's home.

Timothy Zick has written about this in the context of the First Amendment, what he calls rights pluralism.[54] He argues that the free speech clause both affects and has been affected by other constitutional rights. This section too logs possible intersections in international law, considering a few of the likeliest contestants: the right to property, the right in EU law to trade freely, and the right to privacy.[55] That last might take one of two forms: protection of privacy rights in and about the home—disruptive demonstrations outside, say, the family residence of an arms-dealer (see Kaiser, in this volume)—or privacy rights in the form of bodily autonomy, such as we see with anti-abortion protests outside clinics. In doing so, this section notes the symbiosis: expansion of one likely leads to diminution of other.

While an increasing number of cases placing reliance on the right to peaceful enjoyment of possessions in Article 1 of the First Protocol (A1P1) of the ECHR are starting to come before the UK courts, these offer only apparent succour to businesses seeking protection against protests. These cases involve forms of direct action protests that, either as their deliberate target or as a consequential effect, impact a company's continued, day-to-day use of its land, factory, or offices for lawful activities. An example would be *DPP v Cuciurean*, a sit-in protest against the planned HS2 railway extension on land owned by the developer.[56] This is not the same as a company being able to claim that a long-term assembly by way, say, of a sit-in on the pavement outside has affected its business, its profit-making.[57] Case law of the ECtHR is quite clear on this. No such claim can be maintained, and so no such claim can be prayed in aid to counteract a protester's right to assemble. A1P1 only encompasses possessions which are in existence or where someone has a legitimate expectation an asset or claim will eventuate.[58] Future income constitutes a 'possession' only if the income has been earned or where an enforceable claim to it exists.[59] Furthermore, A1P1 does not insulate from the vicissitudes of business. Only in those rare situations where there is a guarantee of business or turnover, or fixed income, might a company assert it has been deprived of a possession rather than suffering economic loss, simply the 'hazards of economic life'.[60]

Clashes between the right to assemble and business interests might also arise (within Europe) in the context of EU free trade rights, but again are unlikely to found the basis to quell even a disruptive protest. Under Articles 28–29 of the Treaty on the Functioning of the EU (TFEU), a business has the right to have free movement within the Union for its goods. In *Eugen Schmidberger Internationale Transporte Planzuge v Austria*, the Court of Justice held (in a preliminary ruling) that while Austria's decision not to ban an environmental demonstration which closed the Brenner Pass (between it and Italy) for almost thirty hours did constitute a restriction of intra-Community trade in goods, it was objectively justified by the protesters' Article 11 rights.[61] In another case, animal rights activists were trying to end the export of live animals. A Chief Constable decided to reduce manpower at the port where they were protesting. Consequently, officers turned back lorries when there was insufficient policing cover to prevent what they reasonably believed would be a breach of the peace. The UK House of Lords assumed that the policing decision could constitute a restriction on EU imports under Article 34 TFEU which prohibits quantitative restrictions. However, it ultimately decided the wider requirements of public policy, were, under Article 36, provided justification for restrictions, provided the steps taken were proportionate.

The right of privacy is not likelier to prove any more fruitful. The Supreme Court of New Zealand was asked, in *Brooker v Police*, to consider the legality of a protest outside a police officer's house.[62] B believed the officer had acted unlawfully towards him on conducting a search of his house. In response, B decided to hold his protest. The Court, by a majority, overturned his conviction for behaving in a disorderly manner in or within view of a public place. Guided by the protection given to freedom of expression in s.14 of New Zealand's Bill of Rights Act 1990, the Court interpreted the offence as limited to acts which disrupt public order, not merely those which annoy others in public. There was considerable attention by the minority judges to issues of privacy but even the majority addressed the matter: 'Privacy in the home is an important value, recognised by art 17 of the International Covenant. It may properly lead to restrictions on freedom of expression, even if public order is not at risk'.[63] Further, it is 'consistent with the right of freedom of expression that restrictions on that right may be imposed where necessary to protect interests such as privacy or residential quiet, as art 19 of the International Covenant permits'.[64] There have been concerns aired in the United States, similarly thought to offer scant protection to those Supreme Court Justices whose homes have been targeted by protesters.[65]

One of the pinch-points in recent years across the globe has been the regulation of protests outside abortion clinics. This conception of privacy is one that goes to bodily autonomy and the right to access health care in conditions of privacy and dignity.[66] This is the one area where, in general, we can see a marked restriction on the right to assemble founded on the priority accorded to another right. In *P and S v Poland*, the

ECtHR decided that states are under a positive obligation, under article 8, to create a procedural framework enabling a pregnant woman effectively to exercise her right of access to a lawful abortion.[67] From this it follows that 'there is also a positive obligation on states, under article 8, to enable a pregnant woman physically to access the premises where abortion services are lawfully provided, without being hindered or harmed' by protesters.[68]

Constitutional challenges by protesters to what are broadly termed 'safe access' zones outside abortion clinics have thus far failed in the UK, Canada, and Australia.[69] By contrast, the US Supreme Court has interpreted the First Amendment to preclude the imposition of a 35 foot (12m) buffer zone, as being overly broad.[70]

We might here advert to similar concerns raised by those subjected to disruptive gatherings, framed as an affront to their positive right to be protected by the state from inhuman, and so on, treatment (Art 3 ECHR). *Re E (A Child)* arose from the sectarian divide and troubles in Northern Ireland.[71] Catholic parents and children were forced to run a gauntlet of vituperation from Loyalists as they made their way to school: abused, spat at, and missiles thrown at them. The UK House of Lords (the precursor to the Supreme Court) held that the Police Service of Northern Ireland had complied with the qualified duty, to do all that could reasonably be expected of it to avoid a real and immediate risk, once it had, or ought to have had, knowledge of the existence of the risk.

Conclusion

This chapter has explained that as a matter of international human rights law, the fact that a protest is disruptive is not of itself a good reason for the state and its officials to impose restrictions. Not only should police officers demonstrate tolerance, we should require of our fellow citizens that they too tolerate as part and parcel of living in a free society, what David Feldman has termed 'coerced toleration'.[72] Of course, we should not have to put up with such levels of disruption that our right to lead 'the good life' become unlivable. The Strasbourg notion of the 'core' seeks to respond to that concern. We can debate whether that line has been pitched appropriately to balance all the competing interests. Still, in a democratic society *my* right to assemble should not, or should not inevitably and always, extinguish *your* enjoyment of the other valuable rights such a society confers on us. We saw in the chapter how some of those competing tensions have played out.

First, in constructing its notion of 'core' activities, the Court risks reifying certain types of protest—the staged, large-scale march and rally. If so, it risks marginalizing the utility and the prevalence of many other expressive forms. Put simplistically, how would the ECtHR have approached offering the Suffragettes or the African National Congress protection for their disruptive activities, had they been active now? Would it have balked at the tactics, seeing them as (or indeed more) disruptive as the roadblocks in *Kudrevicius*, or would it have developed a more nuanced approach, seeking to weigh in the balance the political value of such obviously counterhegemonic protests? I touch on that latter below. A better approach would be more contextual not the harsh, black and white construction of 'good' protest (and protesters) and 'bad'. After how many hours does slow walking along a main shopping street become sufficiently disruptive that it need no longer be tolerated? A Sunday evening is very different to 22 December, just before Christmas. I would go further. The legitimacy and thus protection we afford to those who assemble and protest must be functions not simply of the level of societal disruption they effect. For example, should our framework for accommodating the competing claims require us to tolerate a greater degree of reprehensible conduct from those whose views run counter to most of us, whose access to the formal institutions of power seem distant?[73] Indeed, we might suggest that protest should always be disruptive, should always disrupt our complacency, jolt us into reassessing (say) the necessity for fossil fuels. Disruptive protest is an agonistic necessity. Simply by being 'out of place',[74] a disruptive assembly forces us into confronting existing understandings through its lack of everyday mundanity. There is a tension then at the heart of laws that seek to impose restrictions: Assemblies are both inevitably and implicitly disruptive—'rights worth having are unruly things'[75]—yet (in most cases) they betoken unwelcome side effects.

The pre-emptive arrests of republican protesters across London on the morning of the coronation of King Charles III in May 2023 show us the problem.[76] The trend of construing certain events as totemic or sacrosanct, such that no dissent is brooked, is worrying.[77] In the build-up, the Metropolitan Police had declared their 'tolerance for any disruption, whether through protest or otherwise, will be low. We will deal robustly with anyone intent on undermining this celebration'.[78] They did so because this was framed as once-in-a-lifetime event, a national coming together. Of course, for many in the UK this was true, but if so, it was equally true for those who wished to mark their opposition. Indeed, where and when better to mark that than in the capital on the day?[79] We forget, to our collective cost, that protest will often need to be visceral in order to remain vital. Those lining the streets marking the occasion were of course exercising their own rights to assemble. It is by no means obvious why those republicans also exercising that same right—save that theirs was more obviously politically expressive, and counter-majoritarian—should not have been accorded the same expanse. No doubt many Londoners were disrupted from their everyday lives by the multi-thousand throng near the Palace—but, it seems, that was the right sort of disruption.

Next, accepting that disruption is essential for the effective enjoyment of the right to assemble, however, requires us to engage with this second-level question: Disruption to whom and for what purpose? We could conceive, quite legitimately, of affording differing protection in different contexts. Unpacking that warrants a book-length exegesis, not some concluding words in one chapter, but perhaps I might frame it like this, as a series of opposites? Let us take fossil fuel extraction. We might ask: Is action aimed at lawmakers to take legislative action? Is it aimed at the wider public designed to engender public support and raise awareness of the environmental harm, or perhaps to mobilize and augment membership?[80] Or is it aimed at Shell, disrupting production such that it ends or adding so greatly to the costs of continuance? This invokes questions of political legitimacy, and the role of disruptive activism within a deliberative democracy and the age-old trope (beyond the scope of this chapter): Does direct action supplant or supplement electoral politics? (see Srinivasan, in this volume and Woolman, in this volume).[81] Clearly, action aimed at invoking leverage against elites or institutional power holders, those groups with, more often than not, the power to effect the desired policy change is the bread and butter of protest and activism, but at what point, if ever, is it right to shift onto producers and commercial targets?[82] Even within that, we might properly distinguish symbolic, short-lived disruption that is still essentially public-facing—such as at the Embassy World Snooker Championship in May 2023—and disruption aimed at bringing about change directly, such as dismantling aircraft that would have been used for internal suppression. There is politically instrumental value in disruptive contention, but at possible cost. There is no guarantee that even a large-scale peaceful staged march will attract any media attention, or garner enough commensurate with the collective investment.[83] For a protest group, there will be a trade-off in deciding on disruption as a tactic: mobilizational publicity versus long-term or even immediate mobilizing harm, undermining support for their claims or cause.[84]

Thirdly, as we saw in the abortion protest cases, disruptive assemblies may require resolving a clash of rights. Care is needed here to distinguish others' rights *strictu sensu* and something better categorized jurisprudentially as a social interest or public good: the prevention of crime, morals, public order, or the impartiality of the judiciary. It is not always the case that courts or policymakers—when announcing a crackdown—see it that way, often positing as equivalent an individual's right to protest and the general public interest in undisturbed social life. Much media discourse too fails properly to disentangle the complexity, simplifying it (usually) to one where the competing concerns are put on a par. It is all too easy to categorize the latter—interests—as types of the former—rights—lumping together all manner of disruption as having the same impact. As one example, on 15 May 2023, the UK's Metropolitan Police tweeted that the rights of Just Stop Oil protesters slow-walking along a main road 'must be balanced against the right of others to go about their everyday business'. UK law affords me no 'right' to go about my everyday business; it is in Hohfeldian terms a liberty. Such elision leads us along false paths, and renders the terrain much more susceptible to incursive measures.

The discourse also suffers from this further identifiable problem. Wrongly assimilating someone's freedom to shop undisturbed with someone suffering a distinct interference with the rights of privacy and peaceful enjoyment of their home risks undervaluing the right to assemble, and, consequently, leading to under-protection. Constructing my desire to go about my weekend shopping business undisturbed as a 'right to shop' (whether or not in those specific terms) underplays the wider, social expressive utility of the right to assemble—the notion that *I* have an interest in *your* ability to demonstrate or go on a march—by configuring both in individualized terms. It confers on shoppers an undeserved priority or parity, at least, and carries echoes of what Blomley termed the overarching 'traffic logic' of much contemporary debate and policymaking.[85] Contrast this view in General Comment No. 37:

> Assemblies are a legitimate use of public and other spaces, and since they may entail by their very nature a certain level of disruption to ordinary life, such disruptions have to be accommodated, unless they impose a disproportionate burden, in which case the authorities must be able to provide detailed justification for any restrictions.[86]

Lastly, this socio-legal observation: Those doubts surrounding the scope of the right become structural impediments to its realization in practice because of the difficulty of effective enforcement on the ground. The power to deny me or to allow me to exercise my right to assemble is one rarely reposed in courts, almost always asked as they are ex post to adjudicate. The primary responsibility rests with decision-makers, the police, and local officials, in advance or at the scene. One of the longest-standing live issues, critical to enjoying the right peacefully to assemble, is in inverse proportion to how much it features in policy debates: What choice is open to us if we are told we cannot now march or have our rally? Even in a Global North, liberal democracy, a demonstrator (whether or not disruptive) confronted with a police demand to stop/never to start but which they believe is unlawful has a very limited choice. They might well choose not to go, for fear of arrest. Even if a court later rules the demand to be unlawful/disproportionate, they will have been chilled from exercising their rights. We too, collectively, have lost the value of their political contribution, disruptive as that might have been. They might instead choose to continue, challenging the officer to arrest them. Only if the officer then backs down has the marcher 'won'. If they are arrested, again ex post vindication several weeks or even months later will do nothing to secure the effective exercise of the right. A court judgment in your favour will still have meant the authoritarian dictator whose presence you objected to some weeks back was able to come and go as they pleased without the inconvenience of your disruptive group objecting to them. The task, then, of creating an *effective* right to disruptive protest is as much a function of surrounding social structures and institutions as it is of strictly delineated human rights laws and norms.

Acknowledgements

I would like to thank the editorial team (Tabatha, Michael, Thomas, and Sharath) and all the contributors who made the series of collaborative workshops leading up to this volume such interesting and thoughtful places to spend online time. I've learned more from them than is evident in this chapter.

Notes

1. B. Morton, 'New Plans to Widen Police Powers for Disruptive Protests', BBC News, 16 January 2023, https://www.bbc.co.uk/news/uk-politics-64282962.
2. S. Khumalo, 'South Africa in Flames: Protests Flare Up across the Country on Monday', *The Citizen*, 16 January 2023, https://www.citizen.co.za/news/south-africa/south-africa-in-flames-protest-action-january-2023/.

3. J. Hill 'Lützerath Eviction: German Police Drag Climate Protesters from Coal Village', BBC News, 12 January 2023, https://www.bbc.co.uk/news/world-europe-64233676.
4. Notably, one of the main US texts on the First Amendment—Geoffrey Stone et al., *The First Amendment*, 6th ed. (New York: Wolters and Kluwer, 2020)—in its almost seven hundred pages of coverage has no section specifically and identifiably discussing the constitutional right 'peaceably to assemble'.
5. *Oxford English Dictionary*, Online ed. (Oxford: Oxford University Press, 2003), continually updated at http://www.oed.com/; *Cambridge English Dictionary*, Online ed. (Cambridge: Cambridge University Press, 2023), continually updated at https://dictionary.cambridge.org/; *The Chambers Dictionary*, 13th ed. (London: Hodder & Stoughton, 2023), continually updated at https://chambers.co.uk/.
6. Tabatha Abu El-Haj, 'How the Liberal First Amendment Under-Protects Democracy', *Minnesota Law Review* 107, no. 2 (2022): 529–604, 561.
7. See e.g. UNHRCtte, *Malei v Belarus* (4 March 2021) UN Doc. CCPR/C/129/D/2404/2014, 9.5; IACommHR, *Graves violaciones a los derechos humanos en el marco de las protestas sociales en Nicaragua*, OEA/Ser.L/V/II. Doc. 86 (21 June 2018) 54; see also *Rangrajan v Jagjivan ram* (1990) LRC (const.) 412 and *Mulundika v The People* [1996] ZMSC 26.
8. Makarau JCC, in *Democratic Assembly for Restoration and Empowerment and Others v Saunyama NO and Others* [2018] ZWCC 9 p. 8.
9. ECtHR, *Kudrevičius and Others v Lithuania* [GC] App. No. 377553/05 (15 October 2015), 91; ECtHR, *Taranenko v Russia* App. No. 19554/05 (15 April 2014), 65; IACtHR, *Caso Mujeres Víctimas de Tortura Sexual en Atenco v México*, Serie C No. 371 (28 November 2018), 171; IACtHR, *Caso López Lone y otros v Honduras*, Serie C No. 302 (5 October 2015), 167.
10. David Mead, *The New Law of Peaceful Protest: Rights and Regulation in the Human Rights Act Era* (Oxford: Hart Publishing, 2010), 106.
11. Abu El-Haj, 'Liberal First Amendment', 560.
12. Ibid., 586.
13. ECtHR, *Schwabe & MG v Germany* App. Nos. 8080/08 and 8577/08 (1 December 2011), 103.
14. UNHRCtte, General Comment 37—Article 21: Right of Peaceful Assembly (17 September 2020) UN Doc. CCPR/C/GC/37, 7.
15. UNHRCtte, *Baytelova v Kazakhstan* CCPR/C/129/D/2520/2015 (18 December 2020) 9.6 (involving a protest by one woman waving lingerie in a public square against devaluation and the rise in prices of women's underwear). States should be put to strictest proof of claims that disruption/obstruction has in fact occurred: ECtHR, *Chumak v Ukraine* App. No. 44529/09 (6 March 2018), 51.
16. UNHRCtte, General Comment 37, 15.
17. ECtHR, *Frumkin v Russia* App. No. 74568/12 (5 January 2016), 99 and also ECtHR, *Knezevic v Montenegro* App. No. 54228/18 (2 February 2021) (finding that an assault on an officer at a time of tension when the police moved to disperse a protest camp did not take K outside the ambit of Article 11 as there was no indication of any initial violent intention). The UK Court of Appeal has recently countenanced that violence to property might be encompassed within the notion of non-peacefulness: *Attorney General's Reference No. 1 of 2022* [2022] EWCA Crim 1259 esp. 87.
18. UNHRCtte, General Comment 37, 44.
19. UNHRCtte, *Toregozhina v Kazakhstan* CCPR/C/129/D/2503/2014, 8.7 (emphasizing UNHRCtte, *Stambrovsky v Belarus* CCPR/C/112/D/1987/2010, 7.6, and UNHRCtte, *Pugach v Belarus* CCPR/C/114/D/1984/2010, 7.8).

20. ECtHR, *Primov v Russia* App. No. 17391/06 (12 June 2014), 146.
21. *Iyakkam v State of Tamil Nadu*, available at https://globalfreedomofexpression.columbia.edu/wp-content/uploads/2018/05/Iyakkam-v.-State-of-Tamil-Nadu.pdf, judgment (15 October 2017).
22. UNHRCtte, General Comment No. 37, 85.
23. ECtHR, *Nurettin Aldemir v Turkey* App. No. 32124/02, Judgment (18 December 2007). *Mlungwana and Others v The State* [2018] ZACC 45 [17]-[19] contains a good analysis of the need to disjoin the legality of organizers giving/failing to give notice and that of the subsequent gathering. This is not the law in the United States.
24. Derived from *Kudrevičius and Others v Lithuania* [GC], 155–157.
25. [2016] ZWHHC 398 p. 6.
26. See e.g. ECtHR, *Guzman v Spain* App. No. 41462/17 (6 October 2020). Wider afield, see *Public Defense Office of Sao Paulo v State of Sao Paulo* (Case No. 1016019-17.2014.8.26.0053 (19 October 2016)) where the state court granted an injunction to prohibit the police using rubber bullets and tear gas to break up public gatherings, such force being incompatible with the constitutional right to assemble and protest, available at https://globalfreedomofexpression.columbia.edu/cases/public-defense-office-sao-paulo-v-state-sao-paulo/.
27. ECtHR, *Chernega v Ukraine* App. No. 74768/10 (18 June 2019), 281.
28. *Kudrevičius and Others v Lithuania* [GC], 146.
29. Ibid.
30. ECtHR, *Ekrem Can v Turkey* App. No. 10613/10 (8 March 2022), 92 (finding a twenty-month prison sentence for a group of PKK supporters who occupied a court building for an hour, disrupting proceedings, was excessive and disproportionate).
31. ECtHR, *Barraco v France* App. No. 31684/05 (5 March 2009).
32. *Chernega v Ukraine*.
33. *Kudrevičius and Others v Lithuania* [GC].
34. *Chernega v Ukraine*, 243; see also *Dzamara and Others v Commissioner General of the Police* [2016] ZWHHC 398 (Judgment of Tsanga J) (stressing alternative remedies and channelling concerns 'through the appropriate political representatives').
35. *Knezevic v Montenegro* (drawing on *Frumkin v Russia*, 97).
36. *Kudrevičius and Others v Lithuania* [GC].
37. Ibid., 97.
38. ECtHR, *Ezelin v France* App. No. 11800/85 (26 April 1991), 53.
39. *Kudrevičius and Others v Lithuania* [GC], 173.
40. *Frumkin v Russia*, and Council of Europe *Guide to Article 11*, 28.
41. *Kudrevičius and Others v Lithuania* [GC], 173.
42. Ibid., [170].
43. ECtHR, *Steel v UK* App. No. 24838/94 (23 September 1998).
44. *Kudrevičius and Others v Lithuania* [GC], 171.
45. Ibid., 98.
46. Ibid., 66.
47. The Court has tended to confer protection as an aspect of the exercise of political expression, rather than of assembly rights *strictu sensu*: *Frumkin v Russia*, 107.
48. ECtHR, *Cisse v France* App. No. 51346/99 (16 January 2001), and *Knezevic v Montenegro* (finding that the removal of some three hundred temporary tents obstructing a major traffic route for twenty days was lawful).
49. ECtHR, *Bumbes v Romania* App. No. 18079/15 (3 May 2022).

50. ECtHR, *Makarashvili v Georgia* App. No. 23158/20 (1 September 2022).
51. Ibid., 103.
52. ECtHR, *Taranenko v Russia* App. No. 19554/05 (15 May 2014).
53. ECtHR, *Annenkov v Russia* App. No. 31475/10 (25 July 2017).
54. Timothy Zick, *The Dynamic Free Speech Clause* (Oxford: Oxford University Press, 2018).
55. We might also think about the prohibition on the destruction of other rights in Article 5 ICCPR/Article 17 ECHR.
56. [2022] EWHC 736 (Admin) [84] (finding that the company's right to exclusive possession of the land, as an aspect of A1P1, trumped an activist's right to protest peacefully).
57. See e.g. *United States v Johnson*, 875 F3d 360 (7th Cir. 2017) (overturning convictions for releasing two thousand mink from a mink farm on grounds that provisions in the Animal Enterprise Terrorism Act 2006 were overbroad in criminalizing speech acts that caused only economic damage such as lost profits); see also Timothy Zick, 'The Costs of Dissent: Protest and Civil Liabilities', *George Washington Law Review* 89, no. 2 (2021): 233–297.
58. ECtHR, *Pressos Compania Naviera S.A. v Belgium* App. No. 17849/91 (3 July 1997), 31.
59. ECtHR, *Ian Edgar (Liverpool) Ltd v the UK* App. No. 37683/97 (25 January 2000).
60. ECHR, *Greek Federation of Customs Officers, Gialouris v Greece* App. No. 24581/94 (6 April 1995), 128, albeit concerning a 'liberal profession' rather than a corporate entity.
61. C-112/00, [2003] ECR I-5659. Whether that same result would now be reached post *Kudrevicius* is moot.
62. (2007) NZSC 30. See also ECtHR, *Király and Dömötör v Hungary* App. No. 10851/13 (17 January 2017) (finding that the failure adequately to protect a Roma community from right-wing demonstrators rampaging violently and threateningly through their neighbourhood constituted a breach of the state's positive obligations under Article 8, to secure citizens' psychological integrity and ethnic identity). In the UK, there are specific prohibitions on certain forms of protests/assemblies outside homes and dwellings: s.42/s.42A Criminal Justice and Police Act 2001 (prohibiting activity seeking to harass, alarm or distress); s.241 Trade Union and Labour Relations (Consolidation) Act 1992 (prohibiting 'watching and besetting' people in their homes).
63. Ibid. [11].
64. Ibid. [41].
65. See *Frisby v Shultz*, 487 US 474 (1988); cf *Carey v Brown*, 447 US 455 (1980).
66. See *A,B,C v Ireland* (2011) EHRR 13 (finding on the facts that the Irish prohibition on abortion pursued the legitimate aim of protecting moral values and did not exceed the broad margin of appreciation, given the availability of the option to travel abroad for an abortion).
67. (2012) 129 BMLR 120 [99].
68. *Reference by the Attorney General for Northern Ireland—Abortion Services (Safe Access Zones) (Northern Ireland) Bill* [2022] UKSC 32 at [115], and consistent with ECommHR, *Van den Dungen v The Netherlands* App. No. 22838/93 (22 February 1995).
69. *Northern Ireland Abortion Reference*; *R v Spratt* 2008 BCCA 34; *R v Lewis* (1996) 24 BCLR (3d) 247 (British Colombia); and *Clubb v Edwards* [2019] HCA 11.
70. *McCullen v Coakley* 573 US 464 (2014) (finding less intrusive means could have been utilized to promote Massachusetts's legitimate state interest).
71. *Re E (A Child)* [2008] UKHL 66, declared inadmissible in ECtHR, *PF & EF v UK*, App. No. 28326/09 (23 November 2010) (finding operational decisions fell within the ambit of

legitimate police discretion and fully complied with the state's positive obligations); cf *Chernega v Ukraine*; see also *Király and Dömötör v Hungary*.

72. David Feldman, 'Protest and Tolerance: Legal Values and the Control of Public-Order Policing', in *Liberal Democracy and the Limits of Tolerance—Essays in Honor and Memory of Yitzhak Rabin*, ed. Raphael Cohen-Almagor (Ann Arbor: University of Michigan Press, 2000).
73. ECtHR, *Berkman v Russia* App. No. 46712/15 (1 December 2020), 46.
74. Tim Cresswell, *In Place/Out of Place* (St. Paul: University of Minnesota Press, 1996).
75. *Tabernacle v Secretary of State for Defence* [2009] EWCA Civ 23 [43].
76. David Mead, 'Coronation Arrests: How the New Public Order Law Disrupted Protesters' Once in a Lifetime Opportunity' (10 May 2023), available at https://theconversation.com/coronation-arrests-how-the-new-public-order-law-disrupted-protesters-once-in-a-lifetime-opportunity-205328.
77. The Olympic Games would be another, such as this in relation to Paris 2024, Texte de la Commission Mixte Paritaire, n° 1066-A0 presented to the National Assembly and the Senate on 4 April 2023, available at https://www.assemblee-nationale.fr/dyn/16/textes/l16b1066_texte-adopte-commission#.
78. Metropolitan Police tweet (@metpoliceuk) 13.57, 3 May 2023, available at https://twitter.com/metpoliceuk/status/1653745710724968448?s=20.
79. In ECtHR, *Sáska v Hungary* App. No. 58050/08 (27 November 2012), the ECtHR stated that 'the right to freedom of assembly includes the right to choose the time, place and modalities of the assembly' (21).
80. Some of the thinking here was prompted by a chance discovery of Gabriela Gonzalez Vaillant and Michael Schwartz, 'Student Movements and the Power of Disruption', *Partecipazione e Conflitto* 12, no. 1 (2019): 112.
81. See e.g. William Smith, 'The Boundaries of a Deliberative System: The Case of Disruptive Protest', *Critical Policy Studies* 10, no. 2 (2016): 152–170; Helen Fenwick and Gavin Phillipson, 'Direct Action, Convention Values and the Human Rights Act', *Legal Studies* 21, no. 4 (2001): 535–568, 540 (providing exceptionally valuable analysis for attempting to disaggregate different forms of activism—obstructive versus symbolic, high- versus low-salience issues).
82. The ECtHR's elision of the two and failure to discuss the distinction in *Kudrevičius and Others v Lithuania* [GC] 171 is, therefore, strange.
83. On which, this tweet by Professor Colin Davies (15 October 2022) is instructive: https://twitter.com/ProfColinDavis/status/1581195809294385152?s=20&t=N_or428Vtb1HpMzoTwwxHw.
84. Dan Wang and Alessandro Piazza, 'The Use of Disruptive Tactics in Protest as a Trade-off: The Role of Social Movement Claims', *Social Forces* 94, no. 4 (2015–16): 1675–1710; Matthew Feinberg, Robb Willer, and Chloe Kovacheff, 'The Activist's Dilemma: Extreme Protest Actions Reduce Popular Support for Social Movements', *Journal of Personality and Social Psychology* 119, no. 5 (2020): 1086–1111; Eric Shuman et al., 'Disrupting the System Constructively: Testing the Effectiveness of Nonnormative Nonviolent Collective Action', *Journal of Personality and Social Psychology* 121, no. 4 (2021): 819–841.
85. Nicholas Blomley, 'Civil Rights Meet Civil Engineering: Urban Public Space and Traffic Logic', *Canadian Journal of Law and Society* 22, no. 2 (2007): 55–72.
86. UNHRCtte, General Comment No. 37, 47, drawing on *Stambrovsky v Belarus*, 7.6, and *Pugach v Belarus* 7.8.

Further Reading

Abu El-Haj, Tabatha. 'All Assemble: Order and Disorder in Law, Politics and Culture'. *University of Pennsylvania Journal of Constitutional Law* 16, no. 4 (2014): 949–1040.
Abu El-Haj, Tabatha. 'Defining Peaceably: Policing the Line Between Constitutionally Protected Protest and Unlawful Assembly'. *Missouri Law Review* 80, no. 4 (2015): 961–986.
Abu El-Haj, Tabatha. 'How the Liberal First Amendment Under-Protects Democracy.' *Minnesota Law Review* 107, no. 2 (2022): 529–604.
Council of Europe. *Case Law Guide: Article 11* (August 2022). https://ks.echr.coe.int/web/echr-ks/article-11.
Council of Europe. *Case Law Guide: Mass Protests* (August 2022). https://ks.echr.coe.int/en/web/echr-ks/mass-protests.
Feldman, David. 'Protest and Tolerance: Legal Values and the Control of Public-Order Policing'. In *Liberal Democracy and the Limits of Tolerance—Essays in Honor and Memory of Yitzhak Rabin*, ed. Raphael Cohen-Almagor, 43–69. Ann Arbor: University of Michigan Press, 2000.
Fenwick, Helen, and Gavin Phillipson. 'Direct Action, Convention Values and the Human Rights Act'. *Legal Studies* 21, no. 4 (2001): 535–568.
Hamilton, Michael. 'The Management of Protest and Dissent'. In *The Routledge Handbook of Illiberalism*, ed. Andras Sajo, Renata Uitz, and Stephen Holmes, 384–402. London: Routledge, 2021.
Hamilton, Michael. 'The Meaning and Scope of "Assembly" in International Human Rights Law'. *International and Comparative Law Quarterly* 69, no. 3 (2020): 521–556.
Inazu, John. *Liberty's Refuge: The Forgotten Freedom of Assembly*. New Haven, CT: Yale University Press, 2012.
Inazu, John. 'Unlawful Assembly as Social Control'. *University of California Law Review* 64, no. 1 (2017): 2–52.
Mead, David. *The New Law of Peaceful Protest: Rights and Regulation in the Human Rights Act Era*. Oxford: Hart Publishing, 2010.
Salát, Orsolya. *The Right to Freedom of Assembly: A Comparative Study*. Oxford: Hart Publishing, 2015.
Smith, William. 'The Boundaries of a Deliberative System: The Case of Disruptive Protest'. *Critical Policy Studies* 10, no. 2 (2016): 152–170.
Wall, Illan Rua. *Law and Disorder: Sovereignty, Protest and Atmosphere*. Abingdon, UK: Routledge, 2020.
Zick, Timothy. *The Dynamic Free Speech Clause*. Oxford: Oxford University Press, 2018.
Zick, Timothy. *Speech out of Doors*. Cambridge: Cambridge University Press, 2009.

CHAPTER 15

ASSEMBLY WITHIN 'SIGHT AND SOUND'

TIMOTHY ZICK

INTRODUCTION

IMAGINE a peaceful assembly gathers to protest the adoption of a government policy that will lead to deforestation in a national park. Park officials inform those seeking to assemble they cannot protest near the site at which trees are now being felled, owing to concerns about obstruction of the scheduled work and 'public safety'. Instead, protesters are informed they may assemble at a remote location—a 'designated free speech zone'—two miles up the road. In this alternative location, no one except the assembled protesters—and a few park officials charged with policing their compliance with the limitation—will see or hear the assembly or its message. If the gathering happens in a forest and no one sees or hears it, does it nevertheless still make a sound? Is it still an 'assembly'?

The scenario raises a fundamental question: Should those seeking to peaceably assemble have a right to gather within 'sight and sound' of specific locations and/or target audiences? The question goes to the very heart of the meaningful exercise of rights of assembly. Peaceable assemblies typically, although they do not always, seek to communicate a public message. Their ability to do so depends to a large degree on access to specific audiences and places. Choice of location may also implicate other values, including group autonomy, solidarity, and self-government.

If indeed 'sight and sound' rights should matter, does the law protect an assembly's right to be seen and heard by others in public places? Some international law sources explicitly support sight and sound rights. For example, the UN Human Rights Committee's General Comment No. 37 states in several paragraphs that assembly participants should be able to conduct assemblies within sight and sound of targeted audiences.[1] Some international courts have begun to recognize sight and sound rights, although there is not yet a robust jurisprudence.[2] Even where sight and sound rights are recognized, they are subject to regulations in the interest of order, safety, and security.[3] As the UN Special Rapporteurs on the rights to freedom of peaceful assembly and of association and on extrajudicial, summary, or arbitrary executions jointly proposed, 'Assemblies, including spontaneous assemblies and counter-protests, should, *as far as possible*, be facilitated to take place within sight and sound of their target'.[4]

In the United States, the Supreme Court has not expressly recognized sight and sound rights under the First Amendment. Partly for this reason, but also owing to First Amendment doctrines that devalue place or location and grant governments broad authority to regulate public assemblies, lower courts in the United States have been reluctant to recognize sight and sound rights.[5] Litigants in the United States have also tended to raise explicit First Amendment sight and sound claims during political conventions and other heightened security events, during which courts are more likely to defer to governmental interests in safety, security, and order.[6] However, as the chapter will explain, under US law there is a foundation for recognizing assemblies' sight and sound rights or strong interests in being seen and heard.

The chapter begins with a review of existing international and US law concerning sight and sound rights. As mentioned, these rights have been embraced by name under some interpretations of international law, while recognition has been slower to materialize in the United States. The chapter then proceeds to argue that strengthening assembly rights to be seen and heard across the globe will require better and deeper understanding of the values associated with acting within sight and sound of places and audiences. Those values include recognizing organizational autonomy, facilitating communication, and supporting democracy-affirming activities. To further these values, international and US law should recognize a meaningful right to peacefully assemble within sight and sound of places and audiences. This can occur through a combination of effectively advocating sight and sound claims, limiting judicial deference to governmental power over place, and overcoming judicial scepticism about the definition and scope of rights to be seen and heard.

The Law of 'Sight and Sound'

As a phrase and concept, 'sight and sound' is no stranger to international human rights and US law. International law has been more explicit about, and more solicitous of, sight and sound rights. However, no body or system of law has developed a strong or sophisticated jurisprudence concerning rights to assemble within sight and sound of chosen audiences or locations. For a variety of reasons, US courts have been sceptical of claims that peaceable assemblies have a First Amendment *right* to gather within sight and sound of target audiences or locations. However, as we will see, US courts have recognized and sometimes supported assemblies' *interests* in access to places and audiences.

International Law

The right of peaceful assembly is recognized in various international charters and most national constitutions. Article 21 of the International Covenant on Civil and Political Rights (ICCPR) states, 'The right of peaceful assembly shall be recognized'.[7] (The right is also recognized in other international and regional instruments.[8]) Article 21 allows for restrictions on the right 'in conformity with the law' and 'in the interests of national security or public safety, public order (ordre public), the protection of public health or morals or the protection of the rights and freedoms of others'.[9]

Under the ICCPR and other instruments, states have the duty to facilitate peaceable assembly subject to necessary restrictions. That duty may extend not just to public places under the government's control, but in some circumstances to private ones as well.[10] Under Article 21, peaceful assemblies generally have a right to choose the place where they can best communicate to intended audiences.[11] The UN Human Rights Council has urged that Article 21 be interpreted to expressly include sight and sound rights. The Council has called upon States 'to facilitate peaceful protests by providing protestors, to the extent possible, with access to public space within sight and sound of their intended target'.[12]

In its General Comment No. 37 on Article 21, the Human Rights Committee observed that 'given the typically expressive nature of assemblies, participants must as far as possible be enabled to conduct assemblies within sight and sound of their target audience'.[13] This includes the rights of counter-demonstrators to gather within sight and sound of the assemblies against which they are directed'.[14] Further, '[p]eaceful assemblies should not be relegated to remote areas where they cannot effectively capture the attention of those who are being addressed, or the general public'.[15] General Comment No. 37 also noted that any time, place, or manner restrictions on assemblies 'should still, as far as possible, allow participants to assemble within sight and sound of their target audience, or at whatever site is otherwise important to their purpose'.[16] Other international law expert opinion, including the UN Special Rapporteur on the rights to freedom of peaceful assembly and of association and the OSCE/ODIHR Panel of Experts on the Freedom of Assembly, likewise recognize sight and sound rights.[17]

In accord with these interpretations, some international case law has expressly recognized a right of assemblies to reach intended audiences. The European Court of Human Rights (ECtHR) has explicitly recognized sight and sound rights in some of its decisions. For example, in a decision striking down restrictions on demonstrations near the Hungarian Parliament building, the ECtHR, interpreting the European Convention on Human Rights, observed that the right of peaceful assembly includes the right to choose the time, place, and manner of conduct of the assembly.[18] However, as the Court explained, the right is qualified by paragraph 2 of Article 11, which allows for restrictions where they are 'prescribed by law and are necessary in a democratic society in the interests of national security or public safety, for the prevention of disorder or crime, for the protection of health or morals or for the protection of the rights and freedoms of others'.[19]

Similarly, in *Lashmankin and Others v Russia* (2017), the ECtHR held the Russian government could not ban peaceable assemblies, including a planned gay rights demonstration, in the vicinity of court buildings. The Court concluded that the government had not justified its general ban by reference to any of the public safety or other interests in paragraph 2 of Article 11.[20] In rendering its decision, the ECtHR recognized that 'the purpose of an assembly is often linked to a certain location and/or time, to allow it to take place *within sight and sound of its target object* and *at a time when the message may have the strongest impact*'.[21]

National courts have sometimes also recognized an assembly's right to effective access to intended audiences. For example, in a case raising assembly rights, the Latvian Constitutional Court held, 'the State has the duty not only to ensure that a meeting, picket or a procession takes place, but also to see to it that freedom of speech and assembly is effective, namely—that the organized activity *shall reach the target audience*'.[22] Like the ECtHR's decisions, the Latvian Court's reasoning appears to recognize sight and sound rights, subject to public safety and other limits.

These decisions make clear that, even when recognized, sight and sound rights are not absolute. The rights of participants in an assembly to be seen and heard are balanced against governmental interests and protected only to the extent possible or practicable. Meanwhile, under Article 21 of the ICCPR and other international instruments, the right of assembly can be restricted when necessary to maintain public order, protect public health, and for other reasons.[23] Thus, whether or to what extent participants in assemblies have a right to be within sight and sound of an audience or place depends on whether the state can demonstrate sufficiently compelling countervailing interests and a proportionate response considering those interests. However, the burden rests on government to justify the need for and proportionality of any limits on sight and sound access.[24] The ECtHR has admonished that time, place, and manner regulations must not be applied in ways that interfere with or burden the expressive content of a peaceful assembly.[25] Relatedly, it has observed that any such restrictions should, as far as possible, allow participants to assemble within sight and sound of their target audiences.[26]

There is not, at present, what one would characterize as 'robust' international case law on the subject of sight and sound rights. Moreover, it is undoubtedly the case that some states do not protect sight and sound rights—even if they are formally obligated to do so. However, two things are notable in the international arena. First, as discussed further in the next section, in contrast to US court decisions, international instruments, interpretative documents, and even some judicial precedents expressly support sight and sound as a central component of the right of peaceful assembly. Second, because of this recognition, European and other courts appear to be less inclined to defer to governmental claims about the general reasonableness of place regulations and, more specifically, the adequacy of 'alternative' places available to assemblies.[27]

US Jurisprudence

The First Amendment to the US Constitution recognizes 'the freedom of speech', the 'right of the people to peaceably assemble', and the right 'to petition the government for a redress of grievances'.[28] However, in US Supreme Court jurisprudence, the assembly right has little force of its own, having generally been overshadowed by the free speech right and transformed to some extent into a right of 'association' linked to expressive activities.[29] Nevertheless, organizers of and participants in public assemblies enjoy First Amendment rights to gather, demonstrate, and engage in expressive activities.

The Supreme Court has not explicitly recognized a First Amendment right to assemble within sight and sound of intended audiences or places. However, as we will see, there is support in its precedents and those of some lower courts for recognizing and enforcing such a right. In general, the claimed right to assemble or speak within sight and sound of intended places or audiences is governed by two First Amendment doctrines: the 'public forum' doctrine, which determines which public areas are available for peaceable assembly, and the 'time, place, and manner' doctrine, which defines the scope of governmental authority to regulate the conditions of assembly.[30] These doctrines significantly limit where, when, and how assembly and expression can occur in places owned or operated by government. Moreover, in contrast to some international regimes, in the United States there is no right to assemble on private property or in places managed by private actors.[31]

The US Supreme Court has recognized a general right to access certain public properties, including public streets, parks, and sidewalks, for the purposes of expression and assembly.[32] However, as explained later in this section, even in these 'quintessential' public fora, government retains broad authority to regulate speech and assembly activities.[33] As far as other public places or properties are concerned, modern public forum doctrine categorizes them based primarily on the government's intent with respect to whether they will be open to expressive activities.[34] As a result, many places that are critically important to protesters and demonstrators are either off limits to assemblies or subject to strict regulation. For example, applying public forum doctrine, lower courts have concluded that national monuments and the plaza in front of the Supreme Court in Washington, DC, are not generally open to expressive activities or are subject to broad restrictions on those activities.[35] The public forum doctrine's categorical approach stands in contrast to interpretations of Article 21 of the ICCPR, which disfavour governmental designations of public places that exclude peaceful assembly.[36]

Under the 'time, place, and manner' doctrine, even in places individuals and groups have a right to access under the public forum doctrine, authorities can restrict location, noise levels, and time of assembly in ways that significantly affect the ability to come within sight and sound of target audiences.[37] Laws regulating peaceful assemblies generally do not violate the First Amendment if they are neutral concerning the speakers' subject and viewpoint, narrowly tailored to address concerns about traffic safety, noise, public order, safety, and other governmental interests, and leave open 'alternative channels' (including other places, means, or times) groups can rely on to deliver their message.[38] An 'alternative channel' is generally considered adequate as long as it allows a group to communicate its message to some audience somewhere—even if the 'channel' does not reach the target audience and is in another location.

US courts have somewhat limited experience adjudicating explicit sight and sound claims. The US Supreme Court has never explicitly recognized sight and sound claims, although as discussed later in this section it has addressed issues relating to locational and audience proximity. Some lower courts have merely used sight and sound descriptively, to indicate the distance between assembly and target audience.[39] Others have held that even if there is a cognizable right to be within sight and sound of target audiences or places, the challenged restrictions did not violate that right.[40] Applying the 'time, place, and manner' doctrine's balancing approach, a few lower federal courts have invalidated restrictions that effectively negated *any* opportunity to come within sight and sound of intended places or audiences or were not supported by important government interests.[41] Thus, some lower US courts have been receptive, in principle, to sight and sound claims.

Nevertheless, in several recent decisions federal courts have rejected explicit sight and sound claims. The cases all involved protesters' claims that they had a First Amendment right to be within sight and sound of delegates and others attending national political conventions. In one case, a federal appeals court upheld the enforcement of a 'demonstration zone' (DZ) at the 2004 Democratic National Convention.[42] The court accepted the district court's finding that the DZ was not *wholly* beyond sight and sound of the target place and audience, but opined in any event that 'there is no constitutional *requirement* that demonstrators be granted that sort of particularized access'.[43] The court conceded that 'the opportunity to interact directly with the body of delegates . . . would doubtless have facilitated the demonstrators' ability to reach their intended audience', but concluded that protesters could still reach their intended audiences through alternative channels of communication including media outlets.[44]

Addressing restrictions at other political conventions, federal district courts have more emphatically rejected sight and sound claims. One court opined that '[w]hatever the legal or practical parameters of the term "sight and sound," the phrase 'appears to find no analytic significance in the First Amendment jurisprudence of the Supreme Court"'.[45] The court observed that 'there is no constitutional entitlement to see the whites of the eyes of one's intended audience'.[46] The court of appeals affirmed, concluding that no case law cited by plaintiffs recognized a First Amendment right to be within sight and sound of the convention site (Madison Square Garden) or the delegates.[47] Another district court similarly concluded that sight and sound is 'not a standard used by the Supreme Court in its First Amendment jurisprudence'.[48] Despite its 'catchy and cogent format', the court observed, the phrase 'does little more than restate the obvious—expressive speech is designed to communicate'.[49] In reaching its conclusion, the court raised (but did not attempt to answer) several questions about the 'legal and practical parameters' of sight and sound claims, including from whose vantage point the right should be measured and how close an assembly had to be to come within sight and sound of its intended audience.[50] Other decisions have similarly rejected sight and sound claims and held that assemblies had ample 'alternative channels' for expression at their disposal.[51] It is worth noting that these cases all arose following the terrorist attacks on 11 September 2001, which created heightened security concerns at public events. They also all involved challenges to access restrictions imposed during national political party conventions—events typically associated with heightened security concerns and subject to heightened security protocols. These factors may have added to the courts' sceptical treatment of sight and sound claims.

The Values of 'Sight' and 'Sound'

In some international forums, the prospects for recognition and enforcement of sight and sound rights are encouraging. However, judicial recognition of such rights is relatively recent and not universal. In the United States, courts have been less willing to explicitly recognize sight and sound rights under the First Amendment. Regardless of legal system, courts and other authorities have not fully elaborated the values associated with sight and sound access. Choosing locations and audiences are core aspects of the autonomy of assembly organizers and participants. Sight and sound access also supports the vocality of place, the expressive benefits of audience proximity, and democratic values.

Organizational Autonomy

As international instruments recognize, choosing a location is a central aspect of organizational autonomy.[52] International law recognizes that the right of peaceful assembly protects 'the ability of people to exercise individual autonomy in solidarity with others'.[53] Under Article 21 of the ICCPR, assembly organizers have a *right* to 'choose the time, place, and modalities of the assembly'.[54] This includes a right 'to choose a location within sight and sound of their target audience'.[55] Although, as discussed, these rights are subject to reasonable restrictions, they are recognized as among the core autonomy rights of those organizing assemblies.

Unfortunately, in the United States the assembly right has been tethered to, and indeed supplanted by, the right to free speech.[56] Among other negative effects, the lack of independent assembly rights has obscured the purpose and scope of the right of peaceful assembly. As a result, First Amendment doctrines and decisions have ignored the connection between choice of location and audience and group autonomy.

Both international and US law connect assembly and expression in ways that can obscure the nature and character of the assembly right.[57] While this problem is perhaps most pronounced in the United States, where assembly is generally considered to be a right relating to 'expressive' forms such as protest or demonstration, it persists in Europe and other parts of the world. As commentators have observed, not all assemblies are forms of communicative 'protest'.[58]

In sum, sight and sound rights are justified by the organizational autonomy values of peaceful assembly that are under-appreciated in both international and US law. People assemble in public and private places for a host of reasons, not just to deliver protest messages. Social scientists have demonstrated 'how experience is embedded in place and how space holds memories that implicate people and events'.[59] Assemblies use place or location to strengthen group solidarity, show intensity of support, emphasize individual and group dignity, and even to provide entertainment.[60] In short, choice of location facilitates aspects of group and individual autonomy that may not pertain to communicating a specific message.

Spatial Vocality

Although assemblies are not *always* about communicating a specific message, choice of location often has symbolic and expressive value. Specific places are chosen for their vocality—how and what they communicate as venues or locations. Peaceful assemblies often speak through the places they choose. Recognizing assemblies' access rights enables them to connect and interact with places; regulatory displacements sever these spatial connections and interactions.

As a general matter, place is a far more complex concept than law tends to recognize.[61] As a legal concept, place tends to be secondary, inert, and fungible. In contrast to social scientific conceptions of place and space, legal conceptions of place-as-property do not recognize or process the *vocality* of public places—how they communicate and how individuals and groups use places to convey and amplify concerns and contentions.[62] Courts do not typically appreciate or address the expressive qualities of place, including the history of specific places such as government buildings and public squares and their contributions to public discourse.

People often seek to assemble near specific places, such as convention centres, abortion clinics, parliament buildings, courts, monuments, and police departments, precisely because such places are an important part of the message they wish to communicate.[63] Because places can be powerfully symbolic, being nearby rather than several or more blocks away allows peaceful assemblies to leverage and amplify spatial symbolism. The vocality of places often relates to the messages they amplify. Places can also be inscribed with broader national memories—for example, of prior movements, contests, and triumphs.[64] Parliament buildings and foreign embassies in many states, as well as the National Mall in Washington, DC, are repositories of such memories. So too are local places connected with specific political and social conflicts. Access to these inscribed places facilitates spatial vocality.

Some interpretations of international assembly law have expressly recognized the vocality of place. Commenting on Article 21 of the ICCPR, the UN Special Rapporteur observed:

> The choice of the venue or location of an assembly by the organizers is an integral part of the right to freedom of peaceful assembly. In many instances the location where an assembly takes part is an important part of its message; a protest demanding accountability for a gas explosion, for example, may be held at the site and exact time of the explosion. Likewise, public areas around iconic buildings are a logical place to convey a message with regard to institutions housed in these buildings.[65]

Similarly, in *Lashmankin*, which was discussed in an earlier section, 'International Law', the Court stressed that the purpose of an assembly is often linked to a certain location such that it must be allowed to take place within sight and sound of its target object and at a time when the message may have the strongest impact.[66]

Although the US Supreme Court has not expressly recognized sight and sound rights, some of its decisions have implicitly recognized the symbolic value of place or location. The Court has generally recognized that the place of expression can affect its meaning.[67] In some cases, it has upheld the right of peaceful assemblies to choose specific locations related to their message.[68] Some lower US courts have likewise acknowledged the importance to assemblies of accessing specific locations.[69] Despite their general lack of spatial sensitivity, US courts have, at times, recognized that access to place can help identify speakers and facilitate communication. However, they have not generally incorporated spatial vocality into First Amendment doctrine.

Place is not an inert or fungible resource. It is dynamic, active, and can be transformed by assemblies in ways that amplify contemporaneous messages and historical memories. By contrast, substantially displacing assemblies from their chosen locations severs symbolic connections between place, speaker, and message.[70] Spatial controls can also communicate something about those being restrained.[71] Thus, requiring an assembly to use a 'free speech zone' located several blocks away from a contested place communicates to audiences that even peaceful assemblies are dangerous, threatening, or a public nuisance. Aggressively policing or 'militarizing' public venues communicates negative messages about peaceable assembly and those who participate in such activities.[72]

The vocality of place offers a strong justification for the sight and sound right formally recognized in international law. It also explains why the assumption, most prominent in US law, that a distant sidewalk or media outlet can somehow serve as an adequate 'alternative' to an assembly within sight and sound of Parliament, the National Mall, or some other symbolic location is flawed. The law should reflect that a peaceful assembly has a strong expression-based interest in choice of location.

Proximity to Audiences

Proximity to audiences is also vital to the effective exercise of assembly rights. Sight and sound access facilitates appeals that are time sensitive. It also allows assemblies to reach target audiences they wish to persuade or dissuade.

As the UN Human Rights Committee has observed, 'Peaceful assemblies should not be relegated to remote areas where they cannot effectively capture the attention of those who are being addressed, or the general public'.[73] Assemblies that occur in a remote forest may indeed make some sound. However, if no audience is there to witness it, the activity fails as an outwardly expressive act—indeed, it may fail altogether as an exercise of the right of 'assembly'.

In some of its decisions, the US Supreme Court has recognized the benefits of proximity to audiences in public places. Addressing restrictions on 'sidewalk counseling' near abortion clinics but making a broader point, the Court stated, 'With respect to other means of communication, an individual confronted with an uncomfortable message can always turn the page, change the channel, or leave the Website. Not so on public streets and sidewalks. There, a listener often encounters speech he might otherwise tune out'.[74] As for sidewalk counselors, so too for many assemblies: Speech that cannot be easily avoided is, by definition, speech that an audience has a reasonable opportunity to see and hear.

In some contexts, capturing the attention of audiences requires that communication occur from close distances. For example, the US Supreme Court has recognized that the right to distribute pamphlets and other materials is only possible within the personal spaces of recipients.[75] The Court has also recognized that abortion clinic 'sidewalk counselors' have a right to engage with clinic patients from a *conversational* distance (i.e. within both sight and sound) of those visiting the facilities.[76] Indeed, the Court observed, it is 'no answer to say that petitioners can still be "seen and heard" by women within the buffer zones. If all that the women can see and hear are vociferous opponents of abortion, then the buffer zones have effectively stifled petitioners' message'.[77]

There is, then, an interest in being not just within sight and sound of the target audience but to engage from a conversational distance. In certain contexts, being close enough to 'see the whites of the eyes' of one's target audience is indeed essential. It is not clear, to be sure, how far the Supreme Court's support for this right to proximate communication extends. The Court has suggested there is a difference between 'normal conversation and leafletting' and 'protest',[78] implying that 'protesters' or perhaps assemblies more generally do not have a right to be within *conversational* distance. Although international courts have not addressed this issue, being able to, in the words of General Comment No. 37, 'effectively capture the attention of those who are being addressed, or the general public', may require close proximity to audiences and places.[79] There is some support in US law for recognizing a right to proximate and immediate expression.[80]

Sight, Sound, and Self-Government

Sight and sound rights are also connected to democratic values. Assembling with others to communicate with or to government officials is an act of self-government.[81] As the Human Rights Committee has explained, together with freedom of speech and other rights, the right of peaceful assembly 'constitutes the very foundation of a system of participatory governance based on democracy, human rights, the rule of law and pluralism'.[82]

Many assemblies seek to communicate with government officials, delegates, and dignitaries—through specific messages, presence, or shows of support. In these instances, sight and sound rights are vitally important to participatory democracy, holding officials accountable, and asserting popular sovereignty.[83]

How governments react to sight and sound claims in moments of political tension also communicates something about their commitment to peaceful assembly rights and popular sovereignty. Broadly restricting or suppressing direct action, including peaceful assemblies, particularly those aimed at public officials, candidates, and delegates, undermines democratic transparency and representational values.

As some interpretations of European law recognize, allowing assemblies to be seen and heard in these moments supports core democratic values.[84] By contrast, US courts have generally failed to support sight and sound claims during critical democratic moments such as national political conventions. The suppressive 'DZ' erected in Boston and other 'time, place, and manner' regulations that have restricted protest at political conventions directly interfered with peaceful assembly precisely when the need for protection was most acute.[85]

Supporting Sight and Sound Rights

While precedent recognizing the right is not yet robust, the previous section demonstrates that there is a strong foundation for recognizing sight and sound rights as core assembly rights. International law authorities and mechanisms already expressly recognize the right of peaceful assemblies to gather, demonstrate, and engage in other activities within sight and sound of intended audiences and places.[86] There is also a foundation for recognizing an assembly's interests in being seen and heard in US constitutional doctrine, even though US courts have not generally considered choice of location or sight and sound as aspects of the right of peaceful assembly.

Under international law, organizations and individuals should continue to invoke and highlight sight and sound rights. Litigants should stress the many values of sight and sound access. International courts should continue to recognize choice of location and access to target audiences and insist on narrow and adequately justified limits on these assembly rights. At the same time, scholars and commentators ought to continue to develop the justifications for recognizing and enforcing sight and sound rights.

Although the challenges for recognizing and enforcing sight and sound rights in the United States are greater, they are not insurmountable. As discussed, Supreme Court precedents have acknowledged both the vocality of place and the importance of access to audiences, especially in cases involving abortion clinic 'sidewalk counselors'.

The Court has also recognized that the location of speech provides information about the identity of speakers and their causes, and has emphasized the general benefits derived from access to public places. Some lower courts have also recognized the strong expressive interests of speakers and groups in gaining access to specific places and audiences.[87]

To be sure, under US law, doctrinal impediments remain. In particular, courts have too readily accepted that as long as assemblies have access to *some* alternative channel of communication, their interests have been adequately protected.[88] Interpretations of European and international law demonstrate the deficiencies of that approach.[89] Talking to reporters (assuming they are even interested) or posting messages on social media are hardly adequate substitutes for assembling peacefully in a chosen public place. Asserting that television and the internet are viable alternative channels to physical locations ignores the values associated with sight and sound access.

Given the scepticism in US law and the underdeveloped scope of the right in international law, one cannot simply ignore questions of definition and scope.[90] However, none of these concerns is unanswerable. For example:

- 'From whose vantage point is "sight" or "sound" measured'—the speaker or the audience?' [*Although both are relevant, because the assembly's rights are directly impacted, the relevant vantage point is that of the assembly. In order to benefit from spatial vocality, proximity to audience, and other values, a peaceable assembly should have a reasonable opportunity to choose a location that allows it to communicate with an intended audience or audiences.*]
- 'Is a speaker within "sight" if she is merely within the range of normal visual perception (potentially thousands of feet under certain conditions)'? [*No. Just as sidewalk counselors are not within 'sight' if they are unable to converse with and pass materials to an intended audience, assembling thousands of feet away deprives assemblies of visual access. Assemblies should have access that enables them to convey messages through signs, banners, placards, and the like. The degree of visual access should allow assemblies to benefit from the vocality of places and proximity to audiences, including government officials.*]
- 'Does the effect of cacophony or background noise change the calculation?' [*No. This is a condition faced by any public speaker or assembly. No one has a right to a tranquil public forum.*]

When determining the scope of any individual right or interest, context obviously matters. However, as far as possible, assemblies should have a meaningful opportunity to choose their locations, gather in the presence of others, and communicate to intended audiences. Courts should rigorously assess government claims that it is not possible, for security or other reasons, to facilitate or grant closer, better, or more meaningful access.[91]

Conclusion

The right to be within 'sight and sound' of intended audiences and places is a central aspect of an assembly's autonomy. As the chapter has explained, respecting choice of location and access to intended audiences also facilitates spatial vocality, expressive proximity, and democratic values. Current European and international law is more expressly committed to these values, although to date this support has not produced a robust jurisprudence of sight and sound or universal agreement. In the United States, by contrast, the lack of a freestanding assembly right, doctrines that devalue place and sharply restrict choice of location, and concerns about security have all combined to hinder recognition of the sight and sound rights of peaceful assemblies.

The general prospects for sight and sound rights will likely improve if courts and other authorities commit to more carefully examining the reasons *why* sight and sound are critical to peaceful assembly. Some European authorities have already highlighted certain of these values. Meanwhile, in the United States, formidable doctrinal and other barriers remain. However, even if the Supreme Court does not explicitly recognize sight and sound rights, its precedents and those of several lower courts support more careful scrutiny of limits on sight and sound access by peaceful assemblies.

Acknowledgements

I would like to thank Sarah Bradley for her diligent research assistance. I would also like to thank the Handbook editors for their insightful comments and suggestions.

Notes

1. See UNHRCtte, General Comment No. 37—Article 21: Right of Peaceful Assembly (17 September 2020), UN Doc. CCPR/C/GC/37, 22, 26, 53, 57.
2. See e.g. ECtHR, *Lashmankin and Others v Russia*, App. No. 57818/09 (7 February 2017), 405 (invalidating ban on demonstrations and other events near public courthouses).
3. See UNHRCtte, *Turchenyak et al. v Belarus* (10 September 2013), UN Doc. CCPR/C/108/D/1948/2010, 7.4 ('The organizers of an assembly generally have the right to choose a location within sight and sound of their target audience and no restriction to this right is permissible, unless (a) imposed in conformity with the law, and (b) necessary in a democratic society, in the interests of national security or public safety, public order, protection of public health or morals or protection of the rights and freedoms of others.').
4. UN Human Rights Council, Joint Report of the Special Rapporteur on the rights to freedom of peaceful assembly and of association and the Special Rapporteur on extrajudicial, summary or arbitrary executions on the proper management of assemblies (4 February 2016) UN Doc. A/HRC/31/66, 24.
5. See Timothy Zick, *Speech Out of Doors: Preserving First Amendment Liberties in Public Places* (New York: Cambridge University Press, 2008), 53–59.

6. Tabatha Abu El-Haj, *The Neglected Right of Assembly, UCLA Law Review* 56, no. 3 (2009): 543–589, 552 ('[S]trategies for securing order often result in situations where protesters are barely within sight or earshot of the challenged officials'.).
7. International Covenant on Civil and Political Rights (ICCPR), article 21 (16 December 1966), 999 UNTS 171.
8. E.g. UN General Assembly, Resolution 217A (III), Universal Declaration of Human Rights article 20 (December 10, 1948) A/RES/217(III); Convention for the Protection of Human Rights and Fundamental Freedoms (European Convention on Human Rights), article 11 (November 1950) 214 U.N.T.S. 221; Organization of American States, American Convention on Human Rights, article 15 (22 November 1969) O.A.S.T.S. No. 36, 1144 U.N.T.S. 123; Organization of African Unity, African Charter on Human and Peoples' Rights, article 11 (27 June 27 1981) O.A.U. Doc. CAB/Leg/67/3 Rev. 5, 1520 U.N.T.S. 217. The right of peaceable assembly has been interpreted and elaborated on by various judicial and non-judicial monitoring bodies.
9. ICCPR, article 21.
10. UN Human Rights Council Resolution 22/10, The promotion and protection of human rights in the context of peaceful protests, (9 April 2013), UN Doc. A/HRC/RES/22/10, operative 4. See also UNHRCtte, General Comment No. 37, 6, 57.
11. See *Turchenyak et al. v Belarus*, 7.4 (noting that the organizers of an assembly have the right to choose a location within sight and sound of their target audience).
12. UN Human Rights Council, The promotion and protection of human rights in the context of peaceful protests, Resolution adopted by the Human Rights Council (6 July 2018), UN Doc. A/HRC/RES/38/11, 4.
13. UNHRCtte, General Comment No. 37, 22.
14. Ibid., 26.
15. Ibid., 55.
16. Ibid., 53.
17. Maina Kiai, Second Thematic Report of the Special Rapporteur on the rights to freedom of peaceful assembly and of association, (24 April 2013) UN Doc. A/HRC/23/39, 60; Office for Democratic Institutions and Human Rights of the Organization for Security and Co-operation in Europe (OSCE/ODIHR) and European Commission for Democracy through Law (Venice Commission) Guidelines on Freedom of Peaceful Assembly, 3rd ed., (2020), 22, 77–78, 82–83, 133, and 147.
18. ECtHR, *Sáska v Hungary*, App. No. 58050/08 (27 November 2012).
19. *Sáska v Hungary*, article 11, 2.
20. *Lashmankin*, 405. See also UNHRCtte, General Comment No. 37, 56 (observing that any restrictions in and around 'places such as courts, parliaments, sites of historical significance or other official buildings' must be 'specially justified and narrowly circumscribed').
21. *Lashmankin*, 405 (emphasis added).
22. Republic of Latvia Constitutional Court, Judgment in the matter No. 2006-03-0106 (23 November 2006), 29.3 (English translation) (emphasis added).
23. *Turchenyak*, 7.4.
24. Ibid., 53.
25. ECtHR, *Stankov & United Macedonia Organisation Ilinden v Bulgaria*, App. Nos. 29221/95 and 29225/95, (2 October 2001), 94, 106–107; ECtHR, *Disk and Kesk v Turkey*, App. No. 38676/08 (27 November 2012), 31.

26. UNHRCtte, *Turchenyak v Belaruse (Communication No. 1948/2010)* (10 September 2013) UN Doc. CCPR/C/108/D/1948/2010, 7.4.
27. OSCE/ODIHR–Venice Commission Guidelines on Freedom of Peaceful Assembly, 147.
28. U.S. Const., amend I.
29. See generally John D. Inazu, *Liberty's Refuge: The Forgotten Freedom of Assembly* (New Haven, CT: Yale University Press, 2012).
30. See *Perry Educ. Ass'n v Perry Local Educators' Ass'n*, 460 U.S. 37, 45 (1983) (describing public forum doctrine); *Ward v Rock against Racism*, 491 U.S. 781, 791 (1989) (explaining government authority to limit the time, place, and manner of speech).
31. *Hudgens v NLRB*, 424 U.S. 507 (1976).
32. *Hague v Comm. for Indus. Org.*, 307 U.S. 496, 515 (1939).
33. *Perry*, 460 U.S. at 45.
34. *Cornelius v NAACP Legal Defense & Educ. Fund*, 473 U.S. 788 (1985).
35. See *Oberwetter v Hilliard*, 639 F.3d 545 (D.C. Cir. 2011) (upholding speech restrictions at Jefferson Memorial, which the court characterized as a 'non-public' forum); *Hodge v Talkin*, 799 F.3d 1145 (D.C. Cir. 2015) (upholding speech and assembly restrictions applicable to Supreme Court plaza).
36. See UNHRCtte, General Comment No. 37, 56 (identifying areas near 'courts, parliaments, sites of historical significance or other official buildings' as prime locations for assembly).
37. See John D. Inazu, 'The First Amendment's Public Forum', *William & Mary Law Review* 56, no. 4 (2015): 1159–1197, 1181 ('One of the problems with the content-neutrality inquiry is that it misses the expressive connection between speech and the time, place, and manner in which it occurs.').
38. *Ward*, 491 U.S. at 791.
39. E.g. *Cologne v Westfarms Assocs.*, 442 A.2d 471, 483 (Conn. Super. Ct. 1982) (describing distance between protesters and potential viewers in a mall); *Olivieri v Ward*, 637 F. Supp. 851 863 (S.D.N.Y. 1986) (raising issue of anti-gay demonstrators being placed within sight and sound of gay activists by the police), *rev'd*, 801 F.2d 602 (2d Cir. 1986).
40. See *Horizon Health Ctr. v Felicissimo*, 622 A.2d 891, 899 (N.J. Super. Ct. App. Div. 1993) (holding that requiring anti-abortion protesters to protest across the street from an abortion clinic was an adequate alternative because '[t]he alternate site permits expression well within ready sight and sound [of clinic users]'); *Johnson v Bax*, 63 F.3d 154, 156 (2d Cir. 1995) ('The parties also dispute whether the "pro" and "anti" demonstration areas afforded equal access, in terms of sight and sound, to Cooper Union and the location where the President entered and exited the building.').
41. See *New Alliance Party v Dinkins*, 743 F. Supp. 1055 (S.D.N.Y. 1990) (concluding assembly had an 'interest' in being within 'sight and sound' of a mayoral mansion which, under the circumstances, 'outweighed any increased security risks'); *Students against Apartheid Coal. v O'Neil*, 660 F. Supp. 333 (W.D. Va. 1987) (voiding a restriction on the construction of a temporary protest structure in public space because there was no adequate alternative channel of access to the protesters' intended audience); *Amnesty Int'l, USA v Battle*, 559 F.3d 1170, 1184–1185 (11th Cir. 2009) (holding that law enforcement violated clearly established First Amendment rights when it prevented protesters from coming within 'sight and sound' of any audience, thus rendering the protest wholly ineffective).
42. *Bl(a)ck Tea Soc'y v City of Boston*, 378 F.3d 8 (1st Cir. 2004).
43. Ibid., 14.

44. Ibid.
45. *Marcavage v City of New York*, 2010 WL 3910355 (S.D. N.Y. 2010), *8.
46. Ibid., *9.
47. *Marcavage v City of New York*, 689 F.3d 98, 101 (2d Cir. 2012).
48. *ACLU of Colo. v City & County of Denver*, 569 F. Supp. 2d 1142, 1180 (D. Colo. 2008).
49. Ibid., 1181.
50. Ibid., 1180–1181.
51. See *Coal. to March on the RNC & Stop the War v City of St. Paul*, 557 F. Supp. 2d 1014, 1016 (D. Minn. 2008) (rejecting anti-war group's First Amendment challenge seeking to modify a parade permit '[t]o come within sight and sound of the convention site'); *Reform Am. v City of Detroit*, 542 F. Supp. 3d 628, 644 (E.D. Mich. 2021) (observing that '[n]othing in the Sixth Circuit jurisprudence suggests that an adequate alternative channel of communication requires that a plaintiff be within sight and sound of his desired audience').
52. See Michael Hamilton, 'The Meaning and Scope of "Assembly" In International Human Rights Law', *International and Comparative Law Quarterly* 69, no. 3 (2020): 540–541, 521.
53. UNHRCtte, General Comment No. 37, 1.
54. *Saska v Hungary*, 21.
55. *Turchenyak*, 7.4.
56. See generally Inazu, *Liberty's Refuge.*
57. See Hamilton, 'Meaning and Scope of "Assembly"', 525–534 (distinguishing assembly from expression and association).
58. Ibid., 527.
59. Setha M. Low and Denise Lawrence-Zuniga, "Locating Culture," in *The Anthropology of Space and Place: Locating Culture*, ed. Setha M. Low and Denise Lawrence-Zuniga (Hoboken, NJ: Wiley-Blackwell, 2003), 18.
60. See Hamilton, 'Meaning and Scope of "Assembly"', 530 ("the right of peaceful assembly protects a range of relational interests quite apart from those deriving from speech"). See also Susan J. Brison, '"No Ways Tired": An Antidote to Protest Fatigue in the Trump Era', in *Protest and Dissent (Nomos LXII)*, ed. Melissa Schwartzberg (New York: New York University Press, 2020), 189–98, 192–195 (observing that assembly dignifies gatherings, energizes participants, and unites movements); Mari Matsuda, *Where Is Your Body? And Other Essays on Race, Gender, and the Law* (New York: Penguin Books, 1996), 75 (discussing dignitary aspects of public protest).
61. Zick, *Speech Out of Doors*, 8–12.
62. Yi-Fu Tuan, *Topophilia: A Study of Environmental Perception, Attitudes, and Values* (New York: Columbia University Press, 1974); Henri Lefebvre, *The Production of Space*, trans. Donald Nicholson-Smith (Hoboken, NJ: Wiley-Blackwell, 1992); Edward Relph, *Place and Placelessness* (Newbury Park, CA: Sage, 2008).
63. Zick, *Speech Out of Doors*, ch. 4.
64. Ibid., 186–189.
65. Written submission prepared by the Special Rapporteur on the rights to freedom of peaceful assembly and of association, Clément Nyaletsossi Voule, on the occasion of the half-day of general discussion in preparation for a General Comment on Article 21 (Right of Peaceful Assembly) of the International Covenant on Civil and Political Rights (Geneva, 20 March 2019).
66. *Lashmankin*, 405. See also ECtHR, *Süleyman Çelebi and Others v Turkey*, Nos. 37273/10 and 17 others (24 May 2016), 109; Council of Europe, European Commission for

Democracy Through Law (Venice Commission), *Compilation of Venice Commission Opinions Concerning Freedom of Assembly*, CDL-PI(2014)003-e (July 1, 2014) 4.2 ('Location is one of the key aspects of freedom of assembly'); OSCE/ ODIHR—Venice Commission, Guidelines on Freedom of Peaceful Assembly, 3.5 ('Public assemblies are held to convey a message to a particular target person, group or organisation. Therefore, as a general rule, assemblies should be facilitated within 'sight and sound' of their target audience').

67. See *City of Ladue v Gilleo*, 512 U.S. 43, 56–57 (1994) ('An espousal of socialism may carry different implications when displayed on the grounds of a stately mansion than when pasted on a factory wall or an ambulatory sandwich board'.).
68. *Brown v Louisiana*, 383 U.S. 131 (1966) (upholding right of civil rights protesters to engage in a silent protest in a public library reading room).
69. See e.g. *Million Youth March, Inc. v Safir*, 18 F. Supp. 2d 334, 348 (S.D.N.Y. 1998) (acknowledging choice of Harlem for protest march was significant because "Harlem enjoys a unique place in the African-American experience").
70. See e.g. UNHRCtte, *Pradad v Belarus (Communication No. 2029/2011)* (10 October 2014) UN Doc. CCPR . . . . , 3.1 (alleging that 'holding the demonstration at any other location [than in front of the Iranian Embassy in Minsk] would have defeated its purpose').
71. Timothy Zick, "Speech and Spatial Tactics," *Texas Law Review* 84, no. 3 (2006): 581–651.
72. Zick, *Speech Out of Doors*, ch. 7.
73. UNHRCtte, General Comment No. 37, 55.
74. *McCullen v Coakley*, 573 U.S. 464, 476 (2014).
75. See *Schneider v State*, 308 U.S. 147, 162 (1939).
76. *McCullen*, 573 U.S. at 490 (invalidating Massachusetts law that prohibited (with some exceptions) standing, walking, or speaking within thirty-five feet of any reproductive health care facilities).
77. Ibid., 490.
78. *McCullen*, 573 U.S. at 489.
79. UNHRCtte, General Comment No. 37, 55.
80. See *Madsen v Women's Health Center, Inc.*, 512 U.S. 753, 774–775 (1994) (invalidating 300-foot buffer zone around clinics and residences of clinic employees).
81. Cf. Alexander Meiklejohn, *Free Speech and Its Relation to Self-Government* (New York: Harper Bros., 1948).
82. UNHRCtte, General Comment No. 37, 1.
83. See Tabatha Abu El-Haj, 'Changing the People: Legal Regulation and American Democracy', *New York University Law Review* 86, no. 1 (2011): 102–166. See also Ronald J. Krotoszynski, Jr., *Reclaiming the Petition Clause* (New Haven, CT: Yale University Press, 2012) (proposing a right of proximate communication with officials, based on the First Amendment's Petition Clause), 183.
84. UNHRCtte, General Comment No. 37, 1, 56.
85. *Bl(a)ck Tea Society*, 378 F.3d at 14–15.
86. Hamilton, 'Meaning and Scope of "Assembly"', 540.
87. See *Wolin v Port Auth.*, 392 F.2d 83, 90 (2d Cir. 1968); *Million Youth March*, 18 F. Supp. 2d at 348; *Galvin v Hay*, 374 F.3d 739, 750–752 (9th Cir. 2004).
88. For a general critique of the 'alternative channels' principle, see Enrique Armijo, 'The Ample Alternative Channels Flaw in First Amendment Doctrine', *Washington & Lee Law Review* 73, no. 4 (2016): 1657–1740.

89. See Republic of Latvia Constitutional Court, Judgment in the matter No. 2006-0-0106 (23 November 2006) [29.1 and 32; English translation]: 'If protesting is envisaged to take place in the centre, then it is not possible to make the procession move through the outskirts so that it does not disrupt the movement of traffic . . . '.
90. See *ACLU of Colo.*, 569 F. Supp. 2d at 1180–81 (raising a number of definitional and practical concerns).
91. Krotoszynski, *Reclaiming the Petition Clause*, 183.

Further Reading

Abu El-Haj, Tabatha. 'Changing the People: Legal Regulation and American Democracy'. *N.Y.U. Law Review* 86, no. 1 (2011): 1–63.

Abu El-Haj, Tabatha. 'The Neglected Right of Assembly'. *UCLA Law Review* 56, no. 3 (2009): 543–586.

Armijo, Enrique. 'The Ample Alternative Channels Flaw in First Amendment Doctrine'. *Washington & Lee Law Review* 73, no. 4 (2016): 1657–1740.

Brison, Susan J. '"No Ways Tired"': An Antidote to Protest Fatigue in the Trump Era'. In *Protest and Dissent (Nomos LXII)*, ed. Melissa Schwartzberg, 189–198. New York: New York University Press, 2020.

Hamilton, Michael. 'The Meaning and Scope of "Assembly" in International Human Rights Law'. *International and Comparative Law Quarterly* 69, no. 3 (2020): 521–556.

Inazu, John D. 'The First Amendment's Public Forum'. *William & Mary Law Review* 56, no. 4 (2015): 1159–1197.

Inazu, John D. *Liberty's Refuge: The Forgotten Freedom of Assembly*. New Haven, CT: Yale University Press, 2012.

Krotoszynski, Ronald K., Jr. *Reclaiming the Petition Clause*. New Haven, CT: Yale University Press, 2012.

Krotoszynski, Ronald J., Jr., and Clint A. Carpenter. 'The Return of Seditious Libel'. *UCLA Law Review* 55, no. 5 (2008): 1239–1315.

Lefebvre, Henri. *The Production of Space*. Donald Nicholson-Smith. Trans. Hoboken, NJ: Wiley-Blackwell, 1992.

Matsuda, Mari. *Where Is Your Body? And Other Essays on Race, Gender, and the Law*. New York: Penguin Books, 1996.

Meiklejohn, Alexander. *Free Speech and Its Relation to Self-Government*. New York: Harper Bros., 1948.

O'Neill, Kevin Francis. 'Disentangling the Law of Public Protest'. *Loyola Law Review* 45, no. 3 (1999): 411–525.

Relph, Edward. *Place and Placelessness*. Newbury Park, CA: Sage, 2008.

Suplina, Nick. 'Crowd Control: The Troubling Mix of First Amendment Law, Political Demonstrations, and Terrorism'. *George Washington. Law Review* 73, no. 2 (2005): 395–428.

Tuan, Yi-Fu. *Topophilia: A Study of Environmental Perception, Attitudes, and Values*. New York: Columbia University Press, 1974.

Zick, Timothy. 'Speech and Spatial Tactics'. *Texas Law Review* 84, no. 3 (2006): 581–651.

Zick, Timothy. *Speech Out of Doors: Preserving First Amendment Liberties in Public Places*. New York: Cambridge University Press, 2008.

CHAPTER 16

RIGHTS TO PARTICIPATE? RIGHTS TO EXCLUDE?

GREGORY P. MAGARIAN

INTRODUCTION

ON 17 March 1993, the heavily Irish-American city of Boston, Massachusetts hosted its annual Saint Patrick's Day parade. The well-attended procession, sponsored by a range of community and civic organizations, featured colourful floats that celebrated Irish-American heritage. One proposed float prompted sharp controversy. The Irish-American Gay, Lesbian, and Bisexual Group of Boston (GLIB) wanted to enter a float in the parade. The parade organizers refused. GLIB then successfully sued the organizers under a Massachusetts statute that barred discrimination based on sexual orientation. The parade organizers appealed to the US Supreme Court, asserting that the law burdened their right of expressive association under the US Constitution's First Amendment.[1] US constitutional doctrine subsumes the right of peaceable assembly within the right of expressive association.

The case of *Hurley v Irish-American Gay, Lesbian, and Bisexual Group of Boston*[2] presented a conflict between two clashing interests in expressive association. GLIB sought to associate with the parade in order to express members' joint Irish-American and LGBTQ identities. The parade organizers sought to exclude GLIB because they wanted to avoid any appearance of endorsing homosexuality. Many observers expected the US Supreme Court, then closely divided between liberals and conservatives, to hand down a fractured, contentious decision. Instead, a unanimous Court ruled firmly in favour of the parade organizers. The Justices held that the organizers had the right to conduct their parade in whatever manner they believed would best express their particular account of Irish-American pride. The First Amendment barred Massachusetts from imposing on the parade, through operation of the state's non-discrimination statute, a message of Irish-American *gay* pride.

Other US Supreme Court cases, which focus mainly on associations, have reinforced the recognition in *Hurley* of a right to exclude unwanted participants,[3] although the Court has recognized some limits on that right.[4] Legal systems outside the United States have paid scant attention to tensions between claimed rights of participation and exclusion in either assemblies or associations. The UN Human Rights Committee has recently stated that '[t]he organizers of an assembly generally have the right to choose whom they wish to invite to participate'.[5] The European Court of Human Rights and the US Supreme Court both recognize a general obligation of governments to protect public assemblies from violence,[6] although the full nature and extent of the obligation remains unsettled.[7] Courts outside the United States have not recognized a right for an assembly or association to exclude participants who might simply interfere with the group's message. In other words, no judicial equivalent to *Hurley* appears to have arisen elsewhere. This divergence amongst liberal legal systems requires explanation.

The analysis and result in *Hurley* depended on several pre-conditions that distinguish US constitutional law from other liberal democratic rights regimes, notably those of Europe and Canada. First, the constitutional requirement of 'state action' compelled the Supreme Court to ignore GLIB's agency and treat Massachusetts as the parade organizers' sole legal adversary. Conversely, despite close ties between the organizers and the Boston city government, GLIB did not contest the organizers' legal posture as an entirely private entity, entitled to claim constitutional rights. Second, the Court conceptualized the parade as an 'expressive association', a distinctive category in US constitutional law that both subsumes the concept of public assembly and requires expressive character in order for any association or assembly to state a constitutional claim. Third, while the Court nominally balanced the parade organizers' expressive association claim against the government's regulatory interest in preventing discrimination, the government interest stood on a categorically lower legal footing than the organizers' constitutionally protected right. The Court did not purport to balance the parade organizers' constitutionally grounded interest in excluding unwanted participants against the GLIB members' constitutionally grounded interest in expressing their identities.

These features of US law diverge from other liberal democratic legal systems in ways that substantially explain why US courts have, and other nations' courts generally have not, recognized a constitutional right of some associations and assemblies to exclude unwanted participants. Rights charters' divergent conceptions of the public-private distinction; conflation or distinction of rights of assembly, association, and speech in determining whether and how to protect groups' autonomy; and willingness or unwillingness to balance competing rights and interests all shed light on legal systems' differing approaches to participation-exclusion disputes.

This chapter discusses the participation-exclusion problem as it pertains to both assemblies and associations. Considering the two contexts together sheds useful light on both. Opposite sets of related qualities characterize the two categories.[8] Assemblies frequently occur on generally accessible public property, while associations generally do not require public resources. Assemblies require physical or virtual proximity of participants, while associations do not. Assemblies are more spontaneous and temporally bounded, while associations are more structured and permanent. Assemblies tend to embody shared immediate concerns, while associations tend to embody shared longer-term interests, affinities, or identities. Assemblies generally require lesser infrastructure and resources than associations require.

Notwithstanding those distinctions between assemblies and associations, some cases about constitutional rights to exclude may combine characteristics of both. Associations frequently engage in assembly, and assemblies may manifest or coalesce into associations. *Hurley* illustrates this dualism. The Boston Saint Patrick's Day parade itself was a classic assembly. It used public space for a physically proximate gathering over a limited period of time. The parade organizers were a classic association. They formed a permanent, private structure, based on a shared identity, supported by substantial resources.

This chapter, following its descriptive analysis, gives normative consideration to how liberal democratic values of equal citizenship, pluralism, and collective self-governance should influence whether liberal rights regimes empower associations and/or assemblies to exclude unwanted participants. The distinction between associations and assemblies matters centrally for the normative analysis. While affirmative rights of both association and assembly can empower socially and politically marginal people and groups, the costlier infrastructural requirements of association mean that a right of non-association tends to benefit powerful, mainstream groups at the expense of social and political outsiders. In contrast, constitutional allowance for letting assemblies exclude unwanted participants can, at least theoretically, extend benefits to less socially and politically powerful groups. However, legal constraints on interference with assemblies, beyond prevention of imminent violence or of wholesale silencing, create serious risks of restricting dynamic public discourse. Therefore, liberal democratic values ultimately counsel against giving assemblies strong rights to exclude unwanted participants.

The Public-Private Distinction

The US Supreme Court's legal analysis in *Hurley* pivoted on the rigid public-private distinction embodied in US constitutional law. Only upon a finding of 'state action' may a rights claim succeed, and only non-state actors have constitutional rights.[9] The Court emphasized that GLIB, despite wanting to express a message of gay Irish pride in the Boston Saint Patrick's Day Parade, was not itself pursuing a First Amendment claim.[10] Rather, the legal dispute set the 'private' parade organizers' First Amendment claim against the state's regulatory interest in protecting GLIB from discrimination. By this logic, the parade organizers enjoyed the same legal status as a natural person who might seek to vindicate a right to privacy or bodily autonomy, while the marginalized identity group's expressive interest collapsed into an asserted act of government coercion.

A strikingly similar conflict to *Hurley* arose in Bonn, Germany in 2019. Every September, Bonn hosts a Culture and Encounter Festival. A wide range of local organizations with international and intercultural orientations exhibit at the festival. In past years, one such exhibitor had been the German-Palestinian Women's Association (GPWA). For the 2019 festival, however, the city government barred GPWA from exhibiting. GPWA had expressed support for the Boycott, Divestment, and Sanctions (BDS) movement against Israel's occupation of Palestine. The city barred GPWA from the festival based on the government's view that BDS, and by extension GPWA, was categorically anti-Semitic. GWPA sued for reinstatement, and a local court sustained the claim, holding that the city's bar violated GPWA's right to free expression under Germany's Basic Law. The court recognized a valid government interest in suppressing anti-Semitism but rejected the city's wholesale branding of the BDS movement as anti-Semitic.[11]

The result in the GPWA case almost perfectly inverts the result in *Hurley*: The unwanted participants, not the event organizers, advanced a free speech claim and prevailed. The public-private distinction seems to explain the divergent outcomes. The government organized the Bonn festival and sought to bar a private speaker, while private speakers organized the Boston parade and sought to resist government power.

Closer consideration, however, reveals the difference made by the public-private distinction to be contingent and contestable. Both the Boston parade and the Bonn festival were major civic events, occurring in public spaces, open to a pluralistic range of participants. Each event depended on substantial government support. In *Hurley*, the City of Boston ran the Saint Patrick's Day parade before granting the nominally private organizers an effectively exclusive license, along with public funds and use of the city's official seal.[12] In light of that arrangement, the Boston parade, like the Bonn festival, implicated government power. Independent speakers in both cases asserted legal rights to resist their exclusion from the events. The US and German legal systems, however, made divergent, decisive choices about how to view the parade and the festival. The US legal system coded a prominent, pluralistic civic event as private and the excluded speakers as public. The German legal system coded a comparable event as substantially public and the excluded speakers as substantially private.

Liberal rights regimes outside the United States generally take nuanced views of the public-private distinction. International human rights law recognizes states' obligation to protect fundamental rights not just from government abridgement but also from private interference. Thus, the International Covenant on Civil and Political Rights requires signatory states not only 'to protect' but also 'to ensure' rights.[13] Following suit, the European Court of Human Rights has recognized that private entities, not just government actors, can undermine constitutional rights.[14] The US Supreme Court has emphatically rejected this approach.[15]

Judicial recognition that private conduct may cause rights violations enables organizers of assemblies to bring constitutional claims against private interference with the assemblies, although few court decisions appear to have considered such claims.[16] Likewise, recognition of private interference with rights can benefit people whom private assemblies or associations exclude from participation. Under a legal regime that remediated private interference, the German-Palestinian case would come out as it did even if the German court treated the Bonn festival as a 'private' event. The government, though not credited with organizing the festival, would have had a legal obligation to prevent the 'private' festival organizers from undermining GPWA's right to expressive freedom.

When courts outside the United States have recognized a right of non-association, they have ascribed the right to individuals who wish to avoid participating in associations, not to associations that wish to exclude individuals. That practice tracks the mandate in the Universal Declaration of Human Rights that '[n]o one may be compelled to belong to an association'.[17] Courts have most commonly recognized rights not to associate in cases where workers resisted legal requirements that they join labour unions. For example, the European Court of Human Rights sustained the non-association claim of a taxi driver who resisted a legal mandate that he pay union dues as a condition of licensure. The driver brought his claim under Article 11 of the European Convention on Human Rights, which protects rights of assembly and association.[18] The Court observed that 'a large number of [EU member states'] domestic systems contain safeguards which, in one way or another, guarantee the negative aspect of the freedom of association, that is the freedom not to join or to withdraw from an association', and it concluded that 'Article 11 must be viewed as encompassing a negative right of association'.[19] The Canadian Supreme Court has reached a similar conclusion.[20] The US Supreme Court has also provided potent constitutional protection for union resisters, but the US doctrine turns on preventing compelled speech, not compelled association.[21]

Nuance in conceptualizing the public-private distinction helps to explain why courts outside the United States more readily ascribe rights of non-association to individuals than to associations. Natural persons, unless positively imbued with state power, are paradigmatic private actors. Associations, in contrast, may achieve levels of civic prominence and significance that enable them to rival or supplement government power.[22] Moreover, government more commonly facilitates or enables the power of associations than of natural persons.

Assemblies have a different relationship to government authority: They often require the availability of public property. This connection of assemblies to government reflects their vulnerability, not their power. Assemblies' dependence on public resources suggests that a nuanced public-private analysis might favour a right of assemblies to exclude unwanted participants. However, assemblies' public locations also encourage broad public engagement and create opportunities for ordinary people to resist powerful actors, including government. That democratic value of assemblies favours a legal regime that facilitates substantial contestation.

The Boston Saint Patrick's Day parade in *Hurley* had a dualistic public character. The parade organizers, as an association, derived substantial power from government support. They commanded an established, influential civic institution with exclusive authority to program the signature celebration of the city's most politically powerful ethnic group. The parade assembly itself created a rich opportunity for broad discourse, in a prominent public setting, about contentious issues of identity and civic membership.[23] The US Supreme Court's rigid state action analysis in *Hurley* failed to acknowledge these layers of the event's public character. A more nuanced view of the public-private distinction might have deterred the Court from giving the parade organizers a constitutional right to exclude GLIB.

Conflation or Distinction of Rights to Assembly, Association, and Speech

The US First Amendment combines in one partial sentence its protections for speech, the press, peaceable assembly, and the right to petition the government.[24] The US Supreme Court has amalgamated those objects of protection, treating speech as the umbrella under which the others shelter. Thus, none of the Court's decisions on participation-exclusion disputes actually rests on the First Amendment's Assembly Clause. Instead, the Court has developed a doctrine of 'expressive association', under which the First Amendment's Speech Clause protects certain groups' autonomy based on their expressive character.[25] The textual right of peaceable assembly gives way to a right of association, which merges into, or submerges beneath, the freedom of speech. The Australian Supreme Court has taken a roughly parallel stance, positing that any constitutional protection for political association must derive from the recognized protection for political communication.[26]

The US emphasis on expressive character as a predicate for a group's right to exclude unwanted participants takes on heightened significance because the First Amendment right of free speech carries exceptional legal potency.[27] In *Hurley*, the US Supreme Court declared that the parade organizers' 'claim to the benefit of th[e] principle of autonomy to control one's own speech is as sound as the South Boston parade is expressive'.[28] That constitutional analysis elevates expressive freedom above other weighty interests, including validation of a group's identity. Thus, the US Court has rejected associations' First Amendment claims to exclude unwanted participants where the conflicts turned more on the associations' and the unwanted participants' identity characteristics than on the contents of their ideas. For example, the Court refused to sustain a professional society's claim of a First Amendment right to exclude women from membership and participation. The Court found that the state government, in applying its nondiscrimination statute to make the group include female members, had not targeted the group's expression and did not appreciably impede its ability to pursue its expressive interests.[29] The lack of a free speech violation neutralized any government encroachment on the group's autonomy.[30]

Outside the United States, most liberal democratic rights charters distinguish rights of speech, assembly, and association in separate provisions, creating parallel entitlements that have independent grounding and may in some cases contradict and compete with one another. For example, the European Convention on Human Rights separately protects the freedom of expression in Article 10 and the freedoms of peaceful assembly and association in Article 11.[31] The EU Charter of Fundamental Rights uses a similar structure, protecting the freedom of expression and information in Article 11 and the freedom of assembly and association in Article 12.[32] The Canadian Charter of Rights and Freedoms distinctly protects freedoms related to expression (including freedoms of thought and of the press), the freedom of peaceable assembly, and the freedom of association.[33] The textual distinctness of these rights requires constitutional courts to assign each one independent weight and to wrestle with tensions between and amongst them, rather than simply treating some rights as adjuncts to others.

Rights regimes that decouple speech from association and assembly have not provided constitutional warrant in the manner of *Hurley* for associations or assemblies to exclude unwanted participants. Some US commentators maintain that the US Supreme Court's failure to recognize a free-standing right of assembly, independent from free speech, has led to under-protection of groups' legal autonomy.[34] These scholars argue that US courts, overly fixated on contestable determinations about whether a given group counts as an 'expressive association', overlook various benefits that diverse groups bring to democratic politics and culture.[35] *Hurley*, however, suggests that the US doctrine of expressive association, compared with other rights regimes' cordoning of speech from association and assembly, enhances at least some groups' autonomy. The US Court's 'stacking' of speech and association atop one another creates a dichotomy of outcomes. On the one hand, non-expressive associations get negligible constitutional protection.[36] On the other hand, where the Court finds that the government has infringed a group's freedom of speech, the group can invoke the right of expressive association—which includes, in cases like *Hurley*, the right to exclude unwanted participants.

In contrast to doctrinal divergences amongst liberal rights regimes about the importance of groups' expressive character, groups' religious character confers strong rights to exclude across most legal systems. The European Court of Human Rights has read the European Convention's protection of religion in conjunction with its protection of association to bar member states from undue interference in religious organizations' terminations of employees for deviations from religious doctrines.[37] Likewise, the UN Human Rights Committee has sustained state educational regulators' allowance for a religious authority to veto an applicant for a position teaching religious doctrine.[38] The Canadian Supreme Court has sustained a religious university's right to require faculty and staff to sign a statement that censured 'biblically condemned' sexual conduct.[39] The US Supreme Court has held that the freedom of religious exercise entails a 'ministerial exception' that protects religious institutions' hiring and firing decisions from generally applicable legal restraints.[40] *Hurley* also has a religious underpinning, given the antipathy of conservative Irish Catholics in Boston to celebrating LGBTQ+ Irish-American pride.[41] Organized religion's historical and cultural distinctiveness seems to explain, not to say justify, most rights regimes' exceptional regard for religious groups' autonomy.[42] In contrast, the High Court of South Africa has sustained a teacher's discrimination claim after a religious school fired him for being in a same-sex relationship.[43]

Non-US legal systems' recognition of assembly as a distinct constitutional right corresponds, perhaps counter-intuitively, with their not granting assemblies a right to exclude unwanted participants. The UN Human Rights Committee defines participation in a protected assembly as 'taking part in a gathering of persons for a purpose such as expressing oneself, conveying a position on a particular issue or exchanging ideas', amongst others.[44] Such appreciation for assemblies' substantial expressive value may undergird the robust affirmative protection that non-US rights regimes tend to provide for assemblies, which likely outstrips US constitutional law's affirmative protection of, say, public political protests.[45] As for the right to exclude, however, the potency of the US right of non-association suggests that US law's absorption of assembly into association, like US law's conflation of association and speech, has—if anything—strengthened constitutional protection for groups' autonomy. To the extent *Hurley* is a case about assembly, the US rights regime distinctively protects a right of non-assembly despite having submerged the textual right of assembly.

Paramount Rights or Balancing of Interests

The US state action doctrine, discussed above, forecloses any possibility of viewing a legal dispute as presenting competing constitutional claims and of thus balancing constitutional rights against one another.[46] An observer unfamiliar with US constitutional formalism easily could view *Hurley* as a clash between constitutionally salient interests. Yet the Supreme Court's *Hurley* opinion focuses almost exclusively on the nature of the parade organizers' overriding constitutional expressive interest. The Court's unanimous, confident decision is hard to imagine without US law's insistence on reifying a paramount legal right on one and only one side of any given constitutional dispute.

Other liberal democratic rights regimes have built very different structures. Most rights charters situate their grants of rights amongst a broader array of important constitutional values. For example, the European Convention subjects its rights protections to restrictions 'necessary in a democratic society', including the safeguarding of other people's rights.[47] The EU Charter, prior to setting out protected freedoms, declares: 'Human dignity is inviolable'.[48] The German legal system likewise elevates human dignity above other freedoms.[49] Moreover, the European rights regime protects a wide range of substantive rights, including rights to personal integrity, to marry and found a family, and to education.[50] Likewise, the Canadian Charter protects 'fundamental freedoms' subject to 'such reasonable limits prescribed by law as can be demonstrably justified in a free and democratic society'.[51] These inclusive structures enable, indeed compel, courts to consider diverse values as they balance competing rights and interests.[52] Judges need not relegate interests that push against rights claims to the status of mere governmental policy choices, as the US Court did in *Hurley*. Instead, individual interests in privacy, dignity, and integrity stand on the same constitutional footing as rights to free speech, association, and assembly.

Balancing calls legal attention to a broad range of constitutional interests. Thus, the European Court of Human Rights pursues 'the fair balance that has to be struck between the general interest of the community and the interests of the individual, the search for which is inherent throughout the Convention'.[53] Free speech protections exemplify the contrast in jurisprudential approaches. Almost all liberal democratic rights regimes allow for greater restrictions on free speech than US constitutional law does, because non-US courts balance free speech against other rights and interests. Thus, the European Court rejected a free expression claim by the director of a film that the British government refused to certify due to a criminal prohibition of blasphemy. The Court found the prohibition 'necessary in a democratic society', and therefore a proper ground for suppressing free expression, because the prohibition served the legitimate (though many would say normatively unappealing) interest of protecting the sanctity of the Christian religion.[54]

The widespread allowance for balancing competing rights and interests provides further explanation of why most liberal democratic legal systems appear to have resisted constitutional rights for associations and assemblies to exclude unwanted participants. A balancing approach would compel a court to analyse a case like *Hurley* very differently than the US Supreme Court did, and the outcome might well be reversed. Assuming a balancing court recognized the parade organizers' right to free expression and/or assembly, the court would likely balance that right against the GLIB members' own expressive and assembly rights as well as their right to human dignity, Massachusetts's democratically weighty interest in preventing discrimination based on sexual orientation, and the public's interest in diverse discourse in public spaces. Balancing compels a rights analysis that takes into account not only associations' and assemblies' rights but also unwanted participants' competing rights and interests.

Participation, Exclusion, and Social Power

Liberal democracies promote a set of core values, centrally including equal citizenship, pluralism, and collective self-governance. Legal rights of association and assembly play a crucial role in advancing those values. Associations and assemblies let disempowered people pursue equality through collective identification and action. Associations and assemblies enhance pluralism by giving form and force to distinctive, sometimes competing values and ideas. Through association and assembly, members of the political community can participate more fully and effectively in collective self-governance. Given the deep importance of associations and assemblies for liberal democracy, legal elaborations of rights to associate and assemble should maximize those collective structures' capacity to promote liberal democratic values while avoiding degradation of those values. Rights regimes should take into account not only association's and assembly's shared liberal democratic benefits but also the ways in which these two rights, particularly in their negative iterations, have divergent implications for liberal democracy.

Associations

Liberal democratic values counsel against a strong constitutional right of associations to exclude unwanted participants. Consider the winners and losers in legal battles over non-association. The strong US non-association right developed slowly through the 1980s, as the US Supreme Court prevented associational interests from undermining the equal citizenship of racial minority groups[55] and women.[56] However, the Court has more recently enforced a right of groups to undermine LGBTQ+ Americans' equal citizenship. *Hurley* and *Boy Scouts of America v Dale,* the high-water marks of non-association in US law, let groups that enjoy substantial government backing subvert LGBTQ+ identities for the dubious purpose of controlling and constraining the broader public's perception of the groups' values.[57] LGBTQ+ Americans have paid a grossly disproportionate share of non-association's steep social cost.[58] The US Court's other signature non-association initiative has enabled the two major political parties, which together enjoy a legally enforced stranglehold on governmental power, to exclude independent and third-party political dissenters from meaningful participation in elections.[59] A more democratically destructive iteration of a right to exclude unwanted participants is hard to imagine.

Why aren't US courts, or for that matter courts anywhere else, vindicating the non-association rights of less powerful groups—arts collectives, dissident political organizations, nascent religious communities? A likely explanation is that socially and politically marginal groups, while benefitting greatly from the affirmative right of association, have little use for the right to exclude unwanted members or participants. Less dominant associations often want to grow, leading them to build bridges rather than walls. Marginal groups that wish to remain small and insular have little cause to fear encroachment by an indifferent or hostile wider world. Claims for non-association only become useful when a group commands social power. Established groups deploy non-association to maintain their power without having to compromise or share it. While those associations draw strength from their coalescence, people whom they block from membership or participation remain literal outsiders, weakened by isolation and atomization.

Some smaller, less powerful associations might conceivably benefit from a right of non-association. Antagonists, in theory, could seek to destroy a marginal group by flooding it with hostile interlopers. However, the dearth of such cases in the US Supreme Court's distinctively potent non-association jurisprudence suggests that marginal groups have not found cause to complain about such unwanted participants. Perhaps

US courts could adjust non-association doctrine to make it more egalitarian. On the other hand, the pretext of such an adjustment might enable courts to reinforce power hierarchies by speciously casting powerful, majoritarian groups as victims of government oppression.[60] Rights regimes that balance competing interests could modulate a non-association right by considering power hierarchies as part of a balancing analysis. Courts in balancing systems, however, have taken the more direct path of simply not recognizing a strong non-association right. No groundswell, or even faint tremor, appears to have emerged in those systems for developing a right of non-association to protect socially and politically marginal groups.

The limited subjects of transnational consensus about non-association strengthen the liberal democratic case against the right. As discussed above, liberal legal systems broadly agree about two tasks that the right to non-association should perform. First, non-association should shield religious groups from legal protections for nonbelievers and dissidents. If a wide variety of religious groups—large and small, mainstream and marginal—shared in that benefit, then non-association might be advancing liberal democracy by promoting religious pluralism and toleration. As the European Court of Human Rights has declared, 'the autonomous existence of religious communities is indispensable for pluralism in a democratic society'.[61] Unfortunately, the religious groups that benefit from non-association are mainly powerful Christian churches. That disparity makes sense, given the political economy of non-association. Only large, mainstream churches tend to control institutions and opportunities in which non-believers might materially benefit from participating. As a result, non-association's solicitude for religion ends up promoting not religious pluralism and toleration but instead religious entrenchment and domination.

The second subject of consensus is that non-association, or the related US First Amendment right against compelled speech, should underwrite workers' desires to avoid joining or supporting labour unions, even as a condition of benefitting from collective bargaining. Unions depend strongly on affirmative rights of association and assembly, as some liberal rights charters specifically emphasize. The right of non-association, however, does organized labour no good. Unions want to attract members, not exclude them. Non-association accelerates the decline in unions' membership by pitting a neo-liberal conception of individual freedom against the labour solidarity that rights of association and assembly are supposed to enable. Unions' decline across the developed world has greatly exacerbated a sharp growth in material inequality.[62] That widening gulf between a small elite of haves and a large mass of have-nots alienates the have-nots from any meaningful stake in collective self-governance.

Disavowal of non-association rights would hardly leave associations bereft of legal protection. Because associations have durable structures, government policies and constitutional jurisprudence can help maintain associations' integrity through structural interventions short of a right to exclude, such as protecting associations' prerogatives to require that members pay dues, attend meetings, and engage in group activities.[63] The availability of structural means to protect associations' autonomy further undermines any justification for a constitutional right of associations to exclude unwanted participants.

Assemblies

Consistent with the affirmative constitutional right of assembly, governments may maintain neutral permit systems for allocating primary access to public expressive spaces.[64] Unbiased arrangements for sharing public expressive resources can facilitate meaningful exchanges of ideas. Even so, C. Edwin Baker made a compelling argument that permit systems should always be voluntary rather than mandatory, offering inducements like reserved access and security assistance in exchange for an assembly's choice to participate in a system of government ordering.[65] Mandatory permit systems can too easily become devices for reinforcing unpopular groups' social and political marginalization, coercing conformity, and squelching dissent. Mandatory systems can also empower government to enforce rigid rules of public order and morality.[66]

Assembly's high value for public discourse and greater utility than association for socially marginal and underfunded groups theoretically justifies greater constitutional protection from unwanted participants for assemblies than for associations. That justification would vary based on an assembly's location, the opportunities it offered for civic participation, the power and status of its organizers, and what if any support it received from government or other institutional actors. However, the democratic importance of dynamic, contentious public discourse ultimately counsels against a strong constitutional right for assemblies on public property to exclude unwanted participants.[67]

The affirmative right of assembly itself compels restraint in constitutionally protecting assemblies from unwanted participants. Rights of assembly generally extend to opposing assemblies, such as counter-protests.[68] Governments frequently attempt to squelch counter-protests either through prior restraint (judicial injunction or denial of a required permit) or through physical separation of groups by law enforcement. However, the only democratically valid reasons to suppress counter-protests are preventing either substantial violence against the initial assembly or wholesale silencing of the initial assembly through encroachment, infiltration, or drowning out.[69] Those reasons could not justify any prior restraint without constitutionally suspect conjecture about the nature of the counter-assembly.[70] The conflict of viewpoints in *Hurley*, for example, posed no threat of violence or silencing. To the contrary, that conflict exemplified assemblies' capacity to encourage dynamic diversity in public discourse.

At most, then, the constitutional right of assembly should justify law enforcement in acting against a counter-protest only during the time when the initial assembly is taking place and only for the purpose of preventing violence against, or wholesale silencing of, the initial assembly. The contours of that justification lack perfect clarity, but so do other standards for adjudicating disputes about constitutional rights. If large, persistent power disparities ever emerged amongst different groups that engaged in public assemblies and counter-protests, then arguments for a stronger right of at least some assemblies to exclude unwanted participants might gain force. No such disparity is apparent now.

Actual or imminent violence between opposing assemblies may, in extreme cases, justify dispersing all participants.[71] However, law enforcement must take great care to avoid confusing or conflating a real threat of violence or silencing with mere offence or disturbance. Some court decisions have enforced that distinction scrupulously,[72] while others regrettably have occluded it.[73] As the European Court of Human Rights has stated: 'If every probability of tension and heated exchange between opposing groups during a demonstration was to warrant its prohibition, society would be faced with being deprived of the opportunity of hearing differing views'.[74]

Denying assemblies a constitutional right to exclude unwanted participants, except in circumstances of violence or silencing, likely decreases assemblies' aggregate ability to express clear, unimpeded messages. That ability advances, to some extent, democratic values of equal citizenship, pluralism, and collective self-governance. This chapter's position, however, is that broad constitutional allowance for counter-protest advances all those values in greater measure. First, legislative policies of maintaining voluntary permit systems for public assemblies can allocate public expressive resources in ways that substantially facilitate many assemblies' clear, unimpeded expression. Second, the absence in most liberal legal systems of a strong right for assemblies to exclude unwanted participants suggests that assemblies generally do not need constitutional protection to achieve their aims. Third, constitutional protection for assemblies against violence and silencing addresses the most severe threats to assemblies' effective communication. Finally, and most importantly, the tumult and disorder of subjecting assemblies to counter-protests enables contention and engagement amongst diverse groups and ideas, encouraging dynamism in public discourse. Such dynamism is essential for a flourishing liberal democracy.

Broader Implications for Liberal Rights Regimes

This normative assessment of the participation-exclusion problem points towards broader insights about trade-offs between different modes of constitutional law. The rest of the liberal democratic world has avoided a strong US-style right of non-association substantially through the legal mechanisms of acknowledging private interference with rights, distinguishing clearly amongst constitutional rights, and balancing competing rights and interests. All those legal practices seem well suited to promoting liberal democratic values and elevating the interests of less powerful people and groups. Letting courts impose constitutional constraints on powerful private actors enables constitutional rights, at least sometimes, to interrupt social and political hierarchies and to redistribute power more broadly. Disaggregating constitutional rights of speech, association, and assembly protects different, valuable means of social and political action and interaction. Letting courts balance competing rights and interests decreases dominant people's and groups' capacity to shield their power behind impregnable structures of legal privilege.

At the same time, strong legal protections for constitutional rights like free speech can substantially advance liberal democratic values. Present US First Amendment jurisprudence reflects an accelerating, retrograde commitment to reifying wealthy, powerful speakers' interests in the name of maintaining social and political stability.[75] At other times, however, First Amendment law has helped socially and politically marginal people and groups pursue political and social change by protecting them from government coercion. The US doctrine of expressive association emerged from just such a moment.[76] Facilitation of political dissent and protest exemplifies the positive contributions that potent rights protections can make to liberal democracy. Liberal legal systems can enhance equal citizenship, pluralism, and collective self-governance by focusing constitutional protections on socially and politically marginal people's and groups' rights to free expression, peaceable assembly, and association.

Conclusion

No legal structure or doctrine can guarantee the survival and flourishing of liberal democracy. Substantive politics ultimately determine whether law will promote or degrade values of equal citizenship, pluralism, and collective self-governance. Even so, rights regimes can contribute positively to liberal democracy by enabling socially and politically marginal people and groups to participate more fully in social processes and collective self-governance. Affirmative constitutional rights of association and assembly enhance opportunities for participation. A strong constitutional right for associations to exclude unwanted participants tends towards the opposite result. Accordingly, liberal democracies' prevalent disinclination to protect a strong right of non-association appears well founded, and the US departure from that tendency appears misguided. Liberal democratic values provide stronger theoretical justification for legal intervention to protect assemblies from unwanted participants. However, the liberal democratic importance of openness and contestation in expressive uses of public spaces should ultimately discourage a strong right of non-assembly.

Notes

1. US Const. Amend. I.
2. 515 U.S. 557 (1995).
3. See *Boy Scouts of America v Dale*, 530 U.S. 640 (2000) (letting a national boys' group exclude gay members and gay adult leaders); *California Democratic Party v Jones*, 530 U.S. 567 (2000) (barring states from subjecting the major political parties to primary elections that allow participation by voters not registered with the party); *Hosanna-Tabor Evangelical Lutheran Church v EEOC*, 565 U.S. 171 (2012) (letting religious institutions discriminate in hiring).
4. See *Christian Legal Soc'y v Martinez*, 561 U.S. 661 (2010) (letting a state university require a religious student group to admit members who violated the group's moral standards);

Roberts v U.S. Jaycees, 468 U.S. 609 (1984) (letting states bar private clubs from excluding members based on identity criteria); *Bob Jones Univ. v United States*, 461 U.S. 574 (1983) (letting the national government withdraw financial aid from a college that barred interracial dating); see also *New York St. Club Ass'n v City of New York*, 487 U.S. 1 (1988) (rejecting a facial First Amendment challenge to a membership non-discrimination ordinance).

5. UN Human Rights Council, Views: Communication No. 2372/2014 (26 September 2018) UN Doc. CCPR/C/123/D/2372/2014 (*Giminez v Paraguay*) [8.3].
6. ECtHR, *Plattform Ärzte für das Leben v Austria* App. No. 10126/82 (21 June 1988); *Forsyth Cty., Ga. v Nationalist Movement*, 505 U.S. 123 (1992).
7. Orsolya Salát, *The Right to Freedom of Assembly: A Comparative Study* (Oxford: Hart Publishing, 2015), 288–289; Frederick Schauer, 'Costs and Challenges of the Hostile Audience', *Notre Dame Law Review* 94, no. 4 (2019): 1671–1698, 1683–1692.
8. Salát, *Right to Freedom of Assembly*, 3–8. This chapter does not consider commercial assemblies, such as audiences at sporting events or entertainment productions, which raise distinctive issues.
9. *Jackson v Metro. Edison Co.*, 419 U.S. 345 (1974).
10. *Hurley*, 515 U.S. at 566.
11. *German-Palestinian Women's Association v Bonn*, Verwaltungsgericht [VG] [Administrative Trial Court] 14 L 1766/19, 13 September 2019.
12. *Hurley*, 515 U.S. at 560–561.
13. International Covenant on Civil and Political Rights, article 6, section 1 (United Nations, 1966).
14. Monika Florczak-Wator, 'The Role of the European Court of Human Rights in Promoting Horizontal Positive Obligations of the State', *International and Comparative Law Review* 17, no. 2 (2017): 39–53. Examples from the European Court of government liability for private interference with rights include ECtHR, *X and Y v Netherlands* App. No. 8978/80 (26 March 1985) (requiring a government to enable prosecution of a rapist where the survivor's incapacity prevented her from making a complaint) and ECtHR, *Young, James, and Webster v United Kingdom* App. No. 7601/76; 7806/77 (13 August 1981) (requiring a government to prevent employers from forcing employees to join unions).
15. *DeShaney v Winnebago Cty.*, 489 U.S. 189 (1989). Legislatures in the United States could of course protect assemblies from private interference, but none appears to have done so. Schauer, 'Costs and Challenges', 1693–1695.
16. See e.g. *Plattform Ärzte für das Leben* App. No. 10126/82.
17. Universal Declaration of Human Rights, article 20.2 (United Nations, 1948).
18. Convention for the Protection of Human Rights and Fundamental Freedoms, articles 11, 4 (November 1950) 214 U.N.T.S. 221.
19. ECtHR, *Sigurjonsson v Iceland*, App. No. 16130/90 (30 June 1993).
20. *Lavigne v Ontario Public Service Employees Union* [1991] 2 SCR 211 (Canada).
21. *Janus v Am. Fed. of St., Cty. & Mun. Emp.*, 138 S. Ct. 2448 (2018). This US doctrine radiates hostility towards labour unions, a stark contrast with other liberal democratic rights charters' recognition of union organizing as central to constitutional rights of assembly and association. For example, Article 12 of the EU Charter protects the rights to assembly and association 'in particular in political, trade union, and civic matters, which implies the right of everyone to form and to join trade unions for the protection of his or her interests'. Charter of Fundamental Rights of the European Union, article 12 (18 December 2000), 2000 O.J. (C 364).

22. Andrew Koppelman, 'Should Noncommercial Associations Have an Absolute Right to Discriminate?', *Law and Contemporary Problems* 67, no. 4 (2004): 27–57, 48–53 (describing the Boy Scouts of America's government backing and market power).
23. Carl F. Stychin, 'Celebration and Consolidation: National Rituals and the Legal Construction of American Identities', *Oxford Journal of Legal Studies* 18, no. 2 (1998): 265–291.
24. US Const. Amend. I.
25. *NAACP v Alabama*, 357 U.S. 449 (1958).
26. *Tajjour v New South Wales* (2014) 254 CLR 508. The Court inferred the right of political communication from the constitutional system of representative government. *Nationwide News Pty Ltd v Wills* (1992) 177 CLR 1; *Australian Capital Television Pty Ltd v Commonwealth* (1992) 177 CLR 106.
27. *See generally* Gregory P. Magarian, *Managed Speech: The Roberts Court's First Amendment* (Oxford: Oxford University Press, 2017).
28. *Hurley*, 515 U.S. at 574.
29. *Roberts*, 468 U.S. at 622–629; see also *Rumsfeld v Forum for Acad. & Inst. Rts., Inc.*, 547 U.S. 47, 68–70 (2006).
30. The lone US Supreme Court victory for unwanted participants who meaningfully undercut an association's expressive interest turned on the Court's special solicitude for a public university's prerogative to manage its educational policies and resources. *Christian Legal Soc'y*, 561 U.S. 661.
31. Convention for the Protection of Human Rights and Fundamental Freedoms, article 11.
32. Charter of Fundamental Rights of the European Union, articles 11, 12.
33. Constitution Act R.S.C. 1982 (Canada).
34. John D. Inazu, 'The Forgotten Freedom of Assembly', *Tulane Law Review* 84, no. 3 (2010): 565–612.
35. Tabatha Abu El-Haj, 'Friends, Associates, and Associations: Theoretically and Empirically Grounding the Freedom of Association', *Arizona Law Review* 56, no. 1 (2014): 53–116; Ashutosh Bhagwat, 'Associational Speech', *Yale Law Journal* 120, no. 5 (2011): 978–1030.
36. The exception to this rule is the category of 'intimate' associations, exemplified by familial bonds, which get strong protection under privacy principles grounded in the Due Process Clause of the Fourteenth Amendment. *Roberts*, 468 U.S. at 617–621.
37. ECtHR, *Fernández Martínez v Spain* [GC] App. No. 56030/07 (12 June 2014); ECtHR, *Obst v Germany* App. No. 425/03 (23 September 2010); ECtHR, *Lombardi Vallauri v Italy* App. No. 39128/05 (20 October 2009).
38. UN Human Rights Council, Views: Communication No. 195/1985 (23 August 1990) UN Doc. CCPR/C/39/D/195/1985 (*Delgado Páez v Colombia*).
39. *Trinity Western University v British Columbia College of Teachers* [2001] 1 SCR 772 (Canada).
40. *Hosanna-Tabor*, 565 U.S. 171.
41. Stychin, 'Celebration and Consolidation', 283.
42. See generally Pamela Slotte and Helge Årsheim, 'The Ministerial Exception—Comparative Perspectives', *Oxford Journal of Law and Religion* 4, no. 2 (2015): 171–198.
43. *Strydom v Nederduitse Gereformeerde Gemeente Moreleta Park* (26926/05) [2008] ZAGPHC 269; (2009) 30 ILJ 868 (EqC) (27 August 2008) (South Africa).
44. UNHRCtte, General Comment No. 37—Article 21: Right of Peaceful Assembly (17 September 2020) UN Doc. CCPR/C/CG/37 [12].

45. Timothy Zick, *Speech Out of Doors: Preserving First Amendment Liberties in Public Places* (Cambridge: Cambridge University Press, 2009); Tabatha Abu El-Haj, 'The Neglected Right of Assembly', *U.C.L.A. Law Review* 56, no. 3 (2009): 543–589.
46. Gregory P. Magarian, 'The Jurisprudence of Colliding First Amendment Interests: From the Dead End of Neutrality to the Open Road of Participation-Enhancing Review', *Notre Dame Law Review* 83, no. 1 (2007): 185–264.
47. Convention for the Protection of Human Rights and Fundamental Freedoms, article 9.
48. Charter of Fundamental Rights of the European Union, article 1.
49. See generally Ronald J. Krotoszynski, Jr., 'A Comparative Perspective on the First Amendment: Free Speech, Militant Democracy, and the Primacy of Dignity as a Preferred Constitutional Value in Germany', *Tulane Law Review* 78, no. 5 (2003): 1549–1609.
50. Charter of Fundamental Rights of the European Union, articles 3, 9, 14.
51. Constitution Act R.S.C. 1982 (Canada).
52. Steven Greer, "Balancing' and the European Court of Human Rights: A Contribution to the Habermas-Alexy Debate', *Cambridge Law Journal* 63, no. 2 (2004): 412–434. A familiar scenario entails balancing rights of religious liberty against rights of sexual autonomy. *Strydom* 30 ILJ 868; *Ontario Human Rights Commission v Brockie* [2002] 222 DLR (4th) 174 (HC) (Canada).
53. ECtHR, *Appleby and Others v United Kingdom* App. No. 44306/98 (6 May 2003).
54. ECtHR, *Wingrove v United Kingdom* App. No. 17419/90 (25 November 1996).
55. *Bob Jones University*, 461 U.S. 574.
56. *Roberts*, 468 U.S. 609.
57. *Hurley*, 515 U.S. at 574; *Boy Scouts*, 530 U.S. at 655–656; Daniel A. Farber, 'Speaking in the First Person Plural: Expressive Associations and the First Amendment', *Minnesota Law Review* 85, no. 6 (2001): 1483–1513, 1503–1512.
58. Koppelman, 'Noncommercial Associations', 43–48.
59. *California Democratic Party*, 530 U.S. 567; Samuel Issacharoff, 'Private Parties with Public Purposes: Political Parties, Associational Freedoms, and Partisan Competition', *Columbia Law Review* 101, no. 2 (2001): 274–313.
60. *Christian Legal Soc'y*, 561 U.S. at 718–721 (Alito, J., dissenting) (likening burdens on a nationwide association of Christian lawyers to those on a radical student group).
61. ECtHR, *Hasan and Chaush v Bulgaria*, App. No. 30985/96 (26 October 2000).
62. Henry S. Farber et al., 'Unions and Inequality over the Twentieth Century: New Evidence from Survey Data', National Bureau of Economic Research Working Paper 24587 (April 2021), https://www.nber.org/system/files/working_papers/w24587/w24587.pdf (documenting a long-term inverse relationship between U.S. income inequality and union density).
63. *Christian Legal Soc'y*, 561 U.S. at 671 n.2.
64. Salát, *Right to Freedom of Assembly*, 285; Zick, *Speech Out of Doors*, 192; Kevin F. O'Neill, 'Disentangling the Law of Public Protest', *Loyola Law Review* 45, no. 3 (1999): 411–526, 450 & n192.
65. C. Edwin Baker, *Human Liberty and Freedom of Speech* (Oxford: Oxford University Press, 1989), 138–160.
66. Ibid.; Zick, *Speech Out of Doors*, 190–196; Abu El-Haj, 'Neglected Right of Assembly', 548–554; Kevin F. O'Neill and Raymond Vasvari, 'Counter-Demonstration as Protected Speech: Finding the Right to Confrontation in Existing First Amendment Law', *Hastings Constitutional Law Quarterly* 23, no. 1 (1995): 77–126.

67. The right of assemblies on private property to exclude unwanted participants lies outside the scope of this chapter.
68. Salát, *Right to Freedom of Assembly*, 288–289.
69. Ibid., 139–140; Schauer, 'Costs and Challenges', 1695.
70. ECtHR, *Christians against Racism and Fascism (CARAF) v United Kingdom* App. No. 8440/78 (16 July 1980); *Forsyth Cty.*, 505 U.S. 123.
71. Salát, *Right to Freedom of Assembly*, 136.
72. ECtHR, *Öllinger v Austria*, App. No. 76900/01 (29 June 2006) (sustaining a claim against the government for barring a public political protest against a commemoration of SS soldiers); *Snyder v Phelps*, 562 U.S. 443 (2011) (holding that the First Amendment barred a tort claim for intentional infliction of emotional distress against a public political protest directed at an outdoor funeral).
73. ECtHR, *Chorherr v Austria* App. No. 13308/87 (25 August 1993) (upholding sanctions against political protesters for impeding some spectators' view of a public military parade).
74. *Öllinger v Austria* App. No. 76900/01 [36].
75. See generally Magarian, *Managed Speech.*
76. *NAACP*, 357 U.S. 449.

Further Reading

Abu El-Haj, Tabatha. 'Friends, Associates, and Associations: Theoretically and Empirically Grounding the Freedom of Association'. *Arizona Law Review* 56, no. 1 (2014): 53–116.

Abu El-Haj, Tabatha. 'The Neglected Right of Assembly'. *U.C.L.A. Law Review* 56, no. 3 (2009): 543–589.

Baker, C. Edwin. *Human Liberty and Freedom of Speech*. Oxford: Oxford University Press, 1989.

Bhagwat, Ashutosh. 'Associational Speech'. *Yale Law Journal* 120, no. 5 (2011): 978–1030.

Farber, Daniel A. 'Speaking in the First Person Plural: Expressive Associations and the First Amendment'. *Minnesota Law Review* 85, no. 6 (2001): 1483–1513.

Florczak-Wator, Monika. 'The Role of the European Court of Human Rights in Promoting Horizontal Positive Obligations of the State'. *International and Comparative Law Review* 17, no. 2 (2017): 39–53.

Greer, Steven. '"Balancing" and the European Court of Human Rights: A Contribution to the Habermas-Alexy Debate'. *Cambridge Law Journal* 63, no. 2 (2004): 412–434.

Inazu, John D. 'The Forgotten Freedom of Assembly'. *Tulane Law Review* 84, no. 3 (2010): 565–612.

Koppelman, Andrew. 'Should Noncommercial Associations Have an Absolute Right to Discriminate?', *Law and Contemporary Problems* 67, no. 4 (2004): 27–57.

Krotoszynski, Ronald J., Jr. 'A Comparative Perspective on the First Amendment: Free Speech, Militant Democracy, and the Primacy of Dignity as a Preferred Constitutional Value in Germany'. *Tulane Law Review* 78, no. 5 (2003): 1549–1609.

Magarian, Gregory P. *Managed Speech: The Roberts Court's First Amendment*. Oxford: Oxford University Press, 2017.

O'Neill, Kevin F. 'Disentangling the Law of Public Protest'. *Loyola Law Review* 45, no. 3 (1999): 411–526.

O'Neill, Kevin F., and Raymond Vasvari. 'Counter-Demonstration as Protected Speech: Finding the Right to Confrontation in Existing First Amendment Law'. *Hastings Constitutional Law Quarterly* 23, no. 1 (1995): 77–126.

Salát, Orsolya. *The Right to Freedom of Assembly: A Comparative Study*. Oxford: Hart Publishing, 2015.

Schauer, Frederick. 'Costs and Challenges of the Hostile Audience'. *Notre Dame Law Review* 94, no. 4 (2019): 1671–1698.

Stychin, Carl F. 'Celebration and Consolidation: National Rituals and the Legal Construction of American Identities'. *Oxford Journal of Legal Studies* 18, no. 2 (1998): 265–291.

Timothy Zick. *Speech Out of Doors: Preserving First Amendment Liberties in Public Places*. Cambridge: Cambridge University Press, 2009.

CHAPTER 17

THE DIGITALLY MEDIATED FREEDOM OF ASSEMBLY

ELLA MCPHERSON

INTRODUCTION

THE freedom of assembly *as practiced online* has been a most misunderstood and misattended manifestation of this particular right. This was clear as I sat in a winter-lit room at the University of Cambridge, where colleagues and I had co-convened an expert meeting on the right of peaceful assembly online. This meeting was to support the UN Human Rights Committee's consultative interpretation and elaboration of the right of peaceful assembly, an exercise the UN undertakes from time to time on particular rights, resulting in published guidance documents called General Comments.

Mind you, this meeting was December 2019—a matter of weeks before COVID-19 really hit the news cycle, and only a few more weeks before most of us were locked down at home with our technological connections as our main pathways to the worlds beyond our walls. It was only a few months before #BLM, as a movement, surged through our social media and our streets in outrage at videos of racially motivated police brutality. Yet, back then, the underlying premise to this meeting was one of seeking assurances about the phenomenon of assembly online.[1] Was it significant enough—or contested enough—to deserve special mention in what would become known as General Comment No. 37? Was it even really assembly—as in deserving of protection as a human right?

As our lives unfolded—or rather, folded in on themselves—in 2020, and as digital places became the only arenas for many of us to assemble to address global and local inequalities, these questions became even more urgent. In this chapter, I start by arguing that online assemblies are, indeed, assemblies that deserve to be protected by human rights conventions, even if they are not conventionally corporeal. I will construct this argument sociologically, drawing on the concept of *mediation*. Mediation is the process of intermediaries connecting communicators and communications across time and space. Building on the idea that even languages and cultures are intermediaries, and thus that face-to-face assemblies involve mediation, I will posit that mediation is a fundamental dimension of assembly. This approach allows us to easily understand more-mediated assemblies, like those occurring online, as assemblies proper. It is for this reason that I prefer to refer to these practices as *digitally mediated assembly* rather than *online assembly*.

Given that digitally mediated assemblies are assemblies, the next important task of this chapter is to investigate why digitally mediated assemblies tend to have been misattended. Here I develop the concept of *visibility backlash*, a widespread public reaction to groups' new visibilities that aims to discredit and thus invisibilize them. The visibility backlash of slacktivism builds on a tradition of subordinating the freedom of assembly in comparison with other communication rights, in part because of its collective and emotional dimensions, and in part because it is a positive liberty less likely to be needed by elites. Understanding discrediting discourses about digitally mediated assemblies—and thus being able to dissemble them—is key to assemblies' present and future, including the possibilities for technologists to design assembly affordances into their digital communication platforms.

In the subsequent chapter section, I draw on media and communications scholarship to outline the concept of *assembly affordance*, which is a normative concept for evaluating or building communication technologies in relation to how they enable assemblies. I outline three assembly affordances: pre-assembly, sight and sound, and gathering. For each of these affordances, I sketch out aspirational ways in which technologies can support these dimensions of the freedom of assembly and provide a snapshot of how actual affordances fall short. Next, I outline three current trends in social media platforms that all have troublesome implications for opportunities to practice the digitally mediated freedom of assembly: the focus on authenticity and consequent depoliticization of new platforms, the fragmentations of networks due to the proliferation of platforms, and user alienation. I conclude by considering what this relatively rigorous approach to understanding the digitally mediated freedom of assembly can do for its protection and understanding, for human rights-centred technology design, and for how we might rethink cognate communication rights like the freedom of expression.

Mediated Assemblies

As at our expert meeting at Cambridge, approaching the freedom of assembly *online* as a special category often happens. On reflection, however, this approach is a bit of a red herring. It sets this kind of assembly out as novel, but also freezes it in time. We should think of it, instead, as the latest in a long tradition of assemblies that have taken place across time and through space.

Consider participants of the same face-to-face assembly—say, a protest extending over several city blocks and hours—who are remote from one another and rely on intermediaries to convey messages, chants, and plans. Think back to the assemblies in the coffee houses of eighteenth-century England, which were sustained across time and space with periodicals, or to the assemblies during the Iranian Revolution in the late 1970s, which relied on cassette tapes, played over phone lines, and photocopied leaflets to share ideas and fuel conversations.[2] Just as it was hard to imagine digitally mediated assembly when the technologies we had were tapes, leaflets, and periodicals, it is hard to imagine the next manifestation of our assembly mediation, even with holograms and the Metaverse emerging. If we think of assembly through the lens of mediation, we can see that the intermediary may change but the mediation remains ever-present.

In fact, mediation is not only a characteristic of assembly—it is at assembly's core. Even co-present, face-to-face assemblies are mediated by language and culture—both of which are intermediaries to our interactions because they have external logics that may distort our meaning and our understanding.[3] Digital mediation, then, is one more layer of a concatenation of mediation through which we assemble. Assembly, because it hinges on meaning and communication, is thus always dependent on mediation. If this is the case, it is quite artificial to cut off digitally mediated assemblies as either not really assemblies or as second-rate assemblies. They are just more obviously mediated. This broader understanding of mediation is analytically and legally useful for those wishing to welcome digitally mediated assembly participants further into the protective human rights fold. This understanding is also particularly crucial given the visibility backlash circulating in public about digitally mediated assembly, which I turn to next.

Slacktivism as a Visibility Backlash

The case I make here about why the digitally mediated freedom of assembly has so often been misunderstood and misattended is built on a scaffolding of discourse, namely, communications made in the pursuit or protection of power.[4] These cases can be hard to definitively prove, in part because of their deniability and in part because of how discourses move between consciousness and subconsciousness. That said, it remains important to interrogate potential discourses so that we are critically aware of their possibility and can work to prevent them. Before addressing the digitally mediated freedom of assembly specifically, however, I will explore why the freedom of assembly in general is considered second-rate in comparison to other communication rights.

Assembly is often an afterthought to concerns for the freedom of expression and the right to privacy, including in technology design.[5] Its subordinate position has at least three causes: Assembly is collective, it is emotional, and its protection requires positive action by the state. In the context of neoliberal societies that emphasize individualism over collectivism, rights that are imagined as relating to individuals, like expression and privacy, are prioritized over those that are exercised collectively, like assembly and association.[6] Rights that convey agency dominate rights that convey solidarity.[7] This hierarchy is exacerbated by the fact that societies' powerful do not often need the freedom of assembly to be seen and heard, as they already have platforms.

In contrast to the freedom of expression, which has its historical links with rational, cool treatises (though less so in the social media age with the rise of hate speech), the freedom of assembly is almost always understood as hot, almost always as emotional. The forms of knowledge conveyed by the expression of these respective rights are ordered in Western knowledge systems, with seemingly rational knowledge ranked above seemingly emotional knowledge. In patriarchal, racist, and classist societies, this is because of the categories of people associated with each norm: rationality with White men of financial means and emotionality with everyone else.[8] Furthermore, because of its reliance on publicly accessible places, which must be created and maintained by states and private institutions, the freedom of assembly is a positive liberty. If we add to these hierarchies the tradition of Western political thought that prioritizes negative liberties over positive ones, we can really start to understand the cultural structures that hold down the right to assembly.[9]

And so, the freedom of assembly is neglected, but it is also actively discredited in its digitally mediated form. We must interrogate the discrediting discourse of 'slacktivism' often applied to what might otherwise be understood as digitally mediated assemblies. To do so, I will outline the slacktivism argument and then make a sociological swerve, moving behind the debate to see what is motivating it by introducing the concept of *visibility backlash*. As we shall see, the slacktivism debate is preceded by a long line of struggles over public visibility.

Slacktivism ('slacker activism' portmanteaued) emerged around the turn of the millennium as a pejorative concept used to describe digitally mediated activism and, by implication, assembly. This concept, and its cognates such as clicktivism, piqued the English-speaking public's interest in the early 2010s.[10] This was when a constellation of what Castells calls 'networked social movements' sprung up around the world, from the Arab Spring to the Occupy movement.[11] It is also when *Kony 2012*, a digital video produced by NGO Invisible Children to gather mass support for the capture of Ugandan war criminal Joseph Kony, went viral; it was, in fact, the first video on YouTube to hit one million likes.[12]

Two authors crystallized the unease of that era about digitally mediated activism, writing in high-profile US publications: Morozov in *Foreign Policy* and Gladwell in *The New Yorker*.[13] Their and other critiques about slacktivism tend to focus on a pair of perceived problematics, both of which compare online activism to offline (now widely accepted as a false dichotomy, given how interpellated our everyday lives are with the digital). First, they see slacktivism as less effectual in achieving social and political change. Second, they worry that online activism substitutes for offline activism, leading to less political commitment overall.[14] The focus of these critiques is on social change and political participation; the changing nature of assembly is implied, and the implication is that digitally mediated assemblies are a lower order of assembly.

Not everyone agreed with Morozov and Gladwell, of course. Using the case study of the marriage equality meme developed by the Human Rights Campaign, Vie wrote a vindication of slacktivism.[15] This meme, a pink equals sign inside a red square, went viral in 2013 as Facebook users across the United States and beyond posted it as profile pictures. As Vie posited, this collective communicative practice might have been dismissed as slacktivism, but that epithet would belie its impact. The meme's catching communication between people on platforms raised the visibility of marriage equality and created solidarity around this common cause.

Although, of course, I have made the argument that digitally mediated assemblies are assemblies, not slacktivism, here is where I take a sociological swerve using a constructivist approach. The swerve moves us away from the trees of arguments and rebuttals and to the forest of the debate. Why has it come about? What is at stake, and for whom? What are its broader consequences? Here, I build on other scholars who have identified slacktivism as a dismissal, but I go further in thinking about why this dismissal might have surfaced and what consequences it might have.[16] To do so, I build on my concept of discrediting discourse and borrow from ideas about moral panics to argue that slacktivism is a visibility backlash.

A visibility backlash is a widespread public reaction to certain groups' new visibility that aims to discredit them, and thus push them out of the limelight. It is a particular manifestation of a *discrediting discourse*, namely, a communicative move in a disagreement that aims to publicly undermine the interlocutor rather than their argument.[17] When your credibility takes a hit, it is harder to get attention. If you want to gain or regain that attention, you need to divert your communicative resources to repairing your reputation. This means you cannot spend as much energy on your original communicative aims.

This distraction, where the public's attention is on the characterization of the person and their practices rather than on their messages and their aims, is redolent of the classic sociological concept of a moral panic.[18] Indeed, the concept of moral panic has been applied to similar digital media-fuelled controversies, like the emergence of the selfie, also in the mid-2010s.[19] Like a moral panic, the visibility backlash is reactionary, pervasive, discrediting, distracting, and fuelled by the media, and it similarly preserves the status quo through diminishing and othering the newly visible. As Marwick points out with her conceptual refinement of 'technopanic', these days, such responses are often to the adoption of new technologies by more marginalized groups.[20]

And yet, I would argue that backlashes like slacktivism and selfie-hating are neither quite about morality nor quite about panics. Instead of challenges to the *moral* status quo, what is at stake is the *visibility* status quo. Backlashes can draw upon morality, as with the accusation against selfie-takers of being narcissistic and the implication of laziness in the epithet of slacktivism. But visibility backlashes are fundamentally responses to challenges to the status quo on who has public visibility and who controls that visibility. Additionally, rather than being about *hyping up*—the panicked, disproportionality element of a moral panic—visibility backlashes are about *playing down*, or belittling.

It is this belittling that has the effect of preserving the status quo. It discredits the messengers, even disciplines them, derailing the debate with ad hominem attacks—and thus turns down the dial on their messages.[21] Consider the mid-2010s uproar over the breastfeeding selfie, which, through the associated hashtag of #brelfie, brings together selfies and digitally mediated assembly. The backlash against brelfies was specifically about the new visibility of a practice traditionally relegated to the private sphere in the West, including whether Facebook should ban these pictures.[22] The public discrediting of brelfie-takers as 'attention-seeking' and of brelfies as 'indecent' diverted attention from brelfies' core challenges to the status quo on how breasts are understood, how women's bodies are policed, and how motherhood is governed.[23] We can understand the visceral discordance between selfie-takers and selfie-haters, as well as between digitally mediated assemblers and their detractors, as symbolic struggles over visibility, because the visibility of new actors and ideas is a pathway to challenging the status quo.[24]

That said, visibility backlashes are not so simple as elites versus the marginalized. As discourses, they are empirical examples of another key—and unresolved—sociological topic, that of how power and knowledge intersect. In determining the source and spread of visibility backlashes, we can certainly consider elites who benefit from maintaining statuses as publicly visible and/or as gatekeepers of public visibility.[25] If we think of the influential authorship and readership of *Foreign Policy* and *The New Yorker*, in which Morozov and Gladwell's criticisms appeared, we can speculate about this group and the threat they might feel about new forms of assembly challenging the status quo from below.

Additionally, we can consider institutions like the media and how their political, economic, and cultural structures tend to favour the status quo.[26] Media pay more attention to the powerful, but the media also are looking for newsworthy stories; just like the moral panic, the visibility backlash is a story that sells.[27] Consider, for example, *The Telegraph*'s breathless 2015 headline about selfies: 'More people have died by taking selfies this year than by shark attacks: It seems that taking a selfie is actually quite a dangerous endeavor, and many people have died while doing so' (we are talking about twelve fatal selfies versus eight lethal sharks in the first nine months of 2015, worldwide).[28]

Another way that visibility backlashes may spread is through becoming common sense.[29] When something is common sense, if you ask people how they know it, they might reply, 'Come on, everyone knows that!' A discourse becomes common sense when it begins to free-float, separated from its source and thus from critical engagement with its sources' motives. If it chimes with widely held sentiments, like unease about new technologies or worries about instability, common sense can move out broadly in society beyond those who benefit more directly from the discourse. A commonsense visibility backlash, as it becomes naturalized, further invisibilizes; all of a sudden, we are talking about how people are assembling rather than what they are assembling about.

This exposition on visibility backlashes has two purposes. The first is theoretical. Visibility backlash is a concept that helps us see slacktivism as part of a history of discursive struggles over visibility—more recently manifested in the current culture war's co-opted and critical use of 'woke'. The second is political. If digitally mediated assemblies are assemblies proper, and if these have been discredited through backlash attacks, then proponents of the freedom of assembly must do discursive work to rename and reclaim these digitally mediated assembly practices. Without this discursive work, we might under-evaluate and under-design how intermediary digital platforms can support digitally mediated assembly.

Assembly Affordances

It is one thing to argue that the digitally mediated freedom of assembly exists; it is another to enable it. Regulation is a key mechanism, though efforts to date have proven platform regulation to be a snarled knot.[30] Instead, I wish to focus on how technology projects can voluntarily enable human rights through their own institutional change, an approach bolstered by the UN Guiding Principles on Business and Human Rights.[31] In the early twenty-first century, this culture proliferated in the corporate technology sector, though it still has a long way to go, as evidenced by conflicts pitting human rights against profit at Google and the eradication of Twitter's human rights team before it was rebranded as X.[32] While some might see the volatility in importance of human rights at Big Tech as the inevitable outcome of rights-washing or ethics-washing, I prefer the more optimistic view that sees struggles as openings for change.[33] This section thus lends support to the besieged efforts to increase the prominence of human rights in design at Big Tech. It also provides a framework for grassroots efforts to build technologies that support the freedom of assembly—as well as a framework for all of us to evaluate existing technologies.

Human rights-centred design mandates that human rights must be on the agenda at all stages of design, from conception to building to implementing to evaluating.[34] Yet, human rights are notoriously abstract concepts; how do we translate these ideals of human rights into the pragmatics of design? Here, I propose a translation turnkey I call *assembly affordances*. A technology's affordances are the uses made possible through the combination of owners and designers' intentions, users' imaginations, the technology's materiality, and contexts of use.[35] Analysing technologies for their affordances for social change is a productive approach that has been taken vis-à-vis activism, advocacy, and human rights fact-finding.[36] As the concept of affordances focuses us on what the technology *makes possible* rather than what the technology *is*, this approach future-proofs analytical evaluations in the face of rapid technological innovation and obsolescence. Affordances have another analytical utility, and this is a critical one: Evaluating affordances is a way to normatively assess technologies, particularly thinking about the difference between aspirational affordances and actual affordances.

Aspirational affordances are what we would like our technology to afford, while *actual affordances* are either what exists or what is pragmatically possible. Aspirational affordances are ideals. They will vary according to the experiences, identities, and norms of those imagining them. Methodologically, to identify one set of aspirational assembly affordances, I conducted a thematic analysis of General Comment No. 37. I chose this document because it provides so much detail on the scope of the right; because it was written following a global, multi-stakeholder consultation process; and because, pragmatically, the powerful institutions of Big Tech are more likely to listen to another powerful institution.

To think about actual assembly affordances, we can return to the conceptual family of mediation. Intermediation is one such concept, in that the technology in question is the intermediary between participants in the assembly, and this technology has its own actors, logics, norms, cultures, discourses, and features that afford certain practices and not others. A second useful concept is mediatization, which is how people's practices change because of how they imagine intermediary technologies and anticipate being mediated by them.[37] Below, I use these concepts to examine several trends in communication technology for actual assembly affordances. An alternative approach would be to take deep dive into particular technologies using a range of methodologies, including a critical political economy investigation of ownership and control; a critical technocultural discourse analysis of the relationship between technology beliefs, artefacts, and practices by users wishing to pursue assembly; and the walkthrough method for analysing apps.[38] The three assembly affordances I evaluate are pre-assembly, sight and sound, and gathering.

Pre-assembly

Pre-assembly is about the 'would-be' in General Comment No. 37's reference to 'would-be participants in assemblies'.[39] One dimension of pre-assembly is about logistics and awareness-raising, while another is about the conditions that support the potential for assembly, such as community and solidarity. Here, however, I focus on the feeling of freedom to join an assembly without significant negative consequences. Part of the aspiration of this affordance is that this feeling is equal across all people.

General Comment No. 37 speaks of the state facilitating an 'enabling environment' for assembly, and we can infer that platforms must do the same.[40] Of course, an enabling environment is not just about eliminating purposive 'chilling effects' on assembly, but also about considering how these might arise as collateral damage to other purposes.[41] Platforms' profit logics foster surveillance capitalism as the key mechanism for making money through serving up audiences to advertisers. They can also facilitate state surveillance through deals struck to maintain market access. Growth mindsets deliver products and content suited for majorities, including views held by these majorities against minoritized populations.[42] The attention economy, where any attention is good attention, can reward hateful and harmful content. Even if no immediate threats exist, the permanence of digital data means that the security of participating in digitally mediated assemblies cannot be future-proofed. The 'nothing to hide, nothing to fear' discourse about surveillance glosses over real and perceived perils for minoritized populations, whose histories forestall a feeling of freedom to participate in surveilled spaces.[43]

All of this is to say that the actual assembly affordance of pre-assembly is experienced unequally because of the logics of Big Tech intermediaries and how these logics may remediate assembly participation to unknown and threatening audiences. These intermediaries are having a mediatization effect on would-be participants. Often, we think of mediatization as a change to a communicative practice, but sometimes that mediatization effect can be not communicating at all. Closing the gap between this aspirational and actual assembly affordance is no easy feat; it is about alternative business models, better controls against online harms, and facilitating digital evanescence.

Sight and Sound

General Comment No. 37 references communicative purposes of an assembly. These include putting forward and testing ideas and aims, making complaints, conflict resolution, expressing solidarity, and pursuing goals related to entertainment, religion, and the market. We could understand these as expressive acts, but General Comment No. 37 goes beyond this, stating, wonderfully, that assemblies should 'as far as possible' be 'within sight and sound' of their audiences (see also Zick, in this volume).[44]

In assembly, then, communication surpasses the freedom of expression, which (arguably) is limited to expression and its precedents, like forming opinions and gathering information to form these opinions.[45] Many interpret the freedom of expression as not including the right to be heard or seen or, more generally, acknowledged—while the freedom of assembly edges towards this. As such, the aspirational affordance of being within sight and sound is a prerequisite for assembly—both participant-to-participant and participant-to-audience. Ideally, this is visibility or audibility on the assembler's terms. Sometimes, this is recognition of presence but not personhood—in other words, anonymity. According to General Comment No. 37, anonymity is a form of expression that may facilitate participate in assemblies due to the protection it affords.

The actual assembly affordance of sight and sound, however, is significantly inflected by platform intermediaries. All algorithms invisibilize messages that do not conform with their priorities (see also Ashraf, in this volume). Even 'bridging systems' algorithms, which promote content that appeals across audience divides (in contrast to the divisive content favoured by orthodox platform algorithms), may reward apolitical content over political content.[46] The shady practice of shadowbanning, in which targeted users can post as normal but have no indication that their posts are banned from others' view, is another mode of visibility governance. It is not only the posts that are cast in shadow, but also the policies, as platforms regularly disavow them in the face of user evidence.[47] At the time of writing, users of X can pay for visibility through subscribing to X Blue, which bestows a verified veneer as well as 'prioritized rankings in conversations and search'.[48]

Even before assembly participants send messages across time and space in the hopes that they will be seen and heard, their actions are mediatized: Messages' content and style is shaped by anticipation of how intermediary technologies might bestow or withdraw visibility. Returning to the idea of pre-assembly, sometimes this mediatization results in self-censorship because of the conditions of revelation that accompany sight and sound. In many contexts, digitally mediated anonymity is out of reach because of state or platform policies. Users of Chinese social media platform Weibo, long required to register their accounts with real names, now also must relinquish their locational privacy.[49] Facebook asks users 'to use the name they go by in everyday life' to 'keep you and our community safe from impersonation' —though some speculate that the authentic name policy exists because identified users are more valuable to advertisers.[50]

These intermediary and mediatization effects go against the spirit of General Comment No. 37. Extrapolating from the Comment's statements that the regulation of assembly must be content neutral and agnostic to 'technical means', we can infer that intermediary technologies should afford equal opportunities for sight and sound.[51] Of course, intermediary and mediatization effects cannot be entirely avoided. However, understanding their influence on which communications have the potential to be received on whose terms, as well as how this is unequally distributed amongst communicators, is key to human rights-centred design.

Gathering

As General Comment No. 37 explains, 'inherent to the right [of assembly] is an associative element'.[52] What is so refreshing about this right in the context of broad trends towards individualization in many societies is that it does not delineate where one person ends and the other begins; the right only exists for an individual if they can live it with others. It is an 'individual right that is exercised collectively' and the expression of 'individual autonomy in solidarity with others'.[53]

The aspirational assembly affordance of gathering, as designed into platforms that liberate participants from particular times and places, potentially affords many more assemblies as well as many more assemblers. The pandemic made the latter extremely clear, but it has long been the case that technologies have supported the freedom to assemble for those who, for reasons of disability, caregiving, work, resources, location, and context, have not been able to show up in analogue streets and squares. In so doing, these platforms can have an equalizing effect for those who 'may face particular challenges in participating in assemblies'.[54]

The aspirational assembly affordance of gathering requires that people be able to connect with each other. They need to be able to encounter, identify, and reach each other, as well as to sustain their connection in one publicly accessible (if not public) place and/or across time and space. Intermediary stability, in terms of features and underlying norms and aims, is thus key to the assembly affordance of gathering. Over time, social media users invest a significant amount in their social capital on particular platforms.[55] This investment may be about assembly, but often it is about more mundane exchanges and learning about each other. These lower key interactions are part of pre-assembly, as they form the strong web from which gatherings can spring. This benefit of intermediary platforms exists as long as platform owners support user networks through investment and regulation.

As we have seen with Musk's 2022 purchase of Twitter, however, owners or priorities can change, which means that users' networks can be lost in an instant. In the name of free speech, Musk began undoing a lot of the platform's safeguards against online harms, including reducing content moderation and eliminating the independent advisory Trust and Safety Council. Unsurprisingly, hate speech on Twitter escalated significantly.[56] This forced users in minoritized groups to weigh up the value of their established networks and gatherings against their online safety. One such group of groups is known as Black Twitter—African Americans who use Twitter in diverse ways, including building networks, sharing news, and self-representing in the face of misrepresentations and racism in the mainstream media.[57] On the one hand, as journalism and communications professor Dr Meredith Clark explained it to a journalist:

> Among Black Twitter, I see people saying, nope, we're staying. We're digging in our heels. We've been on this platform. We've contributed so much to it that we've made it valuable in the way that it is today [. . .]. I just tweeted the other day that I'll be the last one to turn the lights off if that's what I need to be because I'm certainly not going either.[58]

On the other hand, and in waves corresponding with Musk's destabilizing moves, Black Twitter users have been joining the mass exodus to other platforms. This includes Mastodon, discussed in more detail below, and the new, Black-owned platform called Spill, which is designed to be safety-first for diverse groups.[59]

The choice that Black Twitter users have had to make between gatherings and safety is driven by the platform's shifting culture from one that supported their key norms to one that undermines them.[60] Human rights centred-design would better align intermediary ideals with those of their users. As demonstrated in this section, a wide gulf exists between aspirational and actual assembly affordances as concerns current platforms—but what might the future herald? I turn to this next by examining some new developments in communication technologies.

Emergent Platform Trends

Human rights-centred design is still somewhat niche, in practice even more so than in promise. We can look to emergent platform trends to speculate on the potential of these platforms to support digitally mediated assembly. In this section, I consider three such trends: the focus on authenticity and consequent depoliticization of new platforms, as exemplified by BeReal; the fragmentation of networks due to the proliferation of platforms, like Mastodon; and user alienation, as in the #corecore movement encouraging users to quit TikTok. I evaluate these trends using the assembly affordance of gathering, as it is the affordance most unique to the right to assemble.

At the time of writing, BeReal was having a popularity moment. This platform sends users a simultaneous daily alert at an unpredictable time; users have two minutes to take photos from their phones' front and back cameras, showing what they are doing; they can post after this, but this post is conspicuously marked as 'late'. Only once users have uploaded their own photos can they see and comment on friends' photos, which are visible in their unsearchable timelines until the next day's BeReal alert. Currently funded through investors, this French platform states that its 'core principle is authenticity', as users have neither the time nor the foresight that curation, so characteristic of rival platforms like Instagram, requires.[61] As a result, user networks are very small; as one user described it, 'The key ingredient is adding people you're happy to look shitty in front of'.[62]

Forming a gathering on BeReal is relatively difficult. In addition to small network sizes and the lack of search functionality, the unpredictable and delimited posting window restricts users' abilities to plan gatherings or to extend them across time and space. For example, I attended the British University and College Union National Strike Rally on 30 November 2022 in London, joining other striking workers protesting unequal and unfair working conditions. I hoped and hoped that the 'Time to BeReal' notification would show up on my phone during the rally so I could spread the word about the cause (admittedly, to my five friends). Of course, it only pinged once I was back home. I still got my rally placard into the photo frame, but the setting of my front hallway was not quite the same as the streets streaming with people. In the case of BeReal, then, limitations to the assembly affordance of gathering are collateral damage of the pursuit of authenticity. We can also speculate that BeReal's popularity has to do with disaffection with the politicization of other platforms. All is not lost, however, as the intimacy and regularity of BeReal can support bonds of solidarity so important to pre-assembly.

With the demolition of Twitter as we once knew it, social media users are migrating in different directions, including towards community-owned platforms like Mastodon. Launched by a German non-profit in 2016, Mastodon describes itself as 'social networking that's not for sale. Your home feed should be filled with what matters to you most, not what a corporation thinks you should see. Radically different social media, back in the hands of the people'.[63] Mastodon has no advertisers and no algorithm. It is decentralized, meaning that it is made up of independently governed server communities, and is part of the Fediverse, a network of interoperable social media platforms that allow users to communicate across them.[64] It affords following, searching, hashtagging, trending, and other features that support digitally mediated gathering.

Until the recent uptick in migration to Mastodon, however, gatherings may have been limited by network effects, namely, the phenomenon that people concentrate on platforms where their friends are. Not enough people were on Mastodon. For example, a few years ago, I was browsing a public Google document, authored by a major climate crisis movement, about social media best practices. This document suggested that constituent groups establish accounts on all the mainstream social media platforms. In addition to being publicly available, this document was publicly editable. Someone had interrupted the formal text with a written plea for organizers to consider Mastodon instead. This interjection emphasized how Mastodon servers can be run on clean energy, in contrast to mainstream platforms, which contribute to the climate crisis with energy required for data storage. I visited this document again at the time of writing, and it seemed that this plea had gone unheeded. Even though Mastodon has a normative framework that could align better with the climate crisis movement, the assembly affordance of gathering through network effects probably kept the movement on mainstream platforms. We are currently seeing a proliferation of new platforms, with resulting network fragmentation; it is unclear what the implications are for the critical masses many assemblies need.

The third disaffection trend I refer to in this section is less about migrating platforms and more about quitting them—a trend I consider, with a positive connotation, to be neo-Luddism. A recent example was the movement on TikTok—the Chinese-owned, explosively popular, short-form video app—to quit the social media platform on 3 March 2023. This call for a sort of anti-assembly assembly, a collective sending of a message through not producing or consuming any messages, was related to a hashtag called corecore. The hashtag, which at the time of writing had 2.8 billion views, accompanies a political, cultural, and aesthetic trend on TikTok that manifests in a fast-paced collage of found videos often set to mournful music.[65] The disorienting and dystopian effect is of auto-scrolling through a TikTok feed at speed. Corecore can be deployed with many intents, including producing shared cultural experiences of humour, emotions, and/or critical awareness.[66] Through the splicing of disparate videos, the critical subgenre of corecore emphasizes a structural instead of individualistic interpretation of the problems it critiques. It is 'a dreaming of a better world', as explained by one user in a highly viewed video.[67]

The #corecore videos promoting the 3 March quit TikTok movement were a meta-critique (in the traditional rather than tech behemoth sense of the word); they were self-conscious of the problematic relationship between the platform and its users, as reflected in the doubling of 'core' in their moniker. This doubling referenced the practice of making and sharing 'core' (in the singular) videos on TikTok, which are user-generated memetic tributes to a niche trend—like cottagecore or circuscore—whose consumption is fuelled by TikTok's uncanny algorithm.[68] Consuming TikTok videos can be like falling down the rabbit hole, only to surface, time-warped, hours later.

My cousin shared a #corecore video with me on the 21 February 2023, which had 6.3 million views at the time of writing. It starts with a clip of a baby screaming as a live chicken is put on its highchair tray, then moves as if scrolling to a plate of blue-dusted marshmallows, then a scene from a period drama, an interview with a politician, someone attaching a piece of art to a wall, another person loading an inflatable raft into a truck bed, raw eggs sizzling in a pan—and it scrolls on and on, faster and faster and more and more random, as the soundscape of an MRI scanner builds. Watching it, I feel disoriented, claustrophobic. Then the screen cuts to black, and the words 'Quit tiktok March 3rd 2023' appear. The background becomes the scene of a stream in the forest, and the MRI din is replaced by birdsong.[69]

Student journalist Georgia Mooney captured the sentiment of the 3 March quit TikTok movement, writing, 'If we don't have control and stop now then when will we stop consuming videos like this? We are mindlessly consuming everything on social media and it's rotting our brains'.[70] The repercussions of communication technologies' alienation of publics reverberate; the effects are not just migration and abstention, but also the narrowing of the range of opportunities publics have to exercise their rights.

Conclusion

In this chapter, I have made a case for why we need to need to take the digitally mediated freedom of assembly seriously. I started with a descriptive account of digitally mediated assembly. This hinged on my argument that mediation across time and space—whether the short distances for co-present assemblies or the potentially longer ones for digitally mediated assemblies—is a characteristic of all assemblies. My descriptive account turned into a discursive account meant to counteract the dismissive epithet of slacktivism. I speculated about a range of reasons underpinning the slacktivism smear, including relative neglect of the freedom of assembly compared to other communication rights because of its collective, emotional, and positive liberty dimensions. The traditional subordination of this right dovetailed with the phenomenon of what I called a visibility backlash against the rise of new assemblers and assemblies using digital mediation.

Though pandemic lockdowns highlighted the value of digitally mediated assembly, we proponents still have discursive work to do to repair the damage caused by the idea of slacktivism. Raising the profile of digitally mediated assembly is important for at least four reasons. First, it expands the range of people and practices seen to be protected by this right. Second, it emphasizes the need for further research in the understudied area of digitally mediated assembly, including from sociologies of human rights and technology perspectives. Third, it encourages technologists to consider assembly affordances as design frameworks. In this chapter, I outlined three—pre-assembly, sight and sound, and gathering—and showed that the gulf between aspirational and actual assembly affordances amongst contemporary technologies remains significant. Assembly affordances should be a design priority, particularly given that emergent platform trends are complicating opportunities for digitally mediated assembly. Though the concept of affordances is most associated with technology, I urge policymakers to consider assembly affordances as a framework for evaluating laws, city planners for shaping places, educationalists for designing curricula, and so on.

The fourth reason why we need to raise the profile of assembly, more generally, is because of its communal aspects. Assembly is a right anchored in the collective, and it is easy to see that groups, communities, and societies benefit from its exercise. Further promoting the idea of collective rights may shift the lens a little on other communication rights that are currently understood as being ascribed to the individual. As Solove does with the right to privacy, we have to ask what happens when we think about the freedom of expression in relation to community rather than individual benefits.[71] Rather than pitting one person's freedom of expression against another's—a feature of the current culture wars—this approach considers what policies and platform affordances would best create environments where *everybody* feels free to express themselves.

Even saying all of this, I am not urging assemblers to assemble on platforms, nor insisting that digitally mediated assembly is a substitution for face-to-face assembly. Given all the risks and problems I have identified in this chapter, it is understandable that many people strategically decide not to assemble on platforms, as well as to abandon them wholesale or reject them from the start. It is my hope, however, that the arguments and concepts I have put forward can extend and support the freedom of assembly, should people choose to exercise it through digital mediation.

Acknowledgements

I am very grateful to the editors for astute and helpful comments and many wonderful conversations, as well as to Christof Heyns for the original invitation to consider these topics; the student research team across Cambridge and the University of East Anglia, with whom I initially investigated digitally mediated assembly; and Elise Mathews for her savvy suggestions.

Notes

1. Michael Hamilton, Ella McPherson, and Sharath Srinivasan, '"Deal with Me, Here I Stand!": Presence, Participation and the Equal Protection of Online Assemblies', in *A Life Interrupted: Essays in Honour of the Lives and Legacies of Christof Heyns*, ed. Frans Viljoen et al. (Pretoria: Pretoria University Law Press, 2022), 327–346.
2. Jürgen Habermas, *The Structural Transformation of the Public Sphere: An Inquiry into a Category of Bourgeois Society* (Cambridge, MA: MIT Press, 1989); Annabelle Sreberny-Mohammadi, 'Small Media for a Big Revolution: Iran', *Politics, Culture, and Society* 3, no. 3 (1990): 341–371.
3. Lauren Collins, *When in French: Love in a Second Language* (New York: Penguin Books, 2016); Sonia Livingstone, 'On the Mediation of Everything: ICA Presidential Address 2008', *Journal of Communication* 59, no. 1 (2009): 1–18.
4. John B. Thompson, *Ideology and Modern Culture: Critical Social Theory in the Era of Mass Communication* (Stanford, CA: Stanford University Press, 1990).
5. Rikke Frank Jørgensen, 'Human Rights and Private Actors in the Online Domain', in *New Technologies for Human Rights Law and Practice*, ed. Jay D. Aronson and Molly K. Land (Cambridge: Cambridge University Press, 2018), 243–269; Clément Nyaletsossi Voulé, A/74/349: Report of the Special Rapporteur on the Rights to Freedom of Peaceful Assembly and of Association: Civic Space, Poverty and Exclusion (United Nations General Assembly, 11 September 2019).
6. David Harvey, *A Brief History of Neoliberalism* (Oxford: Oxford University Press, 2005).
7. Virginia Held, *The Ethics of Care: Personal, Political, and Global* (Oxford: Oxford University Press, 2006).
8. Patricia Hill Collins, *Black Feminist Thought: Knowledge, Consciousness, and the Politics of Empowerment* (New York: Routledge, 2002); Catherine D'Ignazio and Lauren Klein, *Data Feminism* (Cambridge, MA: MIT Press, 2019).

9. Danielle Allen, *Justice by Means of Democracy* (Chicago: University of Chicago Press, 2023).
10. See Google Trends: https://trends.google.com/trends/explore?date=all&q=slacktivism.
11. Manuel Castells, *Networks of Outrage and Hope: Social Movements in the Internet Age* (New York: John Wiley & Sons, 2013).
12. James Dennis, *Beyond Slacktivism: Political Participation on Social Media* (Cham, Switzerland: Springer International, 2019); Emma Madden, '"Kony 2012," 10 Years Later', *The New York Times*, 8 March 2022.
13. Malcolm Gladwell, 'Small Change: Why the Revolution Will Not Be Tweeted', *The New Yorker* (2010); Evgeny Morozov, 'The Brave New World of Slacktivism', *Foreign Policy* (2009).
14. Henrik Serup Christensen, 'Political Activities on the Internet: Slacktivism or Political Participation by Other Means?', *First Monday* 16, no. 2 (2011).
15. Stephanie Vie, 'In Defense of "Slacktivism": The Human Rights Campaign Facebook Logo as Digital Activism', *First Monday* 19, no. 4 (2014).
16. Philip N. Howard et al., 'Social Media, Civic Engagement, and the Slacktivism Hypothesis: Lessons from Mexico's "El Bronco"', *SIPA Journal of International Affairs* 70, no. 1 (2016): 55–73; Nora Madison and Mathias Klang, 'The Case for Digital Activism: Refuting the Fallacies of Slacktivism', *Journal of Digital Social Research* 2, no. 2 (2020): 28–47.
17. Ella McPherson, 'Source Credibility as "Information Subsidy": Strategies for Successful NGO Journalism at Mexican Human Rights NGOs', *Journal of Human Rights* 15, no. 3 (2016): 330–346.
18. Stanley Cohen, *Folk Devils and Moral Panics* (London: Routledge, 2011).
19. Theresa M. Senft and Nancy K. Baym, 'What Does the Selfie Say? Investigating a Global Phenomenon', *International Journal of Communication* 9 (2015): 1588–1606.
20. Alice E. Marwick, 'To Catch a Predator? The MySpace Moral Panic', *First Monday* 13, no. 6 (2008).
21. Anne Burns, 'Self(ie)-Discipline: Social Regulation as Enacted through the Discussion of Photographic Practice', *International Journal of Communication* 9 (2015): 1716–1733.
22. For example, see Caitlin Dewey, 'Facebook Is Embroiled in yet Another Breastfeeding Photo Controversy', *Washington Post*, 26 October 2021.
23. Sarah Beach, 'The Embodiment and Discourses of a Taboo: #brelfie', *Kaleidoscope: A Graduate Journal of Qualitative Communication Research* 16 (2017): 43–60, at 49, 50; Vange Holtz-Schramek, 'Post-Brelfie: The Limits of Intersubjectivity & Intersectionality', *Feminist Media Studies*, advance online publication, https://doi.org/10.1080/14680777.2023.2228504.
24. John B. Thompson, 'The New Visibility', *Theory, Culture and Society* 22, no. 6 (2005): 31–51.
25. Erich Goode and Nachman Ben-Yehuda, *Moral Panics: The Social Construction of Deviance*, 2nd ed. (Chichester, UK: Wiley-Blackwell, 2009).
26. Gaye Tuchman, *Making News: A Study in the Construction of Reality* (New York: Free Press, 1978).
27. Stuart Hall et al., *Policing the Crisis: Mugging, the State, and Law and Order*, 2nd ed. (Basingstoke, UK: Palgrave Macmillan, 2013); Angela McRobbie and Sarah L. Thornton, 'Rethinking "Moral Panic" for Multi-Mediated Social Worlds', *British Journal of Sociology* 46, no. 4 (1995): 559–574.
28. Helena Horton, 'More People Have Died by Taking Selfies This Year than by Shark Attacks', *The Telegraph*, 22 September 2015; Cailey Rizzo, 'More People Have Died from Selfies Than Shark Attacks This Year', *Mashable*, 21 September 2015.
29. McRobbie and Thornton, 'Rethinking "Moral Panic"'.

30. Jørgensen, *Human Rights and Private Actors in the Online Domain*.
31. UN Guiding Principles on Business and Human Rights (Office for High Commissioner of Human Rights, 2011).
32. Ross LaJeunesse, 'I Was Google's Head of International Relations. Here's Why I Left', *Medium*, 2 January 2020; Jørgensen, 'Human Rights and Private Actors in the Online Domain'.
33. Karen Yeung, Andrew Howes, and Ganna Pogrebna, 'AI Governance by Human Rights–Centered Design, Deliberation, and Oversight: An End to Ethics Washing', in *The Oxford Handbook of Ethics of AI* (Oxford: Oxford University Press, 2020), 76–106.
34. Ibid.
35. Peter Nagy and Gina Neff, 'Imagined Affordance: Reconstructing a Keyword for Communication Theory', *Social Media + Society* 1, no. 2 (2015): 1–9.
36. Jennifer Earl and Katrina Kimport, *Digitally Enabled Social Change: Activism in the Internet Age* (Cambridge, MA: MIT Press, 2011); Steven Livingston, 'Digital Affordances and Human Rights Advocacy', SFB-Governance Working Paper Series, 2016; Ella McPherson, 'Advocacy Organizations' Evaluation of Social Media Information for NGO Journalism: The Evidence and Engagement Models', *American Behavioral Scientist* 59, no. 1 (2015): 124–148.
37. Livingstone, 'On the Mediation of Everything'.
38. André Brock, 'Critical Technocultural Discourse Analysis', *New Media & Society* 20, no. 3 (2018): 1012–1030; Ben Light, Jean Burgess, and Stefanie Duguay, 'The Walkthrough Method: An Approach to the Study of Apps', *New Media & Society* 20, no. 3 (2018): 881–900.
39. UNHRCtte, General Comment No. 37—Article 21: Right of Peaceful Assembly (17 September 2020) UN Doc. CCPR/C/GC/37, 11.
40. Ibid., 5.
41. Ibid., 11.
42. Safiya Umoja Noble, *Algorithms of Oppression: How Search Engines Reinforce Racism* (New York: New York University Press, 2018).
43. Simone Browne, *Dark Matters: On the Surveillance of Blackness* (Durham, NC: Duke University Press, 2015).
44. UNHRCtte, General Comment No. 37, 4.
45. Convention for the Protection of Human Rights and Fundamental Freedoms, article 10 (November 1950) 214 U.N.T.S. 221.
46. Will Oremus, 'Social Media Can Be Polarizing. A New Type of Algorithm Aims to Change That', *Washington Post*, 11 January 2023.
47. Carolina Are, 'The Shadowban Cycle: An Autoethnography of Pole Dancing, Nudity and Censorship on Instagram', *Feminist Media Studies* 22, no. 8 (2022): 2002–2019.
48. X Corp, 'About Twitter Blue' (2023).
49. 'China's Weibo Shows User Locations to Combat "Bad Behaviour"', Reuters, 28 April 2022.
50. Meta, 'Being Your Authentic Self on Facebook' (2023), https://www.facebook.com/help/186614050293763/.
51. UNHRCtte, General Comment No. 37, 10.
52. Ibid., 2.
53. Ibid., 1, 2.
54. Ibid., 5.
55. Zeynep Tufekci, *Twitter and Tear Gas: The Power and Fragility of Networked Protest* (New Haven, CT: Yale University Press, 2017).

56. Daniel Hickey et al., 'Auditing Elon Musk's Impact on Hate Speech and Bots', *Proceedings of the International AAAI Conference on Web and Social Media* 17, no. 1 (2013): 1133–1137.
57. Allissa V. Richardson, *Bearing Witness While Black: African Americans, Smartphones, & the New Protest #Journalism* (Oxford: Oxford University Press, 2020).
58. National Public Radio, 'What Happens to "Black Twitter" under Musk?', NPR, 12 November 2022.
59. Christopher Smith, 'Black Twitter Exodus: What Is Spill?', *Hip-Hop Wired*, 3 July 2023.
60. André Brock, 'From the Blackhand Side: Twitter as a Cultural Conversation', *Journal of Broadcasting & Electronic Media* 56, no. 4 (2012): 529–549.
61. BeReal, 'UK Users, It's Time for Bonus BeReal!', (2023), https://bereal.com/en/announcement/.
62. Casey Newton, 'Why BeReal Is Breaking Out', *The Verge*, 20 July 2022.
63. Mastodon, 'Decentralized Social Media', (2023), https://joinmastodon.org/.
64. Kalley Huang, 'What Is Mastodon and Why Are People Leaving Twitter for It?', *The New York Times*, 7 November 2022.
65. Chance Townsend, 'Explaining Corecore: How TikTok's Newest Trend May Be a Genuine Gen-Z Art Form', *Mashable*, 14 January 2023.
66. Townsend, 'Explaining Corecore'.
67. littlefreak26, 'Thoughts on Corecore and Nichetok', TikTok, 27 December 2022, https://www.tiktok.com/@littlefreak26/video/7181647126571633962.
68. Townsend, 'Explaining Corecore'.
69. Balldestroyer69, 'Spread the word #corecore #nichetok #fyp✎°viral #xycbca #capcut #march3rd #march3', TikTok, 1 February 2023, https://www.tiktok.com/@cook.e/video/7195087945261518081.
70. Georgia Mooney, 'Explained: Here's the Reason Why People Are Saying They Are Deleting TikTok on 3rd March', *The Tab*, UK, 23 February 2023.
71. Daniel J. Solove, '"I've Got Nothing to Hide" and Other Misunderstandings of Privacy', *San Diego Law Review* 44 (12 July 2007): 745–772.

Further Reading

Hamilton, Michael, Ella McPherson, and Sharath Srinivasan. '"Deal with Me, Here I Stand!": Presence, Participation and the Equal Protection of Online Assemblies'. *A Life Interrupted: Essays in Honour of the Lives and Legacies of Christof Heyns*, ed. Frans Viljoen et al., 327–346. Pretoria: Pretoria University Law Press, 2022.

Livingstone, Sonia. 'On the Mediation of Everything: ICA Presidential Address 2008'. *Journal of Communication* 59, no. 1 (2009): 1–18.

Madison, Nora, and Mathias Klang. 'The Case for Digital Activism: Refuting the Fallacies of Slacktivism'. *Journal of Digital Social Research* 2, no. 2 (2020): 28–47.

McPherson, Ella. 'Advocacy Organizations' Evaluation of Social Media Information for NGO Journalism: The Evidence and Engagement Models'. *American Behavioral Scientist* 59, no. 1 (2015): 124–148.

Nagy, Peter, and Gina Neff. 'Imagined Affordance: Reconstructing a Keyword for Communication Theory'. *Social Media + Society* 1, no. 2 (2015): 1–9.

Vie, Stephanie. 'In Defense of "'Slacktivism'": The Human Rights Campaign Facebook Logo as Digital Activism'. *First Monday* 19, no. 4 (2014). http://firstmonday.org/ojs/index.php/fm/article/view/4961.

PART III

ASSEMBLIES AS EVENTS

CHAPTER 18

THE OCTOBER DAYS

The Women's March on Versailles

MICAH ALPAUGH

Introduction

On Monday 5 October 1789, facing yet another day of bread shortages at the local *boulangeries*, women around the central marketplace of Les Halles took action. Angry at having waited in line since 3 a.m. for insufficient, overpriced bread or finding nothing left (as on many recent days), crowds formed behind a woman beating a tambourine, shouting 'Bread! Bread!' as they snaked from near the grand Saint-Eustache church southwards to city hall. They demanded to speak to their all-male representatives, shouting 'The men have no courage!' and 'we will take over!'[1] Overwhelming the National Guard detachments governing the building, women (and some men) rushed into every room of Paris's grand renaissance Hôtel de Ville, confronting representatives about provisioning and demanding 'bread and arms'. They only left to pillage the municipal armory, taking rifles, pikes, and even cannons.[2]

The women resolved to march on Versailles. They entreated National Guardsmen to join them, shouting 'No delay!' When the men demurred, waiting for orders, women mocked them as 'cowards and bad citizens' and said they would go without them if need be.[3] The demonstration westwards began in 'exuberance' and 'turbulence', with women calling onlookers to join them and even forcing some wealthy ladies from their carriages to make the long walk.[4] After pausing atop the Champs-Elysées to gather the improvised forces streaming westwards from across many neighbourhoods, the demonstration (fearing possible military suppression) strategically split in two: the larger, armed group took a northerly route via Saint-Cloud, while a smaller, unarmed detachment followed the 30 August route via Sèvres.[5] Protester objectives and threats varied: some shouted that 'We'll demand bread from the King!' while others boasted 'We'll carry the Queen's head at the end of a pike!'[6]

Though a paramilitary demonstration, women used their traditional non-combatant status to avoid repression. A mostly unarmed male protest heading to Versailles had been forcibly turned back on 30 August, but no one intervened as the women proceeded. 'We will be heard', one woman shouted from the crowd. 'We shall reach Versailles, for they will not dare to fire on us'.[7] Despite the rain and mud, spirits and ambitions remained high. Thousands more women (joined by some contingents of men) from Paris's eastern and southern extremities marched after them. When the king first heard of the women marching and was asked by his officers for orders, he replied, 'What, for women? You surely jest'.[8] Warning bells rang across Paris for hours, bringing nervous National Guardsmen to their districts.[9] Pressure rose on their commander, the Marquis de Lafayette, to join the demonstration and finally he did, nominally as peacemaker, leading fifty thousand men from the city's massive new revolutionary forces.

By late afternoon, the women's march reached Versailles and first targeted the National Assembly, leaving their rifles and pikes at the door but flooding into the cavernous hall. Women identified and targeted conservative legislators for abuse with surprising acumen, particularly swing-voting First Estate priests, with some shouting 'down with the filthy, skull-cap wearing clergymen!'[10] Some displayed black, mouldy Parisian bread, shouting 'we'll make the Austrian [Marie Antoinette] swallow it, then chop off her neck!'[11] Many began singing, drowning out unwanted orators, and alternately shouting 'Deputy, speak!' or 'Deputy, shut up!' depending on the legislator and their political persuasions. As some orators sought to buy time, women chanted, 'Bread, bread, no long speeches!'[12] When the Assembly's president read the recent decree implementing free circulation of grain throughout the kingdom, some shouted 'What have these measures accomplished? To starve us?'[13] Ultimately, the Assembly agreed to help the protesters lobby the king for new regulations suitable for Paris's uniquely difficult provisioning situation.

Attention turned to the royal château. The women compelled powerful conservative leader Jean-Joseph Mounier to lead a deputation to meet with Louis XVI, who improbably asserted that 'if there is grain or bread', the corpulent king 'would rather deprive himself to give it to them'.[14] With no measures taken, however, tensions flared outside the palace, as protesters shouted invectives at the royal bodyguards and Versailles National Guardsmen. A little before dawn, a rifle shot rang out, killing a protester and inciting others to rush the palace. One group ran for the Queen's apartment, menacing her assassination, before she escaped into the king's rooms. Insurgents soon paraded at least two bodyguards' heads through the streets.[15] With the château now breached and crimes against Parisians avenged, the emboldened crowds now chanted, 'The King to Paris!' Fearing that his family could be enveloped in the worsening disorder, Louis XVI faced the protesters from the royal balcony and consented.[16]

The *Dames des Halles*, carrying aloft the severed bodyguard heads on pikes followed by bread loaves atop others, led the march back to Paris. 'Have courage, friends', some shouted to onlookers, 'we will lack bread no longer'.[17] Humiliated royal bodyguards and troops marched amongst the triumphant Parisian insurgents. One onlooker claimed to have 'never seen such a shocking spectacle', with king and army submitting to Parisian forces.[18] Great crowds (unbroken from Passy onwards) lined the streets for the King's return, often armed with pikes and guns, fired sporadically in celebration. Versailles courtier Comparot de Longsols wrote to his cousin that 'our nephews will never believe this; they will treat it as a fable. How will they ever imagine that the first, greatest, most powerful king in Europe was forced to quit his usual surroundings to go wherever a wild, poorly-armed, half-dressed, miserable populace wanted?'[19] The royals took up residence in the dilapidated Tuileries Palace, from which they would never successfully escape.

Non-Violence and the Age of Revolutions

Despite the richness of the Age of Revolutions for modern political theory and practice, few scholars have traced the origins of peaceful assembly back that far. Still, surveys like Erica Chenoweth's 2021 *Civil Resistance: What Everyone Needs to Know*, after brief nods to ancient Egypt, Greece, Rome, and the Iroquois, jumps immediately to Henry David Thoreau's 1848 foray into civil disobedience.[20] While violent stereotypes of classic revolutions can provide a rhetorically useful foil for describing innovations since the time of Gandhi, such a perspective obscures many of the roots of modern non-violence and leads to historical misinterpretations of the development of democratically oriented protest techniques.

A dedicated minority of scholars have sought to show the importance of alternatives to violence during an age that most remember first for its bloody uprisings and civil war.[21] For the American Revolution, a volume co-edited by famed Peace Studies scholar Gene Sharp, *Resistance, Politics, and the American Struggle for Independence, 1765–1775*, closely examines the predominantly non-violent social movements centred on boycotting, non-cooperation, and protest marches over the decade between the Stamp Act and the Battle of Lexington and Concord. They argue these campaigns provided much of the basis for the American republic, rather than serving as a mere 'prelude' to the War of Independence.[22] More recently, Michael Goode and John Smolenski's edited collection *The Specter of Peace* examines the importance of peacebuilding in early America, particularly how the many efforts aimed at 'mitigating and regulating violence' can offer an alternative frame to focusing on violence itself.[23] Desires for peace, on a new equitable basis of justice, remained common throughout the era's revolutionary movements—while war and terror tended to follow armed intervention from abroad.[24]

Moreover, the eighteenth century—despite the manifold atrocities committed by European governments, empires, and many of their subjects—featured what scholars have increasingly conceptualized as a Humanitarian Revolution. Many Enlightenment-era writers popularized revulsion against 'barbarous' practices, ranging from torture to slavery to cruelty against women, children, and animals, that resulted in cascading waves of abolitions and reforms over the decades and centuries to follow.[25] Hopes arose that war too could be rendered unnecessary through negotiation and enlightened self-interest (indeed, France would promulgate a *Declaration of Peace to the World* only months after its seminal 1789 *Declaration of the Rights of Man and Citizen*).[26] Early French Revolutionaries believed they were eradicating despotism to enable a new era of fraternity and peace.

As my 2015 book *Non-Violence and the French Revolution* demonstrated, more than 87 percent of all 754 identified Parisian collective protests during that period did not involve bloodshed at any point. Most primarily sought to build collaborative relationships with revolutionary authorities, whom they valued as their representatives and wanted to work with to strengthen the new revolutionary order. A significant percentage of those protests which did involve violence (like the October Days) were drawn into fighting during standoffs with authorities, and still sought to minimize their use of physical force.[27] Though willing to utilize confrontation and verbal threats, Parisian activists helped pioneer many of the democratically oriented, predominantly peaceful protest techniques—including demonstrations, mass meetings, and petition campaigns—still broadly used in France and across the world today.

As the Age of Revolutions provided the basis for modern democratization, modern civil resistance techniques grew from the era's popular campaigns. Indeed, on occasions ranging from the American demonstrations against the Stamp Act in 1765–1766, to the massive campaigns against the slave trade convulsing Great Britain after 1787 and the great popular movements that marked 1789 and the succeeding years in France, Ireland, Britain, and elsewhere, collective action created a new order trumpeting human rights and citizen engagement. An historical understanding of peaceful assembly is incomplete without carefully examining the ambitions and complexities of eighteenth-century revolutionary movements.

Conflict Resolution in the Early French Revolution

The October Days remains an important case study for scholars of both non-violence and violence. Market women's strategic intervention in the political crisis prevented massive bloodshed, breaking a political stalemate that could possibly have degenerated into civil war. Conversely, the protest does not fit the modern definition of a peaceful assembly—women raided municipal armouries to equip themselves with pikes, guns, knives, and cannons, and used them against several offending members of the king's bodyguard. The threat of greater violence helped bring the crisis to a conclusion—yet in practical terms, few great changes had ever been achieved through collective action with so little blood spilt.

Women had long played an integral role in the 'moral economy' across France and Europe. As household buyers, they believed the government had a responsibility to provide them with life's necessities, and intervened when prices reached unaffordable levels to denounce authorities and merchants considered corrupt or incompetent, mobilize large protests, and occasionally pillage or carry out retribution against offenders. Waves of disorder over high food prices struck France in 1708–1709, 1725–1726, 1738–1741, 1757, 1768–1771, 1775 (the famed 'Flour War'), and 1784.[28] The *Dames des Halles* who led the October Days march had for generations possessed the Old Regime privilege of direct access to the monarch, to tell him about issues directly affecting the common people of Paris, in hopes of avoiding crises in France's largest and most precariously governed city.[29] Now, they felt more drastic action necessary to prevent what they feared would become an abject disaster for their city and nation—building from traditional actions but risking their influence through a radical confrontation.

The women's march occurred amidst the profound revolution in political representation that marked the early French Revolution. The absolutist order which had governed France for a millennium in recent months had been forced to accept first an Estates General turned-National Assembly, then (in the wake of the uprising that captured the Bastille) municipal revolutions across the nation that overthrew royal administrators in favour of elected city councils and created citizen militias to replace the Old Regime police. Most of the year's greatest changes came through direct action by France's citizens: advocating for new proposals, dialoguing with new authorities, destroying hated symbols and structures of despotism (occasionally but not usually using physical violence), and participating in the new governing structures.[30] August's Declaration of the Rights of Man and Citizen significantly, but ambiguously, contained a right of 'Resistance to Oppression' in its Article II, adapted from the Lockean social contract tradition emphasizing the need to oppose tyranny with collective force. Authorities deliberately declined to define or limit what resistance could include, rejecting proposals for a specific right to petition or right to bear arms as in the Bill of Rights the US Congress approved that September.[31]

Women remained formally excluded from electoral politics and National Guard participation but nevertheless played important roles in the developing revolution. Many females attended National Assembly and local municipal meetings, rising to speak or heckle from the galleries, particularly on issues they felt concerned them directly. Most revolutionary protests remained gender-inclusive, with women often playing a central role in demanding lower food prices and sometimes seeking the overthrow of hated royal administrators. The revolution became a major ignition point for modern feminism, as many women (particularly by the revolution's most radical phases) began openly to demand the full freedoms the Declaration of the Rights of Man and Citizen promised.[32] A rising spirit of fraternity (ambiguously applicable to women as well as men) replaced exclusion with tantalizing semi-inclusion in the revolution's expanding public sphere, creating contradictions never satisfactorily resolved but opening manifold possibilities.

The October Days occurred at a fraught moment in the early revolution, as the revolutionary summer of 1789's gains faced erosion from moderates and attacks from absolutist conservatives. Revolutionaries became divided during the August–September debates over a royal veto, which ultimately granted the king the ability to suspend National Assembly legislation for up to five years. Many wondered the extent to which the *Monarchien* faction, concerned with reestablishing a strong executive power, would erode the Assembly's newfound sovereignty. Meanwhile, many believed that the monarchy—perhaps with the military support of Europe's other crowned heads—would try to re-implement absolutism by force (as they had already unsuccessfully attempted to do in July). A banquet thrown for the arriving Flanders Regiment at Versailles on 1 October became a direct provocation, as drunken soldiers shouted 'The Assembly to the Devil!' and stomped on revolutionary symbols when the royal family appeared.[33] Letting conspiracies ferment unchecked at Versailles could threaten the entire revolution.

The women's march also responded to a dire provisioning crisis in Paris. Despite the strong harvest across France (in contrast to 1788's ecological disasters that had helped to spark a year of dearth and revolt), prices remained high and many feared speculators and/or counterrevolutionaries conspired to create an artificial famine. 'The lack of bread, sooner or later, will make the people rise', the popular *Révolutions de Paris* newspaper prognosticated the last day of September.[34] Rumours of both a counterrevolutionary rising and immediate lack of bread convulsed Paris on Sunday 4 October, making action essential against an aristocratic 'hydra' existentially menacing revolutionaries' lives and freedom.[35]

Female intercession on 5 October thus served as a form of conflict resolution as well as a new revolutionary offensive. French military intervention to massacre marching women would have been an unprecedented atrocity, likely bringing Louis XVI condemnation across Europe and massive revolts across France (which had responded to his firing of reformist minister Jacques Necker in July with a vast wave of popular uprisings). Moreover, the women knew of the troubled monarch's irresolution and desire to maintain his personal popularity, which had led him to fold during numerous recent crises. By demonstrating their commitment to the cause and willingness to fight, while ably applying political pressure against targeted authorities, the women enabled the peaceful resolution of a crisis menacing potential civil war.

Removing the king from Versailles to Paris, with all its heavy symbolism, reset the revolution's political geography. Instead of the royal court remaining in their heavily fortified complex twenty kilometres from radical Paris, free to manoeuvre or escape, now the king would be physically accountable for his decisions and could only oppose the revolution at his family's peril. The National Assembly followed, taking new residence at an old horseback riding school outside the new royal Tuileries Palace residence, eliminating the distance between them and Parisian radicals. Indeed, popular revolutionaries packed the visitors' gallery and would increasingly gain admission to petition, thereby helping to shape policy. Now, pressure could be exerted on national authorities with unprecedented regularity in the densely packed urban centre.

Far from necessarily advancing the protesters' cause, violence often hurt it, weakening the fragile collaborative bonds with authorities that protesters usually needed to succeed. With authorities seeking to reassert their power in the aftermath of the women's march, impulsive protester violence brought repression. On 21 October, renewed subsistence riots in Paris targeted Ile de la Cité baker Denis François, with angry crowds accusing him of hoarding sixty to eighty loaves amidst continued shortages. Taken to City Hall for interrogation, insurgents broke in and dragged the baker outside, hanging him on Place de Grève. The corpse's head was then severed to be paraded on a pike—soon shoved in the face of his pregnant wife—while others dragged his gushing body through the central districts' open sewers.[36] In response, the National Assembly passed an aggressive Martial Law decree. When invoked, a red flag would fly from City Hall and National Guard units carry such banners through the streets, warning 'good citizens' to return home. Those defying the final order (after three warnings) would receive no quarter: 'Every gathering, with or without arms, becomes criminal and must be dispersed by force'.[37] Few significant Parisian protests occurred over the following months. Despite the revolutionary order's creation from collective action, the new authorities now demanded to control of Paris and the nation themselves, seeking to end the revolution on their own terms.

Despite the many attempts to contain them, Parisian protesters nevertheless continued to play pivotal roles across the rest of the radical revolution. Authorities forcibly suppressed a massive, predominantly non-violent protest movement against Louis XVI's rule with the Massacre of the Champ de Mars in 1791, but proved unable to contain republicanism's resurgence in 1792, which motivated the monarchy's abolition after the king's Swiss Guards fired on a large demonstration on 10 August. The early First Republic featured enhanced collaboration between Parisian activists and Jacobin authorities—including, in an event reminiscent of the October Days, tens of thousands marching on the re-named National Convention for three days between 31 May and 2 June 1793 to successfully pressure for Girondin legislators' resignation. While protest lost much of its subversive content across the terror-ridden Year II (Summer 1793–1794), major movements re-surfaced as bread prices rose again and protesters demanded the continuation of the price protections the Jacobins had promised them. Though ultimately suppressed after the slaying of a National Assemblyman during the Prairial Uprising of Year III, Parisian protesters had created a new model of citizen engagement and government accountability that future generations would adapt across many revolutions to follow.

Conclusion

The October Days proved amongst the most astounding of a shocking revolution's events. Women and men rejected antique deference to seize the opportunity to intervene amidst a worsening revolutionary crisis and pressure authorities to follow their demands. Ordinary women, out of concern for procuring basic necessities, incited an uprising that mobilized tens of thousands, subverted the armed forces, and brought the royal government to the precipice of annihilation. Their core demand for affordable foodstuffs was not immediately soluble (though 1789's good harvest largely accomplished that by November), but forcing the monarch's removal from Versailles significantly decreased counterrevolutionary conspirators' scope of action and made Paris, with its volatile crowds, the revolution's unquestioned political centre.

Amidst a complex and ongoing revolution filled with varying interests, ambitions, and conspiracies, peace could only be achieved through struggle. Though marching armed, shouting threats, risking massacre, and engaging in limited retaliatory violence, the women and men of the October Days effected a massive shift in revolutionary politics with a low body count. Pragmatically working within a violent society, the demonstrators nevertheless sought to avoid violence that would imperil their cause and themselves. Indeed, across 1789, revolutionaries repeatedly achieved massive changes with the cumulative national casualty list of only a mid-sized battle. Over the centuries since, the women's march has remained a striking symbol of empowerment—evoked and echoed in events from massive suffragette marches to the International Women's Day protests that began February 1917's Russian Revolution, to the 2017 Women's Marches against Donald Trump—showing how collective action by the disenfranchised can alter the parameters of government and society.

Notes

1. *Révolutions de Versailles et de Paris*, no. 1; *Révolutions de Paris*, no. 13; Henri Leclercq, *Les journées d'octobre et la fin de l'année 1789* (Paris: Letouzey and Ane, 1924), 46; Philippe-Joseph Buchez and P.-C. Roux, *Histoire parlementaire de al Révolution française*, Vol. 3 (Paris: Paulin, 1834–1838), 71.
2. *Patriote français*, 8 October 1789; François-Marie Kerverseau, *Histoire de la Révolution de 1789, et de l'établissement d'une constitution en France*, Vol. 3 (Paris: Clavelin, 1790), 291–294; *Révolutions de Versailles et de Paris*, no. 1.
3. *Patriote français*, 8 October 1789; *Révolutions de Versailles et de Paris*, no. 1, Leclercq, *Les journées d'octobre*, 44.
4. Charles François, de. *Essais historiques sur les causes et les effets de la Révolution en France* (Paris, 1801), Vol. 2, 178; William Auckland, *Journal and Correspondence of William, Lord Auckland*, Vol. 2 (London: Bentley, 1861), 361; Timothy Tackett, *The Coming of the Terror in the French Revolution* (Cambridge, MA: Harvard University Press, 2015), 66.
5. Bertrand de Moleville, *Histoire de la Révolution de France pendant les dernières années du règne de Louis XVI*, Vol. 2 (Paris: Guiget and Michel, 1802), 196; *Révolutions de Paris*, no. 13; R. B. Rose, 'The French Revolution and the Grain Supply', *Bulletin of the John Rylands Library* 39 (1956): 172.

6. Abbé Papon, *Histoire du gouvernement françois, depuis l'assemblée des notables tenue le 22 février 1787, jusqu'à la fin de décembre de la même année*, Vol. 1 (London, 1788), 267.
7. *London Chronicle*, 8 October 1789.
8. Charles Hereford, *History of France, from the First Establishment of that Monarchy to the Present Revolution* (London: Kearsley, 1791), Vol. 3, 471.
9. Leclercq, *Les journées d'octobre*, 50.
10. Timothy Tackett, *Becoming a Revolutionary: The Deputies of the French National Assembly and the Emergence of a Revolutionary Culture (1789–1790)* (Princeton, NJ: Princeton University Press, 1996), 197; Suzanne Desan, 'Gender, Radicalization, and the October Days: Occupying the National Assembly', *French Historical Studies* 43, no. 3 (2020): 372; *Courier provincial*, no. 18.
11. Étienne Hocquart de Turtot, *La Conquête des communes (mai-juillet 1789)* (Paris: Perrin, 1910), 234.
12. Jean-Joseph Mounier, *Exposé de la conduit de M. Mounier dans l'Assemblée nationale* (Paris: Dessene, 1789), 77.
13. *Fouet national*, 6 October 1789.
14. Armand-Gaston Camus, 'La journée du 5 octobre 1789', *Révue de la Révolution* 6 (1885): 87–89; Rudolf Reuss, 'L'Alsace pendant la Révolution française: Correspondance des députés de Strasbourg à l'Assemblée nationale', *Révue d'Alsace* 30, no. 1 (1879): 208.
15. Jean-Baptiste Poncet-Delpech, 'Documents sur les premiers mois de la Révolution: La suite des papiers de Poncet Delpech', *Annales historiques de la Révolution française* 185 (1966): 104; Pierre de Vaissière, *Lettres d'aristocrates: La Révolution racontée par des correspondances privées, 1789–1794* (Paris: Perrin, 1907), 25; *Oracle*, 13 October 1789.
16. *Révolutions de Paris*, no. 13; *Moniteur universel*, 12 October 1789.
17. A. M. Lorient, BB 16; *Moniteur universel*, 12 October 1789; Olwen Hufton, *Women and the Limits of Citizenship in the French Revolution* (Toronto: University of Toronto Press, 1992), 12.
18. Françoise Brunel and Sylvain Goujon, eds., *Les Martyrs de Prairial: Textes et documents inédits* (Genève: Georg, 1992), 243; Hereford, *History of France*, 489.
19. Etienne Georges, *La Révolution de 1789 à Troyes* (Troyes: Nouvel, 1895), 23.
20. Erika Chenoweth, *Civil Resistance: What Everyone Needs to Know* (Oxford: Oxford University Press, 2021), 18.
21. They encounter a popular and scholarly historiography often focused on the theme of violence: Russell Bourne, *Cradle of Violence: How Boston's Waterfront Mobs Ignited the American Revolution* (New York: Wiley, 2006); Holger Hoock, *Scars of Independence: America's Violent Birth* (New York: Crown, 2017); Simon Schama, *Citizens: A Chronicle of the French Revolution* (New York: Knopf, 1989); Jean-Clément Martin, *Violence et révolution: Essai sur la naissance d'un mythe national* (Paris: Seuil, 2006).
22. Walter H. Conser, Jr., et al., eds., *Resistance, Politics, and the American Struggle for Independence, 1765–1775* (Boulder, CO: Lynne Rienner, 1986), 472.
23. Michael Goode, 'The Relevance of Peace in Early American History', in *The Specter of Peace: Rethinking Violence and Power in the Colonial Atlantic*, ed. Michael Goode and John Smolenski (Leiden: Brill, 2018), 5.
24. See my *Friends of Freedom: The Rise of Social Movements in the Age of Atlantic Revolutions* (Cambridge: Cambridge University Press, 2022).
25. Lynn Hunt, *Inventing Human Rights* (New York: Norton, 2007); Steven Pinker, *The Better Angels of Our Nature: Why Violence Has Declined* (New York: Penguin Books, 2011); Pierre

Serna, *Comme des bêtes: Histoire politique de l'animal en révolutions, 1750–1840* (Paris: Fayard, 2017).
26. David Bell, *The First Total War: Napoleon's Europe and the Birth of War as We Know It* (Boston: Houghton Mifflin, 2007).
27. Micah Alpaugh, *Non-Violence and the French Revolution: Political Demonstrations in Paris, 1787–1795* (Cambridge: Cambridge University Press, 2015), 5.
28. Judith A. Miller, *Mastering the Market: The State and the Grain Trade in Northern France, 1700–1860* (Cambridge: Cambridge University Press, 1999), 2, 25–26, 43; Cynthia Bouton, *The Flour War: Gender, Class, and Community in Late Old Regime France* (University Park: Penn State University Press, 1993); E. P. Thompson, 'The Moral Economy of the English Crowd in the Eighteenth Century', *Past & Present* 50 (1971): 76–136.
29. Katie Jarvis, *Politics in the Marketplace: Work, Gender, and Citizenship in Revolutionary France* (Oxford: Oxford University Press, 2019).
30. See John Markoff, *The Abolition of Feudalism: Peasants, Lords and Legislators in the French Revolution* (University Park: Penn State University Press, 1996).
31. See Micah Alpough, 'The Right of Resistance to Oppression: Protest and Authority in the French Revolutionary World', *French Historical Studies* 39, no. 3 (2016): 567–598.
32. Dominique Godineau, *The Women of Paris and Their French Revolution*, trans. Katherine Streip (Berkeley: University of California Press, 1998); Joan B. Landes, *Women and the Public Sphere in the Age of the French Revolution* (Ithaca, NY: Cornell University Press, 1988).
33. Francisque Mège, *Gaultier de Miauzat, député du tiers-état aux Etats-généraux de 1789, vie et correspondence*, Vol. 2 (Paris: Lechevalier, 1890), 281; Adrien Duquesnoy, *Journal d'Adrien Duquesnoy, député du Tiers état de Bar-le-Duc*, Vol. 1 (Paris: Picard, 1894), 397.
34. *Révolutions de Paris*, no. 12.
35. *Parisien nouvelliste*, 10 October 1789.
36. *Moniteur universel*, 26 October 1789; *Chronique de Paris*, 22 October 1789; Riho Hayakawa, 'L'assassinat du boulanger Denis François le 21 octobre 1789', *Annales historiques de la Révolution française* 333 (2003): 1–19; George Rudé, *The Crowd in the French Revolution* (Oxford: Clarendon, 1959), 78.
37. Marquis de Ferrières, *Correspondance inédite, 1789, 1790, 1791* (Paris: Colin, 1932), 181; *Moniteur universel*, 20 and 26 October 1789.

Further Reading

Alpaugh, Micah. *Non-Violence and the French Revolution: Political Demonstrations in Paris, 1787–1795*. Cambridge: Cambridge University Press, 2015.

Bouton, Cynthia A. *The Flour War: Gender, Class, and Community in Late Old Regime France*. University Park: Penn State University Press, 1993.

Desan, Suzanne. 'Gender, Radicalization, and the October Days: Occupying the National Assembly'. *French Historical Studies* 43, no. 3 (2020): 359–390.

Hufton, Olwen. *Women and the Limits of Citizenship in the French Revolution*. Toronto: University of Toronto Press, 1992.

Jarvis, Katie. *Politics in the Marketplace: Work, Gender, and Citizenship in Revolutionary France*. Oxford: Oxford University Press, 2019.

Leclercq, Henri. *Les journées d'octobre et la fin de l'année 1789*. Paris: Letouzey and Ane, 1924.

Martin, Jean-Clément. *Violence et révolution: Essai sur la naissance d'un mythe national.* Paris: Seuil, 2006.
Rudé, George. *The Crowd in the French Revolution.* Oxford: Clarendon Press, 1959.
Tackett, Timothy. *Becoming a Revolutionary: The Deputies of the French National Assembly and the Emergence of a Revolutionary Culture (1789–1790).* Princeton, NJ: Princeton University Press, 1996.

CHAPTER 19

PETERLOO

IAIN CHANNING

INTRODUCTION

THE Peterloo massacre was one of the bloodiest political events of nineteenth-century British political history and remains central to the story of the labour movement in the UK today. It has come to exemplify the nadir of respect for the right of peaceful assembly. On 16 August 1819 at St Peter's Field, Manchester, a Parliamentary reform meeting where protesters met to demand the vote and to abolish the Corn Laws was violently dispersed by the sabres of the volunteer Manchester Yeomanry and the regular Hussars.[1] Seventeen people including women and children were killed and more than 650 were injured.[2] Since the end of the Napoleonic Wars in 1815, local societies had formed across the growing manufacturing towns to demand political change in a time of economic depression. The meeting was part of a national plan, and meetings had already been held at Leeds, Birmingham, and London. Henry 'Orator' Hunt, a well-known radical reformer was due to speak to a crowd estimated to have been sixty-thousand-strong.

The events that unfolded in Manchester have been fiercely contested both by those who witnessed the disorder and in the subsequent historiography. Moreover, Peterloo has remained alive in social memory—particularly within working-class activism—more than two hundred years later. Historian Robert Poole stated that 'the Peterloo massacre is one of the best-documented events in British history. It was the bloodiest political event of the nineteenth century on English soil'.[3] This examination demonstrates that the Peterloo massacre signifies an important juncture in time which came to influence structural transformation.

The chapter applies the Flashpoints Model of Public Disorder (hereinafter 'Flashpoints Model')[4] to the event, elaborating some of the significant factors that contributed to its outcome. This will demonstrate how the build-up to the Manchester meeting, and the decision-making on the day, had created a scenario where the risk of disorder was dramatically increased. The discussion will also utilize the historiography, where there is common consensus that those meeting at Peterloo had constituted a peaceful and lawful assembly before they were dispersed. Finally, the chapter will assess the influence of the Peterloo massacre upon the period that followed, including political reform and the use of public order tactics.

The Road to Peterloo

Any study of an incident of disorder and the responses to it must also take into account their contemporary social, political, and economic contexts. For instance, previous experiences of disorder and the methods used to control or prevent them as well as the contemporary law become vital to understanding state responses to public assemblies. Historian Adrian Randall has highlighted the prevalence of riot and disorder across the eighteenth century, arguing that notions of liberty and the free-born Englishman played an important role in disorder, but has also reminded us that riot was often the final line of defence when traditional rights and customs were threatened (see Randall, in this volume).[5] Historian George Rudé also noted how the French Revolution had inspired new ideological notions of the Rights of Man and the Sovereignty of the People while the Industrial Revolution provided new directions for popular protest and created a polarized working class that displaced the old domestic system.[6] Nonetheless, even when crowds gathered to protest, this has never inevitably meant disorder was certain. When riot or disorder did occur, it may have done so for a variety of reasons. In his analysis on popular disturbances in the eighteenth and nineteenth centuries, historian John Stevenson argued that in each event, a moment could often be identified when things may have turned out quite differently.[7] While this may typically refer to a specific incident immediately before the disorder, the pre-history to an event such as a riot must also consider a range of broader cultural, economic, social, and political factors.

The Flashpoints Model conceptualizes a framework that can be applied to an event that exhibits preconditions to disorder.[8] It deposes previous psychological explanations that disorder happens because of the allegedly irregular and irrational nature of the crowd and emphasizes the importance of police behaviour and legitimacy (see Adang, in this volume). Coercive tactics such as *escalated force* are seen to provoke disorder while *negotiated management* can de-escalate it. The Flashpoint Model consists of the structural, cultural, political/ideological, contextual, situational, and interactional levels. Applying this model to the disorder at Peterloo not only helps to examine the preconditions for disorder, but also provides important historical context. It is also worth noting that while the model was developed in the era of the modern public police, it is also applicable to all systems of 'policing' more generally and in this case will apply to the use of discretion by the magistrates and the actions of the yeomanry and the Hussars who were present in a 'policing' capacity.

The *structural level* of the theory relates to marginalization, inequality, and disadvantage experienced by some groups and communities. This can include the lack of political power or influence held by people who feel collective grievances but are powerless to improve their own quality of life.[9] Where such marginalization exists, groups will feel as though they have no real stake in the social order. In the years before Peterloo, poverty, poor labour conditions, and the lack of political representation created a marginalized and exploited working class that demanded change. Furthermore, food prices were high due to the Corn Laws and, since the end of the Napoleonic wars in 1815, the demobilization of soldiers was contributing to high unemployment. The cotton industry was already in depression, yet, despite this, people were still migrating to Manchester to seek employment.[10]

Distress in the emerging towns and cities that developed through the Industrial Revolution was exacerbated by lack of political representation in Parliament. Political reform in England was slow, working men still did not have the right to vote, and Parliamentary representation was significantly uneven as the urban areas became more densely populated. In fact, despite growing to the second largest city in the country, Manchester did not have a Member of Parliament while many rural areas were overrepresented.[11] Although it may seem inconsequential to a disenfranchised working class that there was no Parliamentary representation in their area, E. P. Thompson reminds us that the working class were still engaged in politics and made their voice heard as they could still 'parade, huzza and jeer on the hustings', typically providing radical candidates with vast support.[12] Indeed, earlier in 1819, in Birmingham, an attempt had been made to remedy this structural inequality by appointing Sir Charles Wolseley as a 'legislatorial attorney' at a reform meeting.[13] Prior to the ill-fated meeting in Manchester on 16 August, the Manchester Patriotic Union were due to follow suit.

At the *political/ideological level*, the actions of key political figures and the voices of others with authority or power to control public discourses such as the media and magistrates become prominent. When such discourses highlight a view that delegitimizes the actions or demands of a protesting group, then the theory predicts the results will not only fuel resentment towards the authorities but will also help legitimize more robust police responses. Reflecting on the period from the late eighteenth century to the mid-nineteenth century, historian F. M. Leventhal argued that 'respectable Englishmen lived in periodic fear of working-class insurrection'.[14] This periodic fear and suspicion contributed to an eagerness to control the working class to maintain their social position.

Applying this to Peterloo, it is worth observing that when Wolseley was acclaimed as 'legislatorial attorney' in Birmingham, and a meeting had been organized for 2 August 1819 in Manchester to appoint a representative there, the authorities acted swiftly. Fuelled by fear of the French revolutionary model, the appointment of what was seen as an unofficial MP, prompted the attorney general to stress his opinion that to elect an MP without the King's writ was illegal.[15] The reformers acquiesced by postponing their meeting. They also changed the wording of the rearranged meeting, stating it was being called to 'consider the propriety of adopting the most LEGAL and EFFECTUAL means of obtaining a reform in the Common House of Parliament'.[16]

The authorities used the law to restrict the reformers freedom to assemble in public. Despite the lawful intentions of the meeting, and Henry Hunt's further calls for attendees to not allow themselves to become excited and commit a breach of the peace, the authorities still deemed the proposed meeting unlawful.[17] While there was no positive, legally defined right of public assembly at this moment, under the concept of residual freedom, organizers and protesters believed they had the liberty to exercise the freedom to assemble in public as long as they did not contravene any existing law. In an attempt to control the ideological debate, the authorities called upon the working class to abstain from the 'illegal meeting' and urged them to contemplate the intentions of the 'wicked and seditious men' whose actions threatened the 'JUST and EQUAL LAWS of your COUNTRY, which protect alike the Poor and the Rich'.[18] The language used here is certainly an attempt to vilify the reformers as well as to delegitimize both their demands and their strategies.

The *cultural level* relates to the cultures or subcultures within both the group that is being policed and the police themselves. There is an increased risk of disorder when those responsible for policing the assembly are from outside the local area, are unfamiliar with local customs, and are ill-trained or inexperienced.[19] The likelihood of conflict is also increased when the dissenting group and those policing them view each other in negative stereotypes and no accommodation is made for cultural norms. At Peterloo, one of the key cultural aspects of the event that was misconstrued by the authorities was the culture of festivity that included processions, music, flags, banners, and rushcarts. During the prosecution of the meeting organizers, witnesses for the defence testified that it was part of the culture and became common practice to parade with music and flags.[20] Conversely, the prosecution described the march as a military procession where clubs and sticks were carried as weapons and the banners contained seditious and inflammatory inscriptions that caused alarm and terror. Countering this claim the defendant Samuel Bamford testified, 'We went in the greatest hilarity and good humour, preceded by a band of music playing several loyal and national airs; and . . . our fathers and mothers, sweethearts and children were with us. And this was the dreadful military array'.[21]

The misunderstanding of cultural norms, whether born from genuine fear of violent insurrection or cynically created to discredit the reformers' agenda, still had the same effect. Negative stereotyping was deployed that presented the reformers as either violent revolutionaries or a ragged mob. To combat these perceptions, the reformers organized the drilling of their members so they could form an orderly and unarmed procession to the meeting place. Many reformers spent evenings on the moors learning how to march in rank instructed by former soldiers. Samuel Bamford declared their intention to 'disarm the bitterness of our political opponents by a display of cleanliness, sobriety, and decorum, such as we never before had exhibited'.[22] Despite this, the fear continued as well as the rhetoric that referred to the crowd as 'mob', a term which when used, as it was by the magistrate William Hay, identifies a position that sees them and their protest as illegitimate.[23]

At the *contextual level*, the Flashpoints Model focuses on the processes of communication prior to the event. This may include direct communication and liaison between authorities and organizers, but also other dynamic processes such as rumour, previous negative relations, and media coverage.[24] Prior to Peterloo, there was little communication between the authorities and the reformers. The authorities gathered their information through a system of informers while communication on planned demonstrations and the authority's response to them was largely carried out through newspapers.

In 1817, the reformers had planned a hunger march from St Peter's Field in Manchester to London, each with a blanket on their back and a petition on their arm requesting that the Prince Regent remedy the poor conditions suffered as a consequence of the decline of the cotton trade. They became known as the Blanketeers. There were no specific political demands, the marchers were unarmed, and they were not riotous. The Riot Act was read, the speakers at St Peter's Field were arrested, and of the six hundred to seven hundred marchers, only one made it to London, many were arrested before they even reached Stockport, others were ordered to turn back. Despite the peaceable nature of the march, the authorities feared that the marching men could grow into an army as they continued south.[25] The relationship between reformer and authority then had a recent history of suspicion and fear that continued up to the event of Peterloo and thwarted meaningful communication.

Following the failed march of the Blanketeers, the reformers began to operate in a more open, and constitutional way to legitimize their activism.[26] The change in tactics frustrated the authorities whose lack of official intelligence from spies now meant that 'absence of evidence was construed as evidence of conspiracy'.[27] This deduction only heightened fear and tension relating to the reform movement. Where direct communication had occurred at meetings that preceded Peterloo, such as the meetings at Manchester and Stockport in June, the reformers demonstrated their peaceful intentions by requesting that the magistrates helped maintain order. This was refused.[28]

The *situational level* refers to spatial or social causes of disorder. For example, there may be symbolic significance of the location where the event is held. Also, the spatial prominence of the policing authorities may itself be a cause of disorder, especially when riot police are physically visible, rather than kept discreetly out of view. The authorities anticipated insurrection and disorder at the meeting at St Peter's Field. In a letter to James Norris (Lancashire magistrate) on 5 August 1819, Henry Hobhouse (Permanent Undersecretary to the Home Office) warned that prosecuting for treason was difficult and the use of force that could be used at the meeting depended on the discretion of the local authorities on the day.[29]

Historian R. J. White highlighted the ambiguity of the reformers' activism stating that those 'who watched the fruit of all this painstaking preparation . . . such "beautiful order" was in itself a symptom of untold menace'.[30] Furthermore, George Rudé suggested that the colour and the vast numbers present at St Peter's Field would have alarmed the authorities and propertied class as much as acts of violence.[31] Furthermore, the recent experiences between the magistrates and the reformers also contributed to the events that unfolded at Peterloo. Following the perceived threat that came from the Blanketeers, the Manchester and Salford Yeomanry Cavalry was formed to assist the magistrates to maintain order as further radical activism was anticipated. They were an amateur force, they were ill-trained, and White stated they were local tradesmen, consisting 'almost exclusively of cheese mongers, ironmongers and newly enriched manufacturers, and the people of Manchester and district thought them a joke, and not a very good joke'.[32]

The magistrates may have anticipated disorder on the day of Peterloo, yet, the formation of the assembling crowd was not consistent with one preparing for violence, but as Poole reminds us, one preparing for festivities.[33] As they were assembling, the only policing agency visible were the special constables, acting under Deputy Constable Joseph Nadine. A warrant for Hunt's arrest was signed before the event; nonetheless, this was not executed until Hunt began to address the crowd. White stated that the magistrates wanted to see how the meeting was going to turn out, but such a delay only created a more incendiary situation. The magistrates then ordered the arrest of Hunt as they anticipated that his presence would cause a breach of the peace.[34] Although the Manchester and Salford Yeomanry were initially out of sight, they were called upon to assist with the arrest. Even at this stage, the crowd jeered, but disorder was not inevitable.

Finally, the *interactional level* highlights the final face-to-face interactions between policing authorities and the crowd. With respect to Peterloo, historians have debated the causes for the disorder as well as the notions of 'battle' or 'massacre' with questions such as 'did the yeomanry attack before or after they were provoked?' As previously mentioned, the crowds were unarmed, consisted of women and children, and were in good humour. Certainly, this does not conjure the image of a crowd set for battle or violent insurrection. Yet, the decision to send the amateur yeomanry to support the constables' arrest of Henry Hunt created an interaction that led to bloodshed. Firstly, the yeomanry were not fully in control of their horses. On their arrival to the scene, the first death occurred when a child was killed after being knocked to the ground along with their mother. This may have caused some dissent and disorder from the crowd who witnessed the sight, but even then, many of the yeomanry were able to get to the husting and support the arrest. At this stage, the yeomanry found themselves trapped in a densely packed crowd and, upon witnessing the spectacle, the magistrates continued with a tactic of *escalated force* and ordered Colonel Guy L'Estrange to disperse the crowd as their perception was that the crowd were attacking the yeomanry. At this point, there was likely some resistance towards the yeomanry, but also, as St Peter's Field was so densely packed, it was difficult for the crowd to disperse. The Hussars, some wearing their medals from the battle of Waterloo, advanced into the crowd with their swords drawn. It is reported that the Hussars used the flats of their swords to disperse the crowd, if not the casualty list would have been much longer.

The decision to send in the amateur yeomanry, was certainly a moment at the interactional level that led to disorder. The *Manchester Observer*, a pro-Parliamentary reform newspaper, claimed that the Riot Act was not read and that:

> Had the military only attacked robust men . . . much less infamy would have been their lot. But it is notorious, that some of our gentlemen not only struck the quickest but the heaviest on those who were the most defenceless. The women seemed to be the special objects of the rage of these bastard soldiers.[35]

The historiography of the unfolding of events at Peterloo then presents us with a difficult conundrum. They are contested not just through the historians' gaze, but also in the contemporary accounts that have survived. M. L. Bush stated that radical reformers saw the event as an 'unprovoked massacre of the innocent . . . [while to those] loyal to the old regime it was revolution quashed and order restored'.[36] In the historiography, Robert Walmsley offered an alternative view that attempted to clear the magistrates from blame while dismissing the accounts of reformers as prejudiced, and Philip Lawson presented the view of a pitched battle rather than a massacre.[37] These accounts have been challenged and rebutted numerous times since their publication.[38] Poole's authoritative account in *Peterloo: The English Uprising*, further vilifies the authorities, arguing that it was 'not a clumsy exercise in crowd control . . . [but a riot] and it was the forces of order that rioted'.[39]

Applying the Flashpoint model to the events at Peterloo provides a framework for analysing the event and demonstrates the ways the authorities unwittingly created the conditions for disorder. It also shows that the question at the heart of Walmsley's thesis of whether it was the crowd or the yeomanry that struck the first blow also becomes immaterial. The conditions for disorder had been planted before the crowds started to march to St Peter's Field on 16 August 1819. The different levels of the model demonstrate how the exploitation and neglect of the needs of the working-class people, the increasing fear and suspicion harnessed by the magistrates, the use of the largely untrained amateur yeomanry, and poor discretionary decision-making by the authorities on the day created an environment where the likelihood of disorder was increased. Even if the assembly was lawful, these conditions—as well as the use of the four hundred volunteer yeomanry who had a vested interest in suppressing reform—created a scenario where the forces of order felt empowered to use deadly force as they had the support of the local magistrates, who were in turn supported by the Home Office.[40] When disorder did transpire, it was not a pitched battle—but a massacre.

The Legacy of Peterloo

As a seminal event in the history of British politics and political activism, the influence of Peterloo, and the lessons learnt from it are still part of our cultural memory over two hundred years later. From the ballads and poems that were published in the months after the event which included Percy Shelley's *The Mask of Anarchy* (1819), to the release of Mike Leigh's historical epic motion picture *Peterloo* in 2019, the massacre on St Peter's Field in 1819 has been continually retold to new generations.[41] Meanwhile, in case law, the important lessons from Peterloo were recited by Lord Denning in *Hubbard v Pitt* (1976)[42] as a warning against the suppression of the rights to peaceful assembly.

However, that lesson of restraint was not learnt in the immediate aftermath of Peterloo. The prosecution of the ten reformers became a public spectacle with the newspapers covering the trial in detail. Poole stated that the prosecution faced great difficulty in proving the crowd to have been riotous, as the defence was able to muster numerous witnesses ready to testify on their peaceable nature. Yet, despite the evidence weighted in the defendants' favour, the guilty verdict for five of the ten defendants came as a shock, even to the prosecution.[43] They were found guilty on only one count of seditious conspiracy despite the seven charges they faced—which included three counts of seditious conspiracy, two counts of unlawful assembly, and two counts of riot. Here, the judge's summing up may have influenced the jury as he brought their attention to the 'wording of the banners, and to Hunt's inflammatory words at the earlier reform meeting at London's Smithfield'.[44] Hunt received a two-year prison sentence and the others who were found guilty received one-year sentences.

The trial was also to have longer-lasting impacts on the British legal system. It was in the trial that the notion of unlawful assembly was discussed and elaborated. This would go on strongly to influence the state's response to political radicals at a time when prosecution for seditious libel was becoming more difficult. Following the Napoleonic Wars, it became more accepted that one could debate constitutional matters without committing a libellous offence. Legal Historian Michael Lobban argued that, as a result of the Peterloo trials, the doctrine of unlawful assembly, 'would serve to divert the prime attention of government prosecutors from charges of seditious libel, to charges of unlawful and unruly behaviour whose unlawfulness rested on the political signification of the behaviour'.[45] Furthermore, the trials helped establish the concepts of breach of the peace, obstruction, and nuisance which were then to become staples of the authorities' suppression of political activity which now more commonly used the mass public platform.[46]

Legal repression also came when Parliament reassembled in November 1819, and passed the notorious and repressive 'Six Acts'. The powers included 'restricting meetings and the press, empowering the seizure of arms in disturbed districts, preventing delays in trials for misdemeanours, and preventing military training'.[47]

In the long term, the state's actions at Peterloo 'helped discredit the Government as an increasingly self-conscious middle class began to demand greater representation'.[48] Following splits within the Tory Party and the ascension of Charles Grey in 1830 as Prime Minister, the Whigs were able to implement their pledge to reform. The first Reform Act 1832 created sixty-seven new constituencies and widened the property qualifications for the voting franchise. Manchester received Parliamentary representation for the first time. Additionally, with the creation of the Metropolitan Police Force in 1829, which was followed by County and Borough forces later in the century, the public police became more prominent in the maintaining of public order.[49] Furthermore, since the massacre at Peterloo, calls to arm the police throughout the nineteenth century were resisted, and policing with moderation prevailed.[50]

Conclusion

This chapter has revealed how, despite the perceived threats of radical reformers, the meeting at Peterloo constituted a peaceful assembly, and that, following Robert Poole, '[w]hatever the causes of Peterloo, it was not a battle but a massacre'.[51] As an event, we have also witnessed how Peterloo became a turning point in political, social, and legal history in a number of ways. Of course, there are other factors that also influence historical change, but the significance of Peterloo in the way that public order policing has evolved should not be understated. From the continued use of unarmed police in the nineteenth century, to the more recent common-law judgments that evoke the events of Peterloo[52] as warnings against the violent suppression of democratic right of freedom of peaceful assembly. Moreover, the actions of the reformers and the national importance of the events at Peterloo should also be seen as a significant part of the progression of political reform. It is part of a wider history of protest that includes the Chartists and the Suffragettes. The activism and the sacrifice of those gathered on St Peter's Field in 1819 should not be underestimated or forgotten.

Notes

1. The Corn Laws were passed in 1815 and placed tariffs on imported grain to favour British agriculture, but this also led to higher domestic food prices and increased cost of living.
2. See Michael Bush, *The Casualties of Peterloo* (Manchester, UK: Manchester Centre for Regional History, 2005).
3. See Robert Poole, '"By the Law or the Sword": Peterloo Revisited', *History* 91, no. 2 (2006): 254–276.
4. D. P. Waddington, K. Jones, and C. Critcher, *Flashpoints: Studies in Public Disorder* (London: Routledge, 1989).
5. Adrian Randall, *Riotous Assemblies: Popular Protest in Hanoverian England* (Oxford: Oxford University Press, 2006).
6. George Rudé, *Ideology and Popular Protest* (London: Lawrence and Wishart, 1980).
7. John Stevenson, *Popular Disturbances in England, 1700–1870* (London: Longman, 1979).
8. Waddington et al., *Flashpoints*.
9. Mike King and David Waddington, 'Flashpoints Revisited: A Critical Application to the Policing of Anti-globalization Protest', *Policing and Society* 15, no. 3 (2005): 255–282.
10. Joyce Marlow, *The Peterloo Massacre* (London: Rapp and Whiting, 1969), 90–91.
11. Ibid.
12. E. P. Thompson, *The Making of the English Working Class* (London: Penguin Books, 1991), 85–86.
13. Sir Charles Wolseley was a baronet who delivered radical speeches in England following his presence at the storming of the Bastille in Paris. See Poole, 'By the Law or the Sword', 267.
14. F. M. Leventhal, 'Why a Massacre? The Responsibility of Peterloo', *Journal of Interdisciplinary History* 2, no. 1 (1971): 109–118, 109.
15. Poole, 'By the Law or the Sword', 267.
16. 'Manchester Public Meeting,' *Manchester Observer*, Saturday, 7 August 1819, quoted in Marco Canani, 'Perspectives on Peterloo at 200: Construing and Representing the Event', *The Keats-Shelley Review* 35, no. 2 (2021): 116–124, 121.
17. See Michael Lobban, 'From Seditious Libel to Unlawful Assembly: Peterloo and the Changing Face of Political Crime c1770-1820', *Oxford Journal of Legal Studies* 10, no. 3 (1990): 307–352.

18. Public notice issued by the magistrates, reproduced in Canani, 'Perspectives on Peterloo', 123.
19. David Waddington, *Policing Public Disorder: Theory and Practice* (Cullompton, UK: Willan, 2007).
20. Robert Poole, 'The March to Peterloo: Politics and Festivity in Late Georgian England', *Past and Present* 192 (2006): 109–153.
21. Ibid., 110–111.
22. Leventhal, 'Why a Massacre?', 113.
23. Poole, 'By the Law or the Sword', 276.
24. Waddington, *Policing Public Disorder*.
25. R. J. White, *Waterloo to Peterloo* (London: William Heinemann, 1957).
26. Poole, 'March to Peterloo'.
27. Poole, 'By the Law or the Sword', 266.
28. Ibid., 267.
29. Ibid., 270.
30. White, *Waterloo to Peterloo*, 182.
31. George Rudé, *The Crowd in History 1730–1848* (London: Lawrence and Wishart, 1981), 239.
32. White, *Waterloo to Peterloo*, 185.
33. Poole, 'March to Peterloo'.
34. White, *Waterloo to Peterloo*.
35. *Manchester Observer*, 21 August 1819.
36. M. L. Bush, 'The Women at Peterloo: Impact of Female Reform on the Manchester Meeting of 16 August 1819', *History* 89 no. 2 (2004): 209–232.
37. Robert Walmsley, *Peterloo: The Case Re-opened* (Manchester, UK: Manchester University Press, 1969); Philip Lawson, 'Reassessing Peterloo', *History Today* 38, no. 3 (1988): 24–29.
38. E. P. Thompson, 'Thompson on Peterloo', *Manchester Region History Review* (1993). Leventhal, 'Why a Massacre?' and Poole, 'By the Law or the Sword'.
39. Robert Poole, *Peterloo: The English Uprising* (Oxford: Oxford University Press, 2019), 1.
40. Ibid.
41. For more on the ballads and songs, see Alison Morgan, ' "Rise Now from Your Slumber": Ballads and Songs of Peterloo', *The Keats-Shelley Review* 35, no. 2 (2021): 138–148. For an interesting discussion of Mike Leigh's Peterloo, see Richard Wells, 'Class Politics and the Filmmaker's Craft in Mike Leigh's *Peterloo*', *Labor: Studies in Working-Class History of the Americas*, 19, no. 3 (2022): 57–74.
42. *Hubbard v Pitt* [1976] QB 142 (CA).
43. Poole, 'By the Law or the Sword'.
44. Ibid., 275.
45. Lobban, 'From Seditious Libel'.
46. Nadine El Enany, 'Innocence Charged with Guilt, the Criminalisation of Protest from Peterloo to Millbank', in *Riot, Unrest and Protest on the Global Stage*, ed. D. Pritchard and E. Pakes (Basingstoke, UK: Palgrave Macmillan, 2014), 72–97.
47. Stevenson, *Popular Disturbances in England*, 216.
48. Ibid., 217.
49. Iain Channing, *The Police and the Expansion of Public Order Law in Britain, 1829-2014* (London: Routledge, 2015).
50. Clive Emsley, *The English Police: A Political and Social History* (Harlow, UK: Pearson Education, 1996), 121.

51. Poole, 'By the Law or the Sword', 263.
52. For example, see *Hubbard v Pitt* [1976] and Lord Denning's judgment here is further cited in *DPP v Jones (Margaret)* [1999] 2 A.C. 240, *Kent v Commissioner of Police of the Metropolis* [1981] 5 WLUK 116 and others.

Further Reading

Canani, Marco. 'Perspectives on Peterloo at 200: Construing and Representing the Event'. *The Keats-Shelley Review* 35, no. 2 (2021): 116–124.
Lobban, Michael. 'From Seditious Libel to Unlawful Assembly: Peterloo and the Changing Face of Political Crime c1770-1820'. *Oxford Journal of Legal Studies* 10, no. 3 (1990): 307–352.
Poole, Robert. '"By the Law or the Sword": Peterloo Revisited'. *History* 91, no. 2 (2006): 254–276.
Poole, Robert. *Peterloo: The English Uprising*. Oxford: Oxford University Press, 2019.
Thompson, E. P. *The Making of the English Working Class*. London: Penguin Books, 1991, 85–86.

CHAPTER 20

FROM NATAL TO THE TRANSVAAL

Women in the Front Lines of the Satyagraha March of 1913

LOUISE DU TOIT

Introduction

The Satyagraha march of 1913 of several thousand striking mine and plantation workers, illegally crossing the border between the provinces of Natal and the Transvaal was a milestone event in the early days of anti-colonial rebellion everywhere. It was also a turning point in the life of Mohandas Karamchand Gandhi, who left South Africa for India shortly afterwards, there to pursue his anti-colonial struggle against the British. While this bare-bones version of the march is widely known, what is less well known is the central role that women played. As Gandhi biographer Ramachandra Guha writes, 'They were breaking a boundary far more rigid or sacrosanct than [transgressing a provincial border], in that, for the first time, some of the protesters were women. In South Africa and in India alike, at this time, it had been unthinkable that women could mingle with men and participate in protests.'[1] The one woman who stands out in this regard is Kasturba Gandhi, the wife of Mohandas. The focus of this chapter is on those events surrounding Kasturba's persuasion of her husband that she had to take a leading role in the front lines of the struggle. These events raise the question of whether women's front-line participation in non-violent direct action can throw new light on the established meanings of assembly and its degree of peacefulness and effectiveness.

Early Days of Satyagraha in the Transvaal

It is clear from Gandhi's monograph, *Satyagraha in South Africa*, that he was inspired in his own activism by the example of women's rebellions—the resolute Suffragettes (whom he had encountered in London in 1906 and 1909), the dignified behaviour of the Boer women in the British concentration camps (1899–1902) and the resistance by the Irish Ladies' Land League (1881–1882).[2] Nevertheless, since the start of the Satyagraha campaigns in the Transvaal Republic in 1906, aimed against the proposed 'Black Act' meant to control Indian influx, movement, and trade in the country, the resistance was an unquestioned all-male affair. Until 1913, Gandhi and his group held that women should not participate directly in openly transgressive acts. He wrote in retrospect about this stance:

> Some brave women had already offered to participate, and when Satyagrahis went to jail for hawking without a licence, their wives had expressed a desire to follow suit. But we did not then think it proper to send women to jail in a foreign land. There seemed to be no adequate reason for sending them into the firing line, and I for my part could not summon courage enough to take them to the front. Another argument was, that it would be derogatory to our manhood if we sacrificed our women in resisting a law, which was directed only against men.[3]

Several aspects of this explanation are important for our theme. The first is the assumption that Satyagrahis are always men, and that women are only relevant insofar as they appear or speak as 'wives' of Satyagrahis. The limitation of women's role to a wifely one moreover reinscribes an assumption that women would resist only for private rather than social or political reasons, whether out of love, loyalty, or dependency, rather than out of an independent sense of (in)justice. Second, the use of the terms 'firing line' and 'the front' draws an analogy with war, and we know that women are often positioned as 'the other of war'—those who stand outside the violence, excluded from the action, unless they are targeted for violation as the 'innocents' of war.[4] Thirdly, Gandhi's reference to women being jailed 'in a foreign land' evokes the spectre of sexual violence perpetrated by ethnic and religious male strangers. The employment of these terms emphasizes that women would be out of place there, taking unnecessary risks and even impeding 'their' men's effective actions. Gandhi's second argument, namely, that women's presence would detract from Indian 'manhood', similarly rests on a problematic association of masculinity with war and violence, together with an assumption that if women were to participate it would be (seen as) essentially a masculine act—insofar as women's participation would be seen as men 'sacrificing [their!] women' without good reason. It is possible to overinterpret Gandhi's words here but finally note also how he qualifies 'women' with the terms 'some brave', as if courage is exceptional in women but the norm in men.

Gandhi's notion of Satyagraha was from the beginning plagued by a certain gender ambiguity. Inspired by the women's examples of non-violent resistance, he was nevertheless adamant from the start that Satyagraha (which he viewed as a new form of direct action) was not a 'weapon of the weak' and also not a form of 'passive resistance'.[5] Therefore, he built the word for force or insistence (*agraha*) into his new name, 'Satyagraha', which means the insistence upon, or force of, truth or love (*satya*).[6] It is equally important to him to repeatedly insist upon the 'manliness' of engaging in Satyagraha, and to distinguish it clearly from (feminized) acquiescence, or cowardice. Calling Satyagraha 'manly', he aims to distinguish it from helplessness and the pity that helplessness evokes: more courage and strength of character is required for its practice, he claims, than for the practice of violence or 'brute force'.[7]

This need for exceptional courage is also raised in the first, all-male, meeting in 1906 in Johannesburg, of what would later become the Satyagraha movement. There, Gandhi insisted that each person must 'search his own heart' to ensure 'he has the requisite strength to carry him through', before pledging allegiance to the movement.[8] Everyone must understand that participation in Satyagraha might entail the suffering of a range of harms, from imprisonment, to insult, hunger, hard labour, flogging, illness, to deportation and even death, and they must ensure that they have the internal strength to stay the course through such hardship. Until this point one can thus see that Gandhi held a conventional view of courage in the face of violence as a masculine attribute and he additionally justified the exclusion of women on the basis that the men were the primary targets of the proposed legislation in Transvaal. Emphasizing the signs of women's activism as springing from personal, familial ties ('wives of Satyagrahi'), Gandhi moreover at this point reinscribed women as domestic, pre-political beings. In his defence, however, it must be noted that some women used the same kind of argument to demand participation. Already in 1909, the Tamil wives of Satyagrahis in prison held a meeting in a temple in Germiston and passed the following resolution: 'As our religion tells us that a wife may not be separated from her husband, we pray the Government to send us to gaol with our husbands'.[9]

Women's Leadership Leading up to the 1913 Satyagraha March

Individual female support behind the scenes of the Satyagraha movement had been critical and constant in the first seven years, as personified, for example, in Sonja Schlesin, Gandhi's secretary, who was also an activist in her own right. However, the catalyst for the direct participation of women in the 1913 march itself was a court decision. Remarkably shortly after the end of the bitter South African War between Boer and Brit, these same two groups started to find common ground to unify the former colonies and create a White South African nation by repressing the darker-skinned majority population. Soon after the 1910 creation of the Union of South Africa, the Immigration Acts of the Union (into which the former Transvaal Republic had been absorbed) 'were being administered with an ever-growing severity',[10] due to the prejudices and fears of the White population. In this climate, in March 1913, the Cape Supreme Court (justice Searle) refused to recognize the marriage of a South African Indian man to an Indian woman, and thereby refused permission for her to enter the country. Gandhi immediately understood the dire implications of this decision, writing in *Indian Opinion*, 'a Hindu, Muslim or Parsi wife can live in this country only by the grace of the Government. . . . The remedy is entirely in our hands. . . . Any nation that fails to protect the honour of its women, any individual who fails to protect the honour of his wife is considered lower in level than a brute'.[11] Whereas before, Gandhi had felt that the discriminatory legislation mainly affected men (e.g. as traders), now he saw that '[t]he Searle judgment, if interpreted literally and implemented vigorously, threatened to sunder husband from wife, mother from children. This would seriously damage the life of the Indian community in South Africa'.[12]

A mass meeting in Johannesburg eight days after the judgment, again consisted only of men. The 1913 campaign could thus easily have been another men-only affair, with the men intent upon defending the honour of 'their wives'. That is, if it wasn't for Kasturba, who asked Gandhi whether Searle implied 'that I am not your wife according to the laws of this country'. When he answered in the affirmative, she first suggested they move back to India. He replied that would be cowardly, upon which she said, 'Could I not, then, join the struggle and be imprisoned myself?'[13] Guha reads these words as 'a mark of deep loyalty to her husband, and of her acquired understanding of *his* cause'.[14] I would instead say that this moment is indicative of Kasturba's emergent political agency. Recall that one of the reasons Gandhi gave for the earlier exclusion of women from the front lines was that the legislation targeted men—that reason now no longer held. As the Gandhis realized, the new legislation rendered all Indian customary marriages illegal. This outraged the women who were thereby 'degraded to the rank of concubines',[15] while their children lost their inheritance rights. Clearly this went to the heart of women's own dignity, status, and power, both within and beyond their families and communities.

A further indication of Kasturba's awakening political self-determination is reflected in a conversation between them that Mohandas recounted. He explained to her regarding her wish to participate: 'In matters like this everyone should act relying solely upon one's own strength and courage. If I asked you, you might be inclined to go just for the sake of complying with my request'.[16] These comments combine his mistrust of women's courage with his concern about undue pressure on a wife to participate. Her somewhat irritated response was: 'You may have nothing to do with me if being unable to stand jail I secure my release by an apology. If you can endure hardships and so can my boys, why cannot I? I am bound to join the struggle'.[17] Kasturba here explicitly insists upon her own independent conviction, commitment, strength, and courage. From her intimate knowledge of her husband and sons, she knows that she does not lack endurance in comparison. Her words may even be read as a reminder to Gandhi that she is the mother of the brave boys and thus not only brought them into the world and raised them as courageous men, but that her authority over them should also bestow some authority upon her. In a sense, she demonstrates here the feminist principle 'the personal is political' and insists upon familial recognition of her civic status as much as upon state recognition of the same. This was a turning point for the Gandhis, for the Indians in South Africa and for the later anti-colonial struggle in India. Upon relaying their conversation to Gokhale, Gandhi said, with a clean conscience, 'the womenfolk will join the struggle' because they 'feel they can no longer refrain from facing the gaol no matter what it may mean in a place like this. Mrs Gandhi made the offer on her own initiative, and I do not want to debar her'.[18]

In April 1913, the Union Government released the draft of a new Immigration Bill, which rendered 'the status of [Indian] wives and children uncertain and insecure', in the name of 'the self-preservation of the white race in South Africa'.[19] Throughout 1912 and 1913, Mohandas Gandhi and Sonja Schlesin wrote hundreds of letters and petitions to the government and sought audiences with Smuts and others, Schlesin stating inter alia that 'the [Indian women] would offer passive resistance along with their menfolk' if Indian marriages were not recognized.[20] Clearly, Kasturba breaking through to Mohandas led to more women volunteering for the struggle, and their participation becoming a recognized strategy. By September 1913, when all other attempts had failed, the Indians started to prepare for offering Satyagraha.

Guha explains why at the time it had been 'unthinkable' that women could participate in public protests, in South Africa and India alike.[21] It would be doubly problematic from the Indian point of view in that women would mingle with men not of their family (in the protest) and they would encounter 'male jailors not of their kin or caste'. We have already seen how this fear raised the spectre of sexual contact and sexual violence from ethnic and other strangers—as Gandhi also hints at above when he says, 'no matter what it may mean in a place like this'.[22] The salience of these fears underscores the unprecedented nature of the gender composition of the 1913 march. At the same time, we should recognize the then recent African women's resistance in the Orange Free State—quite likely, there was mutual influence and inspiration between their event and the Satyagraha march. In August 1913, African women in the Orange Free State en masse 'turned in their passes to the authorities, pledging never to carry them again'.[23] This was the earliest of a long series of women's acts of mass non-violent resistance in the history of modern South Africa.

On 15 September 1913, a group of four women (including Kasturba and two of her nieces) plus twelve young men, started the campaign by setting out to illegally cross the border by mail train, from the Phoenix settlement in Natal via Volksrust into Transvaal. Gandhi asked Kallenbach to meet the party at the border, but that he should only 'watch as a spectator'. He further instructed: 'They are not to speak English. One of them only will speak in that tongue, interpret for the others. They will not give fingerprints. If the police arrest them, they must ask for shelter at the police station. If the police do not arrest them, you should . . . proceed [with them] to Johannesburg'.[24] They were subsequently detained, tried, and sentenced to three months in prison, with hard labour. Guha notes that Gandhi's activism in the meanwhile had also taken another new turn—towards the poor.[25] Although Gandhi had previously campaigned on their behalf, indentured labourers had not before 1913 participated in the vanguard of Satyagraha. Yet another boundary (caste and class) was being crossed, with one of the key demands of the campaign being the abolition of the tax that hit the poor hardest. In Durban in October 1913, Gandhi met with and found great support amongst the workers in mines and plantations. His support amongst the miners was partly due to the mobilization work of eleven Tamil women, whom he had sent to illegally cross the border from Transvaal to Natal, roughly at the same time as the Kasturba party went in the opposite direction. If the Tamil group were not arrested, they were to continue to Newcastle, where they were to encourage the miners to strike in support of the campaign.[26] Unlike Kasturba's group, these women were not arrested.

The front-line activism of these two parties of women, both how they conducted themselves, and their effectiveness, caught Gandhi off guard. The Tamil women's work in Natal was particularly effective—thousands of mostly male workers went on strike in response to their provocations. Gandhi writes, 'Their influence spread like wildfire . . . I was not prepared for this marvellous awakening'.[27] The women's determination and courage in the face of state violence and detention was the prelude to the great success of the 1913 march. It opened Gandhi's eyes to women's physical and moral strength, and the capacity of women's front-line participation to inspire mass participation. Later, in India, he writes, 'To call woman the weaker sex is a libel; it is man's injustice to woman . . . If non-violence is the law of our being [as he proclaimed], the future is with women'.[28] Clearly, where Gandhi was initially reluctant about women's 'front-line' participation, this 'experiment with truth' resulted in a new understanding of the very nature of Satyagraha. Although Gandhi admitted that it was the difference between the South African and Indian societies at the time that created the freedom for more social experimentation, he left South Africa for India firmly convinced of the key importance of women's frontline work in the struggle against racism and colonialism.

The Satyagraha March

The 1913 march proper started in early November when the mine and plantation owners reached Dundee and Newcastle in Natal with the aim to coerce the striking workers to return to work. The Satyagrahis decided to move the workers to Charlestown, thirty-five miles away, and the only way was on foot. Upon reaching Charlestown, however, the leadership decided to march all the way to Tolstoy Farm south of Johannesburg in Transvaal province. About two thousand non-violent resisters joined them in Charlestown. Meanwhile, Indians and supporters were assembling in Johannesburg to mourn the sufferings of the community, to support the Satyagrahi, and to celebrate specifically the women resisters in jail. A photograph of the Johannesburg (Tamil) women in jail was flashed on a screen, and donations flowed in. Schlesin then travelled down to Charlestown particularly to assist the women gathering for the march, a further indication that women's participation had by now become an organized part of the action.[29] On the morning of 6 November, the protesters walked from Charlestown and crossed illegally into the Transvaal. Gandhi and the other two leaders Polak and Kallenbach were arrested and jailed. However, the march continued, with thousands of workers still joining in the strike. From prison, Gandhi asked government assistance for the 'nearly 150 men, women and children' who were 'footsore and otherwise disabled' at Paardekop. Around fifteen thousand sugar workers were on strike by the middle of November, in solidarity with the miners and the march, and other workers (in railways, ships, shops, etc.) joined in besides. African reformer John Dube[30] and Cape Coloured leader Dr Abdurahman were sympathetic and impressed, expressing new respect for the Indian community. Support also swelled in India, where there was even a play performed of Gandhi's life in South Africa.[31] Guha comments: 'At a time when Indian women of all castes and creeds were confined to the home, or in purdah, that Kasturba and her colleagues went to jail in protest against discriminatory laws was a fact—or achievement—noted [across India] with not a little admiration'.[32]

By November, there were one thousand Indians in jail. The scale of participation in the non-violent resistance and its unprecedentedly broad alliance (finally breaching the boundaries of province, economic sector, class and gender) are what resulted in high-level responses from both India and Britain, according to Guha.[33] It led to the Viceroy of India and the Governor-General of South Africa to call upon Smuts to establish a commission of enquiry to investigate the marriage and tax questions. Mohandas Gandhi was finally released from prison on 18 December; Kasturba Gandhi on 22 December 1913. Gandhi came to Pietermaritzburg to meet Kasturba and her fellow prisoners as they emerged from jail after three months, where they were 'pulled in a flower-strewn carriage through the streets'. Kasturba's health was very poor, with Polak wiring to Gokhale, 'Reduced skeleton tottering appearance old woman heartbreaking sight'.[34] At a subsequent public meeting, Millie Polak said:

> This was essentially a women's movement, and there was no question that had it not been for the women taking the lead, there would have been no strike. When women once realized the enormous power they had they would rise up and make their own lives and the world that they wished. (loud applause)[35]

Gandhi always worked to establish broad alliances, and the solidarity and sympathy that the methods of Satyagraha inspired in opponents, allies, and otherwise affected groups and individuals formed an integral part of the effective force of truth that he promoted. The 1913 march with its mass participation by cross-cutting sectors of the Indian population was particularly effective in inspiring broad-based sympathy. In responding to women's and workers' participation in the campaign, some influential White women in South Africa played a crucial role in the successful conclusion of the campaign of 1913. By early 1914, Smuts appointed a biased Commission of Enquiry and Gandhi threatened more marches, this time to Pretoria. Betty Molteno, daughter of the first Prime Minister of the Cape Colony, had left South Africa in protest of the treatment of the Boers during the South African War and had met Gandhi in 1909 in London.[36] After the Gandhis' release from prison in December 1913, Molteno travelled to Natal to meet with them. 'She was moved by their stories of jail life, and by the cross-class support for the satyagraha'.[37] Molteno introduced Emily Hobhouse to Gandhi—Hobhouse, who brought the plight of the Boer women and children under the attention of the British public, played a key role in ending that war. This meeting prompted her to write to Smuts on 29 December, urging him to 'readjust the marriage question and abolish that stupid £3 tax',[38] and to address the Indian grievances before the next planned march on 15 January. She further wrote that the Indians' cause 'is really moral not material and so, having all the power of the spiritual[39] behind him, he [Gandhi] and you are like [the British suffragette] Mrs Pankhurst and [the British Home Secretary Reginald] McKenna and never, never will governmental physical force prevail against a great moral and spiritual upheaval'.[40]

Hobhouse thereby closed the circle that had started with Gandhi's early admiration for the Suffragettes, and his associated understanding of the efficacy of moral, rather than physical force. The new-found inclusive, mass nature of the 1913 campaign, and the key role played by women Satyagrahi, led these White women to caution Smuts that despite White support he was unlikely to prevail against the Indians in the long run. The pressure they exerted on Smuts contributed to him re-entering talks with Gandhi on 13 January, which led to the release of all remaining prisoners and an agreement on the Commission's recommendation to Government. In June 1914, the Indians' Relief Bill was passed through Parliament that conceded to all Gandhi's demands, against significant opposition by the White population and MPs. On 19 July, the Gandhis left South Africa for good.

In retrospect, speaking to a group of women students in Lahore in July 1934, Gandhi said, 'When I was in South Africa, I had realized that if I did not serve the cause of women, all my work would remain unfinished'.[41] These words reveal a profound inversion of Guha's idea that Kasturba wanted to participate out of a deep loyalty to *Gandhi's cause*. The women's participation led Gandhi to revise his conception of Satyagraha and showed him how important it was that the moral force and energetic indignation of a whole community—all genders and classes—be mobilized for effective change.

Conclusion

Of course, the women's role in the 1913 Satyagraha march was not unique. Time and again, focused feminist research reveals crucial work done by women to bring about world historical changes—work that had mostly been erased in the dominant narratives. So, for instance, we now know that the October 1789 Women's March on Versailles was a turning point in the French Revolution (see Alpaugh, in this volume); that women activists started and sustained the civil rights movement;[42] that women's protests, boycotts, and other forms of non-cooperation over many decades kept the struggle alive for Africans fighting against colonialism. Women often contribute much in terms of 'eco-systems of assembly' (see Inazu, in this volume, and Page and Robinson, in this volume), supplying the material, labour, and other support needed for assemblies, and in terms of the social movements that often undergird assemblies (see Zhelnina and Jasper, in this volume). A good example in the context of Gandhi's campaigns in South Africa is Sonja Schlesin, who ran the movement behind the scenes in his absence.

In this chapter, however, the focus was on women's front-line work, high visibility in openly transgressive acts, including mobilizing male workers to strike. Recent work of authors such as Erica Chenoweth and Danielle McGuire has drawn renewed attention to the public role of women in mass movements for change, including the organization and execution of peaceful assemblies.[43] The history of the mutual inspiration of Gandhi's 1913 march and the activism of African women also since 1913 must, to the best of my knowledge, still be written, and the question of the rootedness of these instances of women's activism in older forms of indigenous resistance to colonial and pre-colonial patriarchal excesses must also still be investigated.[44] If indeed the success of the 1913 campaign had much to do with the visibility of women, one might well wonder why. The first impression is that the front-line involvement of women seemed to have inspired broad-based participation and sympathy with the cause. The role played by the first parties of women inspired thousands of male workers to strike or join the march, both at great personal risk. The symbolic impact of the woman resisters is attested to by the fact that their photos were shown at rallies. There seems to have been a direct link between the women's front-line activism and the extension of the movement from the professional elites to the working masses, even into the sugar fields of southern Natal, a place never visited by Gandhi. As we have seen, the initiative and leadership displayed by women sparked interest in India and political concerns in Britain and led to pressure upon the South African Government to investigate the grievances related to marriage and taxes—the two issues that hit women and the poor the hardest. The broad-based and peaceful nature of the protests and the sufferings endured, inspired many observers, including influential local White women, to exert pressure on the White male leadership to concede the Indians' moral victory. This phenomenon must be a key part of what Gandhi meant by Satyagraha as the force of truth or love, even if its precise manifestation in 1913–4 caught him off-guard.

Erica Chenoweth's wide-ranging research into revolutionary movements from 1900 to today has shown that when women are around half or more of the assemblers publicly visible, then peaceful assemblies increase significantly in size (up to seven times), presumably because women's mass presence stamps assemblies as (likely to be) peaceful, as well as enjoying mass support.[45] Chenoweth notes a correlation between women's visible participation on the front lines, increased support, non-violence, and the success of revolutionary movements, where success is measured in terms of the achievement of regime change, coupled with sustained democratic transformation. Chenoweth further shows that women bring more horizontal and larger social networks into the political domain than men, and that this greatly affects regime defections, and law enforcement reluctance to shoot into crowds. This concept of broad sympathy, which correlates with Gandhi's idea of the force of love, again translates into greater stability after a transition. The role played by women activists in the 1913 campaign, especially in relation to motivating male workers to join the struggle, illustrates this claim. The fact that the 1913 campaign breached gender, class, caste, and other boundaries, resulted in both national and international, both official and personal, pressure placed on the Union Government. Later in his life, because of his experience with male activists' propensity for violence and women activists' resistance to it, Gandhi even started to envisage an all-female 'army' of Satyagrahi as the future ideal.[46]

Notes

1. R. Guha, *Gandhi before India* (London: Allen Lane, 2013), 464.
2. M. K. Gandhi, *Satyagraha in South Africa* (Ahmedabad: Navajivan Publishing House, 2006).
3. Ibid., 255.
4. L. Sjoberg, *Gendering Global Conflict: Toward a Feminist Theory of War* (New York: Columbia University Press, 2013).
5. Gandhi, *Satyagraha*, 121.
6. Ibid., 119.
7. M. K. Gandhi, *The Collected Works of Mahatma Gandhi*, Vol. 10 (New Delhi: Publications Division, 1958–1994), 93.
8. Gandhi, *Satyagraha*, 115.
9. Guha, *Gandhi before India*, 465.
10. Ibid., 446.
11. Ibid., 446–447.
12. Ibid., 447.
13. Ibid., 447.
14. Ibid., 447 (emphasis added).
15. Gandhi, *Satyagraha*, 256.
16. Ibid., 259.
17. Ibid., 260.
18. Guha, *Gandhi before India*, 448.
19. Ibid., 449.
20. Ibid., 450.
21. Ibid., 465.
22. Such fears are not unfounded, because examples abound. Philippa Levine described how anti-colonial women activists and militants in both Algeria and Kenya were subjected in jail to sexual torture, rape, and threat of rape, in P. Levine, 'Gendering Decolonisation', *Histoire@Politique. Politique, culture, société*, 11 (May–August 2010): 8–9.
23. Guha, *Gandhi before India*, 465.
24. Gandhi, *Collected Works*, Vol. 96, 142.
25. Guha, *Gandhi before India*, 465.
26. Gandhi, *Satyagraha*, 257–258.
27. Ibid., 261.
28. M. K. Gandhi. *The Women* (Karachi: Anand T Hingorani, 1941), 36.
29. Guha, *Gandhi before India*, 475.

30. Dube was also the first President of the African National Congress, and a neighbour and friend of the Gandhis at Phoenix in Durban.
31. Guha, *Gandhi before India*, 487–488.
32. Ibid., 536.
33. Ibid., 493.
34. Ibid., 496.
35. *Natal Mercury*, 23 December 1913, quoted in Guha, *Gandhi before India*, 495.
36. C. Corder and M. Plaut, 'Gandhi's Decisive South African 1913 Campaign: A Personal Perspective the Letters of Betty Molteno', *South African Historical Journal* 66 (2014): 22–54.
37. Guha, *Gandhi before India*, 497.
38. Ibid., 497.
39. '[A]ll the power of the spiritual'—this phrase is a literal translation of Satyagraha.
40. Ibid., 498.
41. Ibid., 534.
42. D. McGuire, *At the Dark End of the Street: Black Women, Rape and Resistance—A New History of the Civil Rights Movement from Rosa Parks to the Rise of Black Power* (New York: Knopf, 2010).
43. E. Chenoweth and M. Stephan. *Why Civil Resistance Works: The Strategic Logic of Nonviolent Conflict* (New York: Columbia University Press, 2013); McGuire, *At the Dark End of the Street.*
44. J. van Allen, '"Sitting on a Man": Colonialism and the Lost Political Institutions of Igbo Women', *Canadian Journal of African Studies* [*Revue Canadienne des Études Africaines*] 6, no. 2 (1972): 165–181.
45. Chenoweth and Stephan, *Why Civil Resistance Works*, 220.
46. Gandhi, *Women*, 175.

Further Reading

Bhalla, B. M. *Kasturba Gandhi: A Biography*. New Delhi: The Lotus Collection, Roli Books, 2020.

Chenoweth, Erica, and Maria Stephan. *Why Civil Resistance Works: The Strategic Logic of Nonviolent Conflict*. New York: Columbia University Press, 2013.

Corder, Catherine, and Martin Plaut. 'Gandhi's Decisive South African 1913 Campaign: A Personal Perspective the Letters of Betty Molteno'. *South African Historical Journal* 66 (2014): 22–54.

Du Toit, Louise. 'Gandhi and the Gender of Nonviolent Resistance'. *Religions* 13, no. 5 (2022): 467. https://doi.org/10.3390/rel13050467.

Du Toit, Louise, and Jana L. Vosloo. 'When Bodies Speak Differently: Putting Judith Butler in conversation with Mahatma Gandhi on Nonviolent Resistance'. *Religions* 12 (2021): 627. https://doi.org/10.3390/rel12080627.

Gandhi, Mohandas Karamchand. *Satyagraha in South Africa*. Printed and published by Jitendra T. Desai. Ahmedabad: Navajivan Publishing House, 1928.

Hiralal, Kalpana. 'Rethinking Gender and Agency in the Satyagraha Movement of 1913'. *Journal of Social Sciences* 25 (2017): 1–3, 71–80.

Tarlo, Emma. 'Married to the Mahatma: The Predicament of Kasturba Gandhi'. *Women: A Cultural Review* 8, no. 3 (1997): 264–277.

CHAPTER 21

ORANGE PARADES IN NORTHERN IRELAND

Impacting 'the Life of the Community'

DOMINIC BRYAN

INTRODUCTION

On Sunday 9 July 1995, the Royal Ulster Constabulary (RUC), the police in Northern Ireland, took the decision to block the brethren of Portadown Orange District No. 1, in County Armagh, from parading from Drumcree parish church back to their Orange Hall in the centre of town. The route the Orangemen wanted to take was along the Garvaghy Road, an area that has a predominantly Catholic population. This church parade has been held annually since 1807 on the Sunday before the Twelfth of July, commemorating the Battle of the Boyne of 1690 when the Protestant King William defeated Catholic King James. The decision made by the police came after many years of contestation over the Drumcree parade and resulted in more years of bitter confrontations. In July 1995, 1996, and 1997 the parade eventually proceeded down the Garvaghy Road after days of sometimes-violent protest.

During that period, from 1995 to 1998, five people, three of them children, died in incidents related to the protests, many millions of pounds were spent in policing, and it is no exaggeration to suggest that the peace process in Northern Ireland, which culminated in an Agreement on 10 April 1998, was put under severe strain.[1] That same year, new legislation was passed to empower the Northern Ireland Parades Commission (hereafter the Parades Commission) to make determinations on processions, and the parade was re-routed away from the Garvaghy Road. Orange Lodges have been handing in a letter of protest to the police every Sunday since July 1998.

Taking an anthropological approach to ritual events and using an ethnographic methodology, the chapter examines the structure of the ritual 'Orange' processions in Northern Ireland and the complex understandings of participation held by individuals and constitutive groups. It highlights the complexities in understanding who is participating in the events, why they participate, and the tension this presents for the state in facilitating the events.

The chapter contrasts the complexity of these ritual events compared with the relative simplicity of the legislation, Public Processions Act (Northern Ireland) 1998, which seeks to codify how the Parades Commission can place restrictions on a procession. Crucial here is the role the event or events play in the ethnic identity of the group that views itself as British, Protestant, and Unionist. As such, the criteria in the Public Processions Act that the Parades Commission use to make determinations, 'disruption to the life of the community which the procession may cause' and 'impact which the procession may have on relationships within the community', have significance well beyond those participating on the parade and those living and working on the route of the parade.[2] Given the role played by these parades in ethnic identity politics, and the defence of a particular group's 'traditions' and 'cultural heritage', tensions around the duty of the state to facilitate freedom of assembly become particularly apparent, even acute. The chapter concludes that placing restrictions based upon judging the impact upon 'the community', as required by the Public Processions Act, is hampered by the difficulty in defining what 'community' might mean.

The 'Tradition' of Orange Parades

Parades and demonstrations in 'the north of Ireland', 'Northern Ireland' since 1921, have played an important role in the defining of ethnic group identities and the control of public space through most of the nineteenth and twentieth centuries.[3] The nature of policing and the rule of law have been in a constant conflictual relationship with claims to a 'traditional' right to parade, claims of rights to religious practice, and ultimately claims to the right of peaceful assembly. Periods in nineteenth century Ireland saw legislation on processions that completely banned people's right to parade and in the twentieth-century groups representing Irish, Catholic, and Republican identity, as well as civil rights marches in the 1960s and 1970s, have been significantly restricted.[4] The two largest cities in the north of Ireland, Derry/Londonderry and Belfast, have histories with civil disorder linked to parades and demonstrations leading to the use of high levels of physical force by the state and playing a role in residential areas being constituted as 'Protestant' and 'Catholic'. The events in Derry on 30 January 1972 when British soldiers opened fire on civil rights protesters, killing fourteen people, known as Bloody Sunday, was a defining moment in the violent conflict, as was the stand-off between Orangemen and the RUC and British Army over the disputed Drumcree Church parade in Portadown in 1995. The street confrontations between Loyal Orange Lodges and the RUC (which was the predominantly Protestant police force of Northern Ireland), seemed to defy the simple sectarian polarized logic of the violent conflict. A police force that was seen as the last line of defence for the state was pitched in confrontation with Orangemen professing loyalty to that same state.

The Twelfth of July in Belfast

On the Twelfth of July, Orangemen remember the victory of Protestant King William of Orange over the deposed Catholic King James II at the Battle of the Boyne in 1690. It is a complex series of parades with participants expressing a range of identities. Annually, at 10.00 am on the morning of the Twelfth of July, the Orange Lodges in Belfast and their associated bands gather at Carlisle Circus in north Belfast to start a parade of 4.5 miles that, in recent years, has finished in the south of the city, where a religious ceremony and political speeches take place. After around two hours in 'the field', the parade forms up again and marches back through the centre of the city.

On top of the round trip of nine miles, many of the Orange lodges and their associated bands will have marched in their local area before getting to the meeting point for the parade, and they will march back to their local area at the conclusion of the main parade. Some participants, many of whom are quite elderly, and their supporters might have walked fifteen miles during the day. The historical divisions of the city of Belfast into residential areas that are Protestant or Catholic has made the routing of these parades deeply contentious. Their policing has presented significant challenges since the middle of the nineteenth century.[5]

The parade has been organized by the Belfast County Grand Orange Lodge (see fig. 21.1) and is one of about eighteen venues around Northern Ireland.[6] The media depict the Twelfth of July as the day the Protestants march on the streets, although the majority of Protestants do not participate, and the event is more diverse than such a simple depiction suggests. If we take an anthropological approach to how ritual works and an ethnographic look at the content and activities in the ritual, then a much more complicated picture arises.

The 'lodges' each have a distinct number which is displayed on the sashes worn by the men of the Lodge and on the banner which each lodge will carry, often depicting William of Orange on his white horse (see figs. 21.1 and 21.2). Lodges may reflect different types of Protestant churches; different focuses of employment; a particular local history; temperance or abstinence in relation to alcohol; a link to the British armed forces or local security forces (RUC and the Ulster Defence Regiment); particularly important moments of history for unionists such as the Battle of the Somme (1916); particular individuals of historic or religious importance (such as Oliver Cromwell); social class differences; and sometimes political differences within Unionism. As well as the Orange sashes (or collarets) worn by the men participating, a lodge will usually carry ornate banners, some with pictures of King William at the Battle of the Boyne, but many with symbols and pictures reflecting the localized diversity of different lodges.[7] As such, this is a parade of local and particular identities.

There will be up to one hundred lodges represented on parade in Belfast, although many have suffered from declining numbers and ageing brethren.

FIGURE 21.1. Members of the Belfast County Grand Lodge and guests Orangemen form up to head the Twelfth of July parade in 2023. Note that they are wearing Orange sashes (collarets) displaying the number of their Lodge. They are being led by the Millar Memorial flute band.

(Picture by Dominic Bryan)

Most of the lodges hire a marching band to accompany the lodge (fig. 21.3). Whilst some of these bandsmen will be Orangemen, most will not be, and each band also reflects the histories, identities, and the politics of where they come from. The bands are independent from the Orange Institution and they organize many of their own parades as well as participating in parades organized by the 'loyal orders': the Orange Order, Royal Black Preceptories, and the Apprentice Boys of Derry. There are different types of bands although most are flute bands, some of which are known for their 'rowdy' carnivalesque performances and are locally termed 'blood and thunder' bands. As the bands pass various parts of the city, alcohol-filled celebrating results in joyous dancing, often led by women spectators dressed in patriotic colours. The focus of each band is a bass drummer who will often dance and weave down the road as young men lead from the front hurling batons into the air (figs. 21.3 and 21.5).

Many of the flute bands have formed since the 1970s, the onset of the conflict, and reflect militia groups from Irish history with names like 'Defenders', 'Volunteers', and 'Conquerors'.[8] They come from predominantly working-class areas and some have

FIGURE 21.2. Orangemen from the Sons of Belfast LOL 743 carry their banner of King William III on the Lisburn Road in Belfast 12 July 2023 led by a flute band.

(Picture by Dominic Bryan)

direct connections with Loyalist paramilitary groups the Ulster Volunteer Force (UVF) and the Ulster Defence Association (UDA), both proscribed organizations under the Terrorism Act 2000. All these bandsmen wear colourful military-type uniforms, and bands display symbols on their drums and carry flags and bannerets. Symbols displayed will include many connecting them to forms of Britishness and to an Ulster identity (in this case, an alternative term for Northern Ireland); many reflecting a marshal or military history including many references to the World War I particularly with displays of the poppy, and sometimes including symbols representing the UVF or the UDA (figs. 21.5 and 21.7).

FIGURE 21.3. The Sons of Ulster flute band parade down Donegall Street on the Twelfth of July parade in Belfast 2022. Note the police vehicle on the left that marks the point at which the bands are allowed to start playing music again. In the background is St Patrick's Roman Catholic Church, which the Northern Ireland Parades Commission has determined that all bands must pass playing just a drumbeat.

(Picture by Dominic Bryan)

There is a wide repertoire of music, played vigorously by many of the bands, from the long-standing historic tunes like 'The Sash My Father Wore' and 'Billy Boys' to marching tunes, hymns, movie theme tunes such as the Dam Busters, popular songs such as Bridge over Trouble Waters (Simon and Garfunkel), and Sloop John B (The Beach Boys).[9] Some songs, such as Sloop John B (with a version known as the Famine song), are associated with adapted lyrics that are sectarian. The music is played in a range of styles, from the very formal to the carnivalesque. Some bandsmen weave and dance down the road in stark contrast to the formalized walk of the Orangemen. In recent years, I have counted around seventy bands in the Belfast Twelfth parade, of which some come from local areas around Belfast, others from rural parts of Northern Ireland, and over a dozen are from the west of Scotland.

The Twelfth parade in Belfast is predominantly made up of men. Up until 1990, no women were allowed to participate in the Belfast parade, but the rules were changed to accommodate women coming from other parts of the world to the special Tercentenary of the Battle of the Boyne held in the city. Women's Orange lodges have slowly increased

FIGURE 21.4. July Twelfth 2021, displaying the determination by the Parades Commission that supporters and the playing of music is restricted whilst passing St Patrick's Roman Catholic Church on Clifton Street, north Belfast.

(Picture by Dominic Bryan)

in number and more women and girls are in the marching bands, sometimes carrying the flags at the front of the band.[10] That said, even before they were formally given a role, women were present as vociferous spectators known as 'Orange Lills'. Some dress in Union Jacks and dance to the music, whilst teenage girls walked alongside the band from their area.

At the Twelfth parade in Belfast there are a large number of animated supporters along the route with the road lined with families seated in deck chairs often with food and drink, including alcohol, to sustain their day. They often get up and greet those in the parade whom they know and erupt as the bands perform loudly and energetically in front of them. Younger people follow their local band along the routes, again often carrying alcohol. It is a day for dressing up, cheering your favourite band, and meeting friends. Some of the conflicts at parades stem from the behaviour of spectators who are colloquially described as the 'hangers-on'. Both organizers, lodges, and bands argue that it is not their job to control the behaviour of these groups of people.

It should be clear from the above that despite falling under the term 'Orange Parade' there is a good deal of diversity of identity and behaviour. For some, it is religious and

FIGURE 21.5. Bridgeton Loyalist flute band, Twelfth of July in Belfast 2022, one of more than a dozen flute bands that come over from Scotland. The base drummer of a flute band often performs vigorously weaving up the road. Note also the use of the phrase 'Quis Separabit' translated as 'who will separate us', a motto used by a number of British Army Regiments and the illegal Ulster Defence Association (UDA) in Northern Ireland.

(Picture by Dominic Bryan)

they maintain a formality about what they do, carrying banners with the bible depicted, abstaining from alcohol, standing and listening to the religious service at the field, or going to a tent of lodge for tea and sandwiches (see fig. 21.6).

For others, the day is political, a ritual of Britishness parading through the centre of Belfast, stopping at a War memorial to remember those who have fought and died fighting for the United Kingdom. At the halfway stage of the parade they listen to speeches made by Unionist politicians at 'the field'. When the Ulster Unionist Party

FIGURE 21.6. The banner of the Ark of Freedom Temperence Loyal Orange Lodge 592. The avoidance of alcohol in the form of Temperance and Abstinence movements have an important part in the history of Belfast and are reflected in a number of lodges.

(Picture by Dominic Bryan)

governed Northern Ireland (1921–1972) the Twelfth could be a day for heckling a government minister for not 'defending' the Protestant people. In more recent decades the parade has become a place for rallying the brethren, resisting the state, confronting police officers, holding banners protesting at the Anglo-Irish Agreement (1986), or the rerouting of parades (1995–2000), or the Brexit Protocol (2020–2023).

Most importantly the parade is an acknowledgement of their cultural identity shared with friends from their local area, often fun, sometimes defiant, and with a sense of pride. It is the annual day of renewing relationships with family and friends. Younger members relish it as carnivalesque, dressing up, dancing to music through the celebrations with copious amounts of alcohol consumed (notwithstanding the averred temperance of some of the lodges), and having fun. The contrast between the sombre, sober abstinence lodges and the drunken and carnivalesque behaviour of many participants is one of the long-standing contradictions of the Twelfth of July in Belfast.

Whilst the parades are seen as exclusively Protestant from the outside, The Twelfth has worked as a set of events because it encompasses a diversity within that identity. So the Twelfth of July parade through the centre of Belfast has banners professing abstinence from alcohol (fig. 21.6) and spectators and participants drink lots of alcohol; it has decorum and respectability and people dressing up in fancy dress costumes dancing down the road; it has bands dressed in the simplest of uniforms and others that are as regimented as any military band; it has hymns and sectarian tunes; it is dominated by men and yet sometimes young women proudly carry the flags of the bands; it has groups from different parts of the city coming together to acknowledge their common Unionism, Loyalism, and Protestantism, but support competing political parties; and it even has a tension, found in the symbols and the speeches, between a loyalty to Ulster and a loyalty to the United Kingdom.

Bibles, battles, and bottles everywhere express Britishness but not in a way that many in the rest of Britain understand it. Internal tensions run through the event, in particular, tensions between the law-abiding mainstream unionists and considerable numbers of working-class loyalists supporting paramilitary groups. Among those in mainstream political parties, there is tension between those in the formerly dominant Ulster Unionist Party and the now dominant Democratic Unionist Party. And then there have been ongoing tensions between the UDA and the UVF reflected in years of bloody feuding meaning the bands supporting the different groups can compete to the point of fights.

The critics of these events accuse it of sectarian 'coat-trailing'. The Orange Order is viewed as an organization explicitly in existence to bind together different forms of Protestantism to oppose the doctrines of the Roman Catholic Church. Marches in Belfast pass near and through areas of the city that are predominantly Catholic in population sometimes leading to determinations by the Parades Commission over the route, timing, or conduct of that section of the procession (fig. 21.4). The Orange Order's interpretation of a Protestantism, explicitly linked to their loyalty to the British monarch, head of the Church of England and defender of 'the' faith, stands in opposition to an imagined Irishness that is both Catholic and Republican. This is captured in some of the music and songs performed such as the Sash My Father Wore.

> It is old but it is beautiful, and its colours they are fine
> It was worn at Derry, Aughrim, Enniskillen and the Boyne.
> My father wore it as a youth in bygone days of yore,
> And on the Twelfth, I love to wear the sash my father wore.
>
> For those brave men who crossed the Boyne have not fought or died in vain
> Our Unity, Religion, Laws, and Freedom to maintain,
> If the call should come we'll follow the drum, and cross that river once more

FIGURE 21.7. Flags carried by a band in the 2022 Twelfth of July parade referencing the Ulster Volunteer Force (UVF).

(Picture by Dominic Bryan)

> That tomorrow's Ulsterman may wear the sash my father wore!

In addition, quite of number of the songs and tunes played are derogatory or apparently threatening, such as the Billy Boys containing the term 'Fenian'—a nineteenth-century republican brotherhood but also understood as derogatory word for Catholic.

> Hoorah, Hoorah, we are the Billy Boys,
> Hoorah, Hoorah, we are the Billy Boys,
> Up tae yer knees in Fenian blood—surrender or ye'll die.
> We are the Brigtown Billie Boys.

This of course is on top of the numerous symbolic references to loyalist paramilitary groups, responsible for many sectarian killings (fig. 21.7). The enmity and fear that the Twelfth of July creates for people holding Irish and Catholic identities is easy to understand. In addition, recall that from the time the state of Northern Ireland was set up until the proroguing of Stormont Parliament in 1972, all but three Government ministers had been members of the Orange Order. There is also a clear link between the power of the UUP and the widespread development of the 'tradition' of Orange Parades. This has been particularly true since 1926 when the Twelfth of July was made a public holiday and over some of the following years the commemorative cycle of parades, now often called 'the marching season' increased. Factored into this is also the nature of policing in Northern Ireland during this period with the RUC being predominantly Protestant. For many Catholics in Ireland the Orange Order is inextricably linked with the sectarian discrimination and policing of 'Unionist rule'. The parades are experienced as a direct extension of that power.

Ritual, 'Tradition', 'Community', and Regulating Parades

The Twelfth of July parades are often described as 'traditional', a claim of legitimacy that the event has a long history and is particularly connected to a group of people. In this sense they could be viewed as a cultural right, 'our culture', closely related to the ethnic identity of unionists in Northern Ireland often termed as 'Protestants'. Consequently, this type of assembly has an emotional resonance well beyond those taking part and crucially any potential restriction on the parade is treated as a potential attack upon the wider group.

As has been evidenced by much historical research since the work on the 'invention of tradition' by Hobsbawm and Ranger, what are commonly termed 'traditions' are usually in a process of adaptation depending upon the context in which they exist.[11] This is clearly the case with the Twelfth of July where the complex set of groups and social relationships involved in the ritual have shifted over time.[12] Indeed, you could argue that the Twelfth parades have remained popular because they have adapted.

At points in the nineteenth century such a procession in Ireland was against the law, yet, in 1926, the processions were granted the status of a public and bank holiday. In the first half of the nineteenth century, parades were predominantly rural, yet by the end of the nineteenth century large parades were organized within the urban working classes. From the 1870s to the 1970s the Orange Order was patronized by the landed and business classes but by the later part of the twentieth century most had left. At points in its history many police officers have been members of the Orange Order, but there is also a long history of parades confronting the police. More recently, displays of paramilitary symbols by the marching bands, mixed in with references to World War I, have added a significant text to the 'traditional' parade.

Anthropological approaches to ritual and identity can provide a useful model for understanding the role played by such assemblies in society.[13] At the core of understanding the role of ritual is the affect it has on both participants and the wider social groups. How does it impact the social relationships involved? Or, to put it another way, how does it impact the individuals and their communities? One way of modelling this is the debate over action versus meaning.[14] Early sociological theory exploring elementary forms of religious life highlights that human beings who participate in rituals experience 'effervescence'.[15] Or to put it another way, the function or the outcome of the event is not the meaning it is the participation. It is the feeling of 'communitas', as Turner puts it, that is so vital in giving cohesion and a sense of belonging.[16] One's identity in the social world is partly driven by participation rather than derived from the meaning of the event. This aspect of participation raises the legitimate question as to whether participants 'mean' what they are doing. Examples in Northern Ireland have included the behaviour of loyalist bands or the singing of IRA songs by people from an Irish nationalist background such as the chanting of 'ooh ah up the RA'.[17] Participation, it can be argued, is about social cohesion and given the complex divisions that I have discussed in the Twelfth of July this provides one answer of why it holds people together. Those participating do not spend much time analysing the contradictions within the events because participation points towards a sense of social cohesion and a broad identity.

In contrast, these events are clearly also texts or narratives with complex, if often contested, meanings. Symbols carrying multiple meanings impacted by the context in which they are used. Thirty years of violence in Northern Ireland (1969–1998) perpetrated by forces of the State, Loyalists, and Republican paramilitary groups leave even the national flags, the Irish Tricolour and the Union (Jack) flag, with a problematic legacy. Most significantly, some symbols carry with them heavy emotional responses linked to people's identities. Flags, commemorative days, anthems, and a range of symbols work because they give a sense of belonging and cohesion to different groups of people. In that sense what we often term a 'community' is constructed around the imagination linked by symbols that are commonly used and experienced, even when people in the group might infer different meanings.[18]

The role of processions such as the Twelfth of July are thus a part of what Pierre Bourdieu described as the labour of representation.[19] They represent a sense of consciousness for a complex set of identities within groups through changes over time imagined as 'tradition'. And the identity politics within the event impact other groups, in this case those with a Catholic identity, thus maintaining the ethnic boundary between the two groups. This is locally understood as the relationship between the 'two communities'.[20]

The word 'community' has a long philosophical history used to describe, in a quite positive way, groups of people that share a form of cohesion.[21] Policies surrounding 'community relations' have been part of the peace-building repertoire in Northern Ireland since the early 1970s. Processions, important in the labour of representation for these communities, have been a central focus for community relations policies. The management of civic space or 'shared space', as it is sometimes termed in Northern Ireland, has been recognized in any number of policies since the Good Friday Agreement was reached in 1998.[22] As such, despite the obvious problem in defining what sort of social group might be designated as a 'community' and recognizing that there might be many groups in a society that might process the traits of a community, the term in Northern Ireland predominantly refers rhetorically to those viewed as ethnically Catholic and ethnically Protestant.

The regulation of these assemblies since the 1998 Agreement has been so controversial that it was kept out of the talks that led to the Agreement. The Public Processions (Northern Ireland) Act 1998 gave legal power to make determinations on parades to the Parades Commission, a quasi-judicial non-departmental public body with independent commissioners picked to represent the 'two communities'. In making determinations, under the Act, the Parades Commission should have, inter alia, with regard to:

> '(b) any disruption to the life of the community which the procession may cause;
> (c) any impact which the procession may have on relationships within the community; . . .'[23]

Given the problem of defining what a 'community' is, and given the way these events are woven into ethnic relations in Northern Ireland, making judgments on 'disruption to the life of the community' raises all sorts of difficulties. The criteria look anodyne and readily applicable but are in practice difficult to interpret.

Conclusion

An anthropological or ethnographic approach to events reveals the level of sociological and political complexity that is being engaged with in the facilitation or regulation of freedom of assembly. Northern Ireland is a deeply divided society in which a range of symbols and rituals play an important role in the labour of representation of the two politically predominant ethno-national groups. We might note that the start of a period of violent conflict in Northern Ireland in 1969, sometimes called 'the Troubles', was precipitated by confrontations over civil rights marchers being blocked from accessing the civic space of towns and cities, setting up a range of confrontations with the RUC and then the British Army. And the end of that period of violence in 1998, after more than 3,500 people had been killed, was likewise precipitated by confrontations over parades, this time over the predominant use of public spaces by the Orange Order and other loyal order organizations in a society with residential ethnic boundaries. The role of parades and protests in such a divided society asks the most acute questions about the facilitation of freedom of assembly.

The ethnographic account of the Twelfth of July parade in Belfast reveals an event that is linked to much broader social relationships, part of the labour of representation, or validation, of the Protestant community, a British ethno-national identity that in Northern Ireland is oppositional to the identity of Catholics. It is difficult to view the parade as an individual event as it exists in a broader social context of parades and the access to public space in a society with significant residential, territorial divisions. And the parade also shows significant internal diversity whilst providing a level of 'communitas' or social cohesion to the social group. In this context, regulation of such events by the Parades Commission and the Police Service of Northern Ireland is a difficult job. Indeed, twenty-five years since it began its role in regulating processions in Northern Ireland, it remains the policy of the Grand Orange Lodge of Ireland not to recognize the legitimacy of the Parades Commission.

Notes

1. Dominic Bryan, T. G. Fraser, and Seamus Dunn, *Political Rituals: Loyalist Parades in Portadown* (Coleraine: Centre for the Study of Conflict, 1995).
2. Public Processions (Northern Ireland) Act 1998 §§ 6(6)b and 6(6)c.
3. Neil Jarman, *Material Conflicts: Parades and Visual Displays in Northern Ireland* (Oxford: Berg, 1997); Dominic Bryan, *Orange Parades: The Politics of Ritual Tradition and Control* (London: Pluto Press, 2000).
4. Jarman, *Material Conflict*, 46–61; Bryan, *Orange Parades*, 44–59.

5. Jarman, *Material Conflict*, 46–61; Bryan, *Orange Parades*, 44–59.
6. In 2019–2020 there were 3,793 processions of which the Parades Commission defined 2,312 as ' Protestant/Unionist/Loyalist', 99 as 'Catholic/Republican/Nationalist', and 1,382 as 'other'. Northern Ireland Parades Commission Annual Report, March 2020. https://www.paradescommission.org/Publications.aspx.
7. Neil Jarman, *Displaying Faith: Orange, Green and Trade Union Banners* (Belfast: Institute of Irish Studies, 1999).
8. Gordon Ramsey, *Music, Emotion and Identity in Ulster Marching Bands; Flutes, Drums and Loyal Sons* (London: Peter Lang, 2011).
9. Ibid.
10. Bryan, *Orange Parades*, 142
11. Eric Hobsbawm and Terrence Ranger, eds., *The Invention of Tradition* (Cambridge: Cambridge University Press, 1983).
12. Bryan, *Orange Parades.*
13. For a classic statement of the role of ritual in politics and identity, see David Kertzer, *Ritual, Politics and Power* (New Haven, CT: Yale University Press, 1988).
14. Caroline Humphrey and James Laidlaw, *The Archetypal Actions of Ritual: A Theory of Ritual Illustrated by the Jain Rite of Worship* (Oxford: Oxford University Press, 1994).
15. Emile Durkheim, *The Elementary Forms of Religious Life* (London: Allen and Unwin, 1915).
16. Victor Turner, *The Ritual Process: Structure and Anti-Structure* (Chicago: Aldine, 1969).
17. Ivan Little 'Ooh, ah, up the "Ra" is sung almost like a new national anthem across Ireland . . . songs of the saddos won't be easily binned', *Belfast Telegraph* 16 October 2022, https://www.belfasttelegraph.co.uk/opinion/comment/ooh-ah-up-the-ra-is-sung-almost-like-a-new-national-anthem-across-ireland-songs-of-the-saddos-wont-be-easily-binned/42069613.html.
18. Anthony Cohen, *The Symbolic Construction of Community* (London: Tavistock, 1985).
19. Pierre Bourdieu, *Language and Symbolic Power* (Cambridge: Cambridge University Press), 130.
20. Dominic Bryan, 'The Politics of Community', *Critical Review of International Social and Political Philosophy* 9, no. 4 (2006): 603–617.
21. Gerard Delanty, *Community* (London: Routledge, 2003).
22. Dominic Bryan, Sean Connolly, with John Nagle, *Civic Identity and Public Space: Belfast since 1780* (Manchester, UK: Manchester University Press, 2019), 180–227.
23. Public Processions (Northern Ireland) Act 1998 §§ 6(6)b and 6(6)c.

Further Reading

Blake, Jonathan. *Contentious Rituals: Parading the Nation in Northern Ireland.* Oxford: Oxford University Press, 2019.

Bryan, Dominic. '"Drumcree" and "The Right to March": Orangeism, Ritual and Politics in Northern Ireland'. In *The Irish Parading Tradition: Follow the Drum*, ed. T. G. Fraser, 119–207. London: Palgrave Macmillan, 2000. https://doi.org/10.1057/9780333993859_13.

Bryan, Dominic. 'Drumcree: Marching Towards Peace in Northern Ireland?' In *Peace at Last: The Impact of the Good Friday Agreement on Northern Ireland*, ed. Jörg Neuheiser and Stefan Wolff, 94–110. Oxford: Berghahn Books, 2003.

Bryan, Dominic. *Orange Parades: The Politics of Ritual Tradition and Control.* London: Pluto Press, 2000.
Hamilton, Michael, and Dominic Bryan. 'Deepening Democracy—Dispute System Design and the Mediation of Contested Parades in Northern Ireland'. *Ohio State Journal on Dispute Resolution* 22, no. 1 (2006): 133–187.
Jarman, Neil. *Material Conflicts: Parades and Visual Displays in Northern Ireland.* Oxford: Berg, 1997.
Jarman, Neil. 'Regulating Parades and Managing Public Order: Parade Disputes and the Peace Process 1995–1998'. *Fordham International Law Journal* 22, no. 4 (1999): 1415–1439.
Jarman, Neil, and Dominic Bryan. *Parade and Protest: A Discussion of Parading Disputes in Northern Ireland.* Coleraine: Centre for the Study of Conflict, 1996.
Ryder, Chris. *Drumcree: Orange Orders Last Stand.* London: A&C Black, 2002.

CHAPTER 22

LOOKING BACK AT THE SKOKIE CASE

A Personal Reflection

DAVID GOLDBERGER

INTRODUCTION

I am the Jewish lawyer who represented a group of self-styled Nazis in the controversial Skokie case which arose during the late 1970s. This chapter describes that case, remembered today because it involved the efforts Nazis took to hold a lawful demonstration in Skokie, Illinois, the home of an estimated thirty thousand Jews, including seven thousand Holocaust survivors and their families.[1] The case is a useful example because it exposes the tensions generated when a lawful but extremely controversial demonstration was faced with government-imposed delays and litigation that ultimately enabled the planning of a large potentially violent counter-demonstration.

THE SKOKIE CASE REALLY STARTED IN A CHICAGO PARK

'The Skokie case' was not a single case. Instead, it involved several events and court cases starting in Chicago, shifting to Skokie, a Chicago suburb, then later back to Chicago. However, for purposes of simplicity I will refer to this aggregate of events and cases as the Skokie case.

The case arose from the activities of Frank Collin, the leader of the National Socialist Party of America (NSPA), a neo-Nazi group that had splintered off from the American Nazi Party, and in the early 1970s, under Collin's leadership, established itself in a small storefront building, dubbed Rockwell Hall, in Marquette Park, a southwest-side Chicago neighbourhood.[2] On one wall of the NSPA building, in huge letters, were the words 'Nigger Beware'. As the Skokie case proceeded, there were allegations that Collin's father was a Holocaust survivor. Collin denied this.

The NSPA received financial and political support from some White residents who lived in the Marquette Park neighbourhood and were anxious about the growing possibility that African Americans from an adjacent neighbourhood would move into the Marquette Park neighbourhood. To reach potential supporters, the NSPA, wearing Nazi-style, storm trooper uniforms, held demonstrations in the neighbourhood's local park, also named Marquette Park. Like all other Chicago public parks, it was operated by the Chicago Park District.

After the NSPA began their demonstrations in the park, the Park District began to search for ways to stop them. First, the Park District informed Collin that the NSPA could no longer use Marquette Park because of a new policy banning public assemblies in all Chicago parks except for four parks it had designated as public forums. All were distant from the Marquette Park neighbourhood, so the policy made it impossible for the NSPA to reach its target audience.

In response, Collin sought the assistance of the Illinois American Civil Liberties Union (ACLU) headquartered in downtown Chicago, where I served as the legal director. Collin knew that the ACLU's policy was to defend the First Amendment rights of all persons no matter their identity or viewpoint. He also knew that the New York ACLU had previously represented Nazis seeking to hold demonstrations in New York City parks.[3]

Collin's request for representation was simple and straightforward. He wanted to hold demonstrations in the Chicago Park District's Marquette Park (a quintessential public forum) and the Park District's new ban on assemblies prevented this. We agreed to take the case on the ground that it raised the basic First Amendment right of speakers to have access to their audience.[4]

The terms of our representation were clear. Collin had to agree to fully disclose all information relevant to our representation; he had to be completely honest with counsel about relevant activities by him or the NSPA; and he had to accept the fact that I, a Jew, would be representing him and NSPA in court. In addition, he had to agree to let me and any other ACLU lawyers on the case express our disagreement with Collin's views and his group's message as long we made clear that we were representing them because their First Amendment rights were being violated. Finally, Collin had to agree that he and his group would follow any appropriate legal advice we gave him. In return, it was understood that neither I nor any other ACLU representative would make insulting statements directed at the NSPA or its members.

A short time later, with the help of long-time ACLU volunteer attorney Barbara O'Toole, I filed suit in Chicago's federal district court challenging the constitutionality of the policy denying the NSPA access to Marquette Park.[5] The Park District fought back aggressively, appealed an initial ruling against it, and delayed at every available opportunity. As a result, it took nearly two years to get a final court decision invalidating the ban.[6] Following the final court decision, the Park District immediately imposed a new requirement that anyone seeking a permit to hold an assembly in a Chicago park must obtain a $300,000 liability insurance policy. Predictably, no insurance company would provide insurance coverage for a Nazi demonstration.

Again, Collin and the NSPA asked for the ACLU's legal assistance. Because it was clear that the requirement would ban the NSPA from its parks, we again agreed to represent Collin and the NSPA. We feared that if the Park District insurance requirement stood, insurance requirements would quickly spread to park districts and public forums elsewhere. Such requirements were particularly dangerous to protest groups without assets because they would be unable to afford the insurance premiums and would need lawyers or other resources to challenge them.

We then filed suit challenging the insurance requirement. The federal judge hearing the case found the insurance requirement imposed an impermissible burden on speech. However, the Chicago Park District appealed, causing an additional delay. In the meantime, Collin's quest for access to the Marquette Park public forum and other Chicago parks came to a standstill that lasted for a further two years.

Up to this point, the NSPA's activities had focused on access to Marquette Park. So outside of sporadic news coverage, Collin and the NSPA were paid little attention outside of the Marquette Park area. Anxious to find a location for a NSPA demonstration, Collin probed the suburbs outside of Chicago to find a site where there was no ban on NSPA demonstrations—probes that would have been unlikely if the NSPA had access to Marquette Park.

The Nazis Choose Skokie and Skokie Responds

In October 1976, Collin sent letters to park districts located in the north suburbs of Chicago, including the Skokie Park District requesting a permit for an assembly.[7] The letters were typed on NSPA stationery that had a large swastika across the top.[8] All the park districts except Skokie ignored Collin's letters. The Skokie Park District responded with a letter stating that a permit would not be granted unless a $350,000 insurance bond was posted. Although the Skokie Park District had no insurance requirement at the time, it hastily enacted one.[9]

Collin then sent a letter to the Skokie chief of police announcing that the NSPA would hold a demonstration on the public sidewalk in front of the village hall for thirty minutes on 1 May 1977. The letter said that the demonstration was to protest the Skokie Park District's imposition of an insurance requirement instead of granting the NSPA a permit. It also said there would be about twenty-five NSPA demonstrators in Nazi-style uniforms carrying signs saying, 'White Free Speech' and 'Free Speech for White Americans'. There would be no speeches. At the time, Skokie had no regulations governing demonstrations held on village sidewalks.

Upon learning of NSPA plans to demonstrate in front of the village hall, Skokie officials determined that, in all likelihood, Collin's plans were protected by the First Amendment.[10] At the suggestion of the Anti-Defamation League, a national Jewish organization fighting anti-Semitism, village officials initially pursued a 'quarantine policy', strongly urging village residents to stay home and ignore the demonstration, thus depriving the NSPA of the publicity it sought.[11]

However, as word of the proposed quarantine circulated, Skokie's Holocaust survivors and other Jewish community leaders pushed back. For them, ignoring the Nazi demonstration was completely out of the question. Soon swamped by opponents of the quarantine policy, Skokie officials reversed course and decided to seek an injunction that would prevent the Nazis from coming.[12]

Skokie filed its injunction suit in state court on 27 April 1977. This lawsuit not only triggered additional delays of the NSPA demonstration but also drew national attention to the demonstration that triggered the mobilization of a potentially violent counter-demonstration much larger than the proposed NSPA demonstration itself.

After being served with Skokie's lawsuit, Collin called my office and requested ACLU representation. Illinois ACLU Executive Director David Hamlin, general counsel Edwin Rothschild, and I agreed that the ACLU should represent the NSPA because Skokie's case raised classic First Amendment issues—the NSPA neither planned nor advocated anything violent or unlawful. However, Rothschild warned me that he thought the case would be far more controversial than I anticipated. His warning proved to be prescient.

Next, I made calls to several ACLU volunteer attorneys. The response to each of my calls was the same. 'I would like to help this time, but, frankly, this case is too hot to handle, and would be too offensive to my firm's private clients. Call me back when you have another case'. Therefore, I asked Barbara O'Toole to be my co-counsel. While the two of us felt we had had our fill of representing Collin and the NSPA in the Chicago Park District cases, we felt that, if they went unrepresented, the case could result in a potentially disastrous First Amendment legal precedent.

The Court Hearing and the Injunction against the Nazi Assembly

From the ACLU's perspective, Skokie's legal effort to obtain an injunction against the proposed NSPA demonstration was, at best, a longshot. Collin had intuitively understood that if demonstrators silently carried signs alleging denials of freedom of speech for a short time, in this case thirty minutes, and they stayed on the public sidewalks, it would be difficult, if not impossible, for Skokie to stop them without violating the First Amendment.

The injunction hearing began the morning after the NSPA was served. I appeared along with Barbara O'Toole to represent Collin and the NSPA. Executive Director David

Hamlin, who was not a lawyer, was present in the courtroom to handle the press. The case was heard by Chicago Judge Joseph Wosik.

At the pretrial conference, it was clear that Skokie's attorneys had an uphill battle. They had to overcome the well-established First Amendment doctrine prohibiting courts from entering an injunction order banning speakers from speaking. Such an order, known in American law as a prior restraint, was presumed to be unconstitutional.[13]

Once the hearing started, Skokie strenuously argued that the NSPA's display of the swastika and their Nazi-style uniforms were hate speech and therefore unprotected speech under the 'fighting words' doctrine. I responded that the fighting words doctrine only applied to a personal, face-to-face, personal insult likely to generate reflexive physical retaliation and was inapplicable to the display of a swastika at a public demonstration.[14] Those who were offended by the Nazi regalia did not need to watch the demonstration.

Skokie also argued that the NSPA's uniforms, symbols though political in nature, were offensive hate speech that was unprotected by the First Amendment. In response, I pointed to Supreme Court decisions that protected offensive, non threatening, political statements as well as the wearing of a military-style uniform to make a political statement.[15]

Finally, Skokie argued that NSPA's assembly would provoke violence. However, it submitted minimal evidence to support this argument. Skokie evidence showed that, if there were to be violence, it would come from hostile counter-demonstrators. Indeed, it was clear that the NSPA plans were for a peaceful assembly and contained no indication that the NSPA intended any violence. Moreover, Skokie submitted no evidence that police would have difficulty maintaining order.[16] Many months later, Skokie's lead attorney told me that Skokie did not have Skokie's police chief testify about possible uncontrollable violence because the village did not want him publicly stating that they were incapable of successfully managing the assembly were it to occur.

Soon after the hearing started, it became clear that Judge Wosik felt strong personal sympathy towards Skokie's case and tremendous antipathy towards the NSPA; his comments made clear that he was giving the NSPA's First Amendment defence little heed. This was underscored when, during the morning proceedings, we learned that Judge Wosik had briefly left the bench to take a telephone call from the county sheriff. (He made no effort to hide it.) Because the sheriff had law enforcement authority in Skokie, everyone in the courtroom felt that the call was probably about the case. However, after the case was over, Harvey Schwartz, Skokie's lawyer, opined that the call probably did not actually impact the judge's final ruling because he had obviously been sympathetic to Skokie's case anyway.[17]

At the end of the hearing that day, the judge entered an injunction barring the NSPA from appearing in Skokie on the next Sunday, the day Collin had scheduled for the demonstration. It specifically prohibited 'Marching, walking or parading in the uniform of the National Socialist Party of America . . . [or] otherwise displaying the swastika on or off their person; Distributing pamphlets or displaying any materials which incite or promote hatred against persons of Jewish faith or ancestry or hatred against persons of any faith or ancestry, race or religion'.[18]

After the hearing, Barbara O'Toole and I returned to our nearby ACLU office with David Hamlin where we found our telephones jammed with press inquiries and calls from members of the public angry that the ACLU was providing counsel to the Nazis. Hamlin and I promptly began our months-long effort to explain the freedom of speech and assembly principles at stake to the press and public alike. No matter how many times we repeated the fact that the NSPA demonstration was to be an assembly in front of the village hall, we could not dispel the erroneous rumour constantly spread by the media that the Nazi demonstration was really a march through Skokie—a rumour that reinforced existing anger and helped attract additional hostile counter-demonstrators. By the end of the day, Barbara O'Toole and I initiated an expedited appeal. Unfortunately, because of stalling by the state courts, it would not be ruled on for months. Meanwhile, the day after the original injunction, Collin announced to the press that he would hold a demonstration in front of Skokie's village hall the following day, a day not explicitly covered by the terms of the injunction. Skokie responded by having an available local judge broaden the injunction to completely ban all NSPA attempts to demonstrate in Skokie. (I was not told about this attempt until after Skokie police had turned back the NSPA pursuant to the broadened injunction.)

The delay created by the injunction, and the slow-moving appellate process that followed, led to intense and constant media coverage. It also provided unanticipated publicity for the NSPA and its views. However, while the publicity was a boon to the NSPA, it never ceased its effort to regain access to Marquette Park, where everything had started.

The appellate process was so slow that at one point the US Supreme Court entered an order requiring the Illinois courts to expedite determination of the validity of the injunction or to immediately allow the Nazi demonstration to go forward.[19] Initially, I hoped the prestige of a Supreme Court ruling would help the public understand that the ACLU was defending important First Amendment issues applicable to everyone, even though Nazis were involved. Instead, all the ruling did was to focus more public attention on the case, increase antagonism towards the Nazis and the ACLU, and focus anger on me personally as lead attorney and because I was a Jew.

New Efforts to Block the Nazis and Final Court Responses

A few days after the injunction was issued, Skokie's city council added to the growing delay by enacting three new ordinances designed to block the Nazis. They were soon followed by the introduction of legislation in the Illinois legislature directed at the NSPA. Skokie's new ordinances made any Nazi-styled demonstration illegal anywhere in

Skokie. The legislation introduced in the legislature sought to make the 'public display of racial hatred' a criminal offence. If passed, this bill would provide a basis for prosecuting Nazis and other racists for holding any demonstrations under a statewide law.

The passage of the new ordinances and the proposed statewide legislation signaled that the battle to prevent the neo-Nazis from coming to Skokie had extended far beyond the original injunction case. After discussions within the Illinois ACLU, a decision was made to represent the NSPA against all the obstacles being thrown in the path of the Skokie demonstration. The organization felt that the new ordinances, along with two additional private lawsuits filed by Holocaust survivors and a north suburb-area resident, were inseparable parts of the original case. So, we filed suit in federal district court challenging Skokie's new ordinances and filed appearances in the two private lawsuits.

Because the new cases required additional legal resources, I asked several ACLU volunteer attorneys from top Chicago law firms to help. The attorneys agreed but, because the Skokie case was so controversial, these attorneys worked on the cases behind the scenes. To protect their firms against any retaliatory loss of business, the attorneys promised their law firms that they would never appear in court and that their names would not be on any legal documents.

Finally, in January 1977, nine months after Collin announced the Nazi plan to go to Skokie, the Illinois Supreme Court ruled that Skokie's injunction violated the First Amendment, and simultaneously dismissed the privately initiated state court cases for the same reason.[20] A month later the federal district court judge in the case challenging Skokie's ordinances ruled that all the ordinances, including the $350,000 insurance requirement, violated the NSPA's right to freedom of assembly and freedom of speech. The decision against the ordinances was upheld by a federal appellate court, and Skokie's request for a stay in the US Supreme Court was denied.[21]

After these court rulings, all the legal obstacles directly impeding the NSPA demonstration in Skokie were gone. The only remaining legal obstacle was the proposed legislation pending in the Illinois legislature.

Plans for a Potentially Violent Counter-demonstration

While the Skokie litigation worked its way through the courts, planning for hostile counter-demonstrations had continued locally and nationally. Even in the absence of the internet, constant, widespread news coverage spurred planning by counter-demonstrators. The Jewish Defense League and a radical left-wing group publicly advocated violent action against the NSPA demonstration. The Jewish Defense League held a sit-in at the New York ACLU office. When some anti-Nazi protesters engaged in a sit-in at my Chicago ACLU office, one swung a baseball bat near some ACLU staff members to send a message of animosity. (The office staff was careful to close my office door so the protesters could not see I was there.) More temperate supporters of Skokie's Jewish community also planned a large counter-demonstration, but at a sufficient distance from the Nazi demonstration to avoid direct contact with it.

In the meantime, I was extremely worried about the policing problems faced by the Skokie police. It was obvious that many police officers would be needed to keep the Nazis separate from counter-demonstrators and maintain order. Skokie's relatively small police department, like most suburban police departments, had little experience with large numbers of hostile counter-demonstrators. My concern was underscored when I was told by a Chicago police commander familiar with the situation that Skokie planned to patch together contingents of equally inexperienced officers from other suburban police departments, along with some county sheriff's deputies and Illinois state police officers.

Ironically, Skokie's rejection of the original plan to 'quarantine' the Nazi demonstration had generated the opposite of its intended effect. Rather than protecting Skokie from the Nazis, the injunction, the court cases, the ordinances, and the possibility of state legislation created an extended delay that enabled potentially violent counter-demonstrators to plan and to expand their numbers. All this in the face of law enforcement resources that appeared to be unlikely to manage possible violence.

Animosity Grows towards the ACLU and towards Me

The slow pace of litigation enabled word about the case and accompanying anger to spread worldwide. Thousands of angry telephone calls and letters poured into ACLU offices all over the country, particularly into the Illinois ACLU office and ACLU's national office in New York. Some were threatening, others merely angry. Many ACLU members resigned. According to National ACLU board member Philippa Strum, 'The ACLU lost thirty thousand members—15 per cent of those who had belonged. The income that disappeared with them amounted to some $500,000 a year'.[22]

In response to the outpouring of anger, both Illinois ACLU Executive Director Hamlin and I accepted invitations to give speeches throughout the Chicago area to explain ACLU's civil liberties principles and its reasons for taking the case. Both of us received threatening phone calls at home. Both of us faced threats that required special security at some of our speaking events. At two of my speaking engagements, some hostile members of the audience aggressively approached the lectern where I was speaking and had to be forcibly escorted out by security. Members of the ACLU national staff and affiliate staffs around the country met with similar hostility.[23]

Many personal attacks focused on the fact that I was a Jew. At one point, a rabbi at my family's long-time congregation gave a sermon excoriating me personally for my work on the Skokie case. I knew how painful the case was for the entire Jewish community, especially Skokie's survivor community, so the distressing personal attacks were no surprise. Fortunately, my family was steadfast in its support.

The Unexpected Success of Mediation

On 26 May 1978, following its losses in court, Skokie finally issued a permit for an NSPA demonstration in front of the village hall, to be held on 25 June. The grant of the permit focused attention on the risk of potential violence.

Meanwhile, Collin, apparently aware that the anti-Nazi bill working its way through the Illinois legislature could again block his demonstration, issued a press release saying that he would be willing to move the Skokie demonstration under the following circumstances: (1) if the Chicago Park District would drop its insurance requirement and allow the NSPA to have a demonstration in Marquette Park, (2) if they could hold an assembly as a suitable site in downtown Chicago on 25 June as an alternative to the Skokie demonstration, and (3) if the Illinois General Assembly's legislative efforts to block his demonstration were dropped.[24] None of us at the ACLU were aware of this release.

However, unknown to us at the ACLU, Skokie had reached out to the US Department of Justice Community Relations Service (CRS), which offered mediation services in serious community disputes. Skokie's request was referred to two skilled Department of Justice mediators Richard Salem and Werner Patterson.[25]

The CRS mediators then telephoned me to request a meeting with Collin. Two meetings followed. The first was with Hamlin and me; Collin was not present. It set the ground rules for the meeting with Collin that was to follow: (1) the CRS mediators would make no misrepresentations and would not try to pressure Collin, (2) the US Justice Department would not try to interfere with the ongoing litigation, and (3) there would be no public disclosure of the matters discussed unless Collin agreed.

The meeting with Collin followed a short time later, a little more than three weeks prior to the scheduled demonstration in Skokie. At that meeting Collin reiterated the points made in his press release. He also stated that he and his followers did not want violence, and, if it occurred, it would be at the hands of the counter-demonstrators. He repeated that he was going to Skokie as a matter of principle to establish the NSPA's First Amendment rights. But he made clear that he remained anxious to get back access to his Marquette Park audience.

Upon hearing this, I knew that there was a path to a settlement. I knew that the large, downtown Federal Plaza near the downtown federal courthouse was an ideal public forum. Most important, it was often used for political demonstrations, and did not have a permit or notice requirement. All Collin had to do was to show up there with his group. No one had the legal authority to stop them. I also knew that while the case challenging the Chicago Park District insurance requirement was stalled, the judge was finally considering an order that would grant the NSPA access to Marquette Park's public forum. I believed that if pressed he might expedite his ruling. However, I knew of no way to stop the proposed legislation in the state legislature. The mediators said that they would contact sponsors of the legislation to see what could be done.

A short time after the meeting, the CRS mediators confirmed that there would be no obstacle to NSPA access to the Federal Plaza on 25 June. I again requested that the judge considering the validity of the Chicago Park District insurance requirement promptly issue an order requiring the Park District to grant NSPA access to Marquette Park. Upon learning of prospect of settling the Skokie case, he issued an order compelling the Park District to issue permit for the NSPA to hold a demonstration in Marquette Park on 9 July. Then, the CRS and Skokie officials contacted the sponsors of the proposed anti-NSPA law, and it quietly died in committee. Thus, all three of Collin's requirements having been met, he announced the Skokie demonstration was moved to the Federal Plaza in downtown Chicago where it was to be held on 24 June.

The agreement moving the Nazi demonstration from Skokie to downtown Chicago had the immediate impact of scaling down the risk of violence. The drama of a confrontation between the NSPA and Skokie's Holocaust survivors on their home turf was gone. However, when the demonstration moved to Chicago's downtown, the potentially violent counter-demonstrators moved with it. But the worrisome patchwork of police departments to deal with the Skokie demonstration was replaced by the well-resourced, experienced Chicago Police Department which had jurisdiction over demonstrations at the Federal Plaza.

As agreed, the NSPA demonstration was held late in the afternoon of 25 June 1977, on the Federal Plaza and was a far cry from what would have occurred in Skokie. Several hundred Chicago riot helmeted police officers formed a well-coordinated cordon around two dozen Nazi demonstrators to keep them separated from several thousand angry counter-demonstrators.[26] Several hundred more police were present, and more were held in reserve in case of trouble. Collin and his NSPA followers gave brief statements, but drowned out by the counter-demonstrators, they left after fifteen minutes. Some demonstrators threw rocks and bottles, and a limited number of counter-demonstrators were arrested.[27]

Approximately two weeks later, following their demonstration on the Federal Plaza and armed with a court order voiding the Chicago Park District insurance requirement, Collin and the NSPA finally held their long-sought demonstration in the Marquette Park forum near their headquarters on 9 July. It was attended by a several hundred local area residents and a group of angry counter-demonstrators. Like the demonstration on the downtown Federal Plaza, the Chicago police formed a cordon around the NSPA to keep the demonstrators physically separate from the hostile counter-demonstrators. There was scuffling by counter-demonstrators that led to seventy-two arrests, but the Chicago police maintained order overall.[28]

Aftermath

About a year later, the NSPA ejected Collin from the party saying he was 'burned out'. However, the real reason was that he had been charged with engaging in unlawful sexual activities with male minors at the party headquarters. He was later convicted and served time in jail.[29]

In 1981, in response to their confrontation with Collin and his Nazi-style group, Skokie's Jewish community opened a storefront Holocaust memorial in downtown Skokie. In 2009, the storefront memorial was replaced by the Illinois Holocaust Museum and Education Center also located in Skokie. It is now one of the largest Holocaust memorial museums in the world.

Conclusion

There are useful lessons to be learned from the Skokie case. Amongst them are that delays caused by government attempts to ban or forestall a controversial public assembly increases risks and scope of planned violence from counter-demonstrators. Such delays, whether by regulatory devices or by litigation, inevitably draw press attention which, in turn, facilitates planning and organizing of potentially violent counter-demonstrations. They also can trigger an incredibly unpredictable and uncontrollable sequence of events. For example, no one would have predicted obstacles to assemblies in a small park on the south side of Chicago would have led to the Skokie case. On the one hand, delay can create space for mediation and negotiation, but, on the other hand, they increase risks of planned violence by counter-demonstrators. Another important lesson is that skilled, non-directive mediation by outsiders, without attempts to coerce a particular outcome can be invaluable. It can provide a safe space, free from press scrutiny, where all adversaries can explore alternatives that satisfy their interests. Fortunately, in the Skokie case, the space created by the delays enabled such mediation avoiding what may have been serious bloodshed. Perhaps in other cases involving government efforts at bans and delays enabling large, potentially violent counter-demonstrations, things will not turn out so well.

Acknowledgements

The events described here occurred nearly fifty years ago, memories about some of them have faded with time. I therefore owe a debt of gratitude to Philippa Strum's *When the Nazis Came to Skokie*, a detailed history of the Skokie case which helped fill gaps in my recollection. I also want to thank Neil Komesar, Jennifer Jackson, Benjamin Goldberger, and my wife Abbie Harding, who made invaluable editing suggestions.

Notes

1. Philippa Strum, *When the Nazis Came to Skokie: Freedom for Speech We Hate* (Lawrence: University Press of Kansas, 1999), 7.
2. Ibid., 5, 7.
3. See *Rockwell v Morris*, 12 A.D.2d 272 (1961).
4. *Kovacs v Cooper*, 366 U.S. 77, 87 (1949).
5. For purposes of clarity and to avoid undue detail, descriptions of the various legal proceedings have been shortened or omitted.
6. *Collin v Chicago Park Dist.*, 460 F.2d 746 (7th Cir. 1972), *reh'g denied,* 18 May 1972, and 19 June 1972.
7. Strum, *When the Nazis Came to Skokie*, 15–16.
8. Ibid., 16.
9. Ibid.
10. Ibid., 17.
11. Ibid.
12. Ibid., 19–21.
13. See *New York Times v United States*, 403 U.S. 713, 714 (1971).
14. *Chaplinsky v New Hampshire*, 315 U.S. 368 (1942).
15. See *Cohen v California*, 403 U.S. 15 (1971), and *Schacht v United States*, 398 U.S. 58 (1970).
16. *Feiner v New York*, 340 U.S. 315 (1951).
17. Strum, *When the Nazis Came to Skokie*, 55.
18. Ibid., 56.
19. *Nat'l Socialist Party of Am. v Skokie*, 432 U.S. 43 (1971).
20. *Skokie v Nat'l Socialist Party of Am.*, 373 N.E.2d 21 (1978).
21. *Collin v Smith*, 477 F. Supp. 676 (N.D. Ill. 1978), *aff'd*, 578 F.2d 1197 (7th Cir. 1978), *stay denied*, *Smith v Collin*, 436 U.S. 953 (1978).
22. Strum, *When the Nazis Came to Skokie*, 82–87 ($500,000 in 1978 is the equivalent of approximately $2.1 million in 2024 dollars).
23. Ibid., 66, 87.
24. Ibid., 136.
25. See Richard A. Salem, 'Mediating Political and Social Conflicts: The Skokie-Nazi Dispute', *Sociological Practice* 10, no. 1 (1992).
26. Interview of CRS mediator Werner Patterson (12 October 2022).
27. See Strum, *When the Nazis Came to Skokie*, 143.
28. *New York Times*, 10 July 1978, A14.
29. Strum, *When the Nazis Came to Skokie*, 144.

Further Reading

Hamlin, David. *The Nazi-Skokie Conflict: A Civil Liberties Battle*. Boston: Beacon Press, 1981.

Neier, Aryeh. *Defending My Enemy: American Nazis, the Skokie Case, and the Risks of Freedom*. New York: E.P. Dutton, 1979.

Salem, Richard A. 'Mediating Political and Social Conflicts: The Skokie-Nazi Dispute'. *Sociological Practice* 10, no. 1 (1992): 151–163.

Strum, Philippa. *When the Nazis Came to Skokie: Freedom for Speech We Hate*. Lawrence: University Press of Kansas, 1999.

CHAPTER 23

ESCRACHES

Assemblies and Political Memory in Post-Dictatorial Argentina

SUSANA KAISER

INTRODUCTION

ESCRACHES are a communication strategy to challenge impunity and demand justice developed by H.I.J.O.S. (Daughters and Sons for Identity and Justice against Forgetting and Silence), an organization formed by daughters and sons of disappeared and assassinated people, former prisoners, and exiles during the last Argentine dictatorship (1976–1983).[1] The word *escrachar* is an Argentine slang term meaning 'to uncover'. For H.I.J.O.S., *escrachar* is 'to reveal, to make public the face of a person that wants to go unnoticed'. *Escraches* were campaigns of public condemnation through demonstrations that aimed to expose the identities of hundreds of torturers and assassins benefitting from amnesty laws of the 1980s. Protesters invade their neighbourhoods chanting 'Alert, alert, alert neighbours! there's an assassin living next door.' They inform the community about the atrocities the particular individual committed, handing out flyers with the name, address, and photo of the person being *escrachado*, and information about the human rights violations in which they were implicated. The demonstrations end outside the torturers' homes with a brief 'ceremony' of speeches, street theatre, music, and the 'marking' of the torturers' homes by painting slogans on sidewalks and walls.

Being from Buenos Aires, I observed first-hand what unfolded during seven years of state terrorism that left a legacy of an estimated 30,000 'disappeared', including an estimated five hundred children seized as spoils of war. The environment of terror is forever engraved in my memories. The dawn of civilian rule in 1983 was a moment of great expectation. A truth commission investigated disappearances and, in 1985, the military juntas were put on trial. Unfortunately, different steps in the legal formalization of impunity followed these promising beginnings: limited investigations, amnesty laws, and pardons to the few criminals who ended up in prison.[2]

I first researched *escraches* in 1998 and analysed how they contested the legitimization of impunity and constituted a new struggle over memory.[3] I argued that *escraches* presented a new and dynamic twist in the public challenge to political amnesia. Their way of bringing back the past into the public sphere compelled society to face the failure to administer justice and to define its policy towards human rights violations and the struggles for accountability. In what follows, I revisit what I researched twenty years ago guided by a few questions: What was the goal of *escraches* when they emerged? How did peaceful assembly help to achieve their goals? What was their perceived impact on society? What is the significance of the *escraches* as we look back at almost thirty years of H.I.J.O.S.'s activism?

About H.I.J.O.S.

H.I.J.O.S. was created in 1995. During commemorations for disappeared people, some of their daughters and sons, most of them in their early twenties, met for the first time and decided to gather at a countryside campground. This meeting was the space where the group was born. It multiplied rapidly, with regional chapters forming throughout Argentina and beyond among the exiled diaspora. Membership fluctuated over the years, with members joining and leaving. Initially, they were all children of those directly affected by state terrorism—disappeared or assassinated people, ex-prisoners, exiles. Eventually, the organization opened to members who are not biological descendants of such victims.[4] They had different experiences of their parents' disappearance or the repression they suffered. Several had grown up in activist homes and/or were close to the Madres de Plaza de Mayo, the organization of mothers of disappeared people, and the Abuelas de Plaza de Mayo—Madres whose disappeared daughters/daughters-in-law were pregnant, created to search for the disappeared babies. H.I.J.O.S. is an heterogenous group, united by the common goal of challenging impunity and achieving justice. Tensions, as well as political, ideological, and class differences, coexist.

As political heirs of the Madres and Abuelas, H.I.J.O.S. fashioned a new form of protest based on peaceful assembly and a powerful presence in public spaces. The Madres had been the first in taking to the streets in 1977 to denounce state terrorism, to inform society that their children were vanishing, and to demand their reappearance. By turning motherhood into a public activity, they had reset the boundaries of politics and political spaces and reshaped the style and scope of human rights activism. The Madres created a particular style aimed at shocking, disrupting, and galvanizing a paralysed society. Theirs was an assertive conquering of urban territories through marches, mobilizations, and performances, aided by their use of symbols and symbolic spaces. The Madres literally staged performances where witnesses could observe them. If authorities asked one Madre for her ID, other Madres would hand over theirs; if one

Madre was taken to the police station, dozens of them declared themselves jailed. They brought the disappeared to the streets, with enlarged photos and life-size silhouettes. For a Coup's anniversary, the Madres and their children marched together; Madres and cardboard silhouettes holding arms, each one actually filling a physical space in the square. While legislators were discussing impunity laws, they installed replicas of cells where ex-prisoners wearing hoods were chained to each other. The streets facing the Congress became the stage for a performance reminding of the atrocities that thousands had suffered. They defined a style that inspired other activists.

When H.I.J.O.S. emerged, the crimes of state terrorism were well known. Their goal was to expose the identities of torturers and assassins benefitting from impunity laws and eliminate the access to public and societal spaces that they had gained. As shall be shown, H.I.J.O.S. followed the Madres' path and adopted theatrical and performative styles.

Escraches in the Late 1990s

H.I.J.O.S. developed its campaigns within a political and cultural environment of legalized impunity.[5] Hundreds of *represores/genocidas* (generic terms for torturers, assassins, 'disappearers' of people, perpetrators of genocide, and their accomplices) were free to roam public places, invited as guests on television talk shows, elected to office as 'democratic' politicians, and were recognized as kind parents of children whom they had appropriated after torturing and/or disappearing their biological parents. The term 'appropriation' differentiates these cases from legal adoptions.[6] Although not all *represores* appropriated children for themselves, most were accomplices in their stealing. As of August 2023, 133 children, now in their mid to late forties, have recovered their identities. Interestingly, the first time that H.I.J.O.S. uncovered a *repressor* the target was a gynaecologist accused of participating in tortures and the appropriation of babies.[7]

A focused iconization of evil meant that only a few faces and names were well-known–such as dictator Jorge Rafael Videla and other high-ranking members of the military juntas. These were symbols of terror while hundreds of *represores* went unknown to the majority of the population. *Escraches*, thus, contested denial and ignorance by making people realize that those responsible for massive atrocities might be their kind neighbour or the father of their daughter's best friend. In aiming for public exposure and humiliation, H.I.J.O.S.'s actions constituted a metaphorical repossession of the streets by freeing them from these criminals' presence. It was a move to tear off the protective veil of anonymity behind which hundreds hid. In the absence of sentencing, H.I.J.O.S. wanted to curtail the 'peaceful impunity' enjoyed by *represores* by ensuring that their neighbours knew their faces and their crimes.

The *escrache* was a very creative and powerful communication form, a well-planned event quite different from spontaneous demonstrations. *Represores*, neighbours, and the police knew when H.I.J.O.S. was coming. Carefully conducted investigations to track down former *represores* preceded each *escrache*. This was a key 'intelligence' activity that involved locating *represores* and where they currently lived and worked, plus building a 'dossier' detailing the crimes they were accused of. It also included learning about their daily routines, visiting the vicinities beforehand, and talking to neighbours, merchants, and community organizations.

Escraches were publicized demonstrations, well covered by the media. In mobilizing public support and rallying communities to participate actively, H.I.J.O.S. relied on announcements placed in newspapers and flyers circulated around the city. The aim was twofold: both to assemble the crowd and to shape the media narrative, which would multiply its audience. This strategic use of media has been described as *escraches*' 'media boom'.[8]

Escraches follow a script. The H.I.J.O.S. arrive at the neighbourhood and meet their supporters at a pre-established location. The assembled group marches to the torturer's house, touring the streets singing, dancing, and carrying artful banners. It's celebratory; there are speakers playing loud music, drummers and street bands. Their performative style resembles a carnival parade rather than a political march. But their blunt chants warn *represores*: 'Just like the Nazis, it will happen to you; wherever you go, we'll go after you'. For Taylor, who argues that Madres and Abuelas initiated the genre of performance protest, *escraches* are highly theatrical carnivalesque protests that constitute a form of guerrilla performance.[9] But it is a public performance whose participants don't hide in the shadows. Bonaldi highlights *escraches*' festive spirit when giant puppets, jugglers, and flamethrowers join the assembly, further noting that the aim is to express joy for being an act of repudiation or rage for the impunity, never pain or sadness.[10]

Throughout the march, the H.I.J.O.S. give away flyers informing about the *escrache*'s target: his photo, name, code-names, address, current occupation, crimes committed. The march ends at the *represor's* home, where the police will usually be present, and have erected barriers to stop trespassing. The assembly gathers there. Music, chanting, and dancing continue, complemented with a ceremony that includes speeches, the reading of a statement accusing the *represor*, theatre skits parodying military authorities, painting of sidewalks and pavement to mark the *represor* homes. Red paint—symbolising blood—is often thrown at the building.

Evaluating *Escraches*

In 1998, when *escraches* reached their peak, I participated in them and observed the interactions between the marchers and neighbours, many of whom joined the protests and thanked H.I.J.O.S. for alerting them.[11] A few neighbours told me how critical they were of the crimes committed by the *escrachados*. A woman confided that she knew the whereabouts of a *represor* and was considering contacting H.I.J.O.S. Others closed their windows and stayed away but nobody defended the torturers.

I noted that the key issue was how *escraches* impacted the public. At that time, we could only speculate about the consequences of uncovering *represores*. So, I explored the effects by assessing how people judged the strategy. In addition to talking with demonstrators and neighbours, I interviewed and had conversations with activists, including Madres and H.I.J.O.S. I also interviewed some young people born during the dictatorship and/or after the commencement of civilian rule to learn how they 'read' and evaluated *escraches*.[12]

Although most of them rejected impunity and sympathized with H.I.J.O.S., *escraches* were controversial. Some believed that their crimes did not justify harassing these *represores*, even when there was awareness of their cruelty and sadism (e.g. children witnessing their parents' torture, special torments for pregnant women, prisoners being thrown from aeroplanes into the sea). There was inconsistency between a condemnation for the *represores* versus the level of tolerance for them. Many issues were at play: whose interests they serve, their objectives, impact on the torturers' families and neighbours, the style of the demonstrators, concerns over damaging private property, and the relationship between H.I.J.O.S. and society.

Some interviewees perceived that *escraches* were motivated by H.I.J.O.S.'s pain and anger. Other comments showed how the struggle for accountability is often seen as the victims' job and minimized society's responsibility: 'It has to do with memory, so people know. Really; it's the least [H.I.J.O.S.] can do, what's available to them.' However, other remarks indicated that H.I.J.O.S.'s actions were a desperate appeal for society's support, therefore noting activists' isolation and frustration: 'It's [their] way of doing justice, of writing what they feel, the pain that remains in them. Because they're struggling to do something and no one pays attention to them.'

Other interviewees praised *escraches*' strategy, including its originality and effectiveness. They highlighted the critical importance of uncovering *represores* and restricting the spaces where they can circulate without being harassed. *Represores* became prisoners in their own homes, a de facto sentence for officially acquitted individuals. As I was told: 'Now the efforts are to try to exclude them from society. This is the aim of the *escraches*. To know that if you leave your house you have to watch out because a stone might hit your head.' Another comment reinforced the idea of the streets as spaces to force accountability: 'It's street justice. I believe that according to the law they won't ever be jailed, so for as long as they live, let them live like this. Those against whom they do *escraches* would have to move.'

Impact on Torturers' Families and Neighbours

There were debates over *escraches*'s impact on torturers' families and neighbours. Some interviewees indicated that H.I.J.O.S.'s justified motivations conflicted with the rights of the *represores* and those around them. They expressed concern at what they considered unacceptable levels of hostility: 'The guy who was a torturer obviously is a vicious person. But [*escraches*] are very aggressive. That person has children and neighbours, and it seems to me very harsh that they'd go and write: "Your neighbour is a torturer." ' While torturers' families are not responsible for the crimes, these comments showed how people often weighed between the rights of a particular wife and child or the debt that the criminals owed to society. In contrast, some interviewees considered that *represores*'s families should also know about their crimes. There were also divisions about how families were seen—accomplices or ignorant. But there was a generalized belief that it was quite difficult for families, especially wives, to ignore their husbands' activities.

The impact on torturers' neighbours generated disagreement, including with respect to how neighbours should react (i.e. support or rejection). In praising *escraches*, some highlighted that H.I.J.O.S. warned neighbours about assassins living next door. However, some interviewees questioned how *escraches* affected others. Protecting public and private property was a recurrent argument, mainly related to the spraying of graffiti on sidewalks and buildings, or the noise generated by drumming and loud music. One of *escraches*'s goals was that neighbours would isolate the *represores* and force them to move, and the staining of walls had a role to play here. As someone from H.I.J.O.S. told me: 'We hope that those in the building who don't want to keep paying for a paint job would tell the torturer that he should move'. Most interviewees, however, were critical of damaging shared property: 'I don't agree with what was done, it's wrong, obviously. But nor is what [H.I.J.O.S.] are doing right. Besides, they write on the walls.' 'I saw once on the news that someone's neighbours were complaining, "If it were his house and sidewalk and [H.I.J.O.S.] do that it's fine but not in a building where I pay the same maintenance fees." ' Nonetheless, some interviewees noted the absurdity of comparing torture and disappearances with staining walls and equating the right to private property with the right to life. Walls can be repainted; disappeared parents cannot reappear.

Many comments suggested that the media played an important role in portraying how the community responded to *escraches*. Television coverage apparently indicated that many neighbours were more bothered by the disorder than by a torturer living next door. References to neighbours' indignation by demonstrators' banging drums suggested that many were willing to tolerate the *represores*'s presence: 'Neighbours are not to blame for what Videla did. They cannot throw him out of the neighbourhood. "It's OK, it's fair" [to condemn/shame him] is what people said on television. "It's fair but it's not my fault that the guy lives here'." I also heard of neighbours supporting *escraches*: 'I saw on television that one woman who lives in the building went downstairs and joined the demonstrators because she did not know she had a dictator living there'—a proof that the strategy accomplished its goals of 'marking' the *represores*.

Other comments revealed how a legacy of fear was affecting political participation. Fear was founded on the perception that *represores* still had the power to repress those protesting against them. Paradoxically, torturers requested, and received, police protection. Thus, a few *escraches* were suppressed. For example, on the eve of the *escrache* against an infamous torturer, he issued an open letter to his neighbours saying that the police would protect them—implying that demonstrators would be repressed, which is what happened. I participated in it and witnessed the repression. Marching throughout the streets went well. When we arrived at the torturer's house, dozens of cops and infantry soldiers were waiting for us. It was a tense situation while the 'ceremony' took place. Skits and speeches were not interrupted. But when red paint was thrown at the building, a violent repression was unleashed, led by plainclothes police officers who had infiltrated the assembly of mostly young people. Teargas filled the air. Several H.I.J.O.S. and some Madres were brutally beaten; many were taken to police stations.[13] Although H.I.J.O.S. had experienced beatings before, this level of repression against all participants was unusual for an *escrache*.

Escraches's Impact

I concluded that *escraches* illustrated the multiple languages and forms of human rights activism. *Escraches* were disruptive, noisy, provocative, and hard to ignore, a strategy that secured media coverage. They were a strong and loud message telling society 'I won't let you forget'. *Escraches* informed people. Many Argentineans said that they did not know what had gone on during the dictatorship. Now they knew. *Escraches* threatened the *represores*'s impunity by asking that people react to the horror of being surrounded by torturers and assassins. Indeed, many 'uncovered' *represores* were afraid to leave the country and be caught by Interpol or leave their homes and be insulted and harassed by passers-by. *Escraches* trapped torturers and assassins by building metaphorical jails in neighbourhoods throughout Argentina.

H.I.J.O.S. further developed follow-up 'memory activities', so the momentum gained with the *escrache* didn't fizzle out as a one-time affair. One tactic was the 'mobile *escrache*', in which activists revisited the residences of several *represores* who had been already *escrachados*, driving around on bikes, cars, or chartered buses, and briefly stopping at different houses. Another activity was to return to the neighbourhood in the days following an *escrache* to strengthen networks with the community. This 'post-*escrache* day' took place in a public space. H.I.J.O.S. showed photos taken during the *escrache* and organized screenings and/or live music performances. The *escrache* thus became an ongoing event, with active participation of the community, which broadens the territory of protest, including parks or squares as new spaces to stage debates.[14]

H.I.J.O.S. focused on creating spaces for interacting and engaging with society. Theirs is 'not a dialogue with the perpetrator; it's a message from society to that person and to the people who have the power to put him in prison'.[15] Furthermore, *escraches* became H.I.J.O.S.'s distinctive brand and impacted the internal functioning of the organization, which unified by a common activity in spite of differences and conflicts.[16]

H.I.J.O.S. through Evolving Political Environments

In 2003, there was a major transformation regarding accountability: Congress nullified the impunity laws. Then, in 2005, the Supreme Court declared them unconstitutional. Dismantling impunity resulted in revitalized expectations for justice and the reopening of several legal cases. Trials for crimes against humanity mushroomed. Most of those *escrachados* would eventually face justice, be prosecuted, and convicted. By early 2023, more than 1,100 *represores* have been condemned, with several other trials ongoing or imminent.[17] Up until each conviction, H.I.J.O.S. and their *escraches* can be credited with limiting the *represores*'s social and spatial freedom.

Escraches showed the effectiveness of both peaceful assemblies and 'peaceful disruption'. In spite of years of absolute impunity and the slowness of the justice process, not a single member of H.I.J.O.S. took justice into their own hands. In fact, no father, mother, daughter, son, sister, or brother of disappeared has done this—anger and/or sadness never turned into an act of 'vengeance'. We should recognize activists' commitment to justice and the fairness of the trials.

The trials are public; anyone can attend the hearings. H.I.J.O.S. encourage society's participation. As their slogan says: 'A court judges them; we all condemn them'. Many members participate as plaintiffs, witnesses, and/or public. They maintain a visible presence at the tribunals. I have witnessed some of their activities, such as assembling outside the courthouse and staging performances comparable to those at *escraches*.

Furthermore, they carefully monitor and accuse any legal concession granted to *represores*—for example, denouncing a convicted *genocida* serving a life term under house arrest who was allowed to attend his grandchildren's first communion.[18] This surveillance of condemned *represores* is a follow-up activity that enforces the accountability process. Hence, H.I.J.O.S. keep warning when there's a breach and torturers re-enter public spaces where they don't have the right to be. As the say goes, 'prison is the only place for a *genocida*'.

H.I.J.O.S. celebrated its twenty-eighth anniversary in 2023. Over the years, I have continued to observe how their activism adapts to evolving political environments. They are key actors in the unfolding process of dismantling impunity through many activities. Their headquarters is the Casa de la Militancia in Buenos Aires, at the Space for Memory and Human Rights Ex-ESMA (formerly a torture and extermination centre). H.I.J.O.S. hosts multiple events there, ranging from commemorations to film screenings, and offers free educational programmes, such as high school diplomas and certifications in sports journalism and history. Their website keeps records of the trials and links to access live-streaming of the hearings. Their online radio station produces audio reports of the trials.[19]

Even when *escraches*'s main goal has been to uncover *represores* responsible for atrocious crimes, H.I.J.O.S. has also shamed their accomplices, members of those sectors that condoned, collaborated, and benefitted from the repression. For state terrorism was not just a military project. We talk today of a civic-military-ecclesiastic dictatorship. *Escraches*'s targets have ranged from owners of corporations that collaborated with the disappearance of workers to members of the Catholic church hierarchy, including torturers enjoying their impunity overseas and 'recycled' in new professions (e.g. a professor at La Sorbonne in Paris).[20]

Escraches Twenty Years Later: New Layers and Dimensions of Analysis

As times passes, I keep uncovering different dimensions of H.I.J.O.S.'s *escraches.* Exploring their strategies in greater depth generates new layers of analysis. There seem to be endless frameworks to theorize about *escraches* and assess their achievements.

When I first revisited *escraches,* I focused on the struggle for urban territories and the role that Madres and H.I.J.O.S., played in it.[21] I identified strategies aimed at occupying public spaces and expanding territories of disruption. I maintained that H.I.J.O.S.'s *escraches* defined a new style of activism that reshaped the uses of the public places of the city. I argued that taking to the streets is an act aimed at conquering and remapping cultural, political, and ideological zones. Since memory is encoded in places and takes root in spaces, the struggle for urban territories was also a means of enacting memory and writing history. I would now add that by marking the homes and territories where *represores* benefitted from the lack of justice, *escraches* mapped the geography of impunity.

Furthermore, H.I.J.O.S.'s creativity for broadening spaces to assemble illustrates what Miraftab defines as 'invented spaces of citizenship': those 'occupied by the grassroots and claimed by their collective action, directly confronting the authorities and the status quo'.[22] This confrontation is done 'in the hope of larger societal change'. Lacking legal spaces to bring *represores* to justice, H.I.J.O.S. responded with the 'street justice' of their *escraches*. As their motto says: 'If there's no justice, we'll have *escrache*'. They redefined sites of confrontation and kept on inventing spaces of citizenship. For example, for the thirtieth anniversary of the 1976 coup, H.I.J.O.S. *escrached* dictator Videla, then enjoying impunity at home, by metaphorically entering his house. They rented a crane and reached his apartment's floor. A large banner hanging from the crane displayed faces of the disappeared symbolically confronting the dictator hiding behind closed windows.[23]

I engaged again with Pierre Nora's concept of the *lieux de mémoire,* which he uses to discuss those symbolic sites that codify memory as self-referential signs that have a capacity to recycle their meaning endlessly (such as geographical sites, historical figures, or monuments).[24] The concept's breadth includes portable, transitory, and ephemeral sites, and even a more intangible application such as a historical generation. Nora also distinguishes between 'dominant' and 'dominated' sites; the former are generally celebrations officially imposed from above, to which one is summoned; the latter are 'places of refuge, sanctuaries of instinctive devotion'.[25] In analysing *escraches* and the Madres' marches, I made links with the UNESCO World Heritage intangible sites, a category strongly associated with memory that focuses on living cultural heritage (e.g. the Day of the Dead in Mexico, an event that takes place in the same physical spaces [cities, neighbourhoods] but differs year to year). I proposed the notion of rotating *lieux de mémoire*, embodying with meaning particular urban spaces on an ephemeral basis and belonging to a subcategory of memory-centred intangible heritages. And I suggested that we could categorize the H.I.J.O.S. *escraches* and Madres marches as memory-centred intangible heritages and dominated *lieux de mémoire*.[26]

Additionally, I propose to categorize *escraches* as 'human rights memory media', those media strategies and formats for documenting abuses, encouraging intervention to stop them, and using memories as tools to search for truth and demand justice.[27] The concept is inspired by Harlow's idea that 'human rights reporting entails both documentation and intervention'.[28] H.I.J.O.S. trace *represores* and compile an archive of their crimes. *Escraches* use these records to bring state terrorism's atrocities into the public sphere, trigger debates about impunity, encourage society's participation in the struggle for accountability, and influence media and political agendas.

Concluding Remarks

Four decades after the return to civilian rule in Argentina, each gain in the pursuit of memory, truth, and justice has been, to a great extent, the result of activists' relentless efforts. H.I.J.O.S skilfully combined investigations and legal recourse with *escraches*'s powerful street presence and proved that peaceful assemblies can successfully disrupt peaceful impunity. They knew that they had to 'say peacefully what these people had done, so that everyone would know that this person was a rapist, a torturer, a murder, and say it loudly, with flyers, graffiti and a lot of people in the street drumming and chanting'.[29] Moreover, they inspired other groups of daughters and sons who adopted their tactics to shame perpetrators (e.g. in Chile and Uruguay).

Undeniably, H.I.J.O.S. played a key role in challenging impunity and amnesia, made visible the absence of thirty thousand disappeared, kept the issue of human rights in the public sphere and on the politicians' agenda, and influenced policy and action. H.I.J.O.S. and their *escraches* illustrate what Gutman defines as memory activism: the 'strategic commemoration of a contested past outside state channels to influence public debate and policy'.[30] Taking to the streets as a means to achieve 'street justice' is a distinctive characteristic of H.I.J.O.S.'s use of public spaces. Hence, we cannot disregard the forms of participation and debates that result when people peacefully take to the streets and engage in peaceful disorder.

In concluding, I want to re-emphasize the performative connotations and aesthetic dimensions of the *escraches*, including H.I.J.OS.'s striking visual presence. I first saw them marching in 1996. Behind the Madres came H.I.J.O.S. with their big banner. The image suggested that the 'disappeared' were marching in between, behind their mothers and followed by their children. Recently, a younger generation joined them: *Nietes,* an organization of grandchildren of the 'disappeared' created in 2019; grandchildren now march accompanying their disappeared grandparents.[31] We should assume that H.I.J.O.S. will continue to develop communication strategies that will make sure that the thirty thousand 'disappeared' and the demands for justice are present until all the *genocidas* pay for their crimes.

Notes

1. The acronym stands for Hijos e Hijas Por la Identidad y la Justicia Contra el Olvido y el Silencio. 'Hijos' means 'daughters and sons'.
2. 'Full Stop' Law No. 23493 (23 December 1986) established deadlines for prosecutions. 'Due Obedience' Law No. 23521 (4 June 1987) exempted *represores* from punishment for having followed orders. Decrees of Pardon Nos. 2741-43 (30 December 1990) pardoned the few *represores* still in prison.
3. Susana Kaiser, '*Escraches:* Demonstrations, Communication and Political Memory in Post-Dictatorial Argentina', *Media, Culture and Society* 24, no. 4 (2002): 499–516.
4. For a comprehensive history of the organization, see Pablo Daniel Bonaldi, 'Hijos de desaparecidos. Entre la construcción de la política y la construcción de la memoria', in *El Pasado en el futuro: Los movimientos juveniles*, ed. Elizabeth Jelin and Diego Sempol (Buenos Aires: Siglo XXI, 2006), 143–184.
5. Unless noted, all the information in this section is from Kaiser, 'Escraches', and Susana Kaiser, 'The Struggle for Urban Territories: Human Rights Activists in Buenos Aires', in *Ordinary Places/Extraordinary Events: Citizenship, Democracy, and Urban Space in Latin America*, ed. Clara Irazábal (New York: Routledge, 2008), 170–197.
6. The trial against those responsible for this crime was named Systematic Plan for the Appropriation of Children.
7. Bonaldi, 'Hijos de desaparecidos', 164–165.
8. Ibid., 168.
9. Diana Taylor, '"You Are Here": The DNA of Performance', *TDR: The Drama Review* 46, no. 1 (T 173) (Spring 2002): 151.
10. Bonaldi, 'Hijos de desaparecidos', 167.
11. *Escraches* against General Santiago Omar Riveros (June 1998) and torturer Fernando Enrique Peyón (July 1998).
12. None of them had participated in *escraches*; their knowledge about them was mainly based on media coverage. These interviews were for my study identifying memory transmission patterns. See Susana Kaiser, *Postmemories of Terror: A New Generation Copes with the Legacy of the 'Dirty War'* (New York: Palgrave Macmillan, 2005).
13. I left the site helped by a television crew that included a teargassed cameraman. *Escrache* against Peyón (July 1998).
14. Kaiser, 'Struggle for Urban Territories', 186–187.
15. In Sean Mattison's documentary: *Atención! Murderer Next Door* (2020) https://seanmattison.com/project/nyt-op-doc-atencion-murderer-next-door/.

16. Bonaldi, 'Hijos de desaparecidos', 168.
17. Procuraduría de Crímenes contra la Humanidad, https://www.fiscales.gob.ar/lesa-humanidad/.
18. Torturer Juan Carlos Rolón in 2021.
19. H.I.J.O.S. Capital: https://www.hijos-capital.org.ar/.
20. Torturer Sandoval was eventually extradited and convicted.
21. Kaiser, 'Struggle for Urban Territories'.
22. Cited in Clara Irazábal, 'Citizenship, Democracy, and Public Space in Latin America', in *Ordinary Places/Extraordinary Events: Citizenship, Democracy, and Urban Space in Latin America*, ed. Clara Irazábal (New York: Routledge, 2008), 11–34, 19.
23. For images of this and other *escraches*, see Mattison, *Atención!*
24. Pierre Nora, 'General Introduction: Between Memory and History', *Realms of Memory: The Construction of the French Past*, Vol I., ed. Pierre Nora (New York: Columbia University Press, 1996), 1–23.
25. Nora's examples include: non-static and portable sites like the Torah, transitory and ephemeral sites like veterans' organizations, dominant sites as de Gaulle's funeral at Notre Dame, and dominated as Sartre' funeral. Ibid., 19.
26. Kaiser, 'Struggle for Urban Territories', 172–173.
27. See Susana Kaiser, 'Human Rights Memory Media', *Popular Communication* 16, no. 2 (2018): 86–89.
28. Cited in Marilyn Booth, 'Review of *Barred: Women, Writing, and Political Detention*', *Domes* 3, no. 4 (1994): 67.
29. Mattison, *Atención!*
30. Yifat Gutman, *Memory Activism: Reimagining the Past for the Future in Israel-Palestine* (Nashville, TN: Vanderbilt University Press, 2017).
31. *Nietes* means *nietas* (granddaughters) and *nietos* (grandsons) by replacing 'a' and 'o' with gender neutral 'e'.

Further Reading

Druliolle, Vincent. 'H.I.J.O.S. and the Spectacular Denunciation of Impunity: The Struggle for Memory, Truth, and Justice and the (Re-)Construction of Democracy in Argentina'. *Journal of Human Rights* 12, no. 2 (2013): 259–276.

Gelman, Juan, and Mara La Madrid. *Ni el flaco perdón de dios. Hijos de desaparecidos*. Buenos Aires: Planeta, 1997.

Levey, Cara. 'Of HIJOS and Niños: Revisiting Postmemory in Post-Dictatorship Uruguay'. *History and Memory* 26, no. 2 (Fall/Winter 2014): 5–39.

CHAPTER 24

REINVENTING A PUBLIC ASSEMBLY

Pink Dot, Singapore

LYNETTE J. CHUA

INTRODUCTION

ON the sunny afternoon of 16 May 2009, Hong Lim Park in downtown Singapore was buzzing. About 2,500 people were flocking there to participate in Singapore's first gay pride rally. Arriving on foot and by subway, bus, and car, they included teenagers, young adults, parents, and grandparents, some with babies, toddlers, and dogs in tow. Almost every person and their pet were dressed in shades of pink. Amongst them were people who identify as lesbian, gay, bisexual, transgender, or queer (LGBTQ), as well as their friends and allies. As the crowd laid out their picnic mats and settled onto the grass to wait for the event to begin, organizers wearing hats covered in pink disco dust walked around distributing pink cardboard fans, balloons, umbrellas, and flyers.[1]

At 4:45 p.m., one group of organizers called out instructions and guided the crowd to make three consecutive formations: 'LOVE', '4ALL', and a pink dot. Another team took photographs and videos from a hotel room overlooking the park, using walkie talkies to communicate with their counterparts in the park to tweak the formations so that they could get better shots. When each of the three formations was ready, the organizers on the park grounds cued the crowd to hold up whatever pink items they had, such as the cardboard fans, balloons, and umbrellas, and wave them in the direction of the hotel. During the last formation, the pink dot, the person who inspired the creation of Pink Dot, to whom I refer as Nelson, climbed onto a makeshift platform in the centre and raised the Pink Dot flag above his head. And then the crowd burst into the event's theme song, 'All You Need Is Love'.[2]

Since 2009, Pink Dot has been an annually recurring event and the most visible representation of the LGBTQ rights movement in Singapore. If Pink Dot were taking place in a jurisdiction where street protests are commonplace, perhaps it would be less interesting, nothing more than yet another public rally. However, Pink Dot appears and thrives, year after year, in a state known for its strict laws on public assembly and informal political norms against confrontational activist tactics.

To understand Pink Dot and other activities of Singapore's LGBTQ rights movement, in my earlier research I theorized that they were tactics of 'pragmatic resistance'. According to my research, this is an overarching strategy that LGBTQ rights activists in Singapore have formulated and implemented since their movement's inception in the early 1990s. In brief, pragmatic resistance involves simultaneously abiding by Singapore's formal laws and informal political norms ('toeing the line') and testing the boundaries of those laws and norms in a manner that does not attract government retaliation ('pushing the boundaries'). The formal laws include the restriction on forming association without state approval under the Societies Act, and the ban on public assembly, including demonstration by a single protester, under the Public Order Act; the informal norms include the avoidance of confrontational tactics, such as openly opposing the government or the ruling party, or shaming them for their shortcomings. Line-toeing respects the limits of such formal and informal rules in order to ensure the movement's survival. Instead of violating legal restrictions, LGBTQ rights activists obey, circumvent, or take advantage of the law. They also practice non-confrontation and avoid being seen as threatening social harmony, thus keeping in line with informal political norms highly valued by the government. Meanwhile, boundary pushing creatively interprets and uses the formal and informal rules to expand their limits gradually and to build up tolerance by the state for their activities.

Pragmatic resistance, therefore, is a complicated dance. Toeing the line too much achieves little progress, but pushing too aggressively might attract sanctions and retaliation. LGBTQ rights activists constantly refine this dance in response to their prior engagements with the state and their perceptions of shifts to laws and political norms.

Pink Dot vividly illustrates the pragmatic resistance of Singapore's LGBTQ rights movement. The traits of pragmatic resistance shine through right from the event's beginnings. Hong Lim Park, Pink Dot's venue, is the only place in Singapore where prior license approval is not required for a public speaking event (but speakers have to avoid touching on sensitive subjects of race and religion).[3] In 2008, the year before Pink Dot, the government extended the scope of Hong Lim Park's exemption from public speaking to 'performances' and 'exhibitions'. In practical terms, the government carved out a 'notification' regime within an otherwise 'authorization' regime of public assembly: The revised exemption allowed assemblies at Hong Lim Park as long as organizers registered them in advance with the police and agreed to the same pre-conditions regarding race and religion.[4]

In the rest of this chapter, I examine the emergence and development of Pink Dot. I show how activists reinvented a public assembly to suit their political and legal environment, transcended the regulated confines of a physical space, and overcame a public perception in their country that assemblies transgress the political order. I also assess

Pink Dot's impact, particularly how it has contributed to the growth of Singapore's LGBTQ rights movement and its efforts to achieve legal and social change.

Pink Dot through the Years

News of the revised exemption caught Nelson's attention: Why not hold a gay pride parade at Hong Lim Park? Nelson's parade would not come to fruition, but the idea provided the inspiration for Pink Dot. The deliberation process amongst a group of LGBTQ rights activists that led to the invention of Pink Dot highlights the traits of pragmatic resistance, the dance between toeing the line and pushing the boundaries.

First, Nelson wanted to make use of the revised exemption—ultimately a form of legal control—and expand the political norms that had conventionally discouraged large-scale public assemblies by activists. At the same time, he internalized the survival instinct of pragmatic resistance, as illustrated by this excerpt from his interview:

> If the government hadn't liberalized Hong Lim Park . . . then I would think that it would be confrontational, and it would be illegal, and I wouldn't have done it. But because it was legal, that's why I decided to do it. I thought it was a great opportunity to do it in a legal way.

Next, when Nelson broached the idea of a pride parade with other LGBTQ rights activists, they struggled with the question of how to hold a parade in a contained area of approximately 9,300 square metres. Obeying the rules would mean walking in circles around the park, a scenario that did not make sense to them. Activists also doubted that Singaporeans would turn up for a parade. The revised exemption did not necessarily mean that Singaporeans were going to participate in or support public assemblies overnight. These activists thought that Singaporeans would worry about the political stigma attached to protests, having witnessed how activists and dissidents who staged streets protests without permits had been prosecuted, convicted, and consequently delegitimized by the political establishment.

Then one of the activists, Eu-Jin, had a brainwave:

> I said, just have something that is so simple that anybody, all ages, can come, without any preparation. They just need to come knowing why they're there. And why they're there should be so simple that they can say it in one sentence: that it's to support the LGBT community in Singapore . . . If they knew about it an hour before because someone just told them about it, they could still come and do it because there is no need for any prior rehearsal or preparation. It's as simple as that. And then at the same time, it has to be something that will register visually to everyone the next morning and maybe for many years to come.

Thus Pink Dot was born. The event's execution further foregrounds the features of pragmatic resistance. Above all, organizers for the inaugural Pink Dot 2009, and the subsequent annual events since, were and are meticulous about obeying the law—a hallmark of 'toeing the line' to earn and maintain political legitimacy. When publicizing Pink Dot on the internet and social media in 2009, they provided an FAQ sheet (which was also circulated on the day of the event):

Q: Is this event legit or legal?
A: Yes, of course! We have registered for the event and we shall strive to conduct ourselves appropriately, as set out in National Parks' terms and conditions. Who says we can't behave and have fun at the same time!

Every year, Pink Dot leaders not only register their event with the police as a public assembly, as required by the exemption rule, but they also register every person who might be speaking on that day whether to make an announcement or give formation instructions.

Pink Dot organizers also emphasize and obey another important rule: Only Singaporean citizens and permanent residents may participate in the assembly. As Pink Dot grew in popularity and size, the organizers in subsequent years set up checkpoints to confirm the legal status of every individual who wanted to join the assembly. Moreover, from Pink Dot 2011 onwards, they separately obtained entertainment licenses and permissions to use the stage adjacent to Hong Lim Park for bigger musical performances. Although the stage and Hong Lim Park look contiguous, the stage falls outside the park boundaries and is managed by a 'grassroots organization' under the charge of a statutory body.

Besides adhering to formal restrictions, Pink Dot organizers follow informal political norms, another hallmark of 'toeing the line'. They emphasize the event's non-confrontational nature and promotion of social harmony. Their flyers repeatedly stress that the event is not political and is 'not a protest', and remind participants not to confront or engage opponents if they show up. They also promote the message that acceptance of diverse types of sexuality strengthens rather than polarizes Singaporean society. Their publicity videos and on-location activities showcase participants who identify with the major racial and religious groups in Singapore and feature LGBTQ allies, such as parents of LGBTQ persons and local entertainers and celebrities.

In addition, to avoid potential allegations that acceptance of LGBTQ persons harms the social fabric of Singapore, Pink Dot organizers reinterpret the meaning of the colour pink. Instead of connecting the colour to discrimination or gay pride, they link it to domestically resonant signs and symbols. When they launched Pink Dot in 2009, they explained on their website:

> Pink because it's a blend of red and white and the colour of Singapore's national flag. Also, it is the colour of our national identification cards. More importantly, Pink Dot

Sg stands for a Singapore in which all Singaporeans, regardless of their sexual orientation, are free to love and be loved.

Simultaneously, Pink Dot exhibits the other key attribute of pragmatic resistance, 'pushing the boundaries'. The creators of Pink Dot 2009, such as Winston quoted below, do not let the tokenism of an exempted park—something that they clearly recognize—hold them back from transforming it into an opportunity.

[Hong Lim Park is] about restricting the space available for free speech to this tiny corner. So in conceptualizing Pink Dot, we wanted to reverse all that. We wanted to do something that was visually stunning so that it would break out of the confines of that space, something memorable, something iconic.

Most importantly, by capturing Pink Dot's formations on photos and videos and using the internet to distribute the images, its organizers extend its reach—enabling anyone to view the assembly on their website, social media accounts, and YouTube channel anytime, anywhere. Whether these internet users watch Pink Dot videos synchronously or asynchronously, they are perhaps doing more than being passive viewers. Arguably, they are participating in the event (in some cases, repeatedly) beyond the physical constraints of the park and exemption rules.[5]

Since 2009, Pink Dot has also reduced the negative public perception of assemblies. The inaugural Pink Dot attracted about 2,500 participants. In 2010, about four thousand showed up to form a pink heart. In 2011, the crowd swelled to ten thousand. There was no longer any point trying to shape the crowd into a round dot or a heart. From the vantage point of the hotel room where the Pink Dot team took photographs and videos, Hong Lim Park looked like a sea of pulsating pink.

In 2012, Pink Dot organizers moved the event to nighttime to get away from the tropical afternoon heat. They distributed mini pink torchlights and cellophane strips for participants to tape onto their mobile phones to modify the colour of their flashlights. Around 7:30 p.m., fifteen thousand people formed the first-ever nighttime pink dot. The organizers lit a heart-shaped fixture at the hotel window overlooking the park, so that participants in the park could tell where the cameras were. On a countdown from ten, the participants raised their pink light devices, pointed them at the heart in the hotel window, and turned on the lights together. Then they sang the theme song for Pink Dot 2012, 'True Colors'. From 2013 onwards, Pink Dot's annual numbers reached as high as twenty thousand.

During the COVID-19 pandemic in 2020 and 2021 the government prohibited all private and public mass gatherings. Pink Dot leaders had to come up with a new approach to both transcend *and* adhere to legal and physical constraints. They invited supporters to sign up on their website to light up their homes and offices with pink lights throughout June, the month when Pink Dot usually takes place at Hong Lim Park. Using the sign-up information, the organizers generated a 'digital dot', a map of Singapore that indicated the pink light-ups across the island. Anyone can visit the website address, loveliveshere.pinkdot.sg, to look at the digital dot. On the website, when one moves the computer mouse to a lit-up spot on the map, the Pink Dot cartoon berry pops up along with a message left by the participant from that location in Singapore.

In 2022, after the Singaporean government eased COVID-19 restrictions, Pink Dot organizers resumed the annual event in Hong Lim Park. In addition to their usual adherence of assembly laws, they enforced the prevailing COVID-19 measures on vaccination. Participants flocked back, their numbers hitting pre-COVID highs. For the finale, the organizers designated a group to make a formation within the pink dot by holding up light pink umbrellas to spell out, 'Majulah'. This word means 'forward' or 'advance' in Malay and is part of the title of Singapore's national anthem, 'Majulah, Singapura'.

Pink Dot indeed advanced towards a new milestone in 2022: for the first time, a Member of Parliament (MP) from the ruling party accepted Pink Dot's invitation to attend the event in an official capacity. Pink Dot organizers took and circulated through their social media photographs of the MP walking around and talking to other participants at the park.

Pink Dot's Impact

How has Pink Dot fared at helping the LGBTQ rights movement achieve legal and social change in Singapore? Sceptics of tactics of pragmatic resistance will point out that Pink Dot has not led to greater recognition of basic civil-political rights, including the right to assembly. The licensing exemption for public assemblies at Hong Lim Park comprises executive orders pursuant to the Public Order Act. In the weeks leading up to general elections, the government has typically revoked the exemption order—to prevent political campaigning in the park—and then reissued it after the elections. Furthermore, compliance with these formal rules leaves the restrictions unchallenged. Outside the park, assemblies remain forbidden. One LGBTQ rights activist felt proud of Pink Dot, but described it wistfully as a 'party in a prison yard', pointing out the event's containment within a regulated space.

Like most of the LGBTQ rights movement's tactics of pragmatic resistance since the 1990s, Pink Dot's gains involve alterations to practice and the boundaries of informal norms, not changes to formal laws. Critics could argue that Pink Dot pushes boundaries only in particular and restricted ways, stopping short of confrontation or being seen as jeopardizing the ruling party's perception of control, and consequently risks losing creativity to playing safe and routinization. As time passes, the stakes mount for diverging from the routine such that any deviation could disrupt state expectations and attract greater repression. Such routinization of strategy and repression could result in regulating the movement according to the accepted and expected norms heavily controlled by the state.[6]

However, I hold a more sanguine view. LGBTQ rights activists have not simply repeated the same acts of pragmatic resistance but have reshaped their tactics as they interacted with the state through the years. Although each individual tactic of pragmatic resistance may achieve only imperceptible progress; over time, they possess the potential to create powerful social change. As John D'Emilio wrote about the history of the American gay rights movement, the 'long stretches of just creeping along . . . display less drama and excitement; the kind of change that occurs often escapes notice at the time. But the work . . . is critically important nonetheless'.[7] Furthermore, Singapore's strict political conditions—such as the legal curtailment of public assembly and other civil-political liberties and informal norms on non-confrontation and protection of social harmony—already restrict rights activism. LGBTQ rights activists in Singapore not only advocate for changes in their area of concern (i.e. LGBTQ issues), but they also have to overcome limitations on their capacity to mobilize and make those claims in the first place.

To date, Pink Dot is Singapore's LGBTQ rights movement's most visually impactful tactic. Pink Dot organizers have built 'free spaces'[8] that help to generate solidarity and inculcate efficacy amongst the next generation of activists. These gains have contributed significantly to the movement's strength and to its aims of attaining legal and social change. 'Once you give us the space to do this, you cannot take it back. So this process of establishing a beachhead. It's like once we entrench our position, then we stretch the boundaries and push, push, push'.

Of course, the activist who said this is not entirely correct. The government can pull back the boundaries. Nevertheless, with constant and careful 'toeing the line' balanced with 'pushing the boundaries', Pink Dot organizers show that they can cultivate tolerance for and familiarity with their efforts and make reversals of assembly space much harder as time goes by. I have pointed out that Pink Dot had broken Hong Lim Park's physical confines and altered public perception that mass assemblies necessarily transgressed the norms of non-confrontation and preservation of social harmony. In this 'free space' of Pink Dot—on the day of the event at Hong Lim Park and online whenever somebody views the photographs and videos—LGBTQ persons and their allies come together, find connections through shared identities and concerns, and express support for social justice. In fact, Pink Dot organizers have gradually become more outspoken about their wish to repeal the criminal law that penalizes same-sex sexual relations (Section 377A of the Penal Code), openly appealing to the government during the last seven Pink Dots.

I also speculate that, beyond their own event of Pink Dot, these activists might have transformed Hong Lim Park into a place where it is not merely legally permitted but practically viable to assemble and speak out. Since the inaugural Pink Dot 2009, liberals and conservatives alike have held demonstrations on other issues at the park. The most recent was the 2019 climate change rally attended by about two thousand Singaporean youths in solidarity with the global youth climate movement.[9] Of course, it is difficult to draw causal links between Pink Dot and the rise in popularity of public assemblies at Hong Lim Park. Perhaps Pink Dot is part of the trend amongst Singaporeans to slowly expand the constraints on activism. Still, it is nevertheless worth thinking about whether and how the 'free space' of Pink Dot might have opened up the imagination of public assemblies more generally in Singaporean society.

Finally, Pink Dot has also become a home for newcomers to find their footing in the LGBTQ rights movement and learn about doing activism in Singapore. Each generation of Pink Dot organizers instill confidence in the next and teach them how to engage with the government. Pink Dot organizers have gone on to play crucial roles in other efforts of the movement, the most well-known being the litigation campaigns challenging the constitutionality of Section 377A. These multiple litigation campaigns since 2010 drew upon the persistent survival, constant fight, and cumulative gains of the movement, including Pink Dot's. When I first studied the movement in the 2000s, almost no activist could imagine mounting a constitutional challenge. They said constitutional litigation would be too confrontational, because it amounted to shaming the government openly. Yet, by the 2010s, a group of activists, several of them connected to Pink Dot, organized a litigation campaign to challenge Section 377A's constitutionality. This group fronted a pair of litigants, a gay couple who supports various movement activities and participates regularly in Pink Dot. Other Pink Dot organizers worked behind the scenes to raise funds for the lawsuit.

Pink Dot leaders and others involved in the first set of litigation succeeded at widening the scope of pragmatic resistance—by pushing the boundaries of rights activism in Singapore to encompass constitutional litigation and explicit demands for legal reform, actions that seemed unthinkable a decade ago. In line with other tactics in their pragmatic resistance repertoire, these activists consciously toned down the possibly antagonistic aspects of litigation. They hired lawyers whom they deemed acceptable to the political establishment. They also limited their own commentary in mainstream Singaporean media about the potentially unconstitutional nature of Section 377A, focusing instead on the lives and struggles of LGBTQ Singaporeans.[10]

Since 2010, five sets of litigants have filed constitutional challenges against Section 377A. None of them resulted in outcomes in their favour. Their claims and appeals were dismissed by all levels of the Judiciary, including the apex court, the Court of Appeal. However, after the last Court of Appeal dismissal in February 2022, change was in the air. Prominent ministers from the ruling party stated publicly that the government was 'considering best way forward' for the status of Section 377A.[11] Mainstream newspapers, which are heavily regulated by the government, published reports and op-eds that explained Section 377A or discussed in a sympathetic light the experiences of LGBTQ persons in Singapore.

On 21 August 2022, two months following Pink Dot's return to Hong Lim Park since the COVID-19 pandemic, Prime Minister Lee Hsien Loong announced in his annual nationwide speech—which addresses the country's major challenges, plans, and achievements—that Parliament would repeal Section 377A. He said more Singaporeans had shifted their attitudes towards homosexuality and no longer thought that same-sex sexual relations should be criminalized:

> Furthermore, we have seen several court challenges to s377A, seeking to declare the law unconstitutional. None have succeeded, so far. However, following the most recent judgement in the Court of Appeal, the Minister for Law and the Attorney General have advised that in a future court challenge, there is a significant risk of s377A being struck down, on the grounds that it breaches the Equal Protection provision in the Constitution. We have to take that advice seriously. It would be unwise to ignore the risk, and do nothing.[12]

Past and present Pink Dot organizers and other LGBTQ rights activists gathered at a bar to watch the live broadcast. The room fell silent and everyone seemingly held their breath when the Prime Minister arrived at the issue of Section 377A. After he announced that the law would be repealed, they cheered, applauded, turned their eyes away from the television screen, and hugged one another.[13]

But elation over the repeal announcement was tempered by the announcement that immediately followed in the Prime Minister's speech: Alongside the repeal, the government will amend the Constitution so that it states only Parliament may decide on the definition of marriage, currently between a man and a woman.[14] In other words, the government was pre-empting future constitutional challenges on the definition of marriage, which have developed into drawn-out, socially divisive battles in such jurisdictions as the United States. The government wanted to set out the clear position that the legal definition of marriage is a matter for Parliament, a majority-elected organ, to decide and not for people to fight it out in the courts. Although pragmatic resistance expanded the LGBTQ rights movement's tactical repertoire to constitutional litigation, this move signalled that the government wanted to put an end to a tactic that could turn contentious and contravene the norms of non-confrontation and social harmony.

Thus Pink Dot's labours continue. Building confidence, courage, and human resources, Pink Dot organizers have helped the larger movement achieve important milestones, such as being able to openly and collectively express support for LGBTQ rights in Singapore and challenging the criminalization of same-sex sexual relations. Pink Dot's contributions have become part of the movement's history from which current and future generations of LGBTQ rights activists draw inspiration and lessons: By intelligently nurturing, sustaining, and adapting an event, year in, year out, Pink Dot demonstrates that it is possible to overcome, even make use of, seemingly inhospitable legal and political conditions in ways that balance survival, courage, and innovation.

NOTES

1. This chapter draws from the author's book, L. J. Chua, *Mobilizing Gay Singapore: Rights and Resistance in an Authoritarian State* (Philadelphia: Temple University Press, 2014), and, where specifically noted, subsequent publications and additional research.
2. I use pseudonyms for all of my interviewees, as required by my institution's rules on human subjects' research.

3. Executive orders issued under the Public Order Act relating to Hong Lim Park provide that gatherings should not 'speak about a matter that relates, directly or indirectly, to any religious belief or to religion generally' or 'speak about a matter, or a matter in a way, that may cause feelings of enmity, hatred, ill-will or hostility between different racial or religious groups in Singapore'. The most recent version at the time of writing is the Public Order (Unrestricted Area—Speakers' Corner) Order 2020.
4. On notification and authorization regimes, see Hamilton, in this volume.
5. On whether asynchronous co-presence amounts to participation in assembly, also see MacPherson, in this volume, and Ashraf, in this volume.
6. J. Habermas, *Theory of Communicative Action*, trans. Thomas McCarthy (Boston: Beacon Press, 1984).
7. J. D'Emilio, *Sexual Politics, Sexual Communities*, 2nd ed. (Chicago: University of Chicago Press, 1998), 262.
8. Francesca Polletta, '"Free Spaces" in Collective Action', *Theory and Society* 28 (1999): 1–38.
9. Y. Low and N. Elangovan, 'Youths as Young as 11 Lead the Way for Singapore's Inaugural Climate Rally', *Today*, 22 September 2019, https://www.todayonline.com/singapore/youths-young-11-lead-way-singapores-inaugural-climate-rally (accessed 17 November 2022).
10. The analysis on the constitutional challenges are based on the author's article, Lynette J. Chua, 'Collective Litigation and Constitutional Challenges to Decriminalize Homosexuality in Singapore', *Journal of Law & Society* 44, no. 3 (2017): 433–455.
11. J. S. Ng, 'Government "Considering Best Way Forward" on Section 377A While Respecting Different Viewpoints: Shanmugam', *Today*, 3 March 2022, https://www.todayonline.com/singapore/government-considering-best-way-forward-section-377a-while-respecting-different-viewpoints-shanmugam-1834791 (accessed 17 November 2022).
12. National Day Rally speech transcript, https://www.pmo.gov.sg/Newsroom/National-Day-Rally-2022-English (accessed 17 November 2022).
13. Observation on 21 August 2022.
14. Parliament passed a bill to repeal Section 377A and a bill to amend the Constitution on the legal definition of marriage on 29 November 2022. In Singapore, amendment bills for ordinary statutes, such as the Penal Code, pass with a simple majority vote in Parliament, whereas constitutional amendments require two-thirds majority.

Further Reading

Chua, Lynette J. 'Collective Litigation and Constitutional Challenges to Decriminalize Homosexuality in Singapore'. *Journal of Law & Society* 44, no. 3 (2017): 433–455.

Chua, Lynette J. *Mobilizing Gay Singapore: Rights and Resistance in an Authoritarian State*. Philadelphia: Temple University Press, 2014.

D'Emilio, John. *Sexual Politics, Sexual Communities*, 2nd ed. Chicago: University of Chicago Press, 1998.

Polletta, Francesca. '"Free Spaces" in Collective Action'. *Theory and Society* 28 (1999): 1–38.

CHAPTER 25

ANONYMOUS AS ASSEMBLY, ASSOCIATION, AND ASSEMBLAGE

DAVIDE BERALDO

Introduction

Writing about Anonymous is always a challenging task,[1] given that what and/or who constitute Anonymous is up to debate, not only amongst scholars, journalists, and commentators,[2] but also amongst Anonymous's supporters themselves.[3] Often portrayed as a collective of hackers fighting for internet freedom, upon closer examination Anonymous is a much-less-defined entity, that has been signifying different things in different historical and geographical coordinates.

Its origins can be traced to the controversial platform 4chan, an online bulletin board where anyone can post images and comments. A specificity of this website, key to the emergence of Anonymous, is that every user has to post under the same handle: 'anonymous'. Due to this distinctive technical feature, as early as 2004, users on 4chan started referring to 'Anonymous' as some kind of collective entity attributed with agency in its own right. Dubbed initially as 'the Internet Hate Machine',[4] given the debatable and at times straightforwardly deprecable nature of the pranks characterizing its earlier engagement, the Anonymous brand unexpectedly found itself intertwined with major global political turmoil and grassroots activism, making the unexpected transition 'from the lulz[5] to collective action'.[6]

This chapter will reflect upon the implications that the case of Anonymous bears for theories of assembly, focusing on the role that the semiotic layer plays in this *assemblage*. Besides being an historical case, situated in a specific time and space (digital and not), Anonymous is, per participants' own self-descriptions, an idea—and as an idea, it is a rather bizarre yet productive one, judging from the amount and variety of public action that it manages to facilitate. Anonymous, I will argue, is not only interesting because of its *sui generis* nature; rather, as an 'extreme case', it brings to the surface properties that are, to a certain extent, implicit characteristics of any kind of assembly. More particularly, it demonstrates how blurred can be the distinction between contingent forms of assembly and more permanent forms of association. The notions of assemblage will come to the rescue to resolve this seeming contradiction.[7] This chapter is structured as follow. First, a tentative (and necessarily partial) genealogy of this entity is offered, highlighting how the Anonymous brand has been assigned with a stunning variety of meanings in different contexts. The second section will present a brief overview of Anonymous's complex and ever-shifting organizational dimension. In the following section, I will move to the semiotic layer, presenting Anonymous's engagement with meanings and symbols. In the fourth section, I will discuss the relation between Anonymous as an assembly, as an association, and as an assemblage. The conclusion advances some more general implications for theories of assembly.

Complex Genealogy

Anonymous is a complex and multifaceted phenomenon that defies easy categorization. It is not a formal group, organized network, or coherent idea. Rather, it is a diverse collection of actors identifying themselves as part of a loose (non-)collective, tied together by a generic ethos[8] and by a specific symbolism.[9] Anonymous has evolved through various phases, during which it shifted and multiplied its practices and identity, making it difficult to trace a genealogy—let alone drawing a linear timeline. The following selected key events should provide a sense of what Anonymous is (not).[10] Starting somewhere around 2004, Anonymous was 'only' a label used mostly on 4chan to inspire and brand online coordinated pranks, broadly framed in the context of internet trolling.[11] Such actions included coordinated phone pranks, cyberattacks or the spread of private humiliating information for the sole goal of 'the lulz'[12]—an irreverent form of amusement end to itself (and at the expense of others). Whereas these actions lack any political commitment, during this phase Anonymous developed (as) a distinctive culture, language, and symbolism, setting the stage for its evolution into a global force for political contention.

This transformation was sparked by the group's involvement in 'Project Chanology', a sustained campaign against the Church of Scientology which began in 2008 as a response to the Church's attempts to suppress a leaked video featuring Tom Cruise discussing his involvement with Scientology. The campaign quickly evolved into an organized set of cyberattacks, coordinated pranks, as well as offline protests that, besides the contingency of the chosen target, demonstrated a novel focus on collective action and political engagement. Contrary to the largely sporadic and seemingly arbitrary nature of earlier Anonymous's actions, Project Chanology's rationale and goals became the object of explicit elaboration and dissemination, while preserving many elements of the playful and irreverent character of the origins.

The trend escalated in 2010, when Anonymous explicitly aligned itself with the cause of internet freedom and free speech. The Operation Payback campaign started to target anti-piracy organizations and law firms, as retaliation for their efforts in combatting websites, such as Pirate Bay, that offered free file-sharing services. Soon afterwards, the WikiLeaks scandal played a significant role in consolidating the politically active nature of Anonymous: After the release of a number of highly controversial US diplomatic documents, PayPal, Mastercard, and Visa blocked payments towards the whistleblowing organization led by Julian Assange; Anonymous groups responded by expanding Operation Payback into Operation Avenge Assange. This involved launching cyberattacks against the companies' websites, causing multimillion-dollar losses in revenue. In this phase, 'information wants to be free' became Anonymous's (main) defying motto, and it championed the causes of prominent individuals such as Assange himself, the imprisoned former US servicemember-turned-whistleblower Chelsea Manning, or the internet activist Aaron Swartz, who took his life after being convicted by a US court for illegally downloading a database of academic articles.

Starting in 2011, Anonymous inaugurated a new, persistent trend of more or less visible involvement in basically any major grassroots protest movement worldwide. This began with Anonymous providing a notable contribution to the Arab Spring uprisings and the Occupy Wall Street movement, by offering technical assistance, disseminating information, and launching cyberattacks against adversaries' targets, and continued up to the most recent Black Lives Matter protests. Anonymous's new role of facilitator of activism worldwide became its most prominent feature, transforming its symbolism into a universal marker of political contention with sometimes rather cacophonic effects, such as in situations where Anonymous's name has been mobilized both by groups against and by groups in defence of a certain goal or government.[13] This political turn, however, had not been embraced by the totality of people identifying themselves as part of Anonymous. Between May and June 2011, a distinct group named LulzSec gained notoriety for its high-profile cyberattacks against a range of targets, including government agencies, corporations, and media organizations. LulzSec claimed to be motivated by the desire to bring Anonymous back to the original 'lulz'-inspired spirit, allegedly corrupted by the social justice-oriented turn that the most visible sectors of the (non-)group had taken. Despite being largely associated to its online actions, since the very beginning of Operation Chanology Anonymous has also had a direct 'real world' presence. Since 2012, on the occasion of 5 November, Anonymous-related groups have been organizing yearly street demonstrations in dozens of cities around the world, under the banner of the Million Mask March. The date is a reference to Guy Fawkes, the revolutionary who attempted to blow up the British parliament in 1605, popularized by the graphic novel and movie 'V for Vendetta'. The character's rebellious persona, characterized by the aura of an 'anonymous avenger of the people', turned this iconic mask into the most prominent visual component of the Anonymous brand. An interesting point of view from where to gauge Anonymous's contradictory trajectory is its relation to Islamist extremism. Starting in 2013, on 7 April, which coincides with Israeli's Holocaust Remembrance Day, various factions affiliated with Anonymous have been launching intensive attacks against Israeli government and business websites, with the stated aim of erasing Israel from the internet. So called 'Operation Israel' has been endorsed by a number of chapters, including diverse Islamist factions within Anonymous, such as the explicitly pro-Islamic State spin-off AnonGhost. On the other hand, after the ISIS offensive in Paris in November 2015, several Anonymous-related groups declared war to the Islamic State, launching Operation ISIS, mostly tasked with the goal of interfering the Jihadist notorious social media propaganda mastery. The operation gained unprecedented media attention and further popularized Anonymous, but it also sparked internal conflict.

It is important to stress that, except for the very first transition from pranks to political engagement, the vignettes above represent by no means a timeline detailing a linear evolution from point A to point B: Most of the bifurcations highlighted, instead, survive their triggering event and inject a new path into Anonymous's complex trajectory. Moreover, such bird's-eye view fails to account for the long tail of smaller instances that have brought Anonymous to fight for (and, sometimes at the same time, against) the most disparate set of causes:[14] unmasking the Illuminati's plot to destroy America; defending the right to porn on the internet in Australia; supporting Marxist-Leninist revolutionary groups in Turkey; defending dolphins and whales from illegal fishing in Japan; taking down child pornography rings; avenging victims of harassment and bullying.

Logic of Aggregation and Structural Properties

Started as a non-political entity, Anonymous turned into an omnipresent actor of political contention, with a logic of aggregation (or better *assemblage*) that defies common ideas about the dynamics of political assembly and association. In order to understand how this is possible, we shall first look into the pragmatic layer of what Anonymous does, how it is structured, and its organizational logic.

Anonymous's complexity already manifests itself at the level of its repertoire of action. Anonymous mostly (but not exclusively) builds upon a shared online-based repertoire, engaging in a variety of (now) established forms of 'hacktivist' direct action which include Distributed Denial of Service (DDoS) attacks (i.e. 'bombarding' an online service with a volume of requests causing it suspension); websites defacement (i.e. the alteration of the visual appearance of a website); doxxing (i.e. obtaining and publicly revealing personal private information about an individual); information leaks (i.e. acquiring and disclosing confidential information about an organization). Along with these cybertactics, however, Anonymous also engages with more conventional mobilization practices, such as information activism on social media and, in certain cases, the organization of traditional street demonstrations.

It is important to notice that, despite the widespread idea of hacking as an individual and somewhat ethereal activity, Anonymous's cyber-repertoire generally entails forms of synchronous coordination and plural deliberation akin to the form of (digital) assemblies. As a primarily internet phenomenon, its logic of assembly has been influenced by the technical properties of the different platforms that it has appropriated at different stages. On 4chan, a platform renowned as a breeding ground for a number of irreverent internet memes and pseudo-political subcultures,[15] Anonymous was primarily characterized by a storm-like, fully contingent behaviour, due to the properly anonymous and transient nature of interaction on the platform. When some Anonymous groups started coordinating actions on Internet Relay Chat (IRC) channels,[16] chat rooms characterized by distinct usernames, moderating roles, and invitation-only sections, role differentiation emerged, and with it, status and power dynamics of sort.[17] Soon after this, Anonymous accounts have been spreading on not-really-anonymous social media platforms like Twitter, Facebook, and YouTube, which contributed to the emergence of fandom-like dynamics,[18] as well as of more standard information activism strategies—with several, largely independent Twitter accounts acting as hubs for a vast network of news sharing and action claiming,[19] or Facebook pages providing space for online community-like interaction.[20] The migration to 'nonymous' social media platforms likely contributed to Anonymous's proliferation, as well as to its transformation into an even more composite entity when compared to the 'lulz-machine' or the 'guardian of the internet' that it used to be.

In the same vein as other self-proclaimed 'leaderless' movements, within Anonymous informal leadership has always emerged and relied on a 'choreography of assembly'[21] that discursively celebrates horizontality, while not always concretely implementing its principles. For example, tactics such as DDoS attacks (in which thousands of people could in principle participate, even without advanced hacking skills) have been performing a choreography of inclusivity and distributed contribution, whereas the most effective attacks relied on a small group of highly skilled hackers in control of networks of infected computers.[22] Relatedly, in spite of its proclaimed radically inclusive and horizontal nature, internal conflict and power struggles frequently arise within the group, resulting in the emergence of temporary leaders, accusations of inauthenticity, and internal conflict of sort.[23] Besides gathering participants in specific actions, Anonymous provides a framework for political contention suggesting that a logic of association is at play. Nonetheless, this form of association is far from being a stable and cohesive one. Different instances of Anonymous might or might not have any direct links amongst each other: Its network is loosely connected, while its participant base is ever shifting.[24] Anonymous is organized around so-called operations—relatively independent campaigns involved with a specific goal, theme, or enemy. Anonymous operations are generally arranged through a logic of voluntary and contingent association around a common cause—as well as, more often than not, through a logic of dissociation due to the emergence of conflict. Participants sometimes consistently spill over to new operations, while other times new operations emerge because of new recruits joining and bringing their own interests with them.[25] Anonymous's structural dynamics appear to follow a cyclical pattern of concentration and diffusion,[26] alternating between phases in which the network is centralized and (relatively) cohesive, and phases in which the network is greatly fragmented and incohesive.[27] As mentioned, its history is dotted with the creation of spin-offs, such as LulzSec, the Million Mask March, and AnonGhost. Whereas these groups explicitly differentiate their identities, clearly branding themselves as relatively independent entities, they maintain either an explicit or ambiguous reference to Anonymous as a whole, as well as a structural connection through social media networks, further complicating the analytical exercise of tracing the boundaries of this entity.[28]

Anonymous's Semiotic Repertoire

Besides the odd structural and organizational properties, a look at the level of identity and meaning-making is necessary in order to get a better sense of who or what Anonymous is and how that bears on theories of assembly. Originally, Anonymous's spirit coincided with the irreverent ethos of the 'mask culture' characteristics of the niche subcultural web; a culture rooted in impersonal, ephemeral, and vernacular practices.[29] This culture partly survived its politicization phase, when Anonymous repurposed its trickster-like attitude for, amongst, and above others, the cause of internet and information freedom.[30] With the phase of global proliferation, Anonymous turned into a catalyst for activism of all sort—some kind of 'universal marker of contention' adopted or evoked in disparate settings, for disparate causes.

In this sense, Anonymous can be better seen as an 'improper name'[31] or, more broadly, a 'contentious brand',[32] that is, a collection of symbols and signifiers open to be adopted and adapted by various individuals and groups interested in political contention. In order to approach Anonymous's culture and identity, then, one has to look at the level of symbols and signifiers, more than that of the signified/meaning. In contrast with its ever-shifting meanings (i.e. its semantic), indeed, Anonymous's visual aesthetics, symbolic repertoire and labelling collection (i.e. its semiotic) are highly standardized, bold, and conspicuous.

Two symbols, and countless memetic variations around them, accompany almost any Anonymous visual representation: the headless suited man and the Guy Fawkes mask. The first represents the lack of leadership, while the second the fight against corrupted authorities; both recall the power of anonymity and have been adopted and sported in protest setting of various kinds (online and offline) as explicit markers of identity. Slogans and other stylized self-descriptions play an important role in the production of Anonymous's identity, often evoking the tension within the (non-)collective between its internal diversity and its strive for unity.[33] Anonymous actions are in most cases branded with the standard signature: 'We are Anonymous. We are Legion'. The use of the plural pronoun 'we' and other recurrent sloganized self-descriptions ('We are Family'; 'United as one'; 'Everyone is Anonymous') discursively construct a strong 'sense of the we', prerequisite of a collective identity.[34] On the other hand, the specification that 'Anonymous is Legion' is a reference to the multiplicitous nature of this (non-)collective, together with other recurrent expressions such as 'Anonymous is not unanimous'.

Anonymous's participants often explicitly reject the very same idea that a distinction between 'who is' and 'who is not' Anonymous is a valid one. In turn, Anonymous is generally defined in either tautological ('Everyone is Anonymous'; 'Anonymous is everything') or paradoxical terms ('No one is Anonymous'; 'Anonymous does not exist'). Anonymous's intentionally under-/undefined nature, coupled with its radically decentralized structure and the lack of any membership validation procedure, entails that virtually anybody can claim affiliation. This radical openness comes with the paradoxical implication that Anonymous identity is at the centre of constant contention. As a consequence, the categories of authentic and inauthentic fail to determine the boundaries of who 'really is' Anonymous. Nonetheless, (in-)authenticity claims are omnipresent,[35] precisely because, lacking any other organizational vector, Anonymous is a purely semiotic construction: The only evidence of its existence, and the only element to assess its boundaries, is the presence of its brand.

Between Assembly and Association

As noted, Anonymous lacks an integrated structure, a cohesive purpose, and a (non-self-referential) definition of what it actually is. From this point of view, Anonymous embraces a temporality of contingency, characteristic of social formations delimited in space and time such as assemblies. On the other hand, however, the Anonymous brand has been instantiated in countless initiatives across space-time coordinates and social networks, in this resembling the more stable and predictable temporality of associations. In this section, I argue that, in order to resolve this seeming contradiction, one must look at Anonymous as a multiplicity and assemblage.

Anonymous is a contingent assembly, in the sense that it only exists in the 'here and now' of one of its many manifestations. At the same time, however, Anonymous is a permanent association, in the sense that it always exists as a recognizable entity, a *named* repository that various forces of contention can invoke and build upon at any time. Anonymous can be seen as an assembly on two levels: When a number of people get together under the banner of a specific operation, they generate a contingent assembly in the name of Anonymous for a specific cause; at the same time, Anonymous is an immanent 'assembly of assemblies', contingently assembling together various assemblies under a unified brand, attributed with cohesive identity and unified agency.

One could conceptualize Anonymous as one entity, as many entities, or as something in between. As one, Anonymous looks like a defined collective actor, characterized by specific practices, a certain ethos, and a plurality of objectives. As many, Anonymous looks like a collection of distinct initiatives, each with its own distinct identity and purpose. However, Anonymous stands somewhere in between—it is more than one but less than many.[36] The category of 'multiplicity'[37] thus becomes almost essential to characterize the ontological quality of Anonymous. Moving away from the idea that entities can be defined based on the essential properties of their substance, multiplicity emphasizes the way in which reality resists 'counting': Anonymous is 'one' *and* is 'many', a 'family' *and* a 'legion', a permanent association *and* contingent assemblies—all at the same time.

The notion of multiplicity goes hand in hand with that of assemblage,[38] which are networks of relations amongst components in constant flux.[39] Assemblages emerge through the dynamic interplay and connections between multiplicities; as such, they are not simply a collection of parts or a unified totality. They are open and adaptable systems that can change and evolve over time in their components and in their relation with other assemblages, while maintaining a recognizable identity. In the same vein, Anonymous has been in constant flux, changing its components, participants, goals, and even overall significance, while preserving a recognizable identity.

An important characteristic of assemblages is that they are materially heterogeneous, meaning that they are made up of 'stuff' that is different in nature:[40] people, artefacts, natural materials, symbols, ideas. Whereas traditional sociological theories tend to equate assemblies to grouping of human participants, an assemblage perspective emphasizes the role of non-human elements in producing more or less stable social formations. From this perspective, a town square is not a neutral container of assemblies but rather an active participant that produces and shapes the material conditions for gatherings, as well as elements of an imaginary of reappropriation of the public space that can galvanize a protest wave. Countless humans and non-human 'actants' have conspired throughout the years in assembling the puzzling entity named Anonymous. Among these, a special role has been played by its semiotic repertoire—icons, masks, slogans, and the very same name 'Anonymous'.

In the Name of Anonymous

One of the key adjectives that can be used to describe Anonymous is 'weird'. The temptation could be then to relegate Anonymous to the realm of weirdness, understood as a stand-alone category segregated from the normality of 'standard' phenomena. My key tenet here, however, is that Anonymous does not represent a qualitative deviation from the normality of how assemblies really work; rather, it brings to the surface, *giving them a name*, properties which are implicit to any form of assembly-assemblage.

It is no news that contemporary assemblies are inherently performative, in that the grievances, orientations, and meanings they put forward are rarely fixed and predefined, rather continuously redefined in the process of coming together.[41] Similarly, recent protest movements recognize and celebrate their inherent plurality and radical inclusiveness; however, they do so while attempting to synthetize a shared definition of the 'we' and of the course of action.[42] Such shared, representational definition (i.e. a collective identity) is either the premise or, in contemporary 'pluralist' models, the promise of political assemblies and associations: either a pre-existing coherent logic that explains why people get together or an emergent synthesis towards which people getting together aspire to. In Anonymous, it is neither. While references to a sense of 'we' and unity are firmly present and showcased, implying that the collective dimension is not completely diluted into a fully individualized model of digital connectivity,[43] these references are not based on a logic of identity in any representational or traditional sense of the expression.[44]

Abandoning the illusion that some shared transcendent normativity is either the premise or the promise of assemblies, Anonymous embraces the paradox of a 'permanent contingency', providing a reminder for scholars of political contention that assemblies need to be studied as complex assemblages. Anonymous's multiplicity is not denied behind a layer of ideological simplification, nor is it sublimated through a (likewise, ideological) faith in the dialogical power of rational assembly; rather, multiplicity is incorporated in the (non-)group's own imaginary. In other words, Anonymous resists any form of *bona fide* simplification: When approached from perspectives other than that of complexity and multiplicity such assemblage would simply not make sense, because it cannot be even defined. It cannot be defined but, Anonymous teaches us, it can be named. What is left, then, is a purely semiotic definition of this assembly-association-assemblage: The invocation of a certain signifier is the only conceivable marker of its identity. Anonymous is explicitly defined as a multiplicity, and instead of denying or attempting to resolve its multiplicity, it gives it a name—a name which, paradoxically enough, literally means 'nameless'.

Notes

1. This challenge also manifests in that referring to Anonymous with common expressions such as 'group', 'movement', or 'collective' is rather inappropriate. For this reason, the more agnostic term 'entity' will be preferred in most cases. Nonetheless, a certain amount of contradiction seems unavoidable.
2. See Gabriella Coleman, *Hacker, Hoaxer, Whistleblower, Spy: The Many Faces of Anonymous* (London: Verso Books, 2015); Parmy Olson, *We Are Anonymous* (New York: Random House, 2013); Carolin Weidemann, 'Between Swarm, Network, and Multitude: Anonymous and the Infrastructures of the Common', *Distinktion: Journal of Social Theory* 15, no. 3 (2014): 309–326.
3. See Davide Beraldo, 'Dividing by Zero. Tautology and Paradox in the Self-Descriptions of Anonymous', *Journal of Sociocybernetics* 17, no. 1 (2020): 23–49; Leonhard Dobusch and Dennis Schoeneborn, 'Fluidity, Identity, and Organizationality: The Communicative Constitution of Anonymous', *Journal of Management Studies* 52, no. 8 (2015): 1005–1035.
4. See https://knowyourmeme.com/memes/internet-hate-machine.
5. The concept of 'the lulz', a corruption of the popular acronym LOL (Laughing Out Loud), refers to the pleasure that derives from causing mischief at the expense of others.
6. Gabriella Coleman, 'Anonymous: From the Lulz to Collective Action', *The New Everyday: A Media Commons Project* (2011), http://mediacommons.org/tne/pieces/anonymous-traveling-pure-lulz-land-political-territories.
7. This draws upon both Manuel DeLanda's post-deleuzian version and Bruno Latour's Actor-Network Theory one. See Manuel DeLanda, *A New Philosophy of Society: Assemblage Theory and Social Complexity* (London: Continuum, 2006); Bruno Latour,

Reassembling the Social: An Introduction to Actor-Network Theory (Oxford: Oxford University Press, 2005). Whereas the two perspective differs on important ontological points, those differences are not relevant for the present argument.

8. Luke Goode, 'Anonymous and the Political Ethos of Hacktivism', *Popular Communication* 13, no. 1 (2015): 74–86.
9. Davide Beraldo, 'Movements as Multiplicities and Contentious Branding: Lessons from the Digital Exploration of #Occupy and #Anonymous', *Information, Communication & Society* 25, no. 8 (2022): 1098–1114.
10. For a detailed and in-depth overview of Anonymous, albeit delimited to a specific phase, the unavoidable references are the work of Parmy Olson and Gabriella Coleman.
11. Whitney Phillips, *This Is Why We Can't Have Nice Things: Mapping the Relationship between Online Trolling and Mainstream Culture* (Cambridge, MA: MIT Press, 2015).
12. Coleman, 'Anonymous: From the Lulz to Collective Action'.
13. Beraldo, 'Dividing by Zero', 36–37.
14. See Christian Fuchs, 'The Anonymous Movement in the Context of Liberalism and Socialism', *Interface: A Journal for and about Social Movements* 5, no. 2 (2013): 345–376; Beraldo, 'Movements as Multiplicities and Contentious Branding'.
15. Marc Tuters, Emilija Jokubauskaitė, and Daniel Bach, 'Post-Truth Protest: How 4chan Cooked Up the Pizzagate Bullshit', *M/c Journal* 21, no. 3 (2018).
16. Internet Relay Chat (IRC) is a minimalist chatroom system widely adopted in the 1990s, still popular nowadays amongst hacker communities. It plays a crucial coordination and day-to-day discussion role within groups linked to Anonymous.
17. Justus Uitermark, 'Complex Contention: Analyzing Power Dynamics within Anonymous', *Social Movement Studies* 16, no. 4 (2017): 409.
18. Coleman, *Hacker, Hoaxer, Whistleblower, Spy*, 264–267.
19. Davide Beraldo, 'Unfolding #Anonymous on Twitter: The Networks behind the Mask', *First Monday* 27, no. 1 (2022): 26.
20. Beraldo, 'Dividing by Zero'.
21. Paolo Gerbaudo, *Tweets and the Streets: Social Media and Contemporary Activism* (London: Pluto Press, 2012), 18–47.
22. Olson, *We Are Anonymous,* 42.
23. Dobusch and Schoeneborn, 'Fluidity, Identity, and Organizationality'; Uitermark, 'Complex Contention'.
24. Beraldo, 'Unfolding #Anonymous on Twitter', 5.
25. Ibid., 23.
26. Uitermark, 'Complex Contention'.
27. Beraldo, 'Unfolding #Anonymous on Twitter', 6–17.
28. Ibid., 27–31.
29. Daniel De Zeeuw and Marc Tuters, 'The Internet Is Serious Business: On the Deep Vernacular Web and Its Discontents', *Public Culture* 16, no. 2 (2004): 214–232.
30. Coleman, *Hacker, Hoaxer, Whistleblower, Spy*.
31. Marco Deseriis, *Improper Names: Collective Pseudonyms from the Luddites to Anonymous* (Minneapolis: University of Minnesota Press, 2015).
32. Beraldo, 'Movements as Multiplicities and Contentious Branding'.
33. Beraldo, 'Dividing by Zero'.
34. Following Alberto Melucci's theory of collective identity, see Alberto Melucci, *Challenging Codes: Collective Action in the Information Age* (Cambridge: Cambridge University Press, 1996).

35. Dobusch, 'Fluidity, Identity, and Organizationality', 1017–1018.
36. John Law, 'After ANT: Complexity, Naming, and Topology', *The Sociological Review* 47, no. S1 (1999): 12.
37. Gilles Deleuze, *Difference and Repetition* (New York: Columbia University Press, 1994); Manuel DeLanda, *Intensive Science and Virtual Philosophy* (London: A&C Black, 2002).
38. Gilles Deleuze and Félix Guattari, *A Thousand Plateaus: Capitalism and Schizophrenia* (Minneapolis: University of Minnesota Press, 1987), 3–28.
39. DeLanda, *New Philosophy of Society.*
40. John Law, 'Notes on the Theory of the Actor-Network: Ordering, Strategy, and Heterogeneity', *Systems Practice* 5 (1992): 379–393.
41. Judith Butler, *Notes toward a Performative Theory of Assembly* (Cambridge, MA: Harvard University Press, 2015).
42. Melucci, *Challenging Codes.*
43. W. Lance Bennett and Alexandra Segerberg, *Logic of Connective Action* (Cambridge: Cambridge University Press, 2012).
44. Wiedemann, 'Between Swarm, Network, and Multitude'.

Further Reading

Beraldo, Davide. 'Dividing by Zero. Tautology and Paradox in the Self-Descriptions of Anonymous'. *Journal of Sociocybernetics* 17, no. 1 (2020): 32–49. https://doi.org/10.26754/ojs_jos/jos.202014246.

Beraldo, Davide. 'Unfolding #Anonymous on Twitter: The Networks behind the Mask'. *First Monday* 27, no. 1 (2022): 1–36. https://doi.org/10.5210/fm.v27i1.11723.

Butler, Judith. *Notes toward a Performative Theory of Assembly*. Cambridge, MA: Harvard University Press, 2015.

Coleman, Gabriella. 'Anonymous: From the Lulz to Collective Action | The New Everyday'. 2011. http://mediacommons.futureofthebook.org/tne/pieces/anonymous-lulz-collective-action, accessed 5 July 2017.

Coleman, Gabriella. *Hacker, Hoaxer, Whistleblower, Spy: The Many Faces of Anonymous*. Repr. London: Verso Books, 2015.

DeLanda, Manuel. *A New Philosophy of Society: Assemblage Theory and Social Complexity*. London: Continuum, 2006.

Deleuze, Gilles, and Félix Guattari. *A Thousand Plateaus: Capitalism and Schizophrenia*. Minneapolis: University of Minnesota Press, 1987.

Dobusch, Leonhard, and Dennis Schoeneborn. 'Fluidity, Identity, and Organizationality: The Communicative Constitution of Anonymous'. *Journal of Management Studies* 52, no. 8 (2015): 1005–1035.

Fuchs, Christian. 'The Anonymous Movement in the Context of Liberalism and Socialism'. *Interface: A Journal for and about Social Movements* 5, no. 2 (2013): 345–376.

Olson, Parmy. *We Are Anonymous*. New York: Random House, 2013.

Uitermark, Justus. 'Complex Contention: Analyzing Power Dynamics within Anonymous'. *Social Movement Studies* 16, no. 4 (2017): 403–417. https://doi.org/10.1080/14742837.2016.1184136.

Wiedemann, Carolin. 'Between Swarm, Network, and Multitude: Anonymous and the Infrastructures of the Common'. *Distinktion: Journal of Social Theory* 15, no. 3 (2014): 309–326. https://doi.org/10.1080/1600910X.2014.895768.

CHAPTER 26

TAHRIR SQUARE

The Complexity of an Assembly

RABAB EL-MAHDI

INTRODUCTION

ON one of those rare occasions when ordinary people prevail, Tahrir Square was the epicentre of Egypt's 2011 uprising, which ousted Egyptian President Hosni Mubarak. The vibrancy of the assembly stood in stark contrast to an ailing regime of thirty years and its repressive apparatus. The images of a lively and harmonious gathering, with peaceful protesters waving flags and banners, and engaging in artistic expressions, spoke to the 'power of the masses' at its best. Tahrir became a symbol of the broader wave of uprisings known as the Arab Spring, inspiring global protest movements, including Occupy Wall Street. Dismissing a lot of its complexity, the assembly was construed as a peaceful assembly organized by young, educated Egyptian activists using social media to organize which initiated a democratic transition—that eventually failed.

Using participatory observations from the event, and the advantage of hindsight, this chapter reflects on some of these less-discussed aspects of the public assembly in Tahrir Square, highlighting its multi-dimensionality. The chapter sheds light on the multifaceted nature of the assembly, encompassing both expressions of unity and moments of internal tension, highlighting the complexity inherent in collective action. Instead of fitting neatly into dichotomies such as violent versus non-violent, or categorizations of participants as protagonists or bystanders, the Tahrir assembly illustrates the diversity and complexity of some assemblies. While overall it was a peaceful assembly, the use of violence was also part of the making of the Tahrir assembly and later on in protecting it from the state violence.[1] Despite the prevalent emphasis on social media, and the role of middle-class youth in shaping this assembly, the subaltern counter-violence in their dissent to state repression also played a key role in its making. Finally, the assembly was not simply a spontaneous event. Rather, it was in the making for at least a decade earlier, during which different actors developed tools of resistance to combat the dispossession and securitization they experienced in their daily lives.

The following sections first discuss the often-ignored role of violent measures in materializing the assembly and the role of the popular classes. It argues that struggles and forms of resistance in the decade before the assembly came to the fore in 2011. The second section of the chapter reflects on the Tahrir assembly as an exceptional event in Egyptian politics. Particularly, its diversity and inclusivity and how it materialized an alternative reality which many Egyptians aspired to. Finally, the third section addresses how this formative event has distorted actors' perceptions and tactics in the months and years that followed. The revolution was soon characterized as a middle-class affair and the popular classes who brought their resistance to bear for the revolution to happen quickly became invisible in the ensuing political process. The chapter concludes with some observations about the far-reaching and continued impact of this assembly beyond the immediate political outcomes.

The Making of Tahrir Assembly

As the Panoptic Tower of the Egyptian state, protesting in Tahrir Square has always been a formidable challenge.[2] Literally, the centre of Cairo, the capital, and a global metropolis of more than twenty million, the regime has always been adamant about not allowing protesters to reach Tahrir. The 'massive curved rectangle covering about 45,000 square meters' connects 'Downtown and older Cairo to the east, with the river and Giza and the newer districts to the west'.[3] It is home to the Mugamma government building and only a few metres away from the Ministry of Interior.[4] Only on very few occasions did Egyptians manage to defy the repressive apparatus of the state and protest in Tahrir let alone occupy it. Before 2011, it had been the site for a few yet important protests including Egypt's Revolution against the British occupation in 1919; the 1977 Bread uprising when Egyptians protested against former President Anwar Sadat's economic policies; and in March 2003 protests against the US invasion of Iraq.

Thus, overcoming the state-fortified defence and capturing Tahrir in 2011 took more than "tech-savvy" activists, their performativity, and the use of social media, which many accounts of the assembly tend to over-emphasize.[5] In such accounts, 'it was a democratically minded Egyptian youth, armed with new media tools, and disheartened by their lack of socio-economic opportunities or possibilities for political participation, who led the country's eighteen days of revolt'.[6] Specifically, the 'virtual public space' on the internet set in motion the actions that led to the taking over of 'physical public space' (Tahrir) and to the eventual replacement of a despotic government.[7] According to one of the studies in this genre, 'social media in general, and Facebook in particular . . . were crucial in shaping how citizens made individual decisions about participating in protests, the logistics of protest, and the likelihood of success'.[8] But, while youth activists and social media were imperative in disseminating information and mobilizing for the protests at the least possible cost, neither was enough. The state repression was not willed away by social media or the protesters chanting Silmiyya (peaceful).

Rather, it took protesters two attempts to capture the Square in January 2011. Having participated in the protests on both occasions, there was a visible difference in the body of protesters and the dynamics of those landmark days. On the first attempt, the day the protests started—25 January—the majority were the more politicized, middle-class protesters, who responded to the mobilization calls by activist groups such as 6 April Youth Movement (*harakat shabab 6 abril*), the National Association for Change (YNAC), and the Facebook page: We Are All Khaled Said (*Kulina Khaled Said*—KKS). Despite their best efforts, the protesters were not able to defend their foothold when the security forces raided the square with armoured cars and tear gas later that night.

Only on the second attempt on 28 January—known as 'Friday of Fury'—did the protesters capture the Square, when urban poor Egyptians, the popular classes or subalterns, joined the protests and managed to combat the state's physical violence. Simultaneously, during that day police stations in working-class neighbourhoods like Saida Zaynab in Cairo and El-Arbeen, in the city of Suez, were being attacked, increasing the pressure on the security apparatus and pre-empting any chance for reinforcements coming to Tahrir.[9] On that day, I joined thousands of other protesters coming from different mosques in Cairo after the Friday prayer.

At Qasr El-Nile bridge, leading to the square, security forces were camped out in armoured cars blocking access to the Square. With every attempt to cross the bridge, security showered protesters with rubber bullets, tear gas, and water cannons. After a couple of back-and-forth attempts, in which many protesters were injured, the march was scattered into smaller groups. Some took refuge around the bridge, and others just left.

It appeared to be a deadlock until young men from popular classes, identifiable by the modesty of their appearance, body language, slang, and intonation, broke the siege. They came rushing towards the parked security car and used empty bottles to create hand-made Molotovs; they caught the tear-gas bombs and threw them back at the security forces. At one point, one of the young men seized a parked police motorcycle, emptying its fuel into hand-made bottles-turned-grenades and using the vehicle as part of a barricade to stop other security cars from advancing. For hours, they continued these street fights, turning everything they came across into a weapon for combat. Finally, the security forces withdrew and the protesters were able to set camp in Tahrir.

Like a rhizome, the roots of this assembly were entangled in struggles that preceded it and in spaces far beyond its parameters. Despite being unexpected by many analysts, this assembly and the uprising it initiated did not come out of thin air. Rather, the protests of January 2011 were a culmination of a ten-year cycle of contention, in which different movements emerged and developed and gained experience with mobilization. It started with organization in support of the Palestinian Intifada in 2001, followed by protests against the US invasion of Iraq in 2003, and then the emergence of Kifaya (meaning 'enough') in 2005, the first movement calling for regime change.[10] As many have already shown, most of the leading youth activists mobilizing for the protests in 2011, including

6 April, the YNAC, and *Kulina Khaled Said*—KKS, met and became politicized in these episodes.[11]

Similarly, even though less discussed, different sectors of the popular classes and marginalized communities started combatting the state's intensified neoliberal processes of dispossession including forceful land and housing evictions.[12] Starting with labour strikes in the city of Mahalla in 2006, in the few years preceding the uprising, Egypt witnessed a wave of unprecedented labour strikes and workplace sit-ins as well as frequent demand-specific local mobilizations around issues including housing, water, and schools. In doing so, these groups developed the physical skills to resist the entrenched security apparatus that regularly circumscribed their daily lives. It was almost daily incidents to combat forceful evictions, to attack a police station where someone close was being abused, or for informal workers to engage in physical violence to fend off the police harassment on the street.[13] The young men of the popular classes had to develop skills to combat police violence as part of their survival and resistance mechanisms on the periphery of the city years before they brought them to its centre in Tahrir.

Tahrir's Exceptionality

Once the protesters captured the square, they erected barricades and checkpoints on streets leading to the square to protect this newly liberated space from the regime. For the first time in generations, Egyptians claimed a shared 'public' space. Like other securitized states under neoliberalism, in Egypt, the concept of public space does not exist. There is either private property or 'state' property. So, in occupying the square, protesters were 'claiming' the space not just 're'-claiming it. The name of the square reflected the undergoing process: *liberation* (Tahrir) of both space and relations.

The physical space created the ecosystem for an Arendtian *public space of appearance* 'where I appear to others as others appear to me, where men exist not merely like other living or inanimate things, but to make their appearance explicitly' through deliberation and action.[14] One of the common signs in the assembly was: 'Mubarak Leave! Egyptians finally met each other'. Another one was 'Egyptians exchanged phone numbers'. While these phrases were meant to signify the capacity for collective action and the power it generates, the assembly also had people 'seen' and 'heard' in ways they had never experienced before.

For two weeks, Egyptian protesters set up camp in the square; some made tents out of blankets; others just slept in the open. The protesters also established a makeshift hospital to attend to those injured during the multiple attempts by the regime forcefully to end the sit-in. They also set up a stage with a sound system upon which poets and singers performed in between political speeches. Some brought food and water; others took charge of the garbage collection. Some cooked; others brought food from home. Everyone shared. They shared their phone charges, as well as their life stories and experiences. They sang and prayed and made tea. There were discussion groups to develop strategies for social and political change. The people in Tahrir turned the square into an 'extension of their living rooms'.[15]

Marked by its diversity and inclusivity at the same time, the newly liberated space brought together Egyptians who normally lead parallel lives because of the sharp class divisions in Egyptian society. In the absence of public spaces and services, these groups hardly ever cross paths. Tahrir temporarily suspended the pervasive structural inequality and securitization that render many invisible. Homeless children who lived on the street took refuge in the Square, but so did my foreign-educated students. In their daily lives, those two demographics never sit next to each other chatting, even if briefly. But in Tahrir, they did.

All these actions were part of the politics of the assembly. As a liberated island in a sea of regime domination, the protesters developed in Tahrir what Henri Lefebvre called 'spatial practice', ways and routines through which space is experienced in everyday life, not just physically but also socially and culturally, producing and reproducing social relations and power dynamics.[16]

That conducive environment forged a practice of political solidarity by passing many of the pervasive gender and religious polarities. That liberation was reflected in the changing social relations and the ethos of the Square as the protesters called it: Akhlala' El-Midan.[17] It was a code of conduct to govern their newly liberated and self-governed space, whereby there was no sexual harassment or religious bigotry. In a country where gender- and religious-based aggression is not a rarity, the Tahrir assembly codified a different (new) reality. As Judith Butler put it, the protesters 'were breaking down a conventional distinction between public and private in order to establish new relations of equality; in this sense, they were incorporating into the very social form of resistance the principles they were struggling to realize in broader political forms'.[18] The assembly was the space for the protesters to create their own alternative reality away from the state and society as they experience it in their everyday lives.

The Charade of Power and Unity

Prompting the unresolved question of whether public assemblies have durable impacts, soon after the sit-in ended on 11 February 2011, the assumptions of invincibility and unity of the Square soon came crumbling down. The inclusive 'public space of appearance' for all was replaced by a very exclusive political agenda.[19] The grievances of subalterns were sidelined, and their participation—the participation that made the assembly possible in the first place—was criminalized. The revolution became characterized as a middle-class affair, in which activists and their aesthetics were hailed as the true revolutionaries, while working-class aesthetics and actions were villainized as forms of violent 'thuggery'.[20] Issues of social justice, which had been canonized in the revolution's main slogans, 'Bread, Freedom, Social Justice', took a backseat and the public debate spiralled and polarized around the writing of the constitution, the sequencing of plebiscites, and the division of power along a polarized secular-religious binary.[21]

Similarly, the sense of triumphalism that came with the Tahrir assembly was almost an emotional and cognitive entrapment. It blinded some of its protagonists to the fact that this space of appearance, like similar others, was fragile and existed only when actualized through action and presence. Activists over-estimated the threat of public assembly as a powerful antidote against undesirable political outcomes, often using 'El-Tahrir Mawgu'd (Tahrir would always be there) as a euphemism for the ability to mobilize mass protests. But, as Hannah Arendt maintained long ago, 'wherever people gather together, it is potentially there, but only potentially, not necessarily and not forever'.[22] With the political process having become exclusionary and the disintegration of the temporary cross-class alliance that was necessary for the making of Tahrir in 2011, mass mobilization was not easily repeatable.

At the same time, the main strength of Tahrir being a centralized alternative space of resistance became a weakness in the aftermath of the assembly. While the 'enclosure helped create a sense of unity and a shared destiny and facilitated the actualization of a counter-arrangement that critiqued existing systems of power',[23] it also curtailed the spread and growth of resistance and organization outside it. The huge assembly contained in Tahrir became the focal point of attraction for dissent. The community of protesters was contained in that site instead of trying to revolutionize other sites. Except in the final few days of the assembly, when labour strikes prompted the final push in the fall of Mubarak's regime, there were no other sites of contention besides Tahrir.[24] Despite being imperative in the first days of the uprisings, the containment of this space and its exceptionality weakened the prospects of a much-needed decentralization of resistance.

Concomitantly, the political cadres that came out of the assembly did not have the ability to connect to do the kind of political canvassing and organization required outside the new 'centre' that Tahrir had become. As Abdelrahman put it: 'Absence of a centralized organizational structure . . . quickly became a liability in . . . a political process that was reduced to electoral politics, for which centralized organization is paramount and specific skills and tactics essential. They had neither.'[25] Instead, many groups assumed mass mobilization could replace day-in-and-day-out grassroots political work and Tahrir became the short answer for many political groups, and the first tool to which they resorted. Calls to march to Tahrir were overused and exhausted by activists and organizers.

Following two tumultuous years, the uprising that started in the Tahrir assembly in 2011 was aborted by a military takeover supported by mass protests in the same square in 2013. The Tahrir mass assembly of 2013 was the last to date, ushering Egypt into an unprecedented era of authoritarianism. The contradiction left many wondering: 'Can we ever really know who the "we" is who assembles in the street, and whether any given assembly really represents the people as such? And whether any given assembly can represent what we mean by freedom of assembly as such?'[26] Others even rehashed pseudo-Orientalist cultural explanations about the Arab affinity to authoritarianism.

However, the seemingly contradictory outcomes of Tahrir speak more broadly to the limitations of public assemblies as a 'tool', not only the specifics of the Egyptian case. Just like elections that usher in right-wing parties, and mass protests that are deployed by both democratic and non-democratic forces, assemblies can be and are used for different sometimes contradictory outcomes. As a complex form of political intervention, assemblies unlike these other tools can have ramifications past their political outcomes, which was the case of Tahrir.

Conclusion

Tahrir assembly's influence extends beyond immediate political changes. As Alain Badiou, said: 'The Egyptian movement . . . was big . . . was long . . . [and] had many complex compositions'.[27] In contrast to the reversible political outcomes, the dynamics of the assembly, which captured the imagination, minds, and hearts of many, are not necessarily reversible. Friendships, romantic relationships, and political parties were formed during that assembly and outlasted the event. For years, the hundreds of thousands who participated were proud that during the two-week sit-in, there was no theft, assault, or bigotry of any kind. The event was narrated and came to be remembered through a series of powerful images: a young man standing peacefully in front of an armoured police car; Muslim protesters praying while others protecting them; non-veiled women singing next to conservative bearded Islamists; and protesters sharing their food and mopping the streets, along with witty signage and slogans. All these images and the dynamics they reflected were definitely part of the magic of Tahrir, and how it will be remembered.

The enduring significance of Tahrir Square as a touchstone in the collective consciousness underscores the intricate relationship between public assemblies and the enduring impact they can have on social dynamics and individual perspectives long after the assembly itself has concluded. During the 2011 assembly, many were making references to the other few Tahrir sit-ins that they had participated in or read about. Some remembered 30 March 2003 when they managed to camp in the Square following the protests against the US invasion of Iraq. Others were asking older protesters about the 1970s protests. Tahrir Square has become more than a physical space or a moment in time; it has embedded itself in the collective memory of Egyptians. Each of its few yet landmark assemblies created an imprint that together form an intergenerational memory. In songs and poems, the remembrance of the assembly has been immortalized as a reservoir of shared experiences, emotions, and aspirations that can be tapped into during subsequent moments of societal reflection or upheaval.

NOTES

1. On 1 February, the regime hired thugs who raided Tahrir, riding camels and horses in what came to be known as the Battle of Camels. See Farha Ghannam, 'Meanings and Feelings: Local Interpretations of the Use of Violence in the Egyptian Revolution', *American Ethnologist* 39, no. 1 (2012): 32–36.
2. The Panopticon is the metaphor Michel Foucault used to explore the relationship between systems of social control and people in a disciplinary situation. It marked the transition to a disciplinary power, with every movement supervised and all events recorded. Since the tower is the source of surveillance, it has to be protected.
3. Ahdaf Soueif, *Cairo: My City, Our Revolution* (London: Bloomsbury, 2012), 10.
4. A fourteen-story central government building, the labyrinthine home of the monstrous Egyptian bureaucracy.
5. See, for example, Juan Cole, *The New Arabs: How the Millennial Generation Is Changing the Middle East* (New York: Simon & Schuster, 2014); Jeffery Alexander, *Performative Revolution in Egypt: An Essay in Cultural Power* (London: Bloomsbury, 2011).
6. Sarah Rennick, *Politics and Revolution in Egypt Rise and Fall of the Youth Activists* (London: Routledge, 2018), 10.
7. See, for example, Manuel Castells, *Networks of Outrage and Hope: Social Movements in the Internet Age* (Cambridge: Polity Press, 2012).
8. Zeynep Tüfekçi and Christopher Wilson, 'Social Media and the Decision to Participate in Political Protest: Observations from Tahrir Square', *Journal of Communication* 62, no. 2 (2012): 363.
9. For more details, see Neil Ketchley, *Egypt in a Time of Revolution: Contentious Politics and the Arab Spring* (Cambridge: Cambridge University Press, 2017); and Rabab El-Mahdi, 'Orientalising the Egyptian Uprising', *Jadaliyya*, 11 April 2011, https://www.jadaliyya.com/Details/23882.
10. Mona El-Ghobashy, *Bread and Freedom: Egypt's Revolutionary Situation* (Stanford, CA: Stanford University Press, 2021), who dates the rise of this cycle to earlier in the mid-1990s with the start land dispossessions in the countryside.
11. See, for example, Maha Abdelrahman, *Egypt's Long Revolution: Protest Movements and Uprisings* (London: Routledge, 2015).
12. Ray Bush and Habib Ayeb, eds., *Marginality and Exclusion in Egypt* (Chicago: University of Chicago Press, 2012); Joel Beinin, *The Struggle for Workers' Rights in Egypt* (Washington, DC: Solidarity Center, 2010); Anne Alexander and Moustafa Bassiouny, *Bread, Freedom and Social Justice: Workers and the Egyptian Revolution* (London: Zed Books, 2014); Abdelrahman, *Egypt's Long Revolution*; Walter Armbrust, 'The Revolution against Neoliberalism', *Jadaliyya*, 23 February 2011, http://www.jadaliyya.com/pages/index/717/the-revolution-against-neoliberalism-.
13. El-Nadim Center for Rehabilitation of Torture Victims, *Systemic Torture in Egypt* (Cairo, 2010).
14. Hannah Arendt, *The Human Condition* (Chicago: University of Chicago Press, 1958), 198.
15. Lawrence Rosen, 'A Guide to the "Arab Street" ', *Anthropology Now* 3, no. 2 (2011): 41–47.
16. Henri Lefebvre, *The Production of Space* [1974], trans. Donald Nicholson-Smith (Malden, MA: Blackwell, 1991).
17. Transliteration of the colloquial Egyptian pronunciation of the Arabic word Akhlaq meaning manners, ethos, ethics.

18. Judith Butler, *Notes toward a Performative Theory of Assembly* (Cambridge, MA: Harvard University Press, 2015), 90.
19. Ibid., for more on the debate about the durability of Arendt's 'public space of appearance'.
20. Jessica Winegar, 'A Civilized Revolution: Aesthetics and Political Action in Egypt', *American Ethnologist* 43, no. 4 (2016): 609–622.
21. Acknowledging the futility of these debates at the time, the late blogger Muhammad Abu al-Ghayt wrote shortly after the assembly was over, decrying how the process slipped into political parochialism, forgetting the grievances of the majority. 'al-Fuqara' Awwalan Ya Wilad al-Kalb' (the poor first, you sons of bitches), 17 June 2011, http://gedarea.blogspot.com/2011/06/normal-0-false-false-false.html.
22. Arendt, *Human Condition*.
23. Farha Ghannam, 'The Rise and Decline of the Hetrotoptic Space: Views from Midan Al-Tahrir. Jadaliyya', 25 January 2016, https://www.jadaliyya.com/Details/32895/The-Rise-and-Decline-of-a-Heterotopic-Space-Views-from-Midan-al-Tahrir.
24. Alexander and Bassiouny, *Bread, Freedom and Social Justice*, 193.
25. Abdelrahman, *Egypt's Long Revolution*, 74.
26. Butler, *Notes Toward a Performative Theory of Assembly*, 156.
27. https://www.opendemocracy.net/en/north-africa-west-asia/alain-badiou-on-egyptian-revolution-questions/.

Further Reading

Abdelrahman, Maha. *Egypt's Long Revolution: Protest Movements and Uprisings*. London: Routledge, 2015.

Alexander, Anne, and Moustafa Bassiouny. *Bread, Freedom, and Social Justice: Workers and the Egyptian Revolution*. London: Zed Books, 2014.

El-Ghobashy, Mona. *Bread and Freedom: Egypt's Revolutionary Situation*. Stanford, CA: Stanford University Press, 2021.

Ghannam, Farha. 'Meanings and Feelings: Local Interpretations of the Use of Violence in the Egyptian Revolution'. *American Ethnologist* 39, no. 1 (2012): 32–36.

Said, A. 'We Ought to Be Here: Historicizing Space and Mobilization in Tahrir Square'. *International Sociology* 30, no. 4 (2014): 348–366.

CHAPTER 27

MOVEMENT LESSONS AT STANDING ROCK

Protesting the Dakota Access Pipeline

TARA HOUSKA

MIST dusted my eyelashes as I squinted upward, trying to make out the shape of the wings in the swirling grey above. 'Looks like a hawk', I thought. My eyes briefly locked with a man across the loose circle, he had been looking up too. Others in the large camp formed on the border of the Standing Rock Sioux reservation were glancing at the twenty-foot berth that had quietly formed around us amidst the chaos of a camp of thousands at breakfast time. Some walked quickly past, others stared curiously and lingered around our circle.

Two representatives from each of the smaller camps within the main camp opposed to the Dakota Access Pipeline were present. Many of these camps had formed based on geographic region or tribal nation, others on relationships and families. All of us were in various states of outward well-being—some looked like they had access to a shower recently, others not. All looked tired. All looked more vivid, more complete somehow. Living together, tracking the sun instead of the hours, reclaiming old ways of visiting and sharing songs, food, culture; being together for longer than a powwow weekend or a ceremony was changing us all, stirring ancient ways of knowing.

I was pretty sure this meeting had been called to kick our camp out. A few of us were still in jail as of this morning, for blockading yet another pipeline worksite a few days prior. Our camp's social media livestreams were averaging 100,000 viewers and the oil company's CEO (chief executive officer) looked redder and redder at every new press conference. Social media and citizen journalism were overtaking mainstream news on the story of Natives on the Plains staring down big oil. We were telling our own stories for once, and our voices were reaching folks across the world.

The flow of vehicles into the camps never ceased and the story of the Dakota Access Pipeline spilled across both broadcast media and the social media feeds of people all over the globe. Solidarity protests sprang up in communities thousands of miles from the occupation on the prairie. The story of our camp within the broader camp, or rather the lack thereof, as we were largely shrouded in intentional anonymity, was turning heads within our newly created villages.

The rumours flying around were extreme. A few weeks back, two Native women visited our camp, beginning by stating they had heard we were violent, that we had badly harmed someone, and asking for space to say what they came there to say. The pained shock on one of our Lakota matriarch's faces was palpable. 'You're safe here', Olowan said gently, then listened. By the end of that long meeting, those women's faces were red with anger at those by whom they had been misled. One of them hugged us each tightly and told us to stand strong, to keep fighting. We opened the flaps of the tent to the constant presence of federal and state snipers on the hill, helicopters buzzing overhead, the tireless breeze, wood being split, laughter, cooking, chatter. They thanked us again and left.

Some eyes in this morning circle were giving a once-over to me and our other camp representative. Some eyes felt hard; others felt inquisitive.

The night prior, our camp had sat in our largest space together, deciding whom to send to this all-camp meeting called by the Standing Rock chairman as we balanced bowls of hot salmon chowder on our knees. The salmon was a gift from a tribe out of the Pacific Northwest. They had sent us over one thousand pounds of beautiful red gold, a traditional food that was nourishing both our bodies and our spirits in the growing cold. Gifts like these helped us to keep going, to centre why we were here and what was at stake.

After an hour of hemming and hawing, we had agreed to send two of the matriarchs. One was a respected Lakota elder and sun dancer, the other her protégé, Olowan. Deb White Plume smiled carefully and said, 'Well I appreciate your vote of confidence, but this is what I would do', and proceeded to override us all. Her eyes shone brightly in the lantern light as she spoke of us needing to stand up for ourselves, to properly represent our camp of mostly young people by sending young people.

Me and the other voice she picked looked sidelong at each other. 'Okay, I'll find my cleanest Carhartts', he smiled as I gave a brief, uncertain nod to her. She had been directing, guiding, and challenging all I knew over these past months. Maybe she was impressing a lesson upon us about fractionation, about what can happen to a people erased when society notices us, what can happen under enormous pressure and worsening state violence. Maybe she wanted us to stand up and step up.

A small ripple went through one side of the circle. The Standing Rock chairman and another person had arrived. We stood in silence for the briefest moment, the fog of our collective breath whipped away by the relentless prairie wind. Then we were all shaking hands, saying hello to each other. Hellos quickly became a few jokes and easy laughter. My stomach did somersaults, preparing for how to respond to being asked to leave. I was a guest here among the Standing Rock people, like so many others. The elders to whom I was accountable, the fierce Lakota and Dakota women who directed and guided me, were firm in their commitment to continue resisting, to keep fighting for the water.

The laughter quieted. We were on to the serious matter. You could have heard a pin drop were it not for the thick, half-frozen mud we were standing in. One non-governmental organization (NGO) leader grinned at me. Here was the moment he had waited for. The non-violent direction action camp led by matriarchs, the camp of troublemakers who operated outside the NGOs and the tribal council, was finally going to be shut down. I saw his smile falter as the chairman began introducing the man with him, instead. This man was to act in an official liaison capacity, to be the go-between between tribal council and the camps. Some offers of collaboration points for us all were discussed. Folks traded needs and advice. Then we were walking away through what looked like would soon be snow.

'Well, that was unexpected'. I looked up to my fellow 'representative'. 'I thought we were done for, dude'. We both laughed in relief. 'Back to it, then'.

'Go back to main camp!' bellowed over and over through a crackling loudspeaker at top volume. The police officer holding the mic to his lips was heavily armed and wearing a Flak jacket. The main camp was along highway 1806, the primary road between the Standing Rock reservation and Bismarck, just north of the reservation boundary. Now that construction on the pipeline had reached highway 1806, tolerance for the encampment had come to an end. The next step for Dakota Access Pipeline was the under-bore below highway 1806, then on to drilling the Missouri River. The Missouri River was a primary call for many of us—the proposed crossing was just a few miles north of the water intake for the Standing Rock people. It was where relatives and ancestors were buried. It was also the site of government-sponsored flooding and lost land after the building of a dam upstream. These waters were surrounded by prairie that had seen clashes between the United States and Native peoples, land that once held millions of bison and millions of us.

Thousands of people were in the road. Dozens pushed up against the massive line of armed police in riot gear. Voices cried out, police-driven tanks rattled forward, eagle whistles, the bangs of less-lethal munitions, and ear-piercing Long-Range Acoustic Devices cut through the chaos. Most people stood back from the advancing line of police shields, holding selfie sticks and livestreaming the brutality unfolding. Some tried to hold ground against the advancing riot shields.

Tear gas and mace filled the air. The screams and yells of our people being pushed back across the prairie by government agents undulated. I saw a police officer mace a group of young teens point-blank beside me, and my vision went red. These were our future, our children openly harmed for standing up for their drinking water. I came to when Bishop grabbed my arm, pulling me back seconds before a beanbag round exploded by my head; its pellets rained on my cheeks. Some folks were locking their arms to a truck parked in the middle of the road, anything to buy some time, to stop losing ground. I held a bottle of water to my friend's lips as they blinked out mace. 'Go, Tara. You have to go now'.

Police swarmed over the truck and kept pushing forward, grabbing anyone in reach. They reached a circle of elders holding pipes and threw them to the highway pavement, zip-tying their wrists. On the hills around us, young Natives on horseback were chased across the prairie by police on quad-bikes as shots of 'less-lethal' weapons cracked.

Police used pain compliance on our people at the last blockade: twisting and contorting people's limbs as they screamed. Blockades were made of basic materials by those brave few trying to stop Dakota Access Pipeline with their bodies, to offer an act of physical protection to the earth amidst destruction. Blockading is oftentimes controversial or discounted in movement circles. Too often, we are portrayed as violent insurrectionists as if the metal machines possessed more humanity, more rights than a human being blocking its path. Too often folks stick solely to marching and sign-making, as if we lack a diversity of tactics to fight injustice.

The rich foundation of resistance in these United States has become corrupted with the same privilege and extractivism we push back against. It has been further undermined by a narrative shift about protest, leading to a movement ecosystem in which policy change, permitted parade routes, and the least disruptive actions consume significant swaths of energy. Direct actions are often relegated to the fringe, especially if those faces and voices on frontlines belong to people othered and oppressed.

Those brave few gasped for air as police covered their faces with cotton hoods and poured water on them. 'For the sparks', an officer said as a welder began cutting through the metal. One young person refused to let go of the blockade structure. Police zip-tied his hands to his feet, contorting his body until he was screaming in pain. He held on until the metal blockade came apart at the welder's feet.

When the escalations of state violence reached the media, the camps exploded in size. The powwow-like welcoming space in main camp was never silent; a giant dome structure filled with lights, well-meaning folks and shameless hippies alike spewed multi-coloured lights across living structures of all shapes and sizes. The cold and wind grew sharper. Police brought out water cannons in sub-zero temperatures, a young woman named Sophia Wilanksy almost lost an arm, when she was hit by a flash grenade, the shrapnel of which was seized by the FBI at her hospital bed. Hundreds of US veterans arrived. The confrontation between former soldiers and the state was imminent.

At the beginning of December, not long after the veterans poured into camp, President Obama ordered an Environmental Impact Statement ('EIS'). It was the more stringent environmental review that had been sought all along for the pipeline project. The environmental review would ultimately find, years later, that the permits for Dakota Access were invalid. As the camps erupted in cheering and we collectively allowed ourselves a moment of joy to celebrate finally being heard, many of us did so with the sadness of knowing what was to come. Donald Trump had won the election. He would be sworn to office in January. His was an agenda of expanding industry, expanding consumption, expanding endlessly. Indeed, Trump ascended to the Oval Office on a Friday—on Tuesday, he signed orders to move forward both the Dakota Access Pipeline and the Keystone XL pipeline.

Shortly after the EIS announcement, our camp heard we had been formally asked to leave by the Standing Rock tribal council. This call eventually expanded to all camps, to all persons holding space; 'go home' everyone was told. By then—safe in the knowledge that Trump would be President, and absent any meaningful legal enforcement mechanism to prevent them from doing so—construction of the Dakota Access pipeline had fully resumed. A giant drill shook the camps at night as it bore towards the Missouri River. Federal and state snipers sat on hills surrounding the whole of our occupation, alongside an unloaded missile launcher. Drones were regularly spotted near tents and folks were on edge as a growing stream of vehicles drove away from the prairie and wave after wave of blizzards.

'We're tired. I'm tired', Olowan's beautiful face with its big laugh lines and fierce eyes looked hurt, bewildered. 'That drill . . . that goddamned drill. They want us to go'. I lowered my head and she grabbed my hands. 'It's okay, little sister. We've been fighting for 500 years and we're not gonna stop anytime soon'. Her grip was strong.

Years later, I think of her grip, of her defiance. I think of how I stayed on the prairie until the tanks came for those who remained as the camps burned in February 2017. I think of LaDonna Brave Bull Allard, sitting in her hospital bed years later refusing to be still as her body fought a brain tumour, laying out her thoughts on the movement, still guiding and shaping my resistance and so many others. She spoke of how many were woken up during the Dakota Access resistance—the resistance that she helped inspire.

Many of the allies I met during that struggle are the same dear friends I see out in the woods, in the desert, in the old growth forests, in the mountains across Turtle Island today. Many I never saw again. For some, it was impossible to delineate between tribal government and tribal people. Folks left disappointed by activists and elected officials alike. For others, disillusionment with all that effort, all of those voices and campaigns and lawsuits, yet still the pipeline was built was too great to bear. Thinking circularly, thinking in terms of seven generations is not easy when all of us grieved the loss of the fight against the construction of Dakota Access Pipeline—after all that, they still built it through the Missouri River.

Recalling that time, I remember the basics each non-Native person was made to sit through upon entry to main camp. An 'Indians 101' type of crash course on how to be respectful or at least how to try. 'Don't ask to touch folks or their hair'. 'Stop talking about your "spirit animal", that's culturally offensive, especially to those who have clan systems'. 'Be open to listening, be respectful'. 'Remember, you are a guest and this isn't a living museum to gawk at'. Some of it stuck, some of it did not. Many folks came to the fight hoping for an 'Indian experience', wanting and vying for a chance to sit in a tipi, to share space with the mystical noble braves on the Plains, to eat frybread and take a selfie letting their followers know they were there. 'Facebook Hill', the spot with the best internet connection, was consistently busy.

Some folks came to stand in solidarity against Dakota Access Pipeline, which took different forms depending on the camp, on who was giving direction. Some came to stand alongside Native peoples. Some folks came to cook, to chop wood, to haul water. Some came with donations. Some came seeking fame; others sought anonymity. Some came out of sheer curiosity, to see what it might be like to throw off 'normal' for a weekend or two.

The dominant culture of apathy, of individualism, of consumerism as fulfilment is a constant in movement spaces, even as we work to heal our connections with nature, with one another. Those of us in the so-called Westernized world live in a societal structure based on extreme individualism. Communalism lives in idealized theory, personal comfort is the consuming reality. Much of the movement for change is approached via incremental policy shifts, dialogues, investment into 'going green' and that which does not require radical shifts away from individualism and personal comfort.

While there is much to be said about the efficacy and lasting impact of various methodologies of achieving social change, a constant throughout the history of Westernized society is everyday people making personal sacrifices that resonate through time. Rosa Parks refusing to give up her seat, Larry Kramer overtaking the streets, Nelson Mandela cracking the foundations of apartheid—names of people who hold powerful space in the world of making change, all of whom who did so at significant personal cost and risk.

Human beings are now grappling with existential crisis, with mass species extinction and experiencing our only home refusing to compromise. While much of the dialogue visioning climate solutions centres statistical data, a statistic that for some reason seems to hold less weight is that of Native peoples across the globe holding 80 per cent of what remains of earth's biodiversity. Instead of legally empowering Indigenous peoples' land rights and expanding Indigenous models of stewardship and well-being, potentially disastrous policies like '30 By 30' (a plan to expand land conservation that mirrors US National Parks across the globe, policies that would drive out Indigenous peoples, who would then be subject to local nation-state's political agenda), proliferate. Meanwhile, energy models steeped in new mass-scale extraction of precious minerals, mirroring fossil fuel extraction, receive huge government investments.

And in so much of Westernized movement spaces, much of the energy is poured into advocacy streams with little to no risk, streams that largely preserve the systems of individualism that must be undone for a habitable world to exist. It is critical that folks dedicated to protecting our children's chance at a future continue to engage in solution-making processes, in local, national, and international governance systems and institutions that impact climate outcomes. It is equally critical that we recognize we must have balance in our movements, that there must be other ways of thinking and being that step outside of extreme individualism and privilege.

As some push for narrative shift, for a move away from the individualistic consumerism that is tearing away our children's chance at a future, others are fiercely protecting what remains and encouraging others to stand with us. Land defenders are forcing dialogue from the decision-makers and building mass mobilizations, inspiring peoples all over the world via social media platforms that enable new narratives to be told.

We have been able successfully to kick open the doors to the highest levels of government, to force conversation on Dakota Access Pipeline, on Line 3 Pipeline, while simultaneously laying strong foundations and relationships for people's movement building. Project-level fights oftentimes still result in industry wins, yet the social license of both industry and government alike continues to shrink under a wave of civil unrest. While the individual losses hurt, the collective movement and the desire to look to frameworks outside of extraction, outside of individualism, keeps growing.

'Was it really worth it?' my arresting officer said, as I blinked mace out of my eyes. 'Your bosses didn't build Line 3 today and the Army Corps is coming out here, again', I said. His eyes darted back to the road. Zip ties dug into my wrists, my arms and back sang with the pain of rubber bullet wounds and new scar tissue. And past the speeding squad car, the wind rustled the grass, a crowd of land defenders kept chanting next to an unmoving machine, a hawk flew overhead, and a swirl of water in the drought-stricken river danced anew.

Further Reading

ABC News. 'Timeline of the Dakota Access Pipeline Protests'. 28 October 2016. https://abcnews.go.com/US/timeline-dakota-access-pipeline-protests/story?id=43131355.

Bosworth, Kai. 'The Dakota Access Pipeline Struggle: Vulnerability, Security, and Settler Colonialism in the Oil Assemblage'. In *Settling the Boom: The Sites and Subjects of Bakken Oil*, ed. Mary E. Thomas and Bruce Braun. Minneapolis: University of Minnesota Press, 2023.

Montare, Ariadne S. 'Standing Rock: A Case Study in Civil Disobedience'. *GPSolo [American Bar Association]* 35, no. 3 (2018).

Unicorn Riot. 'Black Snake Killaz: A #NoDAPL Story'. 2017. https://www.youtube.com/watch?v=4dWeg_jHdKo.

CHAPTER 28

O-PLATZ IN BERLIN

An 'Eventful' Migrant Protest Camp

MARCO PEROLINI

Introduction

For decades, migrant and anti-racist resistance to the oppression produced by border regimes has been invisibilized, including by scholars. Migrants in West Germany, likewise in other countries, were considered 'guest workers'. The authorities started recruiting them to overcome labour shortages in the late 1950s without expecting that they would remain and become part of the German society.[1] Scholars, politicians, and the society at large often perceived these migrant workers as passive and lacking interest in political mobilization.[2] However, migrants living in shared asylum shelters have been contesting their living conditions since at least the 1990s.[3] Their resistance, similarly to Black German activism and other forms of diaspora activism, contributed to emphasizing the role of racism in the construction of the German identity as a White nation.[4]

The urban occupations that took place in Berlin from 2012 to 2018 are often seen as a turning point for the visibility of migrant resistance. Scholars and activists alike believe that O-Platz, the migrant protest camp on Oranienplatz, a public square in the central Berlin neighbourhood of Kreuzberg, broke through the invisibility that had previously characterized migrant struggles.[5]

O-Platz occurred in a decade where urban occupations constituted the key repertoire for social movements in many countries.[6] Migrant protest camps are, however, characterized, by their own distinctive features (see İkizoğlu Erensü, in this volume). They aspire to constitute a reality opposite to the camps where migrants are often compelled to live as per the policy of encampment. In Germany, migrants claiming asylum must live in shared shelters and are subject to restrictions that prevent them from moving freely within the country (*Residenzplficht*). Activists refer to these shared asylum shelters as 'camps' or, in German, 'Lager', historically a very loaded term.[7] O-Platz, akin to other migrant protest camps such as the one built in Vienna in 2012,[8] was an act of disobedience by activists with precarious legal status who subvert the policy of encampment, by infringing residence requirements and mobility restrictions.

In this chapter, I argue that O-Platz has been constructed as an 'event', especially after its end. Visibility and migrant political agency played a crucial role in shaping the collective memory of O-Platz, which, a decade later, continues to influence the resistance against border regimes. In the rest of this chapter, I will situate the collective memory of O-Platz within the cycle of migrant struggles that followed the protest camp. While accounting for the eventfulness of O-Platz, I will also propose some critical reflections on framing some occurrences of collective resistance as eventful and the limitations of an approach that excessively focuses on visibility and representation.

The Lead-up to the Protest Camp on Oranienplatz

In January 2012, Mohammad Rahsepar, an Iranian asylum seeker who lived in a shared asylum shelter in Würzburg (Southern Germany), took his own life. This tragic event stirred a wave of protests. A group of Iranian asylum seekers first established a protest camp in front of the Würzburg town hall and demanded the abolishment of the policy of encampment.[9] Similar protest camps then sprang up in other cities.

In September 2012, a few dozen activists started marching from Würzburg to Berlin (600 km). After a few weeks, they reached Potsdam (Brandenburg) where they met with other activists who had participated in a bus tour across Germany to stimulate the participation of migrants living in shared asylum shelters in the collective mobilization. On 6 October 2012, several hundred activists erected the protest camp in Oranienplatz, Berlin. In November, also in view of the harsh weather, some activists occupied the building of the former Gerhart Hauptmann school in Ohlauer Straβe, in the same neighbourhood.[10]

The protest camp amplified long-standing demands to abolish the policy of encampment, as it attracted media attention and became a space where many activists involved in different collective initiatives congregated.[11] However, different demands and strategies, mirroring differences amongst migrant activists along nationality and legal status, emerged.[12] For instance, while the 'Lampedusa people' obtained protection in Italy before moving to Germany, other activists claimed asylum in Germany and were either facing the consequences of a rejection or still waiting for a decision. The local authorities initially tolerated the protest camp but then initiated negotiations to put an end to it. They persuaded the 'Lampedusa people' to accept their relocation to shelters and leave the camp. Other activists rejected the offer and continued occupying

Oranienplatz until the authorities evicted them in April 2014.[13] After the end of the protest camp, some activists remained in the former Gerhart Hauptmann school until the beginning of January 2018, when they decided to vacate the building a few days before the planned eviction by police.[14]

Collective Memory Constructing O-Platz as an 'Event'

The protest camp O-Platz was distinct from previous grassroots migrant mobilizations in Germany, mostly taking place in asylum shelters, which are usually located in rural areas or in city suburbs. The protest camp was based in Kreuzberg, a working-class, migrant neighbourhood that became the centre of activism after the fall of the Berlin Wall.[15]

However, its central spatial location cannot, alone, explain why O-Platz continues to be seen as a turning point in the German history of migrant resistance. A key factor, I argue, is that migrant activists took a front-line role. Several years after the end of the protest camp, activists still remember it as an instance where citizen activists took a step back and migrant activists self-organized their resistance.

The connection between claim-making and the collective experiences of racialized migrants is an important aspect of grassroots anti-racism.[16] The protest camp was an experiment of grassroots anti-racist mobilization through which migrants formulated grievances based on their own oppression, which became more visible to mainstream sectors of society. Citizen activists undertook a supporting role and migrant activists were at the centre of the decision-making process. Thus, O-Platz was a departure from representational politics, where pro-migrant citizen activists make demands on the state on behalf of migrants.

In 2018, when I conducted my ethnographic research with grassroots organizations contesting border regimes, migrant activists emphasized the front-line role that they had in O-Platz. For example, when I asked Joanne, a migrant activist from Kenya, to explain the main achievements of the protest camp, she told me: 'We [refugees] got a face, we took a space. The O-Platz movement changed German history because refugees became visible for the first time'.[17]

Brice, an activist involved in setting up the protest camp from its outset, also referred to the notion of visibility when I asked him a similar question. He explained:

> I think Oranienplatz changed the public perception of refugees. Refugees started to be considered as people. The media started talking about us. We had been struggling against the Residenzpflicht [restrictions on freedom of movement for migrants living in camps] since 1998 but no one talked about our struggle before.[18]

Citizen activists shared similar perceptions regarding the impact of O-Platz and the role that migrant activists had played. They also emphasized the shift in their own position and role, which became oriented towards supporting rather than shaping the resistance. In an interview, Rita, a German activist, spoke about the significance of these changes while portraying O-Platz as a unified collective action. She told me:

> For the first time in Oranienplatz refugees raised their voices and articulated their claims. It was not white people who said: 'Refugees want . . .', but refugees who said: 'We want!'[19]

Similar to Rita, many other activists whom I met in 2018 portrayed the cycle of resistance that followed O-Platz as fragmented. However, divisions amongst different groups of migrants, as well as between migrant and citizen activists, marred the protest camp.[20] Power dynamics persisted, despite citizens activists being identified as supporters.[21]

These divisions and challenges were not salient in the collective memory of O-Platz that activists evoked at the time of my research. This absence points to the role that collective memory plays in constructing specific occurrences as 'events'. Memory work can indeed shape the interpretation of past movements as retrospectively eventful as they are seen as turning points that produced critical junctures capable of mobilizing big waves of contention.[22]

This is not to say that memory work operates by cherry-picking occurrences and transforming them into events but to stress that collective memory as a process may enhance the salience of some characteristics of collective action. The present context and circumstances shape memory processes through which past collective actions are remembered, as much as past resistance can have an impact on the present. Polletta has contended that movements' narratives integrate past, present, and future events and that narratives taking shape in the present imply memory work relating to the past.[23] As Haydu has more recently argued, activists pick from the past what is relevant and suitable for the present.[24]

The construction of O-Platz as an 'event' is shaped by its rupture with the prior invisibilization of migrant struggles. However, its eventfulness is also associated with the social and political context after 2014 and the phase of sedimentation that the resistance against border regimes faced until 2018. The demands elaborated by migrant activists against mobility restrictions and the policy of encampment, which O-Platz made more resonant, took ever-increasing importance in the years immediately following the so-called long summer of migration of 2015 when the German authorities temporarily gave in to the movements of people from war-torn Syria. The rise of far-right parties and movements, the harshening of border regimes after 2015–2016, and the emergence of new collective initiatives where migrant activists did not have a front-line role are key in understanding the collective memory of O-Platz.[25]

O-Platz Challenges the Policy of Encampment

O-Platz contested the policy of encampment by providing visibility to the demands centred upon its abolition. This policy became stricter in 2018–2019 and then in 2020, during the COVID-19 pandemic.

In March 2018, an agreement between the social democrats and the conservatives paved the way for the appointment of a new government, and of Horst Seehofer, a Bavarian politician with hawkish views on migration, as Minister of Interior. On 7 June 2019, the Federal Parliament adopted the 'Orderly Return Law' which changed asylum law and further entrenched the encampment policy. Since the adoption of the amendments, migrants claiming asylum have been required to live in a designated reception centre for up to eighteen months. During this period, they cannot leave the district where the reception centre is located. After eighteen months, those who are still waiting for their asylum claim to be processed are moved to a shared accommodation. Those individuals from countries deemed 'safe', including many countries in North Africa and the Balkans, can spend more than eighteen months in the first reception centre.[26]

Framing camps as prisons and calling for their abolition became even more resonant in view of these policy changes. While migrants are not deprived of their liberty in most of these spaces—they could leave them under certain conditions, for example, subjecting themselves to curfews and ID checks—they are, like in a prison, exposed to the ever-present gaze of state bio-power,[27] through which their mobility is contained and their access to rights limited.

'We are living as prisoners or we are prisoners already . . . we are suffering in that camp, honestly, we are suffering, look at our kids, our families . . . the women have no privacy . . . 16 people . . . one toilet one, bedroom [. . .]',[28] said Jane, an activist from Nigeria while speaking against camps in a protest in front of the Federal Office for Migration and Refugees (BAMF) in Nuremberg (South Germany).

The resistance against camps intensified during the COVID-19 pandemic when the police and private securities companies strengthened their grip on migrants by enforcing quarantines in camps, which further restricted freedom of movement. For example, in April 2020, the authorities prevented many migrants living in a shelter in Henningsdorf, a town 25 km northwest of Berlin, from leaving the compound for more than five weeks. They failed to put in place public health measures in the camp, such as the provision of face masks or the prompt separation of migrants who had tested positive for COVID-19 from those who had not contracted the virus.[29] On 8 May 2020, migrant women activists reached the camp to deliver hygiene products and other essential goods to quarantined women and took some photos of themselves holding banners in front of the entrance of the camp. They were met by police who accused them of breaking the restrictions on public assemblies that the authorities had imposed to counter the pandemic.[30]

The pandemic galvanized the resistance against camps as many organizations, including main non-governmental organizations (NGOs) such as Pro-Asyl, the largest refugee rights organization in Germany, demanded their closures. Several courts also requested the transfer of migrants from camps to private housing in view of the health risks they faced.[31]

The demand to abolish camps, which is centred on the lived experiences of migrants, acquired more visibility at the time of the protest camp, partly because O-Platz represented an act of civil disobedience aimed to create a reality opposite to that of isolation, exclusion, and invisibility that migrants lived in the camps where they lived. These demands became more pressing as the policy of encampment became more entrenched after the end of O-Platz, which in turn contributed to shaping the collective memory of O-Platz as a crucial event in the history of migrant resistance.

O-Platz Is an Example of Prefigurative Abolitionist Politics

The COVID-19 pandemic, and the period of intense anti-racist organizing following the killing of George Floyd in the United States in May 2020, brought to the fore abolitionist demands targeting the police.[32] Police also came under increased public scrutiny in the aftermath of the abuses committed against marginalized groups in the enforcement of lockdown measures imposed to counter the pandemic.[33] Undignified detention conditions and prison overcrowding often made the efforts to protect prisoners from COVID-19 void and prompted some governments to take limited measures to release some prisoners on bail or through other non-custodial measures.

While these developments have not fundamentally challenged the logic behind incarceration and mobility restrictions, which continue unabatedly, they have prompted a renewed interest for abolitionism.[34] In considering O-Platz as an example of prefigurative abolitionist politics, we must remember that abolitionism does not entail the immediate end of oppressive institutions such as the police or border regimes but the progressive attempt of replacing, substituting, and subverting the very conditions that enable the existence of those oppressive institutions.[35] O-Platz enabled activists to experiment with modes of organization and social relationships that situated in the then present the type of society in which they aspired to live in the future, free from mobility controls and the policy of encampment. Migrant activists disobeyed the policy of encampment by settling on Oranienplatz, participated in decision-making processes as political subjects, and attempted to establish horizontal social relations amongst themselves and with citizens.

As discussed earlier, the policy of encampment in Germany is intertwined with the asylum system. An abolitionist perspective applied to camps entails the end of the systems underpinning their existence, which include the asylum system and the classificatory system through which the state assigns a multitude of legal status categories, through complex and long bureaucratic procedures, that regulate the differential inclusion of migrants. An abolitionist perspective also implies the end of the isolation and invisibilization of migrants, which the system of camps contributes to reproducing.

O-Platz challenged the spatial and social isolation faced by migrants in camps by providing them with an opportunity to be politically active, as they, for example, participated in assemblies where they attempted to create a horizontal decision-making process. O-Platz also fostered ties and connections with other activists and movements in Kreuzberg, a central neighbourhood with a rich social movement history. The challenges posed by migrant activists to 'police', which Rancière identifies as the system of rules sustaining the existing order, which has historically excluded them, broke the invisibility that had characterized their prior collective acts of resistance.[36] Moreover, as discussed in the previous section, O-Platz also involved an attempt to rebuild social relationships between citizen activists and migrant activists beyond the imbalances along race, nationality, and legal status. O-Platz aimed to overturn those imbalances by centring activism against border regimes upon the lived experiences of migrants, against the attempts of invisibilizing those experiences.

Conceiving O-Platz as an example of prefigurative politics inspired by abolitionism requires overcoming an analysis purely focusing on its policy and structural achievements. O-Platz did not bring about a revolution of social structures, nor did it achieve the abolition of encampment. However, it involved an attempt of creating in the 'here and now' some of the aspired long-term outcomes, such as, for example, challenging the isolation and mobility restrictions that shaped the lives of migrants.

Migrant political agency and visibility, which characterized the prefigurative abolitionist politics of O-Platz, became even more crucial for activists after the end of the protest camp, when the resistance against border regimes entered a phase of sedimentation, which lasted until mid-2018 as new collective actors emerged.[37] These new organizations and initiatives mostly involved citizen activists, in the backdrop of the increasing need to resist the far right.[38] These developments spurred concerns regarding the fading importance of the role of migrant activists and their lived experiences in collective mobilization against border regimes. It is thus its prefigurative character, combined with the social and political contexts following its end, that is central in the construction of O-Platz as an 'eventful' mobilization.

Conclusions: The Limitations of Visibility and Representation

The 'eventfulness' of collective action, conceived of as capable of producing ruptures and reverberations, and catalysing contention, calls for critically reflecting on the actors and the dynamics behind that very characterization. There are indeed numerous examples of uprisings, revolutions, and other resistances led by subaltern groups that have been obliterated, despite their eventfulness.[39]

As discussed in this chapter, migrant activists themselves frame O-Platz as an eventful mobilization while emphasizing why visibility matters for them. Visibility enables migrant activists to contest the very differential inclusion produced by border regimes, which assign them myriad legal status categories associated with a stratified access to rights. O-Platz is eventful for the very subaltern actors that made it possible.

An influential and expanding body of scholarship has emphasized how migrants who participate in protests and other types of collective action in which they claim rights challenge exclusionary notions of citizenship, which tightens the enjoyment of rights to the nation state.[40] However, these perspectives, akin to some approaches within the social movement scholarship, particularly those focusing on contentious politics through which social actors mainly orient their collective action towards the state,[41] tend to turn a blind eye to everyday acts of resistance, which often take place in submerged networks and autonomously from the state.[42]

In the field of migrant activism, scholars who are critical of the excessive focus on state-oriented and visible mobilization have highlighted that migrants engage in a multitude of daily, at times imperceptible, acts of resistance to challenge mobility restrictions.[43] The attempts of migrant activists to challenge the isolation and exclusion produced and reproduced by border regimes are certainly more numerous and varied than the single, spectacular occupation of a central square in the capital of a country, Germany, that has played a crucial role in shaping European border regimes.[44] These less visible acts of collective organizing include, for example, the outreach activities in camps that migrant and citizen activists often carry out to raise the migrants' awareness of their rights and counter their isolation, the efforts to identify and make accessible alternative housing options for migrants living in camps, and the strategies such as the whistle alert system that activists put in place in camps to oppose deportations that are often conducted at night and without any notice.[45]

It would be reductive to consider O-Platz as the quintessential example of mobilization that brought about social change while paying lip service to all the other less visible and spectacular acts of resistance. I realized that myself as I conducted my research in 2018 once the protest camp had already come to an end. My hopes for encountering a similar intense phase of mobilization were confronted with a more fragmented resistance, as it was often described by the activists whom I met. This generated some initial frustration but in the long term made me understand the importance of small acts of daily resistance that not only uphold the hope for a better future but also bring that very future into the present.

Notes

1. Mark E. Spicka, 'The Economic Consequences of the War: West Germany's Growth Miracle after 1945', *Germany History* 37, no. 2 (2019): 269–270.
2. Marco Martiniello, *Political Participation, Mobilisation and Representation of Immigrants and their Offspring in Europe* (Stockholm: School of International Migration and Ethnic Relations, Malmö University, 2005).
3. Gerda Heck, *'Illegale Einwanderung': Eine umkämpfte Konstruktion in Deutschland und den USA* (Münster, Germany: Unrast Verlag, 2008); Abimbola Odugbesan and Helge Schwiertz, '"We Are Here to Stay"—Refugee Struggles in Germany between Unity and Division', in *Protest Movements in Asylum and Deportation*, ed. Sieglinde Rosenberger, Verena Stern, and Nina Merhaut (Cham: Springer, 2018), 185–203; Christian Jakob, *Die bleibenden: Wie flüchtlinge deutschland seit 20 Jahren verändern* (Berlin: Ch. Links Verlag, 2016).
4. Marco Perolini, 'Challenging Oppression: How Grassroots Anti-Racism in Berlin Breaks Borders', *Ethnic and Racial Studies* 45, no. 8 (2022): 1475–1494; Tiffany N. Florvil, *Mobilizing Black Germany: Afro-German Women and the Making of a Transnational Movement* (Champaign: University of Illinois Press, 2020).
5. Fazila Bhimji, 'Visibilities and the Politics of Space: Refugee Activism in Berlin', *Journal of Immigrant & Refugee Studies* 14, no. 4 (2016): 432–450; Elias Steinhilper, *Migrant Protest: Interactive Dynamics in Precarious Mobilizations* (Amsterdam: Amsterdam University Press, 2021), 125–144.
6. Miguel A. Martínez and Ángela García Bernardos, 'Converging Movements: Occupations of Squares and Buildings', in *Crisis and Social Mobilization in Contemporary Spain* (Abingdon-on-Thames, UK: Routledge, 2017), 95–118.
7. 'Lager' also refers to the transit, labour, concentration, and death camps during the Nazi regime.
8. Ilker Ataç and Elias Steinhilper, 'Arenas of Fragile Alliance Making. Space and Interaction in Precarious Migrant Protest in Berlin and Vienna', *Social Movement Studies* 21, no. 1–2 (2022): 152–168.
9. Maurice Stierl, *Migrant Resistance in Contemporary Europe* (Abingdon-on-Thames, UK: Routledge, 2018), 35–58.
10. Napuli Langa, 'About the Refugee Movement in Kreuzberg/Berlin', *Movements. Journal for Critical Migration and Border Regime Studies* 1, no. 2 (2015): 1–10.
11. Marco Perolini, 'We Don't Remember the O-Platz Protest Camp for the Sake of It. Collective Memories and Visibility of Migrant Activism in Berlin', *Sociology Compass* 16, no. 12 (2022): e13009; Langa, 'About the Refugee Movement in Kreuzberg/Berlin'; Stierl, 'Migrant Resistance in Contemporary Europe'.
12. Stierl, 'Migrant Resistance in Contemporary Europe'.
13. Langa, 'About the Refugee Movement in Kreuzberg/Berlin'.
14. Azozomox and IWS, 'Narrating the Challenges of Women-Refugee Activists of Ohlauer Straße 12, International Women's Space (IWS Refugee Women Activists), Berlin', in *Migration, Squatting and Radical Autonomy: Resistance and Destabilization of Racist Regulatory Policies and B/Ordering Mechanisms* (Abingdon-on-Thames, UK: Routledge, 2017), 207–221.
15. Hanno Hochmuth, 'The Return of Berlin-Kreuzberg. Brought Back from the Margins by Memory', *Journal of Contemporary European Studies* 25, no. 4 (2017): 470–480.

16. Alana Lentin, 'Racism, Anti-Racism and the Western State', in Identity, Belonging and Migration, ed. G. Delanty, R. Wodak, and P. Jones (Liverpool: Liverpool University Press, 2008), 101–119; Perolini, 'Challenging Oppression'.
17. Interview with Joanna, 20 September 2018. I refer to all the activists mentioned in this chapter by using a pseudonym to protect their privacy and in line with their informed consent. Migrant activists self-identified themselves as refugees to contest the legal status hierarchies embedded in border regimes and beyond the legal meaning of the notion of refugees. Many of them were waiting for a decision on their asylum claims, some had a precarious legal status which exposed them to the risk of deportation. I refer to them as migrants without making any distinction on the basis of their legal status.
18. Interview with Brice, 29 August 2018.
19. Interview with Rita, 30 August 2018.
20. Stierl, 'Migrant Resistance in Europe'; Nadiye Ünsal, 'Challenging "Refugees" and "Supporters". Intersectional Power Structures in the Refugee Movement in Berlin', *Movements: Journal for Critical Migration and Border Regime Studies* 1, no. 2 (2015): 1–18.
21. Ünsal, 'Challenging "Refugees" and "Supporters" '.
22. Kevin Gillan and Gemma Edwards, 'Time for Change', *Social Movement Studies* 19, no. 5–6 (2020): 501–515.
23. Francesca Polletta, ' "It Was Like a Fever . . . ": Narrative and Identity in Social Protest', *Social Problems* 45, no. 2 (1998): 137–159.
24. Jeffrey Haydu, 'Adding Time to Social Movement Diffusion', *Social Movement Studies* 19, no. 5–6 (2020): 625–639.
25. Marco Perolini, 'Do Human Rights Reinforce Border Regimes? Differential Approaches to Human Rights in the Movement Opposing Border Regimes in Berlin', *Journal of Intercultural Studies* 44, no. 1 (2023): 28–43.
26. European Council on Refugees and Asylum (ECRE), 'Germany Passes Orderly-Return-Law', https://ecre.org/germany-parliament-passes-orderly-return-law/.
27. Michel Foucault, *Histoire de la sexualité. La volonté de savoir* (Paris: Gallimard, 1976).
28. Observation notes, 27 July 2018.
29. Marco Perolini, 'Abolish All Camps in Times of Corona: The Struggle against Shared Accommodation for Refugees in Berlin', *Interface: A Journal for and About Social Movements* 12, no. 1 (2020): 213–224.
30. Ibid.
31. Landesflüchtlingsräte, PRO ASYL and Seebrücken-Initiative, 'Von Politik zweiter Klasse - Niemand darf zurückgelassen werden!', https://fluechtlingsrat-berlin.de/presseerklaerung/11-05-2020-niemand-darf-zurueckgelassen-werden/.
32. Michelle S. Phelps, Anneliese Ward, and Dwjuan Frazier, 'From Police Reform to Police Abolition? How Minneapolis Activists Fought to Make Black Lives Matter', *Mobilization: An International Quarterly* 26, no. 4 (2021): 421–441.
33. Amnesty International, *Policing the Pandemic. Human Rights Violations in the Enforcement of COVID-19 Measures in Europe* (London: Amnesty International, 2020).
34. Martina Tazzioli, *Border Abolitionism: Migrants' Containment and the Genealogies of Struggles and Rescue* (Manchester, UK: Manchester University Press, 2023).
35. Ruth Wilson Gilmore, *Abolition Geography: Essays towards Liberation* (London: Verso Books, 2022).
36. Jacques Rancière, *Disagreement: Politics and Philosophy* (Minneapolis: University of Minnesota Press, 1999).

37. Donatella Della Porta, 'Protests as Critical Junctures: Some Reflections towards a Momentous Approach to Social Movements', *Social Movement Studies* 19, no. 5–6 (2020): 556–575.
38. Perolini, 'Challenging Oppression'.
39. Upendra Baxi, 'What May the "Third World" Expect from International Law?', in *International Law and the Third World*, ed. A. A. Fatourus (Abingdon-on-Thames, UK: Routledge-Cavendish, 2008), 19–32.
40. Ilker Ataç, Kim Rygiel, and Maurice Stierl, 'Introduction: The Contentious Politics of Refugee and Migrant Protest and solidarity Movements: Remaking Citizenship from the Margins', *Citizenship Studies* 20, no. 5 (2016): 527–544.
41. Charles Tilly and Sidney G. Tarrow, *Contentious Politics* (Oxford: Oxford University Press, 2015).
42. Alberto Melucci, *Nomads of the Present: Social Movements and Individual Needs in Contemporary Culture* (Philadelphia: Temple University Press, 1988), 24.
43. Dimitris Papadopoulos, Niamh Stephenson, and Vassilis Tsianos, *Escape Routes: Control and Subversion in the Twenty-First Century* (London: Pluto Press, 2008).
44. Wulf Reiners and Funda Tekin, 'Taking Refuge in Leadership? Facilitators and Constraints of Germany's Influence in EU Migration Policy and EU-Turkey Affairs during the Refugee Crisis (2015–2016)', *German Politics* 29, no. 1 (2020): 115–130.
45. Sophie Hinger, Maren Kirchhoff, and Ricarda Wiese, '"We Belong Together!" Collective Anti-Deportation Protests in Osnabrück', in *Protest Movements in Asylum and Deportation*, ed. Sieglinde Rosenberger, Verena Stern, and Nina Merhaut (Cham, Switzerland: Springer, 2018), 163–184.

Further Reading

Azozomox and IWS. 'Narrating the Challenges of Women-Refugee Activists of Ohlauer Straße 12, International Women's Space (IWS Refugee Women Activists), Berlin'. In *Migration, Squatting and Radical Autonomy: Resistance and Destabilization of Racist Regulatory Policies and B/Ordering Mechanisms*, ed. Pierpaolo Mudu and Sutapa Chattopadhyay, 207–221. Abingdon-on-Thames, UK: Routledge, 2017.

Langa, Napuli. 'About the Refugee Movement in Kreuzberg/Berlin'. *Movements. Journal for Critical Migration and Border Regime Studies*, 1, no. 2 (2015): 1–10.

Perolini, Marco. 'Abolish All Camps in Times of Corona: The Struggle against Shared Accommodation for Refugees in Berlin'. *Interface: A Journal for and About Social Movements* 12, no. 1 (2020): 213–224.

Perolini, Marco. 'We Don't Remember the O-Platz Protest Camp for the Sake of It. Collective Memories and Visibility of Migrant Activism in Berlin'. *Sociology Compass* 16, no. 12 (2022): e13009.

Stierl, Maurice. *Migrant Resistance in Contemporary Europe*. Abingdon-on-Thames: UK: Routledge, 2018.

Tazzioli, Martina. *Border Abolitionism: Migrants' Containment and the Genealogies of Struggles and Rescue*. Manchester, UK: Manchester University Press, 2023.

Ünsal, Nadiye. 'Challenging "Refugees" and "Supporters". Intersectional Power Structures in the Refugee Movement in Berlin'. *Movements. Journal for Critical Migration and Border Regime Studies* 1, no. 2 (2015): 1–18.

CHAPTER 29

'I CAN'T BREATHE'

KAREN J. PITA LOOR

Introduction

This chapter recounts law enforcement's response to community members and racial justice activists in Minneapolis who assembled on the streets to express anguish and protest the police murder of George Floyd in 2020. The account demonstrates the expansive tools and discretion that US law enforcement have at their disposal and use to respond violently to city residents and racial justice activists, whom officers already perceive as adversaries, and thereby stop their protest activity in its tracks. Considering the Minneapolis example, the need to rein in police is evident, particularly in the context of protests where excessive arrests and force infringe not only upon an individual's bodily integrity but also upon their expressive freedom.

George Perry Floyd Jr.'s Murder in Minneapolis, 25 May 2020

In May 2020, the world watched as White police officer Derek Chauvin killed George Floyd, a Black man, in the streets of Minneapolis.[1] As Chauvin knelt on Mr Floyd's neck for nine minutes and twenty-nine seconds, three fellow officers guarded him from bystanders who pleaded for the officer to remove his knee. Mr Floyd cried repeatedly, 'I can't breathe', and before dying, he called out for his mother. Mr Floyd was not the first Black man who died in police custody after his pleas for a breath went unheeded—for the second time in a decade, the words 'I can't breathe' reverberated across social and media outlets, landing on the lips of millions, thus rekindling Black Lives Matter (BLM) demonstrations and leading to the largest protest movement in US history.[2] While demonstrations quickly spread throughout the United States and across the world, it was in Minneapolis where people first assembled in outrage and anger over Mr Floyd's death and were violently confronted by police.

BLM Minneapolis, May through June 2020

On 26 May, the morning after Mr Floyd's death, the Minneapolis Police Department (MPD) released a statement claiming that his death was the result of a medical emergency. The captured video soon went viral, contradicting the police's representation of the incident. By early afternoon, crowds gathered at the site of the murder, 38th Street and Chicago Avenue in the Powderhorn neighbourhood, and at the nearby MPD Third Police Precinct. MPD Chief Medaria Arradondo fired Chauvin and the other three officers involved in the incident. By that night, the crowds had increased to approximately five thousand protesters. Police responded to the protests in riot gear, and after the MPD Chief authorized the use of chemical irritants against protesters, police proceeded to pummel those assembled with rubber bullets and tear gas. Despite this aggressive law enforcement response, thousands of protesters continued taking to the streets each day and night. Admittedly, there were instances of property damage by some at the protests, including vandalizing and even setting fire to buildings like the Third Police Precinct. However, the overwhelming majority of protesters were peaceful. Nevertheless, police consistently responded by ambushing participants, bystanders, and members of the media using less-lethal weapons, in some instances causing serious injuries. Police also conducted mass arrests of demonstrators, sweeping up hundreds for misdemeanors, many of whom remained uncharged for months. The level of protests diminished significantly by Monday, 1 June 2020, but hundreds of protesters continued demonstrating peacefully for some time thereafter.[3]

Since the Minneapolis demonstrations, subsequent investigations at multiple levels of government have concluded that MPD officers violently attacked individuals engaged in peaceful protest.[4]

Racialized Policing

Police violence in the United States is certainly not limited to protests. Instead, as George Floyd's murder and other deaths and incidents of violence, both publicized and not, demonstrate, police routinely act violently towards Black and Brown people and the communities they inhabit. The Department of Justice (DOJ) investigation of the MPD, which included examination of the department's practices before the 2020 protests, concluded that during day-to-day policing, officers discriminated against

Black people and communities.[5] Minneapolis police officers conducted more traffic stops in neighbourhoods with Black and Brown residents, searched Black motorists more readily, stopped Black drivers at six times the rate of their White counterparts, and were nine times more likely to use force against Black people during encounters.[6]

The way that officers treat protesters in a specific community—here the Powderhorn neighbourhood in South Minneapolis[7]—is an extension of how they regularly police its residents. Powderhorn has one of the highest percentages in the city of minoritized people, with Black people accounting for 17 percent of the population and Latine people accounting for 33 percent.[8] Officers who typically engage in violent policing of communities with higher proportions of Black and Brown residents are unlikely to take less aggressive approaches when policing protests in those same communities. In Minneapolis, like in other locations, residents rise in protest in their own city streets[9] and confront the same policing agencies that mistreat them during routine encounters.

Exacerbating the risk for activists in hyper-policed communities, officers are more likely to respond in an aggressive and militarized manner to racial justice protests, and within those protests, more likely to target protesters of colour. Data on nationwide arrests from the 2020 demonstrations suggests that, despite racial justice protesters being demographically diverse, police arrested Black activists at a disproportionate rate.[10] Again, this indicates an extension of the phenomenon of hyper-policing of Black people to the protest context. This does not mean, however, that non-Black racial justice protesters can freely assemble and express public dissent without fear of police retribution. A study of more than 22,000 protests in 2020 demonstrated that police are three times as likely to intervene in racial justice protests than right-leaning protests and are twice as likely to use force.[11] This is despite the fact that racial justice demonstrations are overwhelmingly non-violent, and in the small minority of cases where violence occurred, it was often externally caused, including by the police themselves.[12]

Police Officers' Stance towards BLM

In the context of racial justice protests and, even more specifically, protests objecting to police brutality, officers are unlikely to identify with the ideals espoused by the activists. There is substantial evidence that disturbing numbers of police officers in the United States are members of White supremacist or other right-wing groups.[13] Considering the vast authority and discretion that individual officers possess as they engage with the public, and more relevant for this discussion, with racial justice protesters, this information is devastating. Moreover, police officers are likely to think that viewpoints espoused by left-leaning protesters are extreme, and they are more likely to agree with right-leaning protesters.[14] The DOJ investigation uncovered at least one admittedly racist MPD officer.[15] In response to a Black resident's call to the police station for help surrounding threats to BLM activists, an officer stated that Minneapolis police would 'make sure you and all of the Black Lives supporters are wiped off the face of the Earth'.[16]

Moreover, observations of policing of BLM protests provide evidence that officers are highly sensitive to criticism of policing. Body camera footage from Minneapolis officers during the protests show police officers responding to activists' verbal critiques by spraying them with chemical irritants.[17] This is in contrast to the police response to right-wing militia groups, who often showed up at the 2020 racial justice protests as counter-protesters or even to act as police reinforcements. In such instances, police often welcomed militia members' assistance, referring to them as 'friendly' or even collaborating with them to confront racial justice protesters.[18]

Police Officers Primed, Armed, and Ready for Battle at Protests

Still, despite preexisting police hostility towards particular communities and the views of particular activists, law enforcement officers are situated squarely in the middle of protests with powerful weapons and expansive discretion that they often misuse against racial justice protesters. This unfettered authority and access to weaponry can lead to dire consequences for activists' physical safety and their right to assemble and express dissent.

In terms of the scope of law enforcement's authority, when officers respond to a protest event, they can potentially be executing multiple traditional policing functions including law enforcement, crime fighting, and order maintenance. While enforcing the law includes facilitating protest activity, officers perceive activism by BLM protesters as innately unlawful due to activists' identities and viewpoints. This means that officers neglect any duty to protect BLM activists and interpret their mission as imposing law and order by quashing protests. Police's traditional broad authority to enforce existing law enables officers to use force and mete out arrests freely at protests. An arrest on the scene and a threat of force, particularly when that force is brutal, effectively stops protest activity in its tracks.[19]

Armed with Broad Discretion to Arrest

From the first night of protests, Minneapolis police proceeded to avail themselves of the tools at their disposal to quash protests. One of these tools is criminal law. Police have access to a wide arsenal of criminal offences that they can utilize to effect warrantless arrests of protesters on the streets.[20] While the Fourth Amendment of the US Constitution theoretically protects individuals against unreasonable government seizures, courts consider reasonable an arrest supported by probable cause that a person is committing a crime.[21] Thus, a police officer need only have probable cause that any range of criminal offences has occurred to sweep up activists in mass arrests.[22] Probable cause is a low standard that courts apply with significant deference to police.[23]

I have previously argued that a police-deferential probable cause standard is particularly constitutionally problematic in the context of protests because when an officer arrests a demonstrator, it impacts not only their bodily integrity, as it does during a regular street encounter, but also their freedom of expression. Thus, as I have suggested, courts should strictly scrutinize and restrict law enforcement officers' authority to arrest during protests. However, this is not the case in practice, as courts provide officers the same broad deference to effect warrantless arrests of activists as they do during regular street encounters, meaning a protester's engagement in expressive protest activity currently bears no relevance to the court's analysis of the reasonableness of the officer's conduct. What's more, in the context of protest, probable cause is often not tested by any court because most charges are dismissed prior to arraignment or trial, meaning before a judge would traditionally make a probable cause determination. Therefore, I have advocated both that an officer should not have the authority to make warrantless arrests of protesters for non-violent misdemeanors and, more generally, that when the court is able to review an officer's action during protests, the Fourth Amendment reasonableness calculus should shift from whether their action is reasonable to whether it is *reasonable in light of freedom of expression*.[24]

Considering the wide latitude, however, that courts currently afford police to effect warrantless arrests in and outside the context of demonstrations, officers routinely arrest racial justice activists for what I have previously categorized as traditional crimes and protest crimes.[25] I define traditional crimes as those criminal statutes that police utilize during routine policing. In the context of protests, police often arrest activists for public order crimes like disorderly conduct or failure to obey an officer, and property crimes like trespassing.[26] Reinforcing the point that activists are overwhelmingly non-violent, while officers can also arrest demonstrators for traditional assault crimes, these arrests are few and far between.[27] I define protest crimes as those offences specifically fashioned to respond to civil unrest.[28] Police regularly use these crimes—particularly unlawful assembly and failure to disperse—to arrest protesters.[29]

Moreover, state and local authorities may use their executive powers to declare an emergency when confronting large protests, especially racial justice protests.[30] An emergency declaration expands police arrest power because officers can arrest for conduct that is non-criminal such as just being on the street at a certain time.[31] Curfews that are generally unconstitutional in non-emergency circumstances are commonplace after emergency declarations.[32] During the 2020 racial justice protests emergency declarations with accompanying curfews spread like wind-swept fire.[33] In Minnesota, the governor declared a state of emergency and established a curfew two days after the protests began.[34] Since violating a curfew is a criminal offence in Minnesota like in other states,[35] this provided police with another tool to arrest protesters.

Approximately three weeks after demonstrations began in Minneapolis, about 640 people had been arrested or cited in relation to protests in Minnesota.[36] Beyond the initial Minneapolis protests, six months after George Floyd's murder, police arrested six hundred people in the city on a single night as they marched onto the highway protesting police brutality and other issues. Police kettled protesters, holding them and blocking their exit from the highway, and arrested them en masse for walking on the highway and allegedly being a public nuisance.[37] Beyond Minnesota, the number of arrests nationwide in the summer of 2020 was staggering, with 10,000 people arrested in the first week of demonstrations.[38]

Armed with Military Calibre Weaponry and Broad Discretion to Use Force

The authority to arrest includes the authority to employ force to effect the arrest.[39] The amount of force that police officers can use during arrest is required to be constitutionally reasonable.[40] The recalibrated Fourth Amendment analysis that I have suggested would require courts to determine whether an officer's use of force is reasonable in light of freedom of expression by scrupulously scrutinizing an officer's claim that force was necessary due to a threat posed by an activist.[41] However, in accordance with current doctrine, courts afford great deference to an officer's claims that a prospective arrestee posed a threat, endeavouring to avoid the '20/20 vision of hindsight' since, according to existing jurisprudence, law enforcement officers are 'often forced to make split-second judgments in circumstances that are tense, uncertain and rapidly evolving'.[42] Courts' blanket acceptance of police actors' claims devalues a protester's right to expressive freedom, as well as bodily integrity, and such acceptance is particularly unwarranted when police engage with people primarily involved in protected expression and assembly, rather than suspected of genuine criminal activity.[43]

Whether employing guns, batons, tasers, or brute force, police officers possess various tools to exercise force during routine policing. Beyond these traditional weapons, state and local police departments have surprisingly easy access to military weapons and equipment, which they often wield against racial justice protesters. This access is a by-product of the federal government's effort to arm police departments at all levels to fight what national leaders in the 1980s first termed the 'war on drugs'.[44] It is unclear whether the 'war on drugs' is still raging,[45] but it is clear that police departments' access to military equipment has not ended.[46] Whether the drug war is over, police continue to use military equipment such as battering rams, flashbang grenades, and armored personnel carriers to victimize Black and Brown neighbourhoods during routine policing.[47]

This trend is aggravated during racial justice protests. Lawsuits brought by protesters and journalists have detailed officers pepper-spraying people directly in the face and indiscriminately firing rubber bullets, flashbang grenades, and tear gas canisters without any or sufficient warnings.[48] In the first week of protests in Minneapolis, police officers fired approximately 5,200 of these less-lethal weapons.[49] This excessive display of force terrorized activists and journalists and caused serious injuries. A review of Minneapolis-area hospital records revealed that during the first three weeks of protesting, eighty-nine individuals received treatment for injuries caused by less-lethal weapons.[50] Eighteen percent of those patients injured sustained traumatic brain injuries and 8 percent needed surgery.[51] Police clearly acted in contravention of United Nations recommendations that these weapons not be aimed at the head or torso, considering that about 40 percent of those treated for projectile injuries were hit on the head, face, or neck.[52] Ten percent of patients received eye injuries, and three actually lost an eye.[53] These statistics were not unique to Minneapolis: activists across jurisdictions encountered similar brutality at the hands of police.[54] Across locales, these weapons of war act as force multipliers, boosting the scale and escalating the degree of force that officers exert on affected communities and BLM protesters.[55]

Conclusion

Today, in the Powderhorn neighbourhood, the intersection of 38th and Chicago Avenue has been transformed into George Perry Floyd Square. Considered by many a 'sacred site . . . [and] a place of protest', the square is home to multiple art installations and about five thousand offerings left in memory of Mr Floyd.[56] Members of the community and Mr Floyd's family work to care for the location and to maintain it as a place 'of healing, grieving, reflecting, empowering and planning'.[57] While the intersection where Mr Floyd died certainly looks different three years after his death, it is unclear whether law enforcement in Minneapolis is much changed.[58] Nevertheless, the square displays a colourful six-and-a-half foot high mural of Mr Floyd's face.[59] Behind him are the names of other Black and Brown people who have died at the hands of police.[60] Over his chest are the words 'I can breathe now'.[61]

Acknowledgements

My sincerest gratitude to the editors for the opportunity to contribute to this volume. I am grateful to Madison Erlandson for her research and editing assistance. I am indebted to Penélope Zambrana-Pita and Joseph E. Staska always for their patience and support.

Notes

1. A bystander recorded Mr Floyd's murder on his cell phone and posted it on social media on the evening of his death. The video quickly went viral.
2. See Mike Baker et al., 'Three Words. 70 Cases. The Tragic History of "I Can't Breathe"', *New York Times*, 29 June 2020, https://www.nytimes.com/interactive/2020/06/28/us/i-cant-breathe-police-arrest.html. See also 'Before Floyd, a Black Man Screamed "I Can't Breathe" Then Died', *Al Jazeera*, 17 March 2022, https://www.aljazeera.com/news/2022/3/17/before-floyd-a-black-man-screamed-i-cant-breathe-then-died. See also Larry Buchanan, Quoctrung Bui, and Jugal K. Patel, 'Black Lives Matter May Be the Largest Movement in U.S. History', *New York Times*, 3 July 2020, https://www.nytimes.com/interactive/2020/07/03/us/george-floyd-protests-crowd-size.html (in early July 2020, polls indicated that anywhere from fifteen million to twenty-six million people had participated in protests associated with Mr Floyd's murder).
3. The description offered here is derived from the following sources: Hillard Heintze, *City of Minneapolis: An After-Action Review of City Agencies' Responses to Activities Directly Following George Floyd's Death on May 25, 2020* (Chicago: Jensen Hughes, 2022), https://lims.minneapolismn.gov/Download/RCAV2/26623/2020-Civil-Unrest-After-Action-Review-Report.pdf; 'How George Floyd Died, and What Happened Next', *New York Times*, 22 July 2022, https://www.nytimes.com/article/george-floyd.html; MPR News Staff, '"Unbelievable Devastation": 1 Dead as Floyd Protests Boil Over Again', *MPR News*, 27 May 2020, https://www.mprnews.org/story/2020/05/27/violence-near-south-minneapolis-police-precinct-continues-a-second-day; Anna Granias et al., *An External Review of the State's Response to the Civil Unrest in Minnesota from May 26–June 7, 2020: A Report of Findings and Recommendations Prepared by Wilder Research for the Minnesota Department of Public Safety* (Saint Paul, MN: Wilder Research, 2022), https://www.wilder.org/sites/default/files/imports/DPS_StatesResponseToCivilUnrest_Report_3-22.pdf; Rilyn Eischens, 'Who's Been Charged so Far in Twin Cities Arson and Destruction?', *Minnesota Reformer*, 15 July 2020, https://minnesotareformer.com/2020/07/15/no-arrests-in-most-destructive-arson-following-death-of-george-floyd/; Class Action Complaint and Demand for a Jury Trial, *Goyette v City of Minneapolis*, No. 20-1302 (D. Minn. 2020); Matt Furber et al., 'Minneapolis Police, Long Accused of Racism, Face Wrath of Wounded City', *New York Times*, 27 May 2020, updated 29 October 2021, https://www.nytimes.com/2020/05/27/us/minneapolis-police.html.
4. See US Department of Justice Civil Rights Division and US Attorney's Office District of Minnesota Civil Division, *Investigation of the City of Minneapolis and the Minneapolis Police Department* (2023), 48–50, https://www.justice.gov/opa/press-release/file/1587661/download; Heintze, *City of Minneapolis: An After-Action Review*, 49.
5. US Department of Justice, *Investigation of the City of Minneapolis*, 31–40. The DOJ found comparable and even worse levels of discrimination against American Indian people and communities. Additionally, Minneapolis officials acknowledged that the Minneapolis Police Department engaged in racially discriminatory policing. Minnesota Department of Human Rights, *Investigation into the City of Minneapolis and the Minneapolis Police Department* (2022), 10–18, 68, https://mn.gov/mdhr/assets/Investigation%20into%20the%20City%20of%20Minneapolis%20and%20the%20Minneapolis%20Police%20Department_tcm1061-526417.pdf.
6. U.S. Department of Justice, *Investigation of the City of Minneapolis*, 32–40.

7. See Safy-Hallan Farah, 'George Floyd Was Killed in My Neighborhood', *Vanity Fair*, 11 June 2020, https://www.vanityfair.com/style/2020/06/growing-up-in-george-floyds-minneapolis-neighborhood; Olivia B. Waxman, 'George Floyd's Death and the Long History of Racism in Minneapolis', *TIME*, 28 May 2020, https://time.com/5844030/george-floyd-minneapolis-history/.
8. Caitlin Dickerson, 'A Minneapolis Neighborhood Vowed to Check Its Privilege. It's Already Being Tested', *New York Times*, 24 June 2020, updated 21 July 2020, https://www.nytimes.com/2020/06/24/us/minneapolis-george-floyd-police.html.
9. See Meryl Kornfield et al., 'Swept Up by Police', *Washington Post*, 23 October 2020, https://www.washingtonpost.com/graphics/2020/investigations/george-floyd-protesters-arrests/. See also Louis Jacobson, 'How a False Claim about Out-of-State Protesters Traveled from Minnesota Officials to Trump, Pelosi', *PolitiFact*, 1 June 2020, https://www.politifact.com/article/2020/jun/01/how-false-claim-about-out-state-protesters-travele/.
10. See Melissa Chan, 'These Black Lives Matter Protesters Had No Idea How One Arrest Could Alter Their Lives', *TIME*, 19 August 2020, https://time.com/5880229/arrests-black-lives-matter-protests-impact/. See also Karen Pita Loor, 'An Argument against Unbounded Arrest Power: The Expressive Fourth Amendment and Protesting While Black', *Michigan Law Review* 120, no. 8 (2022): 1581–1627.
11. Roudabeh Kishi et al., 'A Year of Racial Justice Protests: Key Trends in Demonstrations Supporting the BLM Movement', *ACLED*, 25 May 2021, https://acleddata.com/2021/05/25/a-year-of-racial-justice-protests-key-trends-in-demonstrations-supporting-the-blm-movement/; see also Sam Jones, 'US Crisis Monitor Releases Full Data for 2020', *ACLED*, 5 February 2021, https://acleddata.com/2021/02/05/us-crisis-monitor-releases-full-data-for-2020/.
12. Kishi et al., 'Year of Racial Justice Protests'.
13. See Robin D. Barnes, 'Blue by Day and White by (K)night: Regulating the Political Affiliations of Law Enforcement and Military Personnel', *Iowa Law Review* 81, no. 4 (1996): 1079–1172; Vida B. Johnson, 'KKK in the PD: White Supremacist Police and What to Do about It', *Lewis & Clark Law Review* 23, no. 1 (2019): 205–261.
14. See Lesley Wood, 'Policing Counter-Protest', *Sociology Compass* 14, no. 11 (2020): 1–10, 2, 6, https://doi.org/10.1111/soc4.12833.
15. See US Department of Justice, *Investigation of the City of Minneapolis*, 45.
16. US Department of Justice, *Investigation of the City of Minneapolis*, 44–45.
17. Heintze, *City of Minneapolis: An After-Action Review*, 58.
18. Isiah Holmes and Henry Redman, 'Texts Show Kenosha Officers Called Armed Civilians "Very Friendly" Hours before Shooting', *Wisconsin Examiner*, 7 July 2021, https://wisconsinexaminer.com/2021/07/07/kenosha-officers-called-armed-civilians-very-friendly/; Mara Hvistendahl and Alleen Brown, 'Armed Vigilantes Antagonizing Protesters Have Received a Warm Reception from Police', *The Intercept*, 19 June 2020, https://theintercept.com/2020/06/19/militia-vigilantes-police-brutality-protests.
19. Ibid.
20. See Pita Loor, 'Argument against Unbounded Arrest Power'.
21. US Const., amend. 4; *Illinois v Gates*, 462 U.S. 213 (1983).
22. See *Atwater v City of Lago Vista*, 532 U.S. 318, 354 (2001); *United States v Watson*, 423 US 411, 415–417 (1976).
23. See Thomas Y. Davies, 'Recovering the Original Fourth Amendment', *Michigan Law Review* 98, no. 3 (1999): 547–750.

24. I have developed these arguments in detail in my two articles: Karen Pita Loor, 'The Expressive Fourth Amendment', *Southern California Law Review* 94, no. 6 (2021): 1311–1366; and Pita Loor 'Argument against Unbounded Arrest Power', 1621.
25. See Pita Loor, 'Argument against Unbounded Arrest Power', 1588–1589.
26. Ibid., 1589.
27. See Kornfield et al., 'Swept Up by Police'; Anita Snow, 'AP Tally: Arrests at Widespread US Protests Hit 10,000', *AP News*, 4 June 2020, https://apnews.com/article/american-protests-us-news-arrests-minnesota-burglary-bb2404f9b13c8b53b94c73f818f6a0b7.
28. Pita Loor, 'Argument against Unbounded Arrest Power', 1595.
29. Ibid., 1596.
30. See Karen Pita Loor, 'When Protest Is the Disaster: Constitutional Implications of State and Local Emergency Power', *Seattle University Law Review* 43, no. 1 (2019): 1–70. See also US Library of Congress, Congressional Research Service, *Emergency Management and Homeland Security Statutory Authorities in the States, District of Columbia, and Insular Areas: A Summary*, ed. Keith Bea, L. Cheryl Runyon, and Kae M. Warnock (2004), RL32287.
31. Pita Loor, 'Argument against Unbounded Arrest Power', 1589.
32. See Patryk J. Chudy, 'Doctrinal Reconstruction: Reconciling Conflicting Standards in Adjudicating Juvenile Curfew Challenges', *Cornell Law Review* 85, no. 2 (2000): 518–585.
33. Charity L. Scott, 'Did the Curfews Work? Experts Aren't So Sure', *Wall Street Journal*, 9 June 2020, https://www.wsj.com/articles/did-the-curfews-work-experts-arent-so-sure-11591704005.
34. Tim Walz Executive Order 20-64 (Minn. 28 May 2020), https://mn.gov/governor/assets/EO%2020-64%20Final_tcm1055-433855.pdf.
35. See Minn. Stat. § 12.45; Tim Walz Executive Order 20-65 (Minn. 29 May 2020), https://mn.gov/governor/assets/EO%2020-65%20Final_tcm1055-434635.pdf.
36. Eischens, 'Who's Been Charged?'
37. Tony Webster and Max Nesterak, 'State Leaders Face Backlash over Arresting Hundreds of Protesters in Minneapolis', *Minnesota Reformer*, 5 November 2020, https://minnesotareformer.com/2020/11/05/state-leaders-face-backlash-over-arresting-hundreds-of-protesters-in-minneapolis/
38. Snow, 'AP Tally: Arrests'.
39. Karen Pita Loor, 'The Expressive Fourth Amendment,' *Southern California Law Review* 94, no. 6 (September 2021): 1311–1366 (citing *Johnson v Glick*, 481 F2d 1028, 1033 (2d Cir. 1972); *Oberwetter v Hillard*, 639 F.3d 545, 545 (DC Cir. 2011); *White v Jackson*, 865 F.3d 1064, 1080 (8th Cir 2017)).
40. See *Graham v Connor*, 490 U.S. 386, 396–397 (1989).
41. See Pita Loor, 'Expressive Fourth Amendment', 1357–1358.
42. *Graham v Connor*, 490 U.S. 386, 396–397 (1989).
43. See Pita Loor, 'Expressive Fourth Amendment', 1357–1358.
44. See US Congress, Senate, Committee on Homeland Security and Governmental Affairs, *Oversight of Federal Programs for Equipping States and Local Law Enforcement: Hearing before the Committee on Homeland Security and Governmental Affairs*, 113th Cong., 2nd Sess. (2014), 1 (Opening Statement of Honorable Tom Carper, Chairman). See also Peter B. Kraska, 'Militarization and Policing—Its Relevance to the 21st Century Police', *Policing* 1, no. 4 (2007): 1–13, https://doi.org/10.1093/police/pam065; ACLU, *War Comes Home: The*

Excessive Militarization of American Policing (2014), 2, https://www.aclu.org/report/war-comes-home-excessive-militarization-american-police.

45. Since the advent of the opioid epidemic which has predominantly impacted White low-income communities, the approach to substance use in the United States has largely shifted from warfare to public health crisis. Hoag Levins, 'The War on Drugs as Structural Racism', *Leonard Davis Institute of Health Economics*, 7 June 2021, https://ldi.upenn.edu/our-work/research-updates/the-war-on-drugs-as-structural-racism/.
46. Stephen Gandel, 'Brawls during Protests Renew Calls to Halt Police Access to Military Weapons', CBS News, 3 June 2020, https://www.cbsnews.com/news/police-military-weapons-protest-1033-program/; David Welna, 'Twin Cities Area Police Forces Loaded Up on War Surplus under President Trump', NPR, 16 June 2020, https://www.npr.org/2020/06/16/878782600/twin-cities-area-police-forces-loaded-up-on-war-surplus-under-president-trump.
47. ACLU, *War Comes Home*, 21–22, 26. See Nsikan Akpan, 'Police Militarization Fails to Protect Officers and Targets Black Communities, Study Finds', *PBS NewsHour*, 21 August 2018, https://www.pbs.org/newshour/science/police-militarization-fails-to-protect-officers-and-targets-black-communities-study-finds. The militarization of policing is just one of the ways that Black and Brown communities have been primary casualties of the war on drugs. See Michelle Alexander, *The New Jim Crow: Mass Incarceration in the Age of Colorblindness* (New York: New Press, 2010); Dan Baum, *Smoke and Mirrors: The War on Drugs and the Politics of Failure* (Boston: Little, Brown, 1996); Levins, 'War on Drugs'.
48. Second Amended Class Action Complaint and Demand for a Jury Trial at 6, 11, 14–15, 18, 25, 28-29, *Goyette v City of Minneapolis*, No. 20-1302 (D. Minn. 2020); Class Action Complaint at 1–3, *Williams v City of Minneapolis*, No. 20-1303 (D. Minn. 2020); Complaint at 3–4, 6–9, *Stevenson v Doe*, No. 20-2007 (D. Minn. 2020).
49. Dennis Wagner, 'Minneapolis Police Injured Protesters with Rubber Bullets. The City Has Taken Little Action', *MinnPost*, 28 May 2021, https://www.minnpost.com/other-nonprofit-media/2021/05/minneapolis-police-injured-protesters-with-rubber-bullets-the-city-has-taken-little-action/.
50. Erika A. Kaske et al., 'Injuries from Less-Lethal Weapons during the George Floyd Protests in Minneapolis', *New England Journal of Medicine* 384, no. 8 (2021): 774–775, https://doi.org/10.1056/NEJMc2032052.
51. Kaske et al., 'Injuries from Less-Lethal Weapons', 774–775.
52. UN Human Rights Guidance on Less-Lethal Weapons in Law Enforcement (Office of High Commissioner for Human Rights, 2020), 30, 35–36, https://www.ohchr.org/sites/default/files/Documents/HRBodies/CCPR/LLW_Guidance.pdf; Kaske et al., 'Injuries from Less-Lethal Weapons', 774–775.
53. Kaske et al., 'Injuries from Less-Lethal Weapons', 774–775; Matt Sepic, 'Man Who Lost Eye to Mpls. Police Projectile Wins $2.4M from City, Describes Ordeal', *MPR News*, 16 March 2022, https://www.mprnews.org/story/2022/03/16/man-who-won-24m-from-city-of-minneapolis-describes-ordeal. See also Complaint at 7, 21, *Stevenson v Doe*, No. 20-cv-2007 (D. Minn. 2020).
54. *Abay v City of Denver*, 445 F. Supp. 3d 1286, 1290–1292 (D. Colo. 2020); Second Amended Complaint at 1–3, *Black Lives Matter Los Angeles v City of Los Angeles*, No. 20-5027 (C.D. Cal. 2020); Complaint at 3–4, *Black Lives Matter Seattle-King County v City of Seattle*, No. 20-887 (W.D. Wash. 2020).

55. Terry Gross, 'Militarization of Police Means U.S. Protesters Face Weapons Designed for War', NPR, 1 July 2020, https://www.npr.org/2020/07/01/885942130/militarization-of-police-means-u-s-protesters-face-weapons-designed-for-war.
56. Janell Ross and Josiah Bates, 'The Uncertain Future of George Floyd Square', *TIME*, 25 May 2022, https://time.com/6181463/george-floyd-square-memorial-future/.
57. "George Floyd Global Memorial', https://www.georgefloydglobalmemorial.org/ (accessed 30 June 2023).
58. Shaila Dewan and Tim Arango, 'In Minneapolis, Overhaul Efforts Stall as Police Resist Change', *New York Times*, 25 May 2022, updated 22 June 2023, https://www.nytimes.com/2022/05/25/us/minneapolis-police-george-floyd-anniversary.html. See also Memorandum of Law in Support of Motion for Temporary Restraining Order against Defendants John Harrington, Matthew Langer, and John Doe at 1–3, *Goyette v City of Minneapolis*, No. 20-1302 (D. Minn. 2021) (alleging that Minneapolis police, namely, the Minnesota State Patrol, is engaging again with excessive force with journalists reporting on protests after the police killing of Black motorist, Daunte Wright, almost one year after Mr Floyd's murder).
59. Hakim Bishara, 'Artists Create a Mural Honoring George Floyd at the Site of His Murder', *Hyperallergic*, 29 May 2020, https://hyperallergic.com/567663/george-floyd-mural-minneapolis/.
60. Ibid.
61. Ibid.

Further Reading

Cobbina, Jennifer E. *Hands Up Don't Shoot: Why the Protests in Ferguson and Baltimore Matter, and How They Changed America*. New York: New York University Press, 2019.

Hinton, Elizabeth. *America on Fire: The Untold History of Police Violence and Black Rebellion since the 1960s*. New York: Liveright, 2021.

Pita Loor, Karen J. 'An Argument Against Unbounded Arrest Power: The Expressive Fourth Amendment and Protesting While Black'. *Michigan Law Review* 120, no. 8 (2022): 1581–1627.

Pita Loor, Karen J. 'The Expressive Fourth Amendment'. *Southern California Law Review* 94, no. 6 (September 2021): 1311–1366.

Schwartzberg, Melissa, ed. *Protest and Dissent (Nomos LXII)*. New York: New York University Press, 2020.

Zick, Timothy. *Speech out of Doors: Preserving First Amendment Liberties in Public Places*. Cambridge: Cambridge University Press, 2009.

PART IV

THE REGULATION OF ASSEMBLY

CHAPTER 30

LEGAL THREATS TO THE RIGHT TO PROTEST

ELLY PAGE AND NICK ROBINSON

Introduction

Protests have led to important social change, greater public awareness of pressing political issues, and more responsive governance. They are a fundamental form of collective democratic expression and participation, allowing individuals to take part in shaping the world around them.[1] Reflective of this positive historical role, the right of individuals to peacefully protest as part of the freedom of assembly is enshrined in the vast majority of national constitutions and firmly protected under international law (see Inazu, in this volume).[2]

Yet, even as the right to peacefully protest has been included by most countries in their constitutions, this does not mean governments respect the right. A well-documented global decline in democracy over the past two decades has been accompanied by new restraints on civil society and demonstrators.[3] Many of the attributes of protests that make them effective tools for democratic participation—their public physicality, ability to draw diverse participants, and availability as an open forum for promoting even radical social change—also create unique vulnerabilities, allowing the government to justify legal restrictions on protesters in the name of public order, public safety, or national security.

Lawmakers and judges need to be particularly attuned to how justifications for restricting demonstrations are often used in an overbroad or a heavy-handed manner. Protests will invariably create disruptions to daily life; they will frequently push the boundaries of speech; they may include unlawful acts of civil disobedience and even isolated incidents of violence. While governments are justified in taking steps to protect public safety or other clear public interests, demonstrations need to be provided a large buffer of protection. Otherwise, it is far too easy for governments to justify dispersing or significantly restricting almost any type of demonstration.

Indeed, in the face of a record number of protests around the world, governments, including both authoritarian and democratic regimes, have increasingly engaged in illiberal legal practices to control protests, including enacting new laws and aggressively applying older laws to curtail demonstrators.[4] This chapter analyses three of the most common types of legal restrictions on protests: (1) restricting if, where, and when protests occur; (2) criminalizing the activity of non-violent protesters, including through broad application of public order and national security laws; and (3) targeting the ecosystem for protests, including using laws to restrict protest organizing, media coverage of protests, and protesters' access to legal aid.[5] The chapter ends by arguing that a more robust interpretation of the right to protest is needed to address this expanding arsenal of legal threats.

Under international law, states have an obligation to protect and facilitate individuals' right to freedom of peaceful assembly. Restrictions on the right are impermissible unless they are imposed in conformity with the law and are a necessary and proportionate means of achieving a legitimate purpose.[6] Many national legal systems mimic this protective framework, yet legal threats to protests have persisted and evolved in ways that substantially undermine the right.

A research approach that focuses on legal threats to the right to protest, like that developed in this chapter, helps ground efforts to protect the right not in the abstract but rather in conversation with actual, current restrictions on protesters. For instance, it illuminates the impact of overly broad public order laws, which can be used to target non-violent demonstrators, or how disproportionate penalties for minor violations of the law or acts of civil disobedience can deter protests altogether.

A more systematic analysis of legal restrictions on demonstrations also helps judges, lawmakers, and advocates not only to assess current weaknesses in the protection of non-violent protests, but also to point out how they might develop effective protective interventions. For example, it highlights how legitimate concerns around public safety or order are used as a pretext to create overbroad legal restrictions that can be used to suppress dissenting or unpopular views. To guard against this type of abuse, a legal framework that adequately protects non-violent protests needs to tolerate significant disruption to daily life (see Mead, in this volume). A systematic analysis of restrictions also underscores the vast discretion authorities have to disperse, manage, or arrest protesters for even minor violations of the law. Such a significant concentration of power in law enforcement requires significant checks on aggressive policing of demonstrations. And it makes clear that protections are needed not only for protesters, but also for a broader ecosystem of actors and organizing infrastructure that make demonstrations impactful in the first place.

Finally, this approach provides a point of comparison from which to evaluate how legal threats to protests have changed over time. For example, since 9/11 and the global 'war on terror', authorities have increasingly used counterterrorism laws to criminalize and punish protesters. As nationalism and authoritarianism have surged around the world, governments have relied on sweeping national security laws and restrictions on foreign funding to non-profits and activists to undermine protests. And with widespread adoption of internet technology and social media, authorities have leveraged internet shutdowns and takedowns to undermine protest organizing online. In this way, legal threats to protest do not just arise from inherent vulnerabilities of demonstrations to excessive regulation but are also situated in shifting political and social contexts that require an ever-evolving strategy from those working to protect this right.

Of course, there are significant threats other than legal restrictions that are used to unjustifiably curtail protests. These include police violence against peaceful protesters; the deployment of increasingly sophisticated surveillance technologies to track, identify, and harass non-violent protesters; third-party attacks on protesters; and smear campaigns, frequently spurred on by politicians, that erode public support for the right by stigmatizing all protests as violent, unlawful, or seditious.[7] However, these threats are often interlinked with legal restrictions, as protesters' alleged violations of the law are often used to justify aggressive policing, damaging political rhetoric, or even third-party vigilantism against demonstrators.

This chapter uses examples of legal threats to protest rights from around the world, from both democracies and authoritarian governments. These examples are illustrative and not intended to equate restrictions from very different contexts as having the same impact. For example, countries with a political culture of protecting non-violent protest or that have an independent court system can frequently escape the most stifling and destructive impacts of vague or overbroad laws regulating demonstrations.[8] Rather, the goal of these examples is to demonstrate that in response to a desire to control protests, similar types of illiberal legal practices are often deployed by governments of very different character (see Li, in this volume). In other words, while a protester in a democracy may have far more avenues of redress available to them to protect their rights, they still may face some of the same tactics or logics of control used by governments in more repressive environments. These comparisons show the need for constant vigilance in all contexts to protect not only one of the most critical, but also one of the most fragile expressive rights: the right to protest.

Laws Restricting If, When, and Where Protests Happen

Despite the widespread prevalence of a constitutional right of peaceful assembly, governments worldwide have enacted laws that create obstacles for those seeking to exercise their right to protest. In some countries, there is a primary, national law governing protests, while in others the legal regime consists of a patchwork of provisions—often appearing in the penal code, public order laws, and police directives. Federal systems like the United States, India, and Mexico devolve significant parts of the legal regulation of protests to states or provinces, which may adopt their own web of laws and rules.[9]

Many countries' domestic laws enable authorities to ban protests outright in certain situations or impose severe restrictions on when and where protests occur. Authorities frequently invoke such restrictions in the name of public order or national security. In many cases, the laws give authorities expansive discretion to make these determinations, allowing them to suppress disfavoured protests.

Dictating Whether Protests Can Occur at All

Governments can use both ordinary legislation and emergency laws to try to discourage or prevent protests from occurring. Governments may, for instance, seek to prevent or quash protests through curfews and other forms of blanket bans, often in the context of declared emergencies or in the name of maintaining or restoring public order (see Manion, in this volume). In 2022, the Sri Lankan president declared a state of emergency followed by a curfew to suppress massive anti-government protests during an economic crisis.[10] Many governments banned protests in the context of declared public health emergencies in the early months of the COVID-19 pandemic.[11] While targeted restrictions designed to stem the spread of the virus may have been justified in some situations, the pandemic offered a convenient pretext for governments to suppress protests with which they disagreed.[12] Meanwhile, the French government used a state of emergency declared in the name of fighting terrorism to issue more than 155 decrees between November 2015 and May 2017 to prohibit public assemblies.[13]

In many countries, the law also provides authorities the opportunity to excessively burden or even ban disfavoured protests through permitting or notification requirements. Requiring organizers to notify authorities in advance can help the state fulfil its obligation to facilitate protests, for instance by redirecting traffic or providing security to ensure protesters' safety. But these procedural requirements can also operate to wholly preclude the possibility of unplanned or spontaneous protests occurring in response to events (see further 'Constraints on Timing'). Such processes may also effectively require individuals to obtain authorities' approval before they can lawfully gather, and thus unduly enlarge the power of state authorities to effectively choreograph when, where, and how protests occur (see Hamilton, in this volume).

In China, for example, a national law on assemblies requires protesters to apply to the government for authorization well in advance of gathering, and authorities have broad discretion to say whether and how protests may proceed.[14] Similarly in Lebanon, the law which requires protest organizers to obtain a permit from the Ministry of Interior at least three days before a planned protest also gives authorities vast discretion to refuse a permit on broad grounds, including if the event goes against the 'regular and normal course of public interests'.[15] In practice, these provisions allow the government to suppress or ban disfavoured demonstrations.

In some countries, the law allows authorities to prohibit protests if organizers have submitted incomplete or inaccurate information, or otherwise failed to satisfy notification and permitting requirements. Organizers may be forced to obtain approvals from multiple agencies or provide information that may be difficult to obtain or unknowable in advance. Under Indonesia's 1998 'Law on Freedom to Express an Opinion in Public', for instance, authorities can disperse a protest if organizers have omitted any information in their notification, including the protest's duration and number of participants.[16]

Governments have also adopted laws that prevent protests by particular individuals or sectors of society. Under Malaysia's 2012 law on assemblies, the right to protest only extends to citizens and bans foreign nationals, including permanent residents and migrant workers, from participating in a protest.[17] In Jordan, the law bars protests by individuals who have been convicted of crimes.[18]

Regulating When and Where Protests Can Occur

Although international law explicitly disfavours permit requirements, domestic laws in many countries routinely limit the time and place of protests. Time, place, and manner limits may be appropriate in order to protect public safety or avoid unduly infringing the rights and freedoms of non-protesters, but many actual limits on the time and place of protests are overbroad or provide authorities discretion to curtail disfavoured demonstrations.

The choice of when and where to have a protest is frequently essential to the message it is meant to communicate and the audience it is meant to reach (see Zick, in this volume). As such, targeting the timing and location of a protest can significantly undermine the protest's basic function: It can result in a protest being removed from the 'sight and sound' of its target audience or in altering the time or location that is core to the protest's message.[19]

Constraints on Timing

The law often circumscribes the timing and duration of protests. Many countries prohibit, or have a legal presumption against, protests at night.[20] In addition, both authorization and notification requirements can effectively serve to bar protesters from gathering immediately in response to major events, forcing a delay until organizers have submitted proper notification within the required time frame or until they have received official approval. The process of administering such requirements may also allow authorities to effectively postpone protests: In Egypt, police have routinely refused to accept organizers' notification of a planned protest, forcing the organizers to reschedule and thereby blunting the impact of a demonstration.[21] In Morocco, the law allows authorities to change the timing of planned protests, often based on discretionary grounds such as concerns about traffic or security.[22] Such changes can disrupt protest organizing and also frustrate the purpose of the protest, if it is planned for a date or time that is symbolic or otherwise important to the message of the demonstration.

Limits on Location

In principle, people should be able to assemble and protest in any place where the public has access, and to the extent possible within 'sight and sound' of their target audience.[23]

These safeguards help ensure that protesters can easily assemble and that the impact of their message cannot by stifled by confining them to zones away from the public and relevant policymakers. As such, courts including the European Court of Human Rights have recognized that the right to protest 'includes the right to choose the time, place, and modalities of the assembly' within certain clearly prescribed exceptions, like measures needed to protect public safety.[24] However, governments frequently use the law to heavy-handedly preclude or restrict protests in certain public areas. While restrictions may be imposed for a legitimate purpose, they may exceed what is necessary to accomplish that purpose, and in doing so undermine protests.

Amongst the most striking of these location restrictions are those targeting protests and marches on public streets—perhaps the quintessential venue for public demonstrations, due to the disruption they create and consequent attention they garner. Protesters have long struggled with restrictions on access to streets, but governments have increasingly banned street protests altogether or created new draconian penalties for blocking traffic. Some national laws regulating assemblies, like that in Lebanon, specifically prohibit protesters from gathering in the street.[25] In India, authorities in various states may withhold approval of a protest permit on grounds that it would cause 'any obstruction to traffic'.[26] In the United States, many states criminalize protesters for 'blocking traffic' and six states adopted new steeper penalties for doing so in response to widespread street protests for racial justice in 2020.[27]

Countries frequently also limit protests inside or close to government buildings, often invoking national security concerns (see Manion, in this volume) or the need to prevent the disruption of a government function—but muting demonstrators' message in the process. A 2011 ministerial order in Senegal banned 'political demonstrations' in a large swath of Dakar where the National Assembly and presidential residence are located, such that demonstrators protesting the president's attempt to stay in power beyond his constitutional term limits were forced to protest in a neighbourhood on the edge of the capital.[28] In 2017, amidst protests against the government's controversial decision to cede two Red Sea islands to Saudi Arabia, Egypt established an eight hundred metre 'no protest' zone around public buildings including the president's headquarters, the cabinet building, and all courthouses.[29] And as Russian tanks amassed on the borders of Ukraine in March 2022, authorities in Kyrgyzstan prohibited protests around government buildings in the capital Bishkek.[30] As a result, anti-war demonstrators were barred from peacefully protesting in front of the Russian Embassy. Meanwhile, authorities in the United States have repeatedly banned protesters from demonstrating near political party conventions, and Spain has controversially banned spontaneous protests near certain government buildings since the enactment of the 2015 Citizens Security Law (see Zick, in this volume).[31]

Governments have similarly used the law to limit protests around utilities and other public service providers. Thailand's law on public assemblies bars any demonstration that 'obstructs the gateway of, impedes the performance of duties of, or hinders access to the service of public facilities'.[32] Following a prominent protest movement against the Dakota Access Pipeline in the United States, at least seventeen states enacted laws imposing high penalties on protesters that trespass onto gas and oil pipelines and pipeline construction sites or that 'inhibit' construction at these sites.[33] Venezuela and Brazil adopted similar laws in 2014 and 2016, respectively.[34] In the United Kingdom, fossil fuel companies have repeatedly won broad injunctions from UK courts that ban protesters from going near fossil fuel industry property.[35] These types of restrictions, while often adopted in the name of protecting important public services, have in effect made it risky to engage in peaceful protests around certain fossil fuel facilities or infrastructure.

Restrictions on a protest's location, like those on its timing, can undermine its very existence. When Russian authorities have been notified of a planned protest, they routinely require organizers to relocate the protest to a remote location that is not only out of public view but often hard to get to, reducing the number of protesters who are able to attend.[36]

Location restrictions also undermine demonstrators' core message and goals. Barring protests near government buildings can prevent demonstrators from expressing concerns about government decisions within 'sight and sound' of decision-makers. Street protests, which derive much of their messaging power from the attention wrought by disruption, are frustrated by traffic-blocking laws. The growing use of these restrictions has allowed authorities to significantly reduce the visibility of protests or undercut their message, eroding the right to protest.

Criminalizing and Punishing Non-Violent Protesters

Once a protest begins, governments can use a variety of laws to either disperse or arrest protesters. Besides enforcing restrictions concerning if, when, and where protests may occur described in the last section, law enforcement may also target protesters' behaviour, such as through public order laws, or regulate protests based on the content of their message, including through national security and counterterrorism laws.

These laws that can criminalize non-violent protest are frequently both vague and overbroad and carry steep penalties, deterring many peaceful demonstrators from even participating in a protest. Enforcing these laws may not only lead to dispersal of a protest and arrest of demonstrators, but can be used to justify force or violence against non-violent protesters by law enforcement claiming to enforce the law.

Behaviour Restrictions

Public order laws, such as laws against unlawful assembly, disorderly conduct, and rioting, are often a favoured legal tool for governments or law enforcement that want to arrest or disperse non-violent demonstrators. These laws are frequently vague and overbroad. In many cases they can also enable violations of the requirement under international law that authorities assess the conduct of those at a protest on an individual basis, as they can be used to sanction participants for the behaviour of others (see also Salát, in this volume).[37]

Many countries have the offence of 'unlawful assembly', or a similar crime, which can make it illegal for people to gather with the intent to disturb the public peace, if they are perceived to be gathered to commit any criminal offence, if they are blocking a road, or, in some countries, even if they simply did not provide proper notice or receive a permit from the government.[38] Not only does this offence cover non-violent behaviour (that is deserving of protection), the often broad language in such laws provides wide discretion to law enforcement to control and disperse protests, particularly those involving disfavoured voices. For example, in Kenya, where homosexual acts are still illegal, in 2022, sixteen non-violent LGBTQ demonstrators were arrested for unlawful assembly for a procession demanding their rights, despite having properly notified authorities of the protest according to the country's Public Order Act.[39] The same year in Sri Lanka, leaders and participants in protests against the then president were arrested under unlawful assembly charges solely for exercising their right to peaceful protest.[40] In August 2020, after Belarusian President Lukashenko claimed victory in an election independent observers did not find free, thousands of peaceful demonstrators were arbitrarily arrested and detained for 'participation in an unauthorized mass event'.[41] The potential for the offence of 'unlawful assembly' to be used against entirely peaceful demonstrators makes it a blunt but powerful tool of control, at odds with the protection in international human rights law for peaceful assemblies.[42]

Meanwhile, many rioting laws are similarly abused by authorities and used to criminalize individuals for simply attending a protest where isolated property destruction or violence occurs, or where some protesters are perceived merely to pose a threat of violence. In India, for instance, fifteen protesters in Uttar Pradesh were arrested in September 2020 for rioting after burning an effigy of the prime minister while demonstrating against high unemployment, despite effigy-burning being a longstanding practice in Indian protests.[43] In the United States during nationwide racial justice protests in 2020, law enforcement frequently arrested non-violent demonstrators for rioting who had not engaged in any violence themselves.[44] Formal charges were oftentimes never brought, suggesting the purpose was simply to remove demonstrators from the streets.

Similarly, the offence of inciting a crime is often broad enough to apply to organizers of protests in which some participants engage in violence even if that was not the intent of the organizers. For instance, in Hong Kong, the government in 2021 sentenced three activists to jail on incitement to rioting charges despite no evidence that they were involved in rioting, but because the government claimed their presence encouraged others to engage in confrontations with the police.[45] In the Netherlands, seven climate activists were convicted for disseminating calls to join a protest that (illegally) blocked a road under an offence, punishable by up to five years in jail, that made it unlawful to incite someone to commit a crime.[46] These types of inchoate crimes can be used to punish, often severely, those who merely advocate for participation in a protest where some then engage in unlawful activity.

Protesters may face other public order laws that can undermine their ability to demonstrate, such as disorderly conduct, noise ordinances, or face covering laws. For example, confronted with mass pro-democracy protests in Hong Kong in 2019 in which many demonstrators covered their faces in order to protect their identity from police surveillance, the government banned wearing face masks at unauthorized assemblies and arrested dozens of mask-wearing protesters.[47]

Content Restrictions

Governments also use national security, anti-terrorism, and other laws as a means of regulating permissible protest speech and symbols, or even to stop protests on certain issues from taking place at all. These laws differ in their specific provisions, but they often outlaw attempting to undermine the government or national unity. This grants the government wide latitude in bringing often very serious charges against demonstrators. For example, in Thailand, the government used the country's *lèse-majesté* law—which prohibits insulting the royal family—to imprison four prominent protest leaders in 2021 for speeches at a rally. They now face up to fifteen years in prison under the law.[48] Similarly, India's sedition law, which prohibits attempting to bring the government into contempt, has frequently been applied to protesters, including thousands of farmers in the state of Jharkhand in 2020 who were protesting development projects in the area.[49] Myanmar brought high treason charges under the country's anti-terrorism law in 2020 against pro-democracy protesters—including those who demonstrated merely by banging pots, honking horns, or clapping,[50] and Sri Lanka in 2022 used the Prevention of Terrorism Act (1979) to detain student protest leaders.[51] Meanwhile, Israel has periodically restricted or attempted to restrict the display of Palestinian flags, including in a 2022 bill that would have banned Palestinian flags at most university protests.[52] In Jordan, the 2011 Public Assemblies Act prohibits 'slogans, cheers, cartoons, pictures, or symbols that compromise state sovereignty, national unity or law and order'.[53] Meanwhile, in China, protests may not challenge 'party leadership' or infringe upon the 'interests of the state', curtailing many demonstrations.[54]

Other content restrictions include the use of public morality laws to target protesters. These often have disproportionate impacts on women and LGBTQ populations. For example, in Iran in 2018, dozens of women were arrested for violating public morality for removing their headscarves in defiance of a law requiring women to wear headscarves in public, while in 2022 headscarf protesters were charged with 'corruption on earth' and 'being an enemy of God', both punishable by death.[55] In Russia, gay pride parades in Moscow were banned in the late 2000s on public order grounds when people wrote to authorities opposing the demonstrations and the mayor stated he found them to be inappropriate.[56] In Egypt in 2017, seven persons were arrested and prosecuted for 'promoting sexual deviancy' for raising a rainbow flag at a concert.[57]

These types of content restrictions on speech allow governments to selectively target non-violent protesters who are threatening to their power or promoting unpopular causes.[58] Even when those arrested are not convicted, given the seriousness of the penalties involved and the stigmatizing charges, the process of being arrested and tried itself can be a significant punishment.

Targeting the Protest Ecosystem

Protests do not exist in a vacuum but are enabled and made more effective by a broader ecosystem of tools and actors. For a protest to occur at all, participants increasingly rely on the internet to communicate and coordinate. Protests are often facilitated by individual leaders or groups that take a prominent role in organizing and publicizing a demonstration. They often need funding to cover the costs of everything from transportation to security to bottled water, and they depend on external actors, including journalists who can report both on the protesters' message and on law enforcement's response to demonstrations, as well as on lawyers who can aid protesters whose rights are violated.

Increasingly, legal restrictions not only curtail the space for protests and penalize individual protesters, but they target these important elements of the larger protest ecosystem as well. These restrictions allow governments to undermine protests by sapping vital internal and external resources for protesters. As a less visible form of suppression, they may be less likely to elicit public sympathy and support for protest participants. They can be roughly categorized as restrictions on organizing infrastructure, funding, and agents of support.

Undercutting Infrastructure for Protest Organizing

Since the early 2000s, the internet and digital technology have been vital tools in organizing mass protests.[59] Social media, in particular, has allowed movements to communicate concerns to mass audiences; focus the public's attention on important, emerging issues; and manage logistics of planning and coordinating amongst protest participants. It enables huge crowds to assemble on short notice.[60]

But as protest organizing has migrated online, governments have found a new target. Facing an emerging or ongoing protest, authorities have deployed internet shutdowns and network disruptions, relying on ordinary law as well as emergency measures. India's Information Technology Act (2000), for example, gives the government broad power to shut down access to the internet, and in 2021, amidst widespread protests by farmers against new agricultural laws, authorities suspended mobile internet access in specific locations where protests were taking place.[61] Kazakhstan's communications law similarly allows the Prosecutor General's Office to shut down the internet without a court decision, and during widespread protests against rising fuel prices in 2022, the government made use of the so-called kill switch, cutting off internet access to the entire country.[62] In the United Kingdom, law enforcement shut down internet services on the London underground in 2019 in the face of planned climate protests.[63]

Governments have also used the law to go after organizations and individuals involved in protest planning. Authorities in Jordan used the kingdom's 'Crime Prevention Law' to arrest more than 150 activists ahead of planned anti-government protests, only releasing them once the protest date had passed.[64] Individual protest organizers have also faced trumped-up charges. In Russia, for example, a 2018 law made it a crime, punishable by imprisonment, to encourage a minor to join an unauthorized protest. Critics cited the chilling effect of the law on protest organizing amongst young people.[65]

Authorities have also sought to undermine protest organizing by making organizers liable for property damage or other unlawful conduct by protest participants (see further Woolman, in this volume).[66] In the United States, in the years after the Dakota Access oil pipeline protest, nine states enacted laws creating potentially chilling penalties that can be used against organizations involved in pipeline protests where protesters engaged in trespass or property destruction (see Houska, in this volume).[67] In Malaysia, the government sued organizers of a 2012 rally for fair elections, for property damage allegedly committed by rally participants.[68] Such measures can deter protest organizing by placing groups and individuals in fear of facing serious consequences for the unlawful conduct of others.

Restricting Financial Resources

Governments have increasingly sought to undermine protests by going after individual protesters' assets, organizational funding, and other sources of financial support. In 2022, Canada froze more than two hundred accounts of people and businesses that were associated with a protest against COVID measures that blocked streets in Ottawa.[69] Citing an investigation into potential terrorism funding in 2020, Nigerian authorities froze the bank accounts of twenty prominent members of a protest movement against police brutality, including a freelance journalist, a doctor, and several civil society organizations.[70] In some cases, governments have focused on cross-border or foreign funding of protests, cutting off a key source of financial support often while also blaming 'foreign interference' for causing demonstrations. India blocked Greenpeace from receiving foreign funding and froze seven bank accounts after accusing the environmental group of organizing of 'anti-development' protests.[71]

Governments have also sought to quash financial support for disfavoured protests in other ways. In Belarus, authorities seized funds raised via donations to help protesters who had been beaten by police, detained, or fined.[72] In the United States, South Dakota enacted a law allowing the state to sue entities that funded disruptive protests.[73] These types of funding restrictions can significantly inhibit activists' ability to effectively mobilize resources to sustain a protest movement.

Pursuing Agents of Support

Beyond targeting protest organizing and funding, governments undermine protests by targeting lawyers, doctors, protest monitors, and journalists who provide protesters with critical support. Following widespread anti-government protests in Egypt, authorities arrested at least seven lawyers who were defending detained protesters, later charging them with 'spreading false information aiming at disturbing the public and peaceful order' and 'joining a terrorist organization'—charges routinely brought against Egyptian rights activists.[74] In Iran, authorities arbitrarily arrested dozens of doctors who treated wounded protesters involved in the 2022 uprising against clerical rule, as well as more than a dozen lawyers who had provided legal aid to detained demonstrators.[75] Authorities in Nicaragua ordered doctors at public hospitals not to treat injured protesters involved in anti-government demonstrations, and had the doctors fired if they did so.[76]

Governments also use the law to target journalists who report on disfavoured protests. In 2022, authorities arrested a reporter in Kashmir who posted footage of an anti-India protest online, and charged him with inciting public fear or alarm—crimes punishable by life in prison or the death penalty.[77] In Morocco, authorities arrested numerous journalists who were reporting on the Hirak anti-government protest movement in 2017, detaining eight of them for months on charges that included 'shouting'.[78] Journalists play a critical role in raising public awareness about and support for protests, amplifying protesters' message, and documenting state violence or other rights violations against protesters. Like lawyers and doctors, they form a critical part of the ecosystem for protest rights and have increasingly been subject to legal harassment.

Expanding the Conception of the Right of Peaceful Assembly

As this chapter has shown, governments use an array of legal restrictions to limit and target non-violent demonstrators. Protests have unique attributes that make them particularly susceptible to being undermined and even banned through legal restrictions in the name of public safety, protecting against economic disruption, and national security. Demonstrations generally happen in physical places over which there are competing claims on the use of space. They can be disruptive and involve provocative calls for social change, and some participants may engage in civil disobedience or even violence.

Lawmakers and judges need to be particularly sensitive to the fact that protests will almost invariably create disturbances, but while the government can take steps to protect public safety or other legitimate public interests, this does not justify excessive or disproportionate restrictions (see further both Woolman and Mead, in this volume). As General Comment No. 37 states, 'Peaceful assemblies can . . . be inherently or deliberately disruptive and require a significant degree of toleration'.[79] Or as the UN Special Rapporteur on the rights to freedom of peaceful assembly and of association has observed, 'A certain level of disruption to ordinary life caused by assemblies, including disruption of traffic, annoyance and even harm to commercial activities, must be tolerated if the right is not to be deprived of substance'.[80]

It is important for courts and other actors to not only reaffirm the importance of the right to protest to the functioning of a democracy, but also highlight how fragile the exercise of the right can be and take steps to protect it (see Hayes, Cammiss, and Doherty, in this volume). This can be through strong jurisprudence that recognizes the presumptive legality of protests, confirming that protests should not require formal government authorization to proceed, or that they should be able to take place within 'sight and sound' of their intended audience.[81] Courts can contribute to striking down or more careful targeting of public order laws, like unlawful assembly or rioting,[82] or they can intervene to reduce disproportionate penalties on civil disobedience to guard against the chilling effect on the right to protest of such punishment.[83] More robust protections may also be needed to strengthen the ecosystem for protests, including by mitigating legal threats to journalists, lawyers, and doctors who aid protesters, or by banning internet shutdowns.[84]

Judges can and should learn from courts that have already taken steps to strike or read down laws that unduly restrict protest rights.[85] In 2018, civil society activists in South Africa successfully sued to invalidate a law that penalized protesters for failing to notify authorities of a planned protest.[86] In its decision, the Constitutional Court described protest rights as 'simply too important' to permit the restriction introduced by criminalizing a failure to notify.[87] In India, as part of a larger pattern of countries eliminating their colonial era anti-sedition laws,[88] the Supreme Court in 2022 directed officials to suspend all proceedings under a sedition law that had repeatedly been used to quash protests.[89] In the United States, courts have recently struck down provisions of federal and state anti-rioting laws that are overbroad and could capture the conduct of non-violent protesters.[90] And a court in the Netherlands allowed Greenpeace protesters to shut down Shell petrol stations for up to one hour to protest the fossil fuel industry, showing how judges can balance private property rights against the rights of those demonstrating against powerful companies engaged in controversial industries.[91]

Governments themselves have also taken proactive action to create legal regimes that facilitate protests. These reforms have often happened in response to outcry and organization by activists about aggressive policing of protests. For example, following a municipal campaign by civil society organizations (CSOs) in Colombia, in 2019 the cities of Barranquilla and Cali established new protection protocols and guarantees for protests.[92] After the government was accused of using resources meant to combat terrorism to instead target protesters and organizers, Nigeria made changes to a counterterrorism law to better protect organizers.[93] In the aftermath of 2020 racial justice protests in the United States, civil society helped push policymakers at local, state, and national levels to introduce an array of reforms to better protect protest rights.[94]

At times, repressing protests may seem expedient for governments or even popular with some sections of the public, but the use of increasingly wide-ranging legal restrictions to suppress protests comes with limitations and costs for all governments—even authoritarian ones. While protests may have legal vulnerabilities that can be used to curtail or disperse them, it is difficult for governments to stop people from assembling around political causes altogether, and dispersing purely non-violent protests can undermine the legitimacy of a government.[95] Further, when peaceful outlets for collective expression are foreclosed, citizens may instead mobilize in ways that are more likely to lead to violence.[96] As such, heavy-handed legal constraints on protests can lead to instability, or a need for such a high degree of state control that it can undermine the prosperity of a country or public confidence in its leaders.

Surveying legal restrictions used by governments to target protests allows for a deeper analysis of not only how the law can be weaponized to undermine the right to protest, but also how activists and policymakers attempting to protect the right can push back. In doing so, an ongoing analysis of restrictive legal tactics can be an important part of helping shape and expand the right to protest.

Acknowledgements

The authors would like to thank Tabatha Abu El-Haj, Michael Hamilton, Gregory Magarian, Thomas Probert, and Sharath Srinivasan for their comments on this chapter.

Notes

1. UNHRCtte, General Comment No. 37—Article 21: Right of Peaceful Assembly (17 September 2020) UN Doc. CCPR/C/GC/37.
2. A search of the online resource Constitute finds that 181 constitutions that are in force have a freedom of assembly clause. Constitute, Freedom of Assembly, https://www.constituteproject.org/constitutions?lang=en . . . key=assem. Assemblies take many forms other than protests and the right protects those as well.
3. Freedom House, *Freedom in the World* 1 (2023). Finding that global freedom had declined for the seventeenth consecutive year in 2023.
4. Adam Taylor, 'Why Is the World Protesting So Much? A New Study Claims to Have Some Answers', *Washington Post*, 4 November 2021, https://www.washingtonpost.com/world/2021/11/04/protests-global-study/; Michael Hamilton, 'Illiberal Practices and the Management of Protest and Dissent', in *Routledge Handbook of Illiberalism*, ed. András Sajó, Renáta Uitz, and Stephen Holmes (New York: Routledge, 2021) (describing how all regime types have used illiberal protest management practices).
5. These types of restrictions may be used before an assembly to discourage or prohibit an assembly, during an assembly to justify dispersal, or retrospectively to sanction participants.
6. Under Article 21 of the International Covenant on Civil and Political Rights (ICCPR), 'legitimate purposes' include 'national security or public safety, public order (*order public*), the protection of public health or morals or the protection of the rights and freedoms of others'.
7. ICNL, *Defending the Right to Protest* 1–3 (2022), https://www.icnl.org/wp-content/uploads/US-Protecting-Protest-Threats-and-Responses-v2.pdf.

8. See e.g. *Brown and Anor v State of Tasmania* [2017] HCA 43, striking down parts of the Workplaces (Protection from Protesters) Act (2014) in Australia for being unnecessarily overbroad; *SINDIPETRO AL SE v Office of the General Counsel for the Federal Government*, RE 806:339 Sergipe (2020), finding it unconstitutional for law enforcement to ban a protest for failure to receive notification when they were aware of the protest through advertisements.
9. E.g. Vrinda Grover, *Assessing India's Legal Framework on the Right to Peaceful Assembly* (December 2021), https://www.icnl.org/wp-content/uploads/India-freedom-of-assembly-report-2021-final.pdf.
10. Uditha Jayasinghe, 'Sri Lanka Imposes Curfew after President Declares State of Emergency', Reuters, 2 April 2022, https://www.reuters.com/world/asia-pacific/tight-security-sri-lankas-capital-shops-open-after-state-emergency-order-2022-04-02/.
11. ICNL, COVID-19 Civic Freedom Tracker, https://www.icnl.org/covid19tracker/.
12. In Algeria, for instance, the government cited COVID in banning all demonstrations amidst a massive anti-government protest movement, despite there being little evidence protests were leading to new COVID cases. Hamid Ould Ahmed, 'Algeria Bans Street Marches Due to Virus; Some Protesters Unswayed', Reuters, 17 March 2020, https://www.reuters.com/article/us-health-coronavirus-algeria-protests/algeria-bans-street-marches-due-to-virus-some-protesters-unswayed-idUSKBN2143UH.
13. Amnesty International, 'France: Unchecked Clampdown on Protests under Guise of Fighting Terrorism', 31 May 2017, https://www.amnesty.org/en/latest/press-release/2017/05/france-unchecked-clampdown-on-protests-under-guise-of-fighting-terrorism/.
14. China: Barriers to Assembly, ICNL Civic Freedom Monitor, https://www.icnl.org/resources/civic-freedom-monitor/china#analysis.
15. Public Assemblies Law, 1911, article 3 (Lebanon); Ministry of Interior Decree 4082 of 2000.
16. Freedom of Expression in Public, Law 9 of 1998, article 11 (Indonesia).
17. Peaceful Assembly Act, 2012, sec. 4(2) (Malaysia).
18. Jordan: Barriers to Assembly, ICNL Civic Freedom Monitor. https://www.icnl.org/resources/civic-freedom-monitor/jordan#analysis.
19. See UNHRCtte, General Comment No. 37, 22; Timothy Zick, *Speech Out of Doors: Preserving First Amendment Liberties in Public Places* (Cambridge: Cambridge University Press, 2009).
20. E.g. Assembly and Demonstration Act, 2007, article 10 (South Korea); Law on Peaceful Demonstration, 2009, article 14 (Cambodia); Public Order Act, 1950, sec. 5(3) (Kenya).
21. E.g. Sarah El-Sheikh, 'Scheduled Protests against Red Sea Islands Deal Postponed to Saturday', *Daily News Egypt*, 10 January 2017.
22. Loi n° 76-00 B.O du 17 oct 2002 modifiant et complétant le dahir n° 1-58-377 du 3 joumada I 1378 (15 novembre 1958) relatif aux rassemblements publics [Law No. 76 on Public Assemblies (Morocco)], https://www.rightofassembly.info/assets/downloads/1958_Law_on_Assemblies_(French_original).pdf.
23. UNHRCtte, General Comment No. 37, 53, 55.
24. ECtHR, *Sáska v Hungary* App. No. 58050/08 (27 November 2012), 21. But see *Amit Sahni v Commissioner of Police . . . Ors* (2020) 11 SCC 334 where the Indian Supreme Court controversially found that even 'demonstrations expressing dissent have to be in designated places alone'.
25. Public Assemblies Law, 1911, article 3.
26. Grover, *Assessing India's Legal Framework on the Right to Peaceful Assembly*, 22.

27. ICNL, US Protest Law Tracker, https://www.icnl.org/usprotestlawtracker/?location= . . . status=enacted . . . issue=12 . . . date=custom . . . date_from=2020-05-25 . . . date_to=2022-11-30 . . . type=
28. Ministerial Order No. 7580, 20 July 2011 (Senegal); Adam Nossiter, 'Protesters Urge President to Step Down in Senegal', *New York Times*, 23 July 2011, https://www.nytimes.com/2011/07/24/world/africa/24senegal.html.
29. Aswat Masriya, 'Cabinet Creates Protest-Free Zones around Vital Facilities', *Egypt Independent*, 13 January 2017, https://egyptindependent.com/cabinet-creates-protests-free-zone-around-vital-facilites/.
30. Human Rights Watch, 'Kyrgyzstan: Repeal Protest Ban', 24 March 2022, https://www.hrw.org/news/2022/03/24/kyrgyzstan-repeal-protest-ban.
31. These bans have been upheld by courts in the US courts. See *Marcavage and Lefemine v The City of New York and Others* 689 F.3d 98 (2012) (finding that 'sight and sound access is [not] constitutionally compelled' in a case brought by protesters barred from demonstrating near the Republican National Convention in New York City). Heather Galloway, 'Do Proposed Reforms of Spain's Controversial "Gag Law" Go Far Enough?', *EuroNews*, 11 February 2022, https://www.euronews.com/my-europe/2022/02/11/do-proposed-reforms-of-spain-s-controversial-gag-law-go-far-enough.
32. Public Assembly Act, 2015, articles 8 and 27 (Thailand).
33. Elly Page, 'Protecting Peaceful Assembly from "Critical Infrastructure" and Other Anti-Protest Laws', *ICNL*, 14 September 2022, https://www.icnl.org/wp-content/uploads/Elly-Page-Written-Testimony-for-House-Oversight-Subcommittee-Hearing-14-September-2022.pdf.
34. Organic Law on National Security, 2014, articles 48, 51, 56 (Venezuela), http://www.controlciudadano.org/web/wp-content/uploads/Ley-Org%C3%A1nica-de-Seguridad-de-la-Naci%C3%B3n.pdf; Brazil, Law No. 13.260 of 2016 on Terrorism, article 2, §1(IV) http://www.planalto.gov.br/ccivil_03/_ato2015-2018/2016/lei/l13260.htm.
35. Shadia Nasralla, 'Shell Obtains Injunctions against UK Climate Protests', Reuters, 6 May 2022, https://www.reuters.com/business/energy/shell-obtains-injunctions-against-uk-climate-protests-2022-05-06/; Michael Holden, 'Oil Firms Secure Injunctions to Stop UK Climate Protests', Reuters, 15 April 2022, https://www.reuters.com/business/energy/oil-firms-secure-injunctions-stop-uk-climate-protests-2022-04-15/.
36. 'Russia: No Place for Protest', *Amnesty International*, 12 August 2021, https://www.amnesty.org/en/documents/eur46/4328/2021/en/, 10.
37. UNHRCtte, General Comment No. 37, 38.
38. See e.g. Public Order Act, Part III, Sec. 5 (Kenya); Indian Penal Code, Sec. 141; John Inazu, 'Unlawful Assembly as Social Control', *UCLA Law Review* 64 (2017): 2–52.
39. Joseph Ndunda, 'LGBTQ Members Charged with Unlawful Assembly after Holding Demos in Nairobi', *Nairobi News*, 10 September 2022, https://nairobinews.nation.africa/lgbtq-members-charged-with-unlawful-assembly-after-holding-demos-in-nairobi/.
40. 'Sri Lanka Extends State of Emergency as Police Round up Protest Leaders', *The Guardian*, 28 July 2022, https://www.theguardian.com/world/2022/jul/28/sri-lanka-extends-state-of-emergency-as-police-round-up-protest-leaders.
41. Situation of Human Rights in Belarus in the Run-Up to the 2020 Presidential Election and Its Aftermath (Office of the UN High Commissioner for Human Rights, 4 March 2022), https://documents-dds-ny.un.org/doc/UNDOC/GEN/G22/276/97/PDF/G2227697.pdf?OpenElement.

42. UNHRCtte, General Comment No. 37, 38.
43. Grover, *Assessing India's Legal Framework on the Right to Peaceful Assembly*, 38.
44. Nick Robinson, 'Rethinking the Crime of Rioting', *Minnesota Law Review* 107 (2022): 77–138.
45. Helen Davidson, 'Hong Kong Jails Three on Riot Charges despite No Evidence of Rioting', *The Guardian*, 6 May 2021, https://www.theguardian.com/world/2021/may/06/hong-kong-court-jails-riot-charges-joshua-wong-tiananmen-vigil-protest. A court later found that while mere presence is not enough to be convicted of rioting, if the accused 'provides encouragement by words, signs or actions' they can be considered to be 'taking part' in the riot. *HKSAR v Leung Tin Kei*, final appeal no. 6 of 2021, Court of Final Appeal of the Hong Kong Special Administrative Region, https://legalref.judiciary.hk/lrs/common/ju/ju_frame.jsp?DIS=139868 ... currpage=T.
46. 'Taakstraffen voor verdachten Extinction Rebellion na oproepen blockade A12', *de Rechtspraak*, 2 August 2023, https://www.rechtspraak.nl/Organisatie-en-contact/Organisatie/Rechtbanken/Rechtbank-Den-Haag/Nieuws/Paginas/Taakstraffen-voor-verdachten-Extinction-Rebellion-na-oproepen-blokkade-A12.aspx.
47. Victor Ting, 'At Least 77 Arrested over Anti-mask Law', *South China Morning Post*, 8 October 2019, https://www.scmp.com/news/hong-kong/politics/article/3032069/least-77-arrested-over-anti-mask-law-hong-kong-police-say.
48. Human Rights Watch, 'Thailand: Prominent Activists Held in Pre-Trial Detention', 9 February 2021, https://www.hrw.org/news/2021/02/09/thailand-prominent-activists-held-pre-trial-detention.
49. Anumeha Yadav, 'How India Uses Colonial-Era Sedition Law against CAA Protesters', *Al Jazeera*, 21 January 2020, https://www.aljazeera.com/news/2020/1/21/how-india-uses-colonial-era-sedition-law-against-caa-protesters.
50. 'Myanmar Junta Threatens Pot Banging Protesters with Treason', *France 24*, 25 January 2022, https://www.france24.com/en/live-news/20220125-myanmar-junta-threatens-pot-banging-protesters-with-treason.
51. Amnesty International, 'Drop Terror Charges against Student Leaders Detained for 90 Days', 16 November 2022, https://www.amnesty.org/en/latest/news/2022/11/sri-lanka-drop-terror-charges-against-student-leaders-detained-for-90-days/.
52. Isaac Scher, 'Israel Moves to Ban the Palestinian Flag', *Jewish Currents*, 7 June 2022, https://jewishcurrents.org/israel-moves-to-ban-the-palestinian-flag.
53. Jordan, Instructions Regulating Public Assemblies and Demonstrations (2011), article 2(c).
54. US Department of State, '2020 Country Report on Human Rights Practices in China', https://www.state.gov/reports/2020-country-reports-on-human-rights-practices/china.
55. 'Iran Arrests 29 Women for Not Wearing Hijab in Protests', *Al Jazeera*, 2 February 2018, https://www.aljazeera.com/news/2018/2/2/iran-arrests-29-women-for-not-wearing-hijab-in-protests; Farnaz Fassihi, 'Iran Cracks Down as Protests Show No Sign of Easing', *New York Times*, 15 November 2022, https://www.nytimes.com/2022/11/15/world/middleeast/iran-protests-tehran-metro-shooting.html.
56. ECtHR, *Alekseyev v Russia* App. No. 4916/07 (21 October 2010).
57. Ruth Michaelson, 'LGBT People in Egypt Targeted in Wave of Arrests and Violence', *The Guardian*, 8 October 2017, https://www.theguardian.com/world/2017/oct/08/lgbt-people-egypt-targeted-wave-arrests-violence.
58. ECtHR, *Primov v Russia* App. No. 17391/06 (12 June 2014), 134–135.
59. Isabel Ortiz et al., *World Protests: A Study of Key Protest Issues in the 21st Century* (2022), 61.

60. See e.g. Zeynep Tufekci, *Twitter and Tear Gas: The Power and Fragility of Networked Protest* (New Haven, CT: Yale University Press, 2017).
61. Temporary Suspension of Telecom Rules, 2017 and Information Technology Act, 2000 (India); Grover, *Assessing India's Legal Framework on the Right to Peaceful Assembly*, 69; 'India Protests: Internet Cut to Hunger-Striking Farmers in Delhi', BBC, 30 January 2021, https://www.bbc.com/news/world-asia-india-55872480.
62. 'Timeline: Kazakhstan Internet Shutdowns Aim to Crush Protests, Hide State Violence', *AccessNow*, 12 January 2022, https://www.accessnow.org/kazakhstan-internet-shutdowns-protests-almaty-timeline-whats-happening/.
63. And for examples in London and San Francisco, see Giovanni de Gregorio and Nicole Stremlau, 'Internet Shutdowns and the Limits of Law', *International Journal of Communication* 14 (2020): 4225, https://ijoc.org/index.php/ijoc/article/download/13752/3183.
64. 'Jordan: Mass "Preemptive" Arrests to Block Protests against Government', *DAWN*, 6 April 2022, https://dawnmena.org/jordan-mass-preemptive-arrests-to-block-protests-against-government/.
65. 'Activist, 18, Is First Russian Punished under Law against Encouraging Minors to Protest', *Radio Free Europe*, 25 March 2019, https://www.rferl.org/a/activist-18-is-first-russian-punished-under-law-against-encouraging-minors-to-protest/29842797.html.
66. Including discussion of *South African Transport and Allied Workers Union and Another v Garvas and Others* [2012] ZACC 13.
67. ICNL, US Protest Law Tracker. https://www.icnl.org/home/icnl-pattern-library/icnl-pattern-library. Laws enacted in 2002 in Alabama (SB 17), Mississippi (HB 1243), Montana (HB 481), North Dakota (SB 2044), Ohio (SB 33), Oklahoma (HB 1123), South Dakota (SB 151), Texas (HB 3557), and West Virginia (HB 4615) all create new liability for individuals and organizations involved in pipeline protests.
68. 'Malaysia: UN Rights Experts Call for the Protection of NGOs Working for Free and Fair Elections', Office of High Commissioner for Human Rights, 7 June 2012, https://www.ohchr.org/en/press-releases/2012/06/malaysia-un-rights-experts-call-protection-ngos-working-free-and-fair.
69. Ian Austen, 'Canada Ends Its Freeze on Hundreds of Accounts Tied to Protests', *New York Times*, 22 February 2022, https://www.nytimes.com/2022/02/22/world/americas/canada-protest-finances.html.
70. 'Nigeria's Central Bank Freezes Accounts of Police Brutality Protesters', Reuters, 7 November 2020, https://www.reuters.com/article/nigeria-protests-banking/nigerias-central-bank-freezes-accounts-of-police-brutality-protesters-idUSL4N2HT06D.
71. Jason Burke, 'Greenpeace Bank Accounts Frozen by Indian Government', *The Guardian*, 10 April 2015, https://www.theguardian.com/world/2015/apr/10/greenpeace-bank-accounts-frozen-by-indian-government.
72. Shaun Walker, 'Belarus Tells Banks to Seize Money Raised to Help Out Protesters,' *The Guardian*, 13 November 2020, https://www.theguardian.com/world/2020/nov/13/belarus-tells-banks-seize-money-raised-help-protesters-lukashenko.
73. South Dakota House Bill 1117, 2020, https://sdlegislature.gov/Statutes/Session_Laws/Chapter/457.
74. 'Egypt: Amidst the Crackdown, Lawyers Are Also a Target', *International Commission of Jurists*, 10 April 2019, https://www.icj.org/egypt-amidst-the-crackdown-lawyers-are-also-a-target/.

75. 'Iran Protests: Doctors Treating Wounded Protesters Face Deadly State Violence', *Center for Human Rights in Iran*, 31 October 2022, https://iranhumanrights.org/2022/10/iran-protests-doctors-treating-wounded-protesters-face-deadly-state-violence/.
76. Luis Manuel Galeanor, '8 Nicaraguan Doctors Say Fired for Treating Hurt Protesters', *Associated Press*, 27 July 2018, https://apnews.com/article/e9161b17a4e24771a72758ef2cf86d45.
77. 'Kashmir: Journalist Arrested for Posting Video of Protest', *International Press Institute*, 11 January 2022, https://ipi.media/kashmir-journalist-arrested-for-posting-video-of-protest/.
78. Ilhem Rachidi, 'In Morocco, Press Freedom Shrinks with Hirak Protests', *Al-Monitor*, 31 August 2017, https://www.al-monitor.com/originals/2017/08/morocco-rif-hirak-journalists-violations.html.
79. UNHRCtte, General Comment No. 37, 44.
80. Maina Kiai and Christof Heyns, Joint report of the Special Rapporteur on the rights to freedom of peaceful assembly and of association and the Special Rapporteur on extra-judicial, summary or arbitrary executions on the proper management of assemblies (4 February 2016) UN Doc. A/HRC/31/66.
81. See e.g. Tabatha Abu El Haj, 'The Neglected Right of Assembly', *UCLA Law Review* 56 (2009): 543–589.
82. Robinson, 'Rethinking the Crime of Rioting', 77; Inazu, 'Unlawful Assembly as Social Control', 2; Tabatha Abu El-Haj, 'Defining *Peaceably*: Policing the Line between Constitutionally Protected Protest and Unlawful Assembly', *Missouri Law Review* 80 (2015): 961–986.
83. Nick Robinson and Elly Page, 'Protecting Dissent: The Freedom of Peaceful Assembly, Civil Disobedience, and Partial First Amendment Protection', *Cornell Law Review* 107, no. 1 (2021): 229.
84. 'Shutting Down the Internet to Shut Up Critics', *Human Rights Watch* (2020). https://www.hrw.org/world-report/2020/country-chapters/global-5.
85. There are many examples from around the world of judgments on the right to protest, including many protective decisions. Ona Flores, *Case Law on Peaceful Protests Columbia Caselaw on Peaceful Protest* (New York: Global Freedom of Expression at Columbia University, June 2023).
86. Open Society Justice Initiative, South Africa's Constitutional Court Strikes Down Restrictive Protest Law, 29 November 2018, https://www.justiceinitiative.org/voices/case-watch-south-africa-s-constitutional-court-strikes-down-restrictive-protest-law.
87. *Mlungwana and Others v The State and Another* [2018] ZACC 45, https://www.saflii.org/za/cases/ZACC/2018/45.html. In 2022, activists in South Africa successfully had a court bar Johannesburg from charging any fees for holding a protest, see *Right to Know Campaign and Others v City Manager of Johannesburg Metropolitan Municipality and Another* [2022] 3 ALL SA 466 (GJ).
88. Praveen Shekhar, 'How Various Countries Have Junked Sedition Law', *India Today*, 12 May 2022, https://www.indiatoday.in/law/story/how-countries-junked-sedition-law-supreme-court-section-124a-1948152-2022-05-11.
89. Apurva Vishwanath, 'Explained: What Is the Sedition Law, and Why Supreme Court's Fresh Directive Is Important', *Indian Express*, 12 May 2022, https://indianexpress.com/article/explained/sedition-law-explained-origin-history-legal-challenge-supreme-court-7911041/.
90. Robinson, 'Rethinking the Crime of Rioting', 125–126.

91. *Shell Nederland v Greenpeace Nederland* 525686/KG ZA 12-1250 and 526023/KG ZA 12-1271 HJ/JWR (2012), https://wayback.archive-it.org/9650/20200417073746/http://p3-raw.greenpeace.org/international/Global/international/publications/climate/2012/Arctic/final translation%20of%20judgment.pdf.
92. ICNL, Defending the Right to Protest, 6.
93. Brandee M. Butler, 'The Right to Protest Is under Assault. Frontline Activists Show How to Fight Back," *Just Security*, 29 August 2023, https://www.justsecurity.org/87896/the-right-to-protest-is-under-assault-frontline-activists-show-how-to-fight-back/.
94. International Center for Not-for-Profit Law, *Reforms Introduced to Protect the Freedom of Assembly*, 2022. https://www.icnl.org/post/analysis/reforms-introduced-to-protect-the-freedom-of-assembly.
95. For example, recent widespread protests in China and Iran show how difficult it is for even more repressive governments to completely curtail demonstrations and some of the financial and reputational costs of doing so. See e.g. Charles Sullivan, 'Misruling the Masses: The Consequences of Cracking Down in Kyrgyzstan', *Nationalities Papers* (2019), https://www.cambridge.org/core/journals/nationalities-papers/article/abs/misruling-the-masses-the-consequences-of-cracking-down-in-kyrgyzstan/082DC7BB10752219A1E1D9724CD4B946.
96. See e.g. Sabine C. Carey, 'The Dynamic Relationship between Protest and Repression', *Political Research Quarterly* 59, no. 1 (2006), https://journals.sagepub.com/doi/10.1177/106591290605900101.

Further Readings

Amnesty International. Protect the Protest! Why We Must Save Our Right to Protest (ACT 30/5856/2022), July 2022.

Flores, Ona. *Case Law on Peaceful Protests*. New York: Global Freedom of Expression at Columbia University, June 2023. https://globalfreedomofexpression.columbia.edu/wp-content/uploads/2023/06/Case-law-on-peaceful-protests.pdf.

International Center for Not-for-Profit Law. Defending the Right to Protest: Resisting Government Crackdowns on Nonviolent Demonstrators, October 2022. https://www.icnl.org/wp-content/uploads/US-Protecting-Protest-Threats-and-Responses-v2.pdf.

Kiai, Maina. Report of the Special Rapporteur on the rights to freedom of peaceful assembly and of association (24 April 2013) UN Doc. A/HRC/23/39.

CHAPTER 31

(UN)GOVERNING ASSEMBLY

A Manifesto for Voluntary Notification

MICHAEL HAMILTON

INTRODUCTION

MANDATORY notification and authorization procedures have, in many jurisdictions, become established as the conduit through which assemblies either make their way into the public realm and obtain visibility or are instead limited or prevented outright.[1] The domestic legal framework governing the holding of assemblies will generally define the set of events for which prior notification or a permit is required. While such requirements are sometimes regarded as entirely benign, or even as facilitative, it is essential to cast a critical eye on this form of procedural regulation to understand how the law attempts to shape and govern what it means to 'assemble'.

The chapter first presents a summary overview of mandatory notification requirements, explaining both the distinction between notification and authorization and the role of sanctions in differentiating mandatory from voluntary schemes. Then, in critiquing such requirements, the chapter broadly endorses C. Edwin Baker's proposal for a voluntary framework, emphasizing that carrots are, in principle, preferable to sticks to preserve the agency of assembly organizers and participants. The chapter then considers three ways in which international human rights law, in attempting to steer a middle regulatory course, has become confused. International human rights law has sometimes recoiled from addressing the most basic of first-order legal questions—namely, whether or not a notification requirement constitutes an *interference* with the right of peaceful assembly. Conceiving of mandatory notification as an interference is vital—otherwise, it need not even be subject to human rights scrutiny. Second, focusing on the purported justificatory rationales for introducing mandatory notification requirements, it can be seen how the guise of satisfying the state's positive obligations—especially in its role as 'facilitator'—too often undermines the state's negative obligation not to interfere. Third, and finally, having conceded the potential legitimacy of mandatory notification requirements, international human rights law then attempts to backtrack, specifying that any such requirement should never be enforced as an end in itself. However, by calling into question precisely the disciplinary characteristic that distinguishes mandatory from voluntary schemes (the potential for enforcement), insistence on accommodating mandatory requirements becomes all the more incongruous. The chapter concludes that encouraging states to move towards *voluntary* notification is the only coherent position for international human rights law to adopt and the only path capable of adequately protecting the right of peaceful assembly.

Mandatory Notification Requirements and Permit Schemes in Domestic Law

The domestic legal framework that governs public assemblies will generally define what events are notifiable, often simply by a numerical threshold.[2] The law may also enumerate some limited exceptions—and while some leeway may properly be afforded to spontaneous assemblies (events in response to a recent occurrence for which timely notification would not have been possible),[3] exceptions also sometimes privilege more nebulous and arbitrary categories (such as 'sporting', 'cultural', 'religious', or 'customary/traditional' events). The legal schema will also typically establish the requisite time frame(s) for notification[4] and what aspects of the assembly must be notified (though, according to international human rights standards, the level of detail required should not be too onerous).[5] It may also require the relevant authorities to issue a receipt to the organizer (as proof of submission), but this can add a further layer of administrative control that is prone to abuse.[6]

Domestic law tends either to assume or require there to be a named organizer(s).[7] Furthermore, in setting out their responsibilities, the legal framework will usually establish liability for any failure of compliance (possibly extending beyond assembly organizers to participants too).[8] Finally, the domestic framework may set out additional modalities for submitting the notification (e.g. whether this can be done online, or only at a particular police station)[9] and any costs involved (though here again, international human rights law pushes back, emphasizing that notification 'should be free of charge').[10]

The distinction between notification and authorization has often been drawn by constitutional and human rights courts (upholding notification while declaring authorization requirements to be contrary to constitutional guarantees). As the African Commission on Human and Peoples' Rights (amongst others) has emphasized, 'participating in and organizing assemblies is a right and not a privilege, and thus its exercise does not require the authorization of the state'.[11] Aspects of *permit* regimes (or their enforcement) have thus been declared unconstitutional in, for example, Nigeria,[12] Ghana,[13] Sudan,[14] and South Africa.[15] Nonetheless, drawing a bright-line distinction between authorization and notification requirements can be difficult—not least because both procedures may result in the imposition of restrictions—and it is worth clarifying the difference before proceeding further.

It is not the possibility of *restriction* that converts a notification requirement into an authorization regime: restrictions can be imposed on a *notified* assembly (akin to *permission* having been withheld), and unqualified *permission* could be granted within a permissive authorization regime (akin to what might result in a light-touch *notification* process). Instead, the nature of the procedure itself is different: notification entails merely a one-way communiqué and carries no expectation of response from the state, whereas authorization puts on hold any form of assembly (and often, any related mobilization) until permission is granted. While the obligation to notify is fully discharged at the point of submission, compliance with an authorization requirement entails waiting until a permit is issued (or refused). Focusing on these procedural details is especially important in identifying de facto authorization schemes (those masquerading as 'notification'). Prime examples might be the 'notification and endorsement' procedure under the legal framework in the Russian Federation[16] or the requirement for the Commissioner of Police in Hong Kong to issue a 'Letter of No Objection' in relation to notified processions under the (colonial era) Public Order Ordinance.[17]

Towards a Critique: (Un)governing Assembly

The most cogent and persuasive critique of 'mandatory permit schemes' remains a chapter of that title written more than thirty-five years ago by C. Edwin Baker.[18] Baker urged a fundamental 'rethinking of the issue', arguing that an entirely voluntary (and incentivized) scheme would better protect First Amendment rights without any substantial detriment to the state's ability to accommodate other interests at play. Baker observed that mandatory permit systems create 'a bargaining process in which city officials clearly have the upper hand'.[19] He posited that the reasons for their introduction 'may have related less to problems of traffic, policing, and resource allocation'[20] than to 'suppressing the expressive activities and assemblies of unpopular groups, particularly the Salvation Army',[21] 'a generally increased recognition of the need for and acceptability of government regulation',[22] and a decline in judicial activism.[23]

Unfortunately, no radical rewriting of legislative schema (either in the United States or further afield) followed from the publication of Baker's work. Indeed, mandatory notification requirements are today generally viewed as *de rigeur* in public protest law. While Baker's ire was focused on the particularities of the kind of mandatory *permit* schemes prevalent in the United States (and their approbation by the Supreme Court in *Cox v New Hampshire*)[24]—not on mandatory *notification* requirements that exist elsewhere—his arguments have much wider import and have become ever more salient.

Even though mandatory notification requirements may sometimes help forestall more crude and forcible interventions, their coercive potential must not be overlooked. It is suggested here that mandatory requirements are an especially potent weapon—a regulatory trojan horse within the state's wider 'apparatus of public order'.[25] They pave the way for, or directly trigger, other forms of state intervention that patently value public order over public freedom.[26]

In many jurisdictions, mandatory notification or permit requirements give way to asymmetrical spaces of regulation in which those wishing to exercise their rights are abandoned to informal processes of bargaining and where the tactical, territorial, and theatrical dimensions of assemblies can seemingly be renegotiated without comeback. In this vein, mandatory processes of notification or authorization may be argued to unduly choreograph, pacify,[27] script,[28] and stage-manage[29] public assemblies, eliminating spontaneity and surprise in the name of predictability. Just as insidiously, a refusal by assembly organizers to comply with notification requirements has sometimes been read by courts as a means of distinguishing 'good' protesters from 'bad', with police intervention and 'enhanced concern' in relation to the latter being viewed more sympathetically by courts.[30]

More subtly, the very existence of such mandatory requirements (even if applied without arbitrariness or discrimination) recasts access to 'public space' as a benefit capable of being withheld rather than as an entitlement by right. Indeed, the establishment of mandatory notification requirements also informs and conditions how law enforcement (and other public) officials conceive of their own role in relation to assemblies: The legal framework provides a script[31] for regulatory actors and agencies (the police, municipal authorities, courts),[32] setting out definitions, establishing roles, conferring powers and creating offences—thereby normalizing certain understandings of 'assembly' and presuppositions about the assembled subjects.

Carrots over Sticks: Baker's Proposed Voluntary Scheme

Given that the manifesto call for *voluntary* notification rests fundamentally on the distinction between voluntary and mandatory procedures, it is important to be clear about what each involves. While it is possible, in theory, to imagine a binding (mandatory) notification requirement with no penalty attached (where compliance follows from self-interest or other more socially oriented motivations rather than on pain of punishment), our concern here is with the typical form of notification requirement where sanctions generally follow from non-compliance. This potential liability converts a voluntary system into a mandatory one.

As Schauer notes, the word 'voluntary' has 'confusing connotations' since it could conceivably also cover instances where people act, or refrain from acting, to avoid punishment.[33] That, however, is not the kind of 'voluntary' system contemplated here. Rather, voluntary notification involves no threat of sanction—provision of notice is optional and is instead incentivized so that assembly organizers understand the benefits (or losses) that might legitimately accrue from notifying or not.

A mandatory requirement to notify state authorities of an intention to hold an assembly (let alone to obtain prior permission) raises fundamental questions about the place and effectiveness of law in governing human conduct. In probing the utility of such mandatory provisions (and whether a non-coercive system presents a credible alternative), it might be asked whether mandatory notification is epiphenomenal to the decision-making processes of assembly organizers (and to social movements more broadly), such that these procedural requirements are 'causally inert'.[34] While an empirical answer to this question may be beyond reach, it can at least be conjectured that organizers of the most portentous assemblies—those most problematic from the state's perspective, and precisely those that a mandatory system is designed to bring within the regulatory fold—are also those least likely to comply with a mandatory requirement. As the European Court of Human Rights has itself recognized:

> The Court is not convinced, moreover, that a purely obstructive protest action . . . could, in principle and as a practical matter, be subjected to prior notification requirements. Such a requirement would deprive many such actions of much effect and would amount to a requirement to declare the intention to break the law.[35]

Nonetheless, the state's preference for sticks can be straightforwardly understood. The primary regulatory animus is those assemblies that may signal a withdrawal of consent to be governed and thus prefigure some alternative form of self-government (see further Srinivasan, in this volume). These assemblies embody a form of constituent power that exist in 'a gaming relationship'[36] with Hobbesian-style sovereignty and which (on this understanding) the state is continually forced to negate: the state must 'attempt, over and over again, to bring a halt to this ever-threatening conflict'.[37] Mandatory notification procedures can thus be viewed as a play by the state to extract a measure of consent from those who wish to assemble. Such notification schemes (with attendant liability for non-compliance) build in a form of managerialism to the regulatory apparatus, reinforcing the message that state authorities have the dominant hand.[38]

In insisting on the need to rethink the regulatory starting point, Baker argued that the dynamics of a voluntary system are fundamentally different from a mandatory one—the role of public officials 'shifts from that of writing and enforcing restrictions to offering and providing benefits in order to gain the voluntary cooperation of those engaged in first amendment conduct'.[39] He argued that the state could find ways (rewards) that incentivize voluntary notification and that a properly designed voluntary system 'will predictably generate most of the useful information and cooperation that results from a mandatory system . . . while avoiding the great costs . . . in terms of first amendment freedoms, that a mandatory system creates'.[40]

Indeed, the authorities will often already know about non-notified assemblies.[41] As Baker notes, 'the leaflets and advertising designed to notify potential participants of the event will usually provide the police with adequate notice'.[42] If it is accepted that the authorities often already know, the ulterior purpose of notification (to flag to the authorities events whose organizers may already be prepared to break the law by *not* notifying) would still be served by a voluntary system (since the authorities would again be 'on notice' of those assemblies whose convenors have elected not to notify).

Although rarely described in this way, voluntary notification systems already exist in most countries—but they do so for only for a tiny subset of assemblies (e.g. those falling beneath the numerical threshold for the mandatory requirement). For example, if only assemblies of more than one hundred people must be notified, the organizer of an assembly of ninety-nine might nonetheless choose to volunteer notification.[43] If only moving processions but not static assemblies need to be notified, the organizers of a static demonstration could yet decide voluntarily to inform the authorities in advance.

Several of the incentives suggested by Baker—'special parking, first aid, toilets, water, or insurance'—are the kind of perks that might indeed make the provision of notice attractive. Another possible reward Baker points to is the possibility of immunity from forms of police intervention or prosecution for certain offences (incentives that can also exist within a mandatory framework).[44] However, when viewed within the parameters of a human rights framework, some benefits cannot be made entirely conditional on notification being volunteered. If benefits are to be withheld from those who choose not to notify the authorities, either they must be benefits that fall outside the state's obligations (to protect and facilitate the right of peaceful assembly)—or, the state's performance of its obligations must be judged on a sliding scale (depending, amongst other factors, on whether, and to what extent, prior notice was volunteered). This was precisely the reasoning in the key European Court of Human Rights case of *Plattform Ärzte für das Leben v Austria*—where the Strasbourg court declared inadmissible a complaint by organizers of a pro-life procession that Austrian police had failed to sufficiently protect their procession from interruption by pro-choice counter-protesters. The organizer's claim against the police failed, in part, because they had changed the route of the procession at the last minute, leaving the police with insufficient opportunity to redeploy.[45]

In this light, perhaps the most problematic of Baker's suggested incentives is 'to *guarantee* some degree of police protection' to assemblies for which notice has been volunteered.[46] Under international human rights law, state authorities have an obligation to provide protection irrespective of notification (though clearly, there may be many different ways in which this obligation can be satisfied).[47] Furthermore, Baker's suggestion to create a 'reservations system'[48] (whereby those who notify the authorities benefit from a guaranteed space for their event) also obtains little support in international human rights law:[49] first-come, first-served systems can give rise to logistical problems (a race to notify first)[50] and potentially fail to afford sufficient weight to the rights of participants in simultaneous demonstrations.[51]

The primary reason for preferring carrots (incentives) over sticks (sanctions) is the importance of affording effective protection to the *agency* of those who organize and participate in peaceful assemblies—their ability to make strategic choices about how they appear together with others. The procedural requirements of notification and authorization operate as a key background determinant of the capabilities of those who seek to assemble (and as Giddens emphasized, agency is different from intentionality: it 'refers not to the intentions people have in doing things but to their capability of doing those things in the first place (which is why agency implies power . . .)'.[52] As Baker observed, 'mandatory and voluntary systems differ in how they allocate decisional authority with respect to the streets between private citizens and governmental officials'.[53] Moreover, the practices that develop around mandatory notification procedures (including dialogue with the police)[54] can wholly extinguish the decisional authority of assembly organizers—a point acerbically highlighted in a 2013 open letter decrying the overbearing regulation of several antifascist protest events in the UK: '[T]he police have become the protest organisers. It is they who organise what happens on the day, who goes where, what is said and not said, how the protest acts, behaves, moves and demonstrates. We have now not only a state sanctioned but state organised protest.'[55]

Nonetheless, it is argued here that international human rights law has encouraged recourse to sticks over carrots. As the next section outlines, human rights bodies have conceded that states may introduce a mandatory notification requirement—and moreover, have been equivocal about whether such requirements even amount to an interference with the right of peaceful assembly (such that they would need to be justified as provided by law, in pursuit of a legitimate aim, and necessary and proportionate). Second, the state's obligation to facilitate assemblies (as vital as this is) risks being interpreted in ways that conceal the state's coercive power, styling the authorities instead as a partner and overriding the negative obligation to leave well alone. In turn, states are confronted with an enforcement dilemma in cases of non-compliance—and this raises the question of whether a notification requirement (in and of itself) can be a legitimate regulatory endgame. These three factors call into question the coherence of international human rights protections as currently formulated.

The (In)coherence of International Human Rights Law

In seeking to respect and ensure the decisional authority of assembly organizers, human rights law has emphasized that 'the right to freedom of assembly includes the right to choose the time, place and modalities of the assembly'.[56] The starting point for determining the state's response (if any) should be the state's negative obligation not to interfere[57] in combination with 'a presumption in favour of considering assemblies to be peaceful'.[58] Beyond these guardrails, human rights law emphasizes the state's facilitative role ('to make it possible for participants to achieve their objectives').[59] As the following three subsections demonstrate, however, mandatory notification requirements can operate to fatally undermine these ostensibly strong protections.

Mandatory Notification as an Interference

Mandatory notification requirements have commonly been upheld by domestic courts. For example, in Canada, courts in Québec noted (but did not take seriously) that 'the only lesser alternative was to provide no notice at all'.[60] In Hong Kong, the Court of Final Appeal dismissed the idea that mandatory notification could be unconstitutional as 'untenable', one that could not be seriously argued:

> Apart from anything else, notification is required to enable the police to fulfil the positive duty resting on Government to take reasonable and appropriate measures to enable lawful demonstrations to take place peacefully. The statutory requirement for notification is constitutional. A legal requirement for notification is in fact widespread in jurisdictions around the world.[61]

For their part, some human rights bodies have failed to adequately scrutinize the operation of mandatory notification schemes—and in consequence, have not assessed whether other less restrictive means could achieve the same objectives (as or more effectively). The European Court of Human Rights, in particular, has long held that 'subjection to an authorisation or notification procedure does not normally encroach upon the essence of the right as long as the purpose of the procedure is to allow the authorities to take reasonable and appropriate measures in order to guarantee the smooth conduct of any assembly'.[62] The Strasbourg court's approach has echoes of *Cox v New Hampshire* in which the US Supreme Court Chief Justice abruptly dismissed the core of the rights-based challenge to a mandatory permit scheme.[63]

Importantly, and in contrast, the UN Human Rights Committee has regarded a requirement to provide prior notification as a de facto interference with the right to freedom of peaceful assembly, therefore requiring justification.[64] It will be vital for other courts to follow suit, but as the next section highlights, even this critical shift may itself be insufficient to guard against the discretionary excesses that mandatory notification schemes create in the name of satisfying the state's positive obligations.

Facilitation, Not Partnership

Domestic and international courts have tended to view mandatory notification requirements as an innocuous form of administrative planning—serving to facilitate the exercise of the right of peaceful assembly, to coordinate competing and equally legitimate uses of public space (a means of managing scheduling conflicts), to best ensure that the state can uphold the rights and freedoms of others, all the while helping maximize the efficient allocation of public resources by police and municipal authorities (the avoidance of 'resource-depleting guessing games').[65] A further justificatory rationale is that mandatory notification or permit requirements enhance communication and information exchange and incentivize restraint (enabling the police *not* to exercise coercive powers that might otherwise have been utilized).[66]

The purported connection between mandatory notification and the state's obligations to facilitate assembly and as guarantor of the rights and freedoms of others is regularly emphasized.[67] Indeed, mandatory notification requirements have sometimes been enmeshed with a requirement to engage with state authorities in processes of informal dialogue aimed at reaching 'agreement' about how an assembly should (or should not) proceed. Perhaps the most recognized example of such a requirement is the so-called 'safety triangle' under the South African Regulation of Gatherings Act 1993, whereby the convenor of an assembly may be called upon to meet with the police and municipal authority to negotiate an agreed plan for the assembly.[68] Similarly, a new Assembly Act enacted in Hungary in October 2018 imposed a duty on protest organizers to cooperate with the authorities in advance of an assembly.[69]

Such processes have not always passed constitutional muster. For example, in *Sullivan v the City of Augusta* (2005),[70] the organizer of a 2004 march to protest against the war in Iraq challenged a provision in a city ordinance that required, as a condition for being issued a protest permit, the organizer to 'meet with the Police Chief to discuss and attempt to agree on the details of the route and other logistics'.[71] This 'meet and attempt to agree' requirement was deemed by the District Court to be overbroad and not narrowly tailored to a significant government interest:

> By imposing delay for a meeting with the Police Chief as a condition to permitting a parade, the government inhibits spontaneous expression and thus a certain type of speech. Most significantly, the in-person meeting requirement invites subjective assessments, and applicants who are uncomfortable dealing directly with the Police Chief may be discouraged from applying for a parade ordinance altogether. Plaintiffs' example, of an applicant wishing to protest alleged civil rights abuses by police, is well taken. . . . [T]he in-person meeting requirement chills substantially more speech than is necessary to achieve that end.[72]

For the most part, however, such processes of dialogue have been regarded as entirely compatible with international standards—in keeping with the spirit of 'negotiated management' by offering a way of addressing police concerns and thus maximizing protest protections (see further, Probert in this volume). Indeed, in his efforts to convince a US audience of the benefits of moving away from a mandatory permit system, Baker himself strays close to an endorsement of a model premised on negotiation:

> [T]he effect of the voluntary permit system is to require the officials to *secure the cooperation of those exercising first amendment rights through agreement* rather

than through imposition of conditions, such a system changes the dissidents from adversaries into one of the officials' key constituencies.[73]

It is suggested here that an open requirement to enter a process of dialogue is actually another way of 'keeping rules fuzzy',[74] and a mandatory process of negotiation risks substituting the obligation to facilitate and protect peaceful protest with a default position predicated on compromise and on obtaining 'consensus'.[75]

'Facilitation' is a complex and double-edged injunction—one that is undefined and affords significant latitude to state authorities. The duty to facilitate potentially bridges (but often blurs) the state's negative and positive obligations—casting more interventionist and paternalistic forms of regulation (e.g. to ensure the 'smooth conduct' of the event or for the participants' own safety) in a facilitative light. But interpreting 'facilitation' in this way presumes that the optimal relationship between those seeking to assemble and the state is one of partnership. It frames the regulatory goal as being to minimize antagonism and potential confrontation and to channel political action within acceptable bounds.[76] In doing so, mandatory notification requirements significantly chill the exercise of the right of peaceful assembly and can lead to self-censorship.[77] Human rights law thus risks supplying or reinforcing a regulatory logic and apparatus while costuming the state as facilitator. As such, the architecture of facilitation may, in practice (and without further safeguards), become indistinguishable from its regulatory doppelganger. It is argued here, instead, that the obligation of state authorities to seek to engage with assembly organizers[78] ought to be regarded as freestanding—separable from any suggestion that there need be a reciprocal obligation on the part of the organizers.

Enforcement as an End in Itself?

In some jurisdictions, the legal framework leaves open the *possibility* of enforcement for failure to fully comply with the notification requirement (which captures anything from noncompletion to partial completion of the notification requirement).[79] In practice, in many jurisdictions, however, the existence of a mandatory notification requirement is the pretext for imposing liability, and charges of organizing (or even, participating in) an 'unlawful assembly' are commonplace.

As we have seen, by readily conceding the compatibility of mandatory notification schemes, the enforcement dilemma is, to some extent, a problem of international human rights law's own making. International human rights law has itself undermined the scope to push back against such liability through its equivocation over whether mandatory notification amounts to an interference and the heightened focus on the positive facilitative obligations of the state: It might appear somewhat illogical to concede that states can require that assemblies be notified in advance, while simultaneously removing their capacity to do anything about it if this requirement is flouted or ignored. Indeed, for state authorities to refrain from enforcement would not only raise concerns about inconsistency and arbitrariness but would also be potentially self-defeating—undermining the state's claim that the particular mandatory system is necessary in the first place and diminishing the legitimacy of any future enforcement.[80]

All that said, international human rights law has attempted a partial backtrack and has sought to limit the *enforcement* of notification requirements. The African Commission on Human and Peoples' Rights has emphasized that assemblies should 'not be automatically penalized, through dispersal or sanction, due to failure to notify' and a '[l]ack of notification shall not be understood to make an assembly illegal'.[81] UN special procedure mandate holders have stated that '[n]ot giving advance notification or failure to meet other administrative requirements should not render an assembly unlawful nor should it be used as a basis to disperse an assembly, arrest its participants, or impose criminal or administrative sanctions resulting in fines or imprisonment on participants or organizers'.[82] The European Court of Human Rights, in the case of *Oya Ataman v Turkey* (amongst many others), has held that even though organizers may be expected to comply with certain regulations in force, such regulations should not represent a hidden obstacle to the effective enjoyment of the right of peaceful assembly.[83] Moreover, as emphasized by the UN Human Rights Committee, any sanction for non-notification must not be by way of criminal penalty: '[f]ailure to notify the authorities must not in itself be used as a basis for arresting the participants or organizers, or for imposing undue sanctions, such as charging the participants or organizers with criminal offences'.[84]

Most significantly, it has been emphasized that the regulatory endgame should never be to secure *notification* and that '[t]he enforcement of notification requirements must not become an end in itself'.[85] This implies that mandatory notification requirements should not be enforced unless enforcement is itself necessary and proportionate to achieve one or more of the legitimate aims for which notification requirements may be introduced. Ultimately, this would appear to leave very little room at all for enforcement—and if this is so, it essentially pulls the rug from under mandatory notification requirements. As such, the case for having an unenforceable mandatory scheme over a well-designed voluntary one becomes weaker still.

Conclusion

This chapter has sought to highlight the absurdity of regulating rights-protected activities (assembling) in a way that would be considered illegitimate in relation to activities that are not protected as rights. It has been suggested that only a voluntary notification scheme ('with benefits') can properly avoid the normative incoherence in international human rights law.

It is perhaps unsurprising that international human rights law (negotiated and ratified by states) has ceded this regulatory space. But the premises of and justifications for notification have been too readily accepted, and international standards focus merely on attempting to curtail excessive burdens—weakly insisting on notification rather than authorization and emphasizing that notification requirements should be as non-onerous as possible. The chapter has sought to make the case that international human rights scrutiny has not gone far enough—and, as a result, has become part of the problem.

A voluntary system—precisely as a way of implementing the state's obligation to facilitate the right of peaceful assembly—not only properly recognizes the weight that must be attached to the right (and the agency of assembly organizers) but also operates to incentivize the provision of the information actually needed to respond to competing interests (even in those cases where compliance with a mandatory scheme would be unlikely). In this regard, eschewing mandatory procedures that are designed to trigger formal or informal negotiations between assembly organizers and state authorities helps place a thumb on the scale of the right of peaceful assembly—properly casting the authorities in the role of protecting the right (rather than as either licensor or as partner with whom compromise must be reached). State authorities have been too quick to translate 'facilitator' as 'partner'—overlooking the agency of assembly organizers, focusing primarily (or exclusively) on the state's positive obligations (at the expense of its duty to refrain from interfering), and masking, without ever renouncing, its coercive power.

Giving prominence to the state's negative obligation of non-interference enables an openness around the performance of its positive obligations (and what may legitimately be expected from the authorities in different scenarios). Recognizing that the state's response may legitimately correlate with the level of notification (voluntarily) provided opens the path for a more honest discussion about what the state's response ought to be. Indeed, the corollary of a voluntary notification requirement would be to judge the performance of state obligations on a sliding scale, contingent in part on whether the authorities possessed information that could have materially changed the levels of protection and facilitation provided.

While Baker's model may itself require some light modification—in particular, the question of what 'perks' might legitimately be *withheld* under a human rights framework (which requires that states put in place a baseline of protection, an enabling framework for the exercise of the right of peaceful assembly), such a proposal is not as radical as it may first sound. Properly incentivized, and where the police are demonstrably committed to rights-compliant assembly policing, many assembly organizers will recognize that voluntarily notifying the authorities in advance can serve their own interests well.

While it is good that the unbefitting language of '*managing* assemblies' was omitted from General Comment No. 37, there has nonetheless been an abject failure (borrowing Baker's exhortation) to 'rethink the issue'. Courts must recognize the regulatory entry point (and often much more) that notification schemes create. There must be rigorous scrutiny of the nature and operation of notification requirements, assessing what gains actually result from this interference with the right and whether mandatory notification, for the type of assembly concerned, can be justified at all.

Mandatory notification or permit requirements raise critical questions about the role of the state and the (un)governability of assembly. More precisely, such regulatory schemes are a symptom of the existential anxiety assemblies provoke at the heart of the state. Borne of fears of dysfunction (the impotence of regulation in the face of the assembled people), mandatory notification requirements attempt to bring the state back into the game. In structuring the relationship between the assembled people and the state, the very existence of such procedures reserves sovereignty to the latter and diminishes the agency of the former—relegating those who wish to assemble to the position of supplicant. Only a voluntary system of notification recognizes that the role of the state is not to manage assemblies (or to impose an organizational straitjacket) but rather to accommodate their ungovernability.

Notes

1. Similarly, J. Weintraub, 'Varieties and Vicissitudes of Public Space', in *Metropolis: Centre and Symbol of our Times*, ed. Philip Kasinitz (New York: New York University Press, 1995), 280–319, 282.
2. For an overview of permit requirements in the United States, see T. Zick, *Managed Dissent: The Law of Public Protest* (Cambridge: Cambridge University Press, 2023), 69–72; Nathan W. Kellum, 'Permit Schemes: Under Current Jurisprudence, What Permits Are Permitted?', *Drake Law Review* 56 (2008), 381–425.
3. For example, ECtHR, *Éva Molnár v Hungary* App. No. 10346/05 (7 October 2008), 36.
4. This raises an interesting dilemma in relation to counter-demonstrations which tend not to be subject to a different regulatory time frame from other notifiable assemblies (and instead, may be treated as falling within any applicable exemption for spontaneous events). However, see, for example, the fourteen-day notification requirement in Northern Ireland for parade-related protests (in contrast to the twenty-eight-day requirement for parades) under s.7 of the Public Processions (Northern Ireland) Act 1998, as amended.
5. Maina Kiai, Report of the Special Rapporteur on the rights to freedom of peaceful assembly and of association: *Best Practices that Promote and Protect the Rights to Freedom of Peaceful Assembly and of Association* (21 May 2012) UN Doc. A/HRC/20/27, 28.
6. The risk is that the authorities might interpret a receipting process as conferring a power to accept or reject the notification (perhaps for being incomplete), potentially resetting the notification clock and forcing organizers to start the process all over again. Where this happens, the procedure is more appropriately characterized as falling towards the authorization end of the notification-authorization spectrum. In the case of *Boniface Mwangi v Inspector General of Police & 5 others* [2017] eKLR (Petition 544 of 2015), 38–45, the High Court of Kenya emphasized that a notification could not simply be *rejected* by police without reasons being given (since this would violate the right to fair administrative action under Article 47 of the Kenyan constitution).
7. For a stark example, see Article 9 of the Law on Meetings and Demonstrations, 1983 (Türkiye), which requires an organizing committee of seven people. See ICNL, *Freedom of Assembly in Turkey*. https://www.icnl.org/wp-content/uploads/cfr_FoA-in-Turkey.pdf. The imposition of some organizational structure presents a particular problem for those assemblies that have less formal (or less hierarchical) forms of organization—what Paulo Gerbaudo calls the 'choreographing' of assemblies. P. Gerbaudo, *Tweets and the Streets: Social Media and Contemporary Activism* (London: Pluto Press, 2012). In a case

challenging the applicability of the notification requirement under s.11 of the Public Order Act in England and Wales to a Critical Mass Bicycle Ride that had neither an organizer nor a predetermined route (its monthly start time and location being widely known), Lord Brown in the House of Lords argued that only *organized* processions fell within the scope of the Act. See *Kay v Metropolitan Police Commissioner* [2008] UKHL 69.

8. International human rights law emphasizes that *participation* should not be penalized because notification was not submitted. See UNHRCtte, General Comment No. 37—Article 21: Right of Peaceful Assembly (17 September 2020) UN Doc. CCPR/C/GC/37, 17.
9. On this point, international human rights standards emphasize that there should be a single gateway for notification. See Venice Commission and OSCE/ODIHR, Guidelines on Freedom of Peaceful Assembly, 3rd rev. ed. (Strasbourg and Warsaw, 15 July 2020) CDL-AD(2019)017rev, 118.
10. UNHRCtte, General Comment No. 37, 70.
11. African Commission on Human and Peoples' Rights, Guidelines on Freedom of Association and Assembly in Africa (2017), 71. Similarly, UNHRCtte, General Comment No. 37, 70.
12. Nigeria Court of Appeal, *Inspector-General of Police v All Nigeria Peoples Party and Others*, 3PLR/2007/111 (CA) (11 December 2007): requirement of a police permit for the holding of rallies or processions contravenes § 40 of the 1999 Constitution and Article 11 of the African Charter on Human and Peoples' Rights (ACHPR).
13. Supreme Court of Ghana, *New Patriotic Party v Inspector General of Police*, ILDC 2548 (GH 1993) (30 November 1993): striking down provisions of the Public Order Decree (NRCD 68) as contravening Article 21(1)(d) of the Ghanaian Constitution (albeit subsequently reversed by the Public Order Act 491 of 1994). See further Edward Kofi Quashigah, 'The Constitutional Right to Freedom of Assembly and Procession in Ghana in the Light of the Decision in the Public Order Case and the Public Order Act', *University of Ghana Law Journal* 20 (1996–1999): 1–25.
14. African Commission on Human and Peoples' Rights, *Amnesty International and Others v Sudan*, Comm. Nos. 48/90, 50/91, 52/91, and 89/93 (1999), 81–82: holding § 7 of the Process and Transitional Powers Act 1989, which prohibited political assemblies without special permission, to be a measure prone to abuse and a disproportionate interference (albeit misattributed to the right of association under Article 10(1) ACHPR).
15. Constitutional Court of South Africa, *Mlungwana and Others v The State and Another* (CCT32/18) [2018] ZACC 45 (19 November 2018), confirming the constitutional invalidity of § 12(1)(a) of the Regulation of Gatherings Act (1993) to the extent that it makes the failure to give notice, or giving inadequate notice, a criminal offence.
16. ECtHR, *Berladir and Others v Russia* App. No. 34202/06 (10 July 2012), 19–24 and 47–48 (describing the relevant aspects of the procedure under §§ 5 and 7 of the Public Gatherings Act 2004).
17. Sections 13(1) and 14(4) of the Hong Kong Public Order Ordinance (Cap. 245, 1967) provide that a public procession may take place 'if, but only if' the Commissioner of Police has notified the person who submitted the notification 'that he has no objection to the procession taking place.
18. C. E. Baker, 'Mandatory Parade Permits', in *Human Liberty and Freedom of Speech* (New York: Oxford University Press, 1989), 138–160.
19. Ibid., 148.
20. Ibid.
21. Ibid., 140.
22. Ibid.

23. Ibid., 141.
24. *Cox v New Hampshire*, 312 U.S. 569 (1941). Baker maintains *Cox* was 'wrongly decided' (Baker, 'Manadatory Parade Permits', 143). Also David Goldberger, 'Reconsideration of *Cox v New Hampshire*: Can Demonstrators Be Required to Pay the Costs of Using America's Public Forums', *Texas Law Review* 62, no. 3 (November 1983): 403–452.
25. I. Rua Wall, *Law and Disorder: Sovereignty, Protest, Atmosphere* (Oxon, UK: Routledge, 2021), 61–64.
26. Tabatha Abu El-Haj, 'All Assemble: Order and Disorder in Law, Politics and Culture', *Journal of Constitutional Law* 16, no. 4 (2014): 949, 962.
27. J. Duncan, *Protest Nation: The Right to Protest in South Africa* (Pietermaritzburg: University of KwaZulu-Natal Press, 2016), 48.
28. Wall, *Law and Disorder* noting (at 158) that 'when a script has played out, it is usually very difficult to understand what it felt like at the outset'.
29. T. Zick, *Speech Out of Doors: Preserving First Amendment Liberties in Public Places* (Cambridge: Cambridge University Press, 2009), 197–198.
30. For example, justifying the stop and search of a protester en route to an unnotified 'Crude Awakening' protest, a UK High Court judge remarked that 'this was not a case where the organisers of the protest had consulted with the police to assist in the orderly conduct of the event as happens in the case of many peaceful demonstrations today. This was not a protest characterised by the organisers' advance co-operation with the police to ensure mutual facilitation of protest and the preservation of law and order. Enhanced concern was to that extent justified.' *Howarth v MPC* [2011] EWHC 2818 (QB), 33, per McCombe J.
31. For example, R. Martin, *Policing Human Rights: Law, Narratives, and Practice*, Clarendon Studies in Criminology (Oxford: Oxford University Press, 2021), 206. Martin uses the term 'script' to capture the 'carefully constructed template for managing public order events' relied on by the police.
32. See, in particular, the chapters in this volume by Probert; Pita Loor; Casey-Maslen; Adang; and Cammiss, Hayes, and Doherty.
33. Frederick Schauer, *The Force of Law* (Cambridge, MA: Harvard University Press, 2015), 66.
34. Ibid., 59. Schauer challenges the premise in Tom Tyler's assertion (*why* people obey the law) by posing the antecedent question, *do* people obey the law? He asks whether, and if so, how, law makes a difference to the reasoning and decision-making processes of ordinary people (61), arguing that 'when sanctions are removed from the equation, . . . compliance with the law just because it is the law is far less widespread (67). Schauer posits that there is 'substantial support for the hypothesis that unenforced law . . . is often ineffective' (65).
35. ECtHR, *Chernega v Ukraine* App. No. 74768/10 (18 June 2019), 239.
36. James Tully, 'The Imperialism of Modern Constitutional Democracy', in *The Paradox of Constitutionalism: Constituent Power and Constitutional Form*, ed. Martin Loughlin and Neil Walker (Oxford: Oxford University Press: 2008), 315 at 322.
37. A. Honneth, *The Struggle for Recognition* (Cambridge: Polity Press, 1995), 10. See also Duncan Ivison, 'Pluralism and the Hobbesian Logic of Negative Constitutionalism', *Political Studies* 47 (1999): 83; A. Negri, *Insurgencies: Constituent Power and the Modern State* (Minneapolis: University of Minnesota Press, 1999), 304–305.
38. Making the point that the very terms of 'negotiated management' are generally set by the police. See Hugo Gorringe and Michael Rosie, 'It's a Long Way to Auchterarder! 'Negotiated Management' and Mismanagement in the Policing of G8 Protests', *British Journal of Sociology* 59, no. 2 (2008): 187–205; P. A. J. Waddington, 'Negotiating Protest: Policing by Consent?', in *Liberty and Order: Public Order Policing in a Capital City* (London: UCL Press, 1994), 69–103.

39. Baker, 'Mandatory Parade Permits', 156.
40. Ibid., 149.
41. For example, in ECtHR, *Barraco v France* App. No. 31684/05 (5 March 2009), 45: The event had been widely brought to the attention of the public authorities ('d'autant qu'en l'espèce, l'événement avait largement été porté à la connaissance des autorités publiques').
42. Baker, 'Mandatory Parade Permits', 150.
43. For example, a system of authorization exists in Belgium, with only certain small events (which must in any case be notified at least three weeks in advance) falling outside the scope of the authorization requirement: Article 104 of the Antwerp Police Regulation specifies the list of criteria for an event to be exempted, including that it has no more than five hundred participants, lasts for less than a day, will have no amplified music after 10.00 pm, is not organized by a student association and does not involve either percussion instruments or animals.
44. For example, once an assembly has been authorized in Queensland, the police do not then have the power to issue participants with a direction to move on, and certain other offences cannot be prosecuted—there is statutory immunity from prosecution for obstruction (§§ 6 and 10, Queensland Public Assembly Act 1992).
45. ECtHR, *Plattform Ärzte für das Leben v Austria* App. No. 10126/82 (admissibility, 17 October 1985). See also the German Constitutional Court decision in *Brokdorf*, BVerfGE 69, 315 (14 May 1985) (in translation): 'The absence of notification and the resultant lack of information merely make this intervention easier to justify' and 'the more the organisers of a large demonstration are ready . . . to take unilateral confidence-building measures or even for "demonstration-friendly" co-operation, the higher is the threshold for intervention by an authority because of danger to public safety and order.' https://law.utexas.edu/transnational/foreign-law-translations/german/case.php?id=656.
46. Baker, 'Mandatory Parade Permits', 144.
47. UNHRCtte, General Comment No. 37, 71: 'Lack of notification does not absolve the authorities from the obligation, within their abilities, to facilitate the assembly and to protect the participants.'
48. Baker, 'Mandatory Parade Permits', 144.
49. See, for example, *R (Brehony) v Chief Constable of Greater Manchester* [2005] EWHC 640, 15 (per Bean J.).
50. In South Korea in 2015, for example, the organizers of the Seoul Pride parade and counter-protests related to it camped outside the police station for days because of the first-come, first-served system of notification. See Yoonjung Seo and Anna Fifield, 'South Korea, at Behest of Conservative Christians, Bans LGBT March', *Washington Post*, 3 June 2015, https://www.washingtonpost.com/news/worldviews/wp/2015/06/03/south-korea-at-behest-of-conservative-christians-bans-lgbt-march/.
51. Venice Commission and OSCE/ODIHR, *Guidelines on Freedom of Peaceful Assembly*, 3rd rev. ed. (Strasbourg and Warsaw, 15 July 2020) CDL-AD(2019)017rev, 78 and 120.
52. A. Giddens, *The Constitution of Society: Outline of the Theory of Structuration* (Berkeley: University of California Press, 1984), 9.
53. Baker, 'Mandatory Parade Permits', 151.
54. For example, Joanna Gilmore, William Jackson, and Helen Monk, '"That Is Not Facilitating Peaceful Protest. That Is Dismantling the Protest': Anti-Fracking Protesters' Experiences of Dialogue Policing and Mass Arrest', *Policing & Society* 29, no. 1 (2017): 36–51.
55. Refuse to Collaborate, *Open Letter*, 14 September 2013, http://refusetocollaborate.tumblr.com/.
56. ECtHR, *Sáska v Hungary* App. No. 58050/08 (27 November 2012), 21.

57. UNHRCtte, General Comment No. 37, 8 and 23 (no unwarranted interference). See also the joint dissenting opinion of Judges Ziemele, Sajó, Kalaydjiyeva, Vučininć and De Gaetano in ECtHR, *Animal Defenders v UK* App. No. 48876/08 (22 April 2013), 12: 'There is a risk that by developing the notion of positive obligations to protect . . . rights . . . one can lose sight of the fundamental negative obligation of the State to abstain from interfering.'
58. UNHRCtte, General Comment No. 37, 17.
59. Ibid., 8, 24, 71, and 74.
60. Basil S. Alexander, 'Exploring a More Independent Freedom of Peaceful Assembly in Canada', *Western Journal of Legal Studies* 8, no. 1(4) (2017): 10. *Villeneuve c. Montréal (Ville de)* (2016) QCCS 2888, 386–390; Also, *Québec (Ville de) c. Bérubé* (2016) QCCM 122, 133.
61. *Leung Kwok Hung & Ors v HKSAR* [2005] HKCFA 40; [2005] 3 HKLRD 164; (2005) 8 HKCFAR 229; FACC 1/2005 (8 July 2005), 65. https://www.hklii.hk/en/cases/hkcfa/2005/40.
62. See, for example, ECtHR, *Sergey Kuznetsov v The Russian Federation* App. No. 10877/04 (23 October 2008), 42. See also *Patrick Coleman v Australia*, Communication No. 1157/2003, UN Doc. CCPR/C/87/D/1157/2003 (2006), concurring opinion of Mr. Nisuke Ando, Mr. Michael O'Flaherty, and Mr. Walter Kälin, arguing that 'the establishment of such systems, in principle, is wholly consistent with the Covenant, and has additional advantages of fostering clarity, certainty and consistency, as well as providing an easier means of review by the local courts'.
63. *Cox v New Hampshire*, 312 U.S. 569, 578: 'No interference with religious worship or the practice of religion in any proper sense is shown, but only the exercise of local control over the use of streets for parades and processions.'
64. UNHRCtte, General Comment No. 37, 70; Communication No. 412/1990, *Kivenmaa v Finland*, views adopted 31 March 1994, CCPR/C/50/D/412/1990, 9.2. Note also that the State Party sought to rely on the jurisprudence of the European Court of Human Rights to argue (7.8) 'that the right of public assembly *is not restricted* by the requirement of a prior notification to the police'.
65. *Five Borough Bicycle Club v City of New York*, 684 F. Supp. 2d 423, 436–437 (2010).
66. ECtHR, *Oya Ataman v Turkey* App. No. 74552/01 (5 December 2006), 16.
67. For example, UNHRCtte, General Comment No. 37, 70; ECtHR *Bumbeş v Romania* App. No. 18079/15 (May 2022), 94.
68. See § 4 of the South African Regulation of Gatherings Act (1993).
69. A study of the implementation of the 2018 law has shown how, in the absence of express safeguards, informal processes of negotiation create spaces of significant discretionary authority—reliant, in turn, on robust supervision by the courts (and the Budapest-Capital Regional Court has found the process wanting in several cases). See Dalma Dojcsák et al., 'The New Law on the Right to Assembly in Hungary as Applied in Practice' (Friedrich Naumann Foundation for Freedom, 2020), 16–20. https://helsinki.hu/en/research-project-on-the-new-hungarian-assembly-law-as-applied-in-practice-2020/.
70. 406 F. Supp. 2d 92 (D. Me. 2005). The Appeals Court (511 F.3d 16 (1st Cir. 2007)) also held that the 'meet and attempt to agree' provision was overbroad, but noted that it could be remedied if provision was made for reasonable exceptions and alternatives.
71. Ibid. The ordinance provided: '(c) Within ten (10) days of applying for the permit, as a condition to its issuance, the applicant must meet with the Police Chief to discuss and attempt to agree on the details of the route and other logistics'.
72. Ibid.
73. Baker, *Human Liberty*, 156–157 (emphasis added).
74. A. Etzioni, *Demonstration Democracy* (New York: Gordon and Breach, 1970), 98.

75. M. Hamilton, 'The Management of Protest and Dissent', in *The Routledge Handbook of Illiberalism*, ed. András Sajó, Renáta Uitz, and Stephen Holmes (London: Routledge: 2022), 384–402.
76. On agonism and the 'ineradicability of antagonism', see Chantal Mouffe, 'Deliberative Democracy Or Agonistic Pluralism?', *Social Research* 66, no. 3 (Fall 1999): 745–758.
77. See, for example, Pauline Oosterhoff, Tu-Anh Hoang, and Trang Thu Quach, 'Negotiating Public and Legal Spaces: The Emergence of an LGBT Movement in Vietnam' (Institute of Development Studies, IDS, June 2014), 25: 'Through formal and informal communications with city officials, public event organisers know where to draw the line. VietPride organisers adjusted their activities accordingly.'
78. For example, ECtHR, *Frumkin v Russia* App. No. 745678/12 (5 January 2016), 128–129.
79. The court in *Brokdorf* BVerfGE 69, 315 (14 May 1985) noted (in translation): 'It is true that any person who as organiser or leader "conducts" a meeting which has not been notified commits an offence (s.26 Meetings Act). But the Meetings Act merely provides in s.15(2) that the competent authority "can" disperse meetings in the open air and processions if they are not notified. . . . [T]he competent authority is not in any case legally obliged to disperse or ban meetings. It merely has an authority to do so, of which it may, in the light of the great importance of freedom of assembly in general, only make use in accordance with its duty if further prerequisites for an intervention are present.'
80. In relation to the 2011 Occupy protests in the United States, for example, Tabatha Abu El-Haj noted that 'many occupations proceeded without obtaining required permits from local authorities' noting how an initial willingness in some cities not to enforce permit requirements later gave way to more strict enforcement. See Abu El-Haj, 'All Assemble', 958–960, and nn. 34–36.
81. African Commission on Human and Peoples' Rights, Guidelines on Freedom of Association and Assembly in Africa (2017), 71(a), 71(b).
82. Maina Kiai and Christof Heyns, Joint report of the Special Rapporteur on the rights to freedom of peaceful assembly and of association and the Special Rapporteur on extrajudicial, summary or arbitrary executions on the proper management of assemblies (4 February 2016) UN Doc. A/HRC/31/66, 23.
83. ECtHR, *Oya Ataman v Turkey* App. No. 74552/01 (5 December 2006), 38. Similarly, ECtHR, *Mustafa Hajili and Others v Azerbaijan* App. Nos. 69483/13 and 2 others (6 October 2022), 56.
84. UNHRCtte, General Comment No. 37, 71.
85. Ibid., 70.

Further Reading

Baker, C. Edwin. 'Mandatory Parade Permits', in *Human Liberty and Freedom of Speech*, 138–160. Oxford: Oxford University Press, 1989.

Kellum, Nathan W. 'Permit Schemes: Under Current Jurisprudence, What Permits Are Permitted?' *Drake Law Review* 56 (2008): 381–425.

Tertytchnaya, Katerina. '"This Rally Is Not Authorized": Preventive Repression and Public Opinion in Electoral Autocracies'. *World Politics* 75, no. 3 (2023): 482–522.

Waddington, P. A. J. 'Negotiating Protest: Policing by Consent?' In *Liberty and Order: Public Order Policing in a Capital City*, 69–103. London: UCL Press, 1994.

Zenn, Jacob. 'Freedom of Assembly: Procedures of Permission and Notification'. https://www.icnl.org/wp-content/uploads/cfr_Permission-Notification-article.pdf.

CHAPTER 32

ONLINE ASSEMBLIES AND ARTIFICIAL INTELLIGENCE

CAMERAN ASHRAF

INTRODUCTION

THE growing importance of artificial intelligence (AI) has captured the attention of popular media, academics, politicians, multinational businesses, and others. It represents a significant shift in both the capabilities of and our relationship to information and communication technologies. These new challenges and possibilities have prompted vigorous discussion and debate within policy and academic circles on ethical development of AI. Indeed, AI ethics boards and algorithmic impact assessments are increasingly common across industries, with prominent examples including the European Commission's high-level expert group and the Global Partnership on AI and an international secretariat focused on developing human-centric AI hosted by the Organization for Economic Co-operation and Development (OECD).[1] Additionally, Google, Microsoft, and other technology companies have created AI ethics panels to address AI development.[2] At the same time, states around the world are actively seeking to harness AI to gain strategic advantages in business, military affairs, cyberconflict, economic development, and scientific research.

Beyond these initiatives, activists, non-governmental organizations, scholars, and others are examining how AI will interface with international human rights. Many of these interrogations have focused on the impact of AI on the right to privacy and freedom of expression on social media and the internet, with more recent scholarship broadening this scope.[3] In comparison to work on privacy and freedom of expression, the impacts of AI on the right of peaceful assembly online under Article 21 of the International Covenant on Civil and Political Rights (ICCPR) has received comparatively little attention in scholarly literature. This is despite the fact that the UN Human Rights Committee has stated that 'communications technologies offer the opportunity to assemble either wholly or partly online and often play an integral role in organizing, participating in and monitoring physical gatherings'.[4] Indeed, every day, billions of people assemble online for the purpose of expressing themselves, organizing around an issue or topic, or sharing and exchanging information or ideas.

The purpose of this chapter is to contribute to broadening scholarship on AI and human rights by examining the potential harms of AI on the right of peaceful assembly online. Given the nascent state of AI development and deployment, it is critical that the discourse around the impacts of AI be broadened beyond ethics, privacy, and freedom of expression to ensure that AI development incorporates a broader range of fundamental rights as an ethical minimum. This chapter will first describe peaceful assembly online and then define AI, followed by an outline of threats posed by AI to peaceful assembly online.

Understanding Peaceful Assembly Online

For the purposes of this chapter, online assemblies are understood to occur when individuals come together in a certain digital space for an expressive purpose of participating in the social, cultural, and political life of society.[5] For example, when individuals are tweeting the long-running hashtag #IranRevolution, not only are they engaging in an expressive act, but the use of a hashtag creates both a digital space and a common purpose (to comment on the hashtag) and would constitute an online assembly.

Even though the criteria for what counts as an assembly online remains debated amidst fast-paced technological change, that assemblies *do* take place online is now firmly established. General Comment No. 37 by the UN Human Rights Committee on the right of peaceful assembly decisively states that 'Article 21 of the Covenant protects peaceful assemblies wherever they take place: outdoors, indoors and online . . .' The Committee further states that 'Many associated activities happen online or otherwise rely upon digital services. Such activities are also protected under article 21'.[6] The Committee also emphasizes that 'States should ensure that the activities of Internet service providers and intermediaries do not unduly restrict assemblies or the privacy of assembly participants'.[7]

The clarity provided by General Comment No. 37 on recognizing that assembly may occur online followed growing attention within UN bodies during the decade prior. For example, as early as 2013, UN Human Rights Council Resolution 24/5 recognized 'the important role of new information and communications technologies in enabling and facilitating the enjoyment of the rights to freedom of peaceful assembly and of association'.[8] In 2018, UN HRC Resolution A/HRC/RES/38/11 noted 'that although an assembly has generally been understood as a physical gathering of people, human rights protections, including for the rights to freedom of peaceful assembly, of expression and of association, may apply to analogous interactions taking place online'.[9] That same year, UN General Assembly Resolution A/RES/73/173 in 2018 called upon states to grant 'respect to all individuals exercising their rights to freedom of peaceful assembly, of expression and of association, online and offline, in cases of threat, harassment, violence, discrimination, racism and other violations and abuses committed against them'.[10]

The protection afforded by the right of peaceful assembly online is based on a longer history of social media being instrumental for modern peaceful assembly. Social media has played a critical role in peaceful assembly at least since the 2009 Green Movement protests in Iran popularized the phrase 'Twitter Revolution', considered 'the first major world event broadcast worldwide almost entirely via social media'.[11] Twitter and social media were used to organize and disseminate information about these protests, and indeed again in 2022, social media—including Instagram and Telegram—proved vital in the Iranian protests against mandatory hijab (see Liu, in this volume). Social media has been used to organize global climate actions, widespread protests against Donald Trump's election, the global Black Lives Matter movement, delivering more than 6 million signatures to the UK Parliament against Brexit, and numerous other collective mobilizations.[12] Notably, the #MeToo movement saw millions of women assemble synchronously and asynchronously online to share their experiences of sexual harassment and gender-based discrimination, developing into a global movement.[13] In these cases, and more, social media was essential to individuals assembling peacefully online for collective action.

Online peaceful assembly manifests in myriad ways discussed elsewhere in this volume (see both McPherson and Beraldo, in this volume). McPherson et al. outline several key dimensions of the right of peaceful assembly which warrant scrutiny as regards online assemblies: purpose, public/private, presence/participation, and temporary/permanent.[14] Briefly, 'purpose' speaks to individuals coming 'together to communicate, exchange and act to address common concerns'.[15] The distinction between public and private recognizes that most online peaceful assembly occurs in privatized spaces owned by social media companies. Presence and participation emphasize the need to determine what constitutes participation in an online assembly. Temporary and permanent examines the ephemeralities of online assemblies and their relationships to longer-duration 'associations' (see discussion of 'assemblages', Beraldo, in this volume). These dimensions should not be seen as definitional, but rather as conceptual, and thus of heuristic value in helping to better understand assemblies online.

In addition to the definitional debates, conceptual questions, and fast-paced empirical changes in how online assembly manifests and shapes social and political life, increasingly urgent questions have arisen concerning artificial intelligence and its role in online peaceful assemblies. Important here, is how AI might unsettle the assumption that the right of peaceful assembly protects a conscious or intentional act. It is understood that online or offline assemblies involve individuals consciously coming together for an expressive purpose. However, given the role of artificial intelligence in mediating and moderating what content is visible on social media platforms, individuals could be unconsciously 'nudged' into assemblies via promoted advertisements, posts, and groups or participate simply because an assembly is 'trending' on a social media platform. This can happen through the ability of AI to detect unconscious patterns or behaviours in individual actions and serve content or, with generative AI, respond to prompts or generate content which can explicitly target a part of an individual's psychology which is unknown to them. Thus, the intentional nature of assemblies in which individuals consciously decide to participate or have control over visibility and presence is called into question.

Defining Artificial Intelligence

Despite its increasing importance in everyday life, there is no widely accepted definition of AI. However, there is a widespread understanding across scholarly disciplines that AI is powered by algorithms and comprised of two subfields: general and narrow AI.[16] The purpose of narrow AI is to analyse data inputs to generate an output and 'derive a rule or procedure that explains the data or can predict future data'.[17] Examples of this include curated social media feeds and shopping or movie recommendations. Much of the commercial internet utilizes narrow AI to recommend content or goods for consumption or engagement. Other notable examples of narrow AI include the DeepBlue chess engine which defeated the world chess champion Garry Kasparov, Google's AlphaGo which defeated top Go player Ke Jie, and the anti-suicide messages employed in Google searches which provide local psychological support references based on search terms. More recently, rapid developments of 'Large Language Models' (LLMs) for use by AI systems has given rise to popular systems which utilize large databases to generate seemingly human-like responses to queries. Rapidly deployed to billions of individuals by big technology companies, these 'generative AI' systems such as ChatGPT or DALL-E are poised to be enormously influential.[18]

Narrow AI consists of machine learning, deep learning, and reinforcement learning.[19] Machine learning systems are assigned 'a task and given a large amount of data to use as examples of how this task can be achieved or from which to detect patterns. The system then learns how best to achieve the desired output'.[20] David Kaye defines machine learning systems as consisting of 'techniques used to train algorithms to use datasets to recognize and help solve problems'.[21] Machine learning systems are 'trained' using data already interpreted by human beings. For example, AlphaGo was given a database of more than 30 million human Go games to train the system to play the game.[22]

Deep learning differs from machine learning in its algorithmic learning model evolution. In supervised machine learning, a human programmer must intervene to improve the model or modify the results whereas unsupervised involves limited or no human intervention. In contrast, deep learning systems are modelled on neural pathways and consist of algorithms which are self-modifying and self-improving.[23] A deep learning system can 'learn through its own data processing'.[24] Google's AlphaGo system utilized machine learning to learn the 30 million Go game database, then utilized deep learning to play games against itself and learn from its own mistakes until it was sufficiently well trained to defeat top Go players.[25] Self-driving cars are a rapidly improving example of these deep learning systems, with the car improving its driving performance based on interpretation of the data it generates. Finally, reinforcement learning systems generate their own data, learn from their successes and failures, try new methods to achieve results, and require virtually no human input.

Underlying narrow AI are algorithms (sets of instructions) which analyse the generated data and data inputs. Algorithms are 'code designed and written by humans, carrying instructions to translate data into conclusions, information or outputs'.[26] The development of these algorithms reflects the social and cultural practices, classes, races, genders, and unconscious and conscious biases of the human developers.[27] These biases and sociocultural considerations are also present in deep learning systems, despite consisting of self-modifying and improving algorithms. The parameters by which the deep learning systems learn, adapt, and examine inputs as well as the data used to train these systems all continue to reflect the initial human development of these systems, in essence setting a 'boundary' on the types of self-modification and improvement possible. These same biases and sociocultural factors influence not only the development of AI systems, but also the outputs, with implications for peaceful assembly through conscious or unconscious discrimination.

Moving beyond narrow AI, the other subfield is general AI. General AI is an attempt to develop systems which can accurately mimic or substitute human behaviour.[28] General AI models are imagined in popular science fiction, such as the famous AI system 'Samantha' in the 2013 movie *Her* or HAL 9000 in the film *2001: A Space Odyssey*. As a result, imaginings about this form of AI are comparatively widespread among the general public, even though to date no such system exists. Many scholars doubt that AI will ever reach this stage of sophistication, with some optimistic scholars stating that the earliest date for general AI's emergence is 2099.[29]

Understanding Artificial Intelligence and Social Media Online

To understand the impact of AI on the right of peaceful assembly online, it is useful to examine how AI manifests online from a human rights perspective. To date, much of this work has concerned freedom of expression, which forms an important basis for thinking through implications for assembly. In 2018, David Kaye outlined a framework for examining how AI impacts freedom of expression online focusing on content display, content moderation, surveillance, and digital profiling.[30] In 2021, the Organisation for Security and Co-operation in Europe (OSCE) developed its SAIFE (Spotlight on Artificial Intelligence and Freedom of Expression) policy manual which divided manifestations of AI online into content curation and content moderation.[31]

Content curation and display focus on content which an individual sees in their social media feed. These systems seek to personalize content to individuals based on browsing, search, and interaction data and to rank that content by algorithmically determined priority.[32] Content moderation, on the other hand, utilizes AI systems to examine user-generated content to determine if that content is illegal or harmful and should be removed. AI systems, sometimes assisted by humans, will then determine whether such content should exist on the social media platform. Broadly speaking, content curation and display determines what content we *see*, and content moderation determines what content *exists*.

What types of content are seen and by whom are important elements of freedom of expression online, but the structure of social media feeds means what is seen and by whom can be a critical factor in enabling the right of peaceful assembly. Online assemblies can range from those which are publicly visible and actively recruiting for members to those which are private and accessible by invitation only. However, many of the most impactful online assemblies such as Black Lives Matter, the #MeToo movement, and parts of the Arab Spring and Iranian Green Movement relied on online public visibility to garner support. Thus, if an assembly event is not visible online, the opportunity to exercise the right of peaceful assembly by joining assemblies which rely on some element of public visibility becomes constrained or vanishes. In addition, new generative AI systems respond to queries and dynamically generate content in selective ways influenced by sociocultural factors and conscious/unconscious bias present in their algorithms. The implication for the right of peaceful assembly online is that generative AI systems will continue to represent challenges to the right while introducing new risks based on their unique outputs.[33]

Content Curation and Display

In content curation and display, algorithms determine the type of content and its positioning in search results and social media feeds. The purpose of this is to sort and present enormous amounts of data to individuals—for example, in 2022 there were more than 46,000 Instagram posts every minute of every day.[34] Beyond organizing the world's social media data, these systems are designed to learn which content will generate the greatest user interactions and to serve more of that content to enhance and increase user interactivity.[35] Thus, these systems record significant amounts of user-generated data both within these social networks and via outside partners to build a highly focused and personalized profile. These profiles may record unconscious bias and data about the individual, personality tendencies of which users are not aware.

The net result is that these systems determine what content is *seen* online, which occurs not only for the purposes of increasing audience engagement or data collection but also to test new content via dynamic A/B experimentation.[36] To utilize a simplistic example, a system may discover that a user interacts extensively with content related to alpine hiking. The definition of interaction varies: it need not be only liking or subscribing to alpine hiking content but can be when a user likes photos which other alpine hikers have liked, based on types of videos watched and total playtime on various channels, among other variables.[37] Data can come from single browsing sessions, months or years of social media and advertising use and exposure, data generated by 'friends' or connections, or geographical or demographic data aggregates.[38] The Council of Europe summarizes content curation and display succinctly:

> Algorithmic predictions of user preferences deployed by social media platforms guide not only what advertisements individuals might see, but they also personalise search results and dictate the way how social media feeds, including newsfeeds, are arranged.[39]

The OSCE has developed a typology of content curation and display which is useful for understanding this pervasive, 'technological unconscious' of the modern internet.[40] According to the OSCE, there are three broad categories of content curation and display: content-based filtering, collaborative filtering, and hybrid filtering. Content-based filtering works by giving individuals content based on their 'stated or implied preference'.[41] It is the most simplistic and easiest-understood method of content curation and display, operating by giving an individual content aligned with their interactions on the platform, such as someone who is interested in sports receiving more sports-based and allied content.

Collaborative filtering shows individual content based on the interactions of friends or close contacts, or with others who are categorized as belonging to a similar demographic or with similar interests. To continue the sports example from above, collaborative filtering would show an individual other sports content which individuals in their social network have interacted with. Sometimes this can be clearly labelled, as in 'Person X liked Article Y', or by simply appearing in an individual social feed without any prompting. Hybrid filtering is a combination of both methods and this method of filtering would not just display sports content liked by friends or demographic allies but rather would show sports content specific to the individual—for example, a local or regional team or article analysing a previous match.[42]

This ability to curate and display content is reliant upon enormous amounts of data collected and processed by social media platforms: Facebook alone has nearly one hundred data points on each of its nearly three billion active users.[43] According to the *New York Times*, these data points include 'basic stuff like your age and gender, but also more complicated information like whether you own a motorcycle or you recently went on vacation or whether you're a gadget geek'.[44] These data are fed into AI systems which use a filtering typology to serve the content seen by billions every minute of every day.

The impacts on the right of peaceful assembly come from the granularity of targeting that these systems facilitate combined with the biases present within these systems. This means that the visibility of opportunities to engage in peaceful assembly online are limited by how AI systems are developed and deployed. The lack of transparency for the development and deployment of these systems, including generative AI, leaves the right of individuals to peaceful assembly online in the hands of private actors with little oversight, further constrained by developmental opaqueness and little access to remedy.[45] Before examining further the risks to peaceful assembly from these systems posed by AI's influence on content curation and display, its role in content moderation is explained.

Content Moderation

With large amounts of user-generated content each day, social media are reliant on AI to provide moderation.[46] AI-powered content moderation can respond to user reports, mediate comments, and automatically remove offensive content. If the content cannot be adequately evaluated by the system, it can recommend it for review by human moderators. AI content moderation governs online speech on social media platforms, deciding what is acceptable by 'collecting massive amounts of data and applying data analytics techniques to identify patterns and correlations in order to predict trends and outcomes. Such predictions are followed by automatic filtering or removal of expressions'.[47] Broadly speaking, AI moderates illegal content and 'potentially harmful but legal content'.[48] The specific types of content moderated depend on the platforms and the jurisdictions in which the platform is operating.

Leading digital rights, NGO Access Now defines content moderation as the 'practice through which an online service deals with user-generated speech' and thereby can decide what content exists on an online platform.[49] This is notably different from content curation and display which will prioritize but not remove content. Content moderation can remove all types of content—text, videos, photos, and so on—before it is seen, eliminating opportunities for those assemblies online or offline which depend on algorithmic visibility to attract participants. For example, a search for a protest event will eventually result in finding the event whereas with content moderation the same search might yield no results. Here, the visibility and general awareness of opportunities to engage in peaceful assembly are limited by the design and deployment of algorithms. Individuals would be unable to know that assemblies are happening or how to join in and participate. This level of interference with assembly, without disclosure by social media companies and/or AI developers, can be considered a type of infringement on the right of peaceful assembly, with potential implications on other rights.[50] The following sections, therefore, will examine some of the potential risks to the right of peaceful assembly online caused by the use of AI.

Risks for Online Peaceful Assembly from AI

Clément Nyaletsossi Voule, UN Special Rapporteur on the rights to freedom of peaceful assembly and association, stated in 2019 that he 'is concerned about the variety of measures and tactics that are used by states to control and impede access to and use of digital technology for the exercise of the rights to freedom of assembly and of association'.[51] Voule also expressed concerns about social media companies and urged them to share responsibility by following the *Guiding Principles on Business and Human Rights* to protect the human rights of their users. He noted that to protect online peaceful assembly states must address laws which limit or restrict online behaviour and content related to assembly. Voule especially noted content curation and moderation as areas of special concern for social media companies where they can work to ensure that peaceful assembly is protected.[52]

Useful lenses for examining AI and peaceful assembly, and building on the framework provided by McPherson et al., are purpose, presence/participation, and temporary/permanent (temporality).[53] Online assemblies on social media occur largely in privatized public spaces for the explicit purpose of participating in the social, cultural, and political life of a society.[54] Many of these assemblies are created and mediated (for discussion of 'digital mediation' of assemblies see McPherson, in this volume) by private technology actors deploying AI with little transparency into these processes. These assemblies have different forms of participation and presence. Because online assemblies congregate and disperse differently from physical assemblies, their temporality must also be conceived of differently. This can be seen, for example, with the ongoing use of the hashtag #IranRevolution during the numerous social and political protests in Iran since 2009.

These lenses can be further refined by examining potential harms from AI to online peaceful assembly through attention to content curation and display and content moderation. For example, AI-driven content curation and moderation shape possibilities of presence and participation, as being unaware of an event or unsure of how to join has a material impact on the ability to participate in online assemblies. They are also instrumental in the temporality of online assemblies as visibility and discoverability directly impact the duration of online peaceful assemblies. Thus, this section examines potential harms caused by the use of AI for peaceful assembly online by utilizing these lenses to focus on content curation and display and content moderation. While these harms are investigated as 'potential' because it is *possible* for them to occur, the opacity of how AI works means it is likely that such harms have already occurred or are occurring now. What is clear is that AI poses potentially significant challenges to an effective right of peaceful assembly online.

Potential Harms from AI-Driven Content Curation and Display

The algorithms which power content curation and display systems promote certain types of content and user interface features, with behavioural responses to such content and features generating more data to prioritize future content. Here, David Kaye states that 'Artificial intelligence-driven personalization may also minimize exposure to diverse views, interfering with individual agency to seek and share ideas and opinions across ideological, political or societal divisions'.[55]

For online assemblies, these systems, by minimizing exposure and interfering with individual agency, also minimize opportunities to participate in or to encounter issues and topics which may prompt an individual to undertake a collective call to action. Given that the right to freedom of expression is essential for identifying issues and topics which inform the right of peaceful assembly, this opaque limiting of exposure can be detrimental to the full enjoyment of the right of peaceful assembly online. Moreover, these recommendation systems are not just limited to what news topics or content exists in social media feeds, but also recommendations for friends, contacts, or professional connects—thus impacting on the interpersonal connections upon which the act of assembling fundamentally depends.

Algorithms de-prioritize certain types of content which have lower engagement levels while promoting content with higher engagement levels. Understanding how to influence the algorithm means that these systems can be manipulated by sophisticated actors to develop influence or reduce the impact of peaceful assemblies and biasing algorithms towards actors with significant resources.[56] In the absence of publicly documented case studies, this can hypothetically manifest via a well-resourced state actor who can invest significant resources into studying the effect of various actions on how the algorithm engages with content. A hypothetical example here could focus on a planned anti-government protest in a capital city organized on Facebook. The government could create several competing Facebook protest events which are then artificially 'attended' by fake accounts and promoted extensively via automated bots. Since the Facebook algorithm wants to promote events which have a lot of attention and attendance, these fake events begin to 'trend' attracting attention of individuals who would have otherwise gone to the original protest. As there are multiple events, each event will only attract a fraction of what the original event might have attracted, leading to an offline situation in which protesters are dispersed across the capital city making it easier for security services to arrest protesters and avoid protesters achieving critical mass.

For example, during the 2016 US presidential election, Russia's Internet Research Agency utilized Facebook's algorithms to promote dis/misinformation, anti-immigrant, or hate-speech pages gaining hundreds of thousands of followers.[57] Indeed, these efforts were so successful that several of the algorithmically promoted pages held offline events which attracted people to fake protest assemblies in Houston, Texas.[58] Further, it has been argued that media associated with the Russian state, 'used social-media accounts to amplify misleading stories already circulating online, causing news algorithms to identify them as "trending" topics that sometimes prompted coverage from mainstream American news organizations'.[59]

Through the lenses offered by McPherson et al. of purpose, presence/participation, and temporary/permanent, the potential impacts of AI on peaceful assembly become clearer. Manfred Nowak stated that peaceful assemblies must have a specific purpose when they come together.[60] General Comment No. 37 likewise states that the 'right of peaceful assembly protects the non-violent gathering by persons for specific purposes, principally expressive ones'.[61] Thus, peaceful assemblies must have both a specific and possibly expressive purpose, which can be understood as including some element of visibility of action, numbers, and stated purpose.[62] Content curation and display, by opaquely and selectively determining the visibility of peaceful assemblies, significantly influences their expressive purpose—for example, an initial purpose of the #MeToo movement was to highlight the magnitude of the problem of sexual harassment.[63] This peaceful assembly's expressive purpose for millions of people to share experiences of sexual harassment might have been blunted or non-existent if algorithms would not have displayed the posts.

The perspective of presence and participation is likewise impacted by content display and curation. AI systems seek to promote content designed to increase user engagement. While this may include peaceful assemblies, these systems are just as likely to exclude them. Given that algorithmic development is influenced by both the sociocultural context in which algorithms are developed and the social, cultural, political, and economic biases of their developers, content which may act against dominant norms or perspectives could be excluded due to conscious or unconscious bias.[64] This excluded content can make a significant impact on the extent to which online assemblies are visible which in turn influences individual presence in assemblies and audience reach. For example, unconscious bias against African Americans, which has been documented in AI systems, may mean that assemblies geared towards African Americans are difficult to find in social media feeds.[65]

The temporality of online assemblies refers to the long-term preservation and visibility of online assemblies. For an online assembly to achieve the goal of gathering for a specific purpose its temporality is different than an in-person assembly. For example, the #MeToo movement is an ongoing online peaceful assembly which began in 2017. Its temporality is both temporary, as individuals tweet or share content at a specific moment, and permanent in that past tweets and content are engaged with and visible. Thus, content curation and display can consign both past and present movements to irrelevance by ensuring that present content is not displayed or that older content is deprioritized.

Potential Harms from AI-Driven Content Moderation

AI influences whether online peaceful assembly can occur at all by moderating content before it is even seen. This may eliminate entire conversations, pages, videos, events, and all other aspects of modern online peaceful assemblies from social media. The potential harm to the right of peaceful assembly is significant and existential because it can deprive individuals and groups of their ability to exercise their right of peaceful assembly rather than simply making it less accessible or difficult to find as with content curation and display.[66] For example, a search for an online #MeToo event should eventually result in the event being found. However, if the event was moderated out through an AI-driven system, the same search for the event would yield no results. While specific examples do not currently exist, the presence of unconscious bias in the AI systems could lead to this occurring. For example, it is arguable that the presence of unconscious bias resulted in AI developed at Google consistently identifying images of African Americans as gorillas, a long-standing racist trope.[67] It is therefore possible that unconscious bias against Muslims, for example, could lead to events in support of Palestine being moderated out. For peaceful assembly in the context of religion, UN Special Rapporteur on Freedom of Religion or Belief Ahmed Shaheed states that AI content moderation 'can result in the over-policing of certain faith communities and further inhibit communicative action' through conscious or unconscious bias in AI algorithms.[68]

In the same way that AI is trained for content curation, in content moderation the AI system is trained by humans using samples to determine which content should be removed or recommended for human review.[69] The goal of content moderation is to create an online environment which is welcoming for expression, assembly, and other online interactions. The types of content to be removed or otherwise moderated can be harmful online content which could otherwise hinder online peaceful assemblies. For example, racist or homophobic speech can be effectively moderated due to the presence of robust AI content moderation systems, facilitating an online environment conducive to assemblies which might otherwise be inundated by hate speech. However, algorithms and their training data are unavailable for third-party examination, making opacity and lack of access to remedy features of modern online peaceful assembly on social media.[70]

AI also recommends content for review to human content moderators.[71] However, human moderators are often not located in the same jurisdiction as the 'offending' content which they review.[72] They can also lack contextual knowledge and language skills or have social, political, or religious biases which can be detrimental to accurately evaluating content.[73] Further, these human moderators can be exposed to more than 25,000 severely traumatizing images or video every day, leading them to suffer psychological stress, burnout, and post-traumatic stress disorder.[74] The human rights implications of this was highlighted in Facebook's role in the 2017 Rohingya crisis because of AI's inability to understand nuance in hate speech in Myanmar and a critical lack of linguistically or culturally qualified human content moderators.[75]

The potential implications for freedom of assembly are significant. As the Myanmar case demonstrates, human moderators with their sociocultural background alongside the specific biases of the algorithms, can play a significant role in how assemblies manifest online and offline. For the Rohingya, it was not that assemblies were hidden from individuals but rather that assemblies were organized and able to thrive with the purpose of depriving Rohingya of their rights. This occurred due to the lack of effective moderation from both AI and humans.[76] This played a role in more than 700,000 Rohingya fleeing with thousands dead.[77]

How a social media company which uses AI systems develops and deploys those systems is of vital importance for the exercise of the right of peaceful assembly. In this case, the opacity of Facebook's content moderation algorithms, including how they were developed and by whom, the data used to train the systems, and the presence (or lack of) cultural literacy surrounding Myanmar and the Rohingya contributed to a lack of effective moderation of assemblies which were deliberately designed to deprive individuals of their rights and lives.[78]

Despite the insistence of social media companies that AI will be central to efforts at moderating content, Roberts states that human reviewers will continue to play a central and outsized role in content moderation.[79] Scholars like Duarte et al. emphasize that AI content moderation's current state precludes its ability to be the sole content moderator for a platform due to algorithmic inaccuracies and the relative ease by which skilled actors can manipulate algorithms.[80] For these scholars, AI will play a supporting role and human moderators increasingly making final binding decisions. Thus, peaceful assembly online will be subject to both the biases of algorithms and human content moderators, with little access to remedy or transparency regarding processes or policies on content removal. This 'black box' can seriously jeopardize peaceful assembly as organizers and potential and actual participants will be unaware what content was removed and for what reason.

AI content moderation can impact online peaceful assemblies in two ways: removing content before it is visible or after it has been seen. Given the well-documented role of social media in enabling peaceful assemblies online, either case can be detrimental to the exercise of the right of peaceful assembly online. The former case potentially negates peaceful assembly by removing the opportunity to exercise the right online. The latter case of removing assemblies or information during or after participation can have a chilling or discouraging effect on the use of social media platforms as informational reliability and stability are called into question, evidenced by numerous conspiracy theories about how Facebook manipulates content.[81]

Further, content moderation may occur long after an event has occurred, erasing history online. This has a direct and meaningful impact on temporality as well as purpose since evidence of online peaceful assemblies can vanish, leaving participants, historians, human rights advocates, artists, and investigators without evidence of an assembly having occurred. Given that online assemblies can be long-lasting—evidenced by #MeToo or over thirteen years of use of the hashtag #IranRevolution—their expressive and participatory purposes can thus be negated and erased. Vulnerable groups in authoritarian states are especially at risk as these governments often use takedown requests to remove content online.[82] These events have prompted the emergence of digital archives such as the Syrian Archive or Azadi Digital Archive to preserve vulnerable content.[83] These archives can mitigate to some extent the erasure of historical assemblies by ensuring a record of their occurrence. In terms of peaceful assembly, maintaining these collective historical records can both inspire and inform future peaceful assembly online and offline.

Conclusion

Social media platforms offer enormous opportunities for the right of peaceful assembly to be exercised. However, these platforms are mostly moderated by AI systems which curate and moderate social media feeds by determining the types of content that exist and are seen. As a result, these systems play a central role in the ability of individuals to advertise protests, organize groups, and otherwise participate in peaceful assembly online.

The power of these systems is exacerbated by the conscious and unconscious biases present in these systems. These biases can contribute to discrimination against individuals and groups who may be seeking to assemble online. Further, as former UN Special Rapporteur David Kaye has outlined, a lack of transparency and access to remedy means that significant harms can occur and are occurring to the right of peaceful assembly online with no ability to understand the scope of the problem or to seek remedy.

It is impossible for modern social media to exist without some level of curation and moderation by AI. This means that the existence and use of these platforms will entail some limitation of the right of peaceful assembly either through the previously discussed risk factors, error, or simply as part of normal content display and moderation practices. Thus, for the right of peaceful assembly to thrive online, it becomes vital for social media corporations to ensure that AI development and deployment utilize human rights as an ethical minimum standard. This means following the UN Guiding Principles on Business and Human Rights, ensuring that the right of peaceful assembly is respected with an understanding that the realities of modern social media mean that the platforms cannot realistically be obliged to protect the right. Further, they should open some algorithms for outside review and audit by academics and other experts under protection of non-disclosure agreements to protect intellectual property.[84]

These corporations should also provide better access to remedy and transparency about what variables are used to evaluate online content. Finally, they should ensure that their algorithmic tools are subject to thorough Human Rights Impact Assessments alongside Algorithmic Impact Assessments and that the results of these assessments are publicly available.

States can support these private corporate efforts by ensuring timely review of relevant AI code in a way that does not infringe or threaten the intellectual property rights of technology corporations. Further, given the well-documented biases present in AI systems, states can encourage greater diversity and competition in AI development, ensuring that it is not concentrated in the 'Big 5': Meta, Apple, Amazon, Microsoft, and Google. By including individuals and groups in AI development who may be harmed or negatively impacted by algorithms, human rights risks can be more effectively mitigated.

AI content curation and display and moderation are vital to modern social media systems. It is simultaneously vital that individuals, states, corporations, and NGOs be aware of the importance of social media to peaceful assembly and of the risks these systems pose to peaceful online assembly through what content *exists* and is *seen* online. The right of peaceful assembly is a cornerstone right in healthy, rights-respecting societies and essential for functioning democracies. By being aware of threats from AI to this important right, stakeholders and policymakers can more effectively discuss and address the risks and opportunities which AI presents for the right of peaceful assembly.

Notes

1. Laurie Clarke, 'Global Partnership on Artificial Intelligence Founded by UK and Other Nations', *The New Statesman* (blog), 16 June 2020, https://oecd.ai/en/gpai.
2. James Vincent, 'The Problem with AI Ethics', *The Verge*, 3 April 2019, https://www.theverge.com/2019/4/3/18293410/ai-artificial-intelligence-ethics-boards-charters-problem-big-tech.
3. Karl M. Manheim and Lyric Kaplan, 'Artificial Intelligence: Risks to Privacy and Democracy', *Yale Journal of Law & Technology* 21 (2019): 106–188.
4. UNHRCtte, General Comment No. 37—Article 21: The Right of Peaceful Assembly (17 September 2020) UN Doc. CCPR/C/GC/37, 2.
5. Ella McPherson et al., 'The Right of Peaceful Assembly Online: Research Pack' (University of Cambridge Centre of Governance and Human Rights, November 2019), https://www.cghr.polis.cam.ac.uk/system/files/documents/right-to-online-assembly.pdf. The definition of what constitutes an assembly in online or digitally mediated spaces is debated. Further elaboration on the definition and nature of online assemblies is, however, outside the scope of this chapter.
6. Ibid., 6.
7. Ibid.
8. UN Human Rights Council Resolution 24/5, The rights to freedom of peaceful assembly and of association (26 September 2013) UN Doc. A/HRC/RES/24/5, 2.
9. UN Human Rights Council Resolution 38/11, The promotion and protection of human rights in the context of peaceful protests (6 July 2018) UN Doc. A/HRC/RES/38/11, 2.
10. UN General Assembly Resolution 73/173, Promotion and protection of human rights and fundamental freedoms, including the rights to peaceful assembly and freedom of association (17 December 2018) UN Doc. A/RES/73/173, 3.
11. Jared Keller, 'Evaluating Iran's Twitter Revolution', *The Atlantic* 18 (2010).
12. Anne Barnard, '1.1 Million Can Skip School for Climate Protest', *New York Times*, 16 September 2019, https://www.nytimes.com/2019/09/16/nyregion/youth-climate-strike-nyc.html; Anemona Hartocollis and Yamiche Alcindor, 'Women's March Highlights as Huge Crowds Protest Trump: "We're Not Going Away"', *New York Times*, 21 January 2017, https://www.nytimes.com/2017/01/21/us/womens-march.html; Helier Cheung, 'Brexit Debate: Do Petitions Ever Work?', BBC News, 26 March 2019, https://www.bbc.com/news/world-47693506.
13. Farnush Ghadery, '#Metoo—Has the "Sisterhood" Finally Become Global or Just Another Product of Neoliberal Feminism?', *Transnational Legal Theory* 10, no. 2 (2019): 252–274.
14. McPherson et al., 'The Right of Peaceful Assembly Online: Research Pack'.
15. Ibid., 4.
16. David Kaye, Report of the Special Rapporteur on the promotion and protection of the right to freedom of opinion and expression (29 August 2018) UN Doc. A/73/348; Andreas Kaplan and Michael Haenlein, 'Siri, Siri, in My Hand: Who's the Fairest in the Land? On the Interpretations, Illustrations, and Implications of Artificial Intelligence', *Business Horizons* 62, no. 1 (2019): 15–25; Ben Goertzel and Cassio Pennachin, eds., *Artificial General Intelligence* (Heidelberg, Germany: Springer, 2007).
17. White House, 'Preparing for the Future of Artificial Intelligence' (Executive Office of the President, National Science and Technology Council, Committee on Technology, 2016), 8.

18. Sabrina Siddiqui and Deepa Seetharaman, 'White House Says Amazon, Google, Meta, Microsoft Agree to AI Safeguards', *Wall Street Journal*, 21 July 2023, https://www.wsj.com/articles/white-house-says-amazon-google-meta-microsoft-agree-to-ai-safeguards-eabe3680.
19. Steven Livingston and Mathias Risse, 'The Future Impact of Artificial Intelligence on Humans and Human Rights', *Ethics & International Affairs* 33, no. 2 (2019): 141–158.
20. Royal Society, 'Machine Learning: The Power and Promise of Computers That Learn by Example: An Introduction' (2017), 19.
21. Kaye, A/73/348, 4.
22. David Silver and Demis Hassabis, 'AlphaGo: Mastering the Ancient Game of Go with Machine Learning', *Google AI Blog* (blog), 27 January 2016, http://ai.googleblog.com/2016/01/alphago-mastering-ancient-game-of-go.html.
23. Francesca Lazzeri, 'Deep Learning vs. Machine Learning–Azure', *Microsoft Azure Documentation* (blog), 5 March 2020, https://docs.microsoft.com/en-us/azure/machine-learning/concept-deep-learning-vs-machine-learning.
24. Ibid.
25. Silver and Hassabis, 'AlphaGo'.
26. Kaye, A/73/348, 4.
27. Yuri Takhteyev, *Coding Places: Software Practice in a South American City* (Cambridge, MA: MIT Press, 2012); David Golumbia, *The Cultural Logic of Computation* (Cambridge, MA: Harvard University Press, 2009); Safiya Noble, *Algorithms of Oppression: How Search Engines Reinforce Racism* (New York: New York University Press, 2018).
28. Privacy International and Article 19, 'Privacy and Freedom of Expression in the Age of Artificial Intelligence' (2018).
29. James Vincent, 'This Is When AI's Top Researchers Think Artificial General Intelligence Will Be Achieved', *The Verge*, 27 November 2018, https://www.theverge.com/2018/11/27/18114362/ai-artificial-general-intelligence-when-achieved-martin-ford-book; Phillip Boucher, 'How Artificial Intelligence Works' (European Parliament: European Parliamentary Research Service, March 2019), https://www.europarl.europa.eu/thinktank/en/document.html?reference=EPRS_BRI(2019)634420; Anand Ramamoorthy and Roman Yampolskiy, 'Beyond Mad? The Race for Artificial General Intelligence', *ITU Journal* 1 (2018): 1–8.
30. Kaye, A/73/348.
31. Holli Sargeant et al., *Spotlight on Artificial Intelligence and Freedom of Expression: A Policy Manual* (Rochester, NY: Organization for Security and Co-operation in Europe, 17 March 2022, https://www.osce.org/representative-on-freedom-of-media/510332.
32. Kaye, A/73/348; Sargeant et al., 'Spotlight on Artificial Intelligence and Freedom of Expression'.
33. Ramya Srinivasan and Kanji Uchino, 'Biases in Generative Art: A Causal Look from the Lens of Art History', in *Proceedings of the 2021 ACM Conference on Fairness, Accountability, and Transparency* (2021): 41–51.
34. Domo, 'Data Never Sleeps 10.0', *Data Never Sleeps*, https://www.domo.com/data-never-sleeps.
35. Shoshana Zuboff, *The Age of Surveillance Capitalism: The Fight for a Human Future at the New Frontier of Power* (New York: Public Affairs, 2019).
36. Anja Bechmann and Geoffrey C Bowker, 'Unsupervised by Any Other Name: Hidden Layers of Knowledge Production in Artificial Intelligence on Social Media', *Big Data & Society* 6, no. 1 (2019): 2053951718819569.

37. Zeynep Tufekci, 'How Recommendation Algorithms Run the World', *Wired*, 22 April 2019, https://www.wired.com/story/how-recommendation-algorithms-run-the-world/; Ben Smith, 'How TikTok Reads Your Mind', *New York Times*, 6 December 2021, https://www.nytimes.com/2021/12/05/business/media/tiktok-algorithm.html.
38. Renee Diresta, 'The Web's Recommendation Engines Are Broken. Can We Fix Them?', *Wired*, 11 April 2018, https://www.wired.com/story/creating-ethical-recommendation-engines/.
39. Council of Europe, 'Study on the Human Rights Dimensions of Automated Data Processing Techniques (in Particular Algorithms) and Possible Regulatory Implications', *DGI*(2017) 12 (2018): 17.
40. N. Thrift, 'Remembering the Technological Unconscious by Foregrounding Knowledges of Position', *Environment and Planning D: Society and Space* 22, no. 1 (2004): 175–190.
41. Sargeant et al., 'Spotlight on Artificial Intelligence and Freedom of Expression', 62.
42. Ibid.
43. Caitlin Dewey, '98 Personal Data Points That Facebook Uses to Target Ads to You', *Washington Post*, 26 October 2021, https://www.washingtonpost.com/news/the-intersect/wp/2016/08/19/98-personal-data-points-that-facebook-uses-to-target-ads-to-you/.
44. Brian X. Chen, 'I Downloaded the Information That Facebook Has on Me. Yikes', *New York Times*, 11 April 2018, https://www.nytimes.com/2018/04/11/technology/personaltech/i-downloaded-the-information-that-facebook-has-on-me-yikes.html.
45. Kaye, A/73/348.
46. Kirsten Gollatz, Felix Beer, and Christian Katzenbach, 'The Turn to Artificial Intelligence in Governing Communication Online' (Alexander von Humboldt Institute for Internet and Society & Access Now, 2018); David Kaye, *Speech Police: The Global Struggle to Govern the Internet* (New York: Columbia Global Reports, 2019).
47. Niva Elkin-Koren, 'Contesting Algorithms: Restoring the Public Interest in Content Filtering by Artificial Intelligence', *Big Data & Society* 7, no. 2 (2020): 2.
48. Sargeant et al., 'Spotlight on Artificial Intelligence and Freedom of Expression', 24.
49. Access Now, 'Protecting Free Expression in the Era of Online Content Moderation' (May 2019), https://www.accessnow.org/cms/assets/uploads/2019/05/AccessNow-Preliminary-Recommendations-On-Content-Moderation-and-Facebooks-Planned-Oversight-Board.pdf.
50. Ilia Siatitsa, 'Freedom of Assembly under Attack: General and Indiscriminate Surveillance and Interference with Internet Communications', *International Review of the Red Cross* 102, no. 913 (2020): 181–198.
51. Clément Nyaletsossi Voule, Report of the Special Rapporteur on the rights to freedom of peaceful assembly and of association (17 May 2019) UN Doc. A/HRC/41/41, 8.
52. Ibid., 55, 64.
53. McPherson et al., 'The Right of Peaceful Assembly Online: Research Pack'.
54. Ibid.
55. Kaye, A/73/348, 7.
56. Ibid. See also Zeynep Tufekci, 'YouTube's Recommendation Algorithm Has a Dark Side', *Scientific American*, 1 April 2019, https://www.scientificamerican.com/article/youtubes-recommendation-algorithm-has-a-dark-side/.
57. Sheera Frenkel and Katie Benner, 'To Stir Discord in 2016, Russians Turned Most Often to Facebook', *New York Times*, 16 July 2018, https://www.nytimes.com/2018/02/17/technology/indictment-russian-tech-facebook.html; David E. Sanger, *The Perfect Weapon: War, Sabotage, and Fear in the Cyber Age* (New York: Broadway Books, 2019).

58. Ryan Lucas, 'How Russia Used Facebook to Organize 2 Sets of Protesters', NPR, 1 November 2017, https://www.npr.org/2017/11/01/561427876/how-russia-used-facebook-to-organize-two-sets-of-protesters.
59. Craig Timberg, 'Russian Propaganda Effort Helped Spread 'Fake News' during Election, Experts Say', *Washington Post*, 12 April 2023, https://www.washingtonpost.com/business/economy/russian-propaganda-effort-helped-spread-fake-news-during-election-experts-say/2016/11/24/793903b6-8a40-4ca9-b712-716af66098fe_story.html.
60. Manfred Nowak, *UN Covenant on Civil and Political Rights: CCPR Commentary* (NP Engel, 1993).
61. UNHRCtte, General Comment No. 37, 2.
62. Ella McPherson et al., 'The Right of Peaceful Assembly Online: Research Pack'.
63. Nadja Sayej, 'Alyssa Milano on the #MeToo Movement: "We're Not Going to Stand for It Any More"', *The Guardian*, 1 December 2017, https://www.theguardian.com/culture/2017/dec/01/alyssa-milano-mee-too-sexual-harassment-abuse.
64. Nima Kordzadeh and Maryam Ghasemaghaei, 'Algorithmic Bias: Review, Synthesis, and Future Research Directions', *European Journal of Information Systems* 31, no. 3 (2022): 388–409.
65. Noble, *Algorithms of Oppression*.
66. Maina Kiai, Report of the Special Rapporteur on the rights to freedom of peaceful assembly and of association (21 May 2012) UN Doc. A/HRC/20/27, 12.
67. Maggie Zhang, 'Google Photos Tags Two African-Americans As Gorillas through Facial Recognition Software', *Forbes*, 1 July 2015, https://www.forbes.com/sites/mzhang/2015/07/01/google-photos-tags-two-african-americans-as-gorillas-through-facial-recognition-software/.
68. Ahmed Shaheed, Report of the Special Rapporteur on freedom of religion or belief (5 March 2019) UN Doc. A/HRC/40/58, 15; Noble, *Algorithms of Oppression*.
69. Kaye, *Speech Police*.
70. Kaye, A/73/348.
71. Sarah T. Roberts, *Behind the Screen: Content Moderation in the Shadows of Social Media* (New Haven, CT: Yale University Press, 2019).
72. Ibid.
73. Jason Koebler and Joseph Cox, 'Here's How Facebook Is Trying to Moderate Its Two Billion Users', *Vice* (blog), 23 August 2018, https://www.vice.com/en_us/article/xwk9zd/how-facebook-content-moderation-works.
74. Tarleton Gillespie, *Custodians of the Internet: Platforms, Content Moderation, and the Hidden Decisions That Shape Social Media* (New Haven, CT: Yale University Press, 2018); Casey Newton, 'Google and YouTube Moderators Speak out on the Work That Gave Them PTSD', *The Verge*, 16 December 2019, https://www.theverge.com/2019/12/16/21021005/google-youtube-moderators-ptsd-accenture-violent-disturbing-content-interviews-video; Roberts, *Behind the Screen*; Mark Wilson, 'The Hardest Job in Silicon Valley Is a Living Nightmare', *Fast Company*, 8 November 2018, https://www.fastcompany.com/90263921/the-hardest-job-in-silicon-valley-is-a-living-nightmare.
75. Steve Stecklow, 'Why Facebook Is Losing the War on Hate Speech in Myanmar', Reuters, 15 August 2018, https://www.reuters.com/investigates/special-report/myanmar-facebook-hate/.
76. Report of the detailed findings of the independent international fact-finding mission on Myanmar (17 September 2018) UN Doc. A/HRC/39/CRP.2; Victoria Milko and Barbara

Ortutay, '"Kill More": Facebook Fails to Detect Hate against Rohingya', Associated Press, 22 March 2022, https://apnews.com/article/technology-business-bangladesh-myanmar-united-nations-f7d89e38c54f7bae464762fa23bd96b2.

77. A/HRC/39/CRP.2
78. Tom Miles, 'U.N. Investigators Cite Facebook Role in Myanmar Crisis', Reuters, 12 March 2018, https://www.reuters.com/article/us-myanmar-rohingya-facebook-idUSKCN1GO2PN.
79. Roberts, *Behind the Screen*.
80. Natasha Duarte, Emma Llanso, and Anna Loup, 'Mixed Messages? The Limits of Automated Social Media Content Analysis', in *Proceedings of the 1st Conference on Fairness, Accountability and Transparency*: vol. 81. Proceedings of Machine Learning Research, ed. Sorelle A. Friedler and Christo Wilson (New York: PMLR, 2018), 106, http://proceedings.mlr.press/v81/duarte18a.html.
81. Tess Owen, 'What Is the 'New World Order' Conspiracy?', *Vice* (blog), 23 March 2022, https://www.vice.com/en/article/v7dqem/putin-new-world-order-ukraine-conspiracy.
82. McPherson et al., 'The Right of Peaceful Assembly Online: Research Pack'.
83. 'Syrian Archive,' https://syrianarchive.org/; 'The Azadi Digital Archive for Human Rights, Justice, and Accountability,' https://azadiarchive.org/.
84. Danae Metaxa et al., 'Auditing Algorithms: Understanding Algorithmic Systems from the Outside In', *Foundations and Trends® in Human–Computer Interaction* 14, no. 4 (2021): 272–344.

Further Readings

Gillespie, Tarleton. *Custodians of the Internet: Platforms, Content Moderation, and the Hidden Decisions That Shape Social Media*. New Haven, CT: Yale University Press, 2018.

Kaye, David. Report of the Special Rapporteur on the promotion and protection of the right to freedom of opinion and expression (29 August 2018) UN Doc. A/73/348.

Kaye, David. *Speech Police: The Global Struggle to Govern the Internet*. New York: Columbia Global Reports, 2019.

Noble, Safiya. *Algorithms of Oppression: How Search Engines Reinforce Racism*. New York: New York University Press, 2018.

Roberts, Sarah T. *Behind the Screen: Content Moderation in the Shadows of Social Media*. New Haven, CT: Yale University Press, 2019.

Zuboff, Shoshana. *The Age of Surveillance Capitalism: The Fight for a Human Future at the New Frontier of Power*. New York: Public Affairs, 2019.

CHAPTER 33

THE RIGHT TO ASSEMBLE IN TIMES OF EMERGENCY AND THE ENCROACHMENT OF COUNTERTERRORISM

MEGAN L. MANION

INTRODUCTION

STATES, supported by the field of counterterrorism institutions and actors in various contexts, increasingly view the restriction of rights, including the right to freedom of peaceful assembly and association, as a widely acceptable (if not desirable) counterterrorism intervention, one that should be considered with great deference by judiciaries, oversight mechanisms, and international human rights bodies. States have mobilized, and in many cases instrumentalized, the language of 'terrorism' or 'terrorist', allied with broader security powers, to stymie the full 'expressive dimensions'[1] of assemblies and the political power they hold. Furthermore, particular assemblies and protest events have sometimes been singled out as presenting an existential threat to state security such as to justify an emergency response—including efforts to quash opposition or emerging social movements or in response to attempted coup d'états.

Emergency powers (extending beyond counterterrorism measures) have been invoked in a range of situations. Notably, the public health situation created by the COVID-19 pandemic led 110 states, between March and September 2020, to invoke measures limiting the right of peaceful assembly—from explicit restrictions on public gatherings to general stay-at-home orders or quarantine orders. By 2023, this number had risen to 156 countries,[2] including 112 'emergency declarations'.[3] Human Rights Watch (amongst others) documented a trend in abuses purportedly justified on the basis of enforcing COVID-19-related regulations, including 'firing live ammunition at peaceful protesters; beating them at checkpoints; and assaulting them in detention, with apparent impunity'.[4]

Methods of enacting such emergency powers domestically have included executive orders, the activation of dormant provisions in existing laws, regulations, administrative measures, and bureaucratic policies and practices. During the COVID-19 pandemic, only around 10 per cent of the measures restricting assemblies were created through legislation, while the rest were created through 'executive order or administrative regulation'.[5] These too often become regularized in domestic law, notwithstanding being challenged on a range of grounds (including lack of legality or necessity, overbreadth and disproportionality) and being subject to increased scrutiny by international stakeholders.[6]

The right of peaceful assembly is central to what constitutes and sustains a 'democratic society' and is intricately connected to the realization of many other rights.[7] 'Assembly' is thus central to conceptions of what it means to engage in a free and open society. At the most basic level, citizens must be able publicly to decry their government's actions, challenge policies and practices, and do so openly without fear of reprisal or retaliation.[8] Insofar as the act of assembling sometimes seeks to disrupt or upend the status quo, it is predictably cast by those with vested interests as hastening a crisis and requiring emergency pacification (see further Srinivasan and Abu El-Haj, in this volume). Indeed, the qualifier of 'peaceful' means that the protection of this right has too often been contingent on the way in which 'violence' is interpreted.[9] The health of this right is thus affected by a state's (and society's) tolerance for differing views, including those that are structurally disruptive and challenge the state's authority, even peripherally. Therefore, the threshold of 'peaceful' too often depends on executive-level tolerance for dissent.

This chapter explores the legal and political challenges relating to the regulation of the right of peaceful assembly in times of emergency, arguing that the impact on the right of assembly of targeted state repression of dissent, often under the guise of counterterrorism, warrants further exploration. It examines several indicative domestic legal contexts, including France, Sri Lanka, and Egypt, to highlight the ways in which the use of emergency powers (by way of both limitation and derogation), operate to frame those exercising these rights as 'extremists' or 'terrorists'[10] and instantiate broader practices of criminalization to curtail the right to assemble peacefully.

The chapter argues that abusive counterterrorism measures rely heavily on the use of emergency powers, blurring the line between the restriction of rights in normal times and formal derogations in times of emergency. This line is blurred further by the parallel trends of imposing limitations that may meet the legal threshold of derogation but have not been appropriately reported and for derogations that are subsequently found to be noncompliant with international law standards (including for lack of a true emergency). Drawing from the growing literature on the conceptualization, practice, and impact of state use of emergency powers,[11] the chapter shows how overreach at the domestic level is not only well-established but may be consolidating and further emboldened by the lack of accountability enabled by deference to global counterterrorism frameworks.[12]

The chapter draws on specific examples from countries to highlight in its final section how this muddying enables the differential enforcement of restrictions and the discriminatory protection of the right of peaceful assembly.[13] It concludes by suggesting that despite increasingly robust guidance from the Human Rights Committee through its General Comments and periodic review of States Parties reports, further jurisprudence on individual cases may be required to untangle the ways in which limitations/restrictions and derogations are misused, to show explicitly how such misuse is connected to counterterrorism legislation and discourse, and to underscore the imperative of increasing the political costs for ensuing violations.

The Instrumentalization of Counterterrorism Measures to Shrink Civic Space

Terrorism is often conceived as a 'totalitarian form of war and politics'.[14] The moral abhorrence the term evokes can galvanize rhetorical responses cast in the language of 'zero compromise'. However, state instrumentalization of the 'terrorism' lexicon often aligns with the treatment of 'democracy' 'as a strategic discursive term' to thwart political dissent and political movements.[15] These realities have highlighted significant challenges for those seeking to resist such framing, protect civic space, and exercise their right of peaceful assembly.

In countries where counterterrorism and counterextremist narratives are deeply embedded in political or legal discourse, the labelling of groups (and their expressive and associational activities) as 'terrorist' or 'extremist', or characterizing assemblies as non-peaceful, is regularly observed.[16] Although international human rights law asserts a presumption of peacefulness,[17] the limits and boundaries of peacefulness are often contested, particularly in times of emergency and where assemblies are held outside the parameters of domestic law.[18]

Acute definitional questions about what constitutes terrorism complicate the assessment of threats to national security and raise questions as to when the threshold is met for the declaration of emergency or when the restriction of rights might be necessary and proportional to protect national security (insofar as this is itself envisioned by Article 21 of the International Covenant on Civil and Political Rights [ICCPR]). The Siracusa principles purposefully set the 'national security' threshold at a high level—emphasizing that this ground cannot be relied upon in response to 'merely local or relatively isolated threats to law and order', but rather only 'to protect the existence of the nation or its territorial integrity or political independence against force or threat of force'.[19]

Nonetheless, despite the individualized nature of many present-day terrorist attacks (occurring at the level of 'incident' rather than 'campaign'),[20] states continue to respond to terrorist attacks with widely cast and long-lasting measures. Furthermore, while the European Court of Human Rights (ECHR), amongst other bodies, has cautioned against declarations of emergency, which serve merely as a pretext to prevent political expression,[21] state responses still benefit from high levels of deference.[22] In some cases heard by the ECHR, for example, states have specifically leveraged the 'margin of appreciation' (afforded to national authorities under the Convention) by emphasizing the uncertainty that characterizes terrorism-related acts.[23] Similarly, beyond the Council of Europe and EU, states have tended to accentuate the uncertainty of when, where, and how terrorist attacks may occur—often misleading the public as to the nature of the risk and the capacity of the state to thwart such risks and instead shaping the narrative as one requiring vigilance and continuous, preemptive state intervention.[24]

The human rights impact of deference to counterterrorism rationales reaches beyond discrete acts of protest or the civil society, political opposition, or other groups targeted. It imperils not only these groups' interests but also individuals' expressive freedoms. It reshapes the very fabric and health of civic space, undermining key checks and balances and affecting broader futures of democratic governance. This is particularly true in countries where emergency powers have become normalized in domestic law.

Between Limitations, Derogations, and the Blurring Effect of National Security and Counterterrorism Measures

States are obliged not only to protect and facilitate peaceful assemblies but also to respect this right by refraining from its unreasonable curtailment.[25] Curtailments, however, take different forms, ranging from limitations (undertaken in compliance with Article 21 of the Covenant and which may or may not relate to a domestic emergency) to derogations from the obligation to protect the right (in the context of emergencies and as envisaged by Article 4 of the Covenant). It is worth exploring this distinction further because the interplay between using limitations and formally declared derogations is especially important when considering how counterterrorism measures too frequently sidestep human rights treaty protections. This interplay illuminates the increasing use of de facto emergency powers resulting in de facto derogations (not compliant with international law).

Limitations: National Security as a Qualification on the Right of Peaceful Assembly

Article 21 permits the limitation of the right of peaceful assembly under specific circumstances subject to a specific and defined framework.[26] This provides that 'no restrictions may be placed on the exercise of this right other than those imposed in conformity with the law and which are necessary in a democratic society in the interests of national security or public safety, public order (ordre public), the protection of public health or morals or the protection of the rights and freedoms of others'.[27] In addition, the right of peaceful assembly must also be implemented in line with the right to freedom from discrimination.[28]

These grounds for limitation are exhaustive,[29] but their interpretation can be opaque because of the scope for overlap and broader determinations by the state on the presence of an emergency. This was, for example, seen in the restrictions imposed on the exercise of the right of peaceful assembly during the COVID-19 pandemic with prominent cases in the United States in relation to the Black Lives Matter movement, in Chile in relation to women's rights movements and protest, or in Israel in relation to anti-corruption.[30]

The Human Rights Committee has defined public order as 'the sum of the rules that ensure the proper functioning of society, or the set of fundamental principles on which society is founded, which also entails respect for human rights, including the right of peaceful assembly'.[31] While this definition is broad, the Committee has warned that this vagueness should not be used to 'justify overbroad restrictions'.[32] Public safety as a ground for restriction may be used only when 'the assembly creates a real and significant risk to the safety of persons (to the life or security of person) or a similar risk of serious damage to property'.[33] In *Alekseev v Russian Federation* (a case in which the applicant had been denied a permit for his picket on public safety grounds), the Committee noted that neither 'an unspecified and general risk' of violence nor 'the mere possibility that the authorities would be unable to prevent or neutralize such violence' justifies a ban on a demonstration.[34]

Public health, too, is an available rationale for states, but is meant to be invoked in 'exceptional circumstances', such as the spread of 'an infectious disease' that makes gathering 'dangerous' or 'in extreme cases . . . where the sanitary situation during an assembly presents a substantial health risk to the general public or to the participants themselves'.[35] Furthermore, the Committee has emphasized that the restricting authority bears the burden of justifying the restriction,[36] as well as the principled application of the concepts of legality,[37] necessity,[38] and proportionality as the tests against which any measures of the restriction imposed by States Parties should be assessed,[39] and notwithstanding the reality of nondemocratic or backsliding democracies.[40] Necessity means more than 'merely reasonable or expedient',[41] and a disproportionate restriction is one where the negative impact on the right outweighs the corresponding benefit to the permissible ground for its imposition.[42]

Ostensibly therefore, the circumstances in which a state may legitimately limit the right of peaceful assembly may seem somewhat narrow (serving primarily to protect a state's ability to create an optimal rights environment). However, these broad categories of limitation still provide states with significant latitude, enabling nefarious use of limitations in an area where deference to states remains high.[43]

The misuse of emergency powers to curtail rights based on national security has been recognized as a central tactic of states seeking to infringe upon certain fundamental rights for some time.[44] Of particular note are the Siracusa Principles, which recognize the widespread nature of illegal declarations of martial or emergency law in states' efforts to abridge human rights and fundamental freedoms and include four interpretive principles specifically to prevent the misuse of limitations through declarations of martial law or public emergency under the guise of national security (within which counterterrorism responses fall), namely: (1) oft-cited language underscoring that national security limitations may only ever be invoked to protect the 'existence of the nation or its territorial integrity or political independence against force or threat of force';[45] (2) barring invocations of national security for 'merely local or relatively isolated threats to law and order';[46] (3) preventing the use of national security as a 'pretext for imposing vague or arbitrary limitations' along with a prerequisite that, if invoked, there must be 'adequate safeguards and effective remedies against abuse';[47] and (4) a bar on invocation as a 'justification for measures aimed at suppressing opposition' to human rights violations (in recognition of the positive relationship between human rights and national security.[48]

The UN Human Rights Committee regularly addresses purported national security justifications in its periodic reviews of state reports and has made recommendations relating to the enactment of emergency powers and the introduction of counterterrorism measures—critiquing, for example, laws that purport to 'combat *extremism*' but which fail to distinguish between violent extremism and non-violent extremism.[49] The Human Rights Committee's General Comment No. 37 further underscores that restrictions on national security grounds will only exceptionally be permissible in relation to peaceful assemblies.[50] Furthermore, if the very reason for the deterioration of the national security situation is itself 'the suppression of human rights', national security cannot then be invoked as a ground for restriction.[51] This final clause is of great significance for the future promotion and protection of the right of peaceful assembly. It is precisely in those cases where states are repressing fundamental human rights that emergency measures on the grounds of countering terrorism are being misused to halt the realization of the right.

Derogations, Definitions, and De Facto Emergencies

Derogations are specific to exceptional times of emergency and thus differ from the limitations and restrictions (outlined in Limitations: National Security as a Qualification on the Right of Peaceful Assembly) that are permitted even in times of normalcy.[52] Many regional and international human rights law instruments provide a framework for States Parties to derogate from some of their human rights obligations when certain conditions are met.[53] The scope of what constitutes an 'emergency' under international law to permit the legitimate use of derogation remains a pressing debate, particularly, as global crises and the parallel growth of militarization, securitization, and anti-democratic movements strain democratic governance worldwide.

Common among all definitions of emergency is some measure of the depth of exceptionality and imminence of the threat to the general population.[54] In the seminal case of *Lawless v Ireland*,[55] for example, the ECHR defined an emergency as 'a situation of exceptional and imminent danger or crisis affecting the general public, as distinct from particular groups and constituting a threat to the organized life of the community which composes the State in question'. The scope of what constitutes an emergency has continued to be refined, with jurists and scholars articulating alternative and more rigid terms such as 'tantamount to war' or, as stated in the Siracusa Principles, affecting the 'whole of the population and either the whole or part of the territory of the State' and threatening 'the physical integrity of the political independence or the territorial integrity of the State of the existence or basic functioning of institutions indispensable to ensure and protect the rights recognized in the Covenant'.[56]

Even once the existence of such an emergency has been established, the measures taken by states must also meet other key stipulations—they may only be 'to the extent *strictly required* by the exigencies of the situation' and must be consistent with the state's other obligations under international law, including the principle of non-discrimination.[57] The derogation must be 'officially proclaimed'[58] and other States Parties immediately informed of 'the provisions from which it has derogated and of the reasons by which it was actuated',[59] including the 'nature and extent' of such derogations.[60] States must also initiate an additional communication when those reported measures have been terminated.[61]

The interplay between the limitations included in specific provisions of the Covenant and derogations under Article 4 is especially important to determine whether any derogation is justifiable. Importantly, the Committee has stated (with specific reference to the right of peaceful assembly, amongst other rights), that the ability to implement limitations and restrictions often nullifies any rationale for the derogation of such rights.[62] General Comment No. 37 further emphasizes that 'States parties must not rely on derogation from the right of peaceful assembly if they can attain their objectives by imposing restrictions in terms of article 21'.[63]

Today, a new era of emergency powers and counterterrorism laws and policies (often together and by design) are increasingly impacting the right of peaceful assembly.[64] During the COVID-19 pandemic, for example, few states adhered to the protocols of derogation required under Article 4(3) of the ICCPR to notify fellow member states through notification of the UN Secretary-General. Within six months of the beginning of the pandemic, only twenty-one countries had notified the UN Secretary-General of formal derogations from the ICCPR.[65] The Human Rights Committee's Statement in April 2020 documented the growing concern of informal resort to emergency measures that seriously impede the realization of rights.[66]

It remains likely that many states have implemented measures that equate to derogations from the right of peaceful assembly without notifying the Secretary-General or are doing so by claiming that such measures are merely restrictions rather than derogations.[67] In its General Comment No. 29, the Human Rights Committee also noted that domestic legislation in some states appeared to permit derogation in circumstances not envisaged by Article 4.[68] This continues to pose obstacles to the ability of the relevant Treaty Bodies to assess the alignment of these measures with the ICCPR and other treaties, as well as to monitor the continued implementation of these purportedly temporary policies.

The pressures placed on derogation obligations during the COVID-19 pandemic were paralleled many years earlier in the so-called war on terror when the legal limits of derogation 'normalcy-emergency' dichotomy were stretched.[69] Most recently, the UN Special Rapporteur on the promotion and protection of human rights and fundamental freedoms while countering terrorism, joined by many other special procedure mandate holders, made important observations on how the right of peaceful assembly (among other rights) is limited in the context of counterterrorism grounds (whether resulting in the imposition of limitations/restrictions or derogation), noting that de facto states of emergency, which are 'situations of emergency that are frequently hidden by the exercise of restrictive powers without formal acknowledgment of the existence of an emergency', have increased across contexts and in frequency.[70] Moreover, the Special Rapporteur further documented the acceleration of counterterrorism and national security legislation on the tail of the COVID-19 pandemic and the risk of normalization of exceptional and emergency powers that blur the lines between societal challenges, such as public health, and national security, and which result in limited accountability for human rights violations.[71]

The dynamics of state use of emergency powers justified on the grounds of terrorism are opaque and have often involved the integration of 'emergency characteristics'[72] into regular legislation, with some of the most notorious cases found in countries such as Egypt, France, Sri Lanka, El Salvador, and beyond. The core features of such 'integration' include long-term and embedded restrictions on the right to assembly alongside other rights. The consequences have been devastating across the full range of civil and political, as well as economic, social, and cultural, rights with documented and distinct impacts on the right of peaceful assembly.

Many examples predate the growth and deepening of such state practices during COVID-19 where 'terrorism' and 'emergency powers' were closely linked. For example, the imposition of restrictions on assembly and movement to peaceful protests and gatherings in the State of Jammu and Kashmir, with the Government of India citing security concerns related to terrorism;[73] the declaration of a state of emergency in Turkey after the 2016 failed coup d'état, which included measures impacting fair trial rights and protection from arbitrary deprivation of liberty, as well as freedom of expression, assembly, and association;[74] the declaration of a state of emergency in Egypt after the 2013 mass protests, which included measures that purported to justify the excessive, or in some cases wholly unnecessary, use of force;[75] or the suppression of peaceful protests intended to draw attention to the killing of journalists critical of the Russian state's response to the 2004 terrorist attack at the Beslan School, which included the proliferation of federal law and presidential decrees.[76] These few examples illustrate a broader historical pattern, exacerbated by the COVID-19 pandemic, of gross misuse of counterterrorism rhetoric to justify states of emergency or exceptional measures which more nefariously aim to silence political dissent and prevent citizens from exercising their right of peaceful assembly amongst other rights.

The level of discretion that underlies such powers produces discrepancies contingent upon *who is seeking to assemble*. Three loosely defined categories help illustrate this point. States have dealt differently with (1) those generally exercising the right of assembly during current terrorism threats, (2) those exercising their right of assembly in response to terrorism (e.g. victims associations), and (3) those protesting against state responses to terrorism (criticizing, for example, repressive measures, emergency orders, and overly broad definitions of terrorism). Those in the first category, exercising their right of peaceful assembly when there is a heightened risk of terrorist attack, face the reality of increasing hasty resort to emergency powers that fail to comply with the principles of necessity, legality, and proportionality. In contrast, states often respond to the second politicized category with greater leniency, as they are regarded as victims of terrorism, and their actions are viewed as a form of grief and mourning. They may be granted permission to hold peaceful gatherings, and security forces may be more lenient in responding to these gatherings. Those protesting against state responses to terrorism (the third category), however, often face the most resistance from the state, as their actions are seen as challenging the state's authority and its efforts to combat terrorism. They may in turn be met with strict security measures, lowered thresholds on the use of force/excessive force, illegal blanket restrictions on freedom of assembly, and arrest and prosecution. Although the case was declared inadmissible for the nonexhaustion of domestic remedies, in the Case of *Communauté Genevoise D'Action Syndicale (CGAS) v Switzerland*, the French government's intervention provides such an example of a state defence of blanket bans. The following three examples from France, Egypt, and Sri Lanka help to illustrate these discrepancies in the protection of the right.

France has become one of the most notorious examples of the implementation of emergency measures on the grounds of terrorism that directly or indirectly limit freedom of assembly in response to terrorism. For example, after the 2015 terrorist attacks in Paris, France imposed a state of emergency that granted security forces increased powers to monitor and disperse gatherings. Notably, derogations were registered with both the UN Secretary-General and the Council of Europe Secretary-General of its derogation from the ICCPR and ECHR.[77] This led to the ban of several planned demonstrations and protests, including those related to climate change,[78] the restriction of freedom of movement, and the imposition of curfews in some areas.[79] Separately in France, although months prior to the imposition of the official emergency laws, families of victims of terrorism were permitted to organize peaceful gatherings and marches to mourn and honour the victims of the Charlie Hebdo attack through a large national unity march.[80] In contrast, in 2016, thousands of people took to the streets to protest against the government's state of emergency, which they argued was a violation of civil liberties.[81] The protesters were met with a heavy police presence, and several were arrested. To date, the legacy remains: while the Constitution protects the right to assemble, the immediate imposition of stringent measures creates a first-order barrier for those looking to continue to assemble amidst what the state often conveniently term the 'ever-present' threat of terrorism. The hangover from these measures and the embedding into the regular practice of the state can remain a challenge for the realization of the right of peaceful assembly decades on. For example, in France, recent restrictions on planned peaceful protests specific to labour policies have extended to denial of planned labour protest.[82] Restrictions have also now been placed on pro-Palestine protests in the country.[83]

Egypt, too, has become central to the debate around generalized and broad restrictions on human rights and fundamental freedoms in the fight against terrorism, and this applies in equal measure to restrictions on the right of peaceful assembly. The authorities imposed impermissible and overly broad bans on protest without justification and have more broadly sought to criminalize participation in assemblies. These measures, in turn, have emboldened the authorities in resorting to unnecessary and excessive force.[84] Egypt has implemented strict security measures and restrictions on freedom of assembly in response to terrorist attacks. Unique dynamics between and amongst those groups organizing to protest the state's responses to terrorism and the effects of terrorism, however, are present in Egypt. The artificial binaries between victims of terrorism and civil society protesting repressive terrorism responses are blurred in Egypt. For example, after the bombing of a Coptic Christian church in Alexandria in 2011, Egypt imposed a state of emergency, which granted security forces increased powers to monitor and disperse gatherings.[85] At the same time, however, and in contrast to the example of France, restrictions on assembly for victims of the terrorist attacks were also met with heavy police response; the pre-existing forms of discrimination against this victim community and impunity for attacks against them created a differing relation to the state.[86]

In Sri Lanka,[87] for those exercising the right to assembly amidst terrorism threats, the state has implemented strict security measures and restrictions on freedom of assembly in response to terrorist attacks, building upon some of the most long-standing, pre-existing, and broad emergency and counterterrorism legislative measures, including the Public Security Ordinance No. 25 of 1947 and the Prevention of Terrorism Act (PTA) of 1979. The use of these laws, together with regularized additional emergency declarations, such as those enacted in 2019 in response to the Easter Sunday Bombings, have raised concerns for the right of assembly, as well as 'serious human rights violations, including deaths, injuries, arbitrary arrests and detention of protestors and blanket bans on social media'.[88] Those protesting or exercising freedom of peaceful assembly in Sri Lanka in protest at the state's overly broad and discriminatory use of counterterrorism and emergency measures face severe rights violations, as well as regularized bans on their exercise of this right. Notably, however, the state permitted mass funerals, assemblies, and gatherings for victims to mourn and honour the victims.

As these examples illustrate, the lines drawn by states intersect with other pre-existing and perceived relationships with state actors and structural forms of discrimination. For example, contrast the favourable response to the victims' community in France (perceived as being amongst the French majority) with the victims' community in Egypt (inclusive of a large minority group that faced numerous pre-existing forms of discrimination). Indeed, the features of repression of the right to freedom of assembly also depend on the specific context and the government's approach to broader forms of dissent, control, and the use of state violence to enforce particular forms of political power, often through a counterterrorism or emergency lens. Most of the documented cases highlight the misuse of such measures against those critical of the government, creating destabilizing hierarchies and dynamics amongst various civil society and other groups at the national level, including victims of terror attacks. Additionally, different forms of assembly may be met with different levels of repression depending on the perceived threat level, political climate, and the government's human rights record. Nonetheless, in the counterterrorism space, they present distinct ways in which pre-existing political discourse and inequalities can fuel political narratives that shape the categorization of various forms of assembly. These feedback loops create unique pathways for states seeking to curb the right to dissent and the right of peaceful assembly.

Conclusion

Protecting the right of peaceful assembly is frequently undermined by an intricate web of emergency laws and powers embedded in domestic legal frameworks—whether through national security limitations, officially declared derogations, or de facto emergencies. Restrictions and derogations on the grounds of counterterrorism have not only threatened the right of peaceful assembly but appear to be used across contexts in similar ways that actively degrade its protection. There is a growing concern that the replication and regularization of political rationales in relationship to anticipated deference to emergency and counterterrorism are proliferating. Securitized state responses where emergency powers beyond the grounds of terrorism (e.g. in response to global health pandemics, natural disasters, mass migration, or conflict) can reinforce and further embed the desired application of counterterrorism powers in those states. This is particularly true in political climates where broader political rationales of 'countering terrorism' are central to states' national security strategies.

Increasing deference to counterterrorism and terrorism discourses and labelling those expressing viewpoints on the right to rebel, uprise, or violently challenge anti-democratic governance foreclose previously available means for resolving social challenges and achieving the structural change often advocated for through the right of assembly. This is partly evidenced by the normalization and embedding of restrictions on the right of peaceful assembly in regular legislation, prolonged use of limitations/restrictions, and the lack of compliance with the strict requirements for the justification and registration of derogations. At the same time, the growing convergence of rights issues across national contexts that transcend individual territories, such as mass displacement, regionalization of conflict, climate change, and beyond, has meant that some rights activists have begun to use 'emergency' rhetoric to frame the challenges of today.

Some have even called for the use of emergency powers to address such challenges when broader political action evades. The muddying of terminologies in this manner requires further exploration regarding how this advocacy perspective interacts with state misuse of emergency rhetoric towards infringement upon fundamental rights, including the right of peaceful assembly.

The longevity of the existing and protracted states of emergency and the embedded nature of such measures continue to expose the limits of legal safeguards in preventing the misuse of emergency powers on the grounds of terrorism. In particular, the deference provided to states in this space has had a cumulative legal and practical effect. For example, despite the findings of UN human rights bodies on particular countries, UN counterterrorism programming often continues in those countries.[89] The long-standing and growing work of the UN's human rights architecture, including the Human Rights Committee, treaty body mechanisms, and Special Procedures of the Human Rights Council, documenting and aiming to reinforce legal safeguards against this misuse has yet to fully thwart this trend. This is especially the case against the backdrop of a growing international counterterrorism architecture at the United Nations, including the Counterterrorism Executive Directorate of the Counterterrorism Committee of the UN Security Council, as well as the United Nations Office of Counterterrorism, which engages in bolstering counterterrorism governance norms in countries without adequate safeguards. Increasingly, the Human Rights Treaty Bodies as well as Special Procedures have encountered instances where the emergency legislation or de facto imposition of restrictions of emergency character that restrict fundamental rights are directly supported by the UN's capacity-building and technical assistance.[90]

In parallel, in other parts of the United Nations, the colloquialization of language around 'emergency' within the system has also arguably led to the use of emergency nomenclature as a measure to focus attention, to highlight programmes and their urgency to member states. The Secretary-General has, for example, stressed that the world must go into 'emergency mode' to respond to today's top crises—climate, global pandemics, conflict, and more.[91] However, amidst a system-wide undermining of the obligations to promote and protect human rights even amidst emergency, the normalization of these suggestions pose some future challenges for the perceived 'cover' the UN may provide to states seeking to infringe upon human rights through these frames. In the face of this conglomeration of emergencies, some have also questioned the relevance of derogation and limitation frameworks and the particularities of analyses required for each.[92] Just as COVID-19 has sparked new concerns around the infringement on the right to assembly and other rights, so too will the issues of climate change, conflict, and beyond. In a world that continues to expand the category and communities feel the emergent pressures of challenges that go unaddressed—such as climate change, rising economic inequality, and intractable conflict—political rhetoric that exploits such need for legitimate governance and bold action to close civic space may leave a political world without focus on legal meaning and practical steps towards recourse and redress.

Author's Note

The chapter is written in the author's independent capacity. Thank you to Fionnuala Ní Aoláin, Michael Hamilton, and Thomas Probert for their helpful feedback and to Nicole Carter for research assistance. All remaining errors are with the author.

Notes

1. Judith Butler, *Notes toward a Performative Theory of Assembly* (Cambridge, MA: Harvard University Press, 2015), 2, 190.
2. International Center for Not-For-Profit Law (ICNL), 'COVID-19 Civic Freedom Tracker', https://www.icnl.org/covid19tracker/. See also Center for Civil & Political Rights, 'Tracking tool—Impact of States of Emergencies on Civil and political Rights', https://ccprcentre.org/ccprpages/tracking-tool-impact-of-States-of-emergencies-on-civil-and-political-rights. See also Human Rights Watch, 'Covid-19 Triggers Wave of Free Speech Abuse', 11 February 2021, https://www.hrw.org/news/2021/02/11/covid-19-triggers-wave-free-speech-abuse.
3. ICNL, 'COVID-19 Civic Freedom Tracker'. The methodology for the tracker defines 'emergency declaration' as including 'formal declarations of a "state of emergency" . . . as well as variations such as a "state of crisis", "state of disaster", and other terms used by governments to designate exceptional situations that justify some limitations on rights and freedoms'.
4. Human Rights Watch, 'Covid-19 Triggers Wave of Free Speech Abuse'.
5. Eric Richardson and Colleen Devine, 'Emergencies End Eventually: How to Better Analyze Human Rights Restrictions Sparked by the COVID-19 Pandemic Under the International Covenant on Civil and Political Rights', *Michigan Journal of International Law* 42 (2020): 105.
6. United Nations Joint Declaration on Protecting the Right to Freedom of Peaceful Assembly in Times of Emergencies of Special Rapporteur on the rights of freedom of assembly and of association, the Special Rapporteur on freedom of expression of the Inter-American Commission on Human Rights (IACHR), the Special Rapporteur on human rights defenders and focal point for reprisals in Africa and Chairman of the African Commission on Human and Peoples' Rights (ACHPR), and the OSCE Office for Democratic Institutions and Human Rights (ODIHR) (15 September 2022). Although the Joint Declaration does not necessarily specify the frame of counterterrorism, it underscores the ongoing misuse of emergency measures, including the militarization of law enforcement deployments.
7. See Abu El-Haj and Srinivasan, in this volume.
8. One hundred and eighty four of the 193 United Nations member states recognize the right of peaceful assembly in their constitutions. UNHRCtte, General Comment 37—Article 21: Right of Peaceful Assembly (17 September 2020) UN Doc CCPR/C/GC/37, n3. Note too, the Preamble to the Universal Declaration on Human Rights (1948): 'It is essential, if man is not to be compelled to have recourse, as a last resort, to rebellion against tyranny and oppression, that human rights should be protected by the rule of law'. See also Michael Hamilton, 'The Management of Protest and Dissent', in *Routledge Handbook of Illiberalism*, ed. András Sajó, Renáta Uitz, and Stephen Holmes (London: Routledge, 2020), 384–402.
9. See, for example, the discussion related to the use of emergency measures in Canada in 2022. Public Order Emergency Commission, *Report of the Public Inquiry into the 2022*

Public Order Emergency (Canada: Public Order Emergency Commission, 2023), https://publicorderemergencycommission.ca/final-report/.

10. This is made possible through the use of overly broad counterterrorism laws that fail to adequately define terrorism under domestic legislation.
11. See e.g. Fiona De Londras, 'Ever-Expanding Transnational Counter-Terrorism', in *The Practice and Problems of Transnational Counter-Terrorism* (Cambridge: Cambridge University Press, 2022), 88–120; Oren Gross, and Fionnuala Ní Aoláin, *Law in Times of Crisis: Emergency Powers in Theory and Practice*, Cambridge Studies in International and Comparative Law (Cambridge: Cambridge University Press, 2006); A. Greene, *Permanent States of Emergency and the Rule of Law: Constitutions in an Age of Crisis* (Oxford: Hart Publishing, 2018).
12. See e.g. Ní Aoláin, Fionnuala, Report of the Special Rapporteur on the promotion and protection of human rights and fundamental freedoms while countering terrorism (22 December 2017) UN Doc. A/HRC/37/5.
13. See e.g. Julia Hall, 'Peaceful Israel/Gaza Protests Are Not "National Security" Threat', EU Observer. https://euobserver.com/opinion/157668.
14. Michael Walzer, *Just and Unjust Wars: A Moral Argument with Historical Illustrations*, 5th ed. (New York: Basic Books, 2015).
15. Ibid., 3.
16. For example, the recent Global Study on the Impact of Counterterrorism Measures on Civil Society & Civic Space provides a series of documented examples of the labelling of such assemblies as violent, non-peaceful, and thus unlawful in domestic contexts. Fionnuala Ní Aoláin, Megan L. Manion, and Alyssa Yamamoto, *Global Study on the Impact of Counter-Terrorism Measures on Civil Society & Civic Space* (2023), n. 221, https://defendcivicspace.com.
17. UNHRCtte, General Comment No. 37—Article 21: Right of Peaceful Assembly (17 September 2020) UN Doc. CCPR/C/GC/37, 17.
18. See e.g. ECtHR, *Frumkin v Russia* App. No. 74568/12 (5 January 2016), 97–99.
19. American Association for the International Commission of Jurists, *Siracusa Principles on the Limitation and Derogation Provisions in the International Covenant on Civil and Political Rights* (1985) [hereinafter Siracusa Principles], 29–30.
20. See e.g. the comparison between campaigns of attacks perpetrated for example by Jamaat Nusrat Al-Islam wal Muslimeen and the Islamic State in the Sahel region versus the incidents tracked in the "West" as defined by the Global Counterterrorism Index. Institute for Economics & Peace, 'Global Terrorism Index 2023: Measuring the Impact of Terrorism' (Sydney, Australia, 2023), http://visionofhumanity.org/resources.
21. *Mehmet Hasan Altan v Turkey* at 210; *Şahin Alpay v Turkey* at 180. See also, *Barseghyan v Armenia* App. No. 17804/09 (21 September 2021) 47–55 (although the Court finds a violation of Article 11, note the Court's hesitancy in determining claims on the basis of legitimacy of aims and rather looking towards necessity, alongside broad deference to the facts as determined by national courts).
22. Mathias Vermeulen, 'The Impact, Legitimacy and Effectiveness of EU Counter-Terrorism', in *The Impact, Legitimacy and Effectiveness of EU Counter-Terrorism* (London: Routledge, 2017), 74.
23. E.g. *Şahin Alpay v Turkey* App. No. 16538/17 (20 March 2018), 75. Also, *Greece v The United Kingdom* App. No. 176/56 (6 February 1958), 132–138, where the case turned specifically on the presence of an emergency.

24. See e.g. UNHRCtte, Concluding Observations on the Sixth Periodic Report of Sri Lanka (26 April 2023) UN Doc. CCPR/C/LKA/CO/6 (subjection of the right to freedom of peaceful assembly to additional restrictions), and UNHRCtte, Replies of Sri Lanka to the List of Issues in Relation to Its Sixth Periodic Report (11 May 2023) UN Doc. CCPR/C/LKA/RQ/6, 34–36 (Easter Sunday Attacks of 2019 and their continued relationship to emergency law); and UNHRCtte, Concluding Observations on the Fifth Periodic Report of Egypt (14 April 2023) UN Doc. CCPR/C/EGY/CO/5, 11, 40, 47–48 (on use of emergency restrictions and powers during the COVID-19 pandemic without any health grounds, prosecution of individuals within special/counterterrorism courts for exercise of right to freedom of peaceful assembly, and broad violations against the right to freedom of peaceful assembly).
25. UNHRCtte, General Comment No. 37, 23.
26. The abuse of derogation powers under the framing of martial law or emergency powers have been central to human rights discourse and precedent with outlined legal limits of such practices central to human rights litigation and advocacy for decades. See *Siracusa Principles on the Limitation and Derogation Provisions in the International Covenant on Civil and Political Rights* (1985).
27. International Covenant on Civil and Political Rights (ICCPR), adopted by UN General Assembly Resolution 2200A (XXI), 16 December 1966, article 21.
28. E.g. Article 26, ICCPR.
29. UNHRCtte, General Comment No. 37, 41.
30. See e.g. Amnesty International, 'USA: Law enforcement violated Black Lives Matter protesters' human rights', 4 August 2020; Charis McGowan, '"Our role is central": more than 1m Chilean women to march in huge protest', *The Guardian*, 6 March 2020; Mairav Zonszein, 'Israelis Take on Netanyahu and Coronavirus Restrictions in Wave of Civil Disobedience', *The Intercept*, 14 November 2020.
31. UNHRCtte, General Comment No. 37, 44.
32. Ibid.
33. Siracusa Principles, 33.
34. UNHRCtte, *Alekseev v Russian Federation* (Communication No. 1873/2009) (25 October 2013) UN Doc CCPR/C/109/D/1873/2009, 9.6.
35. UNHRCtte, General Comment No. 37, 45.
36. UNHRCtte, *Gryb v Belarus* (Communication No. 1316/2004) (9 July 2004) UN Doc. CCPR/C/103/D/1316/2004.
37. International Covenant on Civil and Political Rights (ICCPR), adopted by UN General Assembly Resolution 2200A (XXI), 16 December 1966, article 21 ('imposed in conformity with the law'); article 19 ('provided by law') UNHRCtte, General Comment No. 34—Article 19: Freedom of Opinion and Expression (12 September 2011) UN Doc. CCPR/C/GC/34, 25.
38. Ibid. ('which are necessary in a democratic society').
39. See further, Siracusa Principles, 10.
40. International Covenant on Civil and Political Rights (ICCPR), adopted by UN General Assembly Resolution 2200A (XXI), 16 December 1966, article 21.
41. UNHRCtte, General Comment No. 37, 40.
42. E.g. UNHRCtte, *Toregozhina v Kazakhstan* (Communication No. 2137/2012) (30 June 2010) UN Doc CCPR/C/112/D/2137/2012, 7.4-7.6. See Martin Scheinin, 'U.N. Human Rights Committee General Comment No. 37 on Freedom of Assembly: An Excellent and

Timely Contribution', *Just Security*, https://www.justsecurity.org/71754/u-n-human-rights-committee-general-comment-no-37-on-freedom-of-assembly-an-excellent-and-timely-contribution/.

43. Evan J. Criddle, 'Protecting Human Rights during Emergencies: Delegation, Derogation, and Deference' (2014), 34, highlighting the idea of states as 'neutral, rights optimizing trustees'.
44. For example, Siracusa Principles, 'Introductory Note'.
45. Siracusa Principles I(B)(vi)(29–32), cited in UNHRCtte, General Comment No. 37, 42, n. 46.
46. Ibid., 30.
47. Ibid., 31.
48. Ibid., 32.
49. See e.g. UNHRCtte, CCPR/C/LKA/CO/6; UNHRCtte, CCPR/C/UZB/CO/5. See also UNHRCtte, *M.T. v Uzbekistan* (Communication No. 2234/2013) (21 October 2015) UN Doc. CCPR/C/114/D/2234/2013.
50. UNHRCtte, General Comment No. 37, 42.
51. Specifically in relation to terrorism, the General Comment states that 'while acts of terrorism must be criminalized in conformity with international law, the definition of such crimes must not be overbroad or discriminatory and must not be applied so as to curtail or discourage the exercise of the right of peaceful assembly. The mere act of organizing or participating in a peaceful assembly cannot be criminalized under counter-terrorism laws'. UNHRCtte, General Comment No. 37, 68.
52. UNHRCtte, General Comment No. 29—Article 4: States of Emergency (12 September 2011) UN Doc. CCPR/C/21/Rev.1/Add.11.
53. See e.g. Article 4(2) of the ICCPR specifically excludes certain rights from derogation, such as the right to life and the prohibition of torture and other cruel, inhuman or degrading treatment or punishment. Notable exceptions include the African Charter on Human and Peoples' Rights; the International Covenant on Economic, Social and Cultural Rights; and the Convention on the Rights of the Child.
54. See e.g. ECtHR, *Lawless v Ireland* App. No. 332/57 (1 July 1961).
55. Ibid.
56. ECtHR, *The Greek Case* App. No. 3321/67, 3322/67, 3323/67, 3344/67 (5 November 1969); Siracusa Principles; see also IACtHR, Habeas Corpus in Emergency Situations, Advisory Opinion (1987).
57. ICCPR article 4(1) (emphasis added).
58. Ibid.
59. ICCPR article 4(3).
60. UNHRCtte, General Comment No. 29.
61. Ibid., 17.
62. Ibid.
63. UNHRCtte, General Comment No. 37, 96.
64. UNHRCttee, 'Statement on derogations from the Covenant in connection with the Covid-19 Pandemic', 30 April 2020, https://www.ohchr.org/Documents/HRBodies/CCPR/COVIDStatementEN.pdf; see also Fionnuala Ní Aoláin, Report of the Special Rapporteur on the promotion and protection of human rights and fundamental freedoms while countering terrorism (1 March 2018) UN Doc. A/HRC/37/52.

65. Human Rights Watch, 'Covid-19 Triggers Wave of Free Speech Abuse', 11 February 2021. https://www.hrw.org/news/2021/02/11/covid-19-triggers-wave-free-speech-abuse.
66. UNHRCtte, Statement on Derogations From the Covenant in Connection With the COVID-19 Pandemic (24 April 2020) UN Doc. CCPR/C/128/2.
67. Ibid., 1.
68. UNHRCtte, General Comment No. 29, 3.
69. Kathleen A. Kavanaugh, 'Policing the Margins: Rights Protection and the European Court of Human Rights', *European Human Rights Law Review* no. 4 (2006): 422–444.
70. Fionnuala Ní Aoláin, Report of the Special Rapporteur on the promotion and protection of human rights and fundamental freedoms while countering terrorism (1 March 2018) UN Doc. A/HRC/37/52, 21–25.
71. Fionnuala Ní Aoláin, 'Covid-19, Counter-Terrorism and Emergency Law' (2023), https://www.ohchr.org/sites/default/files/documents/issues/terrorism/sr/activities/position-paper-sr-ct-Emergency-Powers.pdf.
72. Ní Aoláin, A/HRC/37/52.
73. See e.g. UNHRCtte, List of issues prior to submission of the fourth periodic report of India (22 August 2019) UN Doc. CCPR/C/IND/QPR/4, 26–27; UNHRCtte, Fourth Periodic Report Submitted by India under Article 40 of the Covenant Pursuant to the Optional Reporting Procedure, Due in 2020 (31 May 2022) UN Doc. CCPR/C/IND/4, 77–79, 133–134.
74. Elina Steinerte et al., Special Procedures Urgent Appeal, UN Doc. TUR 6/2017; Elina Steinerte et al., Special Procedures Official Letter, UN Doc. TUR 15/2018.
75. Frank La Rue et al., Special Procedures Urgent Appeal, UN Doc. EGY 3/2013.
76. See e.g. ECtHR, *Tagayeva and Others v Russia* App. No. 26562/07 and six other applications (13 April 2017). UNHRCtte, *Chebotareva v Russian Federation* (Communication No. 1866/2009) (26 August 2012) UN Doc CCPR/C/104/D/1866/2009. See also European Commission on Democracy through Law, *Assemblies, Meetings, Demonstrations, Marches, and Picketing of the Russian Federation* (19 June 2004) Opinion no. 659/2011.
77. See e.g. C.N.703.2015.TREATIES-IV.4 (Depositary Notification), France: Notification under Article 4 (3) (noting that the derogation may involve a derogation from the obligations under the International Covenant on Civil and Political Rights, and particularly its Articles 9, 12, and 17.
78. See e.g. one of the most famous restrictions post-2015 emergency powers in France, which barred protests during the Paris Climate talks. Arthur Neslen, 'Paris Climate Activists Put under House Arrest Using Emergency Laws', *The Guardian*, 27 November 2015, https://www.theguardian.com/environment/2015/nov/27/paris-climate-activists-put-under-house-arrest-using-emergency-laws.
79. Jennifer Fredette, 'The French State of Emergency', *Current History* 116, no. 788 (2017): 101–106.
80. BBC, 'Paris Attacks: Millions Rally for Unity in France', 11 January 2015, https://www.bbc.com/news/world-europe-30765824.
81. Shafik Mandhai, 'France State of Emergency Protest Draws Thousands', *Al Jazeera*, 13 March 2016, https://www.aljazeera.com/news/2016/3/13/france-State-of-emergency-protest-draws-thousands.
82. Mediapart, Jérôme Hourdeaux, 'Liberté d'expression: multiplication des crimes de lèse-Macron', 5 May 2023, https://www.mediapart.fr/journal/france/050523/liberte-d-expression-multiplication-des-crimes-de-lese-macron?utm_source=global&utm_medium=social&utm_campaign=SharingApp&xtor=CS3-5.

83. Pierre Emmanuel Ngendakumana, 'France's pro-Palestine Protest Ban Is OK, Top Court Rules', *Politico*, 18 October 2023, https://www.politico.eu/article/pro-palestine-protest-france-ban-ok-court-rule/.
84. UNHRCtte, Concluding Observations on the Fifth Periodic Report of Egypt, CCPR/C/EGY/CO/5, 48.
85. Special Procedures Communication No. AL EGY 6/2017.
86. UNHRCtte, Concluding Observations on the Fifth Periodic Report of Egypt, CCPR/C/EGY/CO/5, 43.
87. UNHRCtte, Concluding Observations on the Sixth Periodic Report of Sri Lanka, CCPR/C/LKA/CO/6.
88. Ibid., 14.
89. Several examples exist of UN counterterrorism entities engaged in political events and activities advancing counterterrorism activities in states that expressly limit or derogate from the right of peaceful assembly without reform or redress despite UN Special Procedures or Human Rights Committee findings. For example, United Nations Office of Counter-Terrorism (UNOCT), "Press Release: Head of United Nations Counter-Terrorism Office Concludes Official Visit to Nigeria," 2 September 2023, https://www.un.org/counterterrorism/sites/www.un.org.counterterrorism/files/230902_usg_nigeria_end_of_visit_press_release_.pdf. See also the November 2019 conference on counterterrorism in Hungary, following a series of restrictions on protests by the state throughout the year, UNOCT, 'Prevention of Radicalization to Terrorism: Regional Policy Responses and Risk Mitigation', https://www.un.org/counterterrorism/regional-conferences/hungary.
90. Fionnuala Ní Aoláin, Report of the Special Rapporteur on the promotion and protection of human rights and fundamental freedoms while countering terrorism (3 August 2021) UN Doc. (A/76/261).
91. UN News, 'UN Chief Calls for Action to Put Out "5-Alarm Global Fire"', 21 January 2022, https://news.un.org/en/story/2022/01/1110292.
92. See e.g. Kanstantsin Dzehtsiarou, 'Article 15 Derogations: Are They Really Necessary during the COVID-19 Pandemic?', *European Human Rights Law Review* 4 (2020): 359–371.

Further Reading

Criddle, Evan J. *Human Rights in Emergencies*. New York: Cambridge University Press, 2016.

De Londras, Fiona. 'Ever-Expanding Transnational Counter-Terrorism'. In *The Practice and Problems of Transnational Counter-Terrorism, Cambridge Studies in Law and Society*, ed. Fiona de Londras, 88–120. Cambridge: Cambridge University Press, 2022.

Fenwick, Helen, and Gavin Phillipson. 'Covert Derogations and Judicial Deference: Redefining Liberty and Due Process Rights in Counterterrorism Law and Beyond'. *McGill Law Journal* 56, no. 4 (June 2011): 863–918.

Greene, Alan. *Permanent States of Emergency and the Rule of Law: Constitutions in an Age of Crisis*. Oxford: Hart Publishing, 2018.

Gross, Oren, and Fionnuala Ní Aoláin. *Law in Times of Crisis: Emergency Powers in Theory and Practice*. Cambridge: Cambridge University Press, 2006.

Hamilton, Michael. 'The Management of Protest and Dissent'. In *Routledge Handbook of Illiberalism*, ed. András Sajó, Renáta Uitz, and Stephen Holmes, 384–402. New York: Routledge, 2020.

Ní Aoláin, Fionnuala. 'The Cloak and Dagger Game of Derogation'. In *Human Rights in Emergencies*, ed. Evan J. Criddle, 124–147. ASIL Studies in International Legal Theory. Cambridge: Cambridge University Press, 2016.

Vermeulen, Mathias. 'Assessing Counter-Terrorism as a Matter of Human Rights: Perspectives from the European Court of Human Rights'. In *The Impact, Legitimacy and Effectiveness of EU Counter-Terrorism, Routledge Research in Terrorism and the Law*, ed. Fiona de Londras and Josephine Doody, 65–92. New York: Routledge, 2015.

CHAPTER 34

UNDERSTANDING COLLECTIVE VIOLENCE IN ASSEMBLIES AND CROWDS

OTTO ADANG

INTRODUCTION

THIS chapter deals with collective behaviour in assemblies and crowds where people are physically co-present. In human rights law, an assembly is regarded as an occasion where at least two people gather.[1] When larger numbers of people gather, the word 'crowd' is often used—though there is no consensus on the minimum number of people needed. The chapter draws centrally upon insights from the social sciences, specifically crowd psychology, the field that investigates both the behaviour and psychology of *individuals in crowds* and the behaviour of *crowds*, to explore what is known about this collective behaviour and also to reveal how (mis)understandings of collective behaviour have shaped the nature of law enforcement interventions around assemblies.

At the outset, it is worth considering the ways in which this phenomenon of collective behaviour maps onto 'peaceful assembly' as protected in human rights law. The different facets of co-presence that social scientists emphasize have implications for the construction of the notion of 'peaceful assembly'. This has consequences both for the presumptions that may credibly be made regarding the 'peacefulness' of assemblies and for questions about how the heterogeneity or common purpose of a gathering interacts with its organization and coordination. Both deserve further introductory elaboration.

First, a core question that social scientists have sought to address is whether collectivities are in any way predisposed towards violence and, if so, why and in what circumstances? It is important to state from the outset that collective violence (often colloquially called a 'riot', a term that can have a specific meaning in different legal systems) is a rare phenomenon. It is the exception rather than the rule that when large numbers of people gather, violence erupts. Still, administrative and law enforcement interventions are all too often premised on the perceived inherent dangerousness of crowds. In popular parlance, when violence occurs, a crowd is said to turn into an emotional, irrational, and violent mob, but the use of this term is wholly unscientific. The underlying assumptions have all too often shaped, and in many instances still shape, official responses to assemblies in the form of restrictive policies and a repressive, 'escalated force' style of policing (riot control).

It is sometimes suggested that the risks presented by assemblies correlate directly with, and are amplified in proportion to, their size. Gustave Le Bon viewed a 'sentiment of invincible power' as a causal factor for violence, which also resonates with the emphasis in social movement theory of 'strength in numbers'.[2] There is in fact no reason to believe that mere presence in a crowd increases the likelihood of violence. Moreover, by presenting crowd conflict as an expression of simple, primitive drives or a descent into irrationality, such accounts deny the role of groups outside the crowd, such as law enforcement, in the development of violence, and they also deny any meaning or purpose to crowd action. These theories also rationalize the use of coercive force against the crowd as the most appropriate form of state response.[3]

Empirically, the early theories of crowd behaviour failed to explain not only the absence of violence in many crowd events—the vast majority of assemblies are peaceful—but also the patterns and meaningful limits to behaviour found in even the most violent crowd conflicts.[4] Yet these theories still enjoy some form of appeal, as when after collective violence, rioters are referred to as thugs or animals (predisposition), as forming part of a mindless mob, or when the violence is referred to as contagious, viral, or the result of de-individuation (group mind). Alternative modern accounts attempted to move away from notions of primitive drives, irrationality, and mindlessness. Instead, they posited norms,[5] individual decision-making,[6] or situational breakdowns[7] as explanations for collective behaviour.[8]

These different theories are explored further in this chapter, but the starting premise here is that although crowds are sometimes associated all too easily with disorder and (a potential for) collective violence, peaceful assemblies should in fact be considered an integral, valued, and protected part of *order* in democratic societies.

Secondly, in what ways does a common purpose between participants impact organizational coherence and coordination? Reicher and Drury, for example, distinguish between physical crowds (in which people are physically co-present but are not acting as one, such as in a shopping mall or at a train station) and psychological crowds (where they act as one, such as at a protest).[9]

Common purpose, however, does not equate with homogeneity,[10] and this is a critical point in terms of how crowds are perceived to act and the styling of any policing intervention. In crowd psychology, a crowd is seen as a group of people interacting face-to-face, in a novel situation, and with no formal means of collective decision-making.[11] In collective behaviour, by contrast, individuals influence one another and some form of coordination is achieved with respect to location, timing, and type of behaviour. It is sometimes unclear how this coordination occurs in practice.

It is important to make these assessments throughout the temporal life cycle of an assembly, as different moments afford opportunities for disruptive or regulatory intervention. McPhail prefers to speak in more neutral terms about collective behaviour in gatherings, and thus avoid making assumptions about whether people act as one in a psychological sense.[12] In studying assemblies, wherein persons move from disparate points in space to a common location, he distinguishes three phases in the life cycle of temporary gatherings: the process of assembling, the assembled gathering itself, and the dispersal process. In this way, he endeavoured better to describe the diversity of what people do alone, in relation to, and with others within temporary gatherings.

Theoretical Misadventures

For the uninitiated, dipping into the crowd psychology literature can be off-putting because of the complex and fine-spun distinctions between different models, the apparent contradictions between them, and the ways in which certain strands of argument are later resurrected and reinvented. It is nonetheless important to appreciate how these theories can affect the ways in which authorities and the police both perceive and seek to respond to assemblies.[13]

Many studies have sought to explain psychological transformations in the context of conflictual crowds—but since most crowds are not conflictual, such transformations are themselves exceptional. Unfortunately, most of the theories involve unfalsifiable hypotheses and core concepts that cannot be measured in practice. Attempting, for example, to identify and understand the nature and role of agency, rationality, or the role of collective versus individual norms in collective behaviour 'is fraught with epistemological problems' due to the impossibility of measuring the independent variables.[14]

Rational choice theory is a rich source of hypotheses that are precise enough to be falsifiable, but Turner has also identified a number of pitfalls in its application to micro sociological phenomena, including the fact that the approach can only meaningfully be applied 'if the goals of action are identified in a reasonably precise fashion'.[15]

Other theories struggle to establish a clear difference between collective behaviour and routine social behaviour. However, more recent work has examined the role of individual characteristics in collective violence offenders, finding that there are distinct categories of perpetrators of public violence whose behaviour is triggered by different processes. This helps to explain the contradictory findings of previous studies, and points to more nuanced approaches for preventing and dealing with collective violence in assemblies.[16]

With few exceptions,[17] all the different theories about the emergence and escalation of collective violence in crowds were not based on direct observation of crowds,[18] but rather on theoretical conjecturing or on extrapolations from experimental studies in small group settings, computer simulations, or survey studies. In contrast, there are two major authors who have conducted direct systematic observations of crowd behaviour:

McPhail (about crowd behaviour in general)[19] and Adang (specifically about crowd violence).[20] The participant observation studies that have been conducted in the last twenty years provide valuable additional information but also have their own drawbacks and problems.[21] More recently, several studies using video material have been conducted, both using publicly available material[22] and CCTV footage.[23] Obviously, the use of video material has a lot of potential, especially in combination with other methodologies that can compensate for the limited view of cameras or the lack of sound. The following discussion contrasts the various theoretical claims that have been advanced with what is empirically known and established about collective violence (and, in turn, what this means for interventions by law enforcement authorities).

Violence Does Not Occur in Most Collective Situations

Theories of crowd behaviour have proposed different explanations for the emergence of conflict or violence—ranging from assertions of a 'group mind' to 'de-individuation', 'emergent norms', and switching between different social identities. Given this research focus, it is easy to overlook the fact that most collective situations do not ever involve violence.

The earliest debates in crowd psychology concerned whether individuals were 'swept away' and psychologically transformed by being a member of a crowd.[24] The 'group mind' argument, that the crowd subsumed the individual personality, was exemplified in the nineteenth-century work of Gustave Le Bon, who argued that under certain given circumstances, an agglomeration of men presents new characteristics very different from those of the individuals composing it and a man descends several rungs in the ladder of civilization just by being part of a crowd, acting by instinct.[25]

Le Bon described three essential characteristics of crowds—the disappearance of conscious personality and predominance of unconscious personality; the turning by means of suggestion and contagion of feelings and ideas in an identical direction; and the tendency for the suggested ideas to immediately transform into acts.

One modern variant of the idea that crowds exert a negative influence on individuals derives from de-individuation theory.[26] This posited that individuals experience a loss of self-awareness while in crowds and this results in anti-normative behaviour (i.e. in acts that violate established norms of appropriateness).[27] However, many of the assumptions of a 'group mind' have been widely rejected, since they rely upon conceiving of behaviours abstracted from their social context, with violence seen as a characteristic of crowd rather than an intergroup process between, for example, protesters and police. In this way, crowd action is reduced to invariant or fixed behaviour patterns, seen as irrational and exclusively negative.[28]

Furthermore, de-individuating settings do not lead to a loss of personal identity; rather, they can facilitate a transition from a personal to a more social or collective identity.[29] According to Reicher, the so-called anti-normative behaviour found in the crowd is actually a display of what is normative within the crowd.[30] Implicit in this analysis is the distinction between general social norms and situational or group-specific norms. When a person is 'de-individuated' (and hence less accountable or less aware of the personal self), it is the *group's* norms that are important, more so than general social norms.[31]

In developing the elaborated social identity model (ESIM), Reicher pursued the argument that crowd conflict can be understood as normatively structured and shaped by cognition in ways that reflect one's social identity.[32] Where 'group mind' theories suggested that the self was lost or reduced in the crowd, the social identity approach suggests, by contrast, that we have social as well as personal identities, and that the former are based on our group memberships. Each of these categories (e.g. a parent, a football fan, an anti-globalist, or a Protestant) brings along a set of norms and values that determine what behaviour is appropriate and what is not. Norms of the 'parent' category will, for example, differ from that of the 'football fan'. Hence, the model suggests that other than 'losing one's mind' or being governed by a group mind, people shift to a behaviour that relates to the normative structure of their relevant category. So, crowd members do not simply ask 'what is appropriate in this context?' but rather 'what is appropriate for us *as members of this category* in this context?'[33] Thus, the limits and patterns observed in crowd behaviour reflect the social identity shared by participants.[34] This shared social identity makes collective behaviour possible in both collective conflict and other situations.

ESIM suggests two conditions for conflict to emerge and develop in an otherwise peaceful crowd: *an asymmetry of categorical representations* between crowd participants and a relevant outgroup such as the police, and *an asymmetry of power relations* such that the police outgroup is able to impose its definition of legitimate conduct on the ingroup of crowd participants.[35] Where outgroup action is experienced by crowd participants as not only *illegitimate* (thereby legitimizing crowd action against it) but also *indiscriminate* (i.e. as an action against 'everyone' in the crowd), crowd participants come to define themselves through a more inclusive ingroup self-categorization, superseding any previous divisions within the physical crowd.[36] A major contribution of ESIM is the identification of collective violence as an intergroup process. In this way, it becomes clearer how interventions by authorities and law enforcement can contribute to or indeed worsen collective violence.[37] More recent studies support the models' utility in accounting for the *absence* of collective 'violence' and the development of peaceful norms at crowd events.[38]

No Greater Tendency in Crowds to 'Emotional' or 'Irrational' Behaviour

In the 1920s, Allport rejected the idea of a group mind, claiming that 'the individual in the crowd behaves just as he would have alone, only more so'.[39] Accordingly, crowd behaviour is subject to the accumulation of persons with similar traits and therefore crowd disorder would result from a coming together of people with similar traits or criminal, violent, or antisocial personalities. For Allport, the 'course of collective action [is] fairly determined from the start . . . [because of] the fundamental reactions upon which the individuals have been launched'.[40] He termed the process supposed to be responsible for it becoming collective 'social facilitation': the phenomenon that people sometimes show an increased level of effort as a result of the presence of others.

Turner and Killian's 1950s emergent norm theory likewise challenges the idea that crowd behaviour is irrational or governed by a 'group mind', but it proposed instead the rationality of group processes.[41] For them, crowd behaviour is governed by collective norms which emerge during the crowd situation. There is an 'illusion of unanimity'. The crowd situation is seen as distinct from 'normal' social situations: in the crowd people undergo a form of 'crisis' in which traditional norms for action no longer apply. Within this uncertainty and ambivalence people search for meaning and cues to define or create a new normative structure. Turner and Killian describe this communicative phase as a process of 'milling' during which people engage with other crowd participants, looking for clues and 'keynotes' that may provide normative guidance for social action. Also, crowds are not seen as homogeneous, they are characterized 'by differential expression, with some people expressing what they are feeling while others do not'.[42] Persons who are more distinct in their behaviour may then provide a model for new collective norms that emerge within that situation.

With the idea of certain persons differing from others, emergent norm theory has been criticized as being nothing more than a different version of Allport's individualistic approach, explaining crowd behaviour 'tied to the personality of a dominant few'.[43] Further objections concern unanswered questions as to why some follow the crowd behaviour while others do not, or how large group unity can be achieved in a brief period. However, despite these criticisms, the theory is seen as a major step away from the irrationalist view of crowds, with potential consequences for the public order management of assemblies, such as in the more communicative negotiated management approach.[44]

McPhail, who observed and studied many gatherings, approves of the step away from the irrationalist view of crowds but is critical of the norms. It is not clear what norms are: either modal patterns of behaviour or alternatively prescriptions and proscriptions for behaviour. Too often, he argued, they refer to both, with 'a tendency to take regularities in behaviour as the evidence of the norm'.[45] McPhail wonders what the fieldworker is supposed to see or observe and how emergent norm hypotheses can be tested.[46] A similar question would be relevant for law enforcement: How are they supposed to discern what the collective norms are in each assembly and what are they supposed to do in relation to these norms?

The Role of Individual Agency in Collective Violence

Le Bon popularized the concepts of submergence, suggestibility, and contagion (where 'contagion' was itself merely an effect of the increased suggestibility of individuals in a crowd).[47] 'Contagion' draws a parallel with the transfer of infectious diseases (relatively recently theorized at the time Le Bon was writing). By using the word 'contagion', crowd behaviour is labelled as pathological. As the recent COVID-19 pandemic made clear, an approach based on 'contagion' leads to specific types of restrictive measures. Applying such an approach to assemblies as if human beings in an assembly are mindless beings without agency is inappropriate.[48]

Based on decision theory,[49] Berk presents a gaming approach to collective decision-making in crowds whereby individual participants calculate the costs and rewards of pursuing whatever options are available to them in the crowd as well as the perceived social support for those options among other members of the crowd.[50] A novelty of his approach lies in the consideration of context as an impact variable on crowd behaviour. The model suggests that people in crowds act in terms of a 'minimax strategy', making assumptions about outcomes and the likelihood of events, and ultimately choosing a behaviour that most probably will minimize their costs and maximize their rewards. Two dimensions are therefore relevant: probability of support and anticipated payoff.

Berk discusses four variables that affect the probability of support. They are a combination of the number of people acting in ways that support desired actions of a given individual, the visibility of these people, their proximity, and the ease of interpreting actions of others as supportive. The visibility will be affected by the physical characteristics of the environment. The interpretation will depend, among other things, on the role of leaders and the familiarity with people present, with known symbolic components, or with common norms.

Berk recognizes that crowds will differ in the mix of anticipated rewards and costs, in the average gap between rewards and costs for various outcomes as well as in the average probability of supportive behaviour (heterogeneity). They will also differ in the speed with which crowd activities begin: some mill for prolonged periods of time, some initiate actions almost immediately. There will also be differences in which group activities are selected: There are processes through which interactions between crowd members alter expected outcomes and 'agitators' may play a role in this respect.

Unless crowd members arrive at mutually beneficial solutions to their payoff matrices and create common awareness of these solutions, crowd behaviour will not occur. Essential in the gaming approach is the realization that each person's payoff depends fundamentally on the actions of others on the scene. Berk emphasizes that there is nothing fundamentally different about cognitive processes in crowds from those in other circumstances. Crowd members typically must get together and implement goal-directed action on their first and only meeting in circumstances that pose unusual opportunities and constraints: there is incomplete and unreliable information, communication is difficult, prior agreements on what constitutes a decision are rare, and there is time pressure. For authorities and law enforcement, it will be important to take these realities into account in their considerations in communicating with participants, such as through 'dialogue policing'.[51]

Berk sees the gaming perspective as filling important gaps in emergent norm theory. The physical environment and motives of individual crowd members are irrelevant in emergent norm theory, the theoretical emphasis is not on why a particular norm is originally considered. In Berk's view, both perspectives imply different (probably complementary) psychological mechanisms. On the one hand, conscious calculus in which the best anticipated outcomes are selected where concerted action arises because of apparent mutual benefit versus an unconscious tendency to accede to group norms. Concerted action in emergent norm theory involves a kind of self-fulfilling prophesy in which norms shape behaviour because they reflect underlying shared understandings, which are in turn further supported by behavioural conformity.

However, both McPhail and Reicher criticize these rational actor approaches.[52] According to McPhail the minimax principle is only one set of instructions, limited and insufficient in complex situations. Rational actor approaches do not establish problems, formulate solutions, or tell what the behaviour should be, or when, where, how, by, or with whom it will happen. Support may be observable but is not enough of an explanation. McPhail also points to the '*free rider problem*' which renders individual participation in collective action illogical.[53] Nonetheless, McPhail presents an orienting set of assumptions about how individual actors in temporary gatherings make decisions about how to act, conceiving them (in contrast to earlier formulations of crowd mind or emergent norms) as being responsive to short-term purposive calculations about what to do next in such public settings.[54]

Reicher criticizes game theoretical approaches as individualistic: benefits for collective units are not considered as is the possibility that social values and norms might determine utilities, or that the values and norms on which people act, and hence what counts as a utility, might change in collective contexts. According to Reicher, any model that links behaviour to fixed individual tendencies must suppose a commonality of tendencies amongst crowd members and must deny the social character of crowd action.[55]

Turner provides an overall and insightful overview of the use and misuse of rational models in collective behaviour (and social psychology more generally).[56] He usefully identifies arationality (rather than irrationality) as another alternative to rationality. Distinct from Reicher, Turner recognizes that there is no reason individuals cannot pursue altruistic goals in a thoroughly rational manner. Suffice it to say here that the notion that participants in an assembly are not acting irrationally and that implicit cost/benefits calculations (both individually and collectively) play a role in their behaviour should be relevant in any law enforcement decisions.

Assuming that participants in an assembly are irrational leads to the use of more repressive police tactics that emphasize escalated force rather than negotiated management of assemblies.[57]

Fundamentally, people make individual decisions and do not behave uniformly. There are alternative courses of action in collective settings and people do in fact make different choices from others around them. This does not change the fact that individuals are fundamentally social beings and that their decisions are influenced by their social environment. As McPhail indicates, there is constant change from individual to collective behaviour and the crowd as a whole is too crude and cumbersome a unit of analysis.[58] In addition, crowds are not homogeneous, but heterogeneous in their composition, composed as they are of many different subgroups (e.g. groups of friends) and individuals with diverse backgrounds, motivations, and goals. In all types of assemblies, the relevance of the immediate context (both the physical context as well as the social context) and the interactive 'action-reaction' nature of these processes is obvious.

Applications for Understanding Violence in Assemblies

As discussed above, from a crowd-management perspective, it is important to understand these dynamics of decision-making in crowd settings to prevent (escalation of) violence in collective settings. It is crucial to distinguish between the initiation and escalation of violence and to differentiate between those actively seeking violence and others.

Who Actively Seeks Violence?

As already emphasized, the vast majority of people in observed cases of collective violence (even in serious riots) were not violent at all.[59] There are reasons to believe that many of those who actively seek violence in collective settings are also more likely to use violence in other situations.[60] There are a number of approaches, following Allport, that explain collective action in terms of pre-existing individual tendencies. The most obvious would be the expectation that crowd members who take part in violent action or action against the social order might have violent or antisocial personalities—or, at the very least, to be under-socialized or marginal to society. Some researchers, for instance, attribute collective disorder to the convergence of individuals with certain personality traits or dispositions (e.g. abnormal arousal needs which are satisfied through violent activities[61]) while others focus upon the sociological determinants of class-based macro social structures.[62]

In an approach to assemblies based on these theories, there is no need to take participants or their grievances seriously: collective violence is the result of people with criminal intentions, riff-raff, converging. But both McPhail and Reicher have identified several problems with such an approach, the main one being that, so far, no individual attributes have been discovered which reliably predict riot.[63]

On the contrary, even in violent collective situations, people clearly make choices and behave in ways that make sense to themselves. The choices people make seem consistent with the model of (bounded) rationality: they prepare, pursue goals, and clearly consider risks. There is observable variation in the readiness to participate in violence between individuals. In general, the riskier the behaviour (in terms of retaliation or arrest), the lower the number of individuals who participate. Clearly cognition plays a role in the choices people make, and, in addition, it may be useful to acknowledge that sometimes these choices are 'arational', outside the domain of reason, but not irrational.[64]

There is every reason to believe that people's behaviour in collective settings is influenced by the same factors that influence their 'normal' everyday behaviour. Rather than behaving without norms, the data suggest that even in violent situations, certain norms are considered, as shown by restrained behaviour (all-out violence is exceedingly rare), choice of targets that is not random, and examples of self-control. Moreover, violent individuals often adhere to certain rules, the most important being to stick together and support each other during confrontations. In this respect, the results are consistent with findings that convincingly show that (perceived) norms become more rather than less important in collective situations,[65] although the nature of the norms may vary. Crowd behaviour can only meaningfully be understood in the social context in which it occurs as an intergroup process.

Distinguishing How Violence Starts from the Way It Escalates

Collective violence generally starts (or is initiated) in one of two different ways: either as a reaction to a clearly identifiable trigger or as the (often unprovoked) initiative taken by a group of young men.[66] In the 1990 Trafalgar Square poll tax demonstration and riot in London, it was observed that where the early part of the demonstration was overwhelmingly non-violent and good-humoured, the mood changed and violence erupted after the police deployed in the crowd began to push demonstrators.[67] By contrast, the 2009 'beach riot' at a festival in Hoek van Holland, the Netherlands, started as the result of a group of young men collectively and actively starting confrontations, first with fellow party goers and, after that, with (retreating) police.[68] Without resorting to simplistic convergence theories, predispositions and intentions of a part of individuals in an assembly cannot wholly be discarded in explaining (the initiation of) certain instances of collective violence.

The *reactive* violence may be a response to specific frictions in an assembly, be they provocations by opposing groups or third parties, measures taken by police, or some other identifiable trigger. To be sure, not every potential trigger or precipitating event (e.g. an arrest or other police action) is invariably followed by collective violence. Theoretically, this type of violence is easily linked to familiar aggression theories (such as aggression out of frustration, competition for limited resources or as a response to threats). As with other forms of aggression, men are more likely to react aggressively than women, and adolescents or young adults (those ages fifteen to twenty-five) are more likely to react aggressively than individuals from other age groups. Nonetheless, men from other age groups and women may also occasionally react aggressively to certain triggers. The targets of the violence may vary, but they are usually linked with the trigger preceding the behaviour.

However, different mechanisms are responsible for the *escalation* of violence, that is, where more people participate and the violence lasts for a longer time. On the one hand, there is the (perceived) risk of retaliation. Violent individuals regularly take measures to hide their faces to make recognition more difficult and to avoid identification and arrest. In repressive societies, peaceful individuals may wish to hide their faces to avoid being targeted by authorities. These risk-reducing attempts to maintain 'anonymity' are to be distinguished from the so-called de-individuation effect of 'anonymity'.

Bounded rationality and the relevance of *opportunities* to be violent indicate that violence is the result of an interaction between disposition and situation, a basic principle of situational crime prevention.[69] The second important escalation mechanism, is the existence of an 'us versus them' antagonism. The more antagonistic the relationships between different groups, the higher the frequency of observed violence. Collectively applied coercive police measures were often associated with an *escalation* of violence. The collective nature of these measures can exacerbate, or may even create, an 'us vs them' perspective that can lead to more explicit ingroup/outgroup behaviour.

Theoretically, ESIM is relevant here.[70] The defining dimensions of this identity serve to explain the normative limits of collective action (what people do) and the extent of participation (who does and does not join in) during a crowd event. The 'social identity' analysis argues that the dynamics of intergroup interaction are integral to the psychology of widespread 'disorder'. Although collective violence was not *characteristically* triggered by police action, Stott and Reicher indicate that when an initially heterogeneous crowd has come to be treated as a homogeneous whole by the police, this has led crowd members to reconceptualize themselves as members of a common category, thus setting up a cycle of tension and escalating conflict.[71] Policing assemblies as if they present a homogeneous threat may thus create a self-fulfilling prophecy.

Conclusion and Implications for the Policing of Assemblies

It is clear that 'group mind' and individualist theories are deeply ideological in their implications, and that contagion and de-individuation approaches suffer from the same flaws discussed above: They treat human beings in crowds as irrational and lacking agency.

Each assembly and each instance of collective violence represents a unique intergroup context. In terms of the initiation/escalation model, there is a unique and dynamic mix of different (sub)groups with different social identities and with the presence or absence of young men with different inclinations and social backgrounds in situations with (potential) tensions and opportunities. What happens in assemblies, either spontaneously or as a response to specific triggers, is the result of an often implicit decision-making process, where decision-making describes situations in which individuals or groups of individuals can adopt one of two or more alternative behaviours.[72]

Escalation of collective violence is a kind of collective decision-making in a specific social setting: an intergroup context where most individuals do not know each other. This leads to several interesting but as yet unanswered questions: How does individual decision-making take place within the collective decision-making process? What factors influence the decision-making process (e.g. individual variations, emotions, 'situational breakdowns', previous events, intergroup interactions, relations between individuals, relations with other groups, physical context)?

However, it is clear that this decision-making process is not inherently irrational. Old-fashioned ideas, including the idea of group-mind, pathology of crowds or crowd members, mobs and the role of contagion and suggestibility, do not reflect and represent what is known about the behaviour of people in crowds and assemblies.

These theoretical misadventures do nothing to advance our understanding of the collective decision-making process going on in crowds, with important consequences for the policing of assemblies. Policing that is explicitly or (usually) implicitly based on outdated or falsified theories or assumptions leads to assemblies being seen as risky and crowds as inherently dangerous: The focus is on the potential for disorder and criminal activity. This in fact makes collective violence more rather than less likely.

The more psychological distance there is between authorities, including law enforcement, on the one hand and crowd members (often reflected in a physical distance as well), the more the focus will be on restrictive and repressive measures. In these circumstances there is little or no differentiation between different participants and (sub)groups within an assembly that is seen and treated as a homogeneous entity. Deployment of law enforcement units is often high profile with show of force. The emphasis is on (reactive) riot control performed by law enforcement.

A policing approach that takes account of the reality of the fact that the vast majority of assemblies and the vast majority of participants in assemblies are peaceful, takes *order* (rather than disorder) as a starting point. This is also more in line with legal requirements to facilitate peaceful assemblies. Rather than riot control, authorities and law enforcement involve themselves in *public order management*, defined as the systematic planning for and supervision of assemblies and events in the public domain (irrespective of the number of people gathering) where safety or security issues could arise.[73] The emphasis is on interaction and communication between all relevant parties, including organizers and participants. Deployment of law enforcement is low profile. Interventions are targeted and differentiated, focused on individuals (or subgroups) that transgress clearly defined and communicated boundaries, timely, friendly, and firm.

Combining the insights from the systematic observations dealt with above and those from ESIM led to the formulation of four strategic principles for public order (or crowd) management: be informed, facilitate legitimate intentions, communicate and differentiate (based on behaviour, not group membership).[74]

Be informed: Since groups act on the basis of social identities, and gatherings of people typically consist of multiple groups, it is of great practical importance to be informed (and educated) about the respective social identities, including their values and norms, their goals and intentions, their understanding of what is right and appropriate, their prejudices and expectations of other groups, the history of interaction with these groups, and anything (dates, places, objects, forms of action) that has particular symbolic meaning. Information should focus not only on the plans of individuals with a known history of violence (the typical goal of police intelligence), but also on understanding the social identities of the groups that will gather to understand what their goals are, whether and how to support them, what actions would challenge them and make them sympathize with violent individuals in the crowd. The same efforts made to identify potentially violent individuals should be made to understand group identity, and both factors should be given similar priority in briefings.

Facilitate: Rather than preventing people from doing what they want to do and thereby frustrating them, the emphasis should be on support at all stages of the operation: Planning must identify the legitimate goals of the crowd (such as safely attending an event, protesting, expressing opinions or emotions) in order to consider how best to design interventions to help achieve those goals. If potential or actual risks force the police to set limits on the crowd, it is especially important to make this clear. At the same time, alternative ways should be proposed, showing how legitimate goals can still be achieved. Especially when violence breaks out, a clear indication that the police facilitate collective goals and that violence threatens them can make the difference between escalation and de-escalation.

Communicate: One of the contradictions in public order management is that it is increasingly important to communicate with the crowd if you want to avoid a potentially conflictual situation, but that it is in these circumstances that the crowd is least likely to trust what security officials say. Especially if there is a long history of conflict, even attempting to explain facilitating measures can be perceived as dishonest and increase hostility. Therefore, how communication is done is also important. For example, instead of relying solely on police communication teams, one could also use individuals who are trusted and respected by groups within the crowd—preferably as 'one of us'. It is indicative of the balance between repressive and mediating strategies that there are large reserves of armoured vehicles, batons, and so forth that are rarely used, while far less attention is paid to communications technologies. Large screens, mobile communication systems, and social media communications could be more useful than water cannons at many mass events.

Differentiate: It is important to be aware of the different identities of the gathered groups and their different ways of acting and reacting. It is even more important to act on this awareness and not treat all members of a crowd the same. Interventions should be made based on what people actually do rather than on the category to which they (supposedly) belong. It is precisely when some people in the crowd begin to act in a hostile manner that it is important to treat the people in the crowd in a friendly manner. To stop the violence of the few, one has to be lenient towards the many. This is difficult because people tend to view other groups as homogeneous, so if some among them behave negatively, all will be viewed negatively. Differentiation is a consideration that should be incorporated into every tactical or strategic decision, training, planning, equipping, and crowd deployment.

These principles—drawing as they do upon more recent and empirically grounded understandings of collective behaviour—are increasingly being accepted by authorities and law enforcement organizations in different countries as the basis for the policing of assemblies.[75]

Acknowledgement

I am grateful to Nanda Wijermans for stimulating discussions on early drafts of this chapter.

Notes

1. See Shany, in this volume.
2. Gustave Le Bon, *The Crowd: A Study of the Popular Mind* [1895] (Dunwoody, GA: Norman S. Berg, Repr. 1968). See also Tom Postmes and Russel Spears, 'Deindividuation and Antinormative Behavior: A Meta-analysis', *Psychological Bulletin* 123, no. 3 (1998): 238–259. Their review did not show empirical support for the hypothesis that increased group size leads to more anti-normative behaviour.
3. Clifford Stott and Stephen D. Reicher, 'Crowd Action as Intergroup Process: Introducing the Police Perspective', *European Journal of Social Psychology* 26 (1998): 509–529; Clifford Stott and Stephen D. Reicher, 'How Conflict Escalates: The Inter-Group Dynamics of Collective Football Crowd "Violence"', *Sociology* 32 (1998): 353–377.
4. Stephen Reicher, 'The St Pauls Riot: An Explanation of the Limits of Crowd Action in Terms of a Social Identity Model', *European Journal of Social Psychology* 14 (1984): 1–21; Stephen Reicher, 'The Psychology of Crowd Dynamics', in *Blackwell Handbook of Social Psychology: Group Processes*, ed. Michael Hogg and R. Scott Tindale (Oxford: Blackwell, 2001), 182–208.
5. Ralph Turner and Lewis Killian, *Collective Behavior* (Englewood Cliffs, NJ: Prentice-Hall, 1957).
6. Robert Berk, 'A Gaming Approach to Crowd Behaviour', *American Sociological Review* 39 (1974): 355–373.
7. Anne Nassauer, *Situational Breakdowns: Understanding Protest Violence and Other Surprising Outcomes* (Oxford: Oxford University Press, 2019).
8. John Drury, 'Crowd Psychology', in *Encyclopedia of Critical Psychology*, ed. Thomas Teo (New York: Springer, 2014), 341–344.
9. Stephen Reicher and John Drury, 'Collective Identity, Political Participation and the Making of the Social Self', in *Identity and Participation in Culturally Diverse Societies: A Multidisciplinary Perspective*, ed. Assaad E. Azzi, Xenia Chryssochoou, and Bert Klandermans (Oxford: Wiley-Blackwell, 2010), 158–176. It should be understood that a crowd can be composed of different subgroups or psychological crowds.
10. See further the 'illusion of unanimity', in Turner and Killian, *Collective Behavior.*
11. Reicher, 'St Paul's Riot'.
12. Clark McPhail, *The Myth of the Madding Crowd* (New York: Aldine de Gruyter, 1991).
13. Some of these theories concern themselves with collective behaviour in general and have been applied to collective violence as well. Others have been developed specifically to explain the eruption and escalation of collective violence.

14. Berk, 'Gaming Approach', 365. To avoid circular reasoning, for example, measures of anticipated rewards and costs must be made prior to an individual's action.
15. Ralph Turner, 'The Use and Misuse of Rational Models in Collective Behavior and Social Psychology', *European Journal of Sociology* 32, no. 1 (1991): 84–108.
16. Tom van Ham et al., 'Determinants of Persistence in Collective Violence Offending', *Deviant Behavior* 42, no. 1 (2021): 37–53.
17. Berk, 'Gaming Approach'; Robert Berk, 'The Controversy Surrounding Analyses of Collective Violence: Some Methodological Notes', in *Collective Violence*, ed. James Short and Marvin Wolfgang (Chicago: Aldine/Atherton, 1972), 112–118.
18. Otto Adang, 'A Method for Direct Systematic Observation of Collective Violence and Public Order Policing', *Sociological Methods and Research* 47, no. 4 (2018): 761–786.
19. McPhail, *Myth of the Madding Crowd.*
20. Otto Adang, *Hooligans, Autonomen, Agenten: Geweld en politie-optreden in relsituaties* (Alphen aan den Rijn: Samsom, 1998); Otto Adang, 'Initiation and Escalation of Collective Violence', in *Preventing Crowd Violence*, ed. Tamara Madensen and Johannes Knutsson (Boulder, CO: Lynne Rienner, 2011), 47–68.
21. Adang, 'Method for Direct Systematic Observation'. The participant observation studies suffer from a lack of transparency of the methods and definitions used. They also tend to suffer from 'exampling': The practice whereby a researcher addresses a few examples but fails to explain how these examples represent a broader data set or why they were chosen.
22. See, for example, Nassauer, *Situational Breakdowns.*
23. See, for example, Marly van Bruchem et al., 'How Citizens Stop Riots: Analyzing the Case of the 2021 Dutch Curfew Riots', *Deviant Behavior* 44, no. 11 (2023): 1650–1663.
24. Drury, 'Crowd Psychology'.
25. Le Bon, *Crowd.*
26. Ed Diener et al., 'Deindividuation: Effects of Group Size, Density, Number of Observers, and Group Member Similarity on Self-Consciousness and Disinhibited Behavior', *Journal of Personality and Social Psychology* 39, no. 3 (1980): 449–459.
27. All de-individuation studies are experimental: they are based on tests set up by psychologists using (mostly) psychology students, but several explicitly state the relevance of de-individuation theory to crowd behaviour.
28. Stephen Reicher and Jonathan Potter, 'Psychological Theory as Intergroup Perspective: A Comparative Analysis of "Scientific" and "Lay" Accounts of Crowd Events', *Human Relations* 38 (1985): 167–189.
29. Reicher, 'St Paul's Riot'; Stephen Reicher, 'Crowd Behaviour as Social Action', in *Rediscovering the Social Group: A Self-Categorization Theory*, ed. John Turner et al. (Oxford: Blackwell, 1987), 176–178; Stephen Reicher, Russell Spears, and Tom Postmes, 'A Social Identity Model of Deindividuation Phenomena', *European Review of Social Psychology* 6 (1995): 161–198; Russell Spears and Martin Lea, 'Social Influence and the Influence of the "Social" in Computer-Mediated Communication', in *Contexts of Computer-Mediated Communication*, ed. Martin Lea (Hemel Hempstead, UK: Harvester Wheatsheaf, 1992), 30–65; Russell Spears and Martin Lea, 'Panacea or Panopticon? The Hidden Power in Computer-Mediated Communication', *Communication Research* 21 (1994): 427–459.
30. Stephen Reicher, 'The St Pauls Riot: An Explanation of the Limits of Crowd Action in Terms of a Social Identity Model', *European Journal of Social Psychology* 14 (1984): 1–21; Reicher, 'Crowd Behaviour as Social Action'.

31. Reicher, 'Crowd Behaviour as Social Action'. Of course, what is normative to the crowd might contradict what is normative outside the crowd. To an outsider, then, crowd behaviour might seem mindless, anti-normative, and disinhibited; to the crowd, however, it is rational and normative and has its limits.
32. Ibid. Reicher's first formulation of ESIM relied on retrospective accounts to infer the beliefs, perceptions, and categorizations of crowd members. Since then, several authors in the ESIM school have carried out participant observational studies on assemblies, especially protest and football events. See Adang, 'Method for Direct Systematic Observation'.
33. Reicher and Potter, 'Psychological Theory as Intergroup Perspective'.
34. Drury, 'Crowd Psychology'.
35. John Drury and Steve Reicher, 'Collective Action and Psychological Change: The Emergence of New Social Identities', *British Journal of Social Psychology* 39 (2000): 579–604; Stephen Reicher, 'Social Identity and Social Change: Rethinking the Context of Social Psychology', in *Social Groups and Identities: Developing the Legacy of Henri Tajfel*, ed. William P. Robinson (London: Butterworth, 1996), 317–336; Clifford Stott and Stephen D. Reicher, 'How Conflict Escalates: The Inter-Group Dynamics of Collective Football Crowd "Violence"', *Sociology* 32 (1998): 353–377.
36. Drury, 'Crowd Psychology'.
37. See, contrastingly, Stott and Reicher, 'Crowd Action as Intergroup Process', 509f and Adang, 'Initiation and Escalation of Collective Violence'.
38. Clifford Stott and Otto Adang, *Policing Football Matches with an International Dimension in the European Union: Understanding and Managing Risk* (Kopenhagen: Bavnebanke Press, 2009); Clifford Stott et al., 'Variability in the Collective Behaviour of England Fans at Euro 2004: Intergroup Relations, Identity Content and Social Change', *European Journal of Social Psychology* 37, no. 1 (2007): 75–100; Clifford Stott et al., 'Tackling Football Hooliganism: A Quantitative Study of Public Order, Policing and Crowd Psychology', *Psychology, Public Policy, and Law* 14, no. 2 (2008): 115–141; Martina Schreiber and Otto Adang, 'Fiction, Facts and a Summer's Fairy Tale—Mixed Messages at the World Cup 2006', *Policing and Society* 20, no. 2 (2010): 237–255.
39. Floyd Allport, *Social Psychology* (Boston: Houghton Mifflin, 1924), 295.
40. Ibid.
41. Turner and Killian, *Collective Behavior*.
42. Ibid., 26.
43. Reicher, 'Psychology of Crowd Dynamics', 304.
44. Donatella della Porta and Herbert Reiter, 'The Policing of Protest in Contemporary Democracies: An Introduction', in *Policing Protest*, ed. Donatella della Porta and Herbert Reiter (Minneapolis: University of Minnesota Press, 1998), 1–32.
45. McPhail, *Myth of the Madding Crowd*, 100.
46. Ibid.
47. Le Bon, *Crowd*.
48. The notion of contagion (but devoid of suggestibility or irrationality) returns in more recent theories on 'diffusion dynamics', with regard to a wide variety of phenomena that include the coordination of collective action. Damon Centola and Michael Macy, 'Complex Contagions and the Weakness of Long Ties', *American Journal of Sociology* 113, no. 3 (2007): 702–734.
49. See Zhelnina and Jasper, in this volume.
50. Berk, 'Gaming Approach'.

51. Stephan Holgersson and Johannes Knutsson, 'Dialogue Policing: A Means for Less Crowd Violence?', in *Preventing Crowd Violence*, ed. Tamara Madensen and Johannes Knutsson (Boulder, CO: Lynne Rienner, 2011), 191–215.
52. McPhail, *Myth of the Madding Crowd*, 121–126; Reicher, 'Psychology of Crowd Dynamics'.
53. Clark McPhail, 'The Dark Side of Purpose: Individual and collective Violence in Riots', *Sociological Quarterly* 35, no. 1 (1994): 1–32. The free rider problem derives from economics and refers to a situation where people enjoy a shared resource without contributing to it.
54. McPhail, *Myth of the Madding Crowd*.
55. Reicher, 'Psychology of Crowd Dynamics'. As Reicher rightly notes, rational actor or game theoretical approaches to crowd behaviour have generated little research. Having said that, Reicher does not discuss the advances made by Mark Granovetter, 'Threshold Models of Collective Behavior', *American Journal of Sociology* 83 (1978): 1420–1443, or Michael Macy, 'Chains of Cooperation: Threshold Effects in Collective Action', *American Sociological Review* 56 (1991): 730–747. More recently, especially regarding social tipping points, see Marc Wiedermann et al., 'A Network-Based Microfoundation of Granovetter's Threshold Model for Social Tipping', *Scientific Reports* 10 (2020): 11202.
56. Turner, 'Use and Misuse of Rational Models'.
57. David Schweingruber, 'Mob Sociology and Escalated Force: Sociology's Contribution to Repressive Police Tactics', *Sociological Quarterly* 41, no. 3 (2000): 371–389.
58. McPhail, *Myth of the Madding Crowd*.
59. Adang, *Hooligans, Autonomen, Agenten*; Adang, 'Initiation and Escalation'.
60. Van Ham et al., 'Determinants of Persistence.
61. John H. Kerr and Hilde De Kock, 'Aggression, Violence and the Death of a Dutch Soccer Hooligan: A Reversal Theory Explanation', *Aggressive Behavior* 28 (2002): 1–10.
62. Eric Dunning, Patrick Murphy, and John Williams, *The Roots of Football Hooliganism: An Historical and Sociological Study* (London: Routledge, 1988).
63. Clark McPhail, 'Civil Disorder Participation: A Critical Examination of Recent Research', *American Sociological Review* 36 (1971): 1058–1073; Turner and Killian, *Collective Behavior*; Rodney Stark, *Police Riots: Collective Violence and Law Enforcement* (Belmont, CA: Wadsworth, 1972).
64. See McPhail, *Myth of the Madding Crowd*.
65. Turner and Killian, *Collective Behavior*; Reicher, 'St Paul's Riot'; Stephen Reicher, '"The Battle of Westminster": Developing the Social Identity Model of Crowd Behaviour in Order to Explain the Initiation and Development of Collective Conflict', *European Journal of Social Psychology* 6 (1996): 115–134.
66. Adang, 'Initiation and Escalation of Collective Violence'.
67. Clifford Stott and John Drury, 'Crowds, Context and Identity: Dynamic Categorization Processes in the "Poll Tax Riot"', *Human Relations* 53, no. 2 (2000): 247–273.
68. Otto Adang and Tom van Ham, 'Contextual and Individual Factors Determining Escalation of Collective Violence: Case Study of the Project X Riot in Haren, the Netherlands', *British Journal of Criminology* 55, no. 6 (2015): 1226–1244. The same pattern may be observable in the case of the January 6 riot at the US Capitol. See https://www.nytimes.com/2022/07/12/us/politics/proud-boys-jan-6.html.
69. Situational crime prevention focuses on the settings for criminal acts rather than on the characteristics of offenders, see R. V. G. Clarke, 'Situational Crime Prevention', in *Building a Safer Society: Strategic Approaches to Crime Prevention*, ed. Michael Tonry and David P. Farrington (Chicago: University of Chicago Press, 1995), 91–150.

70. Reicher, 'St Paul's Riot'; Reicher, '"Battle of Westminster"'.
71. Stott and Reicher, 'Crowd Action as Intergroup Process'.
72. Andrew King and Cédric Sueur, 'Where Next? Group Coordination and Collective Decision Making by Primates', *International Journal of Primatology* 32 (2011): 1245–1267.
73. Public order management is not just the responsibility of law enforcement, but of all relevant parties (such as local authorities and health services) and is aimed at facilitating legitimate intentions.
74. Stephen Reicher et al., 'An Integrated Approach to Crowd Psychology and Public Order Policing', *Policing: An International Journal of Police Strategies and Management* 27 (2004): 558–572; Stephen Reicher et al., 'Knowledge-Based Public Order Policing: Principles and Practice', *Policing* 1, no. 4 (2007): 403–415.
75. For example, in the United States: Edward Maguire, 'New Directions in Protest Policing', *Saint Louis University Public Law Review* 35, no. 1 (2015); E. R. Maguire and M. Oakley, *Policing Protests: Lessons from the Occupy Movement, Ferguson and Beyond: A Guide for Police* (New York: Harry Frank Guggenheim Foundation, 2020). In the UK, HMIC *Adapting to Protest—Nurturing the British Model of Policing* (2009), https://assets-hmicfrs.justiceinspectorates.gov.uk/uploads/adapting-to-protest-nurturing-the-british-model-of-policing-20091125.pdf. In Sweden, Rikspolisstyrelsen, *Godiac Recommendations for Policing Political Manifestations in Europe* (2013), https://www.recercat.cat/bitstream/handle/2072/220959/GODIAC_BOOKLET_2013_2.pdf.

Further Reading

Adang, Otto. 'A Method for Direct Systematic Observation of Collective Violence and Public Order Policing'. *Sociological Methods and Research* 47, no. 4 (2018): 761–786.

Bürger, Bernd, Tamara D. Herold, and Ryan Lee, eds. *Public Order Policing. A Professional's Guide to International Theories, Case Studies, and Best Practices*. London: Springer Nature, 2023.

Human Rights Handbook on Policing Assemblies. Organization for Security and Co-operation in Europe, 2016. https://www.osce.org/odihr/226981.

Madensen, Tamara D., and John Knutsson, eds. *Preventing Crowd Violence*. Boulder, CO: Lynne Rienner, 2011.

Nassauer, Anne. *Situational Breakdowns: Understanding Protest Violence and Other Surprising Outcomes*. Oxford: Oxford University Press, 2019.

CHAPTER 35

THE ROLE OF THE POLICE AROUND PUBLIC ASSEMBLIES

THOMAS PROBERT

Introduction

As street-level bureaucrats charged with some of the state's most coercive powers, the police often offer a stark insight into the relationships at the heart of the modern state.[1] Unlike a great deal of their other work, policing of assemblies often takes place in the centre of the public's attention. This can make the policing of assemblies particularly important (from the police's point of view) as it is when their performance seems under heightened public scrutiny, and it offers the opportunity for constructive engagement to build legitimacy and trust.

This said, it is worth noting that the policing of assemblies can receive too great an emphasis. It can sometimes be profoundly unrepresentative of broader policing practices. When considering, for example, the number of (lethal) use of force incidents in a jurisdiction, usually only a small proportion will have occurred in the context of public order management, and yet most discussion of 'police brutality' may focus on the often very well-documented examples of abuse occurring in the context of a high-profile public assembly.

Likewise, from a broader human rights perspective, focusing on policing practices during an assembly can often mean overlooking more systemic limitations upon civic space imposed by other state actors. The police act as street-level enforcers of a broader architecture of regulation from which they are sometimes insufficiently distinguished.

How might an analytical review of police practices in relation to assembly be undertaken? One approach, taken in much of the literature, is to adopt a generational model based on evolutions in police tactics. Broadly, as applied to various American police departments, this charts evolutions from the 1960s, where authorities responded to civil rights and other protests with an approach of *escalated force*, using unprovoked arrests and violence to curb assemblies, to an approach of trying to make assemblies more predictable and routine, from the 1970s onwards, via *negotiated management*.[2] The limitations of this routinization were exposed most prolifically during the protests organized around the meeting of the World Trade Organization (WTO) in Seattle in 1999. In the aftermath of those events, and accelerated by the securitization that followed the terrorist attacks of 9/11, police rapidly developed and adopted a new strategy: *strategic incapacitation*, distinguishing between contained ('good') protesters and transgressive ('bad') ones.[3] Sometimes alternatively styled as a *command and control* approach, this involved a variety of tactics, helpfully grouped by Alex Vitale as an aversion to disruption, controlled access, divide and conquer, shock and awe, and zero tolerance.[4] It seems that since the abject failure of these techniques (long criticized by advocacy groups) during the protests of 2020, some police departments have begun to move away from them, back towards the more rights-oriented ('enhanced') negotiated management.[5]

Layered on top of such generational models, usually as a means of comparing them, a number of parameters of 'public order management' (itself a revealing phrase) can be applied. Clark McPhail et al. use five dimensions of policing to define certain of these different approaches: the speech/assembly rights, toleration of disruption, communication, use of arrests, and use of force.[6] John Noakes and Patrick Gillham, analysing the later approach of strategic incapacitation, added surveillance, information sharing, and control of space.[7]

Compared to the generational approach used to analyse US policing, a binary approach, one more frequently applied in globally comparative analyses, is to distinguish between 'democratic policing' and 'regime policing'.[8] The essence of this distinction is the level of agency enjoyed by the police as an institution, which filters down to the level of discretion exercised by individual officers. The distinction can be overly reductive (see Liu, in this volume), but clearly the principles of democratic policing (including, importantly, the nexus between discretion and judicial oversight) will generally be more conducive to the enjoyment of the right of peaceful assembly.[9]

One of the philosophies underlying 'democratic policing' is procedural justice theory. As Clifford Stott and others have summarized,

> [T]he primary pathway by which officers construct legitimacy and compliance is through 'procedural fairness' achieved by enacting four 'rules' in their interactions with members of the public. These are: (1) that police officers should treat people with dignity and respect; (2) that the police should be transparent in their decision-making; (3) that officers should provide citizens the opportunity for voice ('to tell their side of the story'); and (4) that the police should demonstrate that they are acting benevolently and their motives are 'trustworthy'.[10]

For example, the '4Es approach', developed by the UK College of Policing around COVID-19 regulations, suggested that officers first *Engage* in conversation before *Explaining* the guidance. If that dialogue did not work the next stage is to *Encourage* people to comply, and only as a final resort move to *Enforce* through issuing fines, making arrests, or using force.[11] 'Regime policing', by contrast, cannot accommodate such flexibility or discretion, since the police will be organized in such a way as at all times to serve the direction of the executive.

Many of these totalizing theories about the policing of assembly fall into the trap of eliding the distinction between the regime and the police while simultaneously embedding the assumption that it is the police's inherent responsibility to 'respond' to assemblies. In the democratic policing model, to be sure, the assumption is that the primary entity that needs to be 'responding to' the articulated demands of an assembly is the political authority.[12] The police should merely be on hand (in certain circumstances) to ensure that those wanting to engage in violence or other criminal conduct do not compromise the ability of the wider group to assemble peacefully.

There are certain contexts in which the proposition that the police need only be on hand rather than actively intervening seems wholly uncontroversial. In discussions about approaches to policing assembly, I have sometimes presented this as the question of '*why should the police treat a political assembly any differently to the way they treat a football match?*' This is another way of framing an assertion of the importance of content neutrality—in theory it should not matter what the motivation of the gathering.

In reality, of course, political protests can be a good deal less predictable than pre-organized weekly football matches, requiring more flexibility and, hence, more preparation on the part of the police. Moreover, whereas limiting the inconvenience caused by an influx of tens of thousands of people to a particular venue is an agreed objective around, for example, a Premier League match, it can sometimes legitimately be the intention of a far smaller group of people actually to cause disruption in order to make a point.

It is therefore likely that the policing of certain assemblies—howsoever well-guided by principle and well-implemented those principles might be in practice—will prove deeply controversial. The expectations of procedural fairness cannot ultimately change the fundamentally coercive nature of police power.[13]

When considering policing practices globally, whether descriptively or normatively, it seems reductive to try to use one of the totalizing theories introduced above. Moreover, the idea of a prescriptive theory—capable of applying to any and all assemblies—runs contrary to the normative impulse that each assembly should be policed only to the extent necessary. As the Human Rights Committee's General Comment makes clear, *any* policing of an assembly is a limitation upon the enjoyment of the right, albeit sometimes a necessary one.

It is even less helpful to be overly focused on these theories once we recognize that, in practice, the police have a playbook, with different tactics called upon at different times depending on the circumstances. While the improvisational implication should not be taken too far (given the expectation, discussed in the next section, that the public should have 'no surprises' with respect to policing response), this play-by-play approach speaks to the street-level bureaucrat's exercise of explainable discretion, bounded under judicial and other forms of oversight.

In what follows, I shall avoid the array of grand theories of 'protest policing' and instead review the challenges confronting police departments as they endeavour to apply a human rights-based approach during three phases of an assembly: (1) before it takes place, when their role is to mediate the practical challenges the organizers want to overcome (or create) so that in the overwhelming majority of cases an assembly goes ahead (the presumption of facilitation); then (2) during the assembly itself when the police's role is to prevent a number of quite narrowly defined spoilers of the assembly (e.g. participants misbehaving, counter-protesters) and to maintain any restrictions that have been imposed upon the gathering; and (3) the specific set of decisions around ending an assembly, usually by dispersing it, either because it becomes violent or when a proportionality assessment of other relevant interests suggests it should come to a close.

It is important to state at the outset that what follows is a form of normative pragmatism: it does not describe the lived experience of policing in many parts of the world but, drawing upon the most recent comprehensive normative instrument (the General Comment) as well as one of its most influential forerunners (the Joint Report by two UN Special Rapporteurs, Maina Kiai and Christof Heyns), it shows how a balance might be struck, and, critically, how straightforwardly ultra vires are many of excesses observed worldwide (and discussed, for example, by Casey-Maslen, Houska, and Pita Loor, in this volume). In doing so, it makes a case for an approach guided by the objective of facilitation, but understood as tactics aimed at enabling, rather than managing or choreographing, an assembly.

Role and Actions of the Police before an Assembly Takes Place

Notification is addressed elsewhere (see Hamilton, in this volume), but the most persuasive justification of a notification requirement as a sometimes-necessary interference with the right is that it allows the police to prepare for a gathering to be able to facilitate it to the greatest possible extent. That said, the police must also have contingency plans in place to be able to respond effectively to certain assemblies about which they have not received notification.

Facilitation

There is a clear risk, where notification requirements are onerous and overly bureaucratic, that they exert a chilling effect. Likewise, in circumstances where the police do not enjoy trust and legitimacy, especially among the community assembling, a requirement for even quite schematic engagement may aggravate a strained relationship. However, the process can create opportunities for constructive engagement and dialogue if those objectives are centred in a *voluntary* system's design and emphasized by the officials involved. The Human Rights Committee clearly encourages such engagement, noting that 'law enforcement agencies should as far as possible work towards establishing channels for communication and dialogue between the various parties involved in assemblies, before and during the assembly, aimed at promoting preparedness, de-escalating tensions and resolving disputes'.[14]

However, conscious of the community tensions and mistrust that might be implicated, the Committee also observed that 'while it is good practice for organizers and participants to engage in such contact, they cannot be required to do so'.[15] In this way their interpretation of facilitation was clearly one that must be voluntary and enabling, rather than an approach that is coercive and managerial.

It is especially important to bear in mind the priorities of 'sight and sound' when considering effective police facilitation (see Zick, in this volume). While a cardinal principle of policing assemblies should be 'content neutrality', it is important that this not be confused with an expectation that this amount to 'content blindness'. One way in which a notification regime can effectively 'deny' an assembly (and thus act as an authorization regime) is to raise practical policing concerns about the location or timing of a proposed gathering. The fact that policing an assembly would be easier if it took a different form is not in itself a valid reason to vitiate the expressive purpose of a gathering.

That being the case, it must be recognized that the policing arrangements of a public assembly can, in some instances, be complex and burdensome, but these are costs that must be incurred by the public purse.[16] There are limited exceptions, such as large-scale for-profit public gatherings, where it may be appropriate for the organizer, as the entity making a profit from the convening of such a large number of people, to contribute to the cost of the event's impact upon policing resources.[17] However, there is a very delicate balance to strike here, since the neutrality of the police can be compromised, or at the very least appear compromised, where a private party is footing the bill.[18]

Preparation and Training

On the use of force, Casey-Maslen (in this volume) emphasizes the cardinal importance of 'precaution' as a principle underlying police conduct. It is a basic expectation of policing both that authorities have insights into what is likely to happen and that they have in place contingencies for events that are nonetheless unanticipated. Beyond the implications for the use of force, the same principle applies to broader plans for crowd behaviour and 'management', as they can equally impact the right to life and broader public safety.[19] The failure to prepare adequately for the sheer physicality of tens of thousands of people, or preparations that are based upon faulty assumptions about crowd behaviour, have led to tragic outcomes, quite apart from the use-of-force scenario that perhaps most frequently comes to mind—crowd crushes have occurred at sporting events, music concerts, and religious pilgrimages.[20]

These stakes make the policing of assemblies a particular form of policing, and as a general rule, it should only be undertaken by specialist units (or at least only by officers who have received specific training).[21] For tactical decision-making and overall commander-level officers, a certain amount of theory will be essential; for on-the-ground officers, the most meaningful preparation will likely be physical scenario-based role play. It is also important to bear in mind the attitudinal priors that officers bring with them to an assembly. These can be difficult to address through conventional training and do speak to the significance of more holistic human rights sensitization training. Broader discriminatory attitudes may be exacerbated in the case of particular apprehensions about activist groups or enduring tropes about young troublemakers.[22] Respectful content neutrality is a learned skill.

As with all police training, it is important to learn lessons from prior conduct and operations. Casey-Maslen (in this volume) emphasizes the importance of accountability from the perspective of the protection of the right to life, but monitoring and reporting processes, along with comprehensive internal reviews of major operations, can play a formative role in designing training curricula.[23]

There is a certain reluctance to make details of police preparations for assembly public out of a concern that if tactics were publicized in advance, they might be less effective or susceptible to being 'gamed'. There is nonetheless a core content of police training (and—importantly—equipment) that should be subject to clear transparency requirements.[24] Recent normative developments have centred on the 'no surprises' mantra: that organizers and participants can expect predictability from law enforcement responses to an assembly. As conceived, this is a one-directional expectation of predictability; the police must have no similar expectation of organizers, regardless of whether there has been pre-assembly dialogue.[25]

On the subject of equipment, it is important to consider the impact of a highly lucrative marketplace for 'less-lethal' weapons and other police equipment. A significant impetus behind the process of the Office of the United Nations High Commissioner for Human Rights (OHCHR) to develop the UN Human Rights Guidance on Less-Lethal Weapons was to require states to implement a more rigorous process in the procurement of all equipment for law enforcement purposes.[26] Since then, it has further been proposed that a new arms control treaty be negotiated regulating the trade of such equipment.[27]

Police Intelligence and Assemblies

Surveillance will be discussed further in the next section (see also Aston, in this volume), but in addition to observing (and recording) events as they unfold on the ground, the precautionary principle expects a certain amount of foresight on the part of the police about potential risks emanating from an assembly.

The most controversial tactic in this regard has been the deployment of undercover police officers to infiltrate groups responsible for organizing protests. Recent public attention regarding this question in various countries has focused on the way in which certain undercover officers developed intimate relationships, sometimes as a means of infiltrating the group, and sometimes completely incidental to their cover. That public concern has rather overlooked the question of whether or not such an operation is justifiable in the first place.[28] The Special Rapporteurs' Joint Report recommended clear democratic systems of control for undercover policing that explicitly incorporate necessity and proportionality tests and clearly set out how risks of intrusion are to be assessed and managed. They contended that authorization by judicial authority should be required for any undercover policing activity in the context of an assembly.[29]

Of course, in many contexts today, it is perfectly feasible for the police to become aware of an upcoming assembly, especially large-scale ones, through 'open sources'. There should be safeguards, therefore, around how law enforcement agencies monitor social media, especially on sites that are not open-access, and also around what actions they take upon the basis of such monitoring.[30] Nonetheless, using social media as a source to prepare for non-notified assemblies seems consonant with the principle of precaution.

Influence Exercised Prior to an Assembly

In terms of powers the police can exercise before an assembly takes place, the most frequent is likely to be the informal influence to negotiate changes to the plans of the organizers. This can have quite a radical impact upon the assembly, and so ought to be undertaken with caution, and, in the words of the Human Rights Committee 'be guided by the objective of facilitating the right, rather than seeking unnecessary and disproportionate limitations on it'.[31]

The police also have the power to seek a legal injunction against the assembly as a whole, in certain circumstances, including when the negotiations are unsuccessful. They have broader powers to pursue individualized orders in relation to particular participants.[32] With respect to more individualized preventative orders, especially regarding political or other expressive assemblies, there ought to be an extremely high bar to any 'prior restraint' upon participation.[33] In other cases there may be variants of 'stay away' orders, sometimes formalized through a judicial proceeding, or otherwise as an administrative act capable of swift judicial review.[34]

In general, however, the overriding role of the police before an assembly is to understand the intent of the organizers (whether there is dialogue or otherwise), to anticipate potential flashpoints or risks of escalation, and to plan for them in such a way as to minimize their impact, with the minimal possible interference.

Police Tactics during an Ongoing Assembly

Once an assembly is actually taking place, the police have a number of choices to make about how they respond, starting with the question of whether they need to be there at all and, if so, how they present themselves to the public. Thereafter, there are questions about which specific tactics to use: interact with the participants and 'make their presence felt' or rather take a more hands-off role, potentially relying more upon surveillance? There is also a question about whether, even when present, the police ought deliberately to 'under-police' assemblies.

Attending and Making Their Presence Felt

One of the most significant but often overlooked decisions for the police concerning an assembly can be whether they need to attend at all.[35] Their presence may well be unnecessary and, in some cases, could be an escalatory factor. Given the potential 'optics' of having decided not to attend if something goes wrong, it is not an option to be taken lightly. But the potential negative consequences of attendance do favour allowing other actors to play their visible parts while being on hand behind the scenes to step in if needed. One means is to depute the role of direct interaction with a crowd to marshals while they observe from a greater distance or a secondary perimeter. The Human Rights Committee noted that '[i]t is good practice for organizers to appoint stewards or marshals where necessary, but this should not be a legal requirement'.[36] Moreover, it is important to note that the police cannot depute their responsibility for the maintenance of public order, which remains a state obligation.

In a more tactical sense, another means of gaining insight into what is taking place within a crowd and of exerting some kind of control without drawing attention to police action has been to deploy plainclothes officers. These should be distinguished from under-cover officers, though the Human Rights Committee is nonetheless wary of their use, saying that their deployment 'must be strictly necessary in the circumstances'.[37] The Human Rights Committee also notes some well-reasoned expectations for their conduct, namely, that 'before conducting a search, making an arrest or resorting to any use of force, plain-clothed officers must identify themselves to the persons concerned'.[38]

Of course, there will be circumstances in which a police presence needs to be directly visible. Even then there are a range of tactical options about how to present themselves, for example, whether or not front-line officers wear protective equipment. In certain circumstances, while the precautionary principle would dictate that the police have access to more escalated resources, it may be strategic to keep them out of sight.

There is an inherent tension at this point with respect to police equipment. Having the police wear 'riot gear' allows commanders to have a more tolerant attitude towards 'low-level' disturbance, including violent behaviour, such as stone-throwing, but it also potentially encourages such behaviour. There is also the risk of dehumanizing the officers involved in both directions: The risk of officers feeling invincible and hence unaccountable and the risk of the police being perceived as faceless automatons rather than fellow-citizens. More practically, heavy helmets make it hard for officers to hear what is being said and, hence, to communicate with participants and to de-escalate a situation. A balance between these imperatives can be sought through design—for example, the introduction of semi-transparent Perspex shields, through which the police can see participants' hands and also be seen themselves.

Surveillance

As the Human Rights Committee put it, '[t]he mere fact that a particular assembly takes place in public does not mean that participants' privacy cannot be violated'.[39] Police surveillance can exert a chilling effect upon participation. Nonetheless, there may be rare circumstances where it can help deter violence and other criminality and assist in subsequent investigations and prosecution of such offences if they do occur. Indeed, there is some evidence that high-quality surveillance can allow the police to hold back from making arrests for non-violent offences during an assembly, with the potential escalatory risk that might entail, and, instead, pursue offenders after the fact. Meanwhile, other types of surveillance (such as body-worn cameras) can contribute to greater accountability for police conduct at all stages of the assembly. Achieving these positive benefits without risking the chilling effect is a delicate balancing act that will be highly context-dependent.

The recording of crowds, by video or otherwise, is often left to dedicated evidence-gathering teams to document incidents of possible criminal conduct. Given the risks such surveillance poses to a number of human rights, it is important that such evidence gathering takes place well within public view—officers should be uniformed, and should be willing to discuss the purposes for which they are recording an assembly.[40] There should also be robust procedural safeguards around the access to and handling and retention of the resulting data.[41]

Concerns about the surveillance of assemblies are exacerbated by the prospect (indeed in certain jurisdictions, already by the reality) that the footage from such surveillance can, either in retrospect or in real time, be run through facial recognition technology (FRT).[42] Some have called for the use of FRT to be banned in the context of assembly (see Aston, in this volume). There are indeed a wide range of normative and practical concerns around the technology in general, but it is not clear that using such technology in the context of an assembly would be any *more* problematic than its lawful use in other public contexts.

Of course, the use of mere participation in an assembly as a ground for including an individual's record as a search query within an FRT (or any other) database should absolutely be banned. For example, the use of so-called IMSI catchers, which imitate a phone tower in order to identify the mobile phones of all individuals within range, serve no legitimate law enforcement function but rather capture a list of everyone who potentially attended an assembly, regardless of their conduct while present.

It is also worth noting that, in addition to the heightened use of video surveillance for crime detection, in certain jurisdictions, it has become common practice for all officers to be equipped with body-worn cameras to assist in police accountability procedures (amongst other uses). The same kind of safeguards need to exist in terms of the security and potential uses of the resulting footage, but as a general matter, the practice of equipping officers with such cameras seems likely to enhance compliance with good practice, and to assist subsequent investigations.[43] However, it is also important to consider that, given the nature of front-line policing in the context of assemblies, such footage may need to be supplemented with footage recorded from a greater distance to give a wider perspective of an operation.

Moreover, it is tempting in contexts where well-regulated surveillance is less common and body-worn cameras have not been widely introduced to prioritize the policing of assemblies as a sensitive and highly visible policing operation. This seems ill-advised, since introducing new technologies around an assembly is likely, howsoever motivated, to give rise to the suspicion of targeted use.[44]

Stop and Search

The Human Rights Committee applied a fairly high threshold to the use of 'stop and search' or 'stop and frisk' when applied to those who are participating in assemblies or are about to do so, suggesting that they 'must be exercised based on reasonable suspicion of the commission or threat of a serious offence, and must not be used in a discriminatory manner'.[45] Revealing their concern that stop and search can be used to discourage participation (in a 'strategic incapacitation' approach to policing assemblies), the Committee added that 'the mere fact that authorities associate an individual with a peaceful assembly does not constitute reasonable grounds for stopping and searching them'.[46]

It has become commonplace that *all* participants undergo a fairly cursory security inspection before entering many public gatherings. This has proved relatively uncontroversial with respect to ticketed events in privately controlled spaces, where private security usually undertakes this task. It is more difficult to justify this practice in public spaces when conducted by the police, but there may be circumstances in which it could be permissible. Important considerations would be universal application (to the assembly in question and thus non-discriminatory vis-à-vis different participants) and a basis upon a justifiable security concern.

Managing Risks In and Around an Ongoing Assembly

Thus far we have discussed police tactics aimed at policing assemblies in the background or from the margins, avoiding escalatory interactions with a crowd, even if that means overlooking opportunities to make arrests. It is worth underlining that such tactics would be diametrically opposite to those tactics described by Vitale as a 'command and control' approach (which is, in ways, the public-order policing equivalent of the 'broken windows' approach). In discussions around both the Joint Report and the General Comment, this alternative approach was loosely referred to as 'under-policing', sometimes referred to by Francophone law enforcement officials as *opportunité*—namely, that there is a time and a place for enforcing certain kinds of laws, and the middle of a public demonstration may well not be one of them.[47]

However, this approach has limitations. In addition to their responsibility to facilitate an assembly, the police also have a responsibility to protect the participants, which requires them to intervene to prevent acts of interpersonal violence, among other threats.

Despite the plans that may have been laid out beforehand to keep hostile crowds separate, in certain cases, it will be a necessary part of policing an event to have only a 'thin blue line' of police preventing violence between two groups. Likewise, the police may need to protect participants from violence from members of the public not organized as a formal assembly. This can sometimes result in unfortunate optics for the police, where, depending on prevailing legislation concerning hate speech, they can find themselves protecting and thus appearing to endorse the message of assemblies organized by hateful organizations (see Goldberger, in this volume).[48] Those optics are even worse in situations where there may indeed be evidence that officers do in fact endorse such messages of hate (see Pita Loor, in this volume).

Sometimes for protection, but more frequently to prevent a flashpoint somewhere else, the police may limit the movement of participants in an assembly (or a counter-assembly). Commonly referred to by protesters as 'kettling' (and by authorities as 'containment'), this has been a very controversial tactic (see Casey-Maslen, in this volume). The Human Rights Committee imposed a high threshold for its use, saying that it 'may be used only where it is necessary and proportionate to do so, in order to address actual violence or an imminent threat emanating from that section [of a crowd]'.[49] Given the risk of the violation of other human rights, in addition to the right of peaceful assembly, they further noted that '[p]articular care must be taken to contain, as far as possible, only people linked directly to violence and to limit the duration of the containment to the minimum necessary. Where containment is used indiscriminately or punitively, it violates the right of peaceful assembly, and may also violate other rights such as freedom from arbitrary detention and freedom of movement'.[50]

The cardinal problem with containment as a tactic is that it applies to the crowd or a part of the crowd as a whole rather than to specific individuals within the crowd. As discussed by Casey-Maslen, one of the primary considerations related to the use of force in the context of assemblies is that it ought to be targeted as far as possible against specific individuals based on their own conduct.

The most targeted law enforcement tactic, in this regard, is arrest—the ability to remove a potentially violent (or disruptive) element from an assembly. Casey-Maslen considers the practical risks of using 'snatch squads' to arrest participants, but even where the physical opportunity does not present additional risk (e.g. where the targeted participant is already separate from the crowd), there are other risks to using such a coercive power to influence an individual's conduct (see, for example, Pita Loor, in this volume about how the standard of probable cause offers too great a discretion when weighed against a protester's expressive rights).

In some contexts, there are grounds (such as the risk of a breach of the peace related to a time-sensitive event) upon which the police may arrest participants but not charge them and then release (or 'de-arrest') them once the risk of the breach of the peace (or equivalent) has passed. These arrangements may appear to allow for police removal and potential de-escalation without creating a criminal record, but they also bring with them a significant risk of procedural irregularity and abuse that amounts to preventative detention under another name.

More generally, it is important to retain sight of the fact that the primary legal obligation of the police around an assembly is to facilitate it. As such, interventions to remove the potential or actual risk of violence from within or without an assembly should be undertaken only to the extent necessary to allow the assembly to continue. The behaviour of the few should not imperil the continued enjoyment of the right of peaceful assembly by the many.[51] But it also suggests that the police should de-prioritize other forms of enforcement, given the likelihood that active intervention for minor infractions risks doing more harm than good.

Police Decision-Making around the Ending of an Assembly

It has been recognized that 'peaceful assemblies should generally be left to end by themselves'—for both normative and practical reasons.[52] However, there are clearly certain circumstances in which other factors will need to be considered, and this may involve bringing an assembly to a close that is—in the eyes of many of the participants—premature. Broadly speaking these circumstances fall into three categories: those where violence has become serious and widespread, those where the assembly was always technically unlawful but was afforded a degree of tolerance, and those which are causing serious and sustained disruption.

When the Assembly (as a Whole) Is No Longer Peaceful

An assembly remains 'peaceful' (under international law) unless it is 'characterised by widespread and serious violence'.[53] An assembly that crosses this threshold can be dispersed, but—practically—doing so may raise a tactical question for the police because in dispersing such a gathering, one may turn the known problem of violent behaviour by a large number of individuals in one place into the unknown range of problems of violent behaviour by smaller groups of people in unknown other places. Unfortunately, this dynamic likely contributes to the practice of police sometimes using force to subdue rather than to disperse (such as using force without allowing 'escape routes', or the punitive use of chemical irritants)—which is unlawful.

While normatively the clearest case—dispersal is a legitimate response, provided that only minimum necessary force is used—widespread and serious violence is nonetheless a factually disputable trigger. It is rarely straightforward to demonstrate that violence originated within the assembly rather than with the police. Moreover, even where the violence does begin within the crowd, where that is the frustrated consequence of the police refusing to accommodate a facially reasonable expectation, the ultimate responsibility for the breakdown should—from the precautionary and de-escalatory perspective preferred by human rights standards—be evenly distributed.

'Unlawful' Assemblies

In many parts of the world, a distinction is drawn between assemblies that are lawful and those that are unlawful (rather than between peaceful and non-peaceful). From a normative standpoint, this ought to have no impact upon the policing of a gathering. The Human Rights Committee was clear that '[a] failure to notify the authorities of an upcoming assembly, where required, does not render the act of participation in the assembly unlawful, and *must not in itself be used as a basis for dispersing the assembly*'.[54]

But, aside from the technicalities of notification, where legitimate conditions for a gathering have been imposed, in order for them to be meaningful, they must be enforceable. This implies the power to prevent or to respond to conduct on the part of assembly participants, which may be non-violent and which may not pose an immediate or (to the participants) obvious risk to the rights of anybody else. It can often be the deliberate intent of protesters to break laws or violate conditions they view as illegitimate. While dispersal should not be the first choice of tactic to enforce such conditions, it may ultimately need to be resorted to. The mechanism for reaching that stage, after continued refusal to comply with legitimately imposed restrictions or conditions, will often be to declare an ongoing assembly 'unlawful'.[55]

Complexities can also arise when assemblies take place on private land and where the interests of the landowner and the assembly organizers diverge. The police can find themselves with conflicting duties to respond effectively to a complaint of possibly 'aggravated' trespass and their responsibility to use dispersal only as a last resort. This is especially the case if the space in question has an element of public use (such as a shopping mall). Similarly conflicting responsibilities apply where municipal authorities have introduced other forms of 'assembly-free zones', for example, around 'critical infrastructure' or, in some instances, democratic institutions. The Human Rights Committee was clear that such prohibitions 'should generally be avoided' and 'must be specifically justified and narrowly circumscribed'.[56] But, where they exist, they leave the police again called upon to exercise discretion; at the limit of that toleration, they may need to disperse such a gathering.

A likely method of dispersal in this instance is for the police to make clear that the assembly must disperse or they will face arrest. Protesters may well not comply, but making arrests should be tactically preferable to forceful dispersal.

Dispersing Peaceful But Disruptive Gatherings

Whereas it is rarely the original intent for participants in an assembly to behave violently, it can often be the case that their plan is to be disruptive. Indeed, some would contend that this is the whole point of protest. On other occasions, the disruption may be the intent not of the participants but rather those opposed to them.[57] The Human Rights Committee opined that where an assembly, though peaceful, is 'nevertheless causing a high level of disruption, such as the extended blocking of traffic, [it] may be dispersed, as a rule, only if the disruption is "serious and sustained"'.[58]

In reality, the standard applied in a great many domestic laws is lower than this, often left to the complete discretion of a senior police officer (sometimes present on the ground; sometimes a more senior officer off-site). In this instance, like those in the previous subsection, the mechanism will usually be to declare that the assembly will become 'unlawful' from a certain point.

From this point, there are broadly two approaches to disperse physically a group of participants who do not wish to comply: those aimed at using sufficient force to change their minds (which can entail quite significant violence and risk provoking a will to resist) or those using lesser force in such a way as to give the protesters no choice (i.e. by bodily removing individual protesters, often while arresting them). Human rights law requires the use of minimum necessary force in all circumstances (see Casey-Maslen, in this volume). As the Human Rights Committee put it, 'Force that is likely to cause more than negligible injury should not be used against individuals or groups who are passively resisting'.[59] This, then, mandates the latter approach, where techniques that avoid mass confrontation (and that rely more on individualized attrition) are deployed. These tactics can make the police look rather silly, for example, by having to have four officers carry a protester dressed up as a furry animal away from a protest site. That silliness will likely become part of the protesters' messaging strategy ('is this really the State's only response?').

Conclusion

The policing of assemblies in a vibrant civil society will always be messy. By virtue of the often contentious character of peaceful protest, the decisions made by law enforcement will always be unpopular in certain quarters. There can be no one-size-fits-all approach to 'managing' assemblies. However, at least two principles should be uncontroversial. First, content-neutrality is a useful reference point to guide how police anticipate and respond to assemblies. Second, tactical decision-making on the ground should be guided by a presumption in favour of continued facilitation. This can involve the use of discretion not to intervene with respect to low-level criminality, including flexibility with respect to the contravention of imposed restrictions.

Unfortunately, looking around the world, these principles are not often applied in practice. The police too readily enforce 'law and order' at the behest of either explicit political exhortation or an imagined popular will. International human rights standards provide a robust basis upon which to condemn such actions. In many instances, the violations are manifest (and often unusually well-documented). In more marginal cases—where officers have exercised discretion one way or the other—judicial review must act as a check, weighing the proportionality of decisions made on the street.

In the ideal world, the police should be readily available but largely unnoticed. But it remains the case that because of the extent to which the police officers arrayed around the outside of a protest are the most visible and most engaged facet of the state whose policies are in many instances being protested, regardless of how well they facilitate the event, there will always be friction. However much the police may try to employ variants of active facilitation, their efforts will rarely be accepted in good faith (at least during the event), and 'negotiated management' will feel less negotiated and more managed.

Meanwhile, in circumstances in which the policing of assemblies is rightly conducted with a view to minimizing the recourse to force, protesters will increasingly resort to other means of making clear that 'authorities' are not responding to their demands. The policing of peaceful but nonetheless highly disruptive assemblies seems likely to become an increasingly salient challenge. Exercising discretion in those circumstances will be controversial, but a habit of content neutrality and facilitation will stand officers and departments in good stead.

Notes

1. The concept of policing as street-level bureaucracy was developed by Michael Lipsky, dependent on three core characteristics: constant interaction between the public official and the citizenry, the potential of significant impact arising from the interaction, and a very wide-ranging discretion on the part of the official with respect to decision-making. See 'Toward a Theory of Street-Level Bureaucracy', paper for the American Political Science Association, August 1969. For more recent applications in a non-Western context, see Jan Beek et al., *Police in Africa: The Street Level View* (Oxford: Oxford University Press, 2017).
2. See generally Clark McPhail, David Schweingruber, and John McCarthy, 'Policing Protest in the United States: 1960–1995', in *Policing Protest: The Control of Mass Demonstrations in Western Democracies*, ed. Donatella della Porta and Herbert Reiter (Minneapolis: University of Minnesota Press, 1998), 49–69.
3. See Patrick Gillham, 'Securitizing America: Strategic Incapacitation and the Policing of Protest Since the 11 September 2001 Terrorist Attacks', *Sociology Compass* 5, no. 7 (2011): 636–652.
4. Alex Vitale, 'From Negotiated Management to Command and Control: How the New York Police Department Polices Protests', *Policing & Society* 15, no. 3 (2005): 283–304.
5. See, for example, 'Crowd Management: Managing Crowds, Protests and Riots: A Santa Cruz Police Operational Assessment and Training' (2020), https://chiefmillscom.files.wordpress.com/2020/10/sharablepresentation.crowdmanagment1.pdf. Also see National Police Foundation, *A Crisis of Trust: A National Police Foundation Report to the Los*

Angeles Board of Police Commissioners on the Los Angeles Police Department Response to First Amendment Assemblies and Protests Occurring May 27–June 7, 2020 (2021), https://lapdonlinestrgeacc.blob.core.usgovcloudapi.net/lapdonlinemedia/2021/11/A-Crisis-of-Trust.pdf.

6. McPhail et al., 'Policing Protest in the United States'.
7. John Noakes and Patrick Gillham, 'Police and Protester Innovation Since Seattle', *Mobilization* 12, no. 4 (2007): 335–340.
8. David Bayley, *Changing the Guard: Developing Democratic Police Abroad* (Oxford: Oxford University Press, 2006).
9. See generally Lukas Muntingh et al., 'Democratic Policing: A Conceptual Framework', *Law Democracy & Development* 25 (2021): 121–147.
10. Clifford Stott et al., 'Police Powers and Public Assemblies: Learning from the Clapham Common "Vigil" during the Covid-19 Pandemic', *Policing* 16, no. 1 (2021): 75.
11. Ibid.
12. By underling the role and responsibilities of political authorities, as opposed to the police, I am also drawing upon the South African example, pioneered by the Goldstone Commission and later infused into the 1993 Regulation of Gatherings Act, of the 'safety triangle'.
13. See Tim Newburn, 'The Inevitable Fallibility of Policing', *Policing and Society* 32, no. 3 (2022): 434–450.
14. UNHRCtte, General Comment No. 37—Article 21: Right of Peaceful Assembly (17 September 2020) UN Doc. CCPR/C/GC/37, 75.
15. Ibid.
16. Ibid., 64. Also see African Commission on Human and Peoples' Rights (ACHPR), Guidelines on Freedom of Association and Assembly in Africa (2017), 102(b).
17. On the modest contribution made, for example, to the estimated £48m annual cost of policing Premier League football in England and Wales, see Richard Hester and Jon Hobson, 'The True Cost of Policing Football in England & Wales: Freedom of Information Data from 2015–2019', *Police Practice and Research* (2022).
18. See, for example, the exposé by Alleen Brown and John McCracken, 'Documents Show How a Pipeline Company Paid Minnesota Millions to Police Protests', *Grist*, 9 February 2023, https://grist.org/protest/enbridge-line-3-pipeline-minnesota-public-safety-escrow-account-invoices/.
19. Obviously, it is important that evidence justifying these insights is legitimately obtained, and if based on a more theoretical basis (e.g. of crowd behaviour), that it is robustly tested. On the fragility of some evidence in that regard, see further Adang, in this volume.
20. In a retrospective on the 2015 tragedy at Jamarat, Saudi Arabia, William Langeweische notes that in the preceding twenty years there had been fatal crowd crushes in more than forty countries, accounting for nearly eight thousand deaths. See 'The 10-Minute Mecca Stampede That Made History', *Vanity Fair*, 9 January 2018, https://www.vanityfair.com/news/2018/01/the-mecca-stampede-that-made-history-hajj.
21. UNHRCtte, General Comment No. 37, 80.
22. See Duncan Onyango and Petronila Otuya, 'Police Perceptions, Attitude and Preparedness in Managing Public Assemblies', in *Policing Protests in Kenya*, ed. Mutuma Ruteere and Patrick Mutahi (Nairobi: CHRIPS, 2019). Also see Thomas Probert, 'Police Attitudes and Crowd Management in Africa: Exploring the Impact of Soft-Law Instruments and Training in Malawi', APCOF/DIHR Policy Brief (August 2018).

23. UN Basic Principles on the Use of Force and Firearms, endorsed by UN General Assembly Resolution 45/166, 18 December 1990, Principle 20.
24. See UN Human Rights Guidance on Less-Lethal Weapons in Law Enforcement (Office of the High Commissioner for Human Rights, 2020), 4.3 and 4.4.
25. Clément Voule, Model Protocol for Law Enforcement Officials to Promote and Protect Human Rights in the Context of Peaceful Protests, A/HRC/55/60 (31 January 2024), 45.
26. One of the earliest calls for such an instrument within the UN system came in one of Christof Heyns' report as Special Rapporteur in 2014 (A/69/265). This was adapted and repeated in the Joint Report with Maina Kiai (A/HRC/31/66), and then again in Heyns' final report in 2016 (A/71/362). The process to adopt the Guidance began in earnest in 2017.
27. See, for example, Report of the Group of Governmental Experts on torture-free trade, A/76/850, 31 May 2022.
28. In the UK, a broader public inquiry into undercover policing is ongoing, and published its first interim report in 2023. See https://www.ucpi.org.uk/about-the-inquiry/#reports. Also see C. Atkinson, M. McBride, and A. Moore, 'Pitched! Informants and the Covert Policing of Football Fans in Scotland', *Policing and Society* 31, no. 7 (2021): 863–877.
29. Kiai and Heyns, A/HRC/31/66, 78(f). See also, more recently, Voule, A/HRC/55/60, 60(c).
30. It is worth noting that the UNHRCttee lists "the monitoring of social media to glean information about participation in peaceful assemblies" as one of the activities that may infringe the right to privacy. See General Comment No. 37, 62. See also Voule, A/HRC/55/60, 61–62.
31. UNHRCtte, General Comment No. 37, 36.
32. On the potential escalation of 'preventative measures', see William Smith, 'Policing, Protest, and Rights', *Public Affairs Quarterly* 32, no. 3 (2018): 185–204.
33. The UNHRCtte envisions an extremely narrow potential for authorities to use preventative detention to prevent participation; see General Comment No. 37, 82.
34. For a discussion of police officer perceptions of a form of prior restraint in a less politically sensitive setting, and their effectiveness, see Matt Hopkins, 'Ten Seasons of the Football Banning Order: Police Officer Narratives on the Operation of Banning Orders and the Impact on the Behaviour of "Risk Supporters"', *Policing and Society* 24 (2014): 285–301.
35. UNHRCtte, General Comment No. 37, 76, which prefaces a long section on the role of law enforcement with "Where the presence of law enforcement officials is required," to ensure that their presence is not interpreted as a default expectation.
36. UNHRCtte, General Comment No. 37, 65. This is the paragraph of the General Comment that deals with organizer's potential responsibility, which implicitly nods at the idea there is some kind of linkage, explicit in some national practice.
37. UNHRCtte, General Comment No. 37, 92.
38. Ibid.
39. Ibid., 62.
40. The significance of this potential interaction also speaks to the risk of remote surveillance: see Jay Stanley, 'Curbs Needed on Police Drone Surveillance of Public Gatherings', 14 March 2024, https://www.aclu.org/documents/curbs-needed-on-police-drone-surveillance-of-public-gatherings.
41. See Office for Democratic Institutions and Human Rights, Human Rights Handbook on Policing Assemblies (2016) 70–71.
42. See UNHRCtte, General Comment No. 37, 62.

43. An early outpouring of empirical research on the indirect impact of body-worn cameras on phenomena such as the incidence of use of force suggested otherwise. Focussed research concerning more direct impacts, such as the likelihood of an investigation reaching a finding, provides a more reliable measure. See, for example, Suat Cubuku et al., 'The Effect of Body Worn Cameras on the Adjudication of Citizen Complaints of Police Misconduct', *Justice Quarterly* 40, no. 7 (2023): 999–1023.
44. The competing equities of privacy and accountability with respect to police body-worn cameras are widely discussed elsewhere, but further attention should be paid to the public attitude towards their introduction in contexts where the police do not enjoy legitimacy either as individual officers on the street nor as institutional data repositories.
45. UNHRCtte, General Comment No. 37, 83.
46. Ibid., 83. This drew clearly upon language from the Joint Report. See Kiai and Heyns, A/HRC/31/66, 43.
47. Newburn discusses "under-enforcement" as a critical element of police discretion (recognized by scholars such as Egon Bittner and James Q Wilson). See 'The Inevitable Fallibility of Policing', 439f.
48. The shorthand within international norms on this point is to refer to the Rabat Plan of Action (A/HRC/22/17/Add.4). See, for example, Voule, A/HRC/55/60, 69.
49. UNHRCtte, General Comment No. 37, 84.
50. Ibid.
51. This also prompts scepticism about the role that theories of "crowd behaviour" have historically played in devising policing strategies (see Adang, in this volume).
52. UNHRCtte, General Comment No. 37, 54.
53. Ibid., 15. For a problematization of this binary distinction, see Salát, in this volume. Moreover, it should be noted that, just as in deeming an individual's conduct to be violent in cases of imminent violence, intent, or incitement, the same can be true of a whole assembly, albeit with an extremely high threshold, namely where such conduct 'is manifestly widespread within the assembly'. See UNHRCtte, General Comment No. 37, 19.
54. Ibid., 71 (emphasis added). The Committee continued, by highlighting, likewise, that this should also not form the basis for arresting the participants or organizers, or for imposing undue sanctions, such as charging the participants or organizers with criminal offences.
55. In recent years, emergency public health restrictions related to COVID-19 offered an interesting case study of circumstances in which peaceful protest might have been 'unlawful' for other, potentially legitimate, reasons. The use of any significant force for dispersal in such cases would not have been inappropriate.
56. UNHRCtte, General Comment No. 37, 56.
57. See Goldberger, in this volume, and also Frederick Schauer, 'Costs and Challenges of the Hostile Audience', *Notre Dame Law Review* 94, no. 4 (2019): 1671–1698.
58. Ibid., 85. See also Kiai and Heyns, A/HRC/31/66, 62.
59. UNHRCtte, General Comment No. 37, 86, mirroring the UN Guidance on Less-Lethal Weapons, 2.10.

Further Reading

Gillham, Patrick. 'Securitizing America: Strategic Incapacitation and the Policing of Protest Since the 11 September 2001 Terrorist Attacks'. *Sociology Compass* 5, no. 7 (2011): 636–652.

Jackson, Will. 'Researching the Policed: Critical Ethnography and the Study of Protest Policing'. *Policing and Society* 30, no. 2 (2020): 169–185.
Radburn, Matt, Clifford Stott, Ben Bradford, and Mark Robinson. 'When Is Policing Fair? Groups, Identity and Judgements of the Procedural Justice of Coercive Crowd Policing'. *Policing and Society* 28, no. 6 (2018): 647–664.
Stott, Clifford, Matt Radburn, Geoff Pearson, Arabella Kyprianides, Mark Harrison, and David Rowlands. 'Police Powers and Public Assemblies: Learning from the Clapham Common "Vigil" during the Covid-19 Pandemic'. *Policing* 16, no. 1 (2021): 73–94.
Stott, Clifford, Martin Scothern, and Hugo Gorringe. 'Advances in Liaison Based Public Order Policing in England: Human Rights and Negotiating the Management of Protest?' *Policing* 7, no. 2 (2013): 212–226.
Stuurman, Ziyanda. 'Policing Inequality and the Inequality of Policing: A Look at the Militarisation of Policing around the World, Focusing on Brazil and South Africa'. *South African Journal of International Affairs* 27, no. 1 (2021): 43–66.
Vitale, Alex. 'From Negotiated Management to Command and Control: How the New York Police Department Polices Protests'. *Policing & Society* 15, no. 3 (2005): 283–304.

CHAPTER 36

ASSEMBLIES AND TECHNOLOGIES OF SURVEILLANCE

VAL ASTON

Introduction

It has become commonplace for assemblies to be subject to different and multiple forms of public space surveillance. While a particular intensity of surveillance may be reserved for purportedly 'dangerous assemblies' (such as protest events or gatherings of football fans), few assemblies are spared the now ubiquitous deployment of police officers holding cameras or watching remotely from behind closed-circuit television (CCTV). The data being gathered may also be scanned in real time using facial recognition technology.

This chapter will explore the ways in which public space surveillance constrains or 'chills' the exercise of freedom of assembly. It is often argued that the mere act of being observed in a public place—even by police or government bodies—cannot amount to a tangible constraint or interference with assembly or privacy rights. Drawing on an emerging body of empirical data, it is argued here that much depends on the way that surveillance is experienced. Surveillance may amount to a significant constraint if it is intrusive or individualized or results in differentiation and stigmatization.

The legal frameworks used to litigate surveillance in this context—primarily the framework of privacy, but also the framework of freedom of assembly—seem unable to adequately acknowledge or address the particular type of 'chill' that arises from surveillance of this kind. Judicial reasoning has tended to centre on locational concepts (the extent to which privacy has application in the public domain) or issues of informational autonomy (the extent to which privacy has application to the collection and retention of data). Harms that arise at the point of data collection—at the point that people *experience* surveillance—have not been fully acknowledged either within the framework of privacy or as a constraint on freedom of assembly itself.

This chapter proceeds in three parts. It first explores the particular ways in which surveillance operates in the context of public assemblies. Second, noting that surveillance is itself a strategic element of public order policing, the chapter conceptualizes the harms arising from surveillance activity in the context of public assemblies, focusing on impediments to both individual privacy and the collective act of assembly. Thirdly, by further conceptualizing the 'chilling effect' of surveillance, it considers the extent to which courts in two jurisdictions—the United States and the European Court of Human Rights—have acknowledged and recognized the threat to assembly freedoms arising from police and governmental surveillance. Finally, it concludes that there is a need for greater recognition of the way that surveillance operates in the specific and distinct context of assemblies and the particular harms that can result.

Surveillance of Public Assemblies

The surveillance of public assemblies, and the social or political movements associated with them, is far from a new phenomenon. In the UK, there was outcry in 1832, when it came to light that William Popay, an officer with the then nascent Metropolitan Police force, had infiltrated a political organization (the National Political Union of the Working Classes) disguising 'himself as an impoverished revolutionary'.[1]

The modern-day surveillance of public assemblies spans a spectrum of visibility. At the less visible end, policing bodies have an array of hidden or secret technologies available to them that are capable of intercepting communications, tracking movements, and recording conversations and activities without the knowledge of those being monitored. Surveillance of the digital realm, including social media, also takes place largely without our knowledge or awareness.[2] In addition, alongside the modern trappings of electronic and digital surveillance, policing bodies have continued to make use of less technologically sophisticated methods, including the deployment of plain clothes and undercover police officers and informants.[3]

Just as hidden surveillance technologies have advanced in capacity and capability, so too have more visible forms of police surveillance. Police officers will usually have access to CCTV networks, possibly supplemented with facial recognition and other identification technologies. Dedicated intelligence- or evidence-gathering teams may be deployed to gather detailed data from within an assembly, often wielding specialist cameras and recording devices. Camera equipment may also be positioned expressly for the purposes of monitoring an assembly, and mounted on buildings, structures, vehicles, or (increasingly) drones. Police bodycams have also become commonplace, adding greater surveillance agility and proximity. All of this operates within the coercive public order environment often associated with assembly policing, and public order policing strategies (such as containment measures) have themselves been used to enhance or facilitate data-gathering activities.[4]

Overt surveillance measures are not *necessarily* harmful, although the extent to which they promote public safety and police accountability is contested.[5] The question we are concerned with here is whether—or in what circumstances—surveillance activities undertaken by police or government actors are *capable* of harming or constraining the act of public assembly. Participants in a public assembly are, after all, people who are knowingly engaging in an activity that is fundamentally *public* in nature. They will necessarily be seen and heard by those around them, and an audience is often an essential part of the process. In such circumstances, how can assemblies be harmed if, alongside the general public, police officers take photographs, film participants, or record events?

State surveillance must, however, be distinguished from mere watching or observation. Surveillance is best understood as a 'chain or cycle of linked activities' which stretches from the targeting of particular events or people for intelligence gathering, through to the collection of data; the collation, processing, and analysis of data; and the dissemination of information and the actions which can then result.[6] At each stage of this cycle, surveillance can harm those who are subject to it.[7] These harms are explored further below.

The purposes for which surveillance takes place are also integral to conceptions of harm. Public space surveillance may be passive, generalized, and responsive; or they may be active, individualized, and pre-emptive.[8] The former involves the monitoring of public space in order to intervene if 'something happens'—such as if a crime occurs, or there is a need to act to protect public safety. This chapter is concerned with the latter: with a form of surveillance that falls within the broader repertoire of public order controls that have come to typify the experience of gathering with others in public.

This kind of surveillance is concerned with individualizing and differentiating strategies of control. In part, it is disciplinary in nature, in that it is concerned with deterring and evidencing misbehaviour. But it also has an intelligence function, and this is concerned not with what is, or has been, but with what might be. It is predictive and pre-emptive, and centred around probabilistic calculations for the purpose of mitigating potential or possible future risks.[9] While the use of risk-based intelligence gathering and surveillance is not unique to public assemblies, the policing of public assemblies may be one of the areas in which the shift to what Zedner has called a 'pre-crime' society has been most noticeable.[10]

Policing bodies are often under pressure not merely to respond to immediate or imminent threats, but to anticipate or forestall the possibility of future threats.[11] The determination of risk is a matter of crime control, not due process, and risk-averse policing bodies may be quick to attach 'risk' labels to assemblies where there is *any* possibility of disorder or criminality, no matter how remote the risk, and regardless of the nature of the anticipated misdemeanour.[12] Risk evaluations therefore raise the prospect that what is being forestalled is not violence or criminality but legitimate behaviour that falls within the scope of protected activities and fundamental rights.

This is especially troublesome when one considers that assemblies have social and democratic value: They are critical for expressing political dissent, but also for the building of communities and for forging social, cultural, or collective identities. For the right to assembly to be meaningful, there must be respect for autonomy: not as an unrestrained liberty where people can 'do what they want', but a degree of autonomy that enables 'the ability of people to come together as members of their respective community to determine, without coercion, a course of action'.[13] This is the very essence of what it means to have the freedom to assemble, but as we see in the next section, autonomy can be substantially constrained by the operation of police surveillance strategies.

Surveillance Harms: Proximity and Intrusion, Identification, Categorization

This section explores the harms that can arise from surveillance in the particular context of a public assembly. Here, it is argued, surveillance is not used (or at least, not only) for the 'passive' monitoring of public space. Rather surveillance forms part of a strategy of public order policing, and to this end surveillance is concerned with individualization, differentiation, and incapacitation: It is used to identify and classify assembly participants and to determine police interventions. This section explores the various harms that can arise at each stage of the surveillance cycle, including the point of data collection, data processing, and its use.[14]

Proximity and Intrusion

Privacy scholars have long drawn attention to the fact that our individual autonomy can be curtailed by the intrusion or the unwanted proximity of others, or the experience of being watched in what we may feel to be inappropriate ways.[15] It is the function of privacy rights to protect us from such incursions into our 'private sphere', but our expectations of privacy also extend to the public domain. When we go out in public we are necessarily seen and possibly heard by others, but we are still protected from inappropriate intrusion by means of what Westin terms 'reserve'[16] and Goffman 'civil inattention'.[17] While we expect others to see us when we are in public, we expect them to respect social norms[18] and 'conventions of discretion'.[19] We are likely to feel uncomfortable if people come too close, listen to our conversations, track our movements, or follow us from place to place.

It may seem counter-intuitive to talk about proximity and intrusion in the context of a public assembly: This is not a situation where people expect to enjoy seclusion or 'aloneness'. But assemblies give rise to their own expected norms of behaviour, and their contravention can be disruptive and distressing.

Police surveillance of public assemblies is notoriously lacking in respect for social norms. The surveillance of public assemblies may be physically intrusive and 'in-your-face': Participants in public assemblies have often recounted being repeatedly photographed at close range by police camera teams, or being followed for sustained periods by police intelligence officers who stay close enough to listen to conversations.[20] There is no discrete distance to this kind of surveillance: It is not done from the periphery, but deliberately encroaches into space occupied by the assembly itself.

The visibility of this form of surveillance is amplified in order to exaggerate its disciplinary effect: those officers carrying out the surveillance may wear distinctive uniforms; they may carry over-sized cameras; they may act in a way which will make it clear that they are not merely, passively 'watching'. The intended message is that the subject of surveillance has been 'picked out' for special attention: the close scrutiny is intended to make the subject feel 'super-visible'.[21] Those subjected to it may feel uncomfortable, intimidated, and stigmatized.[22]

Identification

The disciplinary impact of surveillance is enhanced if a person is not merely 'picked out' but also *identified*. It is not uncommon for police intelligence officers to be deployed at public assemblies for the purposes of identifying and monitoring selected individuals. Whereas at one time police officers relied on physical images and their own recognition skills,[23] the digital era has significantly enhanced the capacity and capability of policing bodies to identify assembly participants.[24] Facial recognition technology now enables police to scan large crowds and to match individuals, in real time, against a potentially large dataset.[25]

Identification is significant because it enables a connection to be made between the person 'in the flesh' and associated aggregated data, in this case data that has been collated by policing bodies.[26] The impact of identification may be exacerbated by what Amy Stevens has called a strategy of 'intentional chill' whereby police officers make apparent that a person has become a subject—or potential subject—of surveillance.[27] Police officers, to this end, make deliberate and overt use of a person's name. As one protester has put it, 'they just wanted to make sure I knew they knew who I was'.[28]

Such exchanges can leave a person feeling unnerved, unsettled, and perhaps intimidated or scared, regardless of whether or not they have 'something to hide'. Even in democratic states, the implications of being identified are considerable: It indicates that a person has become categorized as a 'person of interest'.

Categorization and Intervention

Surveillance operates as a form of social sorting: It differentiates those assemblies, groups, and individuals that are categorized as posing some form of 'risk' from those who do not.[29] Those categorized in this way are more likely to experience an intensified surveillance regime.[30] They may also experience differentiated policing including preventive or pre-emptive constraints and/or a reduced tolerance for transgression which increases the likelihood of arrest.[31]

Risk categorizations may not accurately indicate criminal intent. They can arise as a result of actuarial analysis of retained data, but they may also be based on subjective judgement influenced by political or policy considerations,[32] or by media representations of the 'dangerousness' of particular groups or populations.[33] They may, nonetheless, carry considerable stigma. In politically expressive assemblies, the designation may involve a politically loaded label such as 'subversion' or 'extremism';[34] meanwhile, sports fans may be labelled 'antisocial' or 'hooligan'.[35]

Cumulative Harms

The combined effects of intrusion, identification, and categorization can have a devastating impact on the exercise of public assembly. If the relevant assembly is part of a wider or ongoing political, social, or cultural movement, surveillance may also have a cumulative and longer-term effect, aggregating over time and affecting a larger, or differently constituted, class of person than those who are directly the focus of surveillance measures. As we have seen, surveillance may damage perceptions of legitimacy, stigmatize participants, and stymie solidarity.[36] It may create obstacles to the building of relationships and networks[37] and may also weaken community bonds and erode interpersonal trust.[38]

The effect of such surveillance may be disproportionately felt by movements that depend on the efforts and energy of unpaid supporters to organize and mobilize assemblies. Surveillance may deplete this essential social capital, making it more difficult for assemblies to happen at all. Protesters may lose motivation or confidence, and their participation and engagement may decline.[39] Surveillance may thus not only constrain individual autonomy; it may also pose a grave threat to the collective exercise of assembly freedoms.

The 'Chilling Effect' of Surveillance on Assembly

The various constraints on assembly freedoms arising from surveillance are often conceptualized as a 'chilling effect', but this is a concept which has proved elusive. The legal concept of 'chilling' equates to measures that have a deterrent effect on the exercise of lawful acts of expression or assembly.[40]

Ostensibly, the purpose of police surveillance of public assemblies is to deter unlawful, rather than lawful activity, something Frederick Schauer has described as a 'benign chill'.[41]

On one conception, assemblies are inherently dangerous: They pose risks of disorderly conduct, criminality, and even violence, and such behaviour is justifiably deterred or discouraged—or 'chilled'—by police surveillance. However, in the sometimes chaotic and often uncertain environment of the public assembly, the distinction between what is and what is not legitimate, permitted, or tolerated is not always evident or easy to determine.

It may not, therefore, be only unlawful acts that are 'chilled' by police monitoring. Daniel J. Solove has highlighted that the ambiguity surrounding surveillance creates a general sense of powerlessness and fear.[42] Further, Jonathon Penney notes that the 'chilling effect' relates not just to compliance with legal norms, but to concerns about reputation, social acceptance, and the capacity for reprisals. This 'conforming effect' involves not just a deterrent but a shaping effect, so that people speak, act, or behave in a way that 'conforms to, or is in compliance with, a perceived social norm.'[43]

As highlighted above, these 'chilling effects' can be accentuated where surveillance is not merely generalized and responsive or passive but is instead pre-emptive, intrusive and individualized. Further, the 'chill' is felt not merely at an individual level—it may have cumulative and sustained implications for the collective process of assembly mobilization. As we shall see below, these broader conceptions of 'chill' have not featured prominently in the reasoning of the courts.

How Law Deals with Surveillance Harms in the Context of Public Assemblies

This section considers the extent to which the harms to assembly posed by surveillance have been acknowledged and addressed by different legal frameworks, drawing on the case law of the European Convention of Human Rights (ECtHR) with reference also to constitutional rights in the United States. Both the United States and the ECtHR emphasize the importance of protecting both individual privacy and the freedom of assembly.

The ECtHR has broadly defined its concept of 'private life' protected under Article 8 of the European Convention of Human Rights, so that it extends to the public domain. The Strasbourg Court has held that private life is a 'broad concept incapable of exhaustive definition' which is not limited to the 'inner circle' of a person's personal life.[44] The United States also protects privacy rights under the Fourth Amendment, which places restrictions on government bodies in carrying out 'unreasonable searches'.[45] Generally, a search take place when there is an official intrusion onto private property or a violation of a person's 'reasonable expectation of privacy'.[46]

The United States and the ECtHR also both place weight on the protection of assembly freedoms. The ECtHR protects, under Article 11 of the Convention, the right to freedom of peaceful assembly and to freedom of association with others. In view of its importance, the Court has held that the right to freedom of assembly should not be interpreted restrictively.[47] In the United States, the First Amendment provides protections for the freedom of expression, association, and assembly. The US Supreme Court has, for example, recognized the 'vital relationship' between the freedom to associate and privacy in one's association.[48] The First Amendment has been found to be relevant to information about a person's political views, beliefs, or associations.[49] It has determined that '[b]road and sweeping state inquiries into' 'a person's beliefs or associations' implicate the First Amendment because they 'discourage citizens from exercising rights protected by the Constitution'.[50]

The US Approach—Privacy

While traditionally 'tied to common-law trespass, the approach of the US courts to government surveillance since the late 1960s has centred around the question of whether a person has a "reasonable expectation of privacy" '.[51] To determine the scope of privacy protections under the Fourth Amendment, the US Supreme Court has utilized a two-part test laid down in the 1967 case of *Katz v United States*. A person has a reasonable expectation of privacy firstly if a person demonstrates an actual (subjective) expectation of privacy, and secondly, that this expectation is one that society is willing to recognize as 'reasonable'.[52] This test has, in the past, been narrowly interpreted to result in a very limited role for privacy rights in the public domain—even where the surveillance in question involved hidden electronic devices. In the case of *United States v Knotts*, for example, the police tracking of a suspect's movements by means of a radio transmitter placed within the suspect's vehicle was not a violation of the Fourth Amendment: A person travelling on a public thoroughfare, the Court held, has no reasonable expectation of privacy as he voluntarily conveys the fact that he is travelling in a particular direction to anyone who cares to look.[53] Given this interpretation, privacy rights would have little application to public assemblies.

In more recent times, however, the US Supreme Court has demonstrated a willingness to interpret a 'reasonable expectation of privacy' more expansively. In *United States v Jones*, the FBI installed a GPS tracking device on Jones's vehicle and remotely monitored the vehicle's movements for twenty-eight days.[54] Ultimately, the Court found that this was unconstitutional based on the physical trespass of the vehicle. But five Justices, in two separate concurring opinions, signalled a potential doctrinal shift and explicitly recognized the 'mosaic effect' of digital surveillance, in which long-term surveillance can build a picture of a person which is greater than the 'sum of its parts'. Justice Sotomayor noted the capacity of this kind of surveillance to create a 'precise, comprehensive record of a person's public movements that reflects a wealth of detail about her familial, political, professional, religious, and sexual associations'.[55] Popular expectations of privacy had, Justice Alito noted in his concurring opinion, shifted with technological advances in surveillance capability.[56]

Jones was followed by the case of *Carpenter v United States* in which the Court held that while a person's location in a public place may not be 'particularly private', privacy concerns could arise from the ability of tracking technologies to build up a chronicle of a person's movements over time.[57] The case concerned access to mobile phone metadata by law enforcement bodies, which was used to track Carpenter's movements over a period of 127 days. In what has been called a landmark decision in the development of privacy law,[58] the Court rejected the government's argument that Carpenter had no reasonable expectation of privacy in relation to this data. The Court, instead, placed emphasis on the revealing nature of the data that could be gathered in this way, the duration of the surveillance and the amount of data that could be collected, and the fact that the data was involuntarily disclosed. The use of modern digital technologies raised particular privacy issues, the Court suggested, because they made possible an intensity of surveillance that would not have been feasible in the past.[59]

Quite how expansive an approach the US courts will take in the post-*Carpenter* world is open to question. For one thing, many of these situations involve the collection of data in private settings, where individuals have a high reasonable expectation of privacy. For another, courts have been noticeably reluctant to apply the 'mosaic effect' idea to less innovative and more familiar forms of surveillance, as well as those which are more limited in scale.[60] Nonetheless, some courts have already expanded the scope of Fourth Amendment protections post-*Carpenter*. For example, in *Leaders of a Beautiful Struggle v Baltimore Police Department*, the Fourth Circuit applied *Carpenter* to the use by police of planes equipped with high-tech cameras to conduct surveillance of Baltimore City.[61] The Court found that the warrantless use of this all-encompassing, prolonged aerial surveillance violated the Fourth Amendment, emphasizing that this type of surveillance transcended 'normal police capabilities', and enabled the compilation of a 'detailed, encyclopaedic' record of 'the whole of' every resident of Baltimore's movements'. However, as Judge Wilkinson detailed in his dissenting opinion, the US Supreme Court has repeatedly sanctioned aerial surveillance of public spaces.[62] Indeed, the Supreme Court has held that, in general, aerial surveillance does not violate the Fourth Amendment because there is no reasonable expectation of privacy in what is readily exposed to the public.[63] The Fourth Circuit distinguished these precedents from the type of surveillance at issue in *Leaders of a Beautiful Struggle* by honing in on the all-encompassing, prolonged nature of the surveillance as opposed to the targeted, limited surveillance in the precedents.[64]

In contrast, courts have not yet reached a settled opinion on the application of Fourth Amendment rights to the use of 'pole cameras' installed in public streets to monitor the exterior and surroundings of suspect's houses for sustained periods. On one side, for example, in *United States v Cuevas-Sanchez*, the Fifth Circuit held that two months of constant surveillance via a pole camera of a fenced-in yard violated defendant's reasonable expectation of privacy.[65] In contrast, most US courts pre- and post-*Carpenter* have held that such surveillance does not violate the Fourth Amendment. A decision of the Seventh Circuit Court in *United States v Tuggle*, for instance, effectively held the use of such cameras to monitor Tuggle's house for a year and a half was lawful.[66] The court, grappling with *Carpenter* and the 'mosiac theory', noted that the surveillance encompassed only the environment surrounding the target house and not the 'whole of' a person's movements over time.[67]

Even in the post-*Carpenter* era, the Fourth Amendment is unlikely to be applicable to surveillance of public assemblies which is limited in duration and geographic scope. Ultimately, the question will turn on whether US courts are convinced that the type or volume of data collected and the nature of the surveillance device might impact an individual's 'reasonable expectation of privacy' when they choose to gather with others in public, including during political protests.

The US Approach—Assembly Rights

The US Constitution also provides for claims to be brought under First Amendment protections for the freedom of expression, association, and assembly.[68] While the US Supreme Court has not construed the right of assembly with much definition, it has recognized the 'vital relationship' between the freedom to associate and privacy in one's association.[69] It has also consistently recognized that sweeping state investigations of a person's associations implicate the First Amendment because they 'discourage citizens from exercising rights protected by the Constitution'.[70]

Where individuals or organizations can show that they have standing, the right of association—potentially—provides a mechanism for addressing collective as well as individual harms, as well as harms to the *process* of assembly mobilization.[71] In *Black Lives Matter v Clarkstown*, for example, the District Court for the Southern District of New York found protesters had plausibly pled a cognizable injury sufficient to prove standing where they had been subjected to electronic surveillance and their risk categorization allegedly resulted in them being targeted by police snipers. The Court recognized such surveillance plausibly constituted a 'chilling effect' on their rights of speech and association: 'When confronted with this threat of violence from the government at a peaceful Black Lives Matter rally, on top of the illegal surveillance targeted against the group and its members, any reasonable person would think twice before continuing to participate in Black Lives Matter'.[72]

The need to be able to convince a court of some tangible harm from police surveillance activities is, however, 'one of the most significant obstacles to challenging the constitutionality of government surveillance activities'.[73] For a First Amendment challenge to succeed, potential claimants must be able to demonstrate that their ability to engage in a constitutionally protected activity was curtailed. There must be evidence of a 'specific present objective harm or a threat of specific future harm':[74] It will not be sufficient for a claimant to demonstrate that a 'chilling effect' has arisen merely from an awareness or fear that surveillance is or may be taking place.[75] Claimants must also demonstrate a causal relationship between that 'chill' and the surveillance activities in question.

The European Court of Human Rights Approach—Privacy

The approach taken by the European Court of Human rights, by contrast, is centred on a broader conception of public privacy (under Article 8 ECHR), and surveillance issues have been litigated almost exclusively within this framework. In determining the scope of privacy rights, the Strasbourg Court has held that the scope of interaction of a person with others, even in a public context, may fall within the scope of 'private life',[76] and that the question of whether a person has a 'reasonable expectation of privacy' is a significant, but not necessarily conclusive, factor.[77] Further, the concept of 'private life' extends to aspects relating to personal identity, such as a person's name, photo, or physical and moral integrity.[78]

In rejecting the 'reasonable expectation' of privacy test as the sole arbiter of privacy rights, the Court has acknowledged that privacy has a role in protecting individuals from harms arising from public space surveillance. This has left the Court with the problem of delineating the scope of privacy rights in the public domain, and of differentiating problematic acts of surveillance from harmless (or even beneficial) observation of public places.

The Court has drawn the line between acceptable observation and potentially problematic surveillance at the point of data *collection and retention*. The observation of public space, even if technologically mediated (e.g. through video cameras), will not amount to an interference with Article 8 because what is observed is, essentially, 'public behaviour'.[79] An interference with Article 8 will arise when personal data are *collected and retained* on police information systems. The following passage in *P.G. & J.H. v UK* is frequently cited:

> A person who walks down the street will, inevitably, be visible to any member of the public who is also present. Monitoring by technological means of the same public scene (for example, a security guard viewing through closed-circuit television) is of a similar character. Private-life considerations may arise, however, once any systematic or permanent record comes into existence of such material from the public domain.[80]

This formulation avoids many of the difficulties faced by the US courts in delineating the scope of a 'reasonable expectation of privacy'. The scope of privacy rights does not here depend on the type or volume of data collected, the nature of the surveillance device, or on the extent to which the data can be used to build a 'picture' of the individual concerned and their movements, although these issues may be relevant to the Court when considering whether an interference with fundamental rights is necessary and proportionate under Article 8(2). Instead, privacy rights become applicable to the public domain simply on the basis that personal data are collected and retained.

This broader conception of privacy means that surveillance of public assemblies may fall within the scope of Article 8. In the case of *Catt v UK*, for example, the claimant was the subject of numerous intelligence reports spanning several years (although the claimant himself had not been suspected of, or implicated in, any criminal activity). The reports were compiled by police intelligence teams overtly deployed to monitor protests, and consisted of notes made of John Catt's appearance, movements, and behaviours. The ECtHR found a violation of Article 8 on the basis that the collection and *retention* of personal data was disproportionate and unjustified. In determining proportionality, emphasis was placed on the lack of appropriate data protection safeguards and retention reviews.[81]

This informational approach to privacy potentially brings any surveillance activity involving the retention of personal data within the scope of Article 8. This appears to be a more expansive approach, but as discussed further below, problems remain.

The European Court of Human Rights Approach: Freedom of Assembly

The European Court of Human Rights has also held that state surveillance may amount to an interference with Article 11, the right to freedom of peaceful assembly and association, but there have been few cases in which this has been considered. Surveillance cases coming before the Court have invariably been heard under the heading of privacy rights, and where it has found a violation of privacy, the Court has not always found it necessary to go on to consider the applicability of Article 11.[82]

For the Court to find a violation of Article 11, there must be a clear and acknowledged link between the exercise of the freedom of peaceful assembly and the measures taken against it.[83] It is, therefore, likely that claimants would need to demonstrate some concrete injury or constraint: that the surveillance measures in question did, in fact, deter or prevent them from engaging in acts of assembly (or association).[84] In the case of *Segerstedt*, the Court suggested surveillance of political mobilizations, which breached Article 8, would *necessarily* amount to a violation of Article 11.[85] This does not, however, appear to have become an established principle, and in other cases involving state surveillance in the context of political protest, the Court has not made a similar observation.[86]

The circumstances in which the Court would recognize surveillance as a constraint on Article 11 are unclear. The Court has suggested in the past that Article 11 issues may arise if there is a likelihood that people will be 'put off' or discouraged from participation in future protest by fear of disciplinary sanction.[87] The Court has also acknowledged the 'chilling effect' of surveillance in relation to the collection and retention of information relating to political activities and opinions.[88] However, recognition of this 'chilling effect' in this context appears to be predicated on the question of whether the surveillance in question would constitute a violation of privacy rights. It is far from certain whether the Court would be willing to recognize the possibility that such a 'chilling effect' may arise from surveillance in the absence of a violation of Article 8.

Conclusion

In neither jurisdiction has privacy rights been interpreted in a way which fully addresses the kinds of surveillance harms discussed above. In the United States, courts have retained a primarily locational approach to privacy. While this has softened a little post-*Carpenter*, the Fourth Amendment still has very limited application to the surveillance of public space. The Strasbourg Court has taken a more expansive approach, and the extension of privacy rights to the circumstances involving the *collection and retention* of data brings a greater range of surveillance activities within the scope of privacy rights. Article 8 rights to respect for private life may have application to surveillance which involves the photography of identified persons, or information about their movements and activities, as long as that data is retained by state authorities.

Although more expansive, the Strasbourg stance is not without limitations. By taking what is fundamentally an informational approach, there is a danger that the courts view potential harms arising from public space surveillance as essentially informational harms, and thus fail to adequately acknowledge or evaluate harms that are not informational in nature—such as proximity and intrusion. Surveillance may come to be seen primarily as a matter of data protection which can be mitigated by informational means (e.g. by ensuring secure storage or limited retention periods) rather than as a potential threat to decisional autonomy and the exercise of fundamental rights.

Because there is a need to define privacy in such a way that it does not over-reach into the public realm, the European Court has determined that for privacy rights to be applicable to data obtained from the public domain, that data must be collected *and permanently or systematically retained* by state authorities. In the context of the surveillance of public assemblies, however, this requirement may be a restrictive one. What constitutes 'permanent or systematic retention' is far from evident and opens the possibility that state authorities may avoid liability by not entering data on a searchable database, or by setting retention regimes with limited duration. Further, the requirement imposes a significant evidential burden on claimants, who may be able to establish that data was collected, but unable to ascertain that the data was permanently or systematically retained. The suggestion by the European Commission in *Friedl*, that Article 8 may extend to data that is 'collected *and recorded*' in relation to an identified individual, has not found favour in subsequent Strasbourg decisions.

Finally, and most importantly, privacy may not, in this context, be the most appropriate framework for recognizing the damage that surveillance may do in the public domain. The harms that are discussed above—the 'chilling effects' of intrusion, identification, and differentiation—are better conceptualized as constraints to freedom of assembly. The surveillance activities encountered by participants in public assemblies may flow from (or lead to) the collection and retention of personal data, but they are *experienced* as an interference in their activities of association and/or mobilization.

A reliance on assembly rights is, however, also problematic. In both jurisdictions, the courts have accepted that surveillance is capable of curtailing assembly freedoms, but the circumstances in which this will amount to a rights violation are limited. In *Strasbourg*, surveillance claims are unlikely to be litigated at all outside the framework of privacy, and the court may be reluctant to consider that surveillance which does not violate privacy rights is capable of undermining assembly freedoms. In the US courts, claimants will not have standing to pursue a claim unless they can provide evidence of a specific and concrete curtailment of their freedom to assemble: A 'chilling effect' resulting from mere awareness or fear of surveillance is unlikely to be sufficient. This imposes a challenging evidential burden. As we have seen, the 'chilling effect' of surveillance can be multi-layered and insidious. The impact of surveillance may not be immediate or direct but rather cumulative and diffuse, aggregating over time and possibly affecting a larger, or differently constituted class of person than those who may be directly the focus of surveillance measures. In these circumstances it may not be possible for claimants to present evidence of a specific and tangible deterrence.

What results then, is a situation where surveillance of public assemblies is in danger of falling between two stools. There is a growing body of evidence that the chilling effect of surveillance—whether intentionally or unintentionally delivered—poses a substantial and possibly long-lasting threat to the freedom of assembly and association. Yet neither the framework of privacy nor that of assembly rights appears capable of acknowledging the range of harms that occur.

Notes

1. C. Emsley, *The English Police: A Political and Social History*, 2nd ed. (Oxford: Routledge, 2014), 104.
2. Arne Hintz, Lina Dencik, and Karin Wahl-Jorgensen, *Digital Citizenship in a Datafied Society* (Cambridge: Polity Press, 2019), 5.
3. Raphael Schlembach, 'Undercover Policing and the Spectre of "Domestic Extremism": The Covert Surveillance of Environmental Activism in Britain', *Social Movement Studies* 17, no. 5 (2018): 491–506, 494.
4. For example, in the UK case of *Mengesha v Commissioner of Police of the Metropolis*, [2013] EWHC 1695 (Admin), the High Court held that it was not lawful for the police to maintain a containment for the purposes of obtaining identification (whether by questioning or by filming).

5. For example, Alexandra Mateescu, Alex Rosenblat, and Danah Boyd, 'Dreams of Accountability, Guaranteed Surveillance: The Promises and Costs of Body-Worn Cameras', *Surveillance & Society* 14, no. 1 (2016): 122–127.
6. P. Gill and M. Phythian, *Intelligence in an Insecure World*, 3rd ed. (Cambridge: Polity Press, 2018), 12.
7. Daniel J. Solove, 'A Taxonomy of Privacy', *University of Pennsylvania Law Review* 154, no. 3 (2006): 477–564, 489 (noting that 'harmful activities' include information collection, information processing, information dissemination, and invasion).
8. Beatrice von Silva-Tarouca Larsen, *Setting the Watch: Privacy and the Ethics of CCTV Surveillance* (London: Bloomsbury, 2011), 156.
9. Susanne Krasmann, 'The Enemy on the Border: Critique of a Programme in Favour of a Preventive State', *Punishment & Society* 9, no. 3 (2007): 301–318, 306.
10. Lucia Zedner, 'Pre-Crime and Post-Criminology?', *Theoretical Criminology* 11, no. 2 (2007): 261–281, 262.
11. Zedner, 'Pre-crime and Post-Criminology?', 267.
12. Herbert L. Packer, 'Two Models of the Criminal Process', *University of Pennsylvania Law Review* 113 (1964): 1.
13. Christina E. Wells, 'Reinvigorating Autonomy: Freedom and Responsibility in the Supreme Court's First Amendment Jurisprudence', *Harvard Civil Rights-Civil Liberties Law Review* 32 (1997): 159.
14. Daniel J. Solove, *Understanding Privacy* (Cambridge, MA: Harvard University Press, 2009), 103.
15. Kirsty Hughes, 'A Behavioural Understanding of Privacy and Its Implications for Privacy Law', *Modern Law Review* 75, no. 5 (2012): 806–836, 812–815.
16. Alan Westin, *Privacy and Freedom* (London: The Bodley Head, 1970), 32.
17. Erving Goffman, *Behavior in Public Relation: Notes on the Social Organization of Gatherings* (New York: Free Press, 1963), 83.
18. Ibid., 193.
19. Larsen, *Setting the Watch*, 21.
20. Valerie Aston, 'State Surveillance of Protest and the Rights to Privacy and Freedom of Assembly: A Comparison of Judicial and Protester Perspectives', *European Journal of Law and Technology* 8, no. 1 (2017): 7–8; Emily Apple, 'Political Policing in the UK: A Personal Perspective', in *Activists and the Surveillance State: Learning from Repression* (London: Pluto Press, 2019), 177–196, 178–181.
21. Andrea Brighenti, 'Visibility: A Category for the Social Sciences', *Current Sociology* 55, no. 3 (2007): 323–342, 330.
22. Niall Hamilton-Smith, Maureen McBride, and Colin Atkinson, 'Lights, Camera, Provocation? Exploring Experiences of Surveillance in the Policing of Scottish Football', *Policing and Society* 31, no. 2 (2021): 179–194, 186.
23. Paul Lewis, 'Spotter Cards: What They Look Like and How They Work', *The Guardian*, October 2009, https://www.theguardian.com/uk/2009/oct/25/spotter-cards.
24. Marc Jonathan Blitz, 'Video Surveillance and the Constitution of Public Space: Fitting the Fourth Amendment to a World that Tracks Image and Identity', *Texas Law Review* 82, no. 6 (2004): 1349–1481, 1383.
25. Zhilong Guo and Lewis Kennedy, 'Policing Based on Automatic Facial Recognition', *Artificial Intelligence and Law* 31, no. 2 (2023): 397–443, 404.
26. Solove, 'Taxonomy', 506.

27. Amy Stevens et al., '"I Started Seeing Shadows Everywhere": The Diverse Chilling Effects of Surveillance in Zimbabwe', *Big Data & Society* 10, no. 1 (2023): 7.
28. Aston, 'State Surveillance', 8.
29. David Lyon, 'Surveillance as Social Sorting: Computer Codes and Mobile Bodies', in *Surveillance as Social Sorting: Privacy, Risk and Discrimination* (London: Routledge, 2003), 13.
30. See, for example, Metropolitan Police, National Domestic Extremism and Disorder Intelligence Unit, *Nominal Creation Policy*, 2013 (referring to a 'step change in a person's status').
31. Joanna Gilmore, Will Jackson, and Helen Monk, 'Keep Moving! Report on the Policing of the Barton Moss Community Protection Camp, November 2013–April 2014', Project Report. Centre for the Study of Crime, Criminalisation & Social Exclusion, LJMU and Centre for Urban Research, University of York, Liverpool (2016), 33–38.
32. Donatella Della Porta, 'Social Movements and the State: Thoughts on the Policing of Protest', Working Paper, European University Institute, 1995, 6.
33. Michael Rosie and Hugo Gorringe, 'What a Difference a Death Makes: Protest, Policing and the Press at the G20', *Sociological Research Online* 14, no. 5 (2009): para. 2.7.
34. Raphael Schlembach, 'Undercover Policing', 499; Stefano Bonino and Lambros George Kaoullas, 'Preventing Political Violence in Britain: An Evaluation of Over Forty Years of Undercover Policing of Political Groups Involved in Protest', *Studies in Conflict & Terrorism* 38, no. 10 (2015): 814–840, 816–825.
35. Clifford Stott, Geoff Pearson, and Owen West, 'Enabling an Evidence-Based Approach to Policing Football in the UK', *Policing: A Journal of Policy and Practice* 14, no. 4 (2020): 977–994, 979–981.
36. Aston, 'State Surveillance', 7.
37. Amory Starr et al., 'The Impacts of State Surveillance on Political Assembly and Association: A Socio-Legal Analysis', *Qualitative Sociology* 31 (2008): 251–270, 267.
38. Nathan Stephens Griffin, '"Everyone Was Questioning Everything": Understanding the Derailing Impact of Undercover Policing on the Lives of UK Environmentalists', *Social Movement Studies* 20, no. 4 (2021): 459–477, 469–472.
39. Aston, 'State Surveillance', 10.
40. Frederick Schauer, 'Fear, Risk and the First Amendment: Unravelling the Chilling Effect', *Boston University Law Review* 58 (1978): 685–729.
41. Ibid., 690.
42. Solove, 'Taxonomy', 522.
43. Jonathon Penney, 'Understanding Chilling Effects', *Minnesota Law Review* 106 (2022): 1451–1529, 1455.
44. ECtHR, *Denisov v Ukraine* [GC] App. No. 76639/11 (25 September 2018), 96.
45. U.S. Const. amend. IV.
46. *Carpenter v United States*, 138 S. Ct. 2206, 2213–2214 (2018).
47. ECtHR, *Kudrevičius and Others v Lithuania* [GC] App. No. 37553/05 (15 October 2015), 91.
48. *NAACP v Alabama ex rel. Patterson*, 357 U.S. 449 (1958).
49. *Shelton v Tucker*, 364 U.S. 479 (1960).
50. *Baird v State Bar of Ariz.*, 401 U.S. 1 (1971).
51. *Carpenter*, 138 S. Ct. at 2213. Traditionally, the Fourth amendment inquiry focused on physical intrusion on a constitutionally protected area. *Katz* rejected that approach. See

Katz v United States, 389 U.S. 347, 351 (1967) ('[T]he Fourth Amendment protects people, not places'). However, there has been a return to considerations in recent cases, such as *United States v Jones* discussed below.

52. *Katz v United States*, 389 U.S. 347, 360 (1967) (Harlan, J., concurring). In his concurrence, Justice Harlan summarized the Court's opinion to create the two-part reasonable expectation of privacy test.
53. *United States v Knotts*, 460 U.S. 276, 281–282 (1983).
54. *United States v Jones*, 565 U.S. 400, 402–403 (2012).
55. Ibid., 415 (Sotomayor, J., concurring).
56. Ibid., 430 (Alito, J., concurring).
57. *Carpenter v United States*, 138 S. Ct. 2206, 2220 (2018).
58. Paul Ohm, 'The Many Revolutions of *Carpenter*', *Harvard Journal of Law & Technology* 32 (2019): 357–416, 358.
59. *Carpenter*, 138 S. Ct. 2206, 2217 (quoting *Jones*, 565 U.S. at 429 (Alito, J., concurring)). See also Matthew Tokson, 'The Aftermath of *Carpenter*: An Empirical Study of Fourth Amendment Law', *Harvard Law Review* 135, no. 7 (2022): 1791–1852, 1804.
60. See e.g. *Carpenter*, 138 S. Ct. at 2220 ('Our decision today is a narrow one. . . . We do not . . . call into question conventional surveillance techniques and tools, such as security cameras').
61. Leaders of a Beautiful Struggle v Balt. Police Department, 2 F.4th 330 (4th Cir. 2021).
62. Ibid., 360–361 (Wilkinson, J., dissenting).
63. *California v Ciraolo*, 476 U.S. 207, 213–214 (1986) (holding aerial surveillance from a plane at one thousand feet did not violate the Fourth Amendment because police are not required to 'shield their eyes when passing by a home on public thoroughfares'); *Dow Chem. Co. v United States*, 476 U.S. 227, 239 (1986); *Florida v Riley*, 488 U.S. 445, 450 (1989); see also *Katz v United States*, 389 U.S. 347, 351 (1967) ('What a person knowingly exposes to the public, even in his own home or office, is not a subject of Fourth Amendment protection').
64. *Leaders of a Beautiful Struggle*, 2 F.4th at 345–346.
65. *United States v Cuevas-Sanchez*, 821 F.2d 248, 250–251 (5th Cir. 1987); see also *People v Tafoya*, 490 P.3d 532 (Colo. Ct. App. 2019), *aff'd*, 494 P.3d 613 (Colo. 2021) (holding, in reliance on *Carpenter and Jones*, that the use of a pole camera for a period of three months violated the Fourth Amendment).
66. See, for discussion, Dana Khabbaz, 'Unmanned Stakeouts: Pole-Camera Surveillance and Privacy After the *Tuggle* Cert Denial', *Yale Law Journal* 132 (2022): 105–135, 107.
67. *United States v Tuggle*, 4 F.4th 505, 524 (7th Cir. 2021); see also *United States v Dennis*, 41 F.4th 732, 740–741 (5th Cir. 2022) ('Although the Supreme Court addressed a form of continuous surveillance in *Carpenter*, unlike cell-site location information, there is nothing inherent in the use of security cameras to cast doubt on their validity').
68. Tyler Valeska, 'First Amendment Limitations on Public Disclosure of Protest Surveillance', *Columbia Law Review Forum* 121 (2021): 241.
69. *NAACP v Alabama ex rel. Patterson*, 357 U.S. 449 (1958).
70. *Baird v State Bar of Ariz.*, 401 U.S. 1 (1971).
71. *Black Lives Matter v Town of Clarkstown*, 354 F. Supp. 3d 313 (2018); see also Isaiah Strong, 'Surveillance of Black Lives as Injury-In-Fact', *Columbia Law Review* 122, no. 4 (2022): 1019–1054, 1034.

72. *Black Lives Matter*, 354 F. Supp. 3d at 324.
73. See, for example, Isaiah Strong, 'Surveillance of Black Lives as Injury-In-Fact', *Columbia Law Review* 122, no. 4 (2022): 1019–1054, 1044.
74. *Laird v Tatum*, 408 U.S. 1, 13–14 (1972).
75. *Clapper v Amnesty Int'l USA*, 568 U.S. 398 (2013).
76. ECtHR, *P.G. & J.H. v the United Kingdom* App. No. 44787/98 (25 September 2001), 56; ECtHR, *Peck v the United Kingdom* App. No. 44647/98 (28 January 2003), 57; ECtHR, *Perry v the United Kingdom* App. No. 63737/00 (17 July 2003), 36.
77. *Perry* App. No. 63737/00, 37.
78. ECtHR, *Vavřička and Others v the Czech Republic* [GC] App. Nos. 47621/13, 3867/14, 73094/14, 19298/15, 19306/15 and 43883/15 (8 April 2021), 261.
79. ECmHR, *Herbecq and Another v Belgium* App. Nos. 32200/96 and 32201/96 (14 January 1998).
80. *P.G. & J.H. v the United Kingdom*, 57.
81. *Catt v United Kingdom* App. No. 43514/15 (24 January 2019), 100–128.
82. See e.g. *Catt v United Kingdom*.
83. ECtHR, *Navalnyy and Yashin v Russia* App. No. 76204/11 (4 December 2014), 52.
84. Cf. *Wilson v Commission of Police for the Metropolis*, [2021] UKIPTrib IPT_11_167_H, 325–326.
85. ECtHR, *Segerstedt-Wiberg and others v Sweden* App. No. 62332/00 (6 June 2006).
86. For example, ECtHR, *Shimovolos v Russia* App. No. 30194/09 (21 June 2011).
87. ECtHR, *Ezelin v France* App. No. 11800/85 (26 April 1991), 52; see also ECtHR, *Navalnyy and Yashin v Russia* App. No. 76204/11 (4 December 2014), 51.
88. For example *Catt v United Kingdom* App. No. 43514/15 (24 January 2019), 123.

Further Reading

Aston, Valerie. 'State Surveillance of Protest and the Rights to Privacy and Freedom of Assembly: A Comparison of Judicial and Protester Perspectives'. *European Journal of Law and Technology* 8, no. 1 (2017): 1–19.

Brighenti, Andrea. 'Visibility: A Category for the Social Sciences'. *Current Sociology* 55, no. 3 (2007): 323–342.

Schlembach, Raphael. 'Undercover Policing and the Spectre of "Domestic Extremism": The Covert Surveillance of Environmental Activism in Britain'. *Social Movement Studies* 17, no. 5 (2018): 491–506.

Starr, Amory, Luis Fernandez, Randall Amster, Lesley Wood, and Manuel Caro. 'The Impacts of State Surveillance on Political Assembly and Association: A Socio-Legal Analysis'. *Qualitative Sociology* 31 (2008): 251–270.

Strong, Isaiah. 'Surveillance of Black Lives as Injury-in-Fact'. *Columbia Law Review* 122, no. 4 (2022): 1019–1054.

CHAPTER 37

POLICING ASSEMBLIES AND THE USE OF FORCE

STUART CASEY-MASLEN

INTRODUCTION

ALTHOUGH peaceful assembly is a 'fundamental' human right,[1] assemblies can be a major flashpoint between the public and the police. This is especially so when participants are convening to criticize the actions of the authorities or their policies, a reality that can be confirmed from even a cursory glance at world news on any chosen day. Protests and demonstrations can and do degenerate into violence, sometimes at the instigation of the assembly participants, sometimes at the hands of the police, and sometimes as a result of the conduct of both. In some cases, protests are directed specifically at the police themselves, accusing individual officers or entire departments of excessive use of force. Global economic and environmental issues can also prompt people to assemble publicly in both a planned and spontaneous manner, with citizens keen to make their views known to the wider public as well as the relevant decision-makers.

Violent repression by the authorities through their law enforcement officers has all too often been the reaction to public gatherings that are deemed illegal or undesirable. While each and every day, thousands of protests pass off without any act of violence on the part of the participants or the police, others do not. As state agents authorized to use force in certain circumstances, a high level of professionalism is naturally demanded of the police and other law enforcement agencies and bodies in the context of assemblies. Some fully comply with their obligations; many do not. At the end of the 1960s, the term 'police riot' entered sociological and criminological discourse, after being coined in the official *Walker Report*[2] which investigated rioting around the 1968 Democratic Convention in Chicago during protests against the Vietnam War.[3] In extreme cases, the unlawful actions of the police may amount not only to human rights violations but also to international crimes.[4]

Given the potential for violence and abuse by a range of state organs and agents, this chapter addresses the constraints imposed by international law on the use of force by the police and other law enforcement agencies in connection with assemblies. The discussion that follows revolves around international legality in three principal respects: when force may be lawful; who may legitimately use force; and how much force may be used where some force is necessary in the prevailing circumstances. While in practice the detailed resolution of each issue depends on the specific context, police use of force is regulated by clear and immutable rules of international law. The rules manifest themselves both through the duty to respect and protect fundamental human rights and by the corresponding obligation to apply general principles of law enforcement to the policing of assemblies.[5] In his report of June 2022 on the situation of human rights in Iran, the Secretary-General of the United Nations (UN) underlined that any use of force must comply with the fundamental principles of legality, necessity, proportionality, precaution, and non-discrimination. He further declared that domestic law on the use of force by law enforcement officials 'must be brought into line with the requirements enshrined under international law'.[6]

The upstream principle of legality thus dictates that the granting of authority to the police to use force must be grounded in existing domestic law and regulation. General principles on use of force and specific regulation of lethal weapons—particularly firearms—must be set forth in domestic law. Detailed rules on the operational use of less-lethal weapons, such as police batons and tear gas, may be put into law or expressed in implementing regulations and standing operating procedures (SOPs). Only weapons that are duly authorized for use by the police should be operationally deployed.

The principle of legality is of course also relevant for both individual and broader institutional responsibility. A failure to provide appropriate and legally binding regulation of any weapons or tactics must then feed into the downstream principle of accountability, along with the actions of law enforcement officials and law enforcement agencies. With respect to Bulgaria, for example, in 2014, after strong criticism by the European Court of Human Rights, particularly its Grand Chamber in the *Nachova* case,[7] Bulgaria adopted a new law on police use of force to improve its compliance with the international rules governing law enforcement.[8]

The two key principles of international law governing the use of force are necessity and proportionality, as this chapter discusses. Only the minimum necessary force may be used in pursuit of a legitimate law enforcement purpose. In most instances, no force at all will be permissible. Moreover, force must be targeted—differentiated—to those in an assembly who are engaged in acts of violence or criminal damage and not generally at the gathering as a whole. Thus, in its judgment in the *Women Victims of Sexual Torture* case, the Inter-American Court of Human Rights called upon state authorities to 'make every effort to distinguish between violent or potentially violent individuals and peaceful demonstrators'. This is on the basis that '[s]poradic acts of violence or crimes committed by certain persons should not be attributed to others whose intentions and behaviour are of a peaceful nature'.[9]

The principle of proportionality adds an additional constraint upon the use of force, dictating that even if a certain level of force may be deemed necessary in the circumstances (e.g. to stop an assembly participant who is escaping after causing criminal damage), if the force used is excessive or indiscriminate when judged with respect to the threat being confronted, it will still be unlawful. International rules on the use of firearms are the obvious—but not the only—manifestation of the principle of proportionality. There is also some evidence that graduated force—where the type and level of force is increased gradually—is also required by international law.

Accountability pertains to the actions and omissions of law enforcement officials and agencies throughout an assembly.[10] If they use excessive or indiscriminate force against participants, they must of course be held to account for this. But accountability is also required by international law when they fail to intervene, for instance, to protect participants against the acts of third parties, whether individual vigilantes, militias, or organized armed groups.[11] Private security companies may sometimes legitimately be delegated by the state to assist in the facilitation of peaceful assemblies, but any such delegation of authority must be tightly constrained and regulated by clear rules and standards for their conduct. Should private security personnel deviate from these rules and standards and/or engage in violent behaviour towards participants, this will obligate law enforcement officials to intervene to stop them.

Police Use of Force in Connection with an Assembly

At the global level, the 1966 International Covenant on Civil and Political Rights expresses the right of peaceful assembly in straightforward terms, declaring that the right of peaceful assembly 'shall be recognized'.[12] A total of 174 states were party to the Covenant at the time of writing, with others similarly bound by the rules of general international law to respect the exercise of the right by those falling under their jurisdiction. The right is also reflected as a general principle of domestic law: no fewer than 184 of the 193 UN Member States recognize the right of peaceful assembly in their national constitutions.[13]

Under treaty and customary law, such recognition of the right of peaceful assembly imposes a corresponding duty on the authorities to facilitate assemblies.[14] Participants must be safeguarded at all times against physical harm, while an assembly as a whole must itself be protected, unless and until it becomes violent as a whole[15] or is otherwise subject to lawful dispersal. These tasks fall primarily to the police (or other relevant law enforcement agencies, when they are duly operating in the context of an assembly). Hence, in a resolution adopted without a vote in July 2022, the forty-seven-seat UN Human Rights Council explicitly recognized 'the critical role that law enforcement plays in respecting and protecting human dignity and maintaining and upholding the human rights of all persons, including in the facilitation of assemblies'.[16]

Ordinarily, no force may be used by the police, other than to protect participants in a peaceful assembly from the unlawful acts of third parties. As stipulated in the 1990 UN Basic Principles on the Use of Force and Firearms by Law Enforcement Officials (the 1990 Basic Principles), this is the case under international law given that 'everyone is allowed to participate in lawful and peaceful assemblies, in accordance with the principles embodied in the Universal Declaration of Human Rights and the International Covenant on Civil and Political Rights'.[17]

At its heart, the notion of a 'lawful' assembly was intended by the states that drafted the provision in the 1990 Basic Principles to refer to adjudication under domestic law. Today, however, the principle is better understood to pertain to legality first and foremost under international law. There is thus a tension between 'peacefulness' (which militates in favour of an assembly being facilitated as a matter of international law) and 'lawfulness' as typically determined by the authorities based on domestic law, which would tend towards the restriction of a protest in which organizers or participants have contravened certain procedural or substantive legal requirements.

The Principle of Necessity

The first general principle of international law governing police use of force is that of necessity. The Code of Conduct for Law Enforcement Officials adopted by the United Nations in 1979 thus stipulates that law enforcement officials may use force 'only when strictly necessary'.[18] This means that the police may only use force where it is necessary in the prevailing circumstances in pursuit of a legitimate law enforcement objective. The UN Human Rights Guidance on Less-Lethal Weapons in Law Enforcement defines this as follows:

> An objective that is recognized in both international and national law, such as protecting members of the public or a law enforcement official from violence, preventing the perpetration of a criminal offence, arresting a person suspected of having committed a criminal offence, or detaining a convicted criminal pursuant to a lawful sentence. The term also refers to the duty of law enforcement agencies and officials to facilitate and protect the right of peaceful assembly.[19]

Dispersal of a peaceful assembly that poses no threat to life or health will thus ordinarily not meet the threshold for any use of force.[20] Hence, if it is not lawful to disperse an assembly, a fortiori it is not lawful to use force with a view to doing so.

International law further dictates that, in the dispersal of assemblies that are unlawful but 'non-violent', the police must avoid the use of force altogether, or, where that is not practicable, must restrict that force 'to the minimum extent necessary'.[21] This notion of minimum necessary force is an integral element of the principle of necessity as it pertains to the actions of law enforcement officials. Moreover, as the European Court of

Human Rights has held, 'where injuries have been sustained at the hands of the police, the burden to show the necessity of the force used lies on the Government'.[22]

Of course, once the need for any use of force has passed, any additional force will be unlawful.[23] This concerns, for instance, the circumstance in which an individual criminal suspect is handcuffed and is not—or is no longer—resisting arrest. But more typically no handcuffing (itself a use of force) will be necessary. Thus, the European Court has reaffirmed that there 'can be no justification' to use pepper spray against a demonstrator who has already been placed under the control of the law enforcement authorities.[24] Where a person in police custody is not acting or threatening to act violently, no force may be lawfully used against them.

Further, the rule also applies more broadly to assemblies, for example, where temporary unrest amongst participants has ceased.[25] If scuffles have ended, the assembly should be allowed to proceed without forcible intervention. In its 2015 judgment in the *Bouyid* case, the Grand Chamber of the European Court of Human Rights reiterated its long-standing position that with respect to any person confronted with law enforcement officers, 'any recourse to physical force which has not been made strictly necessary by his own conduct diminishes human dignity and is, in principle, an infringement' of the right to freedom from inhuman or degrading treatment.[26]

The Precautionary Principle

In adjudging whether the state has complied with the principle of necessity in any given instance, international human rights law will also take into account if adequate precautionary measures were taken to minimize the risk of recourse to the use of force.[27] For, as the UN Special Rapporteur on extrajudicial, summary, or arbitrary executions, Christof Heyns, observed in 2014: 'Once a situation arises where the use of force is considered, it is often too late to rescue the situation'.[28] While the focus of the precautionary principle is on preventing loss of life at the hands of law enforcement officials,[29] it applies more generally to any use of force by the police, including in connection with assemblies.[30] The precautionary principle has particular salience with respect to assemblies whose organization has been notified in advance, but law enforcement officials should also be trained and equipped to facilitate and police spontaneous assemblies and counter-demonstrations in accordance with domestic and international law (see Adang, in this volume, and Probert, in this volume).[31] Contingency plans must be in place for policing operations in both scenarios.

Law Enforcement Actors and Policing of Assemblies

In accordance with the 1979 UN Code of Conduct for Law Enforcement Officials, 'the term "law enforcement officials" includes all officers of the law, whether appointed or elected, who exercise police powers, especially the powers of arrest or detention'.[32] The police are the state agency most likely to be engaged in ensuring that an assembly remains peaceful, especially where there is a perceived risk of an outbreak of violence.

The authorities in many countries have employed private security firms to perform some or all of their law enforcement tasks. While the state incurs responsibility for any unlawful use of force they occasion, the individual security officers themselves do not ordinarily benefit from the same powers of arrest—and therefore the concomitant possibility to use lawful force—that are bestowed by official 'constabulary' powers.[33] The only exception to this general rule is where officers are specifically imbued by the state with such authority in law. International human rights law does not prohibit the use of private security companies and personnel for the performance of law enforcement tasks or for the protection of property or individuals. This is so, whether the tasks relate to an assembly or to other tasks, such as in the criminal justice system. In all such cases, however, private security companies must be strictly regulated by domestic law, and especially the right of any of its employees or agents to use force.

The notion of 'law enforcement official' and 'agency' includes the military, 'whether uniformed or not', as well as other state security forces, whenever and wherever they exercise such powers.[34] In practice, however, the army should not be used to oversee an assembly,[35] as they are rarely well equipped mentally and physically to do so.[36] But if they are so used, soldiers must comply fully with the relevant international rules governing use of force in law enforcement.[37] This will not typically be the case. As just one example among many, on the night of 20 October 2020, members of the Nigerian army opened fire on unarmed protesters calling for the disbandment of a violent police squad at the Lekki toll gate in Lagos. A year later, an officially instituted panel of inquiry found the Nigerian military to be culpable in the shooting and killing of eleven unarmed citizens, during what it described as a 'massacre'.[38]

Militias and similar armed groups should not be used to police assemblies. Their lack of training and accountability makes them wholly unsuitable for such law enforcement tasks, as experiences around the world have clearly demonstrated. The 'Maidan' protests in Ukraine in 2014,[39] for instance, were forcibly repressed by private militia known as 'Titushky' with the authorization, support, or acquiescence of state officials. This included apprehension, ill treatment, and even torture to death of certain protesters, as case law before the European Court of Human Rights has confirmed. In its judgment in *Lutsenko and Verbytskyy v Ukraine*, the Court held that the Titushky had been 'hired' by the police to commit these serious violations of international law.[40]

Constraints on the Use of Force During an Assembly

While the extent of the use of force is of course dependent on the prevailing circumstances (in particular, the behaviour of participants in an assembly), the principles of necessity and proportionality together govern generally how much force may be lawful. According to the principle of necessity, when force is justified by the exigencies of the situation, the force that may lawfully be used is only the minimum necessary in the circumstances. This may be to arrest an individual reasonably believed to be committing an act of violence, whether it is perpetrated against another person or against property. Such targeted arrests may be a suitable—and even a preferable—alternative to dispersing an assembly.

But the minimum necessary force may still be none. In the overwhelming majority of cases, an arrest can readily be effected without any violent action on the part of a police officer, just by using the authority of their office. According to the 1990 Basic Principles, for instance, in carrying out their duty, law enforcement officials 'shall, as far as possible, apply non-violent means before resorting to the use of force'.[41] For, as the US Department of Justice has justly observed, the ability of a police officer to 'bring calm to a situation is a core policing skill'.[42]

The Principle of Proportionality

In addition to the principle of necessity for the use of force, the principle of proportionality always applies (see Robinson and Page, in this volume).[43] As the formal commentary of the 1979 Code of Conduct recalls, domestic law 'ordinarily restricts the use of force by law enforcement officials in accordance with a principle of proportionality'.[44] Indeed, as the commentary further declares, in no case should the use of force be authorized 'which is disproportionate to the legitimate objective to be achieved'.[45] Similarly, according to the 1990 Basic Principles: 'Whenever the lawful use of force and firearms is unavoidable, law enforcement officers shall . . . act in proportion to the seriousness of the offence and legitimate objective to be achieved'.[46]

Proportionality thus fixes an upper limit on when minimum necessary force may be lawful, based on a comparison of the threat posed and the harm inflicted on life or limb and to property by the actions taken to repel the threat.[47] Passive resistance to an order by a police officer to get up from the roadway never justifies a baton strike to the body or an electric shock from a conducted energy device, such as a Taser. While it may be necessary to seek to cause the protester to move, such violent action will not be proportionate. In its report on unrest in Ferguson, Missouri, which followed the shooting to death of Michael Brown in 2015, the Civil Rights Division of the US Department of Justice observed that Ferguson Police Department (FPD) officers' approach to policing involved violation of the US Constitution and the FDP's own policies (see Pita Loor, in this volume).[48] 'Officers across the country encounter drunkenness, passive defiance, and verbal challenges. But in Ferguson, officers have not been trained or incentivized to use de-escalation techniques to avoid or minimize force in these situations. Instead, they respond with impatience, frustration, and disproportionate force'.[49]

Operational Tactics

A range of operational tactics exist for policing assemblies, particularly when an assembly involves violence on the part of certain participants. These are discussed in more detail elsewhere in this volume (see especially Probert, in this volume), but two are considered briefly here: snatch squads and containment (also called kettling).

Snatch squads involve small numbers of law enforcement officials entering an assembly in order to arrest specific individuals who are engaged in acts of violence. If conducted professionally and successfully, this tactic can allow an otherwise peaceful assembly to proceed and avoid the risk of greater violence breaking out later. But it also involves significant risks. In wading into a crowd, police may succumb to the temptation to inflict indiscriminate force on anyone blocking their ingress or egress. Once inside a crowd, there may be a violent reaction from those who were previously peaceful, perceiving an assault by the police on themselves and their rights, thereby endangering the safety of the officers. As with all operational tactics, officers must always be adequately trained and suitably equipped for participating in snatch squads during an assembly.

Containment—often referred to colloquially as 'kettling'—is where law enforcement officials encircle and close in a section of the participants in an assembly. According to the Human Rights Committee, this operational tactic 'may be used only where it is necessary and proportionate to do so, in order to address actual violence or an imminent threat emanating from that section'.[50] Kettling amounts to a use of force by law enforcement officials. Indeed, appropriate measures 'targeted against specific individuals' are often, the Committee says, 'preferable' to containment. In addition, particular care must be taken 'to contain, as far as possible, only people linked directly to violence' as well as 'to limit the duration of the containment to the minimum necessary'.[51] The advantage for the police is that, in contrast to the use of tear gas, which may fragment a group of individuals engaged in acts of violence, kettling may succeed in containing a potentially widespread problem of violence within a defined area. Such preventative tactics may however constitute a deprivation of liberty which must in turn, under the terms of the European Convention on Human Rights, be justifiable under the exhaustive grounds set forth in its Article 5.[52]

Restrictions on the Use of Firearms During an Assembly

An elevated risk during any assembly in which acts of violence are expected or actually committed by some of the participants is that the police will discharge firearms against protesters, leading to loss of life. Firearms are not an appropriate tool for the policing of assemblies, as the UN Human Rights Committee has observed.[53] In particular, firearms must never be used simply to disperse an assembly,[54] and the risk of police killings of protesters during or immediately following forced dispersal may be especially high.[55]

In order to comply with international law, any use of firearms by law enforcement officials in the context of assemblies must be limited to targeted individuals in circumstances in which it is strictly necessary to confront an imminent threat of death or serious injury.[56] The protection of property is therefore not a legitimate ground to discharge a firearm, but only the protection of life or the prevention of life-threatening injury. And as the UN Human Rights Council has confirmed, 'nothing can ever justify the indiscriminate use of lethal force against a crowd, which is unlawful under international human rights law'.[57]

In its 2011 judgment in the *Giuliani and Gaggio* case, the Grand Chamber of the European Court of Human Rights addressed the use of deadly force by a *carabiniere* (an Italian military police officer) in a violent demonstration during the G8 Summit in Genoa in Italy in July 2001. A jeep of carabinieri was suddenly surrounded by rioters and the officers were attacked by stones, sticks, and iron bars. One of the rioters, Carlo Giuliani, tried to throw a fire extinguisher at officers, despite a warning not to do so. The officer, who perceived an imminent threat to his own life and to that of his colleagues, fired his weapon at Mr Giuliani, killing him.[58] The Grand Chamber held that the officer had acted lawfully in doing so.[59] It rejected the applicant's argument that less-lethal ammunition should have been provided to the *carabinieri* since the death had occurred 'not in the course of an operation to disperse demonstrators and control a crowd of marchers, but during a sudden and violent attack' which posed 'an imminent and serious threat' to the lives of three officers.[60]

The fact that officers have not been provided with alternative means to tackle widespread violence does not justify recourse to the use of lethal force. Indeed, this is likely to ground a violation of the right to life on the basis of the failure by the state to take suitable precautionary measures to protect life by equipping its law enforcement officials appropriately. In this regard, dispersal of participants in a riot through the use of firearms has been specifically condemned by the European Court of Human Rights in the *Güleç* case adjudicated in 1998. The case concerned spontaneous and unauthorized demonstrations and attacks on public buildings in the town of Idil in south-eastern Turkey. The son of the applicant to the Court was hit and killed by a ricochet bullet that had been fired by a gendarme with a view to dispersing the demonstrators. The Court held that the authorities should have provided their law enforcement officials with less-lethal alternatives to firearms to disperse the assembly.[61]

The Use of Less-Lethal Weapons During an Assembly

Indeed, the duty of every state to respect and protect life and the right of every person to security implies that the policing of protests should be conducted by law enforcement officials who are suitably equipped with less-lethal weapons. In 2020, the Office of the UN High Commissioner for Human Rights issued *United Nations Human Rights Guidance on Less-Lethal Weapons in Law Enforcement*. The document, which responds to gaps in the regulation of such weapons under the 1990 Basic Principles, supports the use of less-lethal weapons in assemblies where force is both lawful and necessary.[62] But in so doing, it distinguishes between situations where individuals are engaged in acts of violence (where only less-lethal weapons that can be individually aimed may be employed) and weapons such as chemical irritants dispersed at a distance (tear gas) where groups of individuals are engaged in acts of violence (unless it is lawful in the circumstances to disperse the entire assembly). Use of less-lethal weapons, the Guidance clarifies, 'should accord due consideration to the impact on other non-violent participants or bystanders'.[63]

In addition, the use of any less-lethal weapons against assembly participants must pay due attention to the potential for panic in a crowd, including the risk of a stampede.[64] In Guinea, on 28 September 2009, a stampede was caused in a stadium in Conakry as a result of an assault by a combined force of several hundred Presidential Guard troops, gendarmes, officers from the Anti-Riot Police, and dozens of civilian-clothed members of irregular militias. The stadium was packed with tens of thousands of peaceful pro-democracy supporters protesting the military regime and supporting a presumed candidacy in the forthcoming presidential elections. The state forces entered the stadium, sealing off most of the exits, after Anti-Riot Police had fired tear gas canisters into the stadium.[65] The UN-mandated international Commission of Inquiry would later find that many people suffocated or were trampled to death in stampedes, which were compounded by the use of tear gas.[66] Although the precise number of those killed will never be known, as the authorities covered up the scale of the fatalities, at least eighty-nine people were later reported missing.[67] The Commission of Inquiry found that crimes against humanity had been committed.[68]

The circumstances in which the dispersal of an assembly may be lawful are addressed elsewhere in this volume.[69] The 1990 Basic Principles envisage dispersal in unlawful but peaceful assemblies as well as in the case of 'violent' assemblies.[70] While, as discussed above, the use of firearms with conventional ammunition is wholly excluded for such a purpose, employing less-lethal weapons in order to seek to disperse an assembly should also be considered 'a measure of last resort'.[71] In this regard, before approving dispersal, the UN recommends that law enforcement agencies seek rather to identify any violent individuals and to isolate them from the other participants. This may enable the main assembly to continue.[72] It may also prevent an assembly in which acts of violence are occurring from becoming a riot.

But where the decision is taken, in compliance with domestic and international law, to disperse an assembly, authorities in many countries authorize the police to use tear gas with a view to achieving this.[73] Some of the dangers of this approach have already been highlighted, but there are others, as the 2020 *United Nations Human Rights Guidance on Less-Lethal Weapons in Law Enforcement* observes. One is the toxic effects of certain chemical agents, especially when deployed in confined spaces.[74] Another comes from the effects of being struck by a tear-gas canister. For this reason, such projectiles should not be fired directly at people, especially at the head or face, since this generates a significant risk of death or serious injury as a result of impact trauma.[75]

The *Ataykaya* case concerned a worker who found himself in the middle of a demonstration. Mr Ataykaya was struck on the head by a tear-gas grenade fired by the police and died a few minutes later. The government accepted that Mr Ataykaya had just been passing by, but sought to justify his death on the basis that the police had been constrained by circumstances to fire a large number of tear-gas grenades to disperse a group of demonstrators. The autopsy performed on the deceased concluded that death was caused by a haemorrhage and brain damage inflicted by the projectile. The autopsy report further observed that the 'characteristics of the projectile's point of entry show that it had not been fired from a short distance', indicating the significant kinetic energy deposited by tear-gas canisters even when they are fired over a considerable distance.[76] Other risks to participants in an assembly inhere in tactical errors of policing. Thus, if chemical irritants are deployed behind a group of violent individuals, this may cause them to move towards the police, thereby increasing the risk of a violent confrontation.[77]

Accountability for Unlawful Police Use of Force in Connection with Assemblies

The principle of accountability is at the heart of international human rights law and the policing of assemblies is no different from other fundamental human rights. As the Human Rights Committee has stated,

> States have an obligation to investigate effectively, impartially and in a timely manner any allegation or reasonable suspicion of unlawful use of force or other violations by law enforcement officials, including sexual or gender-based violence, in the context of assemblies. Both intentional and negligent action or inaction can amount to a violation of human rights. Individual officials responsible for violations must be held accountable under domestic and, where relevant, international law, and effective remedies must be available to victims.[78]

An after-action report by the authorities following each major assembly, and especially one in which force was used, should consider what went well in policing and what could be improved. Where police use of force has occasioned death or serious injury, a violation of the right to life and/or the right to freedom from torture or inhuman treatment may have occurred.[79]

It remains unsettled whether excessive, extra-custodial use of force by the police during an assembly can amount to torture or only rather inhuman treatment. The better view is that it can, at the least when the victim is powerless to escape from his perpetrator's clutches. The wording of the definition of the UN Convention against Torture and accompanying commentary certainly does not obligate a custodial setting for torture to be inflicted, and the requisite purposes of torture include intimidation and discrimination.[80] Often, however, a human rights body will not distinguish between the different forms of ill-treatment when identifying a human rights violation.[81]

If an initially peaceful assembly escalates into violence and both groups of individuals—participants and police officers—become involved in violent acts, it may be necessary to examine who started the violence.[82] Of course, state agents acting as agents provocateurs engage the international responsibility of the state and obviate necessity for the use of force by police in uniform.[83] Police officers who hide or obscure their identification numbers with a view to avoiding individual accountability for unnecessary or excessive use of force also thereby incur the international responsibility of the state they serve.[84]

In its judgment in the application against Turkey by *Nurettin Aldemir*, the Court observed that there was:

> no evidence to suggest that the group in question initially presented a serious danger to public order. Nevertheless, it is likely that they would have caused some disruption in a particularly busy square in central Ankara. It transpires that the demonstrators, including the applicants, wished to draw attention to a sensitive bill proposed in the Parliament and that their rally was initially peaceful. However, the authorities' intervened swiftly with considerable force in order to disperse them, thereby causing tensions to rise, followed by clashes.[85]

The Court concluded in that case that the forceful intervention of the police officers had been disproportionate. That is so, even though, under domestic law, the assembly in that case was 'unlawful' since it was held in a place where demonstrations were not permitted.

Concluding Remarks

The principles that govern police use of force in connection with an assembly are clear. At the instant of use of force, such force must be both necessary and proportionate. Force applied in a discriminatory manner (based on race, ethnicity, gender, political opinion, or social group) can never be lawful. But to be lawful, force must also respect the principle of legality, meaning that it has been regulated in advance. Accountability demands that every use of force—every baton strike, every use of chemical agents, and of course every shot fired—must be justified and justifiable.

While progress has been made in many countries, there is clearly a long road ahead. Training and equipping law enforcement officials engaged in policing violent or potentially violent assemblies in the appropriate use of tactics and less-lethal weapons and providing them with suitable, personal protective equipment increases everyone's safety. Ensuring a human rights-compliant national legal regime should not be seen as an obstacle to effective policing—because it is not. But a significant change in mindset is still needed in many countries in order to instil all law enforcement personnel with the confidence to practice what governments preach. Ensuring that the use of force against assemblies which have been deemed unlawful by the authorities is not the 'go-to response' assuredly remains a work in progress.

Notes

1. Thus, for instance, the right to assemble peacefully has been duly described as a 'fundamental human right in a democratic society' by the European Court of Human Rights. ECtHR, *Djavit An v Turkey* App. No. 20652/92 (20 February 2003), 56.
2. 'Rights in Conflict: The Violent Confrontation of Demonstrators and Police in the Parks and Streets of Chicago during the Week of the Democratic National Convention of 1968', Report submitted by Daniel Walker, Director of the Chicago Study Team, to the National Commission on the Causes and Prevention of Violence (1 December 1968).
3. The eponymous book by Rodney Stark in the early 1970s on US police actions in countering anti-government and anti-Vietnam War protests would come to popularize the term. Stark defines a police riot as an 'event . . . when roving bands of policemen set upon non-provocative persons and/or property in an excessively violent manner. When only one small group of policemen sets upon citizens and/or property in a single location, it may be useful to call this a police attack. A police riot is any such event involving two or more attacks'. R. Stark, *Police Riots* (Belmont, CA: Wadsworth, 1972), 17.
4. In this regard, in September 2018, a group of States Parties to the Rome Statute of the International Criminal Court (ICC) from the Americas (Argentina, Canada, Chile, Colombia, Paraguay, and Peru), made an unprecedented referral of the situation in Venezuela since 12 February 2014. An English translation of the referral is available at https://www.icc-cpi.int/sites/default/files/itemsDocuments/180925-otp-referral-venezuela_ENG.pdf. On 3 November 2021, the Office of the Prosecutor decided to proceed with investigations, including into allegations 'that State security forces frequently used excessive force to disperse and put down demonstrations'. 'ICC Prosecutor, Mr Karim A A Khan QC, opens an investigation into the Situation in Venezuela and concludes Memorandum of Understanding with the Government', Press release No. ICC-OTP-20211105-PR1625 (5 November 2021), https://www.icc-cpi.int/news/icc-prosecutor-mr-karim-aa-khan-qc-opens-investigation-situation-venezuela-and-concludes.
5. UN Human Rights Council Resolution 50/21, The promotion and protection of human rights in the context of peaceful protests(adopted without a vote on 8 July 2022), 19.
6. Situation of human rights in the Islamic Republic of Iran, Report of the Secretary-General (16 June 2022) UN Doc. A/HRC/50/19, 16.
7. The ECtHR described the 'laxity of the regulations on the use of firearms and the manner in which they tolerated the use of lethal force' and held that the then extant legal framework was 'fundamentally deficient', falling 'well short of the level of protection 'by law' of the right to life that is required by the Convention in present-day democratic societies in Europe'. ECtHR, *Nachova v Bulgaria* [GC] App. Nos. 43577/98 and 43579/98 (6 July 2005), 99, 100.
8. Use of force by law enforcement officials is generally regulated by the 2014 Ministry of Interior Act (especially Articles 85–88). See e.g. University of Pretoria's Law on Police Use of Force website, 'Bulgaria', https://www.policinglaw.info/country/bulgaria.
9. Inter-American Court of Human Rights (IACtHR), *Case of Women Victims of Sexual Torture in Atenco v Mexico*, Judgment (Merits) (28 November 2018), Series C, No. 371, https://www.corteidh.or.cr/docs/casos/articulos/seriec_371_ing.pdf, 175.
10. See generally Report of the Special Rapporteur on the rights to freedom of peaceful assembly and association, Clémont Nyaletsossi Voule, Advancing Accountability and Ending Impunity for Serious Human Rights Violations related to the Exercise of the Rights to Freedom of Peaceful Assembly and of Association (19 May 2023) UN Doc. A/HRC/53/

38, https://www.ohchr.org/en/documents/thematic-reports/ahrc5338-advancing-accountability-serious-human-rights-violations.

11. See e.g. Report by Nils Muižnieks, Commissioner for Human Rights of the Council of Europe, following his visit to Ukraine from 4–10 February 2014, Doc. CommDH(2014)7 (Strasbourg: Council of Europe, 4 March 2014), 70.
12. Article 21: International Covenant on Civil and Political Rights (adopted at New York, 16 December 1966; entered into force, 23 March 1976).
13. UNHRCtte, General Comment No. 37—Article 21: Right of Peaceful Assembly (17 September 2020) UN Doc. CCPR/C/GC/37, 3 and note 3. For details of each state's constitutional provisions see the country profiles on the Laws on the Right of Assembly Worldwide website, https://rightofassembly.info.
14. Ibid., 8. Joint report of the Special Rapporteur on the rights to freedom of peaceful assembly and of association and the Special Rapporteur on extrajudicial, summary or arbitrary executions on the proper management of assemblies (4 February 2016) UN Doc. A/HRC/31/66, 13. See also e.g. Human Rights Council Resolution 50/21, 5 and 10.
15. UNHRCtte, General Comment No. 37, 4 and 15.
16. Human Rights Council Resolution 50/21, 44th preambular para.
17. Basic Principles on the Use of Force and Firearms by Law Enforcement Officials, Principle 12, endorsed by UN General Assembly Resolution 45/166 (8 December 1990), 4, adopted without a vote. Although this was a soft-law instrument without direct legally binding effect, the Basic Principles have come to be regarded as reflective of customary international law, binding on all states. UNHRCtte, General Comment No. 36: Article 6—The Right to Life, UN Doc. CCPR/C/GC/36 (3 September 2019), 14.
18. UN Code of Conduct for Law Enforcement Officials, article 3, adopted by UN General Assembly Resolution 34/169, 17 December 1979, resolution adopted without a vote.
19. UN Human Rights Guidance on Less-Lethal Weapons in Law Enforcement (Office of High Commissioner for Human Rights, 2020), 9, 44.
20. UNHRCtte, General Comment No. 37, 85; Human Rights Council Resolution 50/21, 18; See also, for example, ECtHR, *Laguna Guzman v Spain* App. No. 41462/17 (6 October 2020), 51.
21. 1990 Basic Principles on the Use of Force and Firearms by Law Enforcement Officials, Principle 13.
22. ECtHR, *Anzhelo Georgiev and ors v Bulgaria* App. No. 51284/09 (30 September 2014), 67.
23. S. Casey-Maslen, *The Right to Life under International Law* (Cambridge: Cambridge University Press, 2021), 7.27.
24. ECtHR, *Ali Güneş v Turkey* App. No. 9829/07 (10 April 2012), 41.
25. ECtHR, *İzci v Turkey* App. No. 42606/05 (23 July 2013), 60, 61, 67.
26. ECtHR, *Bouyid v Belgium* [GC] App. No. 23380/09 (28 September 2015), 88, 100. The case is not one directed to the right of peaceful assembly, but the principle holds good with respect to the policing of assemblies.
27. UNHRCtte, General Comment No. 37, 78.
28. Christof Heyns, Report of the Special Rapporteur on extrajudicial, summary or arbitrary executions (1 April 2014) UN Doc. A/HRC/26/36, 63.
29. ECtHR, *McCann and ors v United Kingdom* [GC] App. No. 18984/91 (27 September 1995), 194.
30. See African Commission on Human and Peoples' Rights, General Comment No. 3—Article 4: Charter on Human and Peoples' Rights: The Right to Life (2015), 27.

31. See also Adang and Probert, both in this volume.
32. UN Code of Conduct for Law Enforcement Officials, article 1.
33. See e.g. International Code of Conduct for Private Security Service Providers, as amended (10 December 2021), 34, https://icoca.ch/wp-content/uploads/2022/01/INTERNATIONAL-CODE-OF-CONDUCT_Amended_2021.pdf. See further S. Jerbi, *The International Code of Conduct for Private Security Service Providers*, Academy Briefing No. 4, Geneva Academy of International Humanitarian Law and Human Rights, Geneva, August 2013, https://www.geneva-academy.ch/joomlatools-files/docman-files/Publications/Academy%20Briefings/Icoc_web_final.pdf, 36 and 39.
34. UN Code of Conduct for Law Enforcement Officials, formal commentary to Article 1.
35. UNHRCtte, Concluding observations on the fourth periodic report of the Bolivarian Republic of Venezuela (14 August 2015) UN Doc. CCPR/C/VEN/CO/4, 14; and African Commission on Human and Peoples' Rights, *Guidelines on Policing Assemblies in Africa, Banjul* (2017), 3.2.
36. Thus, the Inter-American Court of Human Rights has reaffirmed that 'the maintenance of internal public order and citizen security must be primarily reserved for civilian police forces'. Only 'exceptionally' should the armed forces intervene in security tasks and any such intervention must be 'justified', 'temporary' and limited to the strict exigencies of the situation. IACtHR, *Alvarado Espinoza and ors v Mexico*, Judgment (Merits) (28 November 2018), Series C, No. 370, https://www.corteidh.or.cr/docs/casos/articulos/seriec_370_ing.pdf, 182.
37. Ibid.; and UNHRCtte, General Comment No. 37, 80.
38. E. Egbejule, 'Panel of Inquiry Finds Nigerian Army Culpable in Lekki "Massacre"', *Aljazeera*, 16 November 2021, https://www.aljazeera.com/news/2021/11/16/panel-of-inquiry-finds-nigerian-army-culpable-in-lekki-massacre.
39. Between 21 November 2013 and 21 February 2014, a series of protests—commonly referred to as 'Euromaidan' and/or 'Maidan'—took place in Ukraine, reportedly in response to the decision of the Cabinet of Ministers to suspend preparations for the signing of the Ukraine-European Union Association Agreement. ECtHR, *Shmorgunov and ors v Ukraine* App. No. 15367/14 and 13 others (21 January 2021), 9.
40. ECtHR, *Lutsenko and Verbytskyy v Ukraine* App. Nos. 12482/14 and 39800/14 (21 January 2021), 19, 68, 82, 93.
41. Basic Principles on the Use of Force and Firearms by Law Enforcement Officials, Principle 4.
42. US Department of Justice, *Investigation of the Ferguson Police Department*, Civil Rights Division (4 March 2015), https://www.justice.gov/sites/default/files/opa/press-releases/attachments/2015/03/04/ferguson_police_department_report.pdf, 26.
43. This notion is distinct from that of proportionality in assessing the legality of restrictions or prohibitions on the holding of an assembly (see Robinson and Page, in this volume).
44. UN Code of Conduct for Law Enforcement Officials, Formal commentary to article 3.
45. Ibid.
46. Basic Principles on the Use of Force and Firearms, Principle 5.
47. Heyns, A/HRC/26/36, 65–66.
48. See further Pita Loor, in this volume.
49. US Department of Justice, *Investigation of the Ferguson Police Department*, 31.
50. UNHRCtte, General Comment No. 37, 84.
51. Ibid.

52. Contrast ECtHR, *Austin and ors v United Kingdom* [GC] App. Nos. 39692/09, 40713/09, 41008/09 (15 March 2012) (finding no deprivation of liberty, but noting the dissenting opinion that the judgment sends 'a bad message to police authorities') with *Eiseman Renyard v United Kingdom* App. No. 57884/17 (5 March 2019) (accepting that a deprivation of liberty had occurred, but holding it was justifiable under ECHR Article 5(1)(c)). Article 5(1) sets out the exhaustive grounds for justification—in particular, Article 5(1)(b) to 'secure the fulfilment of any obligation prescribed by law', and 5(1)(c) 'when it is reasonably considered necessary to prevent his committing an offence'. See further ECtHR, *S., V. and A. v Denmark* [GC] App. Nos. 35553/12, 36678/12, and 36711/12 (22 October 2018).
53. UNHRCtte, General Comment No. 37, 88.
54. Basic Principles on the Use of Force and Firearms, Principle 14.
55. Human Rights Committee, *Florentina Olmedo v Paraguay*, Views (Comm. No. 1828/2008), UN Doc. CCPR/C/104/D/1828/2008, 2012, 2.4–2.7.
56. UNHRCtte, General Comment No. 36, 12; and Basic Principles on the Use of Force and Firearms, Principles 9 and 14.
57. Human Rights Council Resolution 50/21, 20.
58. ECtHR, *Giuliani and Gaggio v Italy* [GC] App. No. 23458/02 (24 March 2011), 21–27.
59. Ibid., 194 and 196.
60. Ibid., 216. For an interesting critique of the judgment, see Stephen Skinner, 'The Right to Life, Democracy and State Responsibility in "Urban Guerrilla" Conflict: The European Court of Human Rights Grand Chamber Judgment in *Giuliani and Gaggio v Italy*', *Human Rights Law Review* 11, no. 3 (2011): 567–577.
61. ECtHR, *Güleç v Turkey* App. No. 21593/93 (27 July 1998), 71.
62. UN Guidance on Less-Lethal Weapons, 6.3.4.
63. Ibid.
64. Ibid., 2.5.
65. Human Rights Watch, 'Guinea: September 28 Massacre Was Premeditated', 27 October 2009, https://www.hrw.org/news/2009/10/27/guinea-september-28-massacre-was-premeditated.
66. Report of the International Commission of Inquiry mandated to establish the facts and circumstances of the events of 28 September 2009 in Guinea, UN Doc. S/2009/693, Annex, 62, 84.
67. Ibid., 198.
68. Ibid., 199.
69. See Probert, in this volume.
70. Basic Principles on the Use of Force and Firearms, Principles 13 and 14.
71. UNHRCtte, General Comment No. 37, 87.
72. UN Guidance on Less-Lethal Weapons, 6.3.3, citing Joint report of the Special Rapporteur on the rights to freedom of peaceful assembly and of association and the Special Rapporteur on extrajudicial, summary or arbitrary executions on the proper management of assemblies, UN Doc. A/HRC/31/66 (4 February 2016), 52.
73. The term 'tear gas' is used to describe a variety of lachrymatory agents launched by police forces against groups in assemblies in many countries. UN Guidance on Less-Lethal Weapons, 7.3.1.
74. Ibid., 7.3.5, citing ECtHR, *Abdullah Yaşa and ors v Turkey* App. No. 44827/08 (16 July 2013), 30.

75. UN Guidance on Less-Lethal Weapons, 7.3.6.
76. ECtHR, *Ataykaya v Turkey* App. No. 50275/08 (22 July 2014), 56–57.
77. UN Guidance on Less-Lethal Weapons, 7.3.4.
78. UNHRCtte, General Comment No. 37, CCPR/C/104/D/1828/2008, 90. Moreover, given that the state authorities may have access to relevant information, the burden of proof cannot rest solely on the individual who is asserting that a violation has occurred. UNHRCtte, *Olmedo v Paraguay*, Views, 7.5.
79. For guidance on an investigation into potentially unlawful death in compliance with international standards, see *The Minnesota Protocol on the Investigation of Potentially Unlawful Death (2016)* (New York: OHCHR, 2017), https://www.ohchr.org/sites/default/files/Documents/Publications/MinnesotaProtocol.pdf. For guidance on an investigation into potential acts of torture or other ill treatment, see *Istanbul Protocol: Manual on the Effective Investigation and Documentation of Torture and Other Cruel, Inhuman or Degrading Treatment or Punishment*, OHCHR, Professional Training Series No. 8/Rev. 2, New York/Geneva, 2022, https://www.ohchr.org/sites/default/files/documents/publications/2022-06-29/Istanbul-Protocol_Rev2_EN.pdf.
80. See e.g. G. Zach, 'Definition of Torture', in *The United Nations Convention against Torture and Its Optional Protocol: A Commentary*, 2nd ed., ed. M. Nowak, M. Birk, and G. Monina (Oxford: Oxford University Press, 2019), 116–120; 'Extra-custodial use of force and the prohibition of torture and other cruel, inhuman or degrading treatment or punishment', Report of the Special Rapporteur on torture and other cruel, inhuman or degrading treatment or punishment, Nils Melzer, UN Doc. A/72/178 (20 July 2017) 47; ECtHR, *Cestaro v Italy* App. No. 6884/11 (7 April 2015), 171–190; and ECtHR, *Bartesaghi Gallo and ors v Italy* App. Nos. 12131/13 and 43390/13 (22 June 2017), 117–120.
81. See e.g. ECtHR, *Annenkov and ors v Russia* App. No. 31475/10 (25 July 2017), 84–91.
82. ECtHR, *Primov and ors v Russia* App. No. 17391/06 (12 June 2014), 157.
83. UNHRCtte, General Comment No. 37, 18.
84. ECtHR, *İzci v Turkey* App. No. 42606/05 (23 July 2013), 68. See further the European Court's judgment in 2022 in the *Boboc* case in which investigators were unable to identify certain officers involved in Mr Boboc's beating because they were wearing balaclavas and 'no means of identification via wearable signs or otherwise had been used, preventing any meaningful attempt to hold each officer responsible for his actions'. ECtHR, *Boboc and ors v Moldova* App. No. 44592/16 (7 June 2022), 54.
85. ECtHR, *Nurettin Aldemir and ors v Turkey* App Nos. 32124/02, 32126/02, 32129/02, 32132/02, 32133/02, 32137/02, and 32138/02 (18 December 2007), 45.

Further Reading

Casey-Maslen, S., and S. Connolly. *Police Use of Force under International Law*. Cambridge: Cambridge University Press, 2017.

Hunton & Williams LLP. *Final Report of the Independent Review of the 2017 Protest Events in Charlottesville, Virginia* (November 2017). https://www.policinginstitute.org/wp-content/uploads/2017/12/Charlottesville-Critical-Incident-Review-2017.pdf.

Office of the Special Rapporteur for Freedom of Expression of the Inter-American Commission on Human Rights. *Protest and Human Rights: Standards on the Rights Involved in Social Protest and the Obligations to Guide the Response of the State*. OAS doc. OEA/SER.L/V/II,

CIDH/RELE/INF.22/19 (September 2019). https://www.oas.org/en/iachr/expression/publications/Protesta/ProtestHumanRights.pdf.

Office of the UN High Commissioner for Human Rights (OHCHR) and UN Office on Drugs and Crime (UNODC). *Resource Book on the Use of Force and Firearms in Law Enforcement.* New York: UN, 2017. https://www.ohchr.org/en/publications/policy-and-methodological-publications/resource-book-use-force-and-firearms-law.

CHAPTER 38

ASSEMBLIES AND THE COURTS

STEVEN CAMMISS, BRIAN DOHERTY, AND GRAEME HAYES

INTRODUCTION

THIS chapter examines an under-researched aspect of peaceful assembly, protest, and direct action: What happens, in the courtroom, to those who are arrested and charged for offences associated with these activities? Recognizing the importance of doctrinal analysis to understanding the options available to defendants in courtroom processes as well as how courtroom processes reify and entrench particular strands of legal doctrine, we are interested in the courtroom as a social space that does, or does not, retain the potential for political contestation. We seek to demonstrate that trials can provide a site of resistance and the means for ongoing struggle and contestation, but they can also be conducted in ways that threaten to repress and restrict protesters' voices. The chapter not only reveals the extent to which some protest trials are more 'political' than others but suggests that one explanation lies in the availability and interpretation of legal defences, which can serve to open up the courtroom as a political site.

As an interdisciplinary team, our observations draw on an ethnography of courtroom processes,[1] and this has influenced our reflections on what we term 'the protest trial'. The title of the chapter (and collection) is focused upon peaceful assembly. Our understanding of the concept is broad, and we therefore engage with a wide range of peaceful protest and direct-action tactics. Partly, this is pragmatic, as it reflects the protest trials that we have observed which cover a range of protest actions and tactics. But our conception of peaceful assembly is also theoretically deliberate: Protest trials can serve precisely to determine the boundaries of 'peaceful' and 'non-peaceful',[2] and by extension, the state's obligation of tolerance. These courtroom processes thus highlight the contingency of human rights protections. The interpretative work of courts renders precarious what the UN Human Rights Committee ostensibly assures—that 'civil disobedience or direct-action campaigns can be covered by article 21 [ICCPR], provided they are peaceful'.[3] Peacefulness is an inherently contested category, and trials of protesters are a key site for such contestation.

With this in mind, we will use a range of terms to describe protests and associated activities involving protesters, whether that be direct action, civil disobedience, or some other form of activism. We acknowledge that these terms have varied meanings, but we are interested in individuals and groups who use protest or direct action to challenge the political status quo and, most importantly, how the law, through the trial, responds to any such challenge.

For the scope of this chapter, we limit our observations to England and Wales. This is a pragmatic choice. Our findings should resonate in other jurisdictions; the courtroom as a possible site of struggle, resistance, and oppression is not limited to England and Wales. The limitations on available defences for protesters will have parallels elsewhere, including the United States[4] and Australia.[5] While our focus on a common law jurisdiction does limit the extent to which our findings apply to civil law countries, previous work by two of the authors suggests that our observations will ring true there too (despite the differences).[6]

Viewing the trial as a normative social process, however, rather than just a legal process, is vital. The chapter's focus on protest trials serves to refocus attention on a critical forum that has received significantly less attention than other means of regulation (such as policing). It illuminates how courts provide opportunities to challenge or entrench the regulatory logics confronting those who assemble to engage in collective action. It shows, that is, how protesters often use (or try to use) their trials to foreground their political claims, to speak truth to power. Ultimately, the chapter explores how the legal and social world of the courtroom operates not only to construct legitimate protest, but to construct the (non)political liberal subject. Consequently, we question the extent to which the trial, and the criminal law, can be conceived as apolitical. There is a strong pull to removing a communicative function for the protest trial to avoid politicizing the trial, but in so doing the (non)political subject thereby created is partial and disconnected from their actions.

Why Protest Trials Matter

There is a long tradition of research on the policing of activism and protest,[7] as evidenced by the range of other works referenced in this volume. However, there is a dearth of research on prosecutorial decision-making or what happens to activists in the courtroom. This is an important gap in the literature because what happens in the courtroom is of vital importance for the strategies of social movements and activist groups; the trial is a possible means of gaining media attention and a potential site of ongoing struggle and contestation. In addition, the trial of activists is an important means of understanding the legal processes by which law exercises its authority and how it constructs *legitimate* protest in modern liberal democratic states.

It is difficult to discuss the trial of activists without considering the ways the legitimacy of civil disobedience and more disruptive forms of protest, especially those at the boundary of peacefulness, are contested in liberal democratic theory. This ambivalence exists despite the rise of activism that embraces such tactics, especially in the environmental context. For example, law breaking is a deliberate tactic to draw attention to environmental concerns, as seen in the UK with Extinction Rebellion (XR), Insulate Britain, and Just Stop Oil.

Discussions in the liberal tradition on the role of civil disobedience, and the response of the law, frequently start with John Rawls.[8] For Rawls, we have a duty to obey the law due to the collective benefit of societal living, and this is the case where injustice occurs, as mistakes are inevitable in political systems. However, there are limits to this obligation and civil disobedience is justified if there are failures to recognize fundamental citizenship rights: 'We are not required to acquiesce in the denial of our own and other's basic rights'.[9] In these circumstances, civil disobedience is potentially rights enhancing; this is important, for instance, in the context of climate justice, given the increasing recognition, in international human rights law, of environmental rights, and the failure of mainstream political processes to address the growing emergency.[10] Nevertheless, Rawls argues that even when civil disobedience is justified, those who break the law for political aims should demonstrate 'fidelity to law' and accept conviction and punishment to evidence their commitment to liberal democracy. We would suggest that this displays a failure in liberal political theory: to recognize that activism is rights enhancing yet still subject to the penalties of the criminal law is a paradox and risks suppressing dissent.[11] Furthermore, the very existence of a constitutional right of peaceful assembly arguably enhances the space for civil disobedience (in ways that challenge the Rawlsian view): A broad definition of 'peaceful', encompassing disruptive behaviour and unlawful acts short of violence (as international human rights law suggests)[12] implies that one might engage in civil disobedience without necessarily accepting punishment.

Rawls's limitations on the justifiability of civil disobedience are based on the idea of the 'nearly just' state: No state will be perfectly just, but limitations on civil disobedience are still acceptable when the state is 'nearly just'. There are strong echoes of this formulation in the law's response to activism; judges state that protest takes place within a 'functioning democratic state' and consequently limit the defences which are available, as activists are expected to rely upon political and democratic processes to raise grievances.[13] This raises the question of the extent to which late modern democratic states are 'nearly just' in Rawls's terms. Crises in democratic governance and failures to address and protect fundamental rights, whether this be in relation to climate change or within the context of the immigration system, raise significant questions about the justness of the state, especially in the eyes of activists.[14] It could be said that the failure of the liberal democratic process is what leads to activism and, insofar as all states are imperfect, deliberate law breaking for political reasons should be understood as a normal, rather than an extraordinary, form of political action in an established democracy.[15]

How the trial deals with activists, therefore, is an important barometer of how the state responds to dissent and resistance.

Turning to the impact of the trial on social movements, trials could be regarded as either an opportunity to continue action by other means or as a repressive moment,[16] and this influences activists' views on the desirability of a trial. In our observations, we see four broad positions on this. For the first, epitomized by the 'Colston 4', any direct action is relatively spontaneous and there is no expectation of a trial (with some attempt to avoid the legal process, at least initially). In this case, defendants were part of a crowd that pulled down the statue of a slave trader and dumped it into the harbour in Bristol. In the second, the focus is on the action as shutting down a site, with the trial regarded as a possible outcome, but not one that is necessarily sought. An example might be the Palestine Action trials we have observed where the aim is to impede production of arms equipment at factories owned by Israeli companies. The third example, seen in the Stansted 15 action, is similarly focused upon shutting down a site (an area of an airport from which migrants were due to be deported), but the means of doing so ('locking on'[17] to maximize the duration of site occupation) and the nature of the site (an airport) means a trial is almost inevitable; in that case, the similarity of the defendants' prepared statements in the police interview suggests that arrest and prosecution had, at least, been contemplated by the defendants. Finally, for some activists, trials are actively sought or accepted as part of the strategy; this is the case for some XR activists, given that getting arrested was a specific aim in some of their actions.[18] As the trial becomes more likely, one would expect that activists contemplate the trial as a continuation of their action and more integral to their political strategy.

For the trial to be a continuation of action, there needs to be a space, or activists need to create a space, to challenge the status quo. This could be through a rejection of the authority of the court and an appeal to some other justificatory discourse for their action. This form of challenge, in our experience, is rare.[19] What is more usual is that activists engage with the process and attempt to challenge the prosecution case. This is usually of a particular type; rather than challenging the prosecution's version of events, activists suggest a different interpretation of these. In other words, they appeal to moral discourses on what is right and attempt to do so in the language of defences; activists claim their acts were necessary or that they had a 'lawful excuse'.

Activists may also see the trial in other ways that are not necessarily focused upon 'winning' the case. In our observations of XR guilty plea hearings,[20] many activists took this as an opportunity to 'speak truth to power', outlining their reasons for acting and how they saw their involvement as a 'moral duty'. The trial is also a means to speak to a constituency outside the courtroom; the Stansted 15 defendants regarded the trial as an opportunity to gain publicity around the harms of the immigration system.[21] Such publicity is also important in building and sustaining social movements.

Protest trials, therefore, are notably different from 'everyday' trials, as activists seek to draw upon political ideals to frame events, and to place motive, ideals, and politics centre stage. Viewing the trial as a binary opportunity or threat is mistaken; our observations show how the trial is always a threat *and* an opportunity; arguments over the admissibility of evidence, or the availability of defences, provide the opportunity to open up the trial as a political space, but also carry the risk that that space will be closed down.

The Courtroom as a Site of Power and Resistance

While the courtroom is a site of legal argument, it is much more than this. There is a rich tradition of understanding the courtroom as a social space where relationships are important in understanding working practices. From Paul Rock's work on the Crown Court,[22] Pat Carlen's examination of power in magistrates' courts,[23] studies which examine local courtroom cultures[24] or workgroups[25] through to ethnomethodological and linguistic studies on courtroom conversations,[26] we learn that we must move beyond legal analysis to fully understand what happens within courts. These studies highlight the social aspect of courtroom interactions, the importance of ongoing working relationships between 'insiders' to the exclusion of 'outsiders', the development of local working practices that can lead to 'justice by geography', and how interactions are ongoing accomplishments framed by language. While these processes operate within a legal framework, they are important in themselves to understand courtroom interactions.

Further, the criminal courtroom is also a normative space where moral judgments are passed on defendants' actions. For Antony Duff, the trial should be seen as a means by which we hold the defendant to account.[27] Criminal responsibility is analogous to moral responsibility, and this is both relational and triadic; individuals are responsible *as* citizens (and, therefore, as members of a moral community), *to* that community, *for* public wrongs. Responsibility, however, is only a necessary, not sufficient, condition for liability. If individuals are responsible, they must answer for their actions. One means of answering is to provide an account which may justify or excuse action. Within the trial, therefore, there could be a moral discussion on the meaning and interpretation of action. As already noted, activists during the trial are unlikely to question 'the facts', but are instead more likely to challenge the interpretation of events. The courtroom should, therefore, operate as a site of ongoing struggle and contestation if the trial is truly to operate, as Duff thinks it should, as a communicative endeavour. In other words, the criminal court is a normatively loaded social space which addresses, through a communicative enterprise, questions of moral wrongdoing.

The protest trial is a space where we see law in action, operationalized by state officials who work in the context of a local court culture, share a similar working outlook with other officials, have a fidelity to law and democratic processes, and where they routinely try (or should try) to hold defendants to account for their wrongdoing. But in the protest trial, these officials are faced with individuals who seek, either explicitly or implicitly, to undermine the credibility or the standing of the state and, possibly, by extension, the very officials who are holding them to account. Activists deny they have breached the norms of the community; instead, they claim to act *on behalf* of the moral community given the reasons that motivate their action. This leads to an important question; how does this actually play out in the particular setting of the courtroom?

In our observations of the trial of the Stansted 15, we documented the extent to which power in the legal process, and the court as a hostile disciplinary space, operated in ways that framed a particular vision of the *legitimate* protester.[28] The Stansted 15 faced terrorism-related charges for entering Stansted airport in March 2017 and halting the departure of a flight chartered by the Home Office to deport sixty immigration detainees to West Africa. As part of their action, they locked on around the parked aircraft, erected a banner ('Mass Deportations Kill—Stop Charter Flights'), and sang protest songs ('No Borders, No Nations, Stop Deportations'). They underwent a ten-week trial in Chelmsford Crown Court in the autumn of 2018. Their defences were necessity related defences of duress of circumstances and prevention of crime, focusing upon the risks of potential harm the detainees would face as part of the deportation process and on their arrival in West Africa. The defendants framed their claims in narrow terms which focused upon this risk and not on wider debates on the operation of the immigration system, its failures, and harms resulting from the 'hostile environment'.[29] As a consequence, their focus was largely an ethics of care and solidarity, rather than a wholesale critique of the system. The choices made were partly a result of legal rulings in the trial—the defendants were denied their request to question Home Office officials on the operation of the immigration process, and the trial judge actively policed the boundary between acceptable and unacceptable testimony, with a particular focus on excluding political statements—and partly a consequence of the high-stakes environment created by the terrorism-related charge—the offence, of endangering the safety of an aerodrome, carries a maximum sentence of life imprisonment, elevating the risks associated with conviction. The defendants were also constrained not just in terms of what they could say; they also felt constrained in how they spoke and how they appeared,[30] thus engaging in 'script compliance',[31] while some felt they could not speak at all due to rulings on bad character evidence.[32] In any event, at the closure of the defence case, the trial judge ruled that a necessity defence was not available on the facts, ironically as this was because their action was driven by their wider political beliefs, not because they wanted to avoid the risk of harm to the detainees.[33] The legal rulings and courtroom environment therefore deprived the defendants of an opportunity to resist the government's narrative and account for their actions. As a consequence, their strong views on immigration policy and practice were silenced. The process was not an open communicative endeavour.

By contrast, the trial of the Colston 4, who were charged with criminal damage after pulling down the statue of Edward Colston (a prominent slave trader) and dumping it in the harbour, operated quite differently. We observed this trial, held in Bristol Crown Court in December 2021 and January 2022, and the contrasts were stark. In particular, the legal defences which were available led to the trial mostly being an effective communicative enterprise, as the defendants were able to raise necessity-based arguments. The defendants asserted multiple defences, but the claim that the defendants were acting to prevent a crime (that the statute of Colston was an indecent display) effectively allowed the defence to put Colston himself in the dock, along with Bristol City Council. Expert evidence was presented by the high-profile historian David Olusoga on the history of slave trade, while citizens of the city gave evidence on what the statue meant to them and how it prolonged the community's pain. Bristol City Council were portrayed as ineffective and unresponsive to citizens' demands that the statue either be removed or be contextualized to highlight Colston's prominent role in the slave trade. As a consequence of the failures of the political system, the defendants were able to portray their behaviour as a moral and civic action on behalf of the community. They claimed they were acting with, not against, the people, and they pointed to the removal of the statue as a positive outcome that would help create a better future for the community.

This freedom to resist the prosecution's narrative, however, also facilitated other acts of resistance. In the trial of the Stansted 15, where the defendants faced a serious terrorism-related charge with the possibility of a long prison sentence, the public gallery was quiet, solemn, and attentive, with defendants themselves sometimes informally policing behaviour, such as through disapproving glances when voices were raised or asking those in the public gallery to move from where they are sitting.[34] Contrastingly, in the Colston 4 trial, where there was less threat of a heavy sentence, the defendant's supporters were vociferous in the public gallery, cheering when they felt that the defence had landed a 'heavy blow' to the prosecution case. Similarly, while the defendants in the Stansted 15 trial made conscious decisions on how they dressed and appeared in the courtroom, some of the Colston 4 defendants resisted conventional means of exerting control. One defendant, for instance, declined the trial judge's 'invitation' to remove a facemask when giving evidence (the trial took place during the COVID-19 pandemic), only relenting when it was made clear, by the trial judge that this was not a request.

These examples are illustrative of how the courtroom is a site of power, a space where the state seeks to exert control over the process and limit the extent to which activists are able to challenge the status quo. But that authority and control can be challenged, particularly if the law creates a space for activists to express their motivations and reasons. We would suggest that if the trial is to be an authentic communicative endeavour, then this space is crucial to allow for defendants to fully account for their actions. This takes us to an examination of the (lack of) availability of defences in protest trials.

Legal Defences in Protest Trials

What is distinctive about the protest trial is the extent to which contestation is not primarily focused upon 'what happened' but rather upon an interpretation of the events that form the basis of criminal proceedings; defendants do not usually dispute their actions, but instead attempt to frame these as legitimate and necessary. One of the means of contesting the interpretation of events is through the raising of defences, particularly necessity or 'lawful/reasonable excuse'.

We refer here to the defence of necessity in broad terms,[35] highlighting how the higher courts in England and Wales have restricted the availability of necessity defences in protest trials (despite instances of successful necessity defences at first instance).[36] For Norrie, a claim of necessity, that breaking the law was required to prevent a greater harm, creates an opening for critique and contestation in the courtroom, as necessity, 'provides the basis for an alternative, politically substantive, account of "the facts" to enter the courtroom and to challenge the law's formalistic defence of the political and economic status quo'.[37] Similarly, Martin suggests that the necessity defence carries the possibility of a 'direct, doctrinally legitimate, and uniquely powerful means through which revolutionary change might be accomplished within prevailing jurisprudential and constitutional structures'.[38] This possibility of critique arises due to the nature of the necessity defence; in claiming that an act was justified, the context of an act (which is usually irrelevant to the question of guilt) can become central. This is the case for protest trials, as defendants point to failures of the state, or the breaching of fundamental rights, as the reason for action.

Doctrinal analysis is therefore important to explore the extent to which these claims—that the actions of protesters are legitimate and necessary—are able to be heard. This then shapes the extent to which the courtroom is a potential site of ongoing contestation and struggle and, therefore, operates as a possible enabler of social change.

Central to the limiting of the defence of necessity in England and Wales is a case concerning twenty protesters who engaged in various acts of civil disobedience (including damage to property) in protest against the Iraq war. In *Jones*, Lord Hoffman paid lip service to the importance of protest and social movements:

> [C]ivil disobedience on conscientious grounds has a long and honourable history in this country. People who break the law to affirm their belief in the injustice of a law or government action are sometimes vindicated by history. The suffragettes are an example which comes immediately to mind. It is the mark of a civilised community that it can accommodate protests and demonstrations of this kind. But there are conventions which are generally accepted by the law-breakers on one side and the law-enforcers on the other. The protesters behave with a sense of proportion and do not cause excessive damage or inconvenience. And they vouch the sincerity of their beliefs by accepting the penalties imposed by the law. The police and prosecutors, on the other hand, behave with restraint and the magistrates impose sentences which take the conscientious motives of the protesters into account.[39]

We have termed this 'Hoffmann's Bargain'. Protesters are expected to act proportionately, thereby limiting the impact of their action on the wider community and accept the law's authority. In return, state officials, be they the police, prosecutors, or courts, will recognize defendants' motives and act 'with restraint' and show leniency in charging and sentencing. However, there is a sting in the tail for protesters: Any defence of necessity will be denied, making conviction probable or inevitable:

> In a case in which the defence requires that the acts of the defendant should in all the circumstances have been reasonable, his acts must be considered in the context of a functioning state in which legal disputes can be peacefully submitted to the courts and disputes over what should be law or government policy can be submitted to the arbitrament of the democratic process. In such circumstances, the apprehension, however honest or reasonable, of acts which are thought to be unlawful or contrary to the public interest, cannot justify the commission of criminal acts and the issue of justification should be withdrawn from the jury.[40]

This is clearly a Rawlsian pact between the protester and state; those who engage in protest, if they are to benefit from Hoffmann's Bargain, must display 'fidelity to law'[41] and accept the consequences of breaking the law.

One outcome of this approach is that trial judges in England and Wales, as a result of their discretion to rule on the availability of defences, can decide that a necessity defence is not operative in protest trials; for instance, in the trial of the 'Frack Free Three' (who climbed on to a truck, thereby blocking access to a fracking site in Lancashire), the trial judge ruled, before any evidence was raised, that a necessity defence was not available.[42] However, in the trial of the Stansted 15, the trial judge delayed ruling on the availability of a necessity defence until the close of the defence case. This allowed the defence some space to contest the meaning of events.[43] Nevertheless, after the closing of the defence case, the judge then ruled that the necessity defence was not available as the risks they were seeking to avoid were not imminent and did not cause them to act; as with Lord Hoffmann's ruling in *Jones*, the judge reflected that the defence 'must be considered in the context of a functioning state in which legal disputes can be peacefully submitted to the Courts and disputes over what should be law or government policy can be submitted to the democratic process'.[44] The door was then firmly slammed shut on the availability of necessity defences in protest trials by the Court of Appeal, holding that the lower court had been right to withdraw the defence from the jury.[45]

The denial of a necessity defence consequently limits the possibility of ongoing critique and contestation of government and private actors. The Frack Free Three, for instance, were unable to call upon their beliefs that fracking is incompatible with net zero environmental obligations and was an imposition upon the local community. Similarly, the Stansted 15 were divested of their political beliefs on the injustice of the immigration system and the extent to which the Home Office were dysfunctional and acting illegally.

A concurrent line of cases has seen the higher courts grappling with lawful and reasonable excuse defences in protest trials. This line of cases explores the extent to which Articles 9, 10, and 11 of the European Convention of Human Rights (ECHR)[46] require a 'proportionality assessment' on the extent to which conviction could be regarded as an unjustified interference with the defendants' ECHR rights. In short, the courts have been grappling with the question of how to balance Articles 9, 10, and 11 rights with the state's obligations to protect the rights of others or prevent crime and disorder. The nature of these rights, particularly freedom of conscience and expression, are such that the beliefs and motivations of protesters could become central to any proportionality assessment in a way that allows protesters to open up the courtroom as a space of dissent and contestation.

In the case of *Director of Public Prosecutions v Ziegler*,[47] the Supreme Court addressed this balancing of rights in the context of the offence of obstructing the highway in the absence of any 'lawful authority or excuse'.[48] The defendants' protest involved blocking a road to an arms fair in London. The Supreme Court held that the defendants did have a lawful excuse, as a conviction would be a disproportionate restriction on their Articles 10 and 11 ECHR rights. While a number of the factors which the court took into account focused upon the nature of the defendants' actions, other relevant factors related to the protesters' reasons for action and, therefore, allowed for them to explain their motivations and their critique of the arms industry. The factors here were that the protest 'clearly related to a "*matter of general concern*"' and the protesters held 'a longstanding commitment to opposing the arms trade' which 'stemmed, at least in part, from their Christian faith'.[49]

A different line of cases, however, has rejected the need for a fact-specific proportionality assessment. In these cases, the courts ruled that the offence itself was such that a conviction would never be a disproportionate restriction of the protesters' rights as the 'necessary balance for proportionality is struck by the terms of the offence-creating provision'.[50] This includes cases where the statutory provision did not include a 'lawful excuse' or 'reasonableness' element,[51] but also cases where there was such a provision.[52] Subsequent decisions of higher courts have affirmed this distinction between offences that must be interpreted to include a proportionality assessment and those where the proportionality assessment is not required, thereby restricting the reach of *Ziegler*.[53]

This has been confirmed by the Supreme Court in *Reference by the Attorney General for Northern Ireland—Abortion Services (Safe Access Zones) (Northern Ireland) Bill*.[54] The court was asked whether the devolved Northern Ireland Assembly was competent to pass a Bill which included an offence of intending to influence patients and staff within a 'safe access zone' around abortion clinics. As the Assembly does not have jurisdiction to pass any Bill in breach of the Human Rights Act 1998, if the proposed offence was a disproportionate interference with protester's Articles 9, 10, and 11 ECHR rights, they would not have competence to pass the Bill. The Court affirmed the distinction that some offences required a case-specific proportionality exercise while others did not, and held that the proposed offence in the Bill did not require a proportionality assessment.

The court, in coming to this conclusion, emphasized the impact that 'pro-life' activists had upon women accessing medical treatment: 'There is a pressing social need for such restrictions to be imposed, in order to protect the rights of women seeking treatment or advice'.[55] Claims that the offence would restrict activists' ability to contribute to public debate were also rejected, because 'the protesters are more focused on influencing the personal decisions of individual women than on the political question of whether abortion law should be amended',[56] adding that other means of advancing their position were available, which focused on making contributions to public debate. In other words, they could engage the organs of a 'functioning democratic state'. This approach can be seen clearly in the court's conclusion (in reasoning that resonates with the 'pacification' of protest described by both Woolman, this volume, and Srinivasan, this volume):

> The right of women in Northern Ireland to access abortion services has now been established in law through the processes of democracy. That legal right should not be obstructed or impaired by the accommodation of claims by opponents of the legislation based, some might think ironically, on the liberal values protected by the Convention. A legal system which enabled those who had lost the political debate to undermine the legislation permitting abortion, by relying on freedom of conscience, freedom of expression and freedom of assembly, would in practice align the law with the values of the opponents of reform and deprive women of the protection of rights which have been legislatively enacted.[57]

While the *outcome* in this case can be supported (to some extent), we lament the limiting of *Ziegler*. We support the outcome based on an important distinction between actions aimed at governmental processes or inaction (as seen in the Stansted 15 and Colston 4 cases) and those targeted at individual women seeking health care or professionals providing care. There is also merit in the court's reflections on the irony of protesters using the liberal principles inherent in the ECHR to seek a space, through targeted acts of gendered harassment,[58] to deny women their right to reproductive health. Nevertheless, the rejection of a *Ziegler* proportionality assessment denies the possibility of any 'hard cases' and limits the ability of the courts to examine the boundaries of offences.[59]

We believe the current state of the law on defences to protest related charges to be unsatisfactory. Much now falls upon the offence charged as to whether the defence can ground their defence, and therefore their actions, in their motivations and reasons for acting. We suspect that prosecutors will opt for offences that do not include a proportionality assessment to exclude justificatory reasons for action. This is the straightforward adoption and extension of Hoffmann's Bargain, an approach that we noted has roots in Rawlsian liberal theory and a demand that protesters display fidelity to law and the mechanisms of democratic governance. Much faith is, therefore, placed in the effective operation of the state and political processes, a level of faith that may well be undeserved.[60] As we have seen in this chapter, the inaction of the state was central to the defence of the Colston 4; Bristol City Council were portrayed as inactive and unwilling to accede to the needs of its electorate.[61]

Conclusion: Politics (and Its Absence) in the Courtroom

One of the central questions in this chapter is the extent to which the protest trial offers an opportunity for ongoing contestation by social movements. To date, there has been insufficient attention to the trial as a social institution that is important in understanding activists, activism, and the response of the state. The trial is something of a 'black box'. Our work aims to throw light on these processes, address the extent to which the trial is a disciplinary space or an opportunity for the continuation of contestation, resistance, and struggle. This is important given that many social movements see arrest, prosecution, and trial as a strategic choice while other activists may see trials as an inevitable consequence of action. In all cases, going to court has the potential to serve other goals, with the associated risk of repression. This speaks to the extent to which defendants in protest trials retain a political voice; the construction of the liberal political subject in the courtroom; and the extent to which the criminal trial is conceived as outside the political realm.

We have referred to the contrast between the trials of the Stansted 15 and the Colston 4. While the trial judge in the Stansted 15 did not immediately rule out a necessity defence, possible lines of questioning (the defence were denied their request to question Home Office Officials on immigration processes) and general admonishments to keep testimony within proper bounds (and, therefore, not overtly political) operated to deny the defendants full voicing of their motivations.[62] Ironically, however, the political views they were able to express were utilized to deny them a necessity defence. Their claim that they acted to avoid harm to the detainees was rejected; in light of their testimony, the trial judge and Court of Appeal ruled a necessity defence was unavailable as they acted on the basis of their wider political motives.[63] The contrast with the Colston 4 was stark. The defendants were able to place Colston on trial as a key player in the slave trade, and Bristol City Council on trial for their unwillingness to accede to popular calls for the statue to be contextualized or removed.

As noted in our exploration of the availability of defences in the protest trial, the substantive criminal law is crucial when assessing the extent to which politics is allowed within the courtroom. However, this is only part of the picture. A significant feature of the trial of the Stansted 15 is the extent to which the trial judge was able to construct the courtroom as an effective disciplinary space, both for the defendants and for the observers in the public gallery.[64] Of importance here is the charge and potential sentence; the Stansted 15 were charged with a terrorism-related offence of endangering the safety of an aerodrome, which carries a maximum sentence of life imprisonment. The upgrading of the charges from aggravated trespass to a terrorism-related offence created a high-stakes environment for the defendants which accentuated the trial judge's disciplinary actions. This construction of disciplinary space was in marked contrast to the Colston 4 trial, where the defendants were more able to assert their political identities and reasons for action and observers (aided by the fact that they were behind a glass screen) were much more animated. Pacification, therefore, of courtroom 'outsiders' is both a product of the law and the courtroom as a social space. This matters to how the process constructs the liberal subject and the extent to which the trial is a truly communicative endeavour.

Some of the Stansted 15 defendants felt constrained in their options as to what they could say (if they felt they could speak at all), how they could say it, and how they presented themselves;[65] the process, therefore, was not a truly communicative endeavour. In Duff's terms, their 'account' of their actions was partial and constrained. As we note elsewhere, this leads to a particular construction of the subject, where the defendants were constructed as 'reasonable' and 'conscientious' and the politics that was allowed into the courtroom was one of 'an ethics of care' limiting a broader questioning of the political status quo.[66] When the trial is framed in this way, defendants must vouch for their sincerity and, drawing upon Weisman,[67] there is a 'separation between act and being', and the defendants' account of their actions is incomplete. Their full motivations, the extent to which their actions derive from their commitments, are lost in the way that the trial constructs their subjectivity. To some extent, therefore, the political actor is reframed as a (non)political subject. For instance, in the Stansted 15 trial, because of the restrictions imposed by the judge, the focus was upon the possible harm to detainees on the flight, rather than the failures of the immigration system and the denial of the detainees' human rights.

Here, Duff's normative construction of the trial as a communicative space does not, therefore, hold good in reality. In the context of the protest trial, it is hardly surprising. As noted above, Martin conceives of the necessity defence as possibly allowing for a 'direct, doctrinally legitimate, and uniquely powerful means through which revolutionary change might be accomplished',[68] but this scarcely fits within common understandings of the criminal law. The mainstream conception of criminal adjudication is that of a value neutral application of an abstract and universal norm to specific facts; the criminal law applies equally to all, and it reflects shared values and moral judgments. To engage in politics is to challenge this orthodoxy; challenging the state's actions in a protest trial is a challenge to the assumption that the criminal law is value neutral. It is also, therefore, an implicit challenge to the authority of the court as a disinterested legal process. For us, the protest trial throws light on the fiction of the criminal law as apolitical; politics is inherent in the criminal process and any action which highlights this is resisted.

Acknowledgements

We would like to thank those who attended the workshops for this collection and the editors for their insightful suggestions. Any errors remain our own.

Notes

1. For a detailed description of our methods, see Graeme Hayes, Steven Cammiss, and Brian Doherty, 'Disciplinary Power and Impression Management in the Trials of the Stansted 15', *Sociology* 55, no. 3 (2021): 561–581.
2. On this boundary, see Tabatha Abu El-Haj, 'Defining *Peaceably*: Policing the Line between Constitutionally Protected Protest and Unlawful Assembly', *Missouri Law Review* 80, no. 4 (2015): 961–986.
3. UNHRCtte, General Comment No. 37—Article 21: The Right of Peaceful Assembly (17 September 2020) UN Doc. CCPR/C/GC/37, 16.

4. James L. Cavallaro, 'The Demise of the Political Necessity Defense: Indirect Civil Disobedience and *United States v Schoon*', *California Law Review* 81 (1993): 351–385.
5. Michael Brogan, 'The Necessity Defence and Anthropogenic Global Warming Protests: The Times They Are a-Changin', *Alternative Law Journal* 46, no. 4 (2021): 268–274.
6. Brian Doherty and Graeme Hayes, 'Having Your Day in Court: Judicial Opportunity and Tactical Choice in Anti-GMO Campaigns in Britain and France', *Comparative Political Studies* 47, no. 1 (2014): 3–29. There are of course other courtroom processes that we do not examine. We do not, for instance, examine cause lawyering which seeks to use the courts as an extra-political means of challenging and shifting policy. Similarly, we do not examine the use of civil injunctions to limit protest and, subsequently, 'punish' those who breach them. This is not to deny that these are important; it is simply an inherent limitation in a chapter of this size. Literature on these omissions can be found in the Further Reading section.
7. Jules Boykoff, 'Limiting Dissent: The Mechanisms of State Repression in the USA', *Social Movement Studies* 6, no. 3 (2007): 281–310; Donatella della Porta and Herbert Reiter, 'Policing Protest', in *The Wiley-Blackwell Encyclopedia of Social and Political Movements*, ed. David A. Snow, Donatella Della Porta, Doug McAdam, and Bert Klandermans, 1577–1583 (London: Wiley-Blackwell, 2022).
8. John Rawls, *A Theory of Justice* (Oxford: Oxford University Press, 1971/1973).
9. Ibid., 355.
10. Kirsten Davies et al., 'The Declaration on Human Rights and Climate Change: A New Legal Tool for Global Policy Change', *Journal of Human Rights and the Environment* 8, no. 2 (2017): 217–253.
11. In contrast to Rawls, both Brownlee and Delmas build a broader rationale for civil disobedience, ones that question whether 'fidelity to law' requires punishment: Kimberley Brownlee, *Conscience and Conviction: The Case for Civil Disobedience* (Oxford: Oxford University Press, 2012); Candice Delmas, *A Duty to Resist: When Disobedience Should Be Uncivil* (Oxford: Oxford University Press, 2018).
12. UNHRCtte, General Comment No. 37, 7, 15–20.
13. Later discussion will focus upon *R v Jones* [2006] UKHL 16, but similar sentiments can be found in *Monsanto v Tilly and Ors* [1999] EWCA Civ 3044. This approach pays insufficient regard to the argument that assembly rights are important to those who are unable or unwilling to engage in conventional politics: see Eric Barendt, 'Freedom of Assembly', in *Freedom of Expression and Freedom of Information: Essays in Honour of Sir David Williams*, ed. Jack Beatson and Yvonne Cripps, 161–176 (Oxford: Oxford University Press, 2000).
14. Steven Cammiss, Graeme Hayes, and Brian Doherty, 'Necessity, Non-Violent Direct Activism, and the Stansted 15: Reasserting "Hoffmann's Bargain"', *Modern Law Review* 85, no. 6 (2022): 1515–1533.
15. Tabatha Abu El-Haj, 'Defining Nonviolence as a Matter of Law and Politics', in *Protest and Dissent (Nomos LXII)*, ed. Melissa Schwartzberg, 201–236 (New York: New York University Press, 2020).
16. Brian Doherty and Graeme Hayes, 'The Courts: Criminal Trials as Strategic Arenas', in *Breaking Down the State: Protesters Engaged*, ed. Jan Willem Duyvendak and James M. Jasper, 27–52 (Amsterdam: Amsterdam University Press, 2015).
17. This is a tactic employed by protesters, using improvised devices, to make it difficult for the police to remove them.

18. As part of their protests, some activists, known as 'arrestables', block roads and glue themselves to the surface making arrest inevitable.
19. There are examples of activists purposely disrupting proceedings by, for instance, gluing themselves to courtroom furniture, as occurred in a trial of XR protesters at St Albans magistrates' court in May 2021: BBC, 'Workers "Stuck" Due to Extinction Rebellion Newspaper Protest', 11 May 2021, https://www.bbc.co.uk/news/uk-england-beds-bucks-herts-57071321.
20. In the summer and autumn of 2019.
21. Ali Tamlit et al., 'The Stansted 15 Have Won: What Can We Learn from their Four-Year Legal Battle?', *Novara Media*, 4 February 2021, https://novaramedia.com/2021/02/04/the-stansted-15-have-won-what-can-we-learn-from-their-four-year-legal-battle/.
22. Paul Rock, *The Social World of an English Crown Court: Witnesses and Professionals in the Crown Court Centre at Wood Green* (Oxford: Oxford University Press, 1993).
23. Pat Carlen, *Magistrates' Justice* (London: Croom Helm, 1976).
24. Anthea Hucklesby, 'Court Culture: An Explanation of Variations in the Use of Bail by Magistrates' Courts', *Howard Journal of Criminal Justice* 36, no. 2 (1997): 129–145.
25. Richard Young, 'Exploring the Boundaries of the Criminal Courtroom Workgroup', *Common Law World Review* 42, no. 3 (2013): 203–296.
26. John M. Atkinson and Paul Drew, *Order in Court: The Organisation of Verbal Interaction in Judicial Settings* (London: McMillan, 1979).
27. Antony Duff, *Answering for Crime: Responsibility and Liability in the Criminal Law* (Oxford: Hart Publishing, 2009).
28. Hayes, Cammiss, and Doherty, 'Disciplinary Power and Impression Management in the Trials of the Stansted 15'.
29. Tamlit et al., 'The Stansted 15 Have Won'.
30. Ibid.
31. Hayes, Cammiss, and Doherty, 'Disciplinary Power and Impression Management in the Trials of the Stansted 15', 574.
32. Ibid.
33. Ibid.
34. Ibid., 576.
35. We have elsewhere noted the extent to which the higher courts are prone to conflate the defences of necessity, prevention of crime and duress of circumstances. Cammiss, Hayes, and Doherty, 'Necessity, Non-Violent Direct Activism, and the Stansted 15'.
36. Doherty and Hayes, 'The Courts: Criminal Trials as Strategic Arenas'.
37. Alan Norrie, *Crime, Reason and History: A Critical Introduction to Criminal Law*, 3rd ed. (Cambridge: Cambridge University Press, 2014), 214.
38. Shaun P. Martin, 'The Radical Necessity Defence', *University of Cincinnati Law Review* 73, no. 4 (2005): 1527–1607, 1530.
39. [2006] UKHL 16, 89.
40. Ibid., 94.
41. Rawls, *A Theory of Justice*, 366.
42. *Roberts and Ors* [2018] EWCA Crim 2739.
43. Hayes, Cammiss, and Doherty, 'Disciplinary Power and Impression Management in the Trials of the Stansted 15'.
44. Cammiss, Hayes, and Doherty, 'Necessity, Non-Violent Direct Activism, and the Stansted 15', 1525.

45. *Thacker and ors* [2021] EWCA Crim 97.
46. Respectively, the rights to freedom of thought, conscience, and religion; freedom of expression; and freedom of peaceful assembly and association.
47. [2021] UKSC 23.
48. Section 137 of the Highways Act 1980. Notably, previous cases suggested that a proportionality assessment should also (similarly) be incorporated into offences with no lawful excuse defence. E.g. *Connolly v DPP* [2007] EWHC 237, 18.
49. [2021] UKSC 23, 21.
50. *James v DPP* [2015] EWHC 3296, 35.
51. E.g. *Bauer and others v DPP* [2013] EWHC 634 (aggravated trespass) and *James v DPP* [2015] EWHC 3296 (failure to comply with conditions imposed on an assembly under s14 of the Public Order Act 1986).
52. E.g. Norwood [2002] EWCH 1564 (aggravated offence of using threatening, abusive or insulting words or behaviour under s.5 of the Public Order Act 1986): such conduct would be 'objectively unreasonable' in any proportionality assessment (39) and a proportionality assessment would not therefore be required.
53. See, for instance, Director of Public Prosecutions v Cuciurean [2022] EWHC 736, where the court declined to read a proportionality assessment into the offence of aggravated trespass, and *Attorney General's Reference (No. 1 of 2022)* where the court held that in cases of high value criminal damage a proportionality assessment would not be required as damage of this type would either result from violence (and therefore outside the scope of ECHR rights) or it would not be disproportionate to convict.
54. [2022] UKSC 32.
55. Ibid., 154.
56. Ibid., 132.
57. Ibid., 156.
58. Pam Lowe and Graeme Hayes, 'Anti-Abortion Activism, Civil Inattention and the Problem of Gendered Harassment', *Sociology* 53, no. 2 (2018): 330–346.
59. Anurag Deb, 'Protest and Proportionality in the Supreme Court', UK Human Rights Blog, 14 December 2022, https://ukhumanrightsblog.com/2022/12/14/protest-and-proportionality-in-the-supreme-court-the-safe-access-zones-bill-reference-2022-uksc-32/.
60. Cammiss, Hayes, and Doherty, 'Necessity, Non-Violent Direct Activism, and the Stansted 15'.
61. After the completion of this chapter and just prior to publication, the Court of Appeal handed down a further ruling which restricts the availability of defences for protesters. In *Attorney General's Reference (No. 1 of 2023)* [2024] EWCA Crim 243 the court ruled on the interpretation of 'lawful excuse' under section 5(2)(a) of the Criminal Damage Act 1971, which provides for a lawful excuse where the defendant holds an honest believe that the owner of the property would have consented had they known of the damage *and its circumstances*. The defendant claimed that she believed that the owners would have consented if they were 'aware that it was carried out to alert those responsible . . . to the nature and extent of man-made climate damage' (14). The court held that the *circumstances* D wanted to rely upon—her motive 'to draw attention to the subject matter of the protest'—'lacked the necessary proximity to the damage' and were therefore too remote and consequently inadmissible (48). This is a further example of the higher courts restricting the extent to which protesters can voice their beliefs in the context of possible defences.
62. Hayes, Cammiss, and Doherty, 'Disciplinary Power and Impression Management in the Trials of the Stansted 15'.

63. Cammiss, Hayes, and Doherty, 'Necessity, Non-Violent Direct Activism, and the Stansted 15'.
64. Hayes, Cammiss, and Doherty, 'Disciplinary Power and Impression Management in the Trials of the Stansted 15'.
65. Ibid.; Tamlit et al., 'The Stansted 15 Have Won'.
66. Hayes, Cammiss, and Doherty, 'Disciplinary Power and Impression Management in the Trials of the Stansted 15'.
67. Richard Weisman, *Showing Remorse: Law and the Social Control of Emotion* (Farnham, UK: Ashgate, 2014).
68. Martin, 'The Radical Necessity Defence', 1530.

Further Reading

Awol, Allo, ed. *The Courtroom as a Space of Resistance: Reflections on the Legacy of the Rivonia Trial*. London: Routledge, 2015.

Boykoff, Jules. 'Limiting Dissent: The Mechanisms of State Repression in the USA'. *Social Movement Studies* 6, no. 3 (2007): 281–310.

Brogan, Michael. 'The Necessity Defence and Anthropogenic Global Warming Protests: The Times They Are a-Changin'. *Alternative Law Journal* 46, no. 4 (2021): 268–274.

Brownlee, Kimberley. *Conscience and Conviction: The Case for Civil Disobedience*. Oxford: Oxford University Press, 2012.

Cammiss, Steven, Graeme Hayes, and Brian Doherty. 'Necessity, Non-Violent Direct Activism, and the Stansted 15: Reasserting "Hoffmann's Bargain"'. *Modern Law Review* 85, no. 6 (2022): 1515–1533.

Cavallaro, James L. 'The Demise of the Political Necessity Defense: Indirect Civil Disobedience and *United States v Schoon*'. *California Law Review* 81 (1993): 351–385.

Ceric, Irina. 'Beyond Contempt: Injunctions, Land Defense, and the Criminalization of Indigenous Resistance'. *South Atlantic Quarterly* 119, no. 2 (2020): 353–369.

Delmas, Candice. *A Duty to Resist: When Disobedience Should Be Uncivil*. Oxford: Oxford University Press, 2018.

Doherty, Brian, and Graeme Hayes. 'The Courts: Criminal Trials as Strategic Arenas'. In *Breaking Down the State: Protestors Engaged*. Amsterdam: Amsterdam University Press, 2015.

Doherty, Brian, and Graeme Hayes. 'Having Your Day in Court: Judicial Opportunity and Tactical Choice in Anti-GMO Campaigns in Britain and France'. *Comparative Political Studies* 47, no. 1 (2014): 3–29.

Hall, Matthew R. 'Guilty but Civilly Disobedient: Reconciling Civil Disobedience and the Rule of Law'. *Cardozo Law Review* 28, no. 5 (2007): 2083–2132.

Hayes, Graeme, Steven Cammiss, and Brian Doherty. 'Disciplinary Power and Impression Management in the Trials of the Stansted 15'. *Sociology* 55, no. 3 (2021): 561–581.

Long, Lance N. 'The Climate Necessity Defence: Proof and Judicial Error in Climate Protest Cases'. *Stanford Environmental Law Journal* 38, no. 1 (2018): 57–116.

Martin, Shaun P. 'The Radical Necessity Defence'. *University of Cincinnati Law Review* 73, no. 4 (2005): 1527–1607.

Sarat, Austin, and Stuart A. Scheingold, eds. *Cause Lawyers and Social Movements* Redwood City, CA: Stanford University Press, 2006.

Index

For the benefit of digital users, indexed terms that span two pages (e.g., 52–53) may, on occasion, appear on only one of those pages.

Figures are indicated by an italic *f* following the page number.